The Essays of

MONTAIGNE

in three volumes

·

VOLUME TWO

containing

the latter half of Book Two

and Book Three

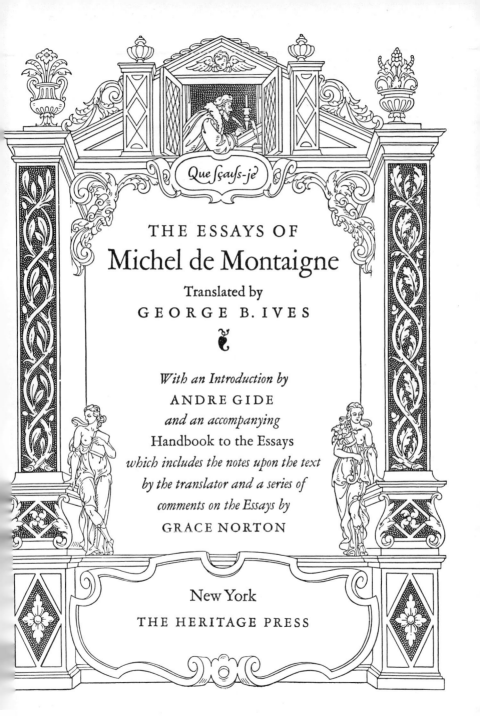

Que sçais-je

THE ESSAYS OF
Michel de Montaigne
Translated by
GEORGE B. IVES

With an Introduction by
ANDRE GIDE
and an accompanying
Handbook to the Essays
which includes the notes upon the text
by the translator and a series of
comments on the Essays by
GRACE NORTON

New York
THE HERITAGE PRESS

Contents

OF BOOK TWO

• •

Contents

Contents
OF BOOK THREE

· ·

The Essays of

MONTAIGNE

.

Book Two

continued from first volume

Chapter XIII

OF JUDGING

THE DEATH OF OTHERS

WHEN we judge the steadiness of men in dying, which is unquestionably the act most worth notice in human life, one thing must be heeded: that we do not easily believe that we have reached that point. Few persons die convinced that it is their last hour; and there is no occasion when the delusion of hope assails us more. It does not cease dinning into the ear: "Others have surely been sicker than you without dying; your case is not so desperate as they think; and, at the worst, God has often performed greater miracles." And this occurs because we account ourselves as too important. It seems as if the universality of things were to some extent affected by our being brought to naught, and were in sympathy with our condition; forasmuch as our vision, changed from what it was, sees things likewise changed; and we believe that they are failing it,[1] in proportion as it is failing them; like those who travel by sea, in whose eyes the mountains, fields, towns, sky, and land move, and at the same rate as themselves.

We sail forth from the harbour, and lands and cities recede.[2]

Of Judging the Death of Others

Who ever saw an old man who did not extol the past and decry the present, holding the world and the morals of mankind responsible for his wretchedness and his discontent?

> And now the aged ploughman shakes his head and sighs; and when he compares present times with times past, he often praises his father's fortune, and prates about the men of old, rich in piety.[3]

We drag every thing along with us.

Whence it follows that we deem our death a weighty matter, and that it does not take place very simply, or without the solemn consultation of the stars—*So many gods excited regarding one man.*[4] And we think so the more, the more highly we value ourselves. How can so much learning be lost, with such great detriment, without special heed taken by the fates? Does so rare and exemplary a mind cost no more in the killing than a commonplace and useless one? This life, which covers so many other lives, upon which so many other lives depend, which employs so many people in its service, and fills so large a place—is it cast out of its place, like that which holds by its single tie? No one of us sufficiently feels that he is only himself. From this sprang these words of Cæsar to his pilot—words more turgid than the waves that threatened him:—

> If you shrink from Italy under the authority of heaven, go thither by my authority; your just ground for timidity is only that you know not who is your passenger. Dash through the storm, confident in my protection.[5]

And these:—

818

Of Judging the Death of Others

Cæsar now believed the peril to be worthy of his destiny. "Is it," he said, "so mighty a task for the gods to overthrow me? Does it need so great a sea against this man sitting in a little bark?"[6]

And that general delusion, that the sun veiled its face in mourning a whole year for his death:—

> Even he, when Cæsar was slain, had pity on Rome, and veiled his luminous head with solemn observances;[7]

and a thousand similar ones, by which the world allows itself to be so easily deceived, believing that our interests affect heaven, and that its infinitude is concerned with paltry doings.[8] *Not so close is the relation between heaven and us, that our mortality is that also of the brightness of the stars.*[9]

Now, to decide that there is resolution and firmness in him who does not yet believe himself to be certainly in danger, however the fact may be, is not reasonable; and it is not enough that he dies in that attitude, since he assumed it to produce precisely this effect. It occurs with the greater number of men, that they strengthen their bearing and their words in order to gain esteem thereby, which they hope to possess while still living. Of all those whom I have seen die, chance has disposed their bearing, not their own purpose.[10] And even regarding those persons who in old days made way with themselves, there is much to discriminate, according as it was by a sudden or a lingering death. That cruel Roman emperor said of his prisoners that he wished to make them feel death; and if one of them killed himself in prison, he said, "That man has escaped me."[11] He desired to stretch death out, and thus to cause it to be felt by torture.

We have seen a body slashed all over, but not given the mortal stroke, and prevented from dying by horrible methods of severe cruelty.[12]

In truth, it is no very difficult matter, when sound in body and composed in mind, to determine to kill oneself; it is very easy to swagger before coming to close quarters; so that the most effeminate man on earth, Heliogabalus, amid his basest debaucheries, carefully planned to put himself to death in a delicate way when the emergency should drive him to it; and to the end that his death might not belie the rest of his life, he built, for the express purpose, a costly tower from which to leap, the lower part and the front of which were sheathed with boards enriched with gold and precious stones; and also he had cords of gold and crimson silk made, wherewith to strangle himself; and a sword of gold forged, to run himself through; and kept poison in caskets of emerald and topaz, to poison himself, according as the desire should come upon him to choose from among all these ways of dying;[13]

Prompt and courageous from necessity.[14]

But, as for him, the effeminacy of his preparations makes it more probable that his heart would have failed him, had he been brought to the reality.[15] But even of those who, more stout of heart, have been undaunted in performance, we must examine, I say, whether it was done with a blow which gave no time to feel its effect; for it may be questioned whether, upon seeing life ebb away little by little, the sensations of the body commingling with those of the soul, if the means of repenting had presented itself, there would have been found steadfastness and persistence in so perilous a purpose.

In Cæsar's civil wars, Lucius Domitius, taken prisoner in the Abruzzi, having poisoned himself, afterward repented of his act.[16] It has happened in our days that a certain man, being resolved to die, and at his first attempt not having struck deep enough, the sensitiveness of the flesh staying his arm, wounded himself twice or thrice again very severely, but could never force himself to drive the blow home. When Plantius Silvanus was under trial, Urgulania, his grandmother, sent him a dagger, with which, not having the courage to kill himself, he had his servants cut his veins.[17] In the time of Tiberius, Albucilla, trying to kill herself, struck too gently and gave her enemies an opportunity to imprison her and put her to death in their way.[18] The same did Demosthenes,[19] after his defeat in Sicily. And C. Fimbria, having struck himself too feebly, prevailed on his servant to despatch him.[20] On the other hand, Ostorius, unable to make use of his own arm, disdained to employ that of his servant otherwise than to hold the dagger straight and firm, and he, flinging himself forward, thrust his breast against it and ran himself through.[21] It is, in truth, a meat that he who has not a well-prepared gullet[22] must gulp down without chewing; but the Emperor Adrianus had his doctor mark and circumscribe around his pap exactly the mortal spot at which the man must aim to whom he should give it in charge to kill him.[23]

It was from such considerations that Cæsar, when he was asked what kind of death he thought most desirable, replied, "The least premeditated and the quickest."[24] If Cæsar

Of Judging the Death of Others

dared to say this, it is no greater cowardice in me to believe it. A quick death, says Pliny, is the supreme fortune of human life.[25] It is grievous to them[26] to recognise death. No one can call himself undaunted by death who fears to argue with it,[27] and who can not meet it with his eyes open. They who are seen, at their executions, to go rapidly to their end, and hasten and urge forward the final act, do this, not from resolution: they want to get rid of time to consider it. The being dead does not distress them, but very much the dying.

> I do not wish to die; but to be dead, I make no account of.[28]

This is a degree of firmness which I have found by experience I could attain to,[29] like those who throw themselves into danger as into the sea, with their eyes shut.

There is nothing, to my thinking, more resplendent in the life of Socrates than the having for thirty long days meditated upon his death sentence; the having accepted it all that time with a very confident hope, without excitement, without change, and with a succession of deeds and words rather lowered and careless in tone, than strained and heightened by the weight of such a cogitation.[30]

That Pomponius Atticus to whom Cicero wrote letters, being ill, summoned Agrippa, his son-in-law, and two or three other friends of his, and said to them that, having found that he gained nothing by trying to be cured, and that all he did to prolong his life prolonged also, and increased, his suffering, he had determined to put an end to the one and the other, begging them to approve his determination and, at the worst, not to waste their pains in dis-

822

suading him from it. Now, having chosen to kill himself by
fasting, lo! his disease was cured by this circumstance: the
remedy that he employed to do away with himself restored
him to health. The physicians and his friends, gladdened by
such a happy result and rejoicing with him thereat, found
themselves greatly mistaken; for it was not possible for
them to make him change his purpose because of this, he
saying that, whether or no, he must cross the line some day
and, being so near it, he desired to avoid the trouble of beginning again another time.[31] This man, having regarded
death at leisure, not only is not discouraged from meeting it,
but is frantic to do so; for, being satisfied about that for
which he had entered into the fight, he daringly spurs himself on to see the end of it. It is very much more than having
no fear of death, to desire to taste it and learn its flavour.
The story of the philosopher Cleanthes is much the same.
His gums were swollen and decayed; the physicians advised
him to be extremely abstinent. Having fasted two days, he
was so much better that they pronounced him cured, and
permitted him to return to his wonted manner of living.
He, on the contrary, having already tasted some sweetness
in his failure of strength, determined to take no backward
step, and to cross the line which he had nearly approached.[32]

Tullius Marcellinus, a young Roman, wishing to anticipate the hour of his destiny, in order to rid himself of a
disease which tormented him more than he was willing to
endure, although the physicians promised him a certain, if
not a very rapid, cure, summoned his friends to deliberate
about this. Some, says Seneca, gave him the advice which,
from cowardice, they themselves would have taken; the
others, to please him, that which they thought would be

Of Judging the Death of Others

most agreeable to him. But a Stoic spoke thus to him: "Do not exert yourself, Marcellinus, as if you were deliberating about something of importance; it is no great matter to live —your servants and the beasts live; but it is a great matter to die worthily, wisely, and firmly. Think how long you have been doing the same thing: eating, drinking, sleeping; drinking, sleeping, and eating. We revolve incessantly in this circle; not only disagreeable and unbearable circumstances, but the mere satiety of living, make us long for death." Marcellinus had need, not of a man to advise him, but of a man to help him. His servants were afraid to meddle in the affair; but this philosopher made them understand that those of a man's household are suspected only when there is some doubt whether the master's death has been voluntary; otherwise, that it would be as bad an example to prevent him from killing himself as to kill him, because

He who against a man's will preserves his life does the same thing as if he killed him.[33]

Later, he advised Marcellinus that just as, when our repasts are ended, the dessert from the table is given to those who serve, so, when life is at an end, it would not be unbecoming to distribute some thing to those who have ministered to us. Now, Marcellinus was open-hearted and liberal; he caused money to be bestowed on his servants and consoled them. For all else, there was no need either of iron or blood; he undertook to depart from this life; not to flee from it; not to escape death, but to experience it. And, to give himself time to deal with it, he refused all nourishment; and on the third day after, having had himself bathed in warm water, he failed little by little, and not without some pleasure, as he

Of Judging the Death of Others

said.[34] In truth, they who have had these faintnesses that come from weakness say that they feel no suffering in them, indeed, rather some pleasure, as of a passage into sleep and rest.

We see in these examples deaths studied and weighed. But to the end that Cato alone might furnish the perfect pattern of courage, it seems that his kind fate weakened the hand with which he dealt himself the blow, so that he might have opportunity to meet death face to face, and embrace it, his courage strengthening instead of weakening in danger. And if it had been for me to represent him in his most superb attitude, it would have been when, all covered with blood, he tore out his entrails, rather than with sword in hand, as did the statuaries of his time.[35] For that second murder was much more savage than the first.

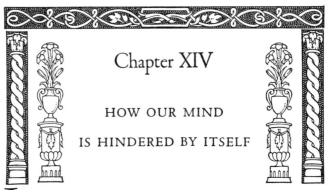

Chapter XIV

HOW OUR MIND

IS HINDERED BY ITSELF

IT is an amusing fancy to imagine a mind exactly balanced between two similar desires. For it is indubitable
that it will never make a choice, because comparison and
selection imply inequality of value; and if we were placed
between the bottle and the ham, with equal appetite for
drink and food, there would be, doubtless, no help save to
die of thirst and hunger. To be prepared for this mishap,
the Stoics, when they are asked whence comes, in our soul,
the choosing between two not differing things, and what
the reason is that, from a large number of crowns, we take
one rather than another, all being alike and there being
nothing about them which inclines us to preference, make
answer that this movement of the soul is out of the ordinary
and is irregular, coming to us from an external, accidental,
and fortuitous impulsion.[1] It might rather be said, it seems
to me, that nothing presents itself to us in which there is
not some difference, however slight it may be; and that,
either to the sight or to the touch, there is always something additional which attracts us, although it be imperceptibly. In like manner, if we imagine a pack-thread
equally strong throughout, it is more than impossible[2] that

How our Mind is Hindered

it should break; for where would you have the fracture[3] begin? and to break everywhere at the same moment, that is not conceivable. If one joined to all this the geometrical propositions which, by the infallibility of their demonstrations, prove the contained to be greater than the container, the centre as great as its circumference, and which find two lines constantly approaching each other and never able to meet, and the philosopher's stone, and the squaring of the circle, wherein reasoning and fact are so opposed, one might perchance derive therefrom some arguments to support that bold saying of Pliny: *The sole certainty is that nothing is certain, and nothing more miserable or more proud than man.*[4]

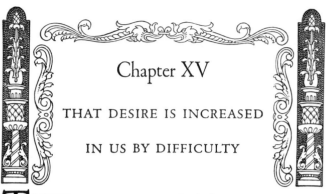

Chapter XV

THAT DESIRE IS INCREASED

IN US BY DIFFICULTY

THERE is no statement which has not its opposite, says the wisest party of philosophers.[1] I was recently ruminating this other notable saying, which one of the ancients brings forward as a reason for contempt of life: No good thing can bring us pleasure, if it be not one for whose loss we are prepared:[2] *equal in pain are the loss of a thing and the fear of losing it;*[3] meaning to prove thereby that the possession of life can not be truly pleasurable to us if we are in fear of losing its enjoyments. It might, however, be said, on the other hand, that we clasp and embrace this good thing so much the more closely and with the more affection, as we see it to be less assured, and fear that it may be taken from us. For it is clearly to be perceived that, as fire is sharper from the presence of cold, so our will is sharpened by contention,—

If Danaë had not been shut up in a brazen tower, she would not have been made a mother by Jove,[4]—

and that there is nothing so naturally opposed to our enjoyment as the satiety that comes from ease, and nothing that so intensifies our enjoyment as rarity and difficulty.

Desire is Increased by Difficulty

Peril increases in all things the very pleasure that we ought to avoid.[5]

Galla, deny me; love is cloyed unless joys torment.[6]

To keep love in breath, Lycurgus decreed that married couples in Sparta should only meet by stealth, and that they should be as much ashamed at being discovered sleeping together as if they had been caught in adultery. The difficulty of assignations, the danger of surprise,

and languor, and silence,
And deep breaths in heavy sighs,[7]—

these things it is that give piquancy to the sauce. How many most lasciviously pleasant sports are the result of the modest and shamefaced style of books on Love! Lust even seeks an additional zest in pain. The pleasure is sweeter when it smarts and scorches. The courtezan Flora used to say that she had never lain with Pompey but she made him carry away the marks of her teeth:

The parts they sought for, those they squeeze so tight,
And pain the body; implant their teeth upon
The lips, and crush the mouth with kisses, yet
Not unalloyed with joy; for there are stings
Which goad them on to hurt the very thing,
Whate'er it be, from whence arise for them
Those gems of frenzy.[8]

This is the same everywhere; difficulty gives value to things. They of the March of Ancona make their vows more readily to Saint-Jacques,[9] and they of Galicia to Our Lady of Loretto; at Liége they make very much of the Baths of Lucca, and in Tuscany of those of Aspa;[10] there are

Desire is Increased by Difficulty

scarcely any Romans to be seen in the fencing-school at Rome, which is full of Frenchmen. The great Cato, like ourselves, found that he did not care for his wife so long as she was his, and desired her when she belonged to another.[11] I have turned an old horse into the stud, as he got quite out of hand when he scented a mare. Facility presently sated him towards his own; but at sight of the first stranger that passed along his paddock, he would neigh as impatiently, and become as hot and furious, as ever.

Our appetite disdains and passes by what is at its hand, to run after what it has not:

> It neglects what is at hand, and would seize what escapes from it.[12]

To forbid us any thing is to give us a desire for it:

> Unless you begin to guard your mistress, she will begin to cease to be mine.[13]

To give it to us completely is to create in us contempt for it. Want and abundance meet with like mishap;

> What is too much troubles you, what is lacking troubles me.[14]

Desire and possession cause us equal discomfort.[15] The aloofness of one's mistress is vexatious, but, in truth, ease and facility of access are even more so; dissatisfaction and wrath are born of the esteem in which we hold the desired object, sharpen love, and rekindle it; but satiety engenders distaste; it is a sluggish, bemused, weary, and drowsy passion.

> She who would reign long, let her be disdainful to her lover;[16]

830

Desire is Increased by Difficulty

be disdainful, O lovers; then will she who denied you yesterday come to you to-day.[17]

What was Poppaea's intention, when she hid her beauty behind a mask, but to enhance it in the eyes of her lovers? Why do they veil, even down to the heels, the beauties that every woman desires to show, and every man to see? Why do they cover with so many obstacles, one on top of another, the parts on which are chiefly concentrated our desires and their own? And what purpose is served by those great bastions which our ladies have recently adopted, to fortify their flanks, except to allure our appetites, and attract us to them by keeping us at a distance?

She flees to willows, and desires discovery.[18]

She delayed by covering with her cloak.[19]

What is the object of that maidenly modesty, that deliberate coolness, that severe expression, that profession of ignorance of things they know better than we who instruct them, but to increase in us the longing to overcome, bear down, and trample upon all those affected airs and those obstacles to our desire? For there is not only a pleasure, but a source of vainglory, in seducing that meek, mild and childlike bashfulness, in inflaming and goading it into madness, and in subduing to our ardour a cool and calculated sternness. It is a matter for boasting, they say, to triumph over rigour, modesty, chastity and temperance; and whoever dissuades the ladies from those attitudes, betrays both them and himself. We are to believe that their hearts shudder with fright, that the sound of our words offends the purity of their ears, that they hate us for them, and yield to our importunities by a forced constraint. Beauty, all powerful

831

Desire is Increased by Difficulty

as it is, has no power to make itself relished without that interposition.

Look at Italy, where there is most beauty on sale, and the most perfect of its kind, and how they are obliged to seek extraneous means and other arts to make it acceptable, and yet, to tell the truth, whatever they may do, being venal and public, it remains feeble and languid. Even in valour, of two similar actions we none the less hold that to be the noblest which offers the most risk.

[20]It is the purpose of divine Providence to allow its holy church to be disturbed by so many troubles and storms as we see it to be, in order to awaken pious souls by this strife, and to rouse them from the slothfulness and sleep in which so long a period of tranquillity has immersed them. If we balance the loss that we have suffered in the number of those who have gone astray with the gain that accrues to us by having been given fresh spirit, and having our zeal and our strength revived by occasion of this combat, I know not if the advantage does not outweigh the injury.

We thought to tie more firmly the knot of our marriages by removing all means of dissolving them; but the knot of inclination and affection has been made light of and loosened in proportion as that of constraint has been tightened. And, on the other hand, that which so long held marriages at Rome in honour and security was the liberty of breaking them at will. They loved their wives the better because they might lose them; and with full permission for divorce, five hundred years and more passed before any man availed himself of it.[21]

> What is permitted is unattractive; what is not permitted the more ardently inflames.[22]

832

Desire is Increased by Difficulty

On this matter we might add the opinion of an ancient, that punishments whet vices rather than dull them;[23] that they do not beget heedfulness to do well,—that is the work of reason and discipline,—but only heedfulness not to be surprised in ill-doing:—

> The plague-spot being cut out, the more widely the contagion spreads.[24]

I know not whether it is true,[25] but this I know as a matter of experience, that no sort of government was ever amended thereby.[26] The ordering and regulation of morals depends upon some other method.[27]

The Greek historians make mention of the Argippæans, neighbours to Scythia, who live with never so much as a stick or a club for offence; yet not only does no one attempt to attack them, but whoever can escape thither is in safety, because of their virtue and sanctity of life; and there is no man so daring as to lay hand on him. Recourse is had to them to settle the differences that arise amongst men elsewhere.[28] There is a nation where the enclosure of the gardens and fields which it is desired to protect is done with a cotton string;[29] and this is much more sure and safe than our ditches and hedges.[30] *Hidden things tempt the thief. . . . The housebreaker passes open doors.*[31]

Perchance the ease of attack serves, among other conditions, to shield my house from the violence of our civil wars. Defence attracts the attempt, and defiance the offence. I have weakened the design of the soldiers, depriving their exploit of risk and of all manner of military glory, which is wont to serve them as pretext and excuse. A brave deed is

Desire is Increased by Difficulty

always an honourable one in times when justice is dead. I render the conquest of my house a dastardly and treacherous act. It is closed to no one who knocks. For all protection there is only a porter of old custom and ceremony, who is employed not so much to defend my door as to open it more courteously and graciously. I have no guard or sentinel other than what the stars keep for me. A gentleman mistakes in appearing to be in a state of defence unless he be completely so. He who is open on one side is open on all. Our fathers did not dream of building frontier strongholds. The means of assailing—that is to say, without artillery and without an army—and of taking our houses by surprise increases every day beyond the means of protection. Men's wits are universally whetted in that direction. Invasion concerns all men; not so defence: that concerns only the rich. My house was strong for the time when it was built. I have added nothing to it in that respect, and I should fear that its strength would turn against me; moreover, a season of peace will require houses to be unfortified. It is dangerous not to be able to regain them. And yet it is difficult to feel secure there. For in time of civil war, your servant may be of the party that you fear. And when religion serves as a pretext, even kinsfolk become untrustworthy under an appearance of justice. The public funds will not provide for our private garrisons; they would be exhausted by so doing. We have not the means to do it without ruining ourselves, or, more unfitly and harmfully, without ruining the common people. My loss of every thing would hardly be worse.[32] Then, too, suppose that you fail? Even your friends busy themselves, more than in pitying you, in blaming your lack of vigilance and forethought, and

Desire is Increased by Difficulty

your ignorance or indifference in the duties of your [military] profession.

The fact that so many garrisoned houses have been destroyed, while this one stands, makes me suspect that they have been destroyed because they were defended. That gives the assailant both the desire and the right: all defence wears the aspect of war. If it be the will of God, some one may attack me; but at least I will not invite him. It is a place of refuge where I can be at rest from the wars. I try to withdraw this corner from the public storm, as I do another corner in my soul. Our war may change its shape as it will, multiply itself and diversify itself into new factions; for my part, I do not stir. Amid so many armed houses, I alone of my rank in France, so far as I know, have trusted entirely to heaven for the protection of mine. And I have never removed from it a silver spoon or a title deed. I prefer neither to be alarmed nor to escape by halves. If a full acknowledgement wins the divine favour, it will continue with me to the end; in any case I have already continued long enough to render my continuance noteworthy and fit to be recorded. How is that? It has been full thirty years.[33]

Chapter XVI

OF FAME[1]

THERE is the name and the thing: the name is a word that denotes and signifies the thing; the name is not a part of the thing and has no substance; it is an extraneous matter added to the thing and outside of it. God, who is in himself complete plenitude and the sum of all perfection, can not in himself be amplified and increased; but his name can be amplified and increased by the blessing and praise which we bestow upon his exterior works. This praise, since we can not embody it in him,—inasmuch as he can have no accession of good,—we ascribe to his name, which is the thing apart from him nearest to him. Thus it is to God alone that glory and honour belong; and there is nothing so remote from reason as for us to go in quest of them for ourselves; for, being indigent and necessitous in ourselves, our essential nature being imperfect and having constantly need of amelioration, there is the ground where we should labour. We are, all, hollow and empty; it is not with wind and words that we should fill ourselves; we need more solid substance to amend us. A hungry man would be very foolish to seek to provide himself with a fine garment rather than a good meal: we must speed to what is most urgent. As our

836

Of Fame

familiar prayers say: *Glory to God in the highest, and on earth peace to men.*[2] We are in dearth of beauty, health, wisdom, virtue, and such essential qualities; let outward adornments be sought for after we have provided for necessary things. Theology treats this subject amply and more pertinently, but I am scarcely versed therein.

Chrysippus and Diogenes were the first and the most assured asserters of contempt of glory;[3] and they said that, among all pleasures, there was none so dangerous, or more to be shunned, than that which we derive from the approbation of others. Truly, experience makes us often perceive therein much harmful perfidiousness. Nothing so corrupts princes as flattery, nor is there any thing whereby bad men more readily gain favour with them; nor any panderism so fitted, and so commonly made use of, to corrupt the chastity of women as to feed them and delight them with their praises. The first charm that the Sirens employed to beguile Ulysses was of this nature:

> Come hither to us, hither, most praiseworthy Ulysses, the greatest honour that gives prosperity to Greece.[4]

These philosophers said that all the glory of the world did not deserve that a man of understanding should even hold out his finger to obtain it.[5]

> What is glory, however great it may be, if it be only glory?[6]

I mean, for itself alone; for it often brings in its train many advantages, for the sake of which it may be desirable. It gains good-will for us; it causes us to be less exposed to the

Of Fame

insults and injuries of others, and the like. This was also among the chief dogmas of Epicurus; for that precept of his sect, "Conceal thy life,"[7] which forbids men to burden themselves with public offices and negotiations, also presupposes necessarily that we despise glory, which is a form of approbation that the world bestows upon the actions which we openly perform. He who bids us conceal ourselves and have no care but of ourselves, and who does not wish us to be known to others, still less wishes us to be honoured and glorified by them. Therefore he counsels Idomeneus to regulate his actions in no wise by common opinion or reputation, unless it be to avoid the other accidental disadvantages that the contempt of men would bring upon him.[8]

These reflections are, in my judgement, infinitely true and reasonable. But we are, I know not how, twofold in ourselves, which is the reason that what we believe we do not believe, and that we can not free ourselves from what we condemn. Observe the last words of Epicurus, which he uttered when dying; noble words and worthy of such a philosopher, yet they have some hint of recommendation of his fame, some touch of that disposition which he had decried by his precepts. Here is a letter which he dictated a little before his last breath.[9]

Epicurus to Hermachus, greeting.

Whilst I was passing the fortunate, and that the last, day of my life, I wrote this, enduring meanwhile such pain in the bladder and the intestines that nothing could have added to its intensity. But it was balanced in equal measure by the pleasure that the remembrance of my discoveries and my doctrines brought to my soul. Do thou now, as due to thy attachment from childhood to me and to philosophy, take upon thyself the protection of the children of Metrodorus.

Such was his letter, and what makes me infer that this pleasure that he says he feels in his soul in regard to his discoveries concerns in some degree the renown that he hoped to acquire from them after his death, is the provision of his will by which he desires that Aminomachus and Thimocrates, his heirs, shall furnish the cost of the celebration of his birthday in January of every year, which Hermachus shall arrange; and, further, of the outlay to be made on the twentieth of every month, for the entertainment of the philosophers, his intimates, who should assemble in honour of his memory and of Metrodorus.[10]

Carneades was the chief upholder of the contrary opinion, and maintained that glory was desirable for its own sake;[11] even as we gladly accept our posthumous children for their own sake, having no knowledge or enjoyment of them. This opinion has not failed to be the more generally followed, as are easily those which are most in accord with our inclinations. Aristotle gives it the highest rank among external goods.[12] Avoid, as two vicious extremes, immoderation both in seeking it and in shunning it. I believe that, if we had the books that Cicero wrote on this subject, he would tell us fine things about it; for he was so out of his wits with this passion that, if he had dared, he would, so I believe, have easily fallen into the extravagant doctrine into which others fell—that virtue itself is desirable only for the glory that always follows after it;[13]

Unseen virtue differs little from forgotten slothfulness.[14]

Of Fame

This is so false an opinion that I am vexed that it ever entered the understanding of a man who had the honour of bearing the name of philosopher. If that were true, there would be no need to be virtuous save in public; and the actions of the soul, where is the true seat of virtue, we should have no reason to keep regular and orderly except so far as they might come to the knowledge of others.

Is it, then, only a matter of erring discreetly and subtly? If you know, says Carneades, a serpent to be hidden in the spot where, unthinking, he is about to sit down by whose death you hope to profit, you do wickedly if you do not warn him thereof; and all the more, if your acts be known only to yourself.[15] If we do not of ourselves abide by the law of well-doing, if to us impunity is justice, to how many kinds of wickedness may we every day abandon ourselves! What Sextus Peducæus did, in faithfully rendering back that portion of his riches which Caius Plotius had entrusted to him with his sole knowledge,[16] and what I have likewise done often, I do not find to be so praiseworthy as I should find it execrable had he failed to do so. And I consider it well worth while and useful to bring to mind, in our days, the instance of Publius Sextilius Rufus, whom Cicero charges with having against his conscience received an inheritance, not only not contrary to law, but by virtue of the law itself.[17] And M. Crassus and Q. Hortensius, who, on account of their authority and power, having been named by a foreigner, because of certain legacies,[18] as joint inheritors under a forged will, to the end that by this means he might secure his own share in it, contented themselves with not being participators in the forgery, and did not refuse to profit by it, being sufficiently under cover if they were

Of Fame

sheltered from the accusations, from witnesses, and from the laws.[19] *Let them remember that they have God as witness; that is (to my thinking), in their own conscience.*[20]

Virtue is a very empty and valueless thing, if it derives its recommendation from fame. To no purpose should we undertake to make that hold a place apart, and disconnect it from fortune; for what is more fortuitous than reputation? *Assuredly fortune governs all matters; she, more from caprice than from truth, brings some things to honour and makes others of no account.*[21]

To cause actions to be known and seen is the pure work of fortune. It is fate that confers fame on us after the fashion of its inconsiderateness. I have very often seen it go in advance of merit, and often outstrip merit by a long distance. He who first bethought himself of the resemblance between a shadow and glory did better than he intended.[22] They are surpassingly vain things. It,[23] too, sometimes precedes its body, and sometimes greatly exceeds it in length. They who teach gentlemen[24] to seek from valour only honour, *as if it were not praiseworthy unless it were renowned,*[25] what do they achieve thereby, save to instruct them never to risk themselves if they be not seen, and to take good heed that there be witnesses who can report news of their valour; whereas a thousand opportunities present themselves of well-doing without its being observed? How many brave individual deeds are buried in the tumult of a battle! Whoever employs himself in spying faults in others in such a confusion is scarcely very busy in it himself, and produces against himself the testimony that he gives of the conduct of his comrades. *True and wise greatness of soul judges that to be worthy of praise and most according to nature which is connected with deeds, not with glory.*[26] All the glory that I claim from my life is having passed it tranquilly—tranquilly, not after the fashion of Metrodorus or Arcesilaus, or Aristippus, but after my own fashion. Since philosophy has been able to find no path to tranquillity which is open to all,[27] let every man seek it for himself!

To what do Cæsar and Alexander owe the infinite greatness of their renown, but to Fortune? How many men has she brought to naught at the outset of their progress, of whom we have no knowledge, who came to it with spirit equal to theirs,[28] if the ill-luck of their fate had not stopped them short on the very threshold of their undertaking! In the course of so many and such extreme perils, I do not remember to have read that Cæsar was ever wounded; but of Hannibal I know that they say that he was, and of Scanderbeg.[29] Thousands have died from lesser perils than the least of those that he passed through. Numberless brave deeds must be lost unwitnessed before one comes to light. A man is not always on the top of a breach or in the forefront of an army, in sight of his general, as on a stage. A man is surprised between the hedge and moat; he must attempt fortune against a beggarly castle;[30] he must dislodge four miserable musketeers from a barn; he must part alone from his company, and alone set about an enterprise according as the necessity presents itself. And if we look closely, we shall find that experience proves that the least brilliant occasions are the most dangerous, and that, in the wars that have occurred in our days, more brave men have been lost in slight and unimportant occasions, and in the struggle for some paltry fort, than in worthy and honourable places.

He who regards his death as ill employed if it happen not

Of Fame

on some noteworthy occasion, instead of making his death illustrious, himself casts a shadow on his life, letting escape meanwhile many fitting occasions to hazard himself. And all fitting occasions are illustrious enough, every man's conscience trumpeting them sufficiently. *Our glory is the testimony of our conscience.*[31] He who is a brave man only because he will be known for such, and because he will be more highly esteemed after it is known; he who has no desire to do well except in such way that his valour shall come to men's knowledge — he is not a man from whom can be obtained much service.

> I believe that, during the rest of that winter, he did things worthy of commemoration; but since that time they are so hidden that it is not my fault if I do not now tell of them; for Orlando was always ready to do noble deeds rather than narrate them; never were any of his exploits made known except when there were witnesses of them.[32]

A man must go to war as his duty, and expect from it that reward which can not fail all brave deeds, however hidden they may be—no, not even virtuous thoughts: the inward satisfaction that a well-ordered conscience reaps from well-doing. We must be valiant for ourselves, and for the advantage there is in having our courage established upon a firm base, secure against the attacks of fortune.

> Virtue, above all ignoble repulses, shines in spotless honours; she neither takes up nor lays down dignities at the gusts of popular favour.[33]

It is not for display that our soul should play her part, but

Of Fame

for ourselves, within, where no eyes penetrate but our own; there she shields us from the fear of death, from suffering, and even from shame; there she strengthens us in the loss of our children, our friends, and our fortunes; and when the opportunity offers, she leads us also into the hazards of war. *Not for any reward, but for the seemliness of honour itself.*[34] This benefit is much greater and much more worth being desired and hoped for than honour and glory, which are nothing but a favourable judgement that others form of us.

We must needs pick from out a whole nation a dozen men to judge about an acre of land; yet judgement of our inclinations and our actions, the most difficult and most important matter there is, we entrust to the voice of the common people, and the rabble, the mother of ignorance, injustice, and inconstancy. Is it reasonable to make the life of a wise man depend upon the judgement of fools?[35] *Is anything more foolish than to think that those whom as individuals you despise are something other when combined into one whole?*[36] Whoever seeks to please them never has done; it is an indefinite mark that can not be hit.[37] *Nothing is so difficult to judge of as the minds of the multitude.*[38] Demetrius said scoffingly of the voice of the people that he made no more account of the wind which issued forth from it above than of that which issued forth from it below.[39] This other goes further: *I think that even if a thing is not base, it is, nevertheless, not* not *base, when it is praised by the multitude.*[40] No skill, no activity of mind could conduct our steps in following a guide so errant and erratic. In this gale of confused rumors, of reports and common opinions that drive us on, no course can be laid down that is worth any thing. Let us not set before ourselves so floating and uncertain an end; let us follow persistently after reason; let public approval follow us on that road if it will; and as this depends altogether on fortune, we have no ground to hope for it more by another road than by that one. Even if I would not follow the right path because of its rightness, I would follow it because I have found by experience that, at the end of the reckoning, it is usually the most fortunate and most advantageous. *Providence has given men this boon, that honourable deeds are the most profitable.*[41] The sailor of old spoke thus to Neptune in a great tempest: "O God, thou mayest save me if thou wilt; thou mayest destroy me if thou wilt; but still I will always hold my rudder true."[42] I have seen in my days a thousand active, two-faced, equivocating men,[43] whom no one doubted to be more worldly-wise than I, ruined where I was saved;

I have laughed that cunning should lack success.[44]

Paulus Æmilius, setting out on his glorious expedition to Macedonia, warned the Roman people above all things to restrain their tongues concerning his actions during his absence.[45] How great a hindrance in great affairs is the license of opinions! inasmuch as every one has not, in with-standing the common clamour, hostile and defamatory, the firmness of Fabius, who preferred to let his authority be mangled by men's idle fancies rather than to do his duty less well, with favourable repute and popular approval.[46]

There is I know not what inborn satisfaction in knowing oneself to be praised; but we yield far too much to it.

I do not shun praise, for my heart is not callous; but I deny that the end and goal of right-doing is, "Well done! Admirable!"[47]

Of Fame

I care not so much what I am in another's judgement, as I care what I am in my own. I wish to be rich of myself, not by borrowing. Strangers see only external matters and appearances; every one can make a good shew outside, full within of trembling and terror. They do not see my heart, they see only my demeanour. We are right in discrediting the forms of pretence seen in war; for what is easier for a skilful man than to avoid dangers, and to swagger when his heart is full of cowardice? There are so many ways of shunning occasions of risking oneself individually, that we shall have deceived the world a thousand times before we are engaged in a dangerous strait; and even when we find ourselves caught in it, we can, for the nonce, cloak our play with a bold countenance and confident speech, although our heart is quaking within us. And those who might have use of the Platonic ring, making him who wore it on his finger invisible if he turned it toward the palm of his hand[48] — many of them often would conceal themselves when they should show themselves most openly, and would be sorry to be placed in so honourable a position wherein necessity would make them bold.

> Who, except a man who is vicious and deceitful, is delighted by undeserved honour, or dreads false calumny?[49]

See how marvellously uncertain and doubtful all these judgements are that are formed from external appearances; and no witness is so trustworthy as each man is to himself. Herein, how many camp-followers[50] have we as companions in our glory? He who steadily stands in an open trench—what does he do that fifty humble pioneers have not done

before him, who open the way for him and protect him with
their bodies, for five sous a day?

> When tumultuous Rome disparages something, do
> do not give your assent, and maintain the false tongue
> of that scale; nor seek your own mind outside your-
> self.[51]

We call it aggrandising our name to spread it abroad
and scatter it in many mouths; our desire is that it may be
everywhere received in good part, and that thus its growth
may be to its advantage; that is what there is most pardonable in this design. But the excess of this disease goes so far
that many seek to get themselves talked about, in whatever
way it may be. Trogus Pompeius says of Herostratus, and
Livy of Manlius Capitolinus, that they were more desirous
of great than of good renown.[52] This is a common vice. We
care more to be talked of than how we are talked of; and it
is enough for us that our name should be often on men's lips,
however it may be there welcomed. It seems that to be
known is, in some sort, to have one'e life and its duration in
others' keeping. For my part, I hold that I exist only in myself; and as to this other life of mine, which lies in the cognisance of my friends, regarding it nakedly and simply in
itself, I know well that I feel neither profit nor enjoyment
from it, save through the foolishness of a fanciful conception. And when I am dead, I shall be even much less sensible of it; and also, I shall completely lose the use of the
real advantages that sometimes accidentally follow it;[53] I
shall have then no means by which to grasp reputation or
by which it can touch or reach me. For, to expect my name
to acquire it, in the first place, I have no name which is

sufficiently mine; of two that I have, one is common to my whole lineage, yes, also to others. There is a family at Paris and at Montpellier surnamed Montaigne; another in Bretagne and in Saintonge, La Montaigne. The removal of a single syllable will confuse our threads[54] so that I shall have a share in their glory, and they, perchance, in my shame. And also, my forbears were formerly surnamed Eyquem, which surname still belongs to a well-known house in England. As for my other name, it goes to any one who likes to take it. So, perhaps, I shall honour a porter in my stead. And then, even if I should have a personal indication for myself, what can it indicate when I am no longer there? Can it designate and grace nothingness?

> But not more lightly will the tombstone press on my bones. Let posterity praise me: still, not from those remains, still, not from the grave and from the favoured ashes, will violets spring.[55]

But I have spoken of this elsewhere.[56]

For the rest, in a whole battle in which ten thousand men are maimed or killed, there are not fifteen who are talked of. There must needs be some very eminent greatness, or some consequence of importance which fortune connects with it, to give estimation to an individual exploit, not only of a musketeer, but of a captain. For, to kill one man, or two, or ten, to offer oneself bravely to death, is in truth something to each of us, for we risk every thing; but to the world they are things so common, so many of them are seen every day, and so many of the like are needed to produce a noteworthy effect, that we can not expect any special commendation for them;

848

Of Fame

This chance is known to many, and is now frequent, and drawn from the middle of fortune's heap.[57]

Of so many thousands of valiant men who have died in France during the last fifteen hundred years, arms in hand, there are not a hundred who have come to our knowledge. The memory, not of the leaders only, but of the battles and victories, is buried. The fortunes of more than half the world, for lack of record, make no stir and vanish without duration. If I had knowledge of unknown events, I should expect very easily to outdo with them those that are known, of all kinds of examples. Why, of the Romans themselves, and the Greeks, with so many writers and witnesses and so many rare and noble exploits, how few have come down to us!

Scarcely has a slight breath of their fame reached us.[58]

It will be much if, a hundred years hence, men remember in a general way that in our day there were civil wars in France.

The Lacedæmonians sacrificed to the Muses when going into battle, to the end that their deeds might be well and worthily chronicled, deeming it a divine favour, and not common, that noble actions should find witnesses who could give them life and memory.[59] Do we think that, at every musket-shot that hits us and at every risk we run, there shall be immediately a clerk to record it? and that a hundred clerks besides shall write of it, whose commentaries shall last but three days, and shall come to the sight of no man? We have not the thousandth part of the writings of the ancients; it is chance which gives them shorter or longer

life, according to its favour; and what we have of them, it
is permissible for us to doubt if it be not the worst, not having seen the rest. Histories are not made of matters of so
little moment; a man must needs have been the leader in
conquering an empire or a kingdom; he must have won
fifty-two pitched battles, always the weaker in numbers,
like Cæsar. Ten thousand brave fellows and many great
captains died in his company, gallantly and bravely, whose
names lasted only as long as their wives and children lived;

Who are shrouded in obscure fame.[60]

Even of those whom we see do well, three months or three
years after they are left on the field they are no more spoken
of than if they had never been.

Whoever shall consider, with just measure and proportion, of what men and deeds the glory is preserved by mention in books, will find that in our time there are very few
actions and very few persons who can claim any right
thereto. How many virtuous men we have seen survive
their own reputation, who have witnessed and permitted
the extinction, in their presence, of the honour and glory
very justly acquired in their youthful days. And for three
years of this unreal and imaginary life, shall we lose our true
and essential life and pledge ourselves to an ever-imminent
death? Wise men of old set before themselves a nobler and
more fitting end of so weighty an undertaking. *The reward
of a good deed is the having done it.*[61] *The fruit of being of
service is the service itself.*[62] It would be excusable, perhaps,
in a painter or other artisan, or even in a rhetorician or
grammarian, to labour to acquire fame by his works; but
the actions of virtue, those are too noble in themselves to

850

seek other reward than from their own worth, and especially to seek it in the vanity of human judgements. If, however, this false belief is of service to the public in holding men to their duty; if the people are awakened by it to virtue; if princes are moved by seeing the world bless the memory of Trajan and detest that of Nero; if it stirs them up to see the name of that villain,[63] once so terrifying and so dreaded, cursed and reviled so freely by every schoolboy who deals with him, may it vigorously increase, and may it be fostered among us as much as possible.

And Plato, employing every means to make his citizens virtuous, advises them, among other things, not to despise a good reputation and estimation in the world; and says that by some divine inspiration it falls out that even the wicked often, as well by word as by thought, can rightly distinguish the good and the bad.[64] This great man and his master[65] are wonderfully skilful and bold workmen in combining divine operations and revelations wherever human power is lacking; *as tragic poets have recourse to a god when they can not achieve the conclusion of their drama.*[66] For this reason, perhaps, Timon, insulting him, called him "the great miracle-worker."[67]

Since men, from their incompetence, can not be satisfied with lawful coin, let them use the false also. This method has been employed by all legislators, and there is no form of government wherein there is not some admixture, either of elaborate pretence or of untrue opinion,[68] which serves as a curb to hold the common people to their duty. It is for this that the greater number have fabulous origins and beginnings, enriched with supernatural mysteries. It is this which has given credit to bastard religions, and has caused them to find favour with men of intelligence; and it was for this that Numa and Sertorius, to make those of their day firmer of faith, fed them with these absurdities: the first, that his nymph Egeria, the other that his white hind, brought to him from the gods all the counsels that he received.[69] And the authority that Numa ascribed to his laws, under the pretext of the patronage of that goddess, Zoroaster, the legislator of the Bactrians and of the Persians, ascribed to his under the name of the god Oromasis; Trismegistus, of the Egyptians, under that of Mercury; Zamolxis, of the Scythians, under that of Vesta; Charondas, of the Chalcideans, under that of Saturn; Minos, of the Candians, under that of Jupiter; Lycurgus, of the Lacedæmonians, under that of Apollo; Draco and Solon, of the Athenians, under that of Minerva. And every government has a god at its head; falsely all others, truly that which Moses framed for the people of Judea coming forth from Egypt.

The religion of the Bedouins, so the sieur de Joinville says,[70] held, among other things, that the soul of those of them who died for their prince passed into another body, happier, fairer, and stronger than the first; wherefore they risk their lives much more freely.

> The minds of men rush on the steel, and their souls
> are prepared for death; and it is faint-hearted to save
> a life that is to be renewed.[71]

This is a very comfortable belief, however vain it may be. Every nation has several such examples of its own; but this subject would deserve a separate discourse.

To add a few more words on my first theme, neither will I advise the ladies to call their duty honour; *just as in*

*common speech that alone is honourable which is glorious
in vulgar opinion;*[72] their duty is the pith, their honour
is but the rind. Nor do I advise them to give us this excuse for payment of their refusal. For I take it for granted
that their intentions, their desire, and their will, with which
honour has nothing to do, since they do not appear on the
surface, are still better regulated than their deeds.

She sins, who but abstains from fear of sin.[73]

Towards God and the conscience the desire would be as
great an offence as the deed. And, besides, they are actions
which are of themselves hidden and secret; it would be
very easy to keep an action, on which honour depends,
from the knowledge of others, if they had no other consideration for their duty and the affection in which they hold
their chastity for its own sake.

Every woman of honour will choose to lose her honour
rather than her conscience.

Chapter XVII

OF PRESUMPTION

THERE is another sort of glory, which is a too high opinion that we conceive of our worth. It is an ill-advised affection with which we flatter ourselves, which represents us to ourselves other than we are; as amorous passion lends beauties and charms to that which it embraces, and causes those who are possessed by it, their judgement being disturbed and diverted, to deem what they love different from what it is, and more perfect. I would not that a man, for fear of erring in that direction, should depreciate himself, or think that he is less than he is. The judgement ought in all things to maintain its prerogative: it is reasonable that he should see in this matter, as in every other, what the truth presents to him. If he be Cæsar, let him boldly deem himself the greatest captain in the world. We are made up of conventions; convention matters much to us, and we neglect the substance of things; we hold by the branches and forego the trunk and the body. We have taught ladies to blush at the mere mention of what they in no wise fear to do; we dare not call our members by their right name, and do not fear to employ them in every sort of dissoluteness. Convention forbids us to express in words

Of Presumption

lawful and natural things, and we obey; reason forbids us to consider any such things unlawful and evil, and no one obeys. I find myself hindered here by the laws of convention; for it permits one to speak neither well nor ill of oneself. We will set it aside for the moment.

Those whom Fortune (good or ill, as one may call it) has made to pass their lives in some eminent station can by their public actions show what they are. But they whom she has employed only in the mass, and of whom no one will talk if they do not talk of themselves, they are to be excused if they have the boldness to talk of themselves to those whom it concerns to know them, after the example of Lucilius:—

> He used to confide his secrets to his books as to
> faithful comrades, and never had other recourse,
> whether he had been successful or unsuccessful; so it
> is that the life of the old man is wholly seen in his
> writings, as it might be in a votive tablet.[1]

He entrusted to his paper his actions and his thoughts, and depicted himself there as he felt himself to be. *Nor for so doing were Rutilius and Scaurus disbelieved or blamed.*[2]

Let me say, then, that I remember that there was observed in me, in my earliest childhood, I know not what carriage of body and demeanour testifying to an empty and foolish pride. I would say about this, in the first place, that it is not unusual[3] to have conditions and propensities so individual and so embodied in us, that we have no means of perceiving them and of recognising them. And from such innate tendencies the body readily retains some habit without our knowledge and volition. It was an affectation in

Of Presumption

harmony with his beauty which made Alexander incline his head slightly,[4] and which made the speech of Alcibiades a little effeminate and lisping;[5] being endowed with extreme beauty, they assisted themselves a little, unintentionally, by foppery.[6] Julius Cæsar was wont to scratch his head with one finger,[7] which is the action of a man full of serious thoughts; and Cicero, methinks, was accustomed to wrinkle his nose, which indicates a natural scoffer. Such notions may come to us imperceptibly. Others there are, intentional, of which I am not speaking, like salutations and bowings, whereby is acquired, oftenest mistakenly, the reputation of being very humble and courteous; a man may be humble vain-gloriously. I am lavish enough in doffing my hat, especially in summer, and am never so saluted without returning it, whatever the man's rank may be, if he is not in my service. I could wish that some princes whom I know were more sparing and judicious dispensers of this courtesy; for being so indiscreetly lavished, it no longer hits the mark; if it is without consideration, it is without effect. Amongst examples of unmannerly demeanour,[8] let us not forget the arrogance of the Emperor Constantius, who, in public, always looked straight before him, without turning his head or bending to one side or the other, not even to look at those close by who saluted him, keeping his body stiff, motionless, not swaying with the motion of his coach, not daring to spit or blow his nose or wipe his face before the lookers-on.[9]

I do not know if the gestures that were observed in me were of this first sort,[10] and if, in truth, I had some hidden propensity to that vice, as may well be the case; and I can not answer for the movements of the body; but as for the

Of Presumption

movements of the soul, I desire to confess here what I feel
with regard to them.

There are two parts in this sort of vain-glory:[11] namely,
the ranking ourselves too high, and the ranking others not
high enough. As for the first, it seems to me, in the first
place, that these considerations should be taken into account: I find myself weighed upon by a mental error that
offends me both as unreasonable and, yet more, as troublesome. I try to correct it, but uproot it I can not. It is that I
diminish the true value of the things that I possess, because
I possess them;[12] and that I increase the value of things in
proportion as they are foreign to me—absent, and not mine.
This disposition stretches far. As their prerogative of authority causes husbands to regard their own wives with unjustifiable disdain, and many fathers their children, so is
it with me; and between two similar works I should always
incline against my own. It is not so much that desire for
my progress and improvement disturbs my judgement and
prevents me from satisfying myself, as that mastership in
itself engenders contempt of that which one holds and
controls. The governments, the manners, and the languages
of distant lands win my admiration; and I perceive that
Latin cheats me, by favour of its dignity, of more than is
its due, as it does with children and the common people.
The domestic management, the house, the horse, of my
neighbour, of equal value with mine, are better because
they are not mine. Moreover, because I am very ignorant
about what concerns me, I admire the confidence and reli-
ance that another man has in himself, when there is almost
nothing which I am sure I know, or which I dare answer to
myself that I can do. I have not my faculties arranged be-

Of Presumption

forehand and at my service,[13] and I am not aided by them until after the thing is done, being as doubtful of myself as of every thing else. Whence it happens, if I acquit myself laudably in some business, that I ascribe it more to my luck than to my ability; inasmuch as I plan them all at hazard and in doubt. For my part, in general, of all the opinions that antiquity has held of mankind in gross, those that I accept most readily, and most adhere to, are those that most contemn and disesteem us, and make naught of us. Philosophy never seems to me to have such good play as when it combats our presumption and emptiness, when it honestly recognises its own hesitation, its weakness, and its ignorance. It seems to me that the nurse-mother of the falsest opinions, both public and private, is the too good opinion that man has of himself. Those people who perch themselves astride the epicycle of Mercury, who see so far into heaven, make me grind my teeth; for in my studies, the subject of which is man, finding so extreme a variety of judgements, so vast a labyrinth of difficulties, one after another, so much diversity and uncertainty in the very school of knowledge of things divine and human,[14] you can think, since those minds have been unable to arrive at the knowledge of themselves and their own condition, which is constantly present to their eyes; since they know not how that moves which themselves set in motion, or how to describe to us and explain the springs which themselves hold and manage—you can think whether I would believe them about the cause of the movement of the eighth sphere and of the rise and fall of the river Nile. The curiosity to know things has been given to men for a scourge, says Holy Writ.[15]

858

Of Presumption

But, to come to my individual case, it would be very hard, it seems to me, for any other man to value himself less, indeed, for any other to value me less, than I value myself. I consider myself to be of the common sort, save in that I do so consider myself; blameworthy of the meanest and most usual failings, but not unacknowledged, not excused; and I rate myself only at what I know to be my worth. If there be vain-glory, it is infused in me superficially by the treachery of my nature, and has no body which is apparent to the sight of my judgement. I am sprinkled with it, but not dyed.[16] For, in truth, as to the conscious actions of my intelligence, nothing has ever gone from me, in whatever fashion, that filled out my wishes; and the approbation of others does not content me. My taste is sensitive and hard to please, and especially in my own case; I incessantly disavow myself, and I perceive that I waver and yield from weakness. I know myself so well that, if there had gone from me any thing which pleased me, I should owe it, doubtless, to fortune.[17] I have nothing of my own with which to satisfy my judgement. My perception is, for the most part, clear and disciplined; but when I am working, it becomes confused; as I experience most evidently in poetry. I love it exceedingly; my insight is excellent about the works of others; but, in truth, I am like a child when I set my hand to it; I can not endure myself. One can play the fool everywhere else, but not in poetry;

> mediocrity in poets is not permitted by the gods, nor by men, nor by the pillars [on which they hang their verses].[18]

Would to God that this sentence were found on the front

Of Presumption

of the shops of all our printers, to forbid the entry of so
many versifiers:—

> But there is nothing more confident than a bad
> poet.[19]

What numbers have we of the tribe![20] Dionysius the
elder valued nothing in himself so much as his poetry. At
the season of the Olympic games, with chariots surpassing
all others in magnificence, he sent also poets and musicians
to present his verses, with tents and pavilions regally gilded
and hung with tapestry.[21] When his verses were brought
forward, the charm and excellence of the delivery attracted
at the outset the attention of the people; but when, later,
they came to weigh the emptiness of the work, they first
became contemptuous, and, their judgement being constantly embittered, they at last became furious, and ran in
anger to pull down and tear to pieces all his pavilions. And
when also his chariots had no success in the races, and the
ship which carried home his attendants failed to reach Sicily, and was driven before the gale and wrecked on the
coast of Tarentum, they held it for certain that it was the
wrath of the gods, irritated, as themselves were, against
that bad poem. And even the sailors who escaped from the
wreck seconded the opinion of the people. To which the
oracle that predicted his death seems in some degree to sub-
scribe. It declared that Dionysius would be near his end
when he had vanquished those who were worth more than
he; which he interpreted to mean the Carthaginians, who
surpassed him in power.[22] And having to do with them, he
frequently avoided victory and lessened it, in order not to
come within the terms of that prediction. But he ill under-

Of Presumption

stood it: for the god indicated the time of the advantage which, by favour and injustice, he gained at Athens over the tragic poets who were better than he, having caused his own tragedy, entitled "The Leneians,"[23] to be acted in competition; immediately after which time he died, partly from the excessive joy that he took in it.[24]

What I find excusable in my poetry is not in itself and in reality, but in comparison with other worse productions to which I see that approval is given. I envy the good-fortune of those who are able to find delight and gratification in their labour, for it is an easy way of giving oneself pleasure, since it is drawn from oneself; especially if there is a little firmness in their persuasion. I know a poet to whom loudly and feebly, in public and in private,[25] both heaven and earth cry out that he has little understanding of the matter. For all that, he does not at all reduce the measure which he has given to himself—always beginning anew, always reconsidering, and always persisting; all the more unyielding in his opinion and more stiff-necked, that he is alone in maintaining it. My works are so far from being agreeable to me, that, whenever I look them over, I am offended by them;

> When I re-read them, I am ashamed of having written them, for I see many things that I, even their author, judge should be erased.[26]

I have always an idea in my mind and a certain confused image, which puts before me, as in a dream, a better form than that which I have made use of; but I can not grasp it and develop it. And this idea itself is only of mediocre quality. From this I conclude that the productions of those

Of Presumption

great and richly endowed minds of the past are very far beyond the extreme bound of my imagination and desire. Their writings do not merely satisfy me and fill me, but they astound me and ravish me with admiration. I appreciate their beauty; I see it, if not to its full extent, at least so far that it is impossible for me to aspire to it.

Whatever I undertake, I ought to pay a sacrifice to the Graces, as Plutarch says, to gain their favour;[27]

> For, if any thing pleases, if any thing sweetly influences men's senses, all is due to the charming Graces.[28]

They abandon me throughout. It is all clumsiness with me; there is a lack of gracefulness and beauty. I know not how to make things show for all they are worth; my fashioning adds nothing to the subject. That is why my subject must be a forcible one, one which has much to take hold of, and which shines by its own light. When I lay hands on popular and lighter themes, it is to follow my bent,—for I myself do not enjoy a formal and sombre wisdom, as the world does,—and to enliven myself, not to enliven my style, which seeks rather those that are serious and grave (if, at least, I may call that a style which is a formless and irregular utterance, a common way of speaking, running on without definition, without division of parts, without any conclusion, vague, after the manner of that of Amafanius and of Rabirius).[29] I know neither how to please, nor how to entertain, nor how to amuse; the best story in the world becomes dry and dull in my hands. I know not how to talk except in sober earnest, and I am altogether without that facility, which I observe in many of my companions, for

862

Of Presumption

conversing with the first-comer and keeping a whole company listening; or for unweariedly amusing the ear of a prince with all sorts of sayings, never lacking matter, by reason of their gift of knowing how to make use of the first subject that comes to hand, and to adapt it to the humour and capacity of those with whom they have to do. Princes do not much enjoy solid talk, nor I, story-telling. What I have to say, I say always with all my strength.[30] The first and simplest arguments, which are commonly the best received, I know not how to make use of; I am a poor preacher of commonplaces. On all matters I say freely the most important things that I know about them. Cicero thinks that in philosophical treatises the most difficult part is the exordium.[31] If it be so, I am wise in undertaking the conclusion.[32]

But we must tune the string to every degree of tone, and the highest is that which comes least often into play. There is at least as much accomplished in lifting high an empty thing as in holding up a heavy one. Sometimes we must handle things superficially, sometimes we must go deep into them. I know well that the greater number of men remain· at a low level, from not conceiving things except on the surface; but I know also that the greatest masters and Xenophon and Plato are often seen, when occasion offers, to let themselves go to this low and common manner of speaking and treating of things, and elevating it by the graces that never fail them.

For the rest, my language has nothing of facility and polish; it is harsh and careless,[33] of free and irregular arrangement; and it pleases me so—if not my judgement, my liking. But I well know that sometimes I let myself go too

far in this, and by dint of trying to avoid art and affectation
I fall into them on another side;

> I strive to be brief, and become obscure.[34]

Plato says that diffuseness and brevity are not properties
which either take away or give value to language.[35]

If I should undertake to follow that other even, smooth,
and regular style, I could not attain it; and although the
breaks and cadences of Sallust are more in accord with my
nature, yet I find Cæsar greater, and also less easy to copy;
and if my bent leads me more to imitation of the style of
Seneca, I do not fail to rate more highly that of Plutarch.
As in deeds,[36] so in words, I follow quite simply my natural
way; whence it is, perhaps, that I am more effective in
talking than in writing. But it may be, also, that gesture
and action give life to words, especially in those persons
who bestir themselves briskly[37] as I do, and grow hot. The
bearing, the face, the voice, the dress, the place, may give
some value to things which in themselves have little, like
idle chatter. Messala, in Tacitus, complains of certain tight
habiliments of his day, and of the arrangement of the
benches where the orators spoke, which enfeebled their
eloquence.[38]

My French tongue is injured, both in pronunciation and
otherwise, by the barbarous speech of my native place; I
have never seen a man of those regions[39] whose speech did
not smack of his native soil,[40] and offend ears purely French.
Yet this does not mean that I am much versed in my Peri-
gordin, for I make no more use of it than of German; and I
take no thought of it. It is an effeminate, languid, feeble
language, like those around me, of one province and an-

864

other—of Poitou, Saintonge, Angoumois, Limousin, and Auvergne. There is, indeed, above us, toward the mountains, a Gascon speech that I find singularly fine, concise, significant, and in truth a more manly and soldier-like tongue than any other that I hear; as vigorous, forcible, and pithy as the French is graceful, refined, and copious. As for the Latin, which was given me as my mother tongue, I have lost by disuse readiness in being able to use it in speaking, yes, and in writing, in which I was formerly called a master. It may be seen how little I am worth in that direction.

Beauty is a thing of great estimation in the intercourse of men; it is the first means of winning good-will among them, and no man is so uncivilised and surly that he may not feel in some degree impressed by its charm. The body has a large part in our existence; it holds a high place there; thus its structure and composition are most worthy of consideration. They who would disunite our two principal parts, and isolate them from one another, are mistaken. On the contrary, we must recouple them and rejoin them. We must bid the soul not to draw aside and maintain herself apart, not to despise and desert the body (indeed, she could not so do save by some false pretence[41]), but to connect herself with it, embrace it, cherish it, help it, guide it, counsel it, correct it, and bring it back when it goes astray—in short, marry it, and assist it as if it were her husband; so that their doings may not seem diverse and opposed, but in accord and uniform. Christians have a special indication of this bond; for they know that the divine justice includes this companionship and union of the body and the soul, to the point of making the body capable of eternal rewards; and

865

that God considers the entire man as acting, and wills that, as a whole, he receive chastisement or praise, according to his deserts.

The Peripatetic school, of all schools the best adapted to human life, considers as an attribute of wisdom[42] this sole care to provide for and procure the common welfare of these two associated parts; and shows that the other schools, by not having paid sufficient heed to the consideration of this conjunction, have taken sides, by a similar error, this one for the body, that one for the soul, and have wandered from their subject, which is man, and their guide, which they declare to be, in general, nature.

It is very probable that superiority of beauty was the first cause of difference among men, and the first consideration that gave the preeminence to some over others.

They divided the fields and gave to each man in proportion to his personal beauty and strength and intellect; for beauty and vigorous strength were much esteemed.[43]

Now I am of a stature a little below the medium. This defect is not only uncomely, but disadvantageous, especially for those who hold high commands and offices; for the authority which is given by a fine presence and bodily majesty is lacking to them. Caius Marius did not willingly accept soldiers who were less than six feet in height.[44] The Courtier[45] is quite right to desire for the gentlemen whom he is educating a usual stature rather than any other, and to object to any peculiarity that attracts attention.[46] But as for choosing, if it is necessary that the height should be rather below than above mediocrity, I would not so do[47] for

Of Presumption

a soldier. Small men, Aristotle says, are very pretty, but not beautiful; and as in a lofty bearing the great soul is recognised, so is beauty in a large and tall body.[48] The Ethiopians and Indians, he says, in choosing their kings and magistrates, had regard to the beauty and height of their person.[49] They were right; for to see a leader of fine and ample stature marching at the head of his troops excites respect in those who follow him, and dread in the enemy.

> Turnus himself, distinguished in appearance, a whole head taller than the rest, marches among the foremost, his arms in his hands.[50]

Our great king, divine and celestial, all of whose conditions should be observed with care, piety, and reverence, did not reject the bodily commendation, *fairer than the sons of men*.[51] And Plato, together with gravity and stoutness of heart, desires beauty for the rulers of his republic.[52]

It is a great annoyance if one speaks to you, amidst your servants, and asks, "Where is your master?" and if you receive only the fag-end of a salutation which is given to your barber or your secretary. As happened to poor Phocion (I can easily make mistakes in the names, but not in the substance).[53] He having arrived before his followers at a lodging where he was expected, his hostess, who did not know him and saw him to be of poor enough appearance, made use of him to help her women draw water, or make a fire, in preparation for Philopœmen. The gentlemen of his suite, having arrived and surprised him busied with this fine occupation (for he had not failed to obey the orders given him), asked him what he was doing. "I am paying the penalty of my ugliness," he answered.[54] Other beauties

867

are for women; beauty of stature is the sole beauty of men. When the figure is small, neither the height *and smoothness*[55] of the brow, nor the clearness *and softness* of the eyes, nor a reasonably well-shaped nose, nor smallness of the ear and mouth, nor regularity and whiteness of the teeth, nor the even closeness of a brown beard, *nor thick hair,*[56] nor a well-shaped head, too large rather than too small, nor a fresh complexion, nor a pleasant expression of the face, *nor an odorless body,*[57] nor the good proportions of the limbs, can make a handsome man.

As for me, my person is strong and thick-set; my face not fat, yet full; my temperament between jovial and melancholy, moderately sanguine and hot,

> And my legs and chest are hairy;[58]

my health was strong and vigorous, seldom impaired by sickness, until late in life, although I made very free use of it.[59] Such I was; for I am not considering myself at the present time, when I have entered into the avenues of old age, being long since past forty;

> Little by little age breaks our powers and our matured strength, and wastes away in decay.[60]

What I shall be henceforth will be only a half existence; it will no longer be myself. Daily I slip away from myself and purloin myself from myself;

> The fleeting years steal from us one thing after another.[61]

Of readiness and activity I have had none; and yet I am the son of a very active father,[62] of an agility that lasted to his extreme old age. There was scarcely to be found a man of his position who equalled him in all bodily exercises; as I have found scarcely any who did not surpass me in them, save in running, at which I was among the moderately good. Of music they have never been able to teach me any thing, either for my voice, which is very unapt, or for instruments. In dancing, in tennis, in wrestling, I have never been able to acquire more than a very slight and ordinary skill; in swimming, in fencing, in vaulting and leaping, none at all. As for my hands, they are so stiff that I can not write, even to be read by myself; so that what I have scribbled, I like better to rewrite than to take the trouble to decipher it. And I read little better; I feel that I weary my hearers. Otherwise, a fair scholar. I can not fold a letter properly,[63] and I never knew how to make a pen, or to carve well at table, or to put on a horse's trappings, or to carry a hawk properly and cast her off, or to train dogs, birds, or horses.

My bodily faculties, in short, are very accordant with those of my soul. There is nothing agile about them; there is only a full and solid vigour. I endure labour very well; but I endure it if I go about it voluntarily, and so far as my appetite leads me to it,—

Eagerness deceptively lightening the severe task.[64]

Otherwise, if I am not allured to it by some enjoyment, and if I have any other guide than my pure free will, I am worth nothing for it. For I have reached the point where, save health and life, there is nothing which I care to purchase at the price of torment of mind, and of constraint,—

Not for me, at such a price, all the sand of the dark Tagus, and all the gold that is in the sea,[65]—

Of Presumption

being extremely idle, extremely free from ties, both by nature and by intention. I would give my blood as readily as my pains.[66]

I have a soul that belongs wholly to herself, accustomed to conduct herself in her own fashion. Having never to this hour had any commanding or enforced master, I have walked as far and at such a pace as pleased me. This has softened me and made me unfit for the service of others, and has made me of use only to myself; and for me there has been no need to put force upon my heavy, indolent, and do-nothing nature. For, finding myself from my birth in such a degree of fortune that I have had reason to stay there, and with such a degree of intelligence as I have felt that I had occasion for, I have sought nothing and have taken nothing.[67]

> My sails are not swollen by the favouring north wind, but my course is not subject to the hostile south wind; in strength, in intelligence, in appearance, in excellence, in position, in fortune, if I am among the last of those of the first rank, I am among the first of those of the last rank.[68]

I have had need, for content, only of a sufficiency; that is, however, when properly understood, a regulation of the mind equally difficult in every sort of condition, and which by experience we see to be found more easily even in want than in abundance, because, perchance, like the course of our other passions, the appetite for riches is more sharpened by their use than by their lack, and the virtue of moderation is more rare than that of long-suffering; and I have needed only to enjoy quietly the goods that God, through his liberality, has placed in my hands. I have had no experience

Of Presumption

of any sort of tedious toil. I have had scarcely any affairs to manage except my own; or, if I have had such, it has been on the condition of managing them at my own time, and in my own way, they being entrusted to me by people who had confidence in me, and who did not importune me and who knew me. For experienced riders obtain some service, even from a stumbling and broken-winded horse. My childhood even was led in a mild, free fashion, and I was exempt from rigorous subjection. All this has endowed me with a sensitive temperament, incapable of caretaking; to such a degree that I like better to have my losses and the irregularities that concern me concealed from me; I set to the account of my expenses what it costs me to support and maintain my negligence.[69]

These are superfluities that are unknown to the master, and that are of profit to thieves.[70]

I like not to know the tale of what I possess, that I may feel a loss less distinctly. I beg those who live with me, when they lack affection and kind deeds, to cheat me, and pay me with pleasant manners. For want of enough firmness to endure the annoyance of the adverse chances to which we are subject, and from not being able to keep myself bent on regulating and ordering my affairs, I foster in myself, as much as I can, this way of thinking, abandoning myself entirely to fortune, to look on the worst side of every thing, and to resolve to endure that worst quietly and patiently. It is for this alone that I labour, and this is the aim to which I direct all my considerations.

About any danger, I do not so much meditate how I shall escape it, as how little it matters whether I escape it. If I

Of Presumption

should come to my end there,[71] what would it amount to? Being unable to regulate events, I regulate myself, and adapt myself to them if they do not adapt themselves to me. I have but little skill in the matter of avoiding Fortune, and escaping from her or overcoming her, and in prudently arranging and conducting affairs to suit me. I have even less endurance in maintaining the keen and painful vigilance that is necessary therefor. And the most painful position for me is to be in suspense about things that are urgent, and agitated between fear and hope. Deliberation, indeed, even in the most trivial things, importunes me; and I feel my mind more pestered in suffering the actions and diverse shocks of doubt and consultation than, after the die is cast, in settling down and resolving upon some course, whatever it may be. Few passions have ever disturbed my sleep, but the least deliberation troubles me. As with roads I by preference avoid steep and slippery hillsides, and take the most muddy and miry beaten path, whence I can not go lower, and there seek safety, so also I like misfortunes unalloyed, which do not work on me and harass me the more from the uncertainty of their being repaired, and which, at the first push, plunge me straightway into suffering:

uncertain evils torture us most.[72]

When the thing happens, I bear myself like a man; while it is approaching, like a child. Dread of the fall depresses me more than the fall itself. It costs more than it is worth. The miser is worse off with his passion than the poor man, and the jealous husband than the cuckold; and often there is less harm in losing one's vineyard than in going to law for it. The lowest step is the most stable; it is the seat of un-

872

Of Presumption

removableness;[73] you have need there only of yourself. It has its own foundation, and leans wholly on itself. Is there not something philosophical in the attitude of a certain gentleman who was well-known? He married when he was well on in years, having spent his youth in convivial company; moreover, great at telling merry tales. Remembering how often he had had occasion to laugh at others who 'wore the horns', he resolved to be safe and under cover, and married a woman whom he picked up in a place where any man could have what he needed for his money, and made a match of it with her. 'How d'ye do, Mistress Whore?'—'How d'ye do, Master Cuckold?' And he was always ready to talk openly about his venture to anybody who came to see him, and so took the wind out of the sails of any would-be scandal-monger or tale-bearer, and the point off their sting.

As to ambition, which is a near neighbour of presumption, or, rather, the daughter, it would have been necessary for my advancement that Fortune should have come and taken me by the hand. Since, to give myself trouble for an uncertain hope, and to subject myself to all the difficulties that wait upon those who try to force themselves into favour at the start of their career—I could not have done it:

I do not buy hope with gold.[74]

I cling to what I see and what I have hold of, and go not far from port;

One oar sweeps through the waves, the other over the sands.[75]

And then one seldom attains these advantages except by

Of Presumption

previously risking what belongs to him; and I am of opinion that, if what one has is sufficient to maintain the condition in which one has been born and brought up, it is folly to let go what is in one's hand, on the uncertainty of increasing it. He to whom Fortune denies a place whereon to set his foot and to establish a tranquil and settled existence is to be forgiven if he ventures what he has, since, in any case, the necessity sends him questing.

> In evil circumstances a dangerous course must be taken.[76]

And I more readily excuse a younger brother for casting his inheritance to the winds than him who has the honour of the family in his keeping, and who can not be in want but by his own fault. I found it, with the counsel of my good friends of past days, a shorter and easier road, to rid myself of such desires, and to keep quiet,—

> Whose agreeable lot it is to receive the palm [of victory] without the dust [of the course],[77]—

judging, too, very truly of my powers, that they were not capable of great things, and recalling that saying of the late Chancellor Olivier, that the French seem like monkeys, who clamber up a tree, from branch to branch, and stay not until they have reached their highest branch, and, when there, show their hinder parts.

> It is shameful to put on one's head a burden it can not carry, when soon, with bent knees, the back gives way.[78]

Even the qualities which are not reprehensible in me, I

874

should have found useless in these days. The pliableness of my character[79] would have been called cowardice and weakness; my loyalty and conscientiousness would have been deemed over-scrupulous and superstitious; my frankness and independence, troublesome, ill considered, and rash. Misfortune is of some use. It is well to be born in a very depraved age; for, in comparison with others, you are reckoned virtuous at small cost. He who, in our days, is merely a parricide and sacrilegious is withal a worthy and honourable man.

> Now, if your friend does not deny the deposit, and returns the old purse, with all the rusty money, it is a prodigious probity, worthy of record in the Tuscan annals, and of the sacrifice of a crowned lamb to the gods.[80]

And never was there a time or place in which, to princes, there was offered more certain and greater reward for goodness and justice. The first who shall consider making his way into favour and influence by this path, I am very much mistaken if he does not honourably outstrip his fellows. Power, violence, can do something, but not always everything. Merchants, village judges, artisans—we see that they are on a par in valour and military ability with the gentry; they conduct themselves honourably, both in public and private combats; they fight, they defend cities in our present wars. A prince finds his fame obscured[81] in such a crowd. Let him shine with humanity, truth, loyalty, temperance, and, above all, with justice: traits rare, unknown, and banished. It is solely by the will of the people that he can succeed, and no other quality can so invite their good-

Of Presumption

will as these, being the most useful to them. *Nothing is so popular as goodness.*[82]

By such a standard I should have seemed to be a great and rare man; whereas I seem puny and ordinary by the standard of some bygone ages, when it was a common thing, even if other stronger qualities did not concur, to see a man moderate in his vengeance, mild in resentment for injuries, religious in the observance of his word, neither two-faced, nor pliable, nor accommodating his faith to the will of others and to circumstances. I would rather let things go to destruction[83] than pervert my faithfulness in their service. For as to this new virtue of hypocrisy and dissimulation, which at this moment is so greatly in favour, I hate it mortally; and of all the vices I find no other that testifies to so much cowardice and baseness of heart. It is a dastardly and servile humour for a man to disguise and conceal himself behind a mask, and not to dare show himself as he is, and not to dare to show his face in public.[84] Thus our men train themselves to perfidy: being accustomed to utter false words, they do not scruple to break them. A generous heart should not belie its thoughts; it desires that there should be seen even what is within just as it is; for there is nothing that is not worthy to be seen.[85] Every thing there is good, or, at least, every thing there is human.

Aristotle considers it the special office of high-mindedness to hate and to love openly, to judge, to speak with entire freedom, and, in comparison with truth, to pay no attention to the approbation or reprobation of others.[86] Apollonius said that it was for slaves to lie and for free men to speak the truth.[87] It is the principal and fundamental part of virtue. It must be loved for itself. He who speaks the truth

876

Of Presumption

because he is elsewise so compelled, and because it is useful, and who does not fear to tell a lie when it matters to no one—he is not sufficiently truthful. My soul, by its nature, shuns falsehood and hates even to think a falsehood. I feel inward shame and sharp remorse if sometimes it escapes me—as sometimes it does, unlooked-for circumstances surprising and moving me. Every thing must not always be said, for that would be folly; but what one says should be what one thinks; otherwise it is knavery. I know not what advantage they expect from incessantly feigning and dissembling unless it be not to be believed even when they speak the truth; it may deceive men once or twice; but to make open profession of concealing one's thoughts, and to boast, as some of our princes have done,[88] that they would throw their shirt into the fire if it were privy to their real intentions (which is a saying of old Metellus Macedonicus),[89] and that he who does not know how to dissemble does not know how to reign, is to give warning to those who have to do with them that what they say is all trickery and falsehood. *The more subtle and astute a man is, the more he is hated and suspected if his reputation for integrity be lost.*[90] It would be great ignorance in one who should allow himself to be misled, either by the face or by the words of him who makes it his business to be always other outside than he is within, as Tiberius did;[91] and I know not what part such persons can have in human intercourse, producing nothing which can be received for current coin. He who is faithless to the truth is so to falsehood also.

Those who, in our day, have considered, in settling the duty of a prince, what is well for his affairs alone, and have placed this before regard for his faith and conscience,[92]

Of Presumption

would mean something to a prince whose affairs fortune had arranged in such a manner that he could settle them for all time by a single failure to keep his word. But it does not happen thus. He often falls again into a similar bargain; he makes more than one peace, more than one treaty, in his life. The profit which tempts them to the first disloyalty (and almost always it appears in the same guise as all other villainies: sacrileges, murders, rebellions, treasons, are undertaken for some kind of benefit), that first profit brings about endless harmful consequences, throwing that prince outside all intercourse and every means of negotiation, by this example of infidelity.

Solyman of the Ottoman race,—a race little heedful of the observance of promises and pacts,—when, in my childhood, he went down to Otranto, having learned that Mercurin de Gratinare and the inhabitants of Castro were held captive after having surrendered the place, contrary to the terms of the capitulation arranged with them, sent word that they should be released and that, as he had in hand other great undertakings in that land, such disloyalty, although it might appear to be of immediate use, would bring upon him in the future an infinitely prejudicial discredit and distrust.[93]

Now, for myself, I prefer to be annoying and indiscreet, rather than flattering and dissembling. I acknowledge that there may be some touch of pride and selfwill in holding oneself so without reserve and candid as I do, without consideration of others; and it seems to me that I become a little more outspoken where I should be less so, and that I wax the hotter in upholding my opinion, the more respect I owe to the person I am talking with.[94] It may be, too, that

878

Of Presumption

I let myself go in accordance with my nature, for lack of skill. Employing with those of high rank the same freedom of language and of bearing that I use in my own house, I feel how it inclines toward indiscretion and incivility. But, besides that I am so made, my mind is not quick enough to evade a sudden claim upon it and to escape by some shift, or to forge a truth;[95] nor is my memory good enough to remember it when thus forged; nor, it is certain, have I assurance enough to uphold it; and I play the braggart from lack of ability. Therefore I abandon myself, both by temperament and by intention, to what is natural to me and to saying always what I think, leaving it to fortune to guide the event. Aristippus said that the chief advantage he had derived from philosophy was that he spoke freely and openly to every one.[96]

The memory is an instrument of wonderful service, and one without which the judgement can hardly perform its office; I altogether lack it.[97] Whatever any one desires to put before me, it must be little by little. For to reply to a discourse in which there are several different heads is not in my power. I could not receive a commission without writing-tablets. And when I have a discourse of importance to make, if it be long, I am reduced to the mean and miserable necessity of learning by heart, word for word, what I have to say; otherwise, I should have neither method nor confidence, being in fear that my memory would play me a bad trick. But this way is no less difficult for me. To learn three lines takes me three hours; and then, in a composition of my own, the liberty and authority to shift the order, to change a word, constantly varying the substance, makes it more difficult to keep in mind. Now, the more I challenge her,[98] the more confused she becomes; she serves me better unexpectedly; I must needs solicit her carelessly, for, if I press her, she is abashed; and when she has begun to stammer, the more I sound her, the more entangled and embarrassed she becomes; she serves me at her own hour, not at mine. This which I am conscious of about memory I am conscious of in many other directions. I shun all command, obligation, and constraint. That which I do easily and naturally, I can no longer do if I order myself to do it by an express and definite order.

Even in my body, the organs which have some freedom and a more special jurisdiction over themselves sometimes refuse to obey me, when I assign and bind them to a fixed point at a fixed hour of necessary service. This constraint and tyrannical foreordaining offends them; they stand still in fright or spite, and stiffen themselves.

In former days, being in a place where it is considered a barbarous discourtesy not to respond to those who invite you to drink, although I was treated there with entire freedom, I tried, in honour of the ladies who were of the party, to play the good fellow according to the custom of the country. But it was matter for mirth; for this being threatened, and prepared to have to force myself contrary to my custom and my inclination, so choked my throat that I could not swallow a single drop, and was deprived of drink, even to the amount necessary for my repast. I found myself satiated and my thirst quenched by all the drinking that my imagination had done in anticipation. This effect is most manifest in those whose imagination is most vigorous and powerful; but it is, however, natural, and there is no one who does not feel it in some degree. An excellent archer,

Of Presumption

condemned to death, was offered his life if he would give a noteworthy proof of his skill; he refused to try to do this, fearing that the too great eagerness of his desire would cause his hand to swerve, and that, instead of saving his life, he would lose also the reputation he had won as a marksman. A man whose thoughts are elsewhere will not fail to take, again and again, the same number and length of steps, almost to an inch, in the place where he is walking; but if he sets himself to measure and count them attentively, he will find that what he did by nature and by chance, he will not do so accurately by design.

My bookroom, which is one of the finest of those not in a city,[99] is situated in a corner of my house; if there comes into my mind something which I wish to go there to find or to write, for fear that, while merely crossing my court yard, it may escape me, I must entrust it to some one else. If I venture, in talking, to turn aside ever so little from my path, I never fail to lose it; which causes me to keep myself, in my talk, restrained, dry, and terse. I am obliged to call the people in my service by the names of their offices or their provinces, for it is very difficult[100] for me to remember a name. I can tell, to be sure, that it has three syllables, that it is harsh-sounding, that it begins or ends with a certain letter. And if my life should last long, I believe that I should not fail to remember my own name, as others have done. Messala Corvinus was for two years without any trace of memory,[101] which is told also of George of Trebizond; and as something that concerns me, I often meditate upon what sort of life theirs was, and whether, without that faculty, I shall have enough left to support me with some comfort; and looking at it closely, I am afraid that that failing, if it be complete, destroys all the activities of the soul. *Certainly memory is the receptacle, not only of philosophy, but especially of all that appertains to the use of life and of all arts.*[102]

I am full of cracks; I leak on every side.[103]

It has happened to me more than once to forget the password which, three hours before, I had given to or received from another; and to forget where I had hidden my purse, whatever Cicero may say.[104] I help myself to lose what I put away with special care.

The memory is the receptacle and envelope of learning; mine being so defective, I have not much right to complain if I know little. I know, in general, the names of the arts and what they treat of, but nothing beyond that. I turn the leaves of books, I do not study them; what I retain of them is something which I do not recognise as coming from another: it is that alone by which my judgements have profited, the reasonings and the imaginations with which it is imbued; the author, the place, the words, and other facts—these I straightway forget. And I am so excellent in forgetfulness that even my own writings and compositions I forget no less than the rest. People frequently quote me to myself without my perceiving it. Whoever might desire to know whence come the verses and examples which I have here piled up would put me in a quandary to tell him; and yet I have craved alms only at well-known and famous doors, not contenting myself with their being rich, if they did not also come from a rich and honourable hand; authority concurs in them with reason. It is no great wonder if my own book has the fate of other books, and if my

Of Presumption

memory loses hold of what I write as of what I read, and of what I give as of what I receive.

In addition to my lack of memory, I have other lacks which greatly contribute to my ignorance. My mind is lazy and not keen; it can not pierce the least cloud,[105] so that, for example, I never proposed to it any riddle easy enough for it to solve. There is no subtlety so foolish that does not embarrass me. In games in which the mind has its share,— chess, cards, draughts, and the like,—I understand only the plainest processes. My apprehension is slow and confused; but what it once grasps, it grasps well, and embraces it very completely, tightly, and profoundly, so long as it grasps it. My sight is long, sound, and perfect, but is easily tired by work and becomes dim; for this reason I can not have long-continued intercourse with books, save by means of another's service. The younger Pliny[106] will inform those who have not tried it how much this hindrance matters to those who devote themselves to this occupation.

There is no soul so needy[107] and so brutish wherein some special faculty may not be seen to shine; there is none so buried that it does not jut out at some point. And how it happens that a soul that is blind and slumbering about all other things is quick and clear-sighted and excelling in a certain special matter, we must enquire of our masters. But the noble souls are the souls of universal powers, open, and thoroughly prepared; instructible at least, if not instructed; which I say, impeaching my own; for, whether from weakness or from indifference (and to be indifferent to what lies at our feet, to what we hold in our hands, which concerns most nearly the habits of life, is far removed from my doctrine),[108] there is none so inept as mine, or so ignorant of

883

many common things of which a man can not without shame be ignorant. I must tell some examples of this.

I was born and brought up in the country, and among husbandmen; I have had business affairs and household matters in my hands since my predecessors in the possession of the property that I enjoy yielded up their place to me. Now I know not how to reckon, either with counters or with the pen; I am not familiar with most of our coins; nor do I know the difference between one kind of grain and another, either in the field or in the granary, unless it is too apparent; nor scarcely that between the cabbages and lettuce of my garden. I do not even know the names of the commonest household utensils, or the most elementary principles of agriculture, which children know; still less of the mechanical arts, about traffic in and knowledge of merchandise, the diversity and nature of fruits, wines, food; nor how to train a bird, or doctor a horse or a dog. And, since I must needs make a clean breast of my shame, it is not a month since I was found ignorant of how leaven is of use in making bread, and the object of putting wine in vats. Anciently, at Athens,[109] an aptitude for mathematics was conjectured in him who was seen ingeniously arranging and binding a bundle of sticks. Truly, one would draw a very opposite conclusion about me; for, give me all the apparatus of a kitchen, I should none the less starve; and I greatly doubt, even if I had a horse and his trappings, whether I should have the intelligence to train him to be of service to me.[110]

From these articles of my confession, others can be imagined at my expense. But, howsoever I make myself known, provided that I make myself known for what I am, I effect my purpose. And therefore I do not apologise

Of Presumption

for venturing to put in writing matters so mean and trivial as these. The meanness of the subject compels me to do it. My project may be blamed, but my treatment of it, no. However that may be, I see plainly enough, without being warned by others, how little value and weight all this has, and the inadvisedness of my design. It is enough that my judgement is not confused, which is here put to proof.

> Let your nose be as keen as you will; be all nose,
> even one that Atlas, being asked, will refuse to bear,
> and deride Latinus himself—you can not speak worse
> of my trifles than I myself have spoken. What pleas-
> ure is there in grinding tooth against tooth? You must
> have food if you would satisfy your hunger. Do not
> waste your labour; on those who admire themselves
> use your venom; I know these things of mine to be
> nothing.[111]

I am under no obligation not to say foolish things, provided that I am not deceived, and recognise them as such. And to fall short consciously is so common with me that I seldom fall short otherwise: I scarcely ever fall short by accident. It is a small matter to make the indiscretion of my disposition responsible for foolish acts, since I can not help ordinarily making it responsible for vicious ones.

I saw one day, at Bar-le-Duc,[112] presented to King Francis II, as a tribute to the memory of King René of Sicily, a portrait that he himself had painted of himself. Why is it not permissible, in like manner, for every man to draw himself with the pen as he drew himself with a pencil? Therefore I do not wish to forget this other blemish, which it is very undesirable to set forth publicly: that is, irreso-

Of Presumption

lution, a very inconvenient defect in the management of the affairs of the world. I know not which side to take in doubtful undertakings,—

Neither yes nor no sounds clearly in my heart.[113]

I know well how to maintain an opinion, but not how to choose it.

Because, in human affairs, to whatever faction one inclines, many aspects present themselves to confirm us in it (and the philosopher Chrysippus said that he desired to learn from Zeno and Cleanthes simply dogmas; for, as for proofs and arguments, he could supply enough of those for himself[114]), to whichever side I turn, I always furnish myself with enough ground and probability to maintain myself in it. Thus I retain within myself doubt and freedom of choice, until I am forced by circumstances. And then, to confess the truth, I generally throw the feather to the wind, as the saying is, and abandon myself to the mercy of fortune; a very slight preference and circumstance wins me over.

When the mind is in doubt, a slight impulse impels it hither and thither.[115]

The uncertainty of my judgement is so evenly balanced in most occurrences that I would readily commit myself to the decision of fate and the dice; and I observe, after giving much thought to our human weakness, the examples that divine history itself has left us of this custom of remitting to fortune and to chance the determination of selection in doubtful matters; *the lot fell upon Mathias*.[116] The human reason is a two-edged and dangerous sword. And even in the hand of Socrates, its closest and most familiar friend, see what a many-ended staff it is!

Thus I am fitted only for following, and I readily allow myself to be carried along by the crowd; I do not enough trust my abilities to undertake to command or to guide; I am very glad to find my steps marked out by others. If the risk of a doubtful choice must be incurred, I prefer that it should be under one who is more certain of his opinions, and more wedded to them than I am to mine, of which I find the substructure and foundation to be unsure. And yet I do not too easily change, inasmuch as I detect a similar weakness in the contrary opinions. *The habit of assenting seems to be dangerous and slippery.*[117] Especially in political affairs there is a fine field open for movement and contestation;

> As when a just balance is pressed upon with equal weights, its scales neither fall on this side nor rise on that.[118]

The reasonings of Machiavelli, for example, were sufficiently solid as to the subject-matter, yet it is very easy to combat them; and they who have done so have left no less facility for combatting theirs. There would always be found in such an argument material for replies, rejoinders, replications, surrejoinders, sur-surrejoinders, and that endless chain of discussions which our chicanery drags out as much as possible in favour of lawsuits,—

> We are struck, and we overwhelm our enemy with as many blows,[119]—

the reasons given having little other foundation than ex-

Of Presumption

perience; and the diversity of human events furnishes us with innumerable examples in every variety of form.

A wise person of our day says that in our almanacs, where they say hot if one should choose to say cold, and damp in lieu of dry, and always set down the contrary of what they predict, were he to wager as to the happening of one or the other, he would not care which side he took, except in matters where no uncertainty can exist, as to promise extreme heat at Christmas and the severities of winter at midsummer. I think the same of these political reasonings: whatever part you assume, you can make as good play as your fellow, provided that you do not run counter to fundamental principles that are recognised and evident.[120] And therefore, to my thinking, there is in public affairs no condition, even a bad one, provided that it is of long standing and persistent, which is not to be preferred to change and commotion. Our morals are exceedingly corrupt, and have a wonderful tendency to grow worse. Of our laws and customs there are many that are barbarous and monstrous; however, because of the difficulty of bringing ourselves into a better condition, and the danger of shaking the structure, if I could put a spoke in our wheel and stop it at this point, I would do so with a good will.

> The examples we make use of are never so foul and so shameful that there are not others that go beyond them.[121]

The worst thing that I find about our state is its instability, and that our laws, no more than our garments, can take permanent form. It is very easy to accuse a government of imperfection, for all mortal things are full of that; it is very

888

Of Presumption

easy to engender in a people contempt for its ancient observ-
ances; no man ever undertakes that, who does not succeed;
but to establish a better state in the place of that which they
have destroyed—in this, many who have undertaken it
have laboured in vain.

I give little heed to circumspection in my conduct; I
readily let myself be guided by the public order of the world.
Happy the people who do what they are commanded better
than they who command, without troubling themselves
about the reasons; who let themselves gently revolve with
the heavenly revolving! Obedience is never pure or un-
troubled in him who reasons and who argues.

In fine, to return to myself, the only thing in which I
deem myself of some account is that in which no man ever
deems himself lacking; what is commendable in me is common, general, and of small account; for who ever thought
that he had not good sense? That would be a proposition
which would in itself imply a contradiction; it is a disease
that never exists when it is seen; it is very tenacious and
powerful, but nevertheless is penetrated and dispersed by
the first ray of the patient's vision, as a dense mist by the
sun's beams. To accuse oneself in this respect would be to
excuse oneself; and to condemn oneself would be to absolve
oneself. There never was a porter or a foolish woman who
was not sure of being sufficiently supplied with good sense.
We easily recognise in others superiority of courage, of bodily
strength, of experience, of activity, of beauty, of rank;
but superiority of judgement we concede to no one; and the
reasonings that proceed from simple natural intelligence in
another, it seems to us that, had we but looked in that direction, we should have found them. The learning, the style,

and such other qualities as we see in works unlike our own,[122] we readily recognise as surpassing our own; but as to the simple products of the understanding, every one thinks that it was in him to meet with the like; and he hardly perceives the effort and difficulty of so doing, unless they be at an extreme and incomparable distance, and scarcely then.[123] Thus it[124] is a sort of exercitation for which very little commendation and praise can be hoped, and a kind of composition of little repute.

And then, too, for whom do you write? The scholars, to whom jurisdiction in bookish matters belongs, recognise no other value than that of learning, and approve no other course in our minds than that of erudition and skill; if you have mistaken one of the Scipios for the other, what have you left to say that is of any value? He who knows nothing of Aristotle, at the same time, according to them, knows nothing of himself. Common and uncultured souls do not see the charm and weight of a lofty and refined discourse. Now these two kinds[125] fill the world. The third kind,— into whose hands your work falls,[126]—of souls well governed and strong in themselves, is so rare that it has consequently neither name nor rank amongst us; it is time half lost to aspire and strive to please it.

It is commonly said that the fairest division of her favours that Nature has made amongst us is that of good sense; for there is no one who is not content with what she has bestowed on him. Is not that natural? He who should see further would see beyond his sight. I think my opinions to be good and sound; but who does not think the same of his? One of the strongest proofs that I have of this is the small value I set upon myself; for if they[127] had not been

Of Presumption

very stable, they would easily have let themselves be cheated by the peculiar affection I bear myself, as one who gathers it all, as it were, unto myself and who scatters it little outside. All that which others distribute among an infinite multitude of friends and acquaintances, to their glory and their greatness, I devote entirely to my health, to my repose of mind, and to myself in general. What of it escapes me elsewhere is not really under the direction of my reason,—

> trained, indeed, to consider myself and live for myself.[128]

Now I find my opinions infinitely bold and unyielding in condemning my own insufficiency. In truth, this also is a subject on which I exercise my judgement as much as on any other. The world looks always outward; for my part, I turn my sight within myself, I fix it and employ it there. Every one looks before himself; I look within myself; I have to do only with myself; I scrutinise myself incessantly; I criticise myself, I taste myself. Others are always going elsewhere if they will but think of it; they are always going forward,—

> no man attempts to enter into himself,—[129]

but as for me, I revolve within myself.

This faculty of culling out the truth, as it exists within myself, and this free propensity not easily to fetter my beliefs, I owe chiefly to myself; for the most stable and general ideas that I have are those which were, so to speak, born with me. They are natural, and wholly my own. I produced them crude and simple, with a bold and vigorous production, but a little confused and imperfect; since then I have established and fortified them by others' authority, and by the sound examples of ancient writers, with whose judgement I have found myself in agreement; these have strengthened my grasp of them and have given me more complete enjoyment and possession of them. The commendation that every one seeks for activity and readiness of mind, I claim for regularity; that which is sought for a brilliant and noteworthy act, I claim for the uniformity, consistency, and equableness of my opinions and morals. *If there be any thing entirely admirable, nothing is more so than equableness in the whole life and in its several acts; and this can not be attained if, imitating the characters of other men, you set aside your own.*[130]

This, then, is as far as I feel myself guilty of that first part[131] which I said existed in the vice of presumption. As for the second, which consists in not valuing others highly enough, I do not know if I can so well excuse myself regarding it; for, whatever it may cost me, I propose to say how the matter stands. Peradventure the constant intercourse that I have with ancient modes of thought, and the conception of those great souls of past times, disgusts me both with others and with myself; or else, in truth, we live in an age which produces only very mediocre things; so it is that I know nothing worthy of great admiration; besides, I know few men as intimately as is necessary to be able to judge them; and those with whom my social position most commonly connects me are, for the most part, persons who pay little heed to cultivation of the soul, and for whom all beatitude lies in honour, all perfection in valour. What I see that is fine in another, that I readily praise and esteem; nay, I often exaggerate what I think about it and give myself leave to lie to that extent. But I do not know how to invent what is wholly false. I readily bear witness about my friends in respect to what I find praiseworthy in them; and of a foot of merit I readily make a foot and a half. But to ascribe to them qualities which are not in them, that I can not do, nor defend them openly in regard to the imperfections they have.

Even to my enemies I frankly render what is due from me of honourable testimony. My feeling changes, not my judgement. And I do not confuse my quarrel with other matters that do not belong with it; and I am so jealous of the independence of my judgement that I can hardly forsake it for any passion whatsoever. I do to myself more injury by lying than I do to him about whom I lie. There is observed in the Persian nation this praiseworthy and generous custom, that they speak of their mortal enemies, with whom they are at deadly war, honourably and fairly, so far as the merit of their valour deserves.

I know men enough who have diverse fine parts: one, the mind; another, the heart; another, authority;[132] another, conscience; another, eloquence; another, one branch of learning; another, another. But a man great as a whole, not perfect, but yet having so many noble qualities combined, or one in such a degree of excellence that he may be wondered at or compared with those men of past time whom we honour—no such man has my fortune shown me. And the greatest man I have known in life—I mean in natural qualities of the mind, and the best trained[133]—was Etienne de la Boëtie: his was truly a well-rounded soul, which presented a noble aspect on all sides; a soul of the old stamp, and one which would have produced great things had his

fortune so willed; for he had added much to that richly endowed nature by learning and study.

But I know not how it happens (and yet it unquestionably does happen), that there is as much emptiness and
weakness of understanding as in any other class of persons, in
those who profess to have the most knowledge, who deal
with lettered occupations, and with offices which have to do
with books and learning; either because more is demanded
and expected from them than from the ignorant, and common faults can not be excused in them; or because their
belief in their knowledge makes them bolder to put themselves forward and lay themselves too open, whereby they
betray and ruin themselves. Just as a craftsman manifests
his lack of skill much more completely on a valuable material that he has in his hands, if he handles it and botches
it stupidly and contrary to the rule of the trade, than on a
mean material, and we are more displeased by a defect in a
statue of gold than in one of plaster, so do these when they
exhibit thoughts which, in themselves and in their place,
would be well; for they make use of them without discretion, doing honour to their memory at the expense of their
understanding: they do honour to Cicero, Galen, Ulpian,
and St. Hierosmus,[134] and make themselves ridiculous.

I recur readily to discourse on the utility of our education:[135] its aim has been to make us, not good men and wise,
but learned; it has succeeded. It has not taught us to follow
and embrace virtue and wisdom, but it has impressed on us
their verbal derivation and etymology. We know how to
decline virtue, if we do not know how to love it; if we do
not know what wisdom is, by results and by experience,
we know it by unmeaning words and by hearsay.[136] Of our

Of Presumption

neighbours we are not content to know the family, the kindred, and the marriages: we wish to have them for friends, and to enter into some intercourse and understanding with them; our education has taught us the definitions, the divisions and the subdivisions of virtue, like the surnames and branches of a genealogy, without taking the further care to bring about any habit of intimacy and personal intercourse between us and it.[137] It[138] has chosen for our instruction, not the books which contain the soundest and truest opinions, but those which speak the purest Greek and Latin; and, amidst fine sayings, has poured into our imagination the idlest fancies of antiquity. A good education changes the judgement and the character; as happened to Polemo, that dissolute young Greek, who, having by chance gone to hear a lecture of Xenocrates, not only remarked the eloquence and ability of the lecturer, but carried home with him, not only learning of fine quality, but a more visible and more substantial fruit, which was the sudden change and improvement in his former life.[139] Who has ever felt such an effect from our education?

> Should you not do what the converted Polemo did?
> Should you not lay aside the tokens of your disease, the
> leg- and the arm- and the neck-wrappings, as he is said
> to have slipped from his neck, unobserved, the
> wreaths, when, drunk, he was sharply reprimanded
> by the voice of a master who was fasting?[140]

The least contemptible kind of man seems to me to be that which, from its naturalness, has the lowest rank, and exhibits to us a more even intercourse. The characters and talk of peasants I find to be commonly more in accordance with the injunctions of true philosophy than are those of our philosophers. *The common people are wiser because they are wise only so much as is needful.*[141]

The most notable men whom I have judged by external appearances (for, to judge them after my fashion, it would be needful to observe them more closely) are, for conduct in war and for military ability, the duc de Guise, who died at Orléans and the late Marshal Strozzi; amongst men of general ability,[142] and of no common goodness, Olivier and L'Hôpital, chancellors of France. It seems to me, too, with respect to poetry, that it has had full vogue in our time. We have abundance of good craftsmen in that trade: Aurat,[143] Bèze, Buchanan, L'Hôpital, Mont-doré, Turnebus. As for the Frenchmen, I think that they have raised it to the highest point which it will ever reach; and in those qualities in which Ronsard and du Bellay excel I find little short of ancient perfection. Adrianus Turnebus knew more, and knew better what he knew, than any man of his day or long before.

The lives of the Duke of Alba, lately deceased, and of our connétable de Montmorency, were famous lives, and had many unusual similarities of fortune; but the beauty and the glory of the death of the latter, before the eyes of Paris and of his king, in their service, against his nearest kindred, at the head of an army victorious through his leadership, and by a surprise, in such extreme old age, seems to me worthy to be placed among the remarkable events of my time. As likewise the unfailing kindness, gentleness of character, and conscientious lenity of Monsieur de la Noue, amidst all the absence of justice of armed factions,—a veritable school of treason, inhumanity, and brigandage, in

Of Presumption

which he had always been brought up,—a great soldier and well proved.

I have taken great pleasure in proclaiming in many places the hopes I have of Marie de Gournay le Jars, my daughter by agreement,[144] and certainly beloved by me much more than paternally, and included in my retirement and solitude as one of the best parts of my own existence. I no longer am interested in any thing in the world save her. If youth can give promise, that soul will be capable some day of the best things, and, among others, of the perfection of that most sacred friendship to which we do not read that her sex has ever yet been able to attain. The sincerity and steadfastness of her character are already sufficient for this; her affection for me is more than superabundant, and such, in fine, that it would leave nothing to be desired, if the dread she has of my death, because of my five-and-fifty years when she met me, disquieted her less cruelly. The judgement that she, a woman, and in those days, and so young and alone in her district, formed of the first Essays, and the wonderful vehemence with which for a long time she loved me and longed to see me, solely from the esteem which she conceived from them for me before having seen me, is a matter well worth consideration.[145]

The other virtues have had little or no currency in this age, but valour has become general from our civil wars; and in this quality there are found among us souls steadfast to perfection, and in great numbers, so that selection among them is impossible. This is all that I have known, to the present moment, of extraordinary and unusual greatness.

Chapter XVIII

OF GIVING THE LIE

YES, but I shall be told that this plan of making use of oneself as a subject to write about would be excusable in exceptional and famous men, who, by their reputation, had caused some desire for their acquaintance. It is beyond question; I admit it; and I know well that, to look at a man of the common sort, an artisan will hardly lift his eyes from his task; whereas, to see a great and renowned personage enter a city, the workrooms and shops are deserted. It is unfitting for any other to make himself known save him who has something to invite imitation, and whose life and opinions may serve as a pattern. Cæsar and Xenophon had the wherewithal to base and strengthen their narratives on the magnitude of their deeds, as on a reasonable and enduring foundation. And it is to be wished that we had the daily records of Alexander the Great, and the notes that Augustus, Cato, Sylla, Brutus, and others may have left of their actions. Of such personages the figures are admired and studied even in copper and in stone.

This remonstrance is very just, but it concerns me very little:—

I do not recite my verses except to friends, and that

898

only when invited; not everywhere, or to every one.
But there are many who, in the middle of the forum,
or when bathing, recite their writings.[1]

I am not erecting here a statue to be set in a city street, or
in a church, or in a public square.

Truly, I do not study to swell my page with pre-
tentious trifles. . . . We talk together privately.[2]

It is for the corner of a library, and for the entertainment
of a neighbour, a kinsman, or a friend, who may have
pleasure in renewing acquaintance and familiarity with me
through this picture. Others have taken courage to speak of
themselves from having found the subject worthy and fruitful; I, on the contrary, from having found it so sterile and
meagre that no suspicion of ostentation can attach to it.

I freely pass judgement on the acts of others; of my own
I give little ground for judgement because of their nullity. I do not find so much good in myself that I can not
tell about it without blushing. What pleasure it would give
me to hear some one thus describe to me the manners, the
appearance, the demeanour, the most ordinary speech, and
the fortunes of my ancestors! How attentively I should
listen! Truly, it would give evidence of a bad nature, to
hold in contempt even the portraits of our friends and predecessors. A dagger, a harness, a sword, which they have
used, I preserve so far as I can from the inroads of time, for
love of them;[3] and I have not banished from my own room
some long staves which my father usually carried in his
hand. *The garment and the ring of a father are dear to
his children in proportion to their love for him.*[4] If, however, my posterity be of another mind, I shall have where-

899

M

with to be revenged; for they can not make less account of me than I shall of them in those days. All the dealing that I have with the public in this matter is that I borrow the tools of their writing as being quicker and more agreeable.[5] As compensation, I shall perhaps prevent a pound of butter in the market-place from spoiling.

That the tunny may not lack a coat, nor the olives hoods.[6]

And I shall often furnish a cloak for the mackerel.[7].

And, if no one shall read me, have I wasted my time in being occupied so many idle hours in such useful and agreeable thoughts? Modelling this figure after myself, I have been obliged so often to trim myself up and arrange myself, in order to give my outline,[8] that the model has consequently strengthened and, in some degree, shaped itself. Painting myself for others, I have painted myself in colours more distinct than were mine originally. I have no more created my book, than my book has created me—a book of the same substance as its author, with an occupation of its own, with its own business,[9] a member of my life; not with an external and alien business, like all other books. Have I wasted my time in taking account of myself so constantly, so minutely? For those who consider themselves in thought only, and in words now and then, do not examine themselves so exactly, or enter into themselves, as he who makes this his study, his business, and his occupation; who binds himself to a lasting record, with all the faithfulness and strength that he has.

The most delightful pleasures, being inwardly recognised, avoid giving any sign of themselves and avoid the observa-

900

tion, not only of the multitude, but of any one. How many times has this occupation diverted me from troublesome thoughts! and all trifling thoughts should be reckoned as troublesome. Nature has endowed us with a great faculty of conversing with ourselves apart; and often invites us to do so, to teach us that we owe ourselves in part to society, but for the most part to ourselves. To the end that I may school my imagination even to muse according to some order and plan, and to keep it from going astray and wandering at random, it is needful only to give shape to all the petty thoughts that offer themselves to it, and place them on record. I listen to my musings because I have to register them. How many times, being vexed by some act which civility and good sense forbade me to reprehend openly, have I here unburdened myself, not without a purpose of public instruction! And indeed these poetic scourges—

> One in the eye, one on the snout,
> One on the back of the pig![10]

make an even greater impression when on paper than when given on the living flesh. What if I lend my ear a little more attentively to books, since I have been on the watch to see if I can filch from them something wherewith to adorn or prop up my own? I have not at all studied to make a book; but I have studied somewhat because I had made it, if it be in any wise studying to select the best,[11] or to catch hold by the head or by the teeth, now of one author, now of another; not at all to form my opinions, but to aid those long ago formed, to second and support them.

But whom shall we believe when speaking of himself in such debased times, seeing that there are few, or none,

Of Giving the Lie

whom we can believe when speaking of others, where there is less to gain by lying? The first feature of corruption of morals is the banishment of truth; for, as Pindar said, being truthful is the beginning of great virtue;[12] and it is the first qualification that Plato requires in the governor of his Republic.[13] Our truth nowadays is not what is, but what others may be persuaded of; as we call coin, not only that which is of good alloy,[14] but also the counterfeit which passes current. Our nation has long been reproached with this vice; for Salvianus Massiliensis, who was of the time of the Emperor Valentinian, said that to the French lying and perjury were not vices, but mere forms of speech.[15] He who would enhance this testimony might say that it is now a virtue in their eyes. Men form and fashion themselves to it as being an honourable practice; for dissimulation is among the most renowned qualities of this age. Consequently, I have often considered whence could arise this habit, which we retained so religiously, of feeling ourselves more bitterly injured by being charged with this vice, which is so common with us, than with any other; and that it is the greatest insult that can be offered us in words, to charge us with falsehood. Whence I conclude that it is natural to defend ourselves most earnestly for the faults to which we are most addicted. It seems that, in resenting the accusation and in being moved by it, we in some measure rid ourselves of the trespass; if we have it in fact, we condemn it to save appearances.

May it not be, also, that this reproach seems to involve cowardice and faint-heartedness? It there any more manifest expression of this than to belie one's word—nay, to belie one's knowledge? Lying is a villainous vice, and an ancient writer depicts it as most shameful when he says that to lie

Of Giving the Lie

is to manifest contempt of God together with fear of man.[16] It is not possible to represent more fully the horror, the vileness, the outrageousness of it. For what can be conceived more villainous than to be cowardly with respect to men, and audacious with respect to God?

Certain nations of the new Indies (there is no need to note their names; they no longer exist; for the desolation of that conquest has extended even to the entire abolition of names and of the former knowledge of places; a wonderful and unheard-of instance) offer to their gods human blood, but no other than that taken from the tongue and ears, by way of expiation of the sin of falsehood, as well listened to as spoken. That Greek worthy[17] said that children play with huckle-bones, men with words.

As for our different methods of giving the lie, and our laws of honour in that matter, and the changes they have undergone, I will postpone to another time saying what I know of them; and I will meanwhile learn, if I can, when this habit began of weighing our words so carefully, and of making our honour dependent upon them. For it is easy to judge that it did not exist of old among the Romans and the Greeks. And it has often seemed to me novel and strange, to see how they gave the lie and insulted one another, without consequently entering into a quarrel. The laws of what was due[18] took some other course than ours. They called Cæsar, to his face, sometimes a thief, sometimes a drunkard.[19] We see the freedom of the invectives they used against one another,—I mean the greatest warchiefs of both nations,—when words were avenged solely by words, and involved no other consequence.

Chapter XIX

OF LIBERTY
OF CONSCIENCE

I T is a common thing to see good intentions, if they are pursued without moderation, impel men to very wrong actions. In this dissension which now agitates France with civil war, the best and sanest party is, doubtless, that which upholds the old-time religion and government of the country. Among the worthy men who follow it, however (for I am not speaking of those who use it only as a pretext, either to wreak their private vengeances, or to gratify their eager desires, or to gain the favour of princes, but of those who follow it from genuine zeal for their religion and from a godly desire to maintain the peace and the good estate of their country), among these, I say, there are seen many whom passion carries beyond the bounds of reason, and sometimes leads to accept unjust, violent, and even reckless counsels.

It is certain that, in those early days when our religion began to gain authority with the laws, zeal armed many men against every sort of pagan books, whereby men of letters suffer an immense loss. I consider that this excess caused more injury to letters than all the fires of the barbarians. Cornelius Tacitus is a good witness to this; for although the

Of Liberty of Conscience

Emperor Tacitus, his kinsman, had by express edict supplied all the libraries in the world with his works, yet not a
single complete copy escaped the careful search of those who
desired to destroy them because of four or five unimportant
sentences opposed to our faith.[1] They have also the habit of
readily ascribing undeserved praise to all the emperors who
favoured us,[2] and of condemning, without exception, all the
acts of those who were our adversaries; as can easily be seen
in the case of the Emperor Julian, surnamed the Apostate.
He was, in truth, a very great and rare man, one whose mind
was deeply imbued with the arguments of philosophy, by
which he professed to order all his acts; and, truly, there is no
kind of virtue of which he did not leave very notable examples. In respect to chastity (of which the course of his life
gives very clear testimony), we read of him an instance
similar to what is told of Alexander and Scipio: that of a number of very beautiful captives he refused to see a single one,
being then in the prime of life;[3] for he was killed by the
Parthians when he was but thirty-one years old.[4] As to his
justice, he took the trouble to listen himself to the contes-
tants; and while, from curiosity, he informed himself about
those who appeared before him of what religion they were,
yet the enmity he bore toward ours gave no counterpoise to
the scale.[5] He himself made many good laws and curtailed
a large part of the subsidies and taxes that his predecessors
had levied.[6] We have two good historians who were eye-
witnesses of his acts, one of whom, Marcellinus, censures
sharply in divers places in his history that edict of the emperor by which he forbade schools to all Christian rhetori-
cians and grammarians, and prohibited them from teaching;
and Marcellinus says that he could wish that act buried in

silence.[7] It is probable that, if he[8] had done any thing more severe against us, he[9] would not have forgotten it, being well affected to our side. He[10] was vehement against us, it is true, but not, for that, a cruel enemy; for our own people tell this story of him, that, as he was walking one day about the city of Chalcedon, Maris, the bishop of that place, dared boldly to call him a wicked traitor to Christ; and that, affecting, they say, philosophic patience, he did no more than reply to him: "Go, poor wretch, and weep for the loss of your eyes." To which the bishop retorted: "I give thanks to Jesus Christ for having deprived me of sight, so that I see not thy brazen face."[11] This incident certainly does not match well with the cruelties that he is said to have exercised against us. He was, says Eutropius, my other witness, an enemy of Christianity, but without bloodshed.[12]

And to recur to his justice, there is nothing that can be alleged against it save the harsh measures that he employed at the beginning of his reign against those who had belonged to the party of his predecssor, Constantius.[13] As to his sobriety, he lived always the life of a soldier, and ate and drank in times of peace like one making ready and accustoming himself to the austerity of war.[14] Vigilance[15] was so great with him that he divided the night into three or four parts, whereof the shortest was that which he gave to sleep;[16] the rest he employed in personally inspecting the condition of his army and his guides, or in study;[17] for, among his other unusual qualities, he excelled in every sort of literature.[18] It is told of Alexander the Great that, when he had gone to bed, for fear that slumber might seduce him from his thoughts and his studies, he had a basin placed beside his bed and held one hand outside, with a copper ball in it, so that, if sleep overcame him and relaxed the grasp of his fingers, the noise of this ball falling into the basin would awaken him.[19] The mind of this man[20] was so bent upon what he desired and, by reason of his singular abstinence, was so little inconvenienced by fumes, that he could very well do without that expedient. As for his military ability, he was admirable in all the qualities of a great captain; and he was, as it were, all his life engaged in waging war, and, for the most part, with us in France against the Germans and Franks. We have scarcely any record of a man who had seen more perils, or who had oftener exposed his person. In his death there was something similar to that of Epaminondas; for he was struck by an arrow, and tried to draw it out, and would have done so but that, the arrow being sharp-edged, he cut himself and weakened his hand.[21] He demanded repeatedly that he should be carried, in this condition, into the thick of the fight, to encourage the soldiers there, who fought very bravely without him, until darkness separated the armies.[22] He owed to philosophy the peculiar contempt in which he held his own life and mortal things.[23] He had a firm belief in the eternity of the soul.

In the matter of religion he was in error throughout; he has been surnamed the Apostate, because he abandoned our form; yet the opinion seems to me more probable, that he had never believed it in his heart, but had pretended to do so, in obedience to the laws, until he held the Empire in his hands. He was, in his own religion, so superstitious, that even those in his day of the same faith made sport of him; and it was said that, if he had won the victory against the Parthians, he would have used up the breed of oxen throughout the world, to fill the measure of his sacrifices; he was besotted, too, with the science of divination, and gave authority to every kind of prognostication.[24] He said, among other things, as he was dying, that he was grateful to the gods, and thanked them, because they had not willed to kill him by surprise,—having long before warned him of the place and hour of his end,—nor by an easy or cowardly death, better suited to idle and delicate persons; nor by a slow and painful one; and because they had found him worthy to die thus nobly, in the full tide of his victories and the flower of his glory.[25] He had had a vision similar to that of Marcus Brutus, which first threatened him in Gaul,[26] and appeared to him later in Persia, at the time of his death.[27] These words, which he is said to have uttered when he felt that he was wounded, "Thou has conquered, Nazarene,"[28] or, as others have it, "Be content, Nazarene,"[29] would scarcely have been forgotten, had they been believed, by my witnesses, who, being present in the army, observed even the least actions and words of his last hours—no more than certain other miracles that have been connected with it.[30]

And, to come to the heart of my subject, he long cherished, Marcellinus says, paganism in his heart; but, all his army being Christians, he dared not let it be known.[31] Finally, when he found himself strong enough to dare to manifest his mind, he caused the temples of the god to be opened, and endeavoured by every means to promote idolatry. To attain his object, having found in Constantinople the people disunited from the dissentient bishops of the Christian Church,[32] having summoned them before him at the palace, he earnestly admonished them to quiet these civil dissensions, and to follow every one his own religion without hindrance and without fear. This he sedulously solicited,

Of Liberty of Conscience

in the hope that this liberty would increase the divisions and contentions of the schism, and would prevent the people from uniting together, and consequently from strengthening themselves against him by their accord and entire agreement; having learned by the cruelty of some Christians that there is no beast in the world so much to be feared by man as man.[33]

These are very nearly his[34] words; wherein this is worthy of reflection, that the Emperor Julian, to kindle the confusion of civil dissension, made use of this same receipt of liberty of conscience which our kings have lately employed to extinguish it. It may be said, on the one hand, that to give the rein to factions to maintain their opinions is to scatter and sow division; is almost to lend a hand in increasing it, there being then neither bar nor coercion by the laws to check and impede its progress. But, on the other hand, it might be said that to give the rein to factions to maintain their opinions is to soften and relax them by facility and ease, and to blunt the spur which is sharpened by rarity, novelty, and difficulty. And therefore I think it is better, for the honour of the piety of our kings, that, not having been able to do what they desire, they have made a show of desiring what they were able to do.

Chapter XX

WE HAVE NO EXPERIENCE

OF ANY SIMPLE THING [1]

THE imperfection of our condition is the cause that things in their natural simplicity and purity can not be used by us. The elements that we profit by are modified; and the metals also; and gold must be debased by some other substance to adapt it to our service. Neither the quite pure virtue, which Aristo and Pyrrho and also the Stoics made the object of life, nor the Cyrenaic and Aristippic pleasure, has been available without alloy. Of the pleasures and goods that we have, there is none exempt from some mixture of evil and unfitness;

> Out of the very well-spring of delights arises something of bitter that gives pain amid the very flowers.[2]

Our keenest pleasure appears, as it were, to groan and lament. Would you not think it mere dying of anguish? Nay, when we compose a picture of it at its highest point; we deck it out with sickly and painful epithets and qualities, languor, softness, weakness, faintness, *morbidezza*; a great testimony to their consanguinity and consubstantiality.

Profound joy is more serious than gay; supreme and perfect contentment more sedate than merry. *Felicity, unless it*

910

moderates itself, is burdensome.[3] Ease eats us up. This[4] is said by an ancient Greek verse, to this effect: "The gods sell us all the goods they give us";[5] that is to say, they give us none pure and perfect, and which we do not purchase at the cost of some ill.

Toil and pleasure, very dissimilar in nature, are nevertheless united by I know not what natural yoke. Socrates says that some god tried to confuse into one mass pain and pleasure; but, being unable to effect this, he decided to couple them together, at least by the tail.[6] Metrodorus said that in sadness there is some mixture of pleasure.[7] I do not know if he meant to say something else; but for my part I readily conceive that there is intention, acquiescence, and satisfaction in fostering melancholy; I mean, besides ambition, which may also be mingled with it.[8] There is a shade of fastidiousness and delicacy, which shines upon us and flatters us in the very lap of melancholy. Are there not temperaments which make it their sustenance?

There is a certain pleasure in tears.[9]

And one Attalus, in Seneca, says that the memory of our lost friends is welcome to us like the bitter taste in wine that is very old,[10]—

Boy, who pourest old Falernian, put the bitterest into my cup,[11]—

and like apples sweetly tart. Nature reveals this confusion to us; painters hold that the same motions and wrinkles of the face that accompany weeping also accompany laughing. And in truth, before either the one or the other expression is completed, observe the action of the picture: you are in

We have no Experience of any Simple Thing

doubt toward which it is proceeding. And the extreme of laughter is mingled with tears. *No evil is without compensation.*[12]

When I imagine man beset with desirable advantages (let us assume that all his members were possessed forever with pleasure as great as that of generation at its extremest climax), I feel him give away under the burden of his delight, and I see him wholly incapable of supporting a pleasure so pure, so constant, and so universal. In truth, he slips away when he reaches that point, and involuntarily hastens to escape thence, as from a place of unstable footing, where he fears to sink. When I devoutly confess myself to myself, I find that the best goodness I have has some tinge of vice. And I fear that Plato, in his most flourishing[13] virtue (I who am as sincere and loyal an admirer thereof, and of virtues of like stamp, as any man can be), if he had listened closely (and he did listen closely), would have heard a sinister note of human intermixture, but a faint note, and audible to himself only. Man, in every thing and everywhere, is but patchwork and motley.

Even the laws of justice can not subsist without some admixture of injustice; and Plato says that they undertake to cut off the heads of Hydra who attempt to remove from the laws all hindrances and unfitnesses.[14] *In every great punishment there is some mixture of injustice toward individuals, which is counterbalanced by the public utility,* [15] says Tacitus.

It is likewise true that for use in life and the service of public intercourse our minds may be too pure and perspicacious; this penetrating clearness has too much of subtlety and inquisitiveness. We must stupefy and blunt them, to make them more obedient to example and experience; and must becloud and obscure their sight, to bring them into relation with this dark and terrestrial life. Therefore, ordinary and less high-pitched minds [16] are more fit to manage affairs happily. And the lofty and choice doctrines of philosophy are found inept in practice. This keen activity of soul and this nimble and restless volubility disturb our negotiations. Human undertakings must be handled more roughly and superficially, and a good and great part of them be left to the laws of fortune. There is no need to search into affairs so deeply and so craftily. We lose ourselves in the consideration of so many opposing lights and varying shapes; *in considering things contrary in themselves, minds were stupefied.*[17] The ancients say of Simonides that, because his imagination brought before him (touching the question that King Hiero had put to him, to reply to which he had several days for reflection) various keen and ingenious arguments, from doubt which was the most reasonable, he despaired altogether of the truth.[18]

He who seeks for and embraces all the circumstances and consequences of action impedes his choice. A medium intelligence[19] is an equally good guide, and suffices for executing matters of great and of little weight. Observe that the best managers of household affairs are those who are least able to tell us how they are so; and that these accomplished talkers oftenest do nothing that is worth while. I know a great discourser and most excellent depicter of every sort of thrift, who has very lamentably let slip through his hands a revenue of a hundred thousand livres.

Chapter XXI

AGAINST SLOTHFULNESS

THE Emperor Vespasian, being sick with the sickness of which he died, did not relinquish his desire to understand the condition of his empire, and even in his bed constantly despatched many affairs of importance. And when his doctor checked him about this, as being something harmful to his health, "An emperor," he said, "should die standing."[1] A fine saying that, to my thinking, and worthy of a great prince. Hadrian the Emperor made use afterward of the same thought;[2] and it should often be recalled to kings, to make them feel that the great office given them, of command over so many men, is no idle office, and that there is nothing which can so justly disincline a subject to expose himself to trouble and danger in the service of his prince as to see the prince himself meanwhile idling in feeble and frivolous occupations; and so disincline the subject from solicitude for the prince's preservation, as to see him so indifferent to ours.

If any one shall choose to maintain that it is better that the prince should conduct his wars by another than by himself, fortune will supply him with examples enough of those princes whose lieutenants have achieved great undertakings, and of those also whose presence has been more harmful than useful. But no worthy and courageous prince could suffer any one to suggest to him such shameful counsels. Under colour of preserving his head, as if he were the statue of a saint, for the good-fortune of his realm, they degrade him from his office, which is military throughout, and declare him incapable of it. I know one[3] who would much rather be cudgelled than sleep while others were fighting for him, and who never saw without jealousy his own subordinates do something great in his absence. And Selim the First said with reason, it seems to me, that victories which are won without the presence of the master are not complete; much more readily would he have said that that master ought to blush for shame to claim a share in it for his renown, having contributed to it only his words and his thought—and not even those, since in such a business the counsels and commands that carry honour are those only that are given on the spot and in the midst of the battle. No pilot does his work standing still on land. The princes of the Ottoman race, the foremost race in the world in military fortune, have warmly embraced this opinion. And Bajazet the Second, with his son, who swerved from it, spending time on book-learning and other retired occupations, thus dealt many great blows to their empire; and he who now reigns, Amurath the Third, following their example, is very evidently beginning to find himself in the same condition. Was it not the King of England, Edward the Third, who said of our Charles the Fifth, "There was never a king who wore armour less, and yet there was never a king who gave me so much to do"?[4] He had reason to deem it strange, as an effect of chance rather than of discretion. And let

those seek some other adherent than myself, who choose to
number among warlike and stouthearted conquerors the
kings of Castile and Portugal, because at twelve hundred
leagues' distance from their abode of sloth, by the direction
of their agents,[5] they have made themselves masters of one
and the other Indies; of whom it is not known whether
they would even have the spirit to go there to enjoy themselves in person.

The Emperor Julian said even more—that a philosopher
and a man, to be admired, should not even take his ease;[6]
that is to say, should grant to bodily necessities only what
can not be denied them, keeping the soul and the body
always employed about good and great and virtuous things.
He was ashamed if he was seen to spit or to sweat in public
(which is said also of the Lacedæmonian youths and by
Xenophon of those of Persia[7]), because he thought that
exercise, constant labour, and sobriety should have digested
and dried up all those superfluities. What Seneca says will
not come amiss in this place: that the ancient Romans kept
their youth standing; they taught nothing to their children,
he said, which could be learned while seated.[8]

It is a noble-hearted desire, to wish even to die usefully
and manfully; but the thing lies not so much in our good
resolution as in our good-fortune. Thousands have determined to conquer or to die fighting, who have missed both
the one and the other; wounds, prisons, baulking that purpose and giving them an enforced life. There are diseases
which overthrow even what we desire and what we know.
Fortune did not second the ambition of the Roman legions,
who bound themselves by an oath to conquer or to die.
Victor, O Marcus Fabius, I shall return from the fight; if

Against Slothfulness

I fail, I will appeal to Father Jupiter and Mars the forth-stepping, and to the other irritated gods.[9] The Portuguese say that, in their conquest of the Indies, they met with soldiers who had condemned themselves, with horrible curses, never to come to terms; [who had vowed] that they would be killed or remain victorious; and in token of this vow they shaved their hair and their beards.[10] To no purpose do we risk our lives and persist in so doing; it seems as if blows avoided those who offer themselves too cheerfully, and they do not willingly fall upon him who offers himself too willingly and spoils their aim. A certain man, failing to achieve the loss of his life at the hands of the enemy after trying every means, in order to carry out his resolution to return with honour or not to return alive, was compelled to give death to himself in the very hottest of the fight. There are other examples; here is one. Philistus, commander of the naval force of the younger Dionysius against the Syracusans, offered battle, which was sharply contested, the forces being equal. At the beginning he had the advantage, from his prowess: but the Syracusans arranging themselves about his galley to invest it, he, having personally performed great feats of arms to extricate himself, and having no longer any hope of succour, deprived himself with his own hand of the life he had in such full measure and unsuccessfully laid open to the hands of the enemy.[11]

Moley Moluch, King of Fez, who has lately won, against Sebastian, King of Portugal, that battle made famous by the death of three kings and by the transmission of that great crown to the King of Castile,[12] chanced to be grievously sick when the Portuguese entered his dominions under arms, and from that time grew ever worse, approaching death and foreseeing it. Never did man make use of his powers more vigorously and bravely. He found himself too weak to undergo the pompous ceremonial of the entry into his camp, which, after their custom, is very magnificent and full of movement, and resigned this honour to his brother. But that was the only office of a leader which he resigned: all the others, necessary and useful, he performed very laboriously and scrupulously, his body lying prostrate, but his mind and his spirit erect and firm even to his last breath and, in a sense, beyond it. He could have worn out his enemies, who had indiscreetly advanced into his territory; and it grievously weighed upon him that, for lack of a little life, and because he had no one to replace him in the conduct of this war and of the affairs of a perturbed realm, he had to seek a bloody and hazardous victory, when he had a different one, pure and spotless, in his hands. However, he miraculously managed during his sickness to use up his enemy, and to draw him far away from his naval force and from the ports he held on the coast of Africa, down to the last day of his life, which he designedly employed and reserved for that great battle. He ranged his forces in a circle, assailing the Portuguese host on all sides; which circle, curving and contracting, not only blocked them in the conflict—which was very hot by reason of the valour of that young invading king, since they had to face on all sides,—but also blocked them in flight after the defeat. And, finding all the issues seized and closed, they were compelled to throw themselves back upon themselves,— *they are heaped up, not only by slaughter, but also by flight*,[13]—and to pile themselves upon one another, thus providing the victors with a very murderous and very complete

918

victory. Dying as he was, he had himself borne hurriedly hither and thither, wherever need called him; and passing along the line, exhorted his officers and soldiers, one troop after another. But, a corner of his array allowing itself to be driven in, he could not be prevented from mounting his horse, sword in hand. He strove to enter into the mellay, those about him holding him back, some by the bridle, some by his robe and by his stirrups. This effort completely overwhelmed the little life he had left. They laid him back on his bed. Reviving suddenly from this swoon, to warn them that they should say nothing of his death, so that the news might not cause discouragement to his troops, which was the most essential command that he had then to give, all other power failing him, he held his finger to his closed lips.—the usual sign to enjoin silence,—and so expired. Who ever lived so long and so deeply in death? Who ever died so erectly?[14]

The extreme degree of treating death courageously, and the most natural, is to view it, not only without amazement, but without concern, freely continuing the tenor of life, even within death.[15] Like Cato, who occupied himself in study and sleep whilst he had present in his head and in his heart a violent and bloody death, and held it in his hand.

Chapter XXII

OF POSTING

I HAVE not been amongst the least able in this exercise, which is adapted to men of my stature, thick set and short; but I am relinquishing the occasions for the use of it;[1] it tries us too much to continue long at it. I was reading just now that King Cyrus, to obtain more readily news from all parts of his empire, which was of very great extent, made enquiry how far a horse could travel in a day without stopping, and at that distance from one another he placed men whose duty it was to have horses ready to supply those who were coming to him.[2] And some say that this swiftness of travel reaches that of the flight of cranes.

Cæsar says that Lucius Vibulus Rufus, being in haste to carry intelligence to Pompeius, travelled day and night, changing horses for greater speed.[3] And he himself,[4] according to Suetonius, made a hundred miles a day in a hired coach. But he was a reckless rider; for when rivers stopped his way, he crossed them by swimming, and never turned from the straight road to seek a bridge or a ford. Tiberius Nero, going to see his brother Drusus, who was ill in Germany, made two hundred miles in twenty-four hours, having three coaches.[5]

Of Posting

In the war of the Romans against King Antiochus, T. Sempronius Gracchus, says Livy, *with relays of horses, by incredible speed, arrived on the third day at Pellæ, from Amphissa.*[6] And it appears, upon observing the place, that they were established posts, not newly arranged for this journey. The invention of Cecinna for sending news to his household was much more speedy: he carried swallows with him, and when he wished to send news of himself, he released them, to go back to their nests, staining them with a spot of colour proper to signify what he desired, as he had concerted with his people.[7] In the theatre at Rome, heads of families carried pigeons in their bosoms, to which they tied letters when they wished to give some order to their people at home; and they were trained to bring back the reply. D. Brutus used them when besieged at Mutina;[8] and others elsewhere. In Peru the couriers rode on men, who took them on their shoulders, in litters,[9] with such skill that, on the run, the first bearers transferred their burden to the next, without any pause.[10] I understand that the Valachi, couriers of the Great Turk, make extreme speed, because it is permitted to them to take the steed of the first traveller they meet on the road, giving to him their jaded horse; and that, to save themselves from weariness, they gird themselves about the middle very tightly with a broad band,[11] as a good many others do. I have found no special locality for this custom.[12]

Chapter XXIII

OF BAD MEANS EMPLOYED

FOR A GOOD END

THERE is a wonderful relation and correspondency in the universal government of the works of nature, which shows clearly that it is neither fortuitous nor conducted by various masters. The diseases and conditions of our bodies are to be seen in states and governments as well; kingdoms and republics are born, flourish, and wither with age, as we do. We are subject to a useless and harmful plethora of humours; whether of benign humours (for even that the doctors are afraid of; and because there is nothing stable in us, they say that perfect health, too active and vigorous, we must enfeeble and diminish by artificial means, for fear lest our nature, being unable to settle down in any one place, and no longer having where to ascend to, to better itself, may retrogress in confusion and too suddenly; to this end they prescribe for athletes purges and bleedings, to withdraw from them this superabundance of health); or whether a plethora of malign humours, which is the common cause of sickness.

From such a plethora states are often seen to be suffering, and they are wont to resort to diverse methods of purging. Sometimes they expel a great multitude of families to re-

lieve the country of them, who go to seek elsewhere a place
to establish themselves at the expense of others. In this way
our ancient Franks, setting out from the depths of Germany, came to seize upon Gaul and drove out its original
inhabitants; thus was set in motion that ceaseless tide of
men which flowed into Italy under Brennus and others;
thus the Goths and the Vandals, as also the peoples who
now possess Greece, abandoned their native countries, to
settle elsewhere, where there was more room; and there are
hardly two or three corners of the world which have not felt
the effects of a like movement. The Romans by this means
built up their colonies; for, perceiving that their city was
becoming over-populous, they relieved it of the least necessary people, and sent these to occupy and cultivate the
lands they had conquered. Sometimes, too, they purposely
fostered wars with some of their enemies, not only to keep
their men in action, for fear that idleness, the mother of
corruption, should bring upon them some worse evils,—

> We suffer the evils of a long peace; luxury, more
> baleful than arms, oppresses us,[1]—

but also to serve as blood-letting for their commonwealth,
and to cool off a little the too vehement heat of their youth;
to prune and thin out the branching of the trunk too lusty
in its growth;[2] to this end they formerly made use of the
war against the Carthaginians.

At the time of the treaty of Brétigny, Edward the Third,
King of England, did not choose to include in the general
peace that he made with our king the controversy about the
duchy of Bretagne, in order that he might have a place
where he could dispose of his troops, and that the multitude

Of Bad Means Employed for a Good End

of English whom he had employed in his affairs on this side of the Channel[3] might not be thrown back into England. The same thing was one of the reasons why our King Philippe consented to send Jean, his son, to the war overseas, in order that he might carry with him a great number of young hot-bloods, who were in his troop of horse.[4]

There are many in these days who reason in like manner, desiring that this heat of emotion which exists among us might be directed to some neighbouring war; for fear that these peccant humours which prevail in our body politic at the present moment, if they are not drawn off elsewhere, will keep our fever still at its height, and finally bring about our total ruin. And, truly, a foreign war is a much milder evil than civil war; but I do not think that God would favour so unjust an enterprise as insulting and quarreling with another nation for our profit.

> O virgin of Rhamnusia, may nothing please me excessively which must be taken from an unwilling possessor.[5]

Nevertheless, the weakness of our condition often urges us to this necessity of making use of evil means for a good end. Lycurgus, the most virtuous and perfect legislator that ever lived, imagined this very unjust method of teaching his people temperance—to make the Helots, who were their slaves, drunk by force, to the end that, seeing them thus lost and buried in wine, the Spartans would hold in horror the excess of that vice.[6] Those were still more to blame who, of old, gave leave for criminals, to whatever sort of death they were condemned, to be torn apart alive by physicians, in order to see the natural condition of our

924

Of Bad Means Employed for a Good End

internal organs, and to establish thereby certainty in the art
of medicine; for, if we must go astray, it is more excusable
to do it in the service of the health of the soul than of that
of the body; as the Romans trained the people to valour
and contempt of danger and death by those furious spectacles of gladiators and fencers pledged to deadly combat,[7]
who fought and gashed and killed one another in their
presence.

> What other end has the impious art of the gladi-
> ator, the slaughter of young men, the pleasure that is
> fed on bloodshed?[8]

And this custom continued to the time of the Emperor
Theodosius:[9]

> Take possession, O prince, of the renown reserved
> for this age, and with the heritage of your father be
> successor to his praise. Let no man in the city fall in
> combat, whose suffering gives pleasure. Henceforth
> let the infamous arena be content with beasts only,
> and let not homicide disport itself with bloody arms.[10]

It was in very truth an admirable example, and of very great
profit for the education of the people, to see every day a
hundred, two hundred, or a thousand pairs of men, armed
against each other, hack each other to pieces in their presence, with such extreme firmness of courage that they were
never known to utter a word of weakness or lamentation,
never to turn their backs, or even to make a cowardly motion to avoid their opponent's blow; but, rather, to expose
their neck to the sword and present themselves to the stroke.
There were not a few instances when one of them, hurt to

Of Bad Means Employed for a Good End

the death and with many wounds, sent to ask the people if they were pleased with his performance, before he lay down to breathe his last on the spot. It was not needful that they should merely fight and die bravely, but cheerfully, too; so that they were hooted and cursed if they were seen to hesitate to welcome death. Even girls egged them on;

> she springs from her seat at each blow; and every time the victor drives his steel into his opponent's throat, she proclaims her delight; and she, a tender maiden, by her turned-down thumb bids the prostrate breast be pierced.[11]

The early Romans employed criminals in this proceeding; but later they employed innocent slaves, and also free men, who sold themselves to that end; even Roman senators and knights, and women as well.

> Now they sell their lives to death, and their corpses lie in the arena; and each one is himself his own enemy, when wars have ceased.[12]

> Amid this din and these new games stands the tender sex, unused to arms, and audaciously joins in men's fights.[13]

Which I should find very strange and incredible, were we not accustomed to see every day in our wars thousands of men from other lands pledging for money their blood and their lives, in broils in which they have no interest.

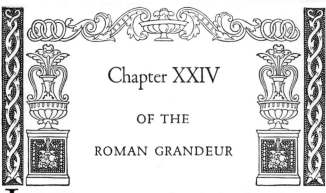

Chapter XXIV

OF THE

ROMAN GRANDEUR

I DESIRE to say just a word on this limitless subject, to show the ignorance of those who compare the paltry grandeurs of the present time with those of Rome. In the seventh book of Cicero's *Familiar Epistles* (and let the grammarians do away with that epithet, "familiar," if they choose, for in truth it is not very appropriate; and those who for "familiar" have substituted *ad familiares* can derive some argument on their side from what Suetonius says in the *Life of Cæsar*, that there was a volume of letters of his *ad familiares*), there is one, addressed to Cæsar, who was then in Gaul, in which Cicero quotes these words, which were at the end of a letter Cæsar had written him: "As for Marcus Furius, whom you have recommended to me, I will make him King of Gaul; and if you would have me advance any other of your friends, send them to me."[1] It was not the first time that a simple Roman citizen, as Cæsar then was, disposed of a kingdom, for he really deprived King Deiotarus of his, to give it to a gentleman of the city of Pergamos named Mithridates.[2] And they who have written his life record the sale by him of several other kingdoms; and Suetonius says that he extorted at one stroke from

Of the Roman Grandeur

King Ptolemy three million six hundred thousand crowns,[3] which was much the same as selling his own:—

Such a sum for Galatia; for so much, Pontus; for so much, Lydia.[4]

Marcus Antonius said that the grandeur of the Roman people was shown not so much by what they took as by what they gave.[5] Yet a century and more before Antonius[6] it took possession of one[7] among others by such an extraordinary exercise of authority, that in all its history I know of no testimony which bears higher the fame of its influence. Antiochus possessed all Egypt, and was about to conquer Cyprus and other appendages of that empire. In the course of his victories, Caius Popilius came to him on the part of the Senate, and on arriving refused to take him by the hand until he had first read the letters that he brought to him. The king having read them and said that he would reflect about them, Popilius drew with his staff a line around the place where he[8] was, saying: "Before you step from out this circle, give me an answer which I can carry back to the Senate." Antiochus, amazed by the harshness of so peremptory a command, after a short meditation said: "I will do what the Senate commands me." Thereupon Popilius saluted him as a friend of the Roman people.[9] To renounce so great a monarchy and a career of such fortunate prosperity because of the impression made by three lines of writing! He had reason, in truth, to send to the Senate, as he afterward did, to say by his ambassadors that he had received its decree with as much respect as if it had come from the immortal gods.

All the kingdoms that Augustus won by force of arms he

928

Of the Roman Grandeur

restored to those who had lost them, or presented them to strangers. And in this connection Tacitus, speaking of the English King Cogidunus, makes us perceive this infinite power by a marvellous touch. "The Romans," he says, "were accustomed from the most ancient times to leave the kings whom they had overcome in possession of their kingdom, under their authority,[10] so that they might have kings themselves, instruments of servitude; *ut haberet instrumenta servitutis et reges*.[11]" It is probable that Solyman, whom we have seen exercise liberality with the kingdom of Hungary and other states, paid more heed to this consideration than to that which he was wont to allege: that he was surfeited and overburdened with so many monarchies and so much power, which his valour, or that of his ancestors, had won for him.[12]

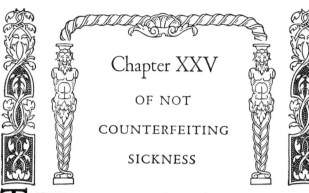

Chapter XXV

OF NOT

COUNTERFEITING

SICKNESS

THERE is an epigram in Martial, which is one of the good ones (for there are all kinds in him), in which he tells amusingly the story of Cœlius, who, to avoid paying court to certain great men at Rome,—being present at their rising, accompanying them, and waiting on them,—pretended to have gout, and, to make his excuse more plausible, had his legs anointed and wrapped up, and in every respect imitated the bearing and appearance of a gouty man; at last fortune gave him the pleasure of being one really:—

So much can painstaking effect, and the art of suffering; Cœlius no longer needs to feign gout.[1]

I have read somewhere in Appian, it seems to me, a similar tale of one who, seeking to evade the proscriptions of the Triumvirs of Rome, by keeping himself hidden and disguised, in order to avoid recognition by those who were pursuing him, added the invention of pretending to be one-eyed; when he had recovered a little more liberty, and when he would have left off the plaster that he had for a long time worn over his eye, he found that his sight had been actually lost behind that mask.[2] It is possible that the action of the eye had been impaired by having been so long without exercise, and that the visual power had all been transferred to the other eye; for we feel distinctly that the eye that we cover passes over to its fellow something of its force, in such wise that this other grows larger and dilates; just as disuse, together with the heat of the swathings and medicaments, might very well have invited some podagric humour to Martial's gouty man. Reading in Froissart of the vow of a party of young English gentlemen to keep a band over the left eye until they had entered France and performed some feat of arms against us, I have often been amused by the thought that it might have happened to them as to that other, and that they might all have found themselves one-eyed on meeting again their mistresses, for whom they had undertaken the enterprise. Mothers do well to reprove their children when they imitate one-eyed people, or lameness, or squinting, or other bodily defects; for besides that the body, then so soft, may thus acquire an ill bent, it seems, I know not how, that fortune delights in taking us at our word; and I have heard of several examples of persons who, having intended only to pretend to be sick, have become so. I have always been in the habit of having a stick or a staff in my hand, both on horseback and on foot, and have even sought elegance in the use of it and in leaning upon it[3] in an artificial manner. Many have warned me that fortune would some day turn this foppery into necessity. I rely upon this, that I should be the first gouty one of my family.

But let us spin out this chapter, and patch on another anecdote about blindness. Pliny tells of a man who, dreaming that he was blind, found himself so on the morrow, without any preceding sickness.[4] The power of the imagination may well assist herein, as I have said elsewhere;[5] and it would seem that Pliny is of this opinion; but it is more probable that the inward agitations which the body perceived, of which the doctors may find the cause if they will, were the occasion of the dream.

Let us add yet another anecdote germane to this subject, which Seneca relates in one of his letters. "You know," he says, writing to Lucilius, "that Harpaste, my wife's fool, has lived in my family as an hereditary burden; for by nature I am averse to these monsters, and if I feel inclined to laugh at a fool, I need not seek very far—I laugh at myself. This fool has suddenly lost her sight. I tell you a strange, but a true thing—she does not perceive that she is blind, and eagerly implores her guardian to take her away; for she says that my house is dark. This that we laugh at in her, I beg you to believe happens to every one of us: no man recognises that he is eager to be better off, no man that he desires wordly things.[6] But the blind ask for a guide, we go astray by ourselves. I am not ambitious, we say, but in Rome one can not live otherwise; I am not extravagant, but the city demands a great expenditure; it is not my fault if I am choleric, if I have not yet established any settled manner of life—it is the fault of youth. Let us not seek outside of ourselves; what is ill with us is in us, is rooted in our bowels. And the very fact that we do not perceive that we are sick makes our cure more difficult. If we do not begin in good season to doctor ourselves, when shall we have attended to so many wounds and so many diseases? Yet we have a very agreeable medicine—philosophy; from other medicines we do not receive pleasure until after the cure; this one pleases and cures at the same time."[7] This is what Seneca says.

Chapter XXVI

OF THUMBS

TACITUS reports that, with certain barbarian kings, their manner of making a binding obligation was to clasp their right hands tightly together and intertwist their thumbs; and when, by dint of squeezing them, the blood came to the tip, they pricked them lightly, and then each sucked the other's.[1] Physicians say that the thumb is the master-finger of the hand, and that the word *pouce* is derived from the Latin *pollere,* which signifies to surpass others in excellence.[2] And it seems that the Latins, too, sometimes use it in the sense of the whole hand:—

> No soft persuasion, or of voice or thumb
> Will make him rise to the occasion.[3]

In Rome it was a sign of favour to put the thumbs together and turn them down,—

> Your companion will applaud your sport with both
> thumbs,[4]—

and of disfavour to raise them and turn them outward,—

> the populace, with thumbs reversed, kill indiscriminately.[5]

Of Thumbs

The Romans released from military service those who were wounded in the thumb, because they were no longer able to grasp their weapons firmly enough. Augustus confiscated the property of a Roman knight who had treacherously cut off the thumbs of his young sons, to excuse them from going into the army;[6] and before that, the Senate, at the time of the Italian war, had condemned Caius Vatienus to life-long imprisonment and had confiscated all his property, for having intentionally cut off the thumb of his left hand, to exempt himself from that expedition.[7] Some one, who it was I do not recall, having won a naval battle, had the thumbs of his vanquished foes cut off, to deprive them of the means of fighting and of handling the oars.[8] The Athenians cut off the thumbs of the Æginetans, to take away their superiority in the art of seamanship.[9] In Lacedæmon the schoolmaster punished the children by biting their thumbs.[10]

934

Chapter XXVII

COWARDICE

THE MOTHER OF CRUELTY

I HAVE often heard it said that cowardice is the mother of cruelty. And I have by experience discovered that the exasperation and fierceness of a malevolent and inhuman heart is commonly accompanied by feminine sensitiveness. I have seen some of the most cruel men prone to weep easily and for trivial reasons. Alexander, tyrant of Pheres, could not bear to listen to tragedies at the theatre, for fear lest his subjects should see him mourn over the misfortune of Hecuba and Andromache—him who, without pity, caused so many persons to be cruelly put to death every day.[1] Can it be weakness of spirit that makes them thus easily moved to every kind of extreme?

True valour (whose intention is to exert itself only against resistance,—

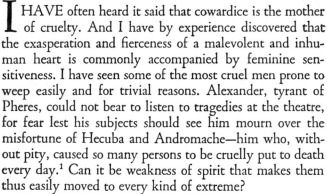

Nor enjoys cutting the throat of a young bull unless it resists[2])—

is stayed by seeing the foe at its mercy. But pusillanimity, assuming that she also is at the feast, not having been able to enter into the first action, takes for her share the second —of massacre and bloodshed. The murders in victories are

935

ordinarily committed by the hangers-on of the army and by those in charge of the baggage-trains; and the reason that there are seen so many acts of unheard-of cruelty in domestic wars is that the rascally rabble is made ready for fight and emboldened[3] by being in blood to the elbows and by mangling a body at its feet, having no comprehension of another sort of valour,—

> And the wolf and the hateful bear and all the less
> noble beasts crowd about the dying,[4]—

like cowardly dogs, which, in the house, tear with their teeth the skins of wild beasts that they dared not attack in the fields.[5] What is it that, in these days, makes our quarrels ever deadly; and that, whereas our fathers had some stages in revenge, we now begin with the extreme degree, and at the outset speak of nothing but killing? What is this, if it is not cowardice? For every one knows that there is more defiance and scorn in whipping an enemy than in putting an end to him, and in making him kiss the dust than in killing him. Furthermore, that the thirst for vengeance is thus better assuaged and satisfied, for it aims only at making itself felt. This is the reason that we do not attack a beast or a stone when it hurts us, because they are incapable of feeling our revenge. And to kill a man is to put him out of reach of our reprisal. And just as Bias exclaimed to a wicked man: "I know that sooner or later you will be punished for this, but I fear that I shall not see it"; and pitied the Orchomenians because the punishment of Lyciscus for his treachery to them came when there was no one left of those who had been affected by it, and who would be touched by the satisfaction of that punishment,[6] so is

Cowardice the Mother of Cruelty

vengeance to be pitied when he against whom it is directed
is without the means of feeling it; for, as the avenger, to
derive pleasure from it, desires to see it, so he upon whom
the revenge is practised must see it also, to receive from it
suffering and repentance. He shall repent it, we say. And
when we give him a pistol-shot in the head, do we think he
repents? On the contrary, if we look closely, we shall find
that he taunts us as he falls; he is not even ungrateful to us;
he is very far from penitence. And we do him the kindest
of all the offices of life, which is to make him die quickly
and painlessly. We have to hide ourselves, and go away, and
fly from the officers of the law who pursue us—and he is at
rest. To kill him is desirable, to avoid future wrongs, but
not to avenge that which is already done; it is an act of fear
rather than of bravery, of precaution rather than of courage,
of defence rather than of attack. It is evident that we thereby
abandon both the true object of vengeance and the care of
our reputation; we fear lest, if he remain in life, he may attack us again in like manner. It is not as against him, it is as
for yourself, that you rid yourself of him.

In the kingdom of Narsingue this expedient would not
be needed by us. There, not only soldiers, but workmen as
well, settle their disputes with the sword. The king never
denies the field to him who wishes to fight; and when they
are persons of rank, he is present and bestows on the victor
a chain of gold. But, to win that from him, the first man
who desires can fight with him who wears it, who, by having rid himself of one combat, has many on his hands.[7]

If we thought to be always masters of our foe by force,
and to domineer over him at our pleasure, we should be very
sorry that he should escape us, as he does by dying: we wish

to conquer, but more safely than honourably; and we seek the result rather than renown in our quarrels. Asinius Pollio, though an honourable man, exhibited a like error; who, having written invectives against Plancus, waited until he was dead to publish them.[8] It was insulting a blind man by gesture, and railing at a deaf man,[9] and wounding a senseless man rather than run the risk of his being sensible of it. So they said regarding him, that it was for ghosts only to contend with the dead. He who waits to see the author depart this life whose writings he desires to dispute, what does he say except that he is weak and contentious? Aristotle was told that some one had spoken ill of him; "Let him do more," he said; "let him whip me, provided I am not there."[10]

Our fathers contented themselves with avenging an insult by giving the lie, giving the lie by a blow, and so on in order. They were valiant enough not to fear their enemy living and outraged. We tremble with fright so long as we see him on his feet. And, to prove that this is so, is it not our fine practice to-day, to pursue to the death, equally, him whom we have wronged and him who has wronged us? It is also a species of cowardice that has introduced into our single combats the custom of being attended by seconds, thirds, and fourths. In old days they were duels; now they are encounters and battles. The loneliness frightened those who first conceived this plan. *For each man had little confidence in himself.*[11] For, naturally, any companionship whatever brings cheer and relief in danger. In old days they made use of third persons to see that there was no confusion or treachery, and to testify to the result of the combat; but since we have adopted this fashion that they themselves

Cowardice the Mother of Cruelty

shall take part in, whoever is invited can not honourably hold himself as a spectator of it, for fear lest this be ascribed to lack of good-will or of courage. Besides the injustice and baseness of such action,—enlisting for the protection of your honour other valour and strength than your own,—I find there is a disadvantage for an able man, who completely trusts himself, to involve his fortune with that of a second. Every one incurs sufficient risk of himself, without incurring it also for another, and has enough to do to safeguard himself in his own valour, for the defence of his life, without entrusting so precious a thing to other hands. For, unless there has been an express agreement to the contrary, it is a joint affair between the four. If your second is down, you have two of them on your hands, with good reason. And if you say that this is outrageous, so indeed it is, even as it is outrageous to attack, well armed, a man who has only a broken sword, or, unhurt, a man who is already badly wounded. But if these are advantages which you have won in fighting, you may make use of them without reproach. Disparity and inequality are weighed and considered only in regard to the conditions in which the fray begins; afterward, accept what fortune gives you. And if you alone have three on your hands, your two companions having been killed, no more wrong is done you than I, with like advantage, should do, in war, by giving a sword-thrust to an enemy whom I saw grappling one of our men. The nature of this fellowship is such that, when there is troop against troop (as when our duc d'Orléans challenged Henry, King of England, a hundred against a hundred;[12] three hundred against a like number, as the Argives against the Lacedæmonians;[13] three against three, as the Horatii against the

Cowardice the Mother of Cruelty

Curiatii),[14] the many on either side are considered as but a single man. Wherever is companionship, there the risk is undefined and involved.

I have a family interest in this subject, for my brother, the sieur de Matecolom, was requested, in Rome, to second a gentleman whom he scarcely knew, who was on his defence, having been challenged by another. In this combat he found himself by chance opposed to one who was more near to him and more known to him (I would that some one would justify to me these laws of honour, which so often run counter to and disquiet those of reason); having disposed of his man, seeing the two principals in the affair still on their feet and unhurt, he went to the relief of his companion. What less could he do? Should he have stood still and looked on at the defeat—if fate had so willed—of him for whose defence he had come thither? What he had done up to that time was of no service in the matter: the brawl was undecided. The courtesy which you can, and certainly ought to, show your enemy when you have brought him to an ill condition and to some great disadvantage, I see not how you can show when another's interest is concerned, when you are only a follower, when the dispute is not yours. He[15] could be neither fair nor courteous at the risk of him to whom he had lent himself. So he was released from Italian prisons by a very prompt and public representation from our king.

Heedless nation! We are not content with making our vices and follies known to the world by report: we go among foreign nations to cause them to be seen in life. Put three Frenchmen in the Libyan deserts—they will not be together a month without provoking and irritating one another; you

Cowardice the Mother of Cruelty

would say that this peregrination is a scheme arranged to give to foreigners the pleasure of witnessing our tragedies; and, in most cases, to those who rejoice in our ills and who make sport of them. We go to Italy to learn to fence, and practise it at the expense of our lives before we know how. Yet it is needful, according to the rules for instruction, to put theory before practice; we betray our lack of skill:[16]

> The unhappy first-fruits of young warriors, and the hard apprenticeship of war to come.[17]

I well know that it is an art useful for its purpose (in the duel between the two princes, cousins-german, in Spain, the elder, Livy says, by skill in arms and by craft easily overcame the paralysed powers of the younger[18]), and, as I have learned by experience, one the knowledge of which sometimes strengthens the heart beyond its natural degree; but that is not properly valour, since it derives its support from skill, and has other foundation than itself. The honour of combat consists in rivalry in courage, not in science; and, consequently, I have seen one of my friends, renowned as a great master in that exercise, choose in his quarrels weapons which deprived him of the means of that advantage, and depend solely on good-fortune and confidence, so that the victory might not be attributed to his fencing rather than to his prowess; and in my childhood gentlemen avoided the reputation of good fencers as insulting, and secreted themselves to learn the art, as being one of cunning, derogatory to genuine and simple valour.

> These do not wish to avoid the combat, or to stop it, or to retreat; nor has skill here any part. They do not give blows now feigned, now full, now few; anger and

rage deprive them of the use of art. Hear their swords clash horribly, blade against blade; their feet do not move from their position; their feet are always firm, their hands always in motion; no blow descends in vain, no thrust is wasted.[19]

Shooting at butts, tourneys, and joustings, the counterfeits of war, were the exercise of our fathers; this other exercise is less noble, inasmuch as it looks only to a private end; it teaches us to destroy one another, contrary to the laws and justice, and in every way always produces harmful results. It is much more meet and becoming to exercise ourselves in things which strengthen, not impair, our government, which concern the public security and the common glory.

Publius Rutilius, consul, was the first who instructed the soldier in handling his weapons with skill and science; who joined art to valour, not for use in private quarrels; it was for war and for the quarrels of the Roman people;[20] a manner of fencing suitable for common people and citizens.[21] And besides the example of Cæsar, who ordered his men to aim chiefly at the faces of Pompey's soldiers in the battle of Pharsalia,[22] a thousand other commanders have likewise bethought themselves to invent new kinds of weapons, new ways of striking and defending, according to the need of the immediate affair. But just as Philopœmen condemned wrestling, in which he excelled, inasmuch as the training employed for that exercise was different from that which pertains to military instruction, to which alone he thought men of worth should apply themselves,[23] so it seems to me that this agility to which limbs are trained, these skilful withdrawals and motions, in which our youth are exercised in this new school, are not only useless, but rather contrary

Cowardice the Mother of Cruelty

and harmful to the conduct of military combat. Besides, our men employ therein[24] special weapons adapted to that particular use. And I have seen the time when it was not thought well for a gentleman, challenged to fight with sword and dagger, to appear equipped as a man-at-arms. It is worthy of consideration that Laches, in Plato, speaking of a training similar to ours in the handling of arms, says that he had never known any great soldier to come from that school, and especially not from the masters thereof.[25] As to them, our own experience says the same. For the rest, we can at least maintain that there are sufficient indications of there being no relation or resemblance. And in the education of children in his system, Plato forbids the art of boxing, introduced by Amycus and Epeius, and that of wrestling, by Antæus and Cercyon, because they have another aim than to render young men fit for military service, and do not contribute thereto.[26] But I find myself not a little distant from my theme.

The Emperor Maurice, being warned by dreams and by many prognostications that one Phocas, a soldier then unknown, would kill him, asked his son-in-law Philippus about this Phocas—his nature, his mode of life, and his character; and when, among other things, Philippus told him that he was cowardly and timid, the emperor forthwith concluded from that that he was capable of murder, and cruel.[27] What makes tyrants so bloodthirsty? It is their solicitude for their safety, and because their cowardly heart suggests to them no other means of ensuring it than by ridding themselves of those who can attack them,—even to women,—for fear of a scratch.

He strikes every thing, fearing every thing.[28]

943

Cowardice the Mother of Cruelty

The first cruelties are committed for their own sake; thence is born the fear of a just revenge, which later produces a long series of fresh cruelties, to stifle the early ones by the later. Philip, King of Macedon, who had so many affairs to settle[29] with the Roman people, agitated by the horror excited by the murders committed at his command, being unable to decide on this method with regard to so many families injured by him at diverse times, took the course of seizing all the children of those whom he had had put to death, in order, day by day, to destroy them one after another, and thus establish his repose.[30]

A subject-matter that is admirable fits well wherever it is placed.[31] I, who am more heedful of the weight and utility of writings than of their order and sequence, am not afraid to give room here, a little by itself, to a most admirable anecdote.[32] Among those condemned by Philip was one Herodicus, Prince of the Thessalians. After him, he had more recently put to death his two sons-in-law, each of whom left a very young son. Theoxena and Archo were the two widows. Theoxena could not be induced to marry again, although much sought after. Archo married Poris, the chief man among the Æneans, and had by him a number of children, and died leaving them all very young. Theoxena, impelled by maternal affection for her nephews, married Poris, to have them under her guidance and protection. And now comes the proclamation of the king's edict. The courageous mother, fearing both Philip's cruelty and the license of his satellites, in respect to those beautiful and tender children, dared to say that she would kill them with her own hands rather than give them up. Poris, alarmed by this declaration, promises her to steal away with them, and carry them

944

Cowardice the Mother of Cruelty

to Athens, to the keeping of some trustworthy and hospitable friends of his. They make use of the opportunity afforded by an annual festival celebrated at Ænia, in honour of Æneas, and go thither. Having been present during the day at the ceremonies and a public banquet, at night they slip off in a vessel made ready for them, to make their way by sea. The wind was adverse to them; and on the morrow, finding themselves in sight of the place from which they had sailed, they were pursued by the guards of the port. As these were approaching, while Poris was labouring to hasten the sailors in flight, Theoxena, frantic with love and vengefulness, reverting to her first idea, brought forward weapons and poison, and, showing them to the children, said: "Hearken, my children; death is now the only resource for your defence and liberty, and will be an occasion for the gods to exercise their sacred justice; these drawn swords, these full cups, open the way into it. Courage! and thou, my son, who are the eldest, grasp this blade, to die the manlier death." Having on one side this vehement persuasion, and on the other the foe at their throat, they wildly seized, each one upon what was nearest at hand, and, half dead, were thrown into the sea. Theoxena, proud of having so gloriously provided for the safety of all her children, clinging closely to her husband, said, "Let us follow those boys, my beloved, and share their place of burial." And thus locked in each other's arms, they threw themselves overboard, so that the vessel was brought back to the shore without its masters.[33]

Tyrants, in order to do both things at once,—to kill and to make their wrath felt,—have exerted all their skill in finding means of prolonging death. They desire their enemies to be gone, but not so quickly that they may not have time to relish their vengeance. Thereupon they are in great perplexity; for, if the tortures are very severe, they are short; if they are long drawn out, they are not painful enough to satisfy them; and to this end, they give rein to their wits. We see a thousand examples of it in ancient times; and I am not sure that we do not, unthinkingly, retain some trace of this barbarity. All that goes beyond simple death seems to me pure cruelty; our justice can not hope that he whom the fear of death, and of being beheaded or hanged, will not keep from wrong-doing will be deterred therefrom by the apprehension of a slow fire, or of pincers, or of the wheel. And it may be that we thus drive them to despair; for what can be the state of a man's mind, awaiting death for twenty-four hours, broken on the wheel, or, after the old manner, nailed to a cross?

Josephus narrates that, during the wars of the Romans in Judæa, on passing a place where, three days before, several Jews had been crucified, he recognised three of his friends, and obtained permission to take them away; two died, he says, the other lived on.[34] Chalcondylas, a trustworthy man, in the memoirs that he left of things that happened in his time and in his neighbourhood, reports, as the worst punishment, that which the Emperor Mohammed often employed—the cutting men into two parts across the middle, at the diaphragm, with a single blow of a scimitar; whence it came about that they died, as it were, two deaths at once; and he says that both parts, full of life, were seen to stir, as moved by great agony, for a long time after.[35] I do not believe that there was much feeling in those movements. The punishments most dreadful to behold are not always the worst to endure. And I find more atrocious what is told by other historians, regarding the Epirote lords, that he[36] had them flayed little by little, with such malicious skill that their life lasted fifteen days in that agony.[37] And these other two: Crœsus, having seized a gentleman, a favourite of his brother Pantaleon, carried him to the shop of a fuller, where he had him scraped and carded by the cards and combs of that trade, till he died of it;[38] George Sechel, leader of those Polish peasants who, under the title of a crusade, committed so many crimes, being defeated in battle by the vayvode of Transylvania, and captured, was for three days bound naked to a raft, exposed to all the varieties of torture that any one could suggest, during which time they kept the other prisoners fasting. At last, he living and beholding, they forced Lucat, his dear brother, for whose safety alone he had entreated, taking upon himself all the blame for their misdeeds, to drink his blood; and they compelled twenty of his most favoured captains to eat his flesh, tearing it apart violently, and swallowing the pieces. The rest of his body and the entrails, when he was dead, were boiled, and others of his following were forced to eat them.[39]

Chapter XXVIII

ALL THINGS

HAVE THEIR SEASON

THEY who compare Cato the Censor with the younger Cato, murderer of himself, compare two noble natures of kindred character.[1] The first displayed his under more aspects, and was the superior in military exploits and in the usefulness of his public functions. But the virtue of the younger, besides that it were blasphemy to compare any other to it in vigour, was much more unspotted. For who could acquit that of the Censor of envy and ambition, since he dared to assail the honour of Scipio, who was much greater than he and than any other man of his time, in rectitude and in all excellent qualities? What, among other things, they tell of him, that in his extreme old age he set about learning the Greek language with eager zest,[2] as if to quench a long thirst, does not seem to me to be very honourable to him. It is really what we call falling into second childhood. All things have their season, good things and all; and I can say my Pater Noster at an unfit moment;[3] as T. Quintius Flaminius was blamed because, being in command of the army, he was seen standing apart, at the very hour of the onset of a battle that he won, busying himself in praying to God.[4]

948

All Things have their Season

The wise man puts limits even to praiseworthy things.[5]

Eudemonidas, seeing Xenocrates, then very old, eagerly listening to the teachings of his school, "When," he said, "will this man know, if he is still learning?"[6] And Philopœmen said to those who extolled King Ptolemy because he daily enured his person to the exercise of arms: "It is not a praiseworthy thing in a king of his years to exercise himself in them; he ought henceforth really to use them."[7] The young man should make his preparations, the old man enjoy them, say the sages.[8] And the greatest defect that they observe in our nature is that our desires constantly renew their youth. We are forever beginning anew to live.[9] Our study and our desire ought some time to give evidence of old age. We have one foot in the grave, and our appetites and our pursuits are newly born.

When your funeral is close at hand, you order the cutting of marbles, and, forgetful of the tomb, you build houses.[10]

The longest of my plans is not of a year's extent; henceforth I think of nothing but coming to an end; I rid myself of all new hopes and undertakings, take my last farewell of all the places I leave, and dispossess myself every day of what I have. *For a long time I have neither lost nor gained any thing. . . . I have more provisions than I have length of way to go.*[11]

I have lived and accomplished the career that fortune allotted me.[12]

It is, in fine, the only solace I find in my old age, that it

949

deadens in me many desires and solicitudes whereby life is disquieted: solicitude about the course of the world, solicitude about riches, rank, knowledge, health, myself. A man is learning to talk when he should be learning to be silent forever.[13] One may always continue to study, but not to go to school; how foolish for an old man to be learning the alphabet![14]

> Different things please different men; not all things are appropriate to all ages.[15]

If we must study, let us study something suited to our condition, so that we may be able to reply as he did who, when he was asked wherefore he thus studied in his decrepitude, replied: "That I may the better and more gladly depart hence." [16] Such study was that of the younger Cato, who, when he felt that his end was near, turned to Plato's discourse on the eternity of the soul.[17] Not, as we must believe, that he had not long been supplied with every sort of provision for such a flitting; of confidence, or firm resolution, and of instruction, he had more than Plato had in his writings; his learning and his courage were in this respect superior to philosophy. He resorted to that occupation, not to make his death easier, but, like one for whom even sleep is not broken because of the importance of some deliberation, thus, without choice and without change, he continued his studies, with the other habitual actions of his life. The night when he had been refused the prætorship he passed playing at games of chance; that on which he was to die; in reading; loss of life or loss of office—it was all one to him.[18]

Chapter XXIX

OF VIGOUR

I FIND by experience that there is much difference between the sudden impulses and outgoings of the mind and a fixed and constant habit; and I see clearly that there is nothing we are not capable of, nay, even to surpassing divinity itself, says some one,[1] inasmuch as it is a greater thing to be made by oneself incapable of suffering than to be so by original condition; and even to combine with the weakness of man a godlike resolution and confidence. But this is only at moments.[2] And in the lives of those heroes of ancient times there are sometimes miraculous passages which seem far to surpass our natural powers; but they are passages only in truth; and it is hard to believe that one can so colour and imbue the mind with these conditions of excitement that they become habitual and as if natural to it. It happens to ourselves, who are but abortions of men, that we sometimes shoot our soul, stimulated by the speech or examples of others, very far beyond its common height; but it is a sort of passion which impels and excites it, and in some wise ravishes it from itself;[3] for, that sudden gust overblown, we find that unconsciously it unbends and relaxes of itself, if not quite to the lowest degree, at least so as to be no more the same; so much that then, on any slight occasion, for a bird lost or a glass broken, we allow ourselves to be moved almost as one of the common people. Except regularity, moderation, and steadiness, I consider that any thing may be achieved by a man who is very imperfect and, as a whole, full of failings. For this reason the sages say that, to judge a man rightly, it is needful to observe chiefly his usual actions, and to surprise him in his every-day dress. Pyrrho, who built upon ignorance so droll a belief, tried, like all other true philosophers, to make his life correspond to his doctrine. And because he maintained that the weakness of the human judgement was so extreme as to be incapable of any choice or inclination, and conceived it as suspended in perpetual equilibrium, regarding and accepting all things as indifferent, it is related that he always maintained the same conduct and bearing: if he had begun a remark, he never failed to finish it, even when he to whom he was speaking had gone away; if he was walking, he did not turn aside for any obstacle that might present itself, and was saved by his friends from precipices, collision with vehicles, and other mishaps. For to fear or to avoid any thing would have been opposition to his assertions, which denied to the very senses[4] all choice and certainty. Sometimes he endured being cut and cauterised with such resolution that he was not seen even to wink his eyes.[5]

It is something to bring the mind to such ideas; it is more to connect with them the desired results; still, this is not impossible; but to connect these with such perseverence and resolution as to establish by them one's ordinary course of conduct, surely it is almost incredible that a man should be able to do this in undertakings so far removed from common

Of Vigour

custom. And for this reason this same philosopher, being sometimes found in his own house scolding his sister very harshly, and being censured for so failing in his indifference, "What!" said he, "must even this foolish woman serve as evidence of my rule?" Another time, when he was seen defending himself from a dog, he said, "It is very difficult to put off man altogether; and we must endeavour and strive to combat things, first by actions, but, at the worst, by reason and arguments."[6]

About seven or eight years ago, a villager, still living some two leagues from here, who had long been vexed by his wife's jealousy, returning one day from his work, and she welcoming him with her usual brawling, he became so frenzied that, on the spot, with the sickle that he still had in his hand, he clean mowed off the parts which were the cause of her heat, and threw them into her face. And it is said that an amorous and lusty young gentleman of our nation, having at length by his perseverance softened the heart of his fair mistress, was thrown into despair because, at the moment of attack, he found that he himself was soft and a weakling, and that

> languidly
> The member raised his head.[7]

When he returned home he immediately stripped himself of it and sent it, a cruel and bloody sacrifice, for the expiation of his offence. If this had been done from religious motives and deliberately, as the priests of Cybele did, what should we not say of so sublime an action?

A few days since, at Bragerac,[8] five leagues from my house, higher up the river Dordogne, a woman who had been maltreated and beaten the night before by her husband, a man of morose and choleric nature, determined to escape from his harshness at the cost of her life; and when she got up in the morning, having greeted her neighbours as usual, she let fall a word or two about her affairs, and taking her sister by the hand, she led her to a bridge; and after she had taken leave of her as if in jest, without showing any sort of change or alteration, threw herself headlong into the river, where she perished. The most notable thing in this is that the scheme was ripening in her brain throughout a whole night. It is quite another thing with the Indian women; for it being customary with them for the husband to have many wives, and for the one who is dearest to kill herself when her husband dies, each one, in the whole plan of her life, aims at gaining this point and this advantage over her companions; and the good offices that they perform for the husband look to no other reward than to be preferred in accompanying him in death.[9]

> When the kindling torch has been thrown on the funeral pile, the crowd of faithful wives, with dishevelled hair, surrounding it, strive to the utmost for death, and while living, to follow their spouse; it is a disgrace not to be allowed to die. The winners take fire and offer their bodies to the flames, and press their scorched lips on their husbands'.[10]

There is a man even in our own day who writes of having seen this custom in practice among those oriental nations; and not only the wife was buried with the husband, but also the female slaves that he had enjoyed. It is done in this fashion. The husband having died, the widow may, if she wishes

Of Vigour

(but few wish it), demand two or three months' delay, to settle her affairs. When the day has come, she mounts her horse, arrayed as for her nuptials, and with a joyous bearing goes, as she says, to sleep with her husband, holding in her left hand a mirror, in the other an arrow. Going on her way thus in state, attended by her friends and kinsmen and by a great concourse of people in holiday mood, she is presently brought to the public place appointed for such spectacles. It is a large space, in the centre of which is a pit filled with wood, and adjoining this a mound four or five steps high, to which she is conducted, and there served with a sumptuous repast. After this she falls to dancing and singing, and, whenever it seems well to her, orders the fire to be lighted. That done, she steps down and, taking by the hand the nearest of her husband's kindred, they go together to the near-by river, where she strips herself naked, and distributes her jewels and garments among her friends, then plunges into the water as if thus to wash away her sins. Coming forth, she envelops herself in a yellow linen cloth fourteen feet[11] long, and, giving her hand again to the same kinsman of her husband, reascends the little hill, whence she speaks to the people and asks their favour for her children if she has any. Between the pit and the mound a curtain may be drawn, to shut out the sight of that glowing furnace; this some forbid, to show more courage. When she has finished what she has to say, a woman presents her with a vessel full of oil, to anoint her head and her whole body; which, having so done, she throws into the fire and at the same moment flings herself in. Immediately the people throw upon her a quantity of logs, to keep her from lingering, and all the joy is changed to wailing and sorrow. If they are persons of meaner condition, the dead man's body is taken to the place where they wish to bury him, and there placed, sitting, the widow on her knees before him, closely embracing him; and she thus remains while they build a wall about them; and when it has reached the height of the woman's shoulders, some one of her kin, taking her head from behind, wrings her neck; and when she has given up the ghost, the wall is quickly built up and closed over, wherein they remain buried.

In this same country, there was something like this among their Gymnosophists; for, not by compulsion from others, nor from the impetuosity of a sudden impulse, but in express acknowledgement of their rule, their custom was, when they had reached a certain age, or found themselves threatened by some disease, to have a funeral pile built, and upon it placed a much-adorned bed; and after having joyously entertained their friends and acquaintances, they lay down on this bed with such resolution that, when it was set on fire, they were not seen to move either foot or hand; and thus died one of them, Calanus, in the presence of the whole army of Alexander the Great.[12] And the man was regarded among them neither as godly nor as blessed, who had not thus destroyed himself, dismissing his soul purged and purified by fire, after all that it had of mortal and terrestrial had been consumed. The steadfast premeditation of this during the whole life is what is marvellous.

Among our other matters of dispute has entered in that of *Fatum;* and, to connect things to come, and even our will, with fixed and inevitable necessity, we still resort to this argument of ancient times: since God foresees that all things will thus happen, as he undoubtedly does, it needs must be that they thus happen. To which our masters reply that the

Of Vigour

seeing that something happens, as we do, and as God likewise does (for every thing being present to him, he sees
rather than foresees), is not to compel it to happen; in truth,
we see because things happen, and things do not happen because we see. The happening makes the knowledge, not the
knowledge the happening. That which we see happen happens; but it might happen differently; and God, in the register of the causes of the events of which he had prescience,
has there also those which are called casual, and the voluntary ones, which depend on the freedom he has given to our
will; and he knows that we shall do amiss because we shall
have chosen to do amiss.

Now, I have seen many men encourage their troops with
this fatal necessity; for, if our death is attached to a certain
moment, neither the enemy's musketry, nor our boldness,
nor our flight and cowardice can bring it nearer or set it
further off. That is all very well to say, but you will not find
the man who will act upon it. And, if it be the fact that a
strong and lively faith draws after it actions of the same
sort, surely this faith of which our mouths are so full is in
our time wonderfully weak, unless it be that the contempt it
has for works makes it scorn their company. Nevertheless,
on this same subject the sire de Joinville, the most credible
of witnesses, tells us of the Bedouins, a nation blended with
the Saracens, with whom King Saint Louis had dealings in
the Holy Land, that they in their faith believed so im-
plicitly that every man's life was from all eternity prescribed
and measured off by unavoidable foreordination, that they
went into battle unarmed save for a Turkish sword, and with
their bodies covered only with a white cloth. And for their
extremist malediction, when they were angry with one an-

other, they had always in their mouths, "Accursed be thou, as he that arms himself for fear of death!"[13] This test of belief and faith is very different from ours. And of this class is also that given by the two friars of Florence in our fathers' day. Being engaged in some learned controversy, they agreed to walk together into a fire, before all the people and in the public square, each as a proof of the truth of his side. And all the preparations for this were already made, and the thing just on the point of execution, when it was interrupted by an unforeseen accident.[14]

A young Turkish nobleman, having performed a distinguished feat of arms, in his own person, in the sight of the two armies, that of Amurath and that of Hunyades, ready to join battle, being asked by Amurath what had inspired him, being so young and inexperienced (for it was the first war that he had seen), with such heroic courage, replied that he had had for chief teacher in valour a hare. "One day," he said, "while hunting, I came across a hare in his form, and although I had two fine greyhounds at my side, still it seemed to me that, to make sure of not missing him, it would be better to use my bow, for he was an excellent mark. I began to discharge my arrows, and let fly the whole forty that there were in my quiver, not only without striking him, but without rousing him. At last I loosed my greyhounds, and they were no more successful. I learned from this that he had been protected by his destiny, and that neither darts nor swords reach their mark except by permission of our fate, which it is not in our power to repel or to advance."[15] This tale should serve in passing to show us how our reason is swayed by all sorts of objects.

A personage great in years, in name, in dignity, and in

Of Vigour

learning boasted to me of having been led to a certain very momentous change of faith by an outside suggestion so odd and, indeed, so far from convincing, that I found it stronger for the contrary effect. He called it a miracle, and so did I, in a different sense. The historians of the Turks say that the conviction generally current among them, of the fatal and inflexible limitation of their days, manifestly assists in giving them confidence in dangers.[16] And I know a great prince who turns this idea nobly to his advantage,[17] if fortune continues to back him.

There has not come to pass within our memory a more wonderful effect of resolution than in those two men who plotted the death of the Prince of Orange.[18] It is marvellous how the second one, who did the deed, could be stimulated to an undertaking in which his companion, who had done his utmost, had such ill success; and, following his steps and with the same weapon, assail a lord armed with so recent a lesson of suspicion, powerful in his following of friends and in bodily strength, in his own hall, amidst his guards, in a city wholly devoted to him. Surely he employed therein a very resolute hand, and a spirit excited by a vehement passion. A dagger is more certain to strike home; but inasmuch as it requires more motion and strength of arm than a pistol, its blow is more likely to be turned aside or hindered. That he rushed to what he knew to be certain death I have not much doubt; for the hope with which they may have thought to beguile him could find no lodgement in a resolute mind; and the manner of his exploit shows that he lacked that no more than courage. The grounds of a conviction so powerful may be various; for our imagination does what it pleases with itself and with us. The deed that was done near

Of Vigour

Orléans[19] was in no wise similar; there was more chance than energy in it; the wound had not been mortal if fortune had not made it so; and the undertaking to fire from horseback and from a distance, at a man moved by the movement of his horse, was the undertaking of one who preferred to fail in his object rather than to fail to escape. What followed after showed this. For he was so dazed and intoxicated by the thought of so great a deed that his wits were completely lost and bemuddled, both as to managing his flight and managing his tongue in his answers. What need he have done save fly back to his friends across a river? That is something to which I have had recourse in less dangers, and which I consider of small risk, however broad may be the stream, provided that your horse finds the entrance easy and that you perceive on the other side a convenient landing-place in relation to the current. The other,[20] when they announced to him his horrible sentence, "I was prepared for this," he said; "I will astonish you by my endurance."

The Assassins, a tribe in the dependence of Phœnicia, are considered among the Mohammedans as having supreme religious zeal and purity of morals. They hold that the most certain means of deserving Paradise is to kill some one of different religious belief. For which reason, scorning all danger to themselves, in favour of so advantageous a deed, one or two are often seen, at the price of certain death, to offer to assassinate (we have borrowed this word from their name) their enemy in the midst of his forces. Thus was slain our Count Raymond of Tripoli in his own city.[21]

Chapter XXX

OF A

CHILD MONSTER

THIS tale shall go without comment, for I leave physicians to discourse of it. I saw the day before yesterday a child whom two men and a nurse (who said they were his father and uncle and aunt) were taking about to get money by exhibiting him, because of his strange appearance. In other respects he was as ordinary children,[1] and stood on his feet, walked, and babbled much like others of the same age; he had not yet been willing to take any other nourishment than from his nurse's breast; and what they tried, in my presence, to put into his mouth, he chewed a little and put it out without swallowing it; his cries seemed to have something peculiar about them; he was just fourteen months old. Below his paps he was caught and fastened to another child without a head, who had the back passage choked, otherwise sound; for, although one arm was shorter than the other, it had been broken by accident at their birth. They were joined face to face, as if a smaller child was trying to embrace a larger one. The ligature and the space between them was only four finger-lengths, or thereabouts, so that, if you lifted up the imperfect child, you saw beneath it the other's navel, since the ligature was between the paps and the navel.

Of a Child Monster

The imperfect one's navel could not be seen, but easily all the rest of his body. So all of the imperfect one that was not attached, as the arms, buttocks, thighs, and legs, was hanging and dangling from the other, and might reach halfway down his legs.

This double body, and these diverse limbs connected with a single head, might well furnish the king[2] with a favourable augury for maintaining the diverse parts and fractions of our realm under the union of his laws; but, lest the event belie this, it is better to let it pass, for divination can be only about things that have happened; *as when facts exist, then, by some kind of interpretation, they may be related to divination.*[3] As they say of Epimenides, that he divined things past.[4] I have just seen a shepherd at Medoc, thirty years of age or thereabouts, who has no show of genital parts. He has three holes from which he continually drops his water. He is bearded, has desires, and readily seeks contact with women.

What we call monsters are not so to God, who sees in the immensity of his work the infinity of forms that he has comprised therein; and it is probable that this figure which astonishes us is related to and connected with some other figure of the same sort unknown to man. From his omniscience nothing comes forth save what is good and common and regular; but we do not see their disposition and relation. *What he often sees he does not wonder at, although he does not know how it comes to pass. What he has not seen before, if it takes place, he ranks as a prodigy.*[5] We call contrary to Nature what comes about contrary to custom; nothing whatsoever exists which is not in accordance with her. Let this universal and natural fact expel from us the error and amazement that novelty brings us.

962

Chapter XXXI

OF ANGER

PLUTARCH is admirable everywhere, but chiefly where he judges of human actions. We may read in the parallel between Lycurgus and Numa excellent things that he says on the subject of our great folly in abandoning children to the governance and care of their fathers. The greater number of our civil governments, as Aristotle says, leave to every man, after the manner of the Cyclops, the guidance of his wife and children, according to his foolish and inconsiderate fancy;[1] and the Lacedæmonians and Cretans were almost alone in entrusting to the laws the schooling of childhood. Who does not see that every thing in a state depends upon its[2] education and nurture? And yet, without any discernment, we leave it at the mercy of parents, however foolish and bad they may be. Among other things, how often, when passing through our streets, have I had a desire to devise something to avenge the little boys whom I saw whipped and knocked down and bruised by some father or mother, furious and mad with anger! You see them sally forth, fire and rage in their eyes,—

agitated by rage, they are carried to an abyss, like

Of Anger

rocks broken from their support, loosened from a mountain, which roll down a steep slope,[3]—

(and according to Hippocrates the most dangerous distempers are those that disfigure the face[4]), with a sharp and violent voice, often against little boys who were but lately at nurse. And afterwards, behold these children maimed and dulled with blows; and our laws make no account of it, as if these maimings and dislocations were not of members of our commonwealth.

It is a cause for gratitude that you have given a citizen to your country and your people, provided that you so act as to make him fit for the country's service, useful in agriculture, useful in the deeds of war and of peace.[5]

There is no passion which so disturbs the honesty of our judgements as anger. No one would hesitate to punish with death the judge who had sentenced his prisoner at the bar in anger; why is it any more permissible for fathers and schoolmasters, when in a passion, to flog children and chastise them? It is no longer correction, it is vengeance. Chastisement takes the place of medicine with children;[6] and should we tolerate a physician who was excited and vexed with his patient?

We ourselves, to do well, should never lay a hand on our servants whilst our anger lasts. When our pulse beats fast and we feel stirred, let us put off the matter; things will seem different to us, in truth, when we have become calm and cool again; it is passion that now rules us; it is passion that speaks; it is not we ourselves.[7] Seen through it, faults seem greater to us, as bodies do when seen through a mist.[8]

Of Anger

He who is hungry makes use of food; but he who desires to make use of chastisement should have neither hunger nor thirst.[9]

Furthermore, chastisements that have been weighed and are made advisedly are received much better and with more profit by him who suffers them. Otherwise he does not think that he was justly condemned by a man moved by wrath and fury; and he alleges in his justification the extraordinary actions of his master, his flushed face, his unwonted oaths, and his disquietude and reckless haste.

> Their faces swell with anger, their veins blacken
> with blood, their eyes flash with more than Gorgonean
> fire.[10]

Suetonius says that, Lucius Saturninus[11] having been condemned by Cæsar, the thing that was of most service to him with the people (to whom he appealed) for gaining his cause was the animosity and harshness that Cæsar brought to that judgement.

Saying is a different thing from doing; the preaching and the preacher must be considered separately. Those persons of our day held good cards[12] who tried to cope with the truth of our Church by setting forth the vices of her ministry; she derives her testimonies from elsewhere;[13] theirs is a foolish way of arguing and would throw every thing into confusion. A man of good morals may have false belief, and a bad man may preach truth, yes, one who does not believe it. It is an admirable harmony, no doubt, when the deed and the word go together; and I do not wish to deny that the word, when deeds follow, is of more authority and efficacy; as Eudamidas said, when he heard a philosopher discoursing of war, "These are fine sayings, but he who utters them is not to be believed, for his ears are not accustomed to the sound of the trumpet."[14] Cleomenes, hearing a rhetorician hold forth concerning valour, began to laugh heartily; and the other taking offence, he said to him: "I should do so if it were a swallow who was talking about it; but if it were an eagle, I should listen to him gladly."[15] I perceive, it seems to me, in the writings of the ancients, that he who says what he thinks strikes home much more vigorously that he who dissembles. Hear Cicero speak of the love of liberty; hear Brutus speak of it; the mere written words of this man tell you that he would purchase it at the cost of his life. Let Cicero, the father of eloquence, treat of contempt of death; let Seneca treat of it also: the first drags himself feebly along, and you feel that he desires to solve for you something he has not solved for himself; he gives you no spirit, for he himself has none about this;[16] the other animates and excites you. I never read an author, especially of those who treat of virtue and of duties, that I do not enquire carefully what manner of man he has been. For the Ephors of Sparta, seeing a dissolute man offer the people useful advice, commanded him to keep silence, and begged a man of worth to claim for himself the idea, and to suggest it.[17]

The writings of Plutarch, if well digested, reveal him to us as much as is needful, and I think that I know him to his soul; yet I could wish that we had some memoirs of his life; and I have been induced to go out of my way into this matter[18] because of my gratitude to Aulus Gellius for having left us in writing that anecdote of his character which bears upon my subject of anger. A slave of his, a bad and vicious man, but one whose ears were in some sort stored with phil-

Of Anger

osophic lessons, having been, by Plutarch's order, stripped for some fault of his, while they were whipping him, complained at first that it was unreasonable, and that he had done nothing; but finally, beginning to cry out and insult his master in good earnest, he reproached him for not being philosophical as he boasted of being; and that he had often heard him say it was uncomely to be angry; indeed, that he had written a book about it; and that now, when head over ears in anger, his causing him to be so cruelly beaten entirely belied his writings. Whereupon Plutarch coolly and temperately replied: "Tell me, knave, from what do you judge that I am at this moment angry? My face, my voice, my colour, my speech—do they give you any evidence that I am excited? I do not think that my eyes are fierce, or my face disturbed, or my voice terrifyingly loud. Am I flushed? Do I foam at the mouth? Do any words escape from me which I may have to repent of? Do I pant? Do I tremble with wrath? For let me tell you these are the true signs of anger." And then, turning to him who was doing the whipping, "Go on with your business," he said, "while this fellow and I argue."[19] Such is the tale.

Architas Tarentinus, returning from a war in which he had been captain-general, found his house all out of order and his land neglected through the bad management of his bailiff; and having summoned him, "Look you," he said; "if I were not angry, I would cudgel you soundly."[20] And Plato likewise, being chafed by one of his slaves, gave Speusippus orders to punish him, excusing himself from laying his own hand on him on the ground that he was vexed.[21] Charillus, a Lacedæmonian, speaking to a Helot who carried himself too insolently and audaciously toward him, "By the gods," he cried, "if I were not angry, I would kill you this very moment!"[22]

It is a passion that takes pleasure in itself and flatters itself. How often, being disturbed without true reason, if we are offered some good defence or excuse, we fall into high dudgeon against the truth itself, and innocence! I remember in this connection a wonderful example in ancient times. Piso, a man in every other respect of notable virtue, being excited against one of his soldiers because, returning alone from foraging, he could give him no account of where he had left a companion of his, held it for certain that he had killed him, and forthwith condemned the other to death. And when he is on the gallows, lo! the lost companion arrives. The whole army was greatly rejoiced; and, after much hugging and embracing between the two companions, the hangman took them both before Piso, every one expecting this to give him great pleasure. But it was far otherwise; for from shame and spleen his violence, which was still at its height, was redoubled; and with a craftiness which his passion suddenly suggested to him he made three guilty men of them, because one of them was found innocent, and ordered them all three to be despatched: the first soldier, because judgement had been passed against him; the second, who had strayed away, because he was the cause of his companion's death; and the hangman, for not obeying the command given him.[23]

They who have to deal with testy women may have learned by experience what a rage they are thrown into when one meets their excitement with silence and composure, and disdains to feed their wrath. The orator Cælius was exceedingly choleric by nature. One who was supping in his company, a man of mild and gentle conversation, in order not to provoke him, adopted the course of approving all he said, and agreeing with it. Cælius, unable to suffer his vexation thus to die away without nutriment, exclaimed: "By the gods, deny something, I say! that there may be two of us."[24] They[25] likewise get into a passion only so that some one may get into a passion with them, in imitation of the laws of love. Phocion, with a man who interrupted his talk by vehemently insulting him, did nothing but keep silence and give him full time to exhaust his anger; that done, without any reference to the hindrance, he resumed his talk at the point at which he had dropped it.[26] There is no retort so stinging as such contempt. Regarding the most choleric man in France (and it is always an imperfection, but more excusable in a military man, for in that profession there are certainly occasions which can not dispense with it[27]), I often see that he makes a greater effort than any other man I know[28] to curb his anger; it moves him so violently and furiously,—

> as when a fire of twigs burns noisily under the sides of a cauldron, and the water dances in boiling; within, the steam mounts and rises high with foam; the water escapes; a dark vapour flies up into the air,[29]—

that he must needs put a cruel constraint upon himself to moderate it. As for me, I know no passion which I could make so great an effort to cloak and bear up against. I would not put so high a price upon wisdom. I do not so much consider what a man does, as what it costs him not to do worse.

Another boasted to me of the composure and gentleness of his deportment, which is, in truth, remarkable. I told him

that it was, indeed, something, especially for those of high
positions like himself, observed by every one, to appear before the world as always discreetly self-governed; but that
the chief thing was to take heed for his inner being and for
himself; and that, in my opinion, it was not managing his
affairs well to fret himself inwardly, which I feared that he
did, in order to maintain that mask and that outward appearance of composure. We incorporate anger in ourselves
by concealing it; as Diogenes said to Demosthenes, who,
fearing to be seen in a tavern, withdrew to the back of it:
"The more you withdraw, the more you enter therein."[30]
It is my opinion that it is better to give one's servant a blow
on the cheek a little unseasonably than to put one's mind
to the trouble of presenting this grave demeanour; and I
should prefer to show forth my passions rather than brood
upon them at my own cost; they lose their strength when
aired, and by expressing themselves; it is better that their
point should be turned away from us than against ourselves.
*All open vices are comparatively unimportant; and those
are most pernicious that lurk under an appearance of
health.*[31]

I warn those in my family whose position authorises displeasure in them, first, that they govern their anger discreetly and do not pour it out recklessly; for that impairs its
effect and weight; hasty and constant noisy scolding becomes a habit, and consequently every one makes light of it;
when you make use of it to a servant for his theft, it is not
felt, inasmuch as it is the same that he has known you to
make use of a hundred times because he has washed a glass
badly, or misplaced a stool; second, that they do not waste
their displeasure on the air, and that they see to it that their

reproof reaches him of whom they complain; for ordinarily they scold before he is in their presence, and continue to scold an age after he has gone;

> And the insane man, seeking [a foe], attacks himself.[32]

They quarrel with their own shadow, and carry this bluster to some place where there is no one either punished or injured by it, save by loud wrangling with their voices to a person who can do nothing about the matter. In like manner, I blame those who swagger and boast without an opponent; we should confine these rodomontades where they take effect,—

> as a bull in beginning the combat bellows terribly, and, exciting himself by the use of his horns, struggles with the trunk of a tree and beats the wind with his blows, scattering the sand in prelude to the fight.[33]

When I show displeasure, it is as sharply, but as briefly and privately, as I can; I let myself go in suddenness and violence, but not in confusion, so that I make no use of any insulting unselected words,[34] and I take heed only to place my darts where I think they will most wound; for I commonly use my tongue only. My servants come off more cheaply in great matters than in small; small ones take me by surprise, and the mischief of it is that, when you go over the precipice, it matters not who gave you the push—you go to the bottom all the same; the fall is enforced, impelled, and hastened by itself. On great occasions it satisfies me if they are so deserving of blame[35] that every one expects to see them produce reasonable anger; I pride myself on disappointing their expectation; I brace and prepare myself against these;[36] they make me uneasy,[37] and threaten to carry me far, should I follow them. I easily restrain myself from entering into them, and am strong enough, if I expect it, to repel the impulse of that passion, whatever violent cause it may have; but if it takes me unawares, and once seizes upon me, it carries me away, however trifling its cause. I bargain thus with those who may dispute with me: "When you feel that I am the first to become heated, let me go, wrong or right; I will do the same in my turn. The tempest is engendered by the meeting of angers which are usually produced one by the other, and do not arise simultaneously. If we let each have its way, we shall always be at peace." A useful prescription, but of difficult execution. Sometimes, too, it happens that I counterfeit displeasure, for the management of my household, without any real emotion. As advancing age sharpens my temper, I study to correct it; and I shall so manage, if I can, that I shall be henceforth so much the less peevish and hard to please as I shall have more excuse and inclination to be so, although heretofore I have been of those who are least so.

One more word, in conclusion. Aristotle says that anger sometimes serves courage and valour as a weapon. That is probable; however, they who deny it reply neatly that it is a weapon of strange use: for we control other weapons, this one controls us; our hand does not guide it, but it guides our hand; it possesses us, not we it.[38]

Chapter XXXII

DEFENCE OF SENECA

AND PLUTARCH

MY familiarity with these personages, and the assistance that they give to my old age, and to my book,
which is constructed wholly of their spoils, compel me to
entertain their honour as my own.

As for Seneca, among a thousand little books that they
of the so-called Reformed religion issue in defence of their
cause, which sometimes come from an able hand,—it is a
great pity that it should not be busied about a better subject,
—I saw one some time ago, which, in order to enlarge and fill
out the parallel that it desires to find between the government of our poor late King Charles IX and that of Nero,
compares the late cardinal de Lorraine with Seneca: their
fortunes, in having both been at the head of the governments of their princes, and also their characters, their conditions, and their conduct. Wherein, in my opinion, he does
much honour to the lord cardinal; for, although I am of
those who rate as high as possible his intellect, his eloquence,
his zeal for his religion and for the service of his king, and
his good-fortune in being born in an age when such a man
was so unheard of and rare, and when, at the same time, it
was so necessary for the public good that an ecclesiastical

973

Defence of Seneca and Plutarch

personage of this nobility and dignity should be a man of ability and qualified for his office, yet, to confess the truth, I do not rate his capacity as nearly so great, or his virtue as so spotless and perfect, or so steadfast, as that of Seneca. Now, this book of which I speak, to attain its end, gives a very contemptuous description of Seneca, having borrowed the strictures of the historian Dion,[1] to whose testimony I give no credit whatsoever; for besides his being inconsistent (since, after having sometimes called Seneca very wise, and again a mortal enemy of Nero's vices, he represents him elsewhere as avaricious, usurious, ambitious, cowardly, and sensual, and by false tokens counterfeiting the character of a philosopher), the virtue of Seneca appears so vivid and vigorous in his writings, and his defence in them about some of these imputations, as of his wealth and excessive expenditure, is so clear, that I should not believe any testimony to the contrary. And, furthermore, it is much more reasonable to believe, in such matters, the Roman historians than the Greeks and foreigners. Now, Tacitus[2] and the other Roman writers speak more honourably of his life and of his death, and describe him to us as in all respects a most excellent and most virtuous person. And I do not desire to cast other blame on Dion's judgement than this, which is inevitable: that his perception about Roman affairs is so faulty that he dares to sustain the cause of Julius Cæsar against Pompeius, and that of Antonius against Cicero.[3]

Let us come to Plutarch. Jean Bodin is an excellent author of our day, and possesses much more judgement than the throng of scribblers of his time, and deserves to be estimated and examined. I find him a little bold in that passage of his *Methode de l'Histoire* in which he not only accuses Plu-

Defence of Seneca and Plutarch

tarch of ignorance,[4]—as to which I should let him say what he would,[5] for that is not for me to deal with,—but also says that this author often writes "incredible and wholly fabulous things" (these are his words). If he had said simply, "things other than they are," that would have been no great reprehension; for what we have not seen we take from the hands of others, and on trust; and I see that he purposely sometimes tells the same story in different ways; as, for instance, the opinion pronounced by Hannibal about the three greatest captains who ever were—it is in one wise in the Life of Flaminius, and otherwise in that of Pyrrhus. But to charge him with having taken for current coin incredible and impossible things is to accuse the most judicious author in the world of lack of judgement. And this is his example: "As when," so he says, "he narrates that a Lacedæmonian boy let his whole belly be torn by a fox-cub that he had stolen, and carried hidden under his garment till it killed him, rather than disclose his theft."[6] I think, in the first place, that this example is ill chosen, inasmuch as it is very difficult to set bounds to the strength of the faculties of the soul, while we have more ability to define and know the bodily powers; and for this reason, if I had been he, I should rather have chosen an example of the second kind;[7] and there are some of these lacking in credibility; as, amongst others, what he narrates of Pyrrhus—that, "severely wounded as he was, he dealt so great a sword-blow to an enemy armed at all points, that he cleft him from the top of his head to his feet, so that the body was divided into two parts."[8] In his example I see no great miracle; nor do I accept the excuse with which he shields Plutarch—that he added this phrase, "as they say," to warn us and curb our belief. For, unless

975

about things accepted by authority and respect for antiquity or religion, he would not have been willing, either to accept himself, or to propose to us to believe, things in themselves incredible; and as to this phrase, "as they say," that he does not employ it in that place for this purpose is easy to see by what he himself relates to us elsewhere on this subject of the endurance of Lacedæmonian children: instances happening in his time, more difficult of belief; something to which Cicero also testified before him (as having been, as he says, on the spot): that even in their day there were children who, in the test of endurance to which they were subjected before the altar of Diana, bore being scourged until they were covered with blood, not only without crying out, but even without lamentation, and some even to the point of voluntarily yielding up their lives.[9] And what Plutarch also narrates,[10] together with a hundred other witnesses, that, during the ceremony of sacrifice, a glowing coal having fallen into the sleeve of a Lacedæmonian child while he was incensing, he let all his arm burn until the smell of the burnt flesh was perceived by the bystanders. According to their custom, there was nothing in which reputation was more concerned, or from which they had to suffer more blame and shame, than the being detected in theft. I am so impressed with the greatness of those men, that not only it does not seem to me, as to Bodin, that his[11] tale is incredible, but I do not even find it to be rare and extraordinary. Spartan history is full of a thousand severer and rarer examples; it is all miraculous in this respect.[12] Marcellinus reports, with regard to this matter of theft, that in his day there had not been found any kind of torture which could force Egyptians detected in that crime, common among them, to tell even their names.[13]

976

Defence of Seneca and Plutarch

A Spanish peasant,[14] being put to the question about the accomplices in the murder of the prætor Lucius Piso, cried out, in the midst of the torture, that his friends should not stir and should stay by him in perfect security; and that it was not in the power of pain to wrest from him a word of confession; and they got nothing else from him the first day. The next day, as they were bringing him back to renew the torture, tearing himself violently from the hands of his guards, he dashed his head against a wall, and so killed himself.[15] Epicharis, having satiated and tired out the cruelty of Nero's officers, and endured fire and beatings and the rack for a whole day, without a word of betrayal of her fellow conspirators, being brought back to torture the next day, her limbs all crushed, she passed a lacing of her garment round an arm of her chair with a running knot, and thrusting therein her head, strangled herself by the weight of her body.[16] Having the spirit to die thus and to evade a renewal of the previous tortures, does it not seem that she deliberately lent her life to this proof of her endurance, in order to mock at that tyrant and to encourage others to like action against him?

And whoever shall enquire of our troopers concerning their experiences in these civil wars will find instances of endurance, persistency, and firmness in these wretched times of ours, and in this rabble, more inert and effeminate than that of Egypt, worthy to be compared with those that we have narrated of Spartan valour. I know that there have been simple peasants who have let the soles of their feet be scorched, their finger-ends crushed with the hammer of a pistol, their bleeding eyes forced out of their heads by their brows being bound with a stout cord, before they chose even to be held for ransom. I have seen one of them left for dead perfectly naked in a ditch, his neck all bruised and swollen by a halter which still hung from it, by which they had dragged him all night at a horse's tail, his body pierced in a hundred places by dagger-thrusts, which had been dealt him, not to kill him, but to cause him pain and terror—who had endured all this, and even to having lost speech and feeling, being resolved, as he told me, rather to die a thousand deaths,—as, indeed, so far as suffering went, he had passed through a full one,—than to promise any thing; and yet he was one of the richest husbandmen in the whole region. How many of them have been seen to submit to be burnt and roasted for opinions borrowed from others, which they neither know nor understand!

I have known hundreds of women,—for they say that Gascon heads have some preëminence in obstinacy,—whom you could more easily induce to take hold of a hot iron than make them let go their hold of an opinion which they had formed in anger. They are exasperated by meeting with blows and compulsion. And he who devised the tale of the woman who, for no correction by threats and cudgelling, would cease calling her husband lousy, and who, having been thrown into the water, raised her hands above her head, even as she was choking, and made the motion of killing lice,[17] devised a tale in which, in very truth, we see the express image of the obstinacy of women. And obstinacy is the sister of constancy, at least in its characteristics of strength and firmness.

We must not decide what is possible and what is not so by what is credible and incredible to our perceptions, as I have said elsewhere;[18] and it is a great mistake, and one which, nevertheless, the majority of men fall into (this I do not say as regards Bodin), to find it difficult to believe of others what they themselves could not do, or would not. It seems to every man that the chief form of human nature is in himself; he tests all others by that, and refers them to it. The proceedings which do not resemble his are false and artificial.[19] What irrational stupidity!

For my own part, I regard some men as very far above me, notably among the ancients; and though I recognise clearly my inability to follow them with my steps, I do not fail to follow them with my eyes, and to imagine the impulses which so lift them up, the seeds whereof I perceive in some degree in myself; as I do also those of the extreme baseness of men's minds, by which I am not astonished, and in which I do not disbelieve. I see clearly the contrivance that the others make use of[20] in order to ascend; I admire their greatness; and those upward soarings that I find so excellent, I comprehend; and if my powers do not go so far, at least my judgement completely accepts them.

The other example that he[21] brings forward of "incredible and wholly fabulous" things told by Plutarch is that Agesilaus was fined by the Ephors for having attracted to himself alone the hearts and wills of his fellow citizens.[22] I know not what mark of falsity he finds in that; but it is evident that Plutarch speaks there of things which must have been much better known to him than to us; and it was no new thing in Greece to see men punished and exiled solely for being too popular with their fellow citizens—witness ostracism and petalism.

There is also, in this same book, another accusation which nettles me on Plutarch's account, where he says that he fairly paralleled Romans with Romans and Greeks with Greeks, but not Romans with Greeks—witness, he says Demosthenes and Cicero, Cato and Aristides, Sylla and Lysander, Marcellus and Pelopidas, Pompeius and Agesilaus; deeming that he has favoured the Greeks in having given them mates so unequal.[23] This is really to attack what is most excellent and praiseworthy in Plutarch; for in his parallels (which are the most admirable portions of his works, and in which, in my opinion, he took much pleasure) the truth and sincerity of his judgements equals their depth and their weight. He is a philosopher who teaches us virtue. Let us see if we can defend him from this reproach of prevarication and falsity. What I think may have given rise to this judgement is the great and dazzling lustre of the Romans' names, as we see them. It does not seem to us that Demosthenes could equal the glory of a consul, proconsul, and quæstor of that great republic. But if the truth of the matter is considered, and the men in themselves, which Plutarch had more in mind, and the comparing of their characters, their natures, and their ability, rather than their fortune, I think, contrary to Bodin, that Cicero and the elder Cato come short of their mates.[24] For his[25] purpose, I should rather have chosen the example of the young Cato compared with Phocion; for in that couple there might be found a more plausible inequality in favour of the Roman. As for Marcellus, Sylla, and Pompeius, I see clearly that their exploits in war are of larger scope, more renowned and stately[26] than those of the Greeks with whom Plato compares them; but the finest and bravest actions, in war as elsewhere, are not always the most famous. I often see the names of those who have been leaders dimmed by the lustre of other names of less merit—witness Labienus, Ventidius, Telesinus, and many others. And, considering him in that respect, if I had to complain on behalf of the Greeks, might I not say that much less is Camillus comparable to Themistocles, the Gracchi to Agis and Cleomenes, Numa to Lycurgus?[27] But it is folly to propose to pronounce with one stroke of the pen upon things of so many aspects. When Plutarch compares them, he does not, in consequence, make them equal. Who could note their differences more eloquently and conscientiously? In comparing the victories, the exploits of arms, and the power of the armies led by Pompeius, and his triumphs, with those of Agesilaus, "I do not believe," he says, "that Xenophon himself, were he living, although he were permitted to write all he pleased in favour of Agesilaus, would dare to put him in comparison."[28] In speaking of paralleling Lysander and Sylla, "There is no comparison," he says, "either in number of victories or in fortune of battles; for Lysander won only two naval battles," etc.[29] This is not to steal any thing from the Romans: by simply bringing them and the Greeks together,[30] he can have put no affront upon them, whatever disparity there may be between them; and Plutarch does not counterpoise them in their entirety; he shows no preference in the mass; he compares the details and the circumstances, one after another, and judges them separately. Therefore, if it were desired to convict him of partiality, it would be necessary to examine carefully some special judgement, or to say, in general, that he mistook in matching a certain Greek with a certain Roman, because there were others among them better adapted for comparison and more resembling each other.

Chapter XXXIII

THE STORY OF SPURINA

PHILOSOPHY does not think that she has made an ill use of her resources when she has given over to the reason the supreme mastery of our soul, and the authority to hold our appetites in check. Those who judge that there is among them none more violent than those to which love gives birth have this support for their belief—that those have hold of both body and soul, and that the whole man is possessed by them, in such wise that even the health is dependent on them, and medicine is sometimes compelled to do them service as a pander. But, on the other hand, it might also be said that the commixture of the body causes abatement and weakening in them; for such desires are subject to satiety and susceptible to material remedies. Many, wishing to rid their soul of the continual restlessness caused by this appetite, have had recourse to incisions and amputation of the disturbed and ravenous parts. Others have quite subdued its strength and ardour by frequent application of cold objects, as snow and vinegar. The sackcloths of our ancestors were used for this purpose; it is a fabric woven of horsehair, of which some wove shirts and others waist-bands to cause them suffering.[1] A prince told me not long ago that in his

The Story of Spurina

youth, on a day of solemn ceremony at the court of King Francis the First, when everybody was fitly habited, the fancy seized him to put on his father's hair-shirt, which is still in his possession; but, devout as he was, he could not muster the endurance to wait till night to take it off, and he was made ill by it for a long time; he added that he did not believe that there is any youthful ardour so vehement that the use of that prescription can not deaden it; perchance, however, he has not experienced the most stinging sort; for experience shows us that such emotion very often endures under rough and rude garments, and that hair-shirts do not always make those chaste who wear them.[2] Xenocrates went more rigorously about it; for his disciples having, to test his continence, smuggled into his bed the famous and beauteous courtesan Laïs, quite bare but for the arms of her beauty and those philters, her wanton charms; he, feeling, in spite of his teachings and rules, his body, usually so hard, beginning to rebel, had those members burned that had lent ear to this rebellion. Whereas the passions which wholly reside in the soul, as ambition, avarice, and others, give much more work to the reason; for there it can be aided only by its own resources, nor are these appetites capable of satiety; indeed, they are whetted and increased by enjoyment.

The single example of Julius Cæsar will suffice to show us the disparity of these appetites; for never was man more addicted to amorous pleasures. Evidence whereof is the scrupulous care he took of his person, making use of the most elaborate[3] methods then employed, even to the point of having the hairs of his body pulled out, and being anointed with perfumes of extreme delicacy.[4] And he was by nature of fine appearance—fair, tall, and lithe in figure, full in the

face, his eyes brown and expressive, if we are to believe
Suetonius; for the statues of him to be seen at Rome do not
quite resemble this description in all points. Besides his
wives, whom he changed four times, to say nothing of his
youthful relations with Nicomedes, King of Bithynia,[5] he
had the maidenhead of the so greatly renowned Queen of
Egypt, Cleopatra—witness the little Cæsarion, who was born
of their commerce.[6] He paid court also to Eunoe, Queen of
Mauretania,[7] and at Rome to Posthumia, wife of Servius
Sulpitius, to Lolla, wife of Gabinius, to Tertulla, wife of
Crassus, and even to Mutia, wife of the great Pompeius;[8]
which was the reason, say the Roman historians, that her
husband repudiated her;[9] as to which Plutarch confesses his
ignorance; and the Curios, father and son, afterward reproached Pompeius when he married Cæsar's daughter, that
he made himself son-in-law to a man who had made him
cuckold, and whom he himself was wont to call Ægisthus.[10]
Besides all these, he had for mistress Servilia, sister of Cato
and mother of Marcus Brutus, whence, every one believes,
proceeded that great affection he bore to Brutus, who was
born at a time when there was a probability that he had begotten him.[11] So that I have reason, it seems to me, to take
him for a man extremely addicted to this form of debauchery
and of a very amorous complexion. But the other passion,
ambition, by which also he was endlessly moved, when it
came into contention with this, immediately forced it to give
place.

In this connection, remembering Mechmet,[12] him who
subjected Constantinople, and brought about the final extermination of the name of Greece, I know not in whom
these two passions can be found more evenly balanced: an

> # The Story of Spurina

equally indefatigable debauchee and soldier. But when they come into his life concurrently, one with the other, the contentious eagerness always imperiously curbs the amorous eagerness. And the latter, though beyond its natural season, does not fully regain supreme authority until he reaches extreme old age, incapable of sustaining longer the burden of wars. That which, as a contrary instance, is told of Ladislas, King of Naples, is worthy of note—that, although he was an excellent soldier, brave and ambitious, he proposed to himself, as the principal aim of his ambition, the consummation of his sensuality and the possession of one and another peculiarly beautiful woman. His death was of the same character. Having by a well-directed siege brought the city of Florence to such straits that the people were ready to compound for his victory, he gave them quittance on condition that they should deliver to him a maiden of their city of whose surpassing beauty he had heard. They had no choice but to give her up to him, and avoid public ruin by a private wrong. She was the daughter of a physician famous in his day, who, finding himself in so hateful a necessity, resolved upon an attempt of high courage.[13] As every one joined in adorning his daughter and bedecking her with ornaments and jewels which would make her charming to this new lover, he also, himself, gave her a handkerchief of exquisite odour and workmanship, which she should make use of at their first meeting, it being an article they never were without in those regions. This handkerchief, filled with poison by the skill of his art, being rubbed against their warm flesh and opened pores, so quickly infused the poison that they expired in one another's arms.[14]

I come back to Cæsar. His pleasures never caused him to

lose a single minute of the hour, or to turn aside one step
from the opportunities that offered themselves for his aggrandisement. This passion[15] in him dominated so master-
fully all others, and possessed his soul with authority so absolute, that it carried him wherever it would. Truly I am
troubled by this, when I consider the greatness of this personage in all else, and the marvellous faculties that were in
him—so much sufficiency in every sort of knowledge that
there is almost no branch of learning of which he has not
written. He was such an orator that many have ranked his
eloquence higher than that of Cicero; and he himself, in my
judgement, did not think that he fell short of him in that
particular.[16] And his two *Anti-Catos* were written chiefly to
counterbalance the admirable style that Cicero had employed in his *Cato*.[17] For the rest, was there ever a soul so
vigilant, so active, and so enduring of hard work as his? And
unquestionably, it was embellished, too, by many rare seeds
of virtue—living and natural, I mean, and not counterfeited.
He was unusually sober, and so far from dainty in his eating
that Oppius narrates that one day, there having been put
before him at the table some sauce of prepared oil, instead
of pure oil, he ate freely of it, in order not to shame his
host.[18] Another time he had his baker whipped for having
supplied him with different bread from that of the common
people.[19] Cato himself was wont to say of him that he was
the first sober man who ever wended his way toward the
ruin of his country.[20] And as to this same Cato calling him
one day a drunkard, it happened in this wise. Both of them
being in the Senate, where there was talk of the conspiracy
of Catiline, about which Cæsar was suspected, there was
brought to him from outside, secretly, a letter. Cato, be-

lieving that it was some warning from the conspirators, called upon him to give it to him; which Cæsar was obliged to do, to avoid more serious suspicion. It chanced to be a love letter, which Servilia, Cato's sister, had written to him. Cato, having read it, threw it back to him, saying: "Take it, drunkard!"[21] This, I say, was rather a word of contempt and anger than an express accusation of that vice; as often we insult those who anger us, with the first insulting words that come to our tongue, although they are in no wise deserved by those to whom we apply them. Moreover, this vice of which Cato accuses him is closely akin to that in which he had surprised Cæsar; for Venus and Bacchus readily go in company, as the proverb has it. But in my own case Venus is much more active when accompanied by sobriety.

The examples of his mildness and his clemency toward those who had offended him are innumerable;[22] I mean, besides those he gave while the civil war was still in progress, which he himself shows clearly in his writings that he made use of to cajole his enemies and make them less dread his future power and victory. And it must be said that these examples, if they are not sufficient to testify to a natural mildness, exhibit at least in this personage a marvellous confidence and greatness of heart. It often befell him to send back whole armies to the enemy after he had vanquished them, without deigning even to bind them by an oath, if not to favour him, at least to restrain themselves from making war upon him. He took prisoner certain officers of Pompeius three and four times, and as often set them at liberty.[23] Pompeius declared all those who did not follow him in war to be his enemies; and he[24] proclaimed that he regarded as friends those who did not stir and who did not actually take arms against him.[25] To those of his officers who secretly left him to take other service, he sent, moreover, their arms and horses and equipment.[26] The towns that he had taken by force he left at liberty to follow such course as they pleased, giving them no other garrison than the memory of his mildness and clemency. On the day of his great battle at Pharsalia, he forbade hands to be laid on Roman citizens except at the utmost need.[27]

These were very hazardous proceedings, in my judgement; and it is no wonder if, in the civil wars which we are in the midst of, those who, like him, are assailing the ancient constitution of their country do not in such ways imitate his example. They are extraordinary methods, which it belongs only to Cæsar's fortune and his wonderful foresight to conduct to a happy result. When I consider the incomparable grandeur of this soul, I excuse Victory for having been unable to disengage herself from him, even in that most unjust and most iniquitous cause.[28]

To return to his clemency, we have several genuine examples of it in the day of his power, when, all things being given into his hands, he had no longer reason for dissimulation. Caius Memmius had written very sharp discourses against him, to which he had replied with great bitterness; yet he did not hesitate, very soon after, to assist in making him consul.[29] Caius Calvus, who had made many offensive epigrams against him, having employed some friends of his to bring about a reconciliation, Cæsar prevailed upon himself to write first to him. And our friend Catullus, who had so rudely handled him under the name of Mamurra, coming to him to excuse himself, Cæsar had him sup at his table

The Story of Spurina

that same day. Having been told of some persons who spoke ill of him, he did no more than declare, in a public speech, that he had been informed about them. He feared his enemies even less than he hated them. Certain conspiracies and gatherings that were formed against his life having been revealed to him, he contented himself with publishing, by an edict, that they were known to him, without otherwise prosecuting the originators of them. As for the consideration he had for his friends, when Caius Oppius was travelling with him and was taken ill, he gave up to him the only lodging he had, and lay all night on the ground and in the open air. As for his justice, he put to death one of his personal attendants whom he especially loved, for having made love to the wife of a Roman knight, although no one made complaint about it. Never did man bring more moderation to victory or more resolution to adverse fortune.

But all these good inclinations were altered and stifled by his madly ambitious disposition, by which he let himself be so carried away that we may easily maintain that it held the helm and the rudder of all his actions. Of an open-handed man it made a public thief, to minister to this profusion and bounty, and led him to utter that vile and very unreasonable saying, that, if the most wicked and disgraced men in the world had been faithful to him in serving his aggrandisement, he would cherish them and advance them to the utmost of his power as readily as the most worthy people. He was so intoxicated by extreme vanity that he dared to pride himself in the presence of his fellow citizens upon having made that great Roman republic a name without form or body, and to declare that what he said should thereafter have the force of laws, and to receive seated the Senate when it came before him, and to allow himself to be adored, and divine honours to be paid him in his presence. In short, that single vice, in my opinion, destroyed in him the finest and richest nature that ever was, and has rendered his memory detestable to all worthy people, forasmuch as he chose to seek his glory in the ruin of his country and the subversion of the most powerful and flourishing commonwealth that the world will ever see.

There might easily be found, on the other hand, many examples of great men whom debauchery has caused to neglect the conduct of their affairs, as Marcus Antonius and others; but where love and ambition are equally balanced, and come into collision with equal forces, I make no doubt that the latter would win the prize of mastery.

Now, to return to my former path,[30] it is much to be able to curb our appetite by the process of reason, or to compel our members, by force, to keep themselves to their duty; but to scourge ourselves for the benefit of our neighbours, and not only to divest ourselves of that gentle perturbation which flatters us by the presence that we feel in seeing that we are agreeable to others and loved and sought by every one, but to conceive even hatred and loathing for our charms which are the cause of this, and to condemn our beauty because some one else is inflamed by it—of this I have seen scarcely any examples. Here is one: Spurina, a young man of Tuscany,—

> As glitters a precious stone set in yellow gold, a neck or head ornament; or as ivory gleams, skilfully mounted in ebony or Orician terebinth,[31]—

being endowed with unusual beauty, so excessive that the

most chaste eyes could not chastely abide its lustre, not content with leaving without furtherance all the fever and fire that he kindled everywhere, entered into violent anger against himself and against these rich gifts that Nature had bestowed upon him,—as if a man were responsible for the fault of others,—and splashed and marred, by dint of wounds deliberately self-inflicted, and scars, the perfect proportion and regularity which Nature had so carefully observed in his face.[32] To express my opinion about this, I wonder at such acts more than I honour them; excesses like this are hostile to my precepts. The design was good and right-minded, but, in my opinion, a little lacking in discretion. What if his ugliness resulted afterward in causing others to fall into the sin of contempt and hatred? or of envy of the glory of so unusual a ground for commendation? or of calumny, attributing this frame of mind to a mad ambition? Is there any subject from which vice may not derive, if it will, opportunity to come into play in some way? It would have been more reasonable, and also more praiseworthy, had he made those gifts of God a subject of exemplary virtue and of discipline.

Those who evade the common duties and that infinite number of thorny rules, with so many faces, which bind a man of scrupulous integrity in civil life, make, to my thinking, a fine saving,[33] whatever degree of special rigour they impose upon themselves. It is, in a sense, dying to avoid the trouble of living worthily. They may win another reward; but the reward for difficulty it has never seemed to me they could have; nor can I see that there is any thing harder than holding oneself erect amid the floods of the crowded world, loyally answering to and satisfying all the parts of one's of-

The Story of Spurina

fice. It is, perchance, easier to do without the sex altogether, than to comport oneself properly in all points in companionship with one's wife; and we are able to slip along less carefully in poverty than in rightly expended abundance. Enjoyment, guided by reason, is more difficult than abstention. The right living of the younger Scipio has a thousand aspects; that of Diogenes has only one. This[34] as much surpasses ordinary lives in innocence as choice and accomplished lives surpass it in usefulness and in strength.

992

Chapter XXXIV

OBSERVATIONS ON

JULIUS CAESAR'S

METHOD OF MAKING WAR

IT is told of several famous warriors that they held certain books in special regard: as the great Alexander, Homer;[1] Scipio Africanus, Xenophon;[2] Marcus Brutus, Polybius;[3] Charles V, Phillippe de Commines;[4] and it is said that, in these days, Machiavelli is still, in another quarter, in repute; but the late Marshal Strozzi, who for his part chose Cæsar, did unquestionably choose much better: for in truth that book ought to be the breviary of every warrior, as being the true and supreme pattern of the military art. And God knows with what charm and what beauty he[5] also adorned that rich material, with a style so pure, so delicate, and so perfect, that to my taste there are no writings in the world which are comparable to his in this respect. I purpose to set down here certain peculiar and unusual qualities in the carrying on of his wars, which have remained in my memory.

His army being somewhat alarmed by the report that was current of the great forces that King Juba was bringing against him, instead of decrying the idea that his soldiers had conceived of this, and belittling the resources of his enemy, having called them together, to reassure them and give them

993

courage, he took a course altogether contrary to that to which we are accustomed; for he told them that they need no longer put themselves to the trouble of enquiring about the forces led by the enemy, for he had had very certain information about them; and then he told them the numbers, going far beyond both the truth and the report about them that was current in his army;[6] following the counsel of Cyrus in Xenophon;[7] forasmuch as delusion is not so important if the enemy is found to be weaker than had been looked for, as when, having from common report believed him to be weak, he is found later to be, in truth, very strong.

He accustomed his soldiers, above all things else, to obey simply, without entering into criticism or talk of the plans of their commander, which he communicated to them only on the point of execution; and it gave him pleasure, if any part of his designs had been discovered by them, to change his mind instantly, in order to deceive them; and often, to this end, having assigned some place for his night's quarters, he went beyond it and lengthened the day's march, particularly if it were bad weather and rainy.[8]

The Swiss, at the beginning of his wars in Gaul, having sent to him to give them passage through territory of the Romans, he, having determined to prevent them by force, nevertheless counterfeited a friendly disposition, and delayed some days before replying to them, in order to make use of that interval to assemble his army. Those unfortunate people did not know how excellent a manager of time this man was: for he often repeats that the highest quality of a commander is knowing how to seize opportunities on the instant, and to use speed, which, in truth, in his exploits is unheard of and incredible in degree.

994

Cæsar's Method of Making War

If he was not very scrupulous in this, the taking advantage of his enemy under colour of a truce, he was as little so in demanding in his soldiers no other virtues than valour; nor did he punish severely any other vices than mutiny and disobedience. Often, after his victories, he turned them loose for every sort of license, dispensing them for some time from the rules of military discipline; boasting that he had soldiers so well trained that, even when all perfumed and anointed, they did not fail to enter furiously into battle. In truth, he liked them to be richly armed, and made them wear graven armour, gilded and silvered, so that care for its preservation might make them more eager to defend themselves.[9] In speaking to them he called them companions,[10] which name we still use; a practice which Augustus his successor abolished, believing that he[11] had done it upon the necessity of his affairs and to flatter the spirit of those who followed him only as volunteers,[12]—

> At the passage of the Rhine, Cæsar was my general;
> here he is my associate; crime places on the same level
> those whom it dishonours;[13]—

but that his style was too mild and familiar[14] for the dignity of an emperor and general of an army; and he brought back the practice of calling them soldiers, simply. With this courteousness, however, Cæsar combined great severity in holding them in restraint. The ninth legion having mutinied near Placentia, he cashiered it ignominiously, although Pompeius was then still on foot; and received it into favour only after many supplications. He quieted them more by authority and by audacity than by mildness.[15]

Where he speaks of his crossing the river Rhine into Ger-

995

many, he says that, deeming it unbefitting the honour of the Roman people that he should take his army across in boats, he had a bridge built, that it might cross with steady footings.[16] It was there that he built that wonderful bridge of which he explains to us the construction in detail; for he does not dwell so long upon any part of his deeds as he does in describing to us the ingenuity of his inventions in manual works of this kind.[17]

I have observed this also, that he regards as of much importance his exhortations to the soldiers before battle: for when he desires to show that he was taken by surprise or was hurried, he always remarks that he had not even time to address his army. Before that great battle against the forces of Tournay, [18] "Cæsar," he says, "having given his orders, quickly hastened wherever chance led him, to exhort his troops; and, falling in with the tenth legion, he had not time to say any thing to them save that they must bear in mind their accustomed valour, that they must not be dismayed, and must sustain bravely the onset of their adversaries; and, because the enemy had already approached within bow-shot, he gave the signal for battle; and thence going quickly elsewhere, to encourage others, he found that they were already fighting." This is what he says in that place. In truth, his tongue did him many times very notable service; and even in his own day his military eloquence was in such repute that many in his army collected his harangues; and by this means volumes were made of them, which existed a long while after his death. His style has peculiar graces, so that his friends, and among others Augustus, hearing his speeches read, distinguished even to sentences and words what was not his.

Cæsar's Method of Making War

The first time that he left Rome on a public mission, he arrived in eight days at the river Rhone, having in his coach, in front of him, a secretary or two, who wrote incessantly, and behind him his sword-bearer.[19] And certainly, if it were a matter of travelling only,[20] it would be difficult to attain the celerity with which, always victorious, having left Gaul, and following Pompeius to Brindisi in eighteen days, he subdued Italy, returned from Brindisi to Rome, from Rome went into the very heart of Spain, where he surmounted extreme difficulties in the war against Affranius and Petreius, and in the long siege of Marseilles. Thence he turned to Macedonia, beat the Roman army at Pharsalia, thence, pursuing Pompeius, passed into Egypt, which he subdued; from Egypt he went into Syria and the territories of Pontus, where he fought Pharnaces; thence into Africa, where he defeated Scipio and Juba, and returned again through Italy to Spain, where he defeated the sons of Pompeius,—

Swifter than lightning from the sky, or the tigress with young.[21]

And like a rock precipitated from the top of a mountain, wrenched from its place by the wind, or loosened by a stormy rain, or detached by the passage of years, its enormous mass falls down with a great rush, and bounds over the earth, dragging with it trees and flocks and men.[22]

Speaking of the siege of Avaricum, he says that it was his custom to remain night and day near the workmen whom he was employing.[23] In every undertaking of importance he always made the investigation himself, and never led his

997

army into a place which he had not first reconnoitred.[24] And, if we believe Suetonius, when he undertook to ferry across to England, he led in exploring the way.[25] He was wont to say that he liked better the victory which was brought on by judgement than by force. And in the war against Petreius and Affranius, when fortune offered him a very manifest occasion of advantage, he refused it, hoping, he says, to get the better of his enemies with a little more delay, but less risk.[26] There, too, he did a wonderful thing in ordering his whole host, without any necessity, to swim across the river;

> And the soldier rushing to the fight hurriedly takes the road that in flight he would have feared; quickly his wet limbs regain warmth, with his newly-taken-on armour, and, by running, his members, frozen by the sea-water, are restored to life.[27]

I find him a little more restrained and deliberate in his enterprises than Alexander; for the latter seems to seek out and give hot chase to dangers, like an impetuous torrent, which rushes on without heed and without choice, assaulting all that it encounters.

> So rolls the two-horned Aufidus, which waters the realms of Apulian Daunus, when it rages and threatens the tilled fields with a dreadful deluge.[28]

Also he was about his work in the prime and first vehemence of his age, while Cæsar began his when already mature and well advanced in years. Moreover, Alexander was of a more sanguine temperament, choleric and ardent, and also inflamed that temperament by wine, about which Cæsar was very abstinent;[29] but when occasions of necessity presented themselves, or when the matter required it, never was there a man who held his life more cheaply. For my own part, it seems to me that I can read in many of his exploits a fixed resolution to be killed, in order to escape the shame of being vanquished. In the great battle that he fought against those of Tournay, seeing the van of his own army wavering, he ran to show himself in front of his enemies, without a shield, just as he was;[30] which befell him many other times. Hearing that his troops were surrounded, he passed in disguise through the hostile army in order to strengthen his men by his presence.[31] Having crossed to Dyrrachium with a very small force, and seeing that the rest of his army, which he had left to the conduct of Antonius, was slow in following him, he undertook alone to repass the sea in a very violent storm, and stole away to resume command of the rest of his forces, the harbours on the other side and the whole sea being in the possession of Pompeius.[32] And as for the enterprises that he achieved by force of arms, there are many that exceed in risk all judgement formed from military calculation; for with what feeble resources did he undertake to subdue the kingdom of Egypt, and afterward to attack the forces of Scipio and Juba, ten times greater than his own! Such men have had I know not what of more than human confidence in their fortune.

And he said that high enterprises should be executed, not pondered.[33] After the battle of Pharsalia, having sent his army in advance into Asia, and crossing the strait of the Hellespont with a single vessel, he fell in at sea with Lucius Cassius with ten great war-vessels; he had the courage, not simply to await him, but to make straight for him, and summon him to surrender; and he was successful.[34] Having undertaken that mad siege of Alesia, where there were eighty thousand men defending it, all Gaul having risen to come down upon him and raise the siege, and having in the field an army of a hundred and nine thousand horse[35] and two hundred and forty thousand foot, what intrepidity and insane confidence there was in choosing not to abandon his enterprise but to disperse at one and the same time two such great obstacles! However, he surmounted them; and after winning that great battle against those outside, he very soon brought to his mercy those whom he held shut up. The same thing happened to Lucullus at the siege of Tigranocerta against King Tigranes, but with unlike conditions, when we consider the lack of energy in the enemies with whom Lucullus had to do.[36]

I desire here to note two unusual and extraordinary occurrences in regard to that siege of Alesia: one, that the Gauls, when assembling to go to meet Cæsar, having made an enumeration of all their forces, determined in their council to cut off a good part of that great multitude, lest they might in consequence fall into confusion.[37] This instance is something strange—to be afraid of being too numerous; but, on reflection, it is very probable that the body of an army should be of moderate size and determined by certain limits, whether because of the difficulty of feeding it, or because of the difficulty of handling it and keeping it in order. At least, it would be easy to prove by examples that armies monstrous in number have seldom done any thing worth while. According to what Cyrus says, in Xenophon, it is not the number of men, but the number of brave men, that gives the advantage, the remainder serving rather as a hindrance than

Cæsar's Method of Making War

a help.[38] And Bajazet based his determination to give battle to Tamburlane, against the advice of all his officers, principally on the fact that the innumerable number of his enemy's men gave him assured hope of conclusion amongst them.[39] Scanderbeg, an excellent judge, and of much experience, was wont to say that ten or twelve thousand reliable fighting men should suffice a competent commander to secure his reputation in every sort of military business.[40]

The other point,[41] which seems to be opposed both to custom and to good judgement in war, is that Vercingetorix, who was named as head and general of all the factions of the rebellious Gauls, adopted the course of shutting himself up in Alesia.[42] For he who commands a whole country should never enter a fortress[43] except in case of such extremity that his last stronghold is at stake, and that there is nothing more to hope for except in its defence; otherwise, he should keep himself at liberty, in order to be able to look after all parts of his government in general.

To return to Cæsar—he became with time a little more deliberate and more given to examination, as his friend Oppius testifies; considering that he should not rashly risk the honour of so many victories which a single mischance might cause him to lose.[44] This is what the Italians mean when they point out that hare-brained boldness which we observe in young men, calling them beggars for honour—*bisognosi d'honore;* and say that, when they are still in so great hunger and dearth of renown, they have reason to seek it at whatever cost; which those should not do, who have already acquired a sufficiency of it. There can be some just moderation in this desire for glory, and some satiety in this appetite, as in others; many people so deal with it. He[45] was far removed from the scruples[46] of the ancient Romans, who desired to get the better in their wars only by virtue of simple and natural valour; but still he brought thereto more conscience then we should to-day, and he did not approve of all sorts of means of obtaining the victory. In the war against Ariovistus, as he was parleying with him, there arose some commotion between the two armies, which began through the fault of the cavalry of Ariovistus. Upon this disturbance, Cæsar found himself in a position of great advantage over his enemy; but he did not choose to benefit by it, for fear that he might be charged with having acted disloyally.[47] He was accustomed to wear, when fighting, rich apparel and of brilliant colour, so as to attract attention to himself. He held the reins the tighter with his soldiers and restrained them the more, when near the enemy.[48]

When the ancient Greeks wished to accuse any one of extreme incompetence, they would say, in a common proverb, that he could neither read nor swim. He had this same opinion, that the art of swimming was very useful in war, and he found several conveniences in it: if he had to make haste, he ordinarily crossed by swimming the rivers that were in the way; for he liked to travel on foot like the great Alexander.[49] In Egypt, being obliged, in order to save himself, to get into a little boat, and so many people having leaped into it with him that he was in danger of going to the bottom, he chose to jump into the sea, and by swimming reached his fleet, which was more than two hundred paces[50] distant, holding his tablets out of the water in his left hand and eagerly dragging after him[51] his coat-armour, in order that the enemy might not obtain it; and he was already well advanced in years.[52] Never was a commander so much in favour with his soldiers; at the beginning of his civil wars the centurions offered to keep in pay, each from his own purse, a man-at-arms; and the foot-soldiers, to serve him at their own expense, those who were the most well-to-do undertaking also to bear all charges of the most needy.[53] The late admiral de Chatillon[54] offered us recently a similar case in our civil wars; for the Frenchmen in his army supplied from their purses the payment of the foreigners who joined him. There would scarcely be found examples of good-will so warm and so ready among those who walk in the old way,[55] under the long-continued government of the laws.

Passion commands us much more vigorously than reason. It did, however, occur in the war against Hannibal that, following the example of the liberality of the Roman people in the city, the soldiers and officers refused their pay; and in the camp of Marcellus they called those who took it mercenaries.[56]

When he[57] was worsted near Dyrrachium, his soldiers came voluntarily to offer themselves to be blamed and punished, so that he had rather to console them than to taunt them.[58] A single cohort of his held out more than four hours against four of Pompeius's legions, until it was almost completely destroyed by bow-shots; and a hundred and thirty thousand arrows were found in the entrenchments.[59] A soldier named Scæva, who commanded at one of the entrances to the fortification, held his ground unflinchingly while an eye was put out, the shoulder and thigh pierced, and his shield struck in two hundred and thirty places.[60] It fell out with many of his[61] soldiers who were taken prisoners, that they chose to accept death rather than promise to join the other side. Granius Petronius being captured by Scipio in Africa, Scipio, having put to death his companions, sent word to him that he gave him his life, for he was a man of rank and a quæstor. Petronius replied that the soldiers of Cæsar were accustomed to grant life to others, not to receive it; and immediately killed himself with his own hands.[62]

There are innumerable examples of their fidelity. Nor should the story be forgotten of those who were besieged at Salona,—a city that took sides with Cæsar against Pompeius, —because an extraordinary occurrence happened there. Marcus Octavius held them besieged; those who were within the walls were reduced to extreme need of every thing, to that degree that, to make up for their lack of men,—the greater number of them being dead or wounded,—they had set free all their slaves, and for the use of their machines they had been compelled to cut off the hair of all the women, to make ropes of it—in addition to an incredible dearth of provisions; this notwithstanding, they were resolved never to surrender. After the siege had dragged along for a great while, whence Octavius had become more careless and less attentive to his undertaking, they, on a chosen day, about noon, having first arranged the women and children on the walls to make a good show, issued forth so furiously on the besiegers that, having routed the first and second and third outer posts,[63] and the fourth, and then all the rest, and having compelled the complete abandonment of the entrenchments, they pursued them even to their ships; and Octavius himself fled to Dyrrachium, where Pompeius was.[64] I do not remember at this moment to have seen any other instance where the besieged fought the whole force of the besiegers and gained possession of the field, nor one in which a sortie brought about pure and complete victory in battle.

Chapter XXXV

OF THREE

GOOD WOMEN [1]

THEY are not to be reckoned by dozens, as every one knows, and especially in respect to the duties of married life; for marriage is a bargain full of so many difficult circumstances that it is not easy for a woman's nature[2] to remain for a long time steadfast therein. Men, although in that state they may be in a somewhat better condition, find that not a little effort is needed.[3] The touchstone of a good marriage, and its true proof, regards the character of the companionship during its existence: whether it has been ever kind, loyal, and meet. In our generation, wives more commonly reserve displaying their good offices and the warmth of their affection for their husbands until they have lost them; they then at least seek to testify to their goodwill. A tardy and unseasonable testimony! They rather prove by that, that they love them only when dead. When living, it is all commotion; when departing, love and courtesy.[4] As fathers conceal their affection from their children, in like manner wives readily conceal theirs from their husbands, by way of maintaining due respect. This absence of expression[5] is not at all to my taste; they may dishevel their hair and tear their faces with their nails: I whisper to a

Of Three Good Women

waiting-woman, or a secretary: "How were they together? How did they live?" I always remember that wise saying: *They who have the least grief weep most ostentatiously.*[6] Their glum looks are hateful to the living and useless to the dead. We will gladly allow them to laugh when we are dead, provided that they laugh with us while we are alive. Is it not enough to bring one back to life with vexation, if she who spat in my face while I lived comes to rub my feet when I am no more?

If there be any thing honourable in weeping for husbands, it is due only to those who have laughed with them; they who have wept during the husband's life, let them laugh when he is dead—outwardly as well as inwardly. Heed not, therefore, the tearful eyes and the pitiful voice; regard the bearing, the colour, and the roundness of the cheeks behind her long veils; it is with those that she speaks clearly.[7] There are few of them whose health does not improve—a thing that can not lie. That conventional demeanour does not look behind so much as before; it is more for acquisition than for payment. In my childhood, a virtuous and very beautiful lady, who is still living, the widow of a prince, had I know not what in her attire other than is allowed by our laws regarding widowhood; to those who blamed her for it, she said: "It is because I no longer enter into new friendships, and have no mind to marry again."

That I may not be wholly out of harmony with our wonted way of thought,[8] I have made choice of three women who, indeed, in connection with the death of their husbands, showed the strength of their tenderness and affection; these are, however, examples of a little different character, and of such weight that they imply the nature of the previous life.

Of Three Good Women

Pliny the younger had, near a house of his in Italy, a neighbour extremely tortured by ulcers which had formed in his private parts. His wife, seeing him suffer so long, begged him to permit her to look carefully and closely into the state of his malady, and said that she would tell him more frankly than any one else what he could hope for. Having obtained her wish, and having carefully examined him, she found that it was impossible that he could be cured, and that all that he had to expect was to drag out for a long time a painful and languishing life; so she advised him, as the most sure and sovereign remedy, to kill himself; and finding him lacking in courage for so pitiless an undertaking, "Do not think, my dear," she said, "that the pain which I see you suffer does not touch me as much as you, and that, to rid myself of it, I am willing myself to use this medicine which I prescribe for you. I desire to accompany you in the cure, as I have done in the sickness; put aside this dread, and think that we shall have naught but pleasure in this passage which is to deliver us from such tortures; we will go hence together, happily." This said, and having kindled her husband's courage, she determined that they should throw themselves into the sea from a window of their house which opened upon it. And to maintain even to his end that faithful and vehement affection in which she had held him during his life, she desired even that he should die in her arms; but for fear that they might fail her, and that the closeness of her embrace might be loosened by the fall and by terror, she had herself tightly bound and attached to him around the waist, and thus gave up her life for her husband's peace of mind.[9]

She was of low station; and amongst people of that con-

Of Three Good Women

dition it is not very unusual to find instances of rare goodness:

It was among such as these that Justice, when she departed from earth, left her last footprints.[10]

The other two women were of noble rank, and rich; amongst such, examples of high qualities rarely have lodgement.

Arria, wife of Cecinna Pætus, a man of consular rank, was the mother of another Arria, wife of Thrasea Pætus, he whose virtue was so renowned in the time of Nero; and through this son-in-law she was grandmother of Fannia; the similarity of the names of these men and women and of their fortunes has caused many persons to make mistakes. Cecinna Pætus, the husband of the first Arria, having been taken prisoner by the soldiers of the Emperor Claudius after the defeat of Scribonianus, whose party he had joined, his wife besought those who were carrying him as a prisoner to Rome to take her into their ship, where she would cause them much less expense and trouble than the number of persons they would need for her husband's service; and she alone would attend to his cabin and his cooking and all other offices. They refused her this; thereupon, having got into the boat of a fisherman, which she immediately hired, she followed him in this way from Sclavonia. When they were at Rome, one day, in the presence of the emperor, Junia, widow of Scribonianus, having accosted her familiarly because of the similarity of their fortunes, she repulsed her harshly with these words: "I," she said, "I speak to you, or listen to you, in whose lap Scribonianus was killed, and you still live!" These words, with many other

1008

indications, made her kinsfolk perceive that she was for doing away with herself, unable to endure her husband's ill-fortune. And Thrasea, her son-in-law, imploring her, consequently, not to seek to destroy herself, and thus saying to her, "What! if I should incur the same ill-fortune as Cecinna, would you desire that my wife, your daughter, should do this thing?" "How can you ask if I should desire it?" she answered. "Yes, yes, I should desire it, if she had lived as long and in as great harmony with you as I have done with my husband." Such answers increased their anxiety about her, and made them watch her actions more closely. One day, after saying to those who were guarding her, "Do your worst; you may indeed make me die a more painful death,[11] but keep me from dying you can not," she sprang madly from a chair on which she was seated, and with all her strength struck her head against the nearest wall. Having fallen to the floor unconscious and sorely hurt from this blow, after they had with great difficulty brought her back to life she said: "I told you that, if you denied me an easy way of killing myself, I would choose some other, however difficult it might be. The conclusion of such wonderful strength of soul[12] was in this wise: her husband, Pætus, not having a firm enough courage of his own to kill himself, to which the emperor's cruelty urged him, she, on one of the following days, after first employing the arguments and exhortations adapted to the advice she was giving him to do this, took the dagger that he wore, and holding it drawn in her hand, said, as the conclusion of her exhortation: "Do thus, Pætus." And instantly, having given herself with it a mortal blow in the breast, drawing it from the wound, she presented it to him, at the same moment ending her life with this noble, generous, and immortal saying: *Pæte, non dolet.* She had time to say only those three words of such fine and lofty significance: "See, Pætus, it does not hurt me."[13]

> As the chaste Arria put in the hand of Pætus the sword she had first drawn from her own breast, "Believe me," she said, "the wound that I have made does not pain me, but the wound that you are to give yourself, that, O Pætus, pains me."[14]

Her words are much more lifelike in their actual form[15] and have a richer meaning; for the wound and the death of her husband and her own were so far from distressing her, that it was she who advised and promoted them; and having done tha lofty and courageous deed for the sole benefit of her husband, she considered only him even in the last breath of her life, and to take from him fear in following her to death. Pætus immediately struck himself with the same blade, ashamed, in my opinion, of having stood in need of so dear and precious a lesson.

Pompeia Paulina, a young and high-born Roman lady, had married Seneca in his extreme old age. Nero, his fine disciple, sent guards to him to announce the decree of his death. (Such deaths were effected in this wise: when the Roman emperors of those days had condemned a man of rank, they sent word to him by their officers to choose some manner of death to his liking, and to execute it within such or such a time, which they assigned to him according to the quality of their anger, sometimes sooner, sometimes later, giving him opportunity to arrange his affairs in the interval, but sometimes depriving him of the power to do so by reason

Of Three Good Women

of the shortness of the time; and if the condemned man resisted their decree, they sent suitable persons to execute it, either by cutting the veins of his arms and legs or by forcing him to swallow poison; but men of reputation did not await that compulsion, but employed their own physicians and surgeons to that end.)

Seneca listened to their message with a calm and resolute countenance, and then asked for paper, to write his will; which having been refused him by the chief official, he turned to his friends and said: "Since I am able to leave you nothing else in recognition of what I owe you, I leave you at least the best I have—that is, the conception of my character and my life, which I beg you to retain in your memory, to the end that, by so doing, you may acquire the glory of sincere and true friends." And then, at one time soothing with gentle words the bitterness of the grief he saw them suffering, and at another time lifting up his voice to chide them, "Where," he said, "are those noble precepts of philosophy? What has become of the provisions we have garnered for so many years against the accidents of fortune? Was Nero's cruelty unknown to us? What could we expect from him who killed his mother and his brother, if not that he would also put to death his tutor, who fostered and educated him?"

Having said these words to them all, he turned toward his wife and, holding her closely in his embrace, since, from the burden of her grief, her courage and her strength failed her, he begged her, for love of him, to endure this mischance a little more patiently, and said that the hour had come when he must show no longer by reasoning and discussions, but by deeds, the profit he had derived from his studies, and

that of a surety he welcomed death, not only without grief,
but with joy. "Wherefore, dear heart," he said, "do not dishonour it by your tears; let it not seem that you love yourself more than my good name; moderate your grief and comfort yourself with the knowledge you have of me and of my
actions, and by leading the rest of your life in the honourable
occupation to which you are devoted."

To which Paulina, having partly recovered her senses
and rekindled by a very noble emotion the magnanimity of
her heart, replied: "No, Seneca, I am not the woman to
leave you in such need without my companionship; I will
not have you think that the virtuous conditions[16] of your
life have not taught me how to die well; and when could I
do it better, or more honourably, or more to my liking, than
with you? Be assured then that I shall depart with you."
Whereupon Seneca, welcoming this resolution of his wife,
so noble and glorious, and which also freed him from the
fear of leaving her after his death to the mercy and cruelty
of his enemies, said to her: "I have counseled you heretofore, Paulina, about what served to guide your life most
happily; but you prefer the honour of death; truly I will
not grudge it to you; firmness and resolution in our common end may be the same with us both, but beauty and
glory are the greater on your side."

Then the veins of their arms were cut at the same time;
but because those of Seneca, contracted by old age as well
as by abstinence, made the flow of blood too slow and too
slight, he ordered the veins of his legs also to be cut; and
for fear lest the agony he thus suffered should impair his
wife's courage, and also to be delivered from the affliction
which he endured to see her in so piteous a state, after taking

leave of her very lovingly, he begged her to allow herself to be taken into the next room; which was done. But all these incisions being still insufficient to cause his death, he ordered Statius Anneus, his physician, to give him a poisonous draught, which had scarcely more effect, for from the weakness and sluggishness of his organs it could not reach his heart. Therefore they placed him in a very hot bath; then, feeling his end to be near, as long as he had breath he continued to make most excellent remarks on the subject of the condition wherein he found himself, which his secretaries wrote down whilst they could hear his voice; and his last words remained long afterward in the hands of men, renowned and honoured (it is a very grievous loss to us that they have not come down to us). As he felt the last touches of death, taking the bloody water of the bath, he sprinkled his head, saying, "I dedicate this water to Jupiter the liberator."

Nero, being advised of all this, fearing that the death of Paulina, who was among the most highly connected Roman ladies and against whom he had no special causes of enmity, might be laid at his door, sent in all haste to have her wounds bound up; which her attendants did without her knowledge, she being already half dead and without consciousness. And thereafter as, contrary to her intent, she lived, it was most honourably and as comported with her virtue, showing by the pallor of her face how much of life had flowed away through her wounds.[17]

These are my three very true tales, which I find as entertaining and as tragic as those which we create at will to give pleasure to the common people; and I am surprised that those who devote themselves to that employment do not bethink themselves rather to choose ten thousand very delightful stories, which are to be found in books, with which they would have less trouble and would provide more pleasure and profit. And he who should choose to construct from them one complete and connected whole would have to supply nothing of his own save the connecting links, like the soldering with another metal; and he could by this means amass many true occurrences of all sorts, arranging them and diversifying them according as the beauty of the work demanded, somewhat as Ovid fastened together that vast number of various fables and pieced out his *Metamorphoses* with them.[18]

In the last couple this point also is worthy to be considered: that Paulina voluntarily offers to relinquish life for love of her husband, even as her husband had in former days relinquished death for love of her. There is not in our eyes much equality of weight in this barter; but I believe that, with his Stoic humour, he thought that he had done as much for her in prolonging his life on her account, as if he had died for her.

In one of the letters that he wrote to Lucilius, after he had informed him that, being attacked by fever at home, he at once took coach to go to a country house of his, against the advice of his wife, who wanted to stop him, and that he replied that the fever that he had was not a fever of the body, but of the place, he continued thus: "She let me go, urgently enjoining upon me to care for my health. Now I, knowing that I contain her life in mine, begin to take care of myself by way of taking care of her; the advantage that my old age has given me, making me firmer and more resolute in many things, I lose when I remember that in this old man there is a young woman who profits by me. Since I can not induce her to love me more courageously, she induces me to love myself more carefully; for something should be granted to honest affection; and sometimes, although events impel us contrariwise, we must summon back life, even a life of torment; we must vigorously detain the soul;[19] for the law, with the good, is not to live as long as they please, but as long as they ought. He who does not value his wife or his friend enough to prolong his life for them, and who persists in dying, is too sensitive and too weak; the soul must give this command to itself when the advantage of those nearest us demands it; it is for us sometimes to lend ourselves to our friends, and, when our wish would be to die, to give up our purpose for their sake. It is a proof of magnanimity to return to life out of consideration for others, as many excellent persons have done; and it is a trait of peculiar kindness to preserve one's old age (whereof the greatest advantage is indifference as to its duration, and a more courageous and contemptuous employment of life), if we feel that our doing this is sweet and agreeable and profitable to some one by whom we are beloved. And one receives from it a delightful reward; for what is sweeter than to be so precious to one's wife that, from regard for her, one becomes more precious to oneself? Thus my Paulina has loaded me, not only with her fear, but with my own also. It has not been enough for me to consider how resolutely I could die, but I have also considered how irresolutely[20] she could endure this. I have forced myself to live, and it is sometimes a magnanimous act to live."[21]

These are his words, admirable, as was his wont.

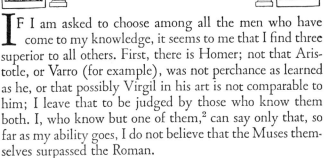

Chapter XXXVI

OF THE

MOST EMINENT MEN[1]

IF I am asked to choose among all the men who have come to my knowledge, it seems to me that I find three superior to all others. First, there is Homer; not that Aristotle, or Varro (for example), was not perchance as learned as he, or that possibly Virgil in his art is not comparable to him; I leave that to be judged by those who know them both. I, who know but one of them,[2] can say only that, so far as my ability goes, I do not believe that the Muses themselves surpassed the Roman.

He sings to his learned lyre such songs as Cynthius [Apollo] modulates with the touch of his fingers.[3]

However, in thus judging, it is not to be forgotten that it is principally from Homer that Virgil derives his learning; that he is his guide and schoolmaster, and that a single passage of the *Iliad* furnished body and substance for that great and divine *Æneid*. But it is not this only that I take into account: I add thereto many other conditions which make that personage marvellous in my eyes almost above the human estate. And in truth I often wonder that he, who created many deities and brought them into favour with the

1016

world by his own authority, has not himself attained the rank of a god. Being blind and poor, living before knowledge had been reduced to regular and fixed laws, he so well understood different branches of knowledge that all those who have since undertaken to establish forms of government, to manage wars, and to write, whether about religion or about philosophy, in whatsoever sect, or about the arts, have made use of him as a master very accomplished in all knowledge, and of his books as a storehouse containing every kind of learning.

> He tells us more clearly and better than Chrysippus and Crantor what is noble, what is base, what is useful, and what is not so.[4]

And, as another says:—

> From which, as from a never-failing spring, the mouths of poets are refreshed by Pierian waters.[5]

And another:—

> Add to these the companions of the Heliconian maids [the Muses], of whom Homer bore the sceptre without a peer.[6]

And another:—

> From this profuse source posterity has drawn for song, and has ventured to turn his river into their streams, enriched by the wealth of one man.[7]

It was contrary to the order of nature that he produced the most perfect work possible; for ordinarily the beginning of things is imperfect; they are enlarged and strengthened by increase; the infancy of poetry and of many other kinds of learning was rendered by him mature, perfect, and complete. For this reason we may call him the first and last of poets, according to that noble testimony to him that antiquity has left us, that there was no one before him whom he could imitate and no one after him who could imitate him.[8] His words, according to Aristotle, are the only words that have motion and action; they are the only substantial words.[9]

Alexander the Great, having found among the spoils of Darius a rich casket, ordered that it should be reserved for him to keep his Homer in, saying that this book was the best and most trustworthy counsellor he had in his military affairs.[10] For this same reason Cleomenes, son of Anaxandridas, said that he was the poet for the Lacedæmonians, because he was a great master of the art of war.[11] The peculiar and special commendation also, in Plutarch's judgement, belonged to him, "that he is the only author in the world with whom mankind has never been surfeited or wearied, as he always showed different sides to his readers, and was always esteemed with fresh favour."[12] That madcap Alcibiades, having sought from one who made profession of letters a book of Homer, gave him a cuff because he had none;[13] as if one of our priests should be caught without his breviary. Xenophanes bewailed himself one day to Hiero, tyrant of Syracuse, because he was so poor that he had not the wherewithal to maintain two attendants. "And yet," was answered him, "Homer, who was much poorer than you, maintains more than ten thousand, dead as he is."[14] What was there not in the saying of Panætius, when he called Plato the Homer of philosophers?[15] Besides all

this, what fame can be compared to his? There is nothing
that so lives in the mouths of men as his name and his works.
Not only some special races, but the greater number of nations, seek their origin in his inventions. Mahomet, the second of that name, Emperor of the Turks, writing to our
Pope Pius II, says: "I am astonished that the Italians oppose
me, seeing that we have our common origin in the Trojans,
and that it is for their interest as well as mine to avenge the
blood of Hector upon the Greeks, whom they are favouring
against me."[16] Is not that a noble drama,[17] of which kings,
republics, and emperors play the characters through so many
ages, and for which all this great universe serves as theatre![18]
Seven Grecian cities disputed his place of birth:—

Smyrna, Rhodos, Colophon, Salamis, Chios, Argos,
Athenæ.[19]

Another[20] is Alexander the Great. For, if we consider his
age when he began his enterprises; the authority which he
acquired in those youthful days among the greatest and
most experienced captains in the world by whom he was
followed; the extraordinary favour with which fortune
embraced and assisted so many of his hazardous and, I may
almost say, audacious exploits—

Sweeping away whatever opposed his lofty ambition, and delighting in making a path through ruins;[21]

that great performance of having, at thirty-three years of
age, victoriously passed over all the habitable earth, and
attained in half a lifetime the whole power of human nature,
so that you can not picture a duration of the usual length
for him, and the continuance of his growth in valour and for-

tune to the ordinary term of years, without picturing something more than man; the having created from amongst
his soldiers so many royal lines, leaving at his death the
world divided amongst four successors known only as commanders of his army, whose descendants have, so long a
time after, continued to maintain that great possession; so
many eminent virtues that existed in him: justice, temperance, liberality, loyalty to his word, love for those near him,
humanity to the conquered, for his conduct seems, in truth,
to be subject to no reproach (yes, certainly, some few of his
infrequent private actions; but it is impossible to carry on
within the rules of justice such great operations; men such
as he are to be judged as a whole, by the controlling aim of
their actions). The destruction of Thebes,[22] the murder of
Menander and of the physician of Ephestion, of so many
Persian captives at one stroke, of a troop of Indian soldiers
not without breach of his word, of the Cossians even to the
little children,[23] are violences somewhat inexcusable. And
as for Clytus,[24] the crime was atoned for beyond its importance, and the quality of his repentance[25] bears witness not
less than other acts to the friendliness of his disposition, and
that his nature was in itself peculiarly inclined to kindness;
and it has been wittily said of him that he had his virtues
by nature, his vices by fortune.[26] As to his being a little
given to boasting, a little too intolerant of hearing himself
spoken ill of; and as to the mangers, weapons, and bits
which he caused to be scattered about in the Indies,[27] all
these things, it seems to me, can be condoned on account
of his age and the unusual prosperity of his fortunes[28] if
we consider at the same time so many military virtues: diligence, foresight, patience, discipline, subtlety, craft, mag-

nanimity, resolution, good-fortune, in which, even if the
authority of Hannibal had not so taught us,[29] he was the
first of men; the rare beauty and qualities of his person,
even bordering on the miraculous;[30] his bearing and awe-
inspiring demeanour, with a face so youthful, ruddy, and
radiant,—

> Like Lucifer, whom Venus delights in more than
> all the other starry luminaries, when he has bathed in
> the waves of Ocean, and lifts his sacred head to heaven,
> and dissipates the darkness,[31]—

the superiority of his knowledge and capacity; the duration and grandeur of his glory, pure, clean, stainless, and
exempt from rivalry; and that, even a long time after his
death, it was a religious belief to think that medals with his
image brought good-fortune to those who wore them; and
that more kings and princes have written of his deeds than
other historians have written of any other king or prince
whatever; and that, even at the present day, the Mohammedans, who despise all other histories, accept and honour
his alone, by special prerogative,[32]—we must confess, all
this taken together, that I have had grounds for placing
him above Cæsar himself, who alone has made me a little
doubtful as to the choice. And it can not be denied that
there is more that is his own in Cæsar's exploits, more fortune in those of Alexander.[33] They were equals in many
respects, and Cæsar, perchance, the greater in some. They
were two flames, or two torrents, that ravaged the world
in divers parts,—

> Like flames kindled in different parts of a dry forest,

and in the whispering laurel thickets, or when foaming
rivers rush noisily down high mountains through the
plains, devastating them on their way.[34]

But, if Cæsar's ambition was in its nature more moderate,
it was so unfortunate in having fastened upon the villainous
object of the ruin of his country and the universal impairing
of the world that, all things collected and put in the scales,
I can not but incline toward the side of Alexander.

The third, and the most eminent in my opinion, is Epaminondas.[35] Of fame he has not nearly so much as others
(which indeed is not a part of the substance of the matter);[36]
of resolution and of valour—not that which is sharpened by
ambition, but that which wisdom and renown can implant
in a well-ordered soul—he had all that can be imagined.
As proof of this virtue in him, he did as much, in my opinion, as Alexander himself and Cæsar; for, although his exploits in war were neither so frequent nor so large in scope,[37]
yet they do not fail, when carefully considered with all their
circumstances, to show as much weight and inflexibility,[38]
and to bear as strong testimony of boldness and of military
ability. The Greeks did him the honour, without gainsay-
ing, of calling him the first man among them;[39] but to be
the first man in Greece is easily to be the first in the world.
As for his learning and ability, this ancient judgement
about it has come down to us, that no man ever knew so
much and said so little as he.[40] For he was a Pythagorean by
sect.[41] And what he said, no one ever said better; an eminent
and very persuasive orator. But as to his character and conscience, he very far surpassed all those who have ever undertaken to manage public affairs. For in that part of a man
which should be chiefly considered, which alone indicates

truly what manner of men we are, and which I hold to outweigh by itself all the others together, he gives place to no philosopher, not to Socrates himself. In this man, innocence is a special quality, sovereign, constant, uniform, incorruptible, in comparison with which it appears in Alexander subordinate, uncertain, many-hued, lax, and fortuitous.

It was judged by the ancients that, in examining part by part all the other great military leaders, there is found in each of them some special quality which makes him illustrious.[42] In this man[43] alone there are power and ability which are even and alike throughout; he, in all the functions of human life, leaves nothing to be desired in him, whether in public or private employment, peaceful or warlike, whether it be in living, or in dying greatly and gloriously. I know neither the figure nor fortune of any man which I regard with so much honour and affection. It is, indeed, true that his persistence in poverty, as it is depicted by his best friends,[44] seems to me somewhat overdone. And this condition alone, albeit lofty and most worthy of admiration, I feel to be a little too bitter for me even to think of wishing to imitate it, to the degree to which he carried it. Scipio Æmilianus alone, could we bestow on him so proud and magnificent an end, and an extent of learning so profound and universal, could make me doubtful as to the choice. Oh, what an ill turn time has done me, to take out of our sight, as of set purpose, amongst the foremost men, precisely the noblest pair of lives in Plutarch, of those two personages who were, by the common consent of the world, one the first of the Greeks, the other, of the Romans.[45] What material—what a workman! For a man who was no saint, but, as we say, a fine fellow, of town-bred and usual ways,[46] of moderate eminence, the richest life that I know to have been lived amongst living men, as the saying is, and most replete with high and desirable conditions, is, all things considered, to my mind, that of Alcibiades.

But, to return to Epaminondas, I desire, as evidencing his extremely good heart, to add here some of his ideas. The sweetest satisfaction that he had in his whole life, he declared, was the pleasure he had given his father and mother by his victory of Leuctra;[47] he plays high,[48] setting their pleasure above his own, so just and complete, in so glorious a deed. He did not think it permissible, even were it to restore liberty to his country, to kill a man without unquestionable justification;[49] this is the reason that he was so slow about the enterprise of his close friend Pelopidas for the deliverance of Thebes. He held also that, in a battle, an encounter with a friend who was on the opposite side must be avoided, and he must be spared.[50] And his consideration for his enemies having even caused him to be suspected by the Bœotians,—forasmuch as, after he had, as by a miracle, forced the Lacedæmonians to open to him the pass they had undertaken to hold at the entrance of the Morea near Corinth, he was content with passing through them,[51] without pursuing them to the utmost,—he was deposed from the office of general-in-chief—most honourably for such a reason, and for the shame which was theirs[52] in being driven by necessity to place him again, soon after, in his command, and to acknowledge how much their glory and their salvation depended upon him, victory following him, like his shadow, wherever he led.[53] The prosperity of his country, indeed, died when he died, even as it was born with him.[54]

Chapter XXXVII

OF THE RESEMBLANCE
OF CHILDREN
TO THEIR FATHERS

THIS fagotting of so many different kinds of sticks is done in these conditions, that I put my hand to it only when a too futile idleness weighs on me, and nowhere but in my own house. So it is compacted with varying pauses and intervals, as matters detain me elsewhere, sometimes for many months. Furthermore, I do not correct my first ideas by later ones—oh, perchance some word, but to give variety, not to take any thing away. I wish to represent the progress of my moods, and that each part shall be seen at its birth. I should find pleasure in having begun sooner and in recognising the course of my mutations. A young man of my household, whom I employed to write at my dictation, thought that he had great booty when he stole from me several pieces, selected at his pleasure.[1] It consoles me that his gain will not be more than my loss.

I am seven or eight years older than when I began, and not without new acquisitions. I have become endowed with the colic[2] by the gift of the years. In commerce and long converse with them[3] some such gain is easily made. I could wish that, of many other presents which they have it in their power to bestow upon those who have long association

Of the Resemblance of Children

with them, they had chosen one that would have been more acceptable to me; for they could not have given me any one. of which from my youth I had more horror; it was precisely, of all the mishaps of old age, the one that I most dreaded. I had thought to myself many a time that I was going too far, and that, travelling so long a road, I should not fail, at last, to be involved in some unpleasant encounter. I felt, and sufficiently declared, that it was time to go hence, and that life should be cut off in the living and sound part, according to the method of surgeons when they have to cut off some limb; that Nature was wont to demand very harsh usury of him who did not quickly pay her. But these were idle propositions. I was far from ready to accept them then; and in the eighteen months or thereabouts that I have been in this disagreeable condition, I have already learned to adapt myself to it. I am already entering into an agreement with this colical life; I find therein the wherewithal to console me and to give me hope. So domesticated are men to their miserable existence, that there is no condition so wretched that they are not prepared to accept it for self-preservation.

Hear Mæcenas:—

> Make me weak of hand, of foot and leg, shake loose
> my teeth; while life remains, it suffices.[4]

And Tamburlane masked with absurd humanity the fantastic cruelty that he practised against lepers, in putting to death as many of them as came to his knowledge, in order, he said, to deliver them from the doleful life they were living. For there was no one of them who would not have liked better to be thrice a leper than not to exist.[5] And Antis-

Of the Resemblance of Children

thenes the Stoic, being very ill, and exclaiming, "Who will deliver me from this suffering?" Diogenes, who had come to see him, gave answer, offering him a knife, "This, if you choose, forthwith."—"I did not say from life," he rejoined, "but from this suffering."[6]

The troubles that affect us simply in the mind afflict me much less than they do the greater number of other men; partly from judgement (for the world deems many things horrible, or to be avoided at the cost of life, which are to me well-nigh indifferent); partly from the dull and insensible nature that I have as regards circumstances which do not touch me directly, which nature I consider one of the best parts of my inborn condition. But the truly essential and bodily sufferings I feel very keenly. Nevertheless, foreseeing them in other days with feeble and sensitive vision, weakened by the enjoyment of the long and fortunate good health and repose which God bestowed on me during the greater part of my life, I had in my imagination conceived them as so intolerable that, in truth, I had more fear of them than I have found evil in them.[7] Wherefore I believe ever more confidently that the greater number of the faculties of our mind, as we employ them, disturb the repose of life more than they promote it.

I am in the clutches of the worst of all diseases, the most violent, the most grievous, the most deadly, and the most irremediable. I have already experienced five or six very long and painful attacks of it; nevertheless, either I flatter myself, or else there is in these conditions ground to sustain him whose soul is free from the fear of death and free from the threatenings, conclusions, and consequences which the art of physic puts into our head. The condition of pain has

Of the Resemblance of Children

not so hard and poignant a bitterness that a man of settled
mind should thereby fall into madness and despair. I have
at least this profit from the colic, that what I have not yet
been able to master for myself—the wholly reconciling myself to death and familiarising myself with it—this malady
will accomplish; for the more it may assail me and torment
me, by so much the less will death be to be feared. I had
already gained this, that I clung to life solely for the sake of
life; this malady will unloose that connection also; and God
grant that finally, if its severity shall surpass my strength, it
may not throw me into the other extreme, not less sinful,
of loving and desiring death!

Neither fear nor desire your last day.[8]

Both these dispositions[9] are to be feared, but one has its
remedy much nearer at hand than the other.

For the rest, I have always found that precept a formal-
ity which commands us so sternly and explicitly to maintain
a steady front and a disdainful and composed demeanour
when enduring discomforts. Why does Philosophy, which
regards only the essential and realities,[10] busy herself with
these external appearances? Let her leave the care of this
to play-actors and teachers of rhetoric, who think our gestures so important. Let her boldly forgive discomfort for
this vocal unmanliness, if it is neither of the heart, nor profound;[11] and place these voluntary lamentations in the same
class as sighs, sobs, palpitations, and pallors, which Nature
has put beyond our control. Provided the spirit be void of
terror, the words void of despair, let her be content! What
matter if we toss about our arms, provided we do not toss
about our thoughts? She trains us for ourselves, not for

Of the Resemblance of Children

others; to be, not to seem. Let her be satisfied with controlling our understanding, which she has undertaken to instruct; let her, while she is in the throes of the colic, keep the soul capable of recognising herself, of following her accustomed course; combatting pain and sustaining it, not shamefully prostrating herself at its feet; excited and heated by the combat, not cast down and overthrown; capable of intercourse, and capable of conversation to a certain extent.

In such extreme conditions it is cruel to demand of us a bearing so composed. If we play the game well, it matters little that we have a doleful countenance.[12] If the body is relieved by complaining, let it complain; if movement gives it pleasure, let it toss and turn as it will; if it seems to it that the pain is in some degree diminished (as some physicians say that this helps in the delivery of pregnant women[13]) by uttering very violent outcries, or if that diverts its pangs, let it scream its loudest. Let us not order this noise to be made, but let us permit it to the body. Epicurus does not merely permit his wise man to cry out in his agony, but advises him to do so.[14] *Pugilists, also, when they strike in throwing the cestus, utter groans, because, by expelling the voice, the whole body is made tense, and the blow comes with more violence.*[15] We have enough labour from the evil circumstance without labouring at these superfluous precepts. Which I say to excuse those who are commonly seen raving under the sudden shocks and assaults of this disease; since, as for myself, I have passed through it up to this time with a somewhat better countenance; not, however, that I give myself trouble to maintain this external decorum, for I make little account of such an advantage; I yield therein to the pain all it demands; but either my sufferings are not so

1029

severe, or I meet them with more steadiness than most
people. I complain, I fume, when the sharp pains seize me,
but I am not beside myself, like this man,—

> With resounding lamentations, groans, sobs, and
> cries, his melancholy voice declares much.[16]

I test myself when the pain is at its worst; and I have always
found that I am able to talk, to think, to reply, as sanely as
at any other time; but not so continuously, the suffering disturbing and distracting me. When I am thought to be most
cast down, and those who are with me demand nothing of
me, I often make trial of my powers, and myself broach subjects furthest removed from my conditions. I can do any
thing by a sudden effort; but let it not last long. O why
have I not the faculty of that dreamer in Cicero, who,
dreaming he was embracing a young girl, found that he had
discharged his stone in the sheets! Mine strangely dis-
wenches me!

In the intervals of this extreme suffering, when my ure-
ters are enfeebled but do not fret me, I quickly recover my
usual form, because my soul feels no alarm at what affects
only the senses and the body; which I owe assuredly to the
care that I have taken to prepare myself by reflection for
such casualties;

> No new or unexpected kind of hardship now is
> presented to me: I have before seen and considered all
> in my mind.[17]

I am pestered, however, somewhat severely for a novice,
and with an extremely sudden and harsh pain, having fallen
abruptly from a very pleasant and very fortunate condition

Of the Resemblance of Children

of life to the most dolorous and painful that can be imagined; for, besides that this is a disease greatly to be dreaded in itself, its beginnings in me are much more sharp and troublesome than they are wont to be. The attacks recur so often that I almost never feel in perfect health. Nevertheless, I maintain my mind up to this hour in such a state that, provided I can persist in it, I find myself in a much better condition of life than a thousand others who have no fever or ill but that which they give themselves by lack of judgement.

There is a certain kind of subtle humility which is born of presumption, as, for instance, this: that we acknowledge our ignorance in many things, and are so courteous as to admit that there are in the works of nature some qualities and conditions which are imperceptible to us, and of which our faculties can not discover the methods and the causes. By this honest and conscientious declaration, we hope to obtain that we shall be believed as to those things that we say we understand. We have no occasion to seek for miracles and unfamiliar difficulties; it seems to me that, amongst the things we see every day, there are some so strange and so incomprehensible that they surpass all the difficulty of miracles. What a wonderful thing it is that that drop of seed from which we are produced bears in it the impressions, not of the bodily form alone, but of the thoughts and inclinations of our fathers! That drop of water—how does it contain this endless number of forms? And how does it convey these resemblances, whose course is so headlong and irregular that the great-grandchild will resemble his great-grandfather, the nephew his uncle? In the family of Lepidus at Rome there were three persons, not in direct succes-

Of the Resemblance of Children

sion but at intervals, who were born with one and the same eye covered by a cartilage.[18] In Thebes there was a family which bore from the mother's womb the mark of a lance-head, and he who bore it not was considered illegitimate.[19] Aristotle says that, in a certain nation where the women were held in common, the children were assigned to their fathers by resemblance.[20]

It is to be believed that I owe to my father this stony condition; for he died terribly tormented by a great stone in his bladder. He perceived nothing of his malady until his sixty-seventh year; and before that he had no threatening of it, and no twinges in the loins or the sides, or elsewhere; and he had lived until that time in excellent health, and very little subject to sickness; and he lived seven years longer with this disease, dragging on a very dolorous close of his life. I was born twenty-five years and more before his sickness, and during his best condition—the third of his children in order of birth. Where, for so long a time, was the proneness to this failing being hatched? And when he was so far from the disease, how did that slight piece of his substance of which he composed me receive for its share so strong an impression of it? And how remain so hidden that forty-five years later I should begin to feel it—I, the only one to this hour among so many brothers and sisters, and all by one mother? Whoever will enlighten me about the happening of this,[21] I will believe him about as many other miracles as he likes, provided that he does not, as some do, give me as satisfaction a belief[22] much more puzzling and fanciful than the thing itself.

Let physicians be a little lenient to my freedom of speech; for by means of this same infusion and fatal penetration, I

Of the Resemblance of Children

have imbibed hatred and contempt of their science.[23] This antipathy that I have for their art is hereditary: my father lived to be seventy-four, my grandfather sixty-nine, my great-grandfather well-nigh eighty, without having tasted any sort of medicine; and with them every thing that was not in common use was regarded as a drug. Medicine is based upon examples and experience; so is my opinion. Is not this a very express and excellent experience? I question if they[24] will find in their records three persons who were born, brought up, and died at the same hearth, under the same roof, who also lived according to their rules.[25] They must needs acknowledge that, if reason is not on my side, at least fortune is; now, with physicians, fortune is of more consequence than reason. Let them not in these days take me at a disadvantage; let them not threaten me, laid by the heels as I am; that would be foul play. And, to tell the truth, I have enough the better of them by my household examples, although they here come to an end. Human affairs have not so great stability; it is two hundred years lacking only eighteen that this experience continued with us; for the first was born in the year 1402.[26] It is, in truth, quite natural that this experience should begin to fail us. Let them not upbraid me with the pains that now have me by the throat; to have lived forty-six years,[27] for my part—is not that enough? If it shall be the end of my career, it is of the longest.

My ancestors held medicine in loathing, from an occult and innate instinct; for the very sight of drugs was abhorrent to my father. The seigneur de Gaviac, my paternal uncle, an ecclesiastic, who was sickly from his birth, and who, nevertheless prolonged his feeble life to sixty-seven years, having fallen once into a violent and continuous fever, the physicians ordered that he should be plainly told that, if he would not help himself (they call help that which most frequently is a hindrance), he was infallibly a dead man. The worthy man, much terrified as he was by that appalling sentence, nevertheless replied: "Then I am a dead man." But God soon after made that prognostic of no account. The youngest of the brothers,—there were four of them,—sieur de Bussaguet (and he was very much the youngest), alone subjected himself to that science, by reason, so I believe, of the commerce he had with other sciences, for he was a councillor in the court of Parliament; and medicine succeeded so ill with him that, though he was apparently of very strong constitution, he died long before the others, except one, sieur de Saint-Michel.

It is possible that I may have derived from my ancestors this natural antipathy to medicine; but if there had been only that ground for it, I would have tried to overcome it. For all those conditions which are born in us without foundation are unsound; it is a sort of sickness to be combatted; perhaps it was thus that I derived this inborn inclination, but I have supported it and strengthened it by arguments which have confirmed in me the opinion that I have of the matter. For I also hate the idea of refusing medicine because of its bitter taste; I should hardly be of that humour, I who hold health worthy of purchase by all the most painful burnings and cuttings that can be used. And in accordance with Epicurus, pleasures seem to me things to be avoided if they bring in their train greater pain, and those pains things to be sought, which bring in their train greater pleasures.[28]

1034

Of the Resemblance of Children

Health is a precious thing, and the only thing which deserves, in truth, that we should expend, not only time, sweat, labour, and wealth, but even life, in its pursuit; because without it life comes to be grievous and harmful to us. Pleasure, wisdom, learning, and virtue, without it, lose their lustre, and vanish; and to the most solid and laboured arguments by which philosophy may desire to impress upon us another view we have only to oppose the figure of Plato stricken by the falling sickness or an apoplexy, and, putting that case, defy him to assist himself with the noble and abundant faculties of his mind. Any road that would lead to health would not be called by me either rough or costly. But I have some other signs that make me strangely distrust all this business.[29] I do not say that there may not be some skill in it; that there may not be, amongst so many of nature's works, things adapted to the preservation of our health—that is certain.[30] I am well aware that there are some simples that create moisture, others dryness; I know from experience both that radishes cause windiness, and that senna leaves relax the bowels. I know of many such facts, as I know that mutton nourishes me and that wine warms me; and Solon said that eating was, like other drugs, a medicine for the disease of hunger.[31] I do not disallow the profit that we derive from the world, nor do I doubt the power and fertility of Nature, and her conformity to our needs. I see clearly that the pike and the swallow fare well with her. I distrust the surmises of our minds, of our learning and skill, in favour of which we have abandoned her and her laws, and in which we know not how to keep within moderation and bounds.

As we call by the name of justice the mixing together[32] of the first laws that fall into our hands, and the dispensing and use of these, which are often very unsuitable and unreasonable; and as those who make mock of this justice, and blame it, do not, nevertheless, mean to insult that noble virtue, but solely to condemn the abuse and profanation of that sacred title; so, in like manner, in medicine, I greatly honour that glorious name, what it suggests, what it promises, so useful to mankind; but what it designates amongst us, I neither honour nor value.

In the first place, experience makes me fear it; for, so far as my knowledge goes, I find no kind of men so quickly sick and so slowly cured as those who are under the jurisdiction of medicine. Their very health is impaired and marred by enforced diet. Physicians are not content to have the control of sickness: they make health sick, in order to make sure that there is no escape from their authority at any time. From constant and perfect health do they not draw occasion for a severe illness to come? I have been sick often enough; without their assistance, I have found my sicknesses—and I have tried almost all kinds—as easy to endure and as brief as any other man; and yet I have not mixed therewith the bitterness of their drugs. My health[33] is free and perfect, without rules and without other schooling than from my habits and my pleasure. Every place is a good one for me to stay at, for I need no other conveniences when I am ill than those which I need when I am well. I am not impatient at being without a doctor, without an apothecary, and without assistance, which I see most men to be more distressed by than by the malady itself. What! they themselves,[34] do they show us, in the fortune and length of their lives, testimony to any manifest effect of their art?[35]

1036

Of the Resemblance of Children

There is no nation which has not existed many ages without medicine, and those the first ages, that is to say, the best and happiest; and the tenth part of the world still makes no use of it to this hour. Countless nations know it not, where people live both more healthfully and longer than they do here; and among us the common people live happily without it. The Romans had existed six hundred years before accepting it;[36] but, after having made trial of it, they expelled it from their city through the management of Cato the Censor, who showed how well he could do without it, having lived eighty-five years, and having kept his wife alive to extreme old age, not without physic, but, indeed, without a physician;[37] for every thing that is healthful for our life may be called physic. He kept his family in health, says Plutarch, by the use, if I remember aright, of hare's meat;[38] as the Arcadians, Pliny says, cure all maladies with cow's milk.[39] And the Libyans, Herodotus says, universally enjoy unusual health, from the custom they have, when children, of cauterising and burning the veins of the head and temples, after they have reached the age of four years, whereby they prevent, for their whole life, all forms of catarrh.[40] And the villagers of this region use for all maladies only the strongest wine they can get, mixed with much saffron and spice; always with the same success. And, to speak the truth, in all this diversity and confusion of prescriptions, what other purpose and effect is there, after all, than to void the bowels? which a thousand household simples can do. And yet I know not whether this is so beneficial as they say, and whether our constitution has not need of the residue of its excrements to a certain degree, as wine has of its lees for its preservation. You often see healthy men

Of the Resemblance of Children

seized with vomiting or diarrhœa in consequence of some external mishap, and make a great discharge of excrement, without any preceding need and without any subsequent benefit, nay, even with impairment and injury to their health. It was from the great Plato that I learned, not long since, that of the three kinds of involuntary bodily actions which belong to us, the last and the worst is that of purging, which no man, if he be not a fool, should undertake except in extreme necessity.[41] We stir up and rouse the disease by opposing it.[42] It should be the manner of living that gently weakens it and guides it to an end; the violent clawings of the drug and the disease are always to our prejudice, since the quarrel is fought out in us and the drug is an untrustworthy helper, by its nature hostile to our health, and which has access to our domain only by disturbance there. Let matters rest a bit. The order of things which takes care of fleas and moles also takes care of men when they have the same patience as fleas and moles in letting themselves be governed. In vain do we shout, "Bihore!"[43] It is a good way to make ourselves hoarse, but not to hasten matters. The order of things is proud and pitiless. Our fear, our despair alienate it and delay its coming to our aid, instead of inviting it to do so. It is bound to let disease as well as health run its course. It will not allow itself to be corrupted in favour of the one to the prejudice of the rights of the other; it would fall into disorder. In God's name, let us follow it! let us follow! It leads those who follow it; those who do not follow, them it drags along,[44] and with them their fury and their physic. Order a purge for your brain; it will be better employed there than in your stomach.

Some one asked a Lacedæmonian what had kept him so

1038

long in health. "Ignorance of medicine," he replied.[45] And
the Emperor Hadrian exclaimed constantly as he was dying, that the crowd of doctors had killed him.[46] A bad
wrestler turned doctor. "Take courage," said Diogenes to
him; "you are wise; you will now put in the ground those
who have heretofore put you there."[47] But they have this
advantage, according to Nicocles,[48] that the sun lights up
their successes and the earth hides their failures; and, more
than that, they have a very profitable way of making use of
all sorts of happenings; for that which Fortune, that which
Nature, or some other external cause (of which the number
is infinite) produces within us of good and salutary, it is the
privilege of Medicine to attribute to herself. All the fortunate results that befall the patient who is under her authority he owes to her. The causes that have cured me, and have
cured many others who do not call physicians to their aid,
they[49] claim as belonging to those subject to them; and as
for the mischances, they either disown them altogether, or
attribute the disaster to the patient by reasonings so futile
that they take care never to fail to have a goodly number of
this kind: "He uncovered his arm"; "He heard the rum-
bling of a coach";

the passing of wheels in the turns of narrow streets;[50]

"His window has been opened"; "He lay on the left side";
or "Some painful thought passed through his head." In
fine, a word, a dream, a glance seems to them a sufficient
excuse to acquit them of mistake. Or, if they choose, they
make use even of our growing worse and worse, and achieve
their ends by this other means that can never fail them,
which is, when the disease is intensified by their administer-

ing, to satisfy us with the assurance they give us that it
would have been very much worse without their remedies.
The man whom, from a cold, they have thrown into a
quotidian fever, but for them would have had a continual
fever. They take no care not to do their work ill, since the
harm they do turns to their profit. Really they are well advised in requiring the sick man to give himself up to a favourable confidence;[51] it must needs be, in truth, sincere,
and very supple, to fit with fancies so difficult of belief.

Plato said very fitly that it belonged only to physicians
to lie with all freedom, since our health is attached to their
empty and false promises.[52] Æsop, an author of very rare
excellence, all whose beauties few persons discover, is delightful when he puts before us the tyrannical authority that
they[53] usurp over those poor souls enfeebled and prostrated
by pain and fear; for he narrates that a sick man, being asked
by his doctor what effect he felt from the drugs that he had
given him, replied: "I have sweated profusely."—"That is
good," said the doctor. Later, he asked him again how he
had felt since. "I have been extremely cold," he said; "indeed, I have shivered violently."—"That is good," again
answered the doctor. Still a third time he asked him how he
was. "I feel," he said, "swollen and puffed up as with
dropsy."—"That is well," declared the doctor. One of his
household presently afterward making enquiry of him as
to his condition, "Of a surety, my friend," he replied, "by
dint of getting better, I am dying." There was in Egypt a
very just law by which the physician took charge of his patient the first three days at the risk and chances of the patient; but when three days had passed, it was at his own
risk;[54] for what sense is there in Æsculapius, their master,

being struck by lightning for having brought Helen from
death to life,[55]—

> Then the omnipotent Father, indignant that a mor-
> tal should rise from the shades of the lower world to
> the light of life, struck with a thunderbolt the son of
> Phœbus, the discoverer of such a remedy and such an
> art, and precipitated him to the waves of the Styx,[56]—

while his disciples are absolved who send so many souls
from life to death? A physician boasted to Nicocles that
his profession enjoyed great authority. "Truly, that is evident,"[57] said Nicocles, "since it can kill so many people
with impunity."[58]

Yet, had I been of their counsel, I should have made my
art more sacred and mysterious; they began well enough,
but they have not ended so.[59]. It was a good beginning to
have made gods and demons the authors of their science, to
have assumed a language of their own, a form of writing
of their own; although philosophy perceives that it is folly
to counsel a man to his advantage in an unintelligible way:

> As if a physician were to order his patient to devour
> an offspring of the earth that creeps on the grass, car-
> ries his house, and is bloodless.[60]

It was a useful rule in their profession, and one which
accompanies all fantastical, vain, and supernatural professions, that the patient's faith must anticipate, with earnest
hope and assurance, their action and operation. Which rule
they follow even to this point, that they deem the most
ignorant and dull physician more fit for the man who has
confidence in him, than the most experienced who is un-

known to him. The choice even of the greater part of their drugs is somewhat mysterious and divinatory: the left foot of a tortoise, the urine of a lizard, the excrement of an elephant, the liver of a mole, blood taken from under the right wing of a white pigeon; and for us who are colical (so disdainfully do they wrong our woeful case), the pulverised dung of a rat, and other such fooleries, which have rather the aspect of magical sorcery than of solid learning. I say nothing of the uneven number of their pills, the setting apart of certain days and festivals in the year, the noting of certain hours to gather the herbs of their compounds, and the austere and circumspect affectation of their bearing and countenance, which Pliny himself derides.[61] But they have failed, I must say, in that they have not added to this fine beginning the making their meetings and consultations more sacred and more secret; no uninitiated man should have access to them, any more than to secret ceremonies of Æsculapius. For it comes to pass from this error that their irresolution, the weakness of their arguments, conjectures, and foundations, the bitterness of their disputes, full of hatred, jealousy, and private considerations, being thereby disclosed to every one, a man must be wonderfully blind if he does not feel in great jeopardy in their hands. Who ever sees a physician make use of another physician's prescription without taking something away from it, or adding something to it?[62] Thereby they evince great distrust of their art, and shew us that they pay more heed to their reputation, and consequently to their profit, than to the welfare of their patient. Of their teachers, that one was wiser who enjoined upon them of old that one physician alone should undertake the treatment of a sick man; for, if he do noth-

Of the Resemblance of Children

ing that avails, the disgrace to the art of medicine will not be very great because of the failure of one man; and, on the other hand, the glory will be great if he meets with success; whereas, when there are many, they discredit the profession[63] at every turn, inasmuch as it happens that they more often do harm than good.[64] They should be content with the perpetual disagreement that exists in the opinions of the chief ancient masters and authors of that science, which is known only to men versed in letters, without displaying also to the people the controversies and instability of judgement which they foster and perpetuate among themselves.

Would you see an example of the ancient disagreement in medicine? Hierophilus places the original cause of disease in the humours of the body;[65] Erasistratus, in the blood of the arteries; Asclepiades, in the invisible atoms passing through our pores; Alcmæon, in the superabundance or lack of corporal forces; Diocles, in the inequality of the elements of the body and in the quality of the air we breath; Strato, in the large amount, rawness, and corruption of the food we eat; Hippocrates places it in the mind.[66] There is one of their friends, whom they know better than I, who declares, on this point, that the most important science that we make use of, that which has charge of our maintenance and our health, is, by ill-luck, the most uncertain, the most confused, and perplexed by the greatest changes.[67] There is no great danger in making a mistake about the height of the sun, or as to a fraction in astronomical computations; but here, where our whole existence is at stake, it is not wise to abandon ourselves to the mercy of the winds blowing from so many quarters.

Of the Resemblance of Children

Before the Peloponnesian War there was not much heard of this science. Hippocrates brought it into credit; all that he had established Chrysippus overturned; later, Erasistratus, Aristotle's grandson, did the same by all that Chrysippus had written. After these came the Empirics, who took a part entirely different from the ancients in the managing of this art. When the credit of these last began to grow stale, Hierophilus put into use another sort of medical practice, which Asclepiades combatted and destroyed in his turn. In their order, the opinions of Themisto gained authority, and then those of Musa, and still later those of Vectius Valens, a physician famous through the relations he had with Messalina. In the time of Nero the sovereignty of medicine fell to Thessalus, who abolished and condemned all that had been maintained concerning it till his day. His doctrine was overthrown by Crinas of Marseilles, who introduced the novelty of regulating all medicinal doings by the ephemerides and the movements of the stars—eating, sleeping, and drinking at such hours as it pleased the moon and Mercury. His authority was very soon supplanted by Charinus, a physician of the same city of Marseilles. The latter opposed, not only the old method of physic, but also the use of public hot baths, a custom for so many previous ages. He made men bathe in cold water, even in winter, and immersed sick persons in the native water of brooks.[68]

Down to the time of Pliny no Roman had ever condescended to practise medicine; it was in the hands of foreigners and Greeks, as it is among us Frenchmen of those who affect Latin;[69] for, as a very great physician says,[70] we do not readily accept the medicine that we understand, any more than the value of the herbs[71] that we gather.[72] If the

Of the Resemblance of Children

nations from which we obtain guaiacum, sarsaparilla, and china-root have physicians, we may suppose that, by reason of this same habit of attaching value to novelty, rarity, and dearness, they eagerly welcome our cabbages and our parsley; for who would dare to disdain things that were sought at such a distance, at the risk of such long and perilous peregrination? Since these mutations of old in medicine, there have been innumerable others, even to our own time; and oftenest complete and universal mutations, like those which Paracelsus, Fioravanti, and Argenterius[73] produced in our day; for they do not change one prescription only, but, as I am told, the whole frame and regimen of the body of physic, accusing of ignorance and imposture those who have practised it before them. I leave it to you to imagine what becomes of the poor patient! If, indeed, we were assured, when they mistake, that, if it does us no good, it does us no harm, it would be a very reasonable arrangement, to risk obtaining some gain without putting ourselves in any danger of loss. Æsop tells this tale: that a man who had bought a Moorish slave, thinking that his colour had come by accident and from ill treatment by his former master, caused him to be medically treated very carefully, with many baths and beverages; the result was that the Moor's dusky hue was in no wise improved, but he wholly lost his former health.[74]

How often it happens that we see physicians imputing to one another the deaths of their patients! I remember a wide-spread malady in the towns in my vicinity a few years ago—deadly and very contagious; this storm having passed over, which had carried away an infinite number of people, one of the most famous physicians in the whole region pub-

lished a pamphlet on this subject, wherein he reconsiders
their having used blood-letting, and confesses that to have
been one of the chief causes of the mischief that had been
done. Furthermore, their authors maintain that there is no
medicine in which there may not be something harmful;
and if even those which are of service to us injure us in some
way, what must those do which they administer to us altogether unseasonably? For my own part, even if there were
nothing else, I think that for those who hate the taste of
medicine it may be a hazardous act and injurious to swallow
it at so annoying a moment, with so much reluctance; and
I believe that so doing greatly tries the sick man at a time
when he has so much need of repose. Moreover, if we consider the incidents to which they[75] commonly ascribe the
cause of our sicknesses, they are so slight and vague, that I
infer therefrom that a very little error in the administration
of their drugs may do us much harm.

Again, if the mistake of the physician be important, we
are badly off, for it is very improbable that he does not fall
into the same mistake often: he requires too many details,
considerations, and circumstances to adjust his purpose accurately.[76] He must learn the sick man's constitution, his
temperament, his humours, his propensities, his actions, his
very thoughts and fancies; he must inform himself as to the
external conditions—the nature of the place, the quality of
the air and of the weather, the position of the planets and
their influences; and he must know, as to the malady, its
causes, its symptoms, its stages, its critical days; as to the
drug, its weight, its strength, its native place, its appearance,
its age, and its compounding; and all these details he must
know how to measure and to conform one to another, so as

to produce a perfect proportion of each part in respect to the whole.[77] Wherein if he fail ever so little, if of so many influences a single one goes awry, behold, that is enough to destroy us. God knows how difficult it is to learn most of these things: for example, how shall he recognise the symptom peculiar to the disease, each disease being capable of an infinite number of symptoms? What discussions and controversies do they not have among themselves, as to the interpretation of the urine! Otherwise, whence would arise the constant altercation we see amongst them in the recognition of diseases? How shall we excuse this error, into which they fall so often, of taking one disease for another?[78] In the sicknesses that I have had, little obscurity as there was in them, I have never found three doctors in agreement. I note more readily the examples that concern myself. Recently, at Paris, a gentleman was cut[79] by order of physicians, in whom no more stone was found in his bladder than in his hand; and there, likewise, a bishop, who was a very warm friend of mine, had been incessantly urged, by most of the physicians he called in counsel, to have himself cut; I joined my persuasions, trusting in others. When he was dead, and his body was opened, they found that his malady was in the kidneys. They are less excusable about this disease, because it is somewhat palpable. It is in this respect that surgery seems to me much more certain, because it sees and touches what it does;[80] there is less conjecturing and guessing, while physicians have no *speculum matricis* which reveals to them the brain, the lungs, and the liver.

The very promises of medicine are incredible; for, having to provide for diverse and opposed contingencies, which often harry us at the same time, and which have an almost necessary relation, as heat in the liver and chill in the stomach, they set about persuading us that, of the ingredients employed, this one will warm the stomach, this other will cool the liver; one is charged to go straight to the kidneys, indeed even to the bladder, without exhibiting its workings elsewhere, and maintaining its strength and virtue in that long road full of obstacles, till it arrives at the place where it is destined, by its occult properties, to be of service; this other will dry the brain; that one will moisten the lungs. Having compounded a potion of all this collection, is it not a kind of delusion to hope that these virtues will divide and separate themselves from this confusion and medley, to carry out such diverse orders? I should immensely fear that they would lose or exchange their billets,[81] and cause disturbance in the lodgings assigned them. And who can believe that, in that liquid mixture, these properties do not vitiate, blend, and alter one another? And consider that the making up of this prescription is another man's office,[82] to whose trustiness and mercy we still again abandon our life.

As we have doublet-makers and breeches-makers to clothe us, and are so much the better served because each undertakes only his special business, and his ability is more restrained and bridled than that of a tailor, who includes every thing; and as, in the matter of food, those of high rank have, for greater ease in their households, distinct offices of soup-makers and roasters, in which a cook who takes charge of every thing can not so perfectly succeed; so, in the matter of curing, the Egyptians did well to reject the profession of medicine in general, and to divide it up;[83] for each disease, for each part of the body, its workman; since this part was much more fitly and less confusedly treated because it was

Of the Resemblance of Children

considered specially by itself. Ours[84] do not consider that he who provides for every thing provides for nothing; that the complete government of this little world is beyond their powers.[85] Fearing to stay the course of a dysentery, lest they cause a fever, they killed a friend of mine who was worth more than the whole pack of them.[86] They balance their conjectures against present ills, and, in order not to cure the brain at the expense of the stomach, they offend the stomach and impair the brain by these disorderly and dissentient drugs.

As for the variety and weakness of the arguments of this profession, they are more evident than in any other. Aperitives are beneficial to a colicky man, inasmuch as, opening the passages and dilating them, they give an exit to that sticky substance of which gravel and stone are formed, and lead downward to the kidneys that which is beginning to harden and collect. Aperitives are dangerous to a colicky man, because, by opening the passages and dilating them, they give entry toward the kidneys of the substance adapted to form gravel, and, the kidneys readily seizing upon it because of their propensity for it, they can not easily be prevented from detaining much of what has been conveyed thither; furthermore, if by chance there is encountered a body a little larger than it should be to pass through all the narrow passages which are still to be traversed in order to eject it, this body, being jogged by these aperitives and forced into these narrow ducts, will, by stopping them up, lead to a certain and very painful death.

They have a like assuredness in the advice they give us as to our regimen of living. It is well to make water often, for we see, as a fact, that by letting it remain we give it time

Of the Resemblance of Children

to deposit its solids and its lees, which will serve as material to form the stone in the bladder; it is well not to make water often, for the heavy solids that it carries with it will not be drained away unless the flow is violent; as we see, in fact, that a torrent that rushes violently sweeps much more completely the place where it passes than does a gentle and sluggish brook. Similarly, it is a good thing to have frequent intercourse with women, for that opens the passages and carries away the gravel and sand; it is also very bad, because it inflames, wearies and weakens the kidneys.[87] It is well to take hot baths, because they relax and soften the places where the gravel and stone remain; it is bad, also, inasmuch as this application of natural heat assists the kidneys in baking and hardening and petrifying the matter that has settled there. For those who are at public baths it is more healthful to eat in the evening, so that the waters which they have to drink the next morning may have more effect, finding the stomach empty and unobstructed; on the other hand, it is better to eat little at dinner, so as not to disturb the working of the water, which is not yet complete, and to burden the stomach so soon after that other labour, and to leave the business of digesting to the night, which can do it better than the day, when the body and the mind are in constant movement and action.[88]

That is the way they idly talk and trifle at our expense in all their utterances. And they could not put before me any proposition against which I could not frame one to the contrary of equal strength. So let there be no more outcry about those who, in this confusion, allow themselves to be quietly guided by their inclination and by the advice of nature, and commit themselves to the common fortune. I have seen,

Of the Resemblance of Children

through the opportunity afforded by my travels, almost all the famous baths of Christendom; and some years since I began to make use of them; for, in general, I think bathing to be healthful, and I believe that we incur our slight discomforts of health from having lost the habit—which was generally followed in times past amongst almost all nations, and still is in many—of washing the body every day; and I can not but believe that we are much less well off for keeping our limbs thus becrusted and our pores checked with dirt. And as for drinking the waters, in the first place, it happens that they are not at all disagreeable to me; in the second place, they are natural and simple, which at least is not dangerous even if it be useless; whereof I take for proof the infinite number of peoples, of all races and constitutions, who flock to them. And although I have not perceived any extraordinary and miraculous effects from them,—rather, by enquiring a little more carefully than is commonly done, I have discovered to be unfounded and false all the rumours of such results which are spread broadcast in those places and which are believed there (as the world is easily cheated about what it desires),—yet I have seen very few persons who have been made worse by these springs; and it can not be honestly denied that they excite the appetite, facilitate digestion, and give us some fresh lustiness, if we go not thither too much broken down, which I advise against doing. They have not the power to rebuild a heavy ruin; they can stay a slight leaning, or provide against the menace of some deterioration. He who does not carry thither sufficient lustiness to be able to take pleasure in the society found there, and in the walks and activities to which he is invited by the beauty of the regions where these springs are com-

Of the Resemblance of Children

monly situated, doubtless loses the best and surest part of
their effect. For this reason I have, to this day, chosen to
abide at, and make use of, those where there is most amen-
ity of situation, most agreeableness of lodgings, of table,
and of company, as in France those of Banieres; those of
Plombieres on the frontiers of Germany and Lorraine; in
Switzerland, those of Baden; in Tuscany, those of Lucca,
and especially Della Villa, which I have made use of oftenest and at different seasons.

Each nation has its own opinion touching their use,[89] and
wholly different rules and methods of making use of them;
and, according to my experience, the result is almost the
same. Drinking the water is not at all thought well of in
Germany; for all diseases they bathe, and lie soaking[90] in the
water almost from sun to sun. In Italy, if they drink nine
days, they bathe at least thirty, and commonly drink the
water mixed with other drugs to aid its operation. Here they
order us to walk, to digest it; there they keep them in bed
when they have taken it, until they have voided it, constantly warming their stomach and feet. As the Germans
have their special custom of being generally scarified all
over with cuppings[91] in the bath, so the Italians have their
doccie, which are certain streams of hot water conveyed
through pipes, by means of which they bathe, during a
month, either the head or the stomach, or such other part of
the body as they are treating, for an hour in the morning,
and the same in the afternoon. There is an infinity of other
differences of custom in each country; or, to say better, there
is almost no resemblance between them. It is evident that
this kind of medical treatment to which alone I have turned,
although it is the least artificial, yet has its fair share of the

Of the Resemblance of Children

Of the Resemblance of Children

confusion and uncertainty which is seen everywhere else in that art.

Poets say whatever they choose, with more significance and grace—witness these two epigrams:—

> Yesterday Alcon touched the statue of Jupiter. Though of marble, it was affected by the physician's force. To-day, behold, he is taken from his ancient temple and carried out to burial, though a god and stone.[92]

And again:

> Andragoras bathed and gaily supped with us; the next morning he was found dead. Do you ask, Faustinus, the cause of so sudden a death? In sleep he had seen the physician Hermocrates.[93]

Hereupon I will relate two stories. The baron of Caupene in Chalosse and I hold in common the right of appointment to a benefice of great extent, at the foot of our mountains, called Lahontan. It is with the people of this corner of the world as it is said to have been with those of the Valley of Angrougne: they had a life of their own, manners, apparel, and morals of their own; they were ruled and governed by certain special regulations and customs handed down from father to son, to which they submitted without other compulsion than that of respect for their long usage. This little community had continued from all antiquity in so fortunate a condition that no neighbouring magistrate had taken the trouble to acquaint himself with their doings, no lawyer was employed to advise them, nor any outsider called upon to adjust their quarrels; and never had any one of that region

1053

been seen asking alms. They avoided alliances and intercourse with the outer world, in order not to impair the purity
of their government; until, as they relate, one amongst
them, within the memory of their fathers, having his soul
spurred by a noble ambition, took it into his head, in order
to bring his name into credit and good repute, to make one
of his children a Maître Jean or Maître Pierre;[94] and having
had him taught to write in some neighbouring town, turned
him at last into a fine village notary. This man, having acquired this dignity,[95] began to disdain their ancient customs
and to put into their heads the ostentatious display of the
region beyond the mountains. The first of his comrades who
had been robbed of the horns of his goat was advised by him
to seek satisfaction from the king's judges thereabouts; and
after this man, another, until he had debased the whole land.
On the heels of this corruption they say that there followed
immediately another, of worse consequence, by means of a
physician who conceived the desire to marry one of their
daughters, and to live amongst them. This man began by
teaching them the names of fevers, of rheums, and of im-
postumes, the location of the heart, of the liver, and of the
intestines, which was knowledge until then very far removed from their ken; and in place of garlic, with which
they had learned to drive away all bodily ills, however severe
and extreme they might be, he accustomed them to take unfamiliar concoctions for a cough or cold, and began to trade,
not on their health only, but also on their death. They swear
that only since then have they perceived that evening damp
made the head dull; that to drink when hot was harmful,
and that autumn winds were more injurious than those of
spring; that after using those new medicines they were over-

whelmed by a legion of unwonted diseases; and that they observed a general falling off in their former vigour, and that their lives were shortened by half. This is the first of my tales.

The other is that, before my subjection to the stone, hearing much value ascribed by many persons to he-goat's blood, as it were a celestial manna sent in these latter ages for the protection and preservation of human life, and hearing it spoken of by men of intelligence as an admirable drug and of infallible operation, I, who have always deemed myself exposed to all the chances that can befall any other man, was pleased, when in perfect health, to provide myself with this miraculous thing, and gave orders to my household that a he-goat should be nurtured for me according to the prescription; for it is necessary that he should be weaned[96] in the hottest months of the summer, and that he should be given only laxative herbs to eat and only white wine to drink. I was, by chance, at home the day of his killing; they came to tell me that my cook had found in his belly two or three large balls, which rattled against one another, amongst what he had eaten. I desired to have all his entrails brought before me, and had that stout large sack opened; there came out of it three great lumps, as light as sponges, so that they seemed to be hollow, and hard and firm outside, and spotted with many dull colours; one perfectly round, of the size of a bowling ball; the other two, a little smaller, imperfectly rounded, as if they were in process of forming. I have found, having made enquiry about this of those who are accustomed to opening these animals, that it is a rare and unusual circumstance. It is probable that they are stones closely related to ours; and, if that be so, it is an idle hope for per-

Of the Resemblance of Children

sons with the stone to derive their cure from the blood of a beast which was on its way to death from a like disease. As for saying that the blood does not feel this contagion, and that its wonted property is not changed by it, it is rather to be believed that nothing is engendered in a body save by the combination and participation of all parts; the mass acts as a whole, although one organ may contribute more than another, according to the diversity of their operation. Wherefore there is a great likelihood that in all the organs of that goat there was some petrifying quality. It was not so much from fear of the future and for myself that I was interested in this experiment, as it was because it happens in my own household, as well as in many others, that the women in it store up such trivial druggeries to aid the common people by them, using the same prescription for fifty diseases, and such a prescription as they do not take themselves, and yet are triumphant over happy results.

In the main, I honour physicians, not, according to the precept, out of necessity,[97]—for to this passage is opposed another, wherein the prophet reproves King Asa for having had recourse to a physician,[98]—but for love of the men themselves, having known many excellent ones and worthy to be loved. It is not they against whom I bear a grudge, it is against their art; nor do I greatly blame them for profiting by our folly, for most of the world does likewise. Many vocations both less and more worthy than theirs have no foundation and support but in public abuses. I call them, when I am ill, to bear me company, if they chance to be at hand at the time, and ask to be entertained by them; and I pay them as others do. I permit them to order me to keep warmly covered if I like better to be so than otherwise; they may choose between leeks and lettuce, of which it pleases them to have my soup made, and prescribe white wine or red for me; and so with all other things that are indifferent to my appetite and habits.

I know well that this is to do nothing for them, because bitterness and strangeness are elements of the very essence of medicine. Lycurgus prescribed wine for sick Spartans. Why? Because, when well, they hated drinking it; just as a gentleman, a neighbour of mine, uses it as a very salutary drug in his fevers because he mortally hates the taste of it. How many of them[99] we find to be of my humour: despising medicine for their own use and adopting an unconstrained manner of life wholly contrary to that which they prescribe for others. What is this if it be not a manifest abuse of our ignorance? For life and health are no less dear to them than to us, and they would adapt their deeds to their doctrine if they were not themselves aware of its falsity.

It is the fear of death and pain, impatience with suffering, a frantic and inconsiderate desire of cure, which thus blind us; it is pure cowardice that makes our belief so easy to be imposed upon[100] and so pliable. For the majority, however, it is not a matter of belief, so much as of toleration; for I hear them complain and talk about it as we do, but finally they conclude: "But what can I do?" As if patience were in itself a better remedy than impatience.[101] Is there any one of those who have acquiesced in this wretched subjection who does not surrender equally to every kind of imposture? who does not put himself at the mercy of any one who has the effrontery to promise him his cure?

The Babylonians took their sick to the public square: the common people served as physician, each passer-by being

Of the Resemblance of Children

obliged by humanity and good citizenship[102] to enquire about their condition and, according to his experience, to give them some salutary advice.[103] We do almost the same. There is not a woman so ignorant that we do not make use of her mumblings and charms; and according to my humour, if I had to accept any remedy, I would accept such a one more readily than any other, inasmuch as, at least, there would be no harm to fear from it. What Homer and Plato said of the Egyptians, that they were all physicians,[104] might be said of all people: there is no one who does not boast of some receipt, and who does not risk trying it on his neighbour if he is ready to trust him about it. The other day I was in company, when one or another of my associates brought news of a sort of pill compounded of a hundred and more ingredients, by actual count. This excited rejoicing and peculiar satisfaction; for what rock could withstand the force of such a numerous battery? I understand, however, from those who tried it, that not the least little gravel deigned to be moved by it.

I can not leave this paper without saying a word touching the fact that they offer us, as warrant of the infallibility of their drugs, the test they have made of them. The greater part, and, as I believe, more than two thirds, of medicinal virtues consists in the quintessence or hidden properties of herbs, as to which we can have no other instruction than from use; for the most essential part[105] is nothing but a quality of which we can not by our intellect discover the cause. Of such proofs, those which they claim to have acquired by the inspiration of some familiar spirit I am content to accept (for about miracles I never concern myself); or, indeed, the proofs derived from things which, for some other con-

sideration, often come into use by us; as when in wool,
wherewith we are accustomed to clothe ourselves, there
happens to be some occult desiccative property which cures
kibes on the heel; and as when in radishes, which we eat for
nourishment, there is found to be some laxative operation.
Galen relates that it befell a leper to be cured by means of
some wine he drank, because by chance a snake had crawled
into the receptacle. We find in this example the method and
a probable guide for attaining knowledge;[106] as also in those
about which physicians say that they have been set in the
way by the example of some animals. But in the greater part
of the different kinds of knowledge[107] to which they say
that they were led by fortune, and had no other guide than
chance, I find incredible the development of this instruction. I imagine man looking about him at the infinite number of things, plants, animals, metals. I do not see how he
would begin his experimenting; and if his first idea fixes itself on the horn of an elk, about which his credulity must be
very pliable and easy, he finds himself no less embarrassed
as to what to do next. There come to his mind so many
diseases and so many circumstances that, before he has
reached certainty as to the point of the completion of his
knowledge, human wit is nonplussed;[108] and before he has
found, amidst that infinity of things, what the quality of the
horn is; amongst that infinite number of diseases, epilepsy;
amongst the many humours, that of melancholy; amongst
the many seasons, winter; amongst the many nations, the
French; amongst the many ages, old age; amongst the many
celestial mutations, that of the conjunction of Venus and
Saturn; amongst the many parts of the body, the finger,[109]
—in all this being guided neither by sure token, nor by con-

Of the Resemblance of Children

jecture, nor by example, nor by divine inspiration, but solely by the action of fortune,—it must needs have been by a perfectly artificial, regulated, and methodical fortune. And still, if the cure should be achieved, how can it be certain that it was not that the disease had come to its end, or the result of chance, or the effect of something he had that day eaten, or drunk, or touched, or the merit of his grand-mother's prayers? Morever, if this proof had been perfect, how many times was it repeated, and this long string of hap-penings and concurrences restrung, to deduce therefrom a certain rule? If it is deduced, by whom? Of all these mil-lions there are but three men who undertake to record their experiences. Will fate have fallen in with one of them at the opportune moment? How if another, and a hundred others, have had contrary experiences? It may be that we should see some light here, if all the judgements and reasonings of men were known to us. But that three witnesses and three doctors should teach mankind is not reasonable; it would be needful that human nature had selected and deputed them, and that they were by express warrant declared our syndics.

To Madame de Duras[110]

Madame, you found me about this writing lately when you came to see me. Because it may happen that these trifles will some time fall into your hands, I desire that they may bear witness that the author feels himself greatly honoured by the favour that you will show them. You will recognise therein the same bearing and the same way of thinking that you have seen in his conversation. Even had I been able to assume some other manner than my usual one, and some other nobler and better appearance, I would not have done so; for I desire to derive from these writings nothing but that they shall present me to your memory as I naturally am. Those same dispositions and faculties, madame, which you have been familiar with, and have welcomed with much more humour and courtesy than they deserve, I desire to lodge (but without alteration or change) in a compact body which may endure for a few years or a few days after me, where you will find them again when it shall be your pleasure to refresh your memory of them, without taking the trouble otherwise to remind yourself of them; for they are not worth it. I desire that you should continue the favour of your friendship to me for the same qualities by which it has arisen. I do not at all seek to be better loved and esteemed when dead than while living.

The humour of Tiberius was absurd, though common. He took, said Tacitus, more pains to spread his renown in future times than he did to make himself estimable and agreeable to the men of his day.[111] If I were one of those to whom the world may owe praise, I would relinquish the debt and have it pay me in advance; let the praises make haste and keep themselves all about me, more profuse than lengthy, more ample than lasting; and let them boldly fade away at the same time with my consciousness, and when their sweet sound can no longer reach my ears.

It would be a foolish humour, at this moment, when I am about to abandon the commerce of men, to set about bringing myself before them by a new recommendation. I make no account of the goods which I have not been able to employ for the service of my life. Whatever I am, I desire to be so elsewhere than on paper. My skill and my diligence have been employed in making myself of value; my studies,

Of the Resemblance of Children

in learning what to do, not how to write. I have devoted all my strength to shaping my life. That is my occupation and my work. I am less a maker of books than of any other affair. I have desired to have sufficient ability for the service of the immediate and essential demands upon me, but not to create from it a storehouse and hoard for my heirs. He who is of value, let him shew it in his conduct, in his every-day talk, in dealing with love or with quarrels, in games, in bed, at table, in the management of his affairs and of his household. They whom I see in ragged breeches writing good books would have first mended their breeches if they had taken my advice. Ask a Spartan whether he prefers to be a good rhetorician rather than a good soldier; for my part, I would rather be a good cook, if I had not already one at my service.

Good God, madame, how I should hate such a commendation as that of being a clever man in writing and a nullity and fool in other things! I would rather be a fool all through than have chosen so ill the way to employ my worth. Therefore, I am so far from expecting to gain any new honour by these dull pages, that I shall do well if I do not lose what little of it I now have. For, besides that this dead and dumb picture will show less than[112] my natural being, it has no relation to my best estate, since I have much fallen away from my former vigour and activity, becoming withered and stale. I am near the bottom of the cask, which smells now of dregs and lees.

For the rest, madame, I should not have dared to touch so boldly on the mysteries of medicine, considering the esteem in which you and so many others hold it, had I not been shown the path by its authors themselves. I believe that

Of the Resemblance of Children

there are of these, among the old Latin writers, but two, Pliny and Celsus. If these some day are in your hands, you will find that they speak much more roughly of their profession that I do; I but pinch it, they cut its throat. Pliny laughs at them,[113] among other things, for this, that, when they were at the end of their rope, they devised that excellent shift of sending the patients whom they had exercised and tormented to no purpose with their drugs and diets, some to the help of prayers and miracles, others to hot baths.[114] (Do not be offended, madame; this is not said of those of our parts, who are under the protection of your family and who are all Gramontoises.)[115] They have a third device for ridding themselves of us, and freeing themselves from the reproaches that we might address to them for the little improvement in our ills, which they have had so long in charge that they have no invention left to hold us with: it is, to send us to seek the goodness of the air of some other region. Enough of this, madame; you will permit me to resume the thread of my discourse, from which I have digressed to talk with you.

It was, I think, Pericles, who, being asked how he was, replied, "You can judge by these," pointing to the amulets he wore on his neck and arms. He meant to imply that he was very sick, since he had gone so far as to have recourse to things so useless, and to allow himself to be arrayed in such fashion.[116] I do not say that I may not be brought some day to this absurd notion of placing my life and my health at the mercy and control of physicians; I may fall into that folly; I can not answer for my future firmness; but at that time, if some one asks me how I am, I shall say to him, like Pericles, "You can judge by this," shewing him in my hand

Of the Resemblance of Children

ten grammes of opium; that will be a very manifest sign of a very violent sickness. My judgement will be strangely unhinged; if any lack of endurance and fright get such an advantage over me, a very acute fever of my mind may be inferred.

I have taken the trouble to plead this cause, which I understand none too well, in order to give a little support and confirmation to the innate aversion to the drugs and methods of our physic which I have derived from my progenitors, to the end that it may not be simply a stupid and inconsiderate prejudice, and that it may have a little more solidity; and also that they who find me so firm against the exhortations and threats that are addressed to me when my sicknesses weigh upon me may not think that it is mere obstinacy—or if there shall be any one so foolish as to judge that there is some spurring from fame in it. What a well-aimed desire it would be, to seek to derive honour from a theme which is common to me with my gardener and my mule-driver! Certainly my heart is not so inflated with wind that I would exchange a solid, material, and marrowy pleasure like good health for an imaginary, spiritual, and unsubstantial pleasure. Fame, even that of the four sons of Aymon,[117] is too dearly bought for a man of my humour, if it costs him three good attacks of colic. Give me health, in God's name! They who like our system of physic may have their good and great and strong reasons also; I feel no ill-will toward opinions contrary to mine. I am so far from being perturbed by seeing the disagreement of my judgement with those of other men, and from becoming incapable of fellowship with men because they are of other minds and parties than mine, that, on the contrary, as the most general

Of the Resemblance of Children

mode that nature has followed is variety,—and more in
men's minds than in their bodies, inasmuch as they are of a
substance more supple and susceptible of variety of form,—
I find it much more unusual to see our humours and our
purposes in agreement. And there were never in the world
two opinions alike, any more than two hairs or two seeds.[118]
Their most universal quality is diversity.

The Essays of

MONTAIGNE

·

Book Three

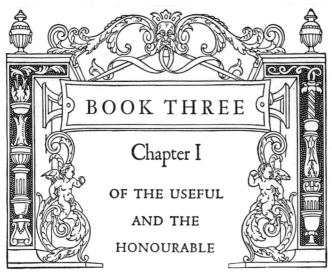

BOOK THREE

Chapter I

OF THE USEFUL
AND THE
HONOURABLE

No one is exempt from saying foolish things; the misfortune is to say them intentionally.[1]

Assuredly this man, with a great effort, will utter great trifles.[2]

That does not touch me; mine fall from me as carelessly as they deserve, which is well for them; I part with them at once, for whatever they may bring, and I neither buy them nor sell them but for what they weigh; I speak to this paper as I speak to the first man I meet. That this is true, here is the proof. To whom should not treachery be detestable since Tiberius spurned it at so great a cost? Word was sent to him from Germany that, if he thought well of it, they would rid him of Arminius by poison (he was the most powerful enemy that the Romans had, who had behaved toward them so villainously by defeating Varus, and who alone

Of the Useful and the Honourable

impeded the extension of his sway in those lands). He[3] replied that the Roman people was accustomed to take vengeance on its foes overtly, arms in hand, and not by deceit and secretly; he set aside the useful for the honourable.[4] He was, you will say, an arrant knave.[5] I think so; that is no great wonder in men of his position.[6] But the acknowledgement of virtue is not diminished in weight by the mouth of him who hates it, inasmuch as truth extorts it from him by force; and, even if he chooses not to welcome it inwardly, he at least clothes himself with it as an adornment.

The edifice of our life, both public and private, is full of imperfection; but there is nothing useless in nature, not even uselessness itself; nothing has found its way into this universe which does not occupy therein a fitting place. Our being is held together by disordered qualities: ambition, jealousy, envy, vindictiveness, superstition, despair abide in us with such natural proprietorship that their likeness is recognisable in the beasts as well; aye, and in us there is cruelty, that unnatural vice; for in the midst of compassion we are inwardly conscious of I know not what bitter-sweet prick of malicious pleasure in seeing others suffer; and children feel this.

It is sweet, when the winds trouble the great sea,
to behold from land the deep distress of another?[7]

Were the seeds of these qualities in man removed, the fundamental conditions of our life would be destroyed. In like manner, in every form of government there are necessary offices which are not only base, but even vicious; the vices here find their place and are employed as connecting links of our union,[8] as poisons are in the conservation of our

1068

Of the Useful and the Honourable

health. If they become excusable, inasmuch as we have need
of them, and general necessity wipes out their true character, this game must be left to be played by the most hardy
and least timid citizens, who sacrifice their honour and their
conscience as the ancients sacrificed their lives, for the salvation of their country. We who are weaker assume less difficult and dangerous parts. The public good demands that
some men betray and lie and kill; let us resign this commission to the more obedient and compliant. Truly, I have often
been wroth to see judges induce the criminal, by deceit
and false hopes of favour or pardon, to disclose his crime,
and employ trickery and shamelessness therein. It would be
well for justice,—and for Plato, too, who approves this
habit,—to find other methods more in accordance with my
way of thinking. It is a treacherous justice, and I think it is
not less wounded by itself than by others. I gave answer not
long ago that I, who should be very sorry to deal treacherously with a private person for the sake of the prince, would
hardly deal treacherously with a prince for the sake of a
private person; and I not only hate to deceive, but I hate
also that any one should deceive himself about me; I am not
willing even to furnish matter and opportunity for dispute.

In the small part that I have had in negotiating between
our princes,[9] in these divisions and subdivisions that tear us
asunder to-day, I have sedulously looked to it that they
should not be mistaken in me and not be deceived by my
rôle.[10] Those who ply that trade[11] keep their thoughts hidden as much as they can, and present themselves with a pretence of being as unbiassed and as acquiescent as possible.
As for me, I show forth my most personal opinions and in
my most characteristic manner; a sensitive and skilled ne-

gotiator, who prefer rather to fail in the business than to be
false to myself. Nevertheless, up to this hour, I have had
such fortune (for luck certainly has had the chief part in it),
that few men have passed between party and party with less
distrust, with more favour and familiarity. I have an open
manner, which easily makes its way and wins confidence
at first acquaintance. Simplicity and pure truthfulness, in
what age so ever, always find their opportuneness, and pass
current.[12] Moreover, freedom of speech is little suspected
and little disliked in those who labour without any interest
of their own, and who can truthfully make use of the reply
of Hyperides to the Athenians, when they complained of
the harshness of his speech: "My masters, do not consider
whether I am free of speech, but whether I am so without
thereby gaining any thing or improving my condition."[13]
My freedom has also relieved me easily from the suspicion
of hypocrisy by its vigour (never refraining from saying
any thing, however weighty and stinging it might be: I
could not have said worse in absence), and because it has a
manifest appearance of simplicity and recklessness. I aim at
no other game in acting than to act, and I connect with that
no long consequences and propositions: each act plays its
own special game; let it succeed if it can.

Furthermore, I am not impelled by emotions, either of
hate or of love, toward the great; nor is my will pinioned by
private injury or obligation. I regard our kings with an affection due simply by law, and from a subject,[14] neither induced nor repelled by any private interest; for which I
thank myself. The general and just cause attaches me to it
only temperately, and without excitement; I am not subjected to its far-reaching and social pledges and engagements;

Of the Useful and the Honourable

anger and hatred are beyond the duty of justice, and are passions of service to those only who are not sufficiently held to their duty by simple reason. *The passions are made use of by him who can not make use of his reason.*[15] All legitimate and equitable intentions are in themselves equable and temperate; otherwise they become seditious and unlawful. It is this that makes me walk everywhere with head erect and an open face and heart. In truth, and I am not afraid to confess it, I would readily, at need, offer a candle to St. Michael and another to his dragon, according to the old woman's idea; I will follow the best side to the point of danger, but no further if I can help it.[16] Let Montaigne be swallowed up in the public ruin if it be necessary; but if it be not necessary, I shall thank fortune if he escapes; and all means that my duty allows me[17] I shall employ for his preservation. Was it not Atticus who, while holding to the right side, and to the side that lost, escaped by his moderation in that universal shipwreck of the world, amidst so many mutations and diversities?[18] For private men, like him, it is an easier matter; and it seems to me that into this sort of business one may rightly not be ambitious to thrust and invite himself. To maintain a wavering attitude, half this and half that,[19] to keep one's feelings unstirred and without preference amidst the troubles of one's country and public divisions, this seems to me neither seemly nor honourable. *That is not a middle course; it is no course at all; it is awaiting the event, to adapt their plans to fortune.*[20]

This may be permitted in relation to the affairs of neighbours; and Gelo, tyrant of Syracuse, held his inclination thus in suspense, in the war of the Barbarians against the Greeks, keeping an embassy at Delphi, with offerings, to be

Of the Useful and the Honourable

on the watch to see on which side fortune would light, and seize the opportunity on the instant to make friends with the victors.[21] It would be a sort of treason so to do in our own affairs, wherein one must necessarily take sides. But I find it more excusable not to employ oneself in the work (and yet I do not make use myself of this excuse) for a man who has neither an office nor an express command to urge him to it, than in foreign wars, in which, however, by our laws, no one takes part who does not choose. At the same time, those who wholly enter into them can do it in such a way and with such temperance that the storm will pass over their heads without injury. Had we not reason to hope this in the case of the late bishop of Orleans, lord of Morvilliers?[22] And I know some, among those who at this hour are thus valiantly working, whose characters are so equable or so mild that they will be left standing, whatever disastrous change and downfall heaven may be preparing for us. I hold that it properly belongs to kings to be roused against kings; and I deride those minds which, from light-heartedness, offer to take part in such disproportioned quarrels; for it is not from a private quarrel with a prince that we proceed against him openly and bravely for our honour and according to our duty; if he[23] does not love such a man, he does better—he esteems him. And notably the cause of the laws and of the defence of the ancient state has always this privilege, that even those who, for their private purposes, oppose this cause forgive its defenders, even if they do not honour them.

But we must not call by the name of duty, as we every day do, a rancorous bitterness and harshness which is born of self-interest and personal affection, nor call treacherous and malicious conduct courage. They give the name of zeal

Of the Useful and the Honourable

to their propensity toward malignity and violence; it is not
the cause that incites them, it is their own interest. They
kindle war, not because it is just, but because it is war.
Nothing hinders you from bearing yourself fittingly and
loyally between men who are enemies; conduct yourself
therein with a good-will which, if not quite the same for
both (for it may be of different degrees), is at least well
governed, and which does not so pledge you to either that
he can demand every thing from you; and content yourself
with a moderate measure of their favour, and swim in rough
water without trying to fish therein.

The other way, that of offering oneself with all one's
strength to both one and the other man, has even less prudence than conscience. He to whom you betray the other,
by whom you were equally well received—does not he know
that with him you will do the like in his turn? He considers
you a bad man; nevertheless, he listens to you, and draws information from you, and profits by your disloyalty, for
double-dealing men are useful for what they bring, but care
must be taken that they carry away as little as possible. I say
nothing to one[24] that I can not say to the other when the time
comes, only with a slight change of tone; and I report only
matters that are unimportant or already known, or that are
of service to both alike. Not for any advantage do I permit
myself to lie to them. What has been entrusted to my silence
I religiously conceal, but I pledge myself to secrecy as little
as possible; the secret of princes is a troublesome care for him
who has no concern with it. I freely offer this bargain, that
they confide little to me, but that they trust boldly in what
I bring them. I have always known more from them than I
have desired to know. Frankness of speech opens the way to

Of the Useful and the Honourable

the like in another and even draws it forth, as wine does.[25]

Philippides replied wisely, in my opinion, to King Lysimachus, who asked him: "What would you have me bestow on you of my goods?"—"Whatever you choose, provided it is not your secrets."[26] I see that most men take offence if the basis of the affairs in which they are employed is concealed from them, and if there is withheld from their knowledge some purpose in the background. For my own part, I am content that nothing more should be told me than what it is wished I should make use of, and I do not desire that my knowledge shall exceed and influence my speech. If I must serve as an instrument of deceit, let it at least be with a clear conscience. I do not desire to be considered either so affectionate or so loyal a servant as to be thought capable of treachery. He who is faithless to himself is excusable in being so to his master.

But there are princes who do not accept the half of a man, and who scorn limited and conditional services. There is no remedy; I tell them frankly how far I can go; for a slave I must not be, save to reason, and consequently I can not well succeed here. And they also are at fault, to exact from a free man a like subjection and obligation to their service as from him whom they have made and bought, or whose fortunes are peculiarly and expressly attached to theirs. The laws have saved me much trouble: they have chosen a party for me and have given me a master; every other authority[27] and obligation must be relative to that and restricted by it. Yet this is not to say that, if my feelings should lead me in another direction, I should still give aid here; our will and our wishes make a law for themselves; our actions have to accept the law of public decree.

Of the Useful and the Honourable

All this procedure of mine is somewhat in disaccord with
our habits; it would not be adapted to produce great results,
or permanent ones; innocence itself could not to-day nego-
tiate without dissimulation, or bargain without lying. And
so public employments are not game for my hunting; so
much of them as my profession demands I supply it with,
in as private a manner as I can. As a youth I was immersed
in them to my ears, and successfully; but I freed myself
from them early in life. I have since often avoided taking
part in them, have rarely consented, never sought, to do so;
keeping my back turned to ambition, but, if not like the
rowers who thus progress backward, still in such wise that I
am less indebted to my resolution than to my good-fortune
for not having embarked in them; for there are ways less opposed to my taste, and more suited to my capacity,[28] by
which if she[29] had formerly summoned me to public service
and to advancement in the world's favour, I know that I
should have trampled down the reasoning of my judgement,
to follow her. They who say usually, in opposition to what
I profess, that what I call frankness, simplicity, and ingenu-
ousness in my manners is art and subtlety, and rather prudence than goodness, rather artifice than nature, rather good
sense than good-fortune, do me more honour than they take
from me. But they certainly make my subtlety too subtle;
and whoever has followed me and watched me closely will
grant that he has the better of me if he does not confess that
there is no rule in their school which could bring about this
natural course and maintain an appearance of liberty and
freedom so uniform and inflexible amidst paths so winding
and diverse; and that all their application and wit[30] could not
lead them to it. The way of truth is one and simple; that of

Of the Useful and the Honourable

private profit and of advantage to the affairs one has in charge is double, unequal, and fortuitous. I have often seen these counterfeit and artificial freedoms made use of, but oftenest without success. They have usually the air of Æsop's ass, who, in emulation of the dog, playfully threw his paws on his master's shoulders; but whilst the dog received caresses for such a greeting, the poor ass received twice as many blows.[31] *That especially becomes each man, which is especially his own.*[32] I do not wish to deprive deception of its due; that would be to understand the world ill; I know that it has often been used with profit and that it maintains and supports most of the vocations of mankind. There are lawful vices, as many acts that are good or excusable are unlawful.

Justice in itself, natural and universal, is otherwise ordered, and more nobly, than this special, national justice, constrained by the needs of our forms of government. *Of true law and genuine justice we have no fixed and complete model; we make use of shadows and images;*[33] so that the sage Dandamys, hearing the lives of Socrates, Pythagoras, and Diogenes narrated, judged them to be great men in all else, but too much subjected to reverence for the laws;[34] since true virtue, to give authority and aid to these, must relinquish much of its native vigour; and not only by their permission, but by their persuasion, do many vicious actions take place. *Crimes are authorized by the senatus consultus and plebiscites.*[35] I follow the common way of speaking, which makes a distinction between what is useful and what is honourable; so that it calls some natural actions, which are not only useful but also necessary, dishonourable and foul.

Of the Useful and the Honourable

But let us pursue our subject of treachery. Two pretenders to the kingdom of Thrace had quarreled about their rights. The emperor[36] prevented them from fighting; but one of them, under colour of bringing about an amicable agreement by an interview, having made an appointment with his competitor to feast at his house, imprisoned and killed him. Justice demanded that the Romans should take account of this crime; there was a difficulty that impeded the ordinary ways: what they could not do lawfully without war and without risk, they undertook to do by treachery; what they could not honourably do, they did profitably. For which task one Pomponius Flaccus was thought fitted; he, by hypocritical words and assurances, having enticed this man into his net, instead of the honour and favour which he promised him, sent him, bound hand and foot, to Rome.[37] One traitor thus betrayed another, contrary to common custom; for they are full of suspicion, and it is hard to surprise them at their own game; witness the burdensome experience that we have just had of this.

Let whoever desires be Pomponius Flaccus—and there are enough who desire it; for my part, both my words and my faith are, like all the rest of me, parts of this common body; their best manifestation[38] is the public service; I hold this as presupposed. But as, in the same way as if I were commanded to take charge of the parliament house and the law courts,[39] I should reply: "I understand nothing of this business";[40] or to take charge as conductor of pioneers, I should say: "I am assigned to a more worthy function"; in like manner, if it were desired to employ me to lie, to betray, and to perjure myself for some important end, not to assassinate or to poison, I should say: "If I have robbed or cheated any one, send me rather to the galleys." For it is permissible for a man of honour to speak as the Lacedæmonians did—when defeated by Antipater—on coming to an agreement: "You can demand of us burdensome and harmful offices as much as you please; but shameful and dishonourable ones, those you will waste your time in demanding of us."[41] Every man should have sworn to himself what the kings of Egypt made their judges solemnly swear: that they would not stray from their conscience for any command they themselves[42] might give them. In such commissions[43] there is an evident note of ignominy and condemnation; and he who so directs you accuses you, and gives you, if you rightly understand him, a burden and a punishment; in proportion as public matters are improved by your performance, your own are impaired; you are the worse in proportion as you do the better. And it will be no strange thing, nor perchance without some appearance of justice, that the same man ruins you who employs you. If treachery can be excusable in any case, it is so only when it is employed to chastise and betray treachery. There are many instances of perfidy, not only rejected, but punished, by those in whose behalf they were undertaken. Who does not know the judgement of Fabricius in the matter of the physician of Pyrrhus?[44] And this also is found, that a thing has been commanded, and afterward he who commanded it has severely avenged it upon him whom he had employed to do it, denying the possession of such unbridled power, and disowning a servitude and obedience so prostituted and so base.

Jaropelc, Duke of Russia, tampered with a Hungarian gentleman to betray Boleslaus, King of Poland, by contriving his death, or by giving the Russians an opportunity

Of the Useful and the Honourable

to do him some notable injury. He[45] bore himself in this business like a wily man: he devoted himself more than before to the service of that king, and succeeded in becoming one of his trusted counsellors. With these advantages, and choosing in good season the opportunity of his master's absence, he betrayed to the Russians Vislicia, a large and rich city, which was completely sacked and burned by them, with slaughter, not only of all the inhabitants of the city, of every age and sex, but of a large number of the nobility of the neighbourhood whom he had assembled there to that end. Jaropelc, his vengeance and his wrath being assuaged (which were not, indeed, without cause, for Boleslaus had greatly wronged him, and by similar conduct), and being sated with the result of this treachery, coming to consider its ugliness, naked and by itself, and to regard it with a sane vision no longer disturbed by passion, was seized with such remorse and loathing that he had the eyes put out and the tongue and privy parts cuts off, of him who had done this.[46]

Antigonus persuaded the Argyraspides soldiers to betray to him Eumenes, their captain-general, his adversary; but, whereas he had him put to death after they had delivered him into his hands, he desired to be himself the agent of divine justice in punishment of so detestable a crime, and he delivered them[47] into the hands of the governor of the province, with express command to destroy them and, in whatever manner, to give them a disgraceful death. And consequently, of the great number of them not one ever afterward saw the soil of Macedonia.[48] The better he had been served by them, the more wickedly and more deserving of punishment he judged their action to have been.

The slave who betrayed the hiding-place of Publius Sul-

1079

picius, his master, was given his liberty in accordance with the promise of Sylla's decree of proscription; but, in accordance with the promise of public justice, being free, he was thrown headlong from the Tarpeian rock.[49] They[50] hang such traitors with the purse of the payment due them round their necks; thus satisfying their own loyalty to their word in its secondary and special sense, they also satisfy it in its general and primal significance.[51]

Mahomet the Second, wishing to rid himself of his brother, from a desire of unquestioned authority according to the custom of their race, employed about this one of his officers, who suffocated him,[52] choking him with a quantity of water poured into him all at once. This done, for expiation of this murder, he[53] delivered the murderer into the hands of the dead man's mother (for they were brothers only on the father's side); she, in his presence, opened the murderer's stomach, and eagerly, with her own hands, searching for and tearing out his heart, threw it to the dogs to eat.[54] And our King Clovis, instead of the golden armour that he had promised them, had the three servants of Cannacre hanged after they had betrayed their master to him; in which matter he had made use of them.[55]

And even to them who are of little worth, it is very agreeable, having derived profit from some wicked act, to be able afterward to attach securely to it some stroke of kindness and justice, as by way of compensation and conscientious correction. Added to this, they regard the agents of such horrible deeds as persons by whom they are branded;[56] and they seek, by the death of these persons, to stifle the knowledge and evidence of such practices. And if, by chance, you are rewarded for what you have done, in order that public neces-

Of the Useful and the Honourable

sity may not lack that extreme and desperate remedy, he
who does this fails not to consider you as an accursed and
execrable man, if he be not himself such a one; and he considers you more treacherous than does he to whom you have
been a traitor; for he is shewn the wickedness of your heart
by the deed of your hands, performed without self-condem-
nation and without personal object.[57] But he employs you in
this business just as outcasts[58] are employed for executing
sentences—an office not less useful than it is dishonourable.
Besides the baseness of such commissions, there is a prosti-
tution of conscience. Sejanus's daughter, who could not be
put to death according to a certain form of sentence at Rome
because she was a virgin, was ravished by the executioner
before he strangled her, that the law might have its course;[59]
not his hand alone, but his soul, is the slave of public utility.

When the first Amurath, to aggravate the punishment
of those of his subjects who had given support to the parricidal rebellion of his son, ordered that their nearest kindred
should assist in their execution, I consider it highly honourable in some of them to have chosen rather to be unjustly
held guilty of another's parricide than to obey the law by
becoming parricides themselves.[60] And when, in some paltry
forts taken in these days, I have seen rascals, to save their
lives, consent to hang their friends and comrades, I have regarded them as of a lower nature than those who were
hanged. It is said that Vuitolde, Prince of the Lithuanians,
introduced into that nation the custom that a criminal condemned to death should kill himself with his own hand,
thinking it unnatural that a third person, innocent of offence, should be employed in, and burdened with, a homicide.[61] A prince, when urgent circumstances and some vio-

Of the Useful and the Honourable

lent and sudden emergency in the needs of his state cause
him to break his word and his faith, or otherwise force him
from his usual duty, should attribute this necessity to a
stroke of the divine rod; crime it is not, for he has put aside
his own sense of what is right for a more universal and potent
rightness;[62] but certainly it is ill-fortune. So that, to some
one who asked me, "What remedy is there?" I answered,
"No remedy; if he were really constrained between those
two extremes,"—(*but let him take heed lest he seek a subter-
fuge for perjury*[63]),—"he must needs so do; but if he did it
without regret, if it did not pain him to do it, it is a sign that
his conscience is in a bad way."

If some prince should be found with so sensitive a conscience that no cure would seem to him worth so burdensome a remedy, I should not think the less highly of him; he
could not be more excusably and beseemingly ruined. Our
ability is not unfailing; however it may be,[64] we must often,
as our last anchorage, commit the protection of our vessels
to the sole guidance of heaven. For what more justifiable
necessity does he reserve himself? What is it less possible for
him to do than that which he can not do save at the cost of
his faith and his honour? things which, peradventure,
should be dearer to him than his own safety and the safety of
his people. If, with folded arms, he simply calls God to his
assistance, may he not hope that it is not in divine bounty to
refuse exceptional favours from its hand to a hand unsullied
and just?

These are dangerous examples, rare and distempered ex-
ceptions to our natural rules; we must yield to them, but
with great moderation and circumspection; no private advantage is worth our putting this strain upon our conscience;

Of the Useful and the Honourable

public advantage, yes, when it is both very evident and very important. Timoleon was fitly defended from the unnaturalness of his deed by the tears he shed, remembering that it was with a brother's hand that he had killed the tyrant; and it rightly stung his conscience that it had been necessary to purchase the public advantage at such a cost of the integrity of his moral character.[65] The Senate itself, delivered from servitude by his means, dared not positively decide concerning a deed so momentous and of which there were two so weighty and opposing aspects; but the Syracusans having opportunely, at that very time, sent to solicit from the Corinthians their protection and a leader competent to restore their city to its former dignity and to rid Sicily of many petty tyrants who oppressed it, Timoleon was sent to them with this strange caution and declaration: that, according as he should conduct himself well or ill in his office, their own sentence would incline to grace him as liberator of his country, or to disgrace him as the murderer of his brother.[66] This fantastic conclusion has some excuse from the danger of the example and the importance of a deed so out of the ordinary. And they did well to disburden their judgement, or to base it elsewhere and upon other considerations. Now, the conduct of Timoleon on this expedition very soon made his cause more clear, he bore himself therein so worthily and virtuously in every respect; and the good-fortune that attended him with the obstacles he had to overcome in that noble enterprise seemed to be sent him by the gods conspiring in favour of his justification.

This man's purpose was his excuse, if any purpose could be. But the profit of the increase of the public revenues, which served the Roman Senate as a pretext for the foul de-

Of the Useful and the Honourable

cision which I am about to relate, is not important enough to warrant such an injustice. Certain cities had bought with money their ransom, and had had their freedom restored at the hands of L. Sylla, by the command and permission of the Senate. The matter having fallen again into judgement, the Senate sentenced them to be taxed as before, and decreed that the money they had used to ransom themselves be forfeited.[67] Civil wars often give birth to such villainous instances, as that we punish private individuals because they believed us when we were other than now; and even a judge makes a man who has no resource suffer the penalty of his opinions; the teacher whips his pupil for his docility, and the guide his blind man: a shocking counterfeit of justice. There are precepts of philosophy both false and weak. The example philosophers set before us, to show that private advantage may prevail over plighted faith, does not acquire enough weight from the circumstances that they attach to it. Robbers have captured you; they have set you at liberty, having made you swear to pay a certain sum. It is wrong to say that a man of worth, when out of their hands, will be released from his word.[68] It is not at all so: what I have once willed through fear I am bound still to will when without fear; and if fear shall have forced only my tongue and not my will, still I am bound to make good my word. For my own part, when my words have indiscreetly gone beyond my thought, I have none the less scrupled to disregard them. Otherwise, step by step, we shall come to abolishing all the claims that another derives from our promises. *As if force could avail against a truly great man.*[69] Only in one case has our private interest the right to excuse us for breach of promise—if we have promised something that is wicked and unjust in itself; for the claim of virtue should prevail over the claim of our bond.

I have heretofore placed Epaminondas in the first rank of eminent men,[70] and I do not retract. How high he held the perception of his private duty, who never killed a man whom he had overcome; who, to gain the inestimable blessing of giving liberty to his country, had scruples about putting to death a tyrant or his accomplices without the forms of law; and who deemed him bad as a man, however good a citizen he might be, who, in the thick of the enemy and in battle, did not spare his friend and his host. This was a soul of rich composition; he united to the most pitiless and violent human deeds kindness and humanity, the most delicate, indeed, that can be found in the school of philosophy. Was it nature or art that softened to such an extreme degree of gentleness and affability of temper that heart so stout, so bold, and so unyielding to suffering, death, and poverty? Terrible in steel and blood, he shatters and crushes a nation invincible by all others than himself alone, and turns aside, in the midst of such a mellay, on meeting with his host and his friend. Truly war was well ruled by him who forced it to submit to the curb of kind feeling at the point of its greatest intensity, so inflamed as it was, and foaming with rage and slaughter. It is wonderful to be able to connect with such actions[71] some appearance of justice; but it belongs only to the strength of Epaminondas to combine with them gentleness and ease of manner and the purest innocence. And whereas one man[72] said to the Mamertines that statutes had no force against armed men; another,[73] to a tribune of the people, that the times of justice and of war were not the same; and a third,[74] that the noise of arms prevented him

Of the Useful and the Honourable

from hearing the voice of the laws—this man[75] was not prevented even from hearing the voice of civilisation[76] and pure courtesy. Did he not borrow from his enemies the custom of sacrificing to the Muses when going forth to war, to soften by their sweetness and gaiety that martial frenzy and fierceness?[77]

Let us not fear, after the example of so great a preceptor, to consider that there is something not lawful, even against enemies;[78] that public interest ought not to require every thing from all men contrary to private interest, *since the memory of private right remains even when public contracts are disputed;*[79]

and no power has force enough to defend doing wrong to a friend;[80]

and that all things are not permissible to a right-minded man in the service of his king or of the general cause and of the laws; *for our duty to the country does not supercede all other duties; and it is of advantage to the country itself that its citizens should be loyal to their parents.*[81] This is a lesson suited to this time; we need not armour our hearts:[82] it is enough that our backs be armoured; it is enough to dip our pens in ink without dipping them in blood. If it be highheartedness, and the result of a rare and surpassing virtue, to despise friendship, private bonds, one's plighted word, and the ties of kindred, in favour of the common welfare and of obedience to authority, it is enough surely to excuse us from it, that this is a sort of loftiness that can find no lodgement in the high-heartedness of Epaminondas. I abhor the frantic exhortations of this other disordered mind,—

When weapons flash, let no thought of filial piety,

1086

Of the Useful and the Honourable

let not even the sight of your fathers opposed to you,
move you; strike with the sword their venerable
heads.[83]

Let us deprive of this pretext of rightness those who are by
nature wicked and blood-thirsty and treacherous; let us turn
our backs on this heinous and insane justice, and hold fast to
more human copies. How great the effect of time and example! In an encounter during the civil war against Cinna,
one of Pompey's soldiers, having unwittingly killed his
brother who was of the opposite faction, immediately killed
himself from shame and grief;[84] and some years later, in
another civil war of this same people, a soldier demanded a
reward from his officers for having killed his brother.[85]

We ill argue the honour and beauty of an act by its usefulness; and it is an ill conclusion to think that every one is
bound to do it, and that it is becoming for every one, if it be
useful.

All things are not equally suited to all men.[86]

If we select what is most necessary and most useful in human
society, it will be marriage; yet the counsel of holy men finds
the contrary course more noble, and excludes therefrom the
most honourable vocation of men, as we assign to the stud
the animals that are of least worth.

Chapter II

OF REPENTING

OTHERS shape the man; I narrate him,[1] and offer to view a special one, very ill-made, and whom, could I fashion him over, I should certainly make very different from what he is; but there is no doing that.[2] Now the lines of my portrait do not err, although they change and are now this, now that. The world is but perpetual motion; all things in it move incessantly,—the earth, the rocks of the Caucasus, the pyramids of Egypt,—both with the universal motion and with their own; fixedness itself is only a more lingering motion. I can not anchor my subject: he is always restless, and staggering with an unsteadiness natural to him.[3] I catch him in the state that he is in at the moment when I turn my attention to him. I do not paint his being; I paint his passing—not the passing from one age to another, or, as the common people say, from seven years to seven years, but from day to day, from moment to moment; my narrative must be in accordance with the hour; I may change immediately, not merely by chance, but also by intention.[4] My narrative is a record of varying and mutable incidents and of uncertain thoughts, and, it may happen, contradictory ones, whether because I am different myself, or because

Of Repenting

I apprehend the subjects by other circumstances and considerations. So it is that, peradventure, I do indeed contradict myself, but the truth, as Demades said, I in no wise contradict.[5] If my soul could find a foothold, I should not exert myself in attempts, I should free myself from perplexity;[6] it is still in pupilage and on trial.

I set forth a life humble and without glory—it comes to the same thing; all moral philosophy may be connected with a common and private life as fitly as with a life of richer substance; every man has in himself the whole form of human nature. Writers of books commune with the world with some special and peculiar badge; I am the first to do this with my general being, as Michel de Montaigne, not as grammarian or poet or jurisconsult. If the world finds the fault that I speak too much of myself, I find the fault that it does not even think of itself.

But is it reasonable that, being so private in my way of life, I undertake to make myself publicly known? Is it reasonable also that I produce to the world, where manner and art have so much influence and authority, results of nature both imperfect and simple, and of a nature, besides, of very little force? Is it not like building a wall without stone, or something of that sort, to build books without learning? The compositions of music are guided by art, mine by chance. I have this at least in accord with doctrine, that never did a man treat a subject which he understood or knew better than I do this that I have undertaken, and that therein I am the most learned man alive; secondly, that no one ever went deeper into his subject, or by full examination of it more distinctly pointed out its different parts and its issues, and

Of Repenting

arrived more exactly and more completely at the end which he had proposed to himself of his work. To perfect it, I have need to bring to it only fidelity; that I give to it, the most sincere and purest that can be found. I tell the truth, not to my full satisfaction, but as much as I venture to utter; and I venture a little more as I grow old; for it would seem that custom concedes to age more liberty of garrulity and indiscretion in speaking of oneself. It can not here happen, as I often see it happen, that there is contrariety between the artisan and his work; a man of such an excellent course of life, can he have written such a foolish book? or, such learned writings, have they proceeded from a man of such weak conduct? If a man be commonplace in intercourse, and his writings remarkable, it means that his ability is somewhere whence he borrows it, and not in himself. A learned person is not learned throughout; but the able man is able throughout, and even in not knowing.

My book and I, we here proceed in conformity with one another and in one course. In other cases, the work may be praised or blamed apart from the workman; in this case, not: who touches the one touches the other. He who shall pass judgement on it without becoming acquainted with the workman will wrong himself more than me; he who comes to know him will wholly satisfy me. Fortunate beyond my deserts if I have only this much of public approbation, that I make people of intelligence feel that I could have profited by learning had I had it, and that I deserve more aid from memory.[7]

Let me be excused for saying here what I often say, that I rarely repent, and that my conscience is content with itself, not as the conscience of an angel or a horse, but as the con-

Of Repenting

science of a man; adding this unfailing qualification,—not a qualification of convention but of true and essential submission,—that I speak as one who is ignorant and seeking, referring myself for decision purely and simply to common and legitimate opinion. I do not teach, I narrate.

There is no sin that is unquestionably sin which does not do harm, and which a sound judgement does not reprove; for it has such manifest vileness and unseemliness that, peradventure, they are right who say that it is chiefly begotten by stupidity and ignorance, so difficult is it to conceive that it can be recognised without being hated. Wickedness swallows the greater part of its own venom, and poisons itself therewith.[8] Vice, like an ulcer in the flesh, leaves repentance in the soul, which is forever scratching and lacerating itself.[9] For reason does away with other sadnesses and pains, but it engenders that of repentance, which is the more grievous inasmuch as it is born within; as the chills and heat of fevers are more severe than those which come from outside. I regard as vices (but each in its degree) not only those which reason and nature condemn, but those also which the opinion of mankind, false and erroneous indeed, has created, if the laws and custom give authority to that opinion. Even so, there is no goodness which does not rejoice a well-dowered nature. There is surely I know not what self-gratification in doing well, which rejoices us ourselves, and a noble pride which attends a good conscience. A boldly vicious character may perhaps obtain for itself security, but it can not supply itself with this complacency and contentment. It is no slight pleasure to feel oneself preserved from the contagion of so rotten an age, and to say within oneself: "Whoever could see me to my very soul would not find me guilty, either of

Of Repenting

causing the affliction or the ruin of any one, or of revenge or
envy, or of public violation of the laws, or of innovation and
disturbance, or of being false to my word; and whatever the
license of the age may permit and teach to every one, yet
have I not laid hands on either the property or the purse of
any Frenchman, and have lived solely upon what is mine,
not less in time of war than in peace, and have made use of
no man's labour without payment." These testimonies of the
conscience are gratifying; and this natural enjoyment is very
beneficial for us, and the only recompense that never fails us.

To base the reward of virtuous actions on the approbation
of others is to choose a too uncertain and obscure foundation.
Especially in a corrupt and ignorant age like this, the good
opinion of the vulgar is offensive; to whom do you trust to
perceive what is praiseworthy? God preserve me from being
a man of worth according to the description which I see
given every day by each one doing honour to himself! *What
were formerly vices have become habits.*[10] Some of my
friends have sometimes undertaken to school me frankly and
spiritedly,[11] either of their own motion or at my invitation,
as a service which, to a well-formed mind, surpasses, not in
utility only, but in kindness as well, all the other services of
friendship. I have always welcomed it with the most open
arms of courtesy and gratitude. But, to speak of it now in all
honesty, I have often found in their reproofs and their praise
so much false measure, that I should hardly have done
wrong to do wrong,[12] rather than do rightly after their
fashion. We especially, who live a private life that is in view
only to ourselves, ought to have a model established within
us, by which to test our actions and, according to it, sometimes make much of ourselves, sometimes correct ourselves.

Of Repenting

I have my laws and my court to judge me, and I resort to them more than elsewhere. I restrain my actions, indeed, according to others, but I enlarge them only according to myself. It is only you who know whether you are cowardly and cruel or loyal and pious; others do not at all see you, they guess about you by uncertain conjectures; they see not your natural disposition so much as your artificial one. Therefore rely not on their judgement; rely on your own. *You must make use of your own judgement about yourself.*[13] *Great is the importance of one's own consciousness of virtues and vices; that discarded, all is laid low.*[14] But this that is said, that repentance follows close on the heels of sin, seems not to regard sin when, armed from head to foot, it dwells within us[15] as in its own abode. We can disown and forbid the vices which surprise us, and to which passions impel us; but those which by long habit are rooted and anchored in a strong and sturdy will are not submissive to being thwarted. Repentance is no other than a forbidding of our will and opposition to our inclinations, which stirs us up on all sides. It makes this man[16] repudiate his past virtue and continence:—

> Why was not my mind the same when I was a boy
> that it is to-day? Or why, with my thoughts of to-day,
> do not my cheeks become as they were?[17]

That is a life of consummate excellence which preserves an orderly bearing even in private. Every one may take part in play-acting, and represent an honourable personage on the stage; but the point is, inwardly and in one's own breast, where all things are permissible, where all things are hidden, there to be subject to rule. The next step is to be so in one's own house, in one's every-day actions, of which we have not

Of Repenting

to render account to any one; where there is nothing studied, nothing artificial. And therefore Bias, describing a surpassingly worthy family condition, says: "The master is the same, when in his house alone, as when out of it, from fear of the law and of men's speech."[18] And that was a fit saying of Julius Drusus to the workmen who offered for three thousand crowns so to arrange his house that his neighbours could no longer look into it as they had done: "I will give you six thousand," he said, "and do you manage so that every one can look into every part of it."[19] We note as honourable the custom of Agesilaus, of taking up his quarters in temples,[20] when he was travelling, so that the people and the gods themselves could witness his private actions. A man may appear wonderful to the world, in whom his wife and his servant see nothing even remarkable; few men have been admired by their household.[21]

No man was ever a prophet, not merely in his own house, but in his native place, declares the teaching of history. Even so with things of naught; and in the following humble instance may be seen the image of greater ones. In my region of Gascony, it seems droll to people to see me in print. In proportion as knowledge of me extends farther from my abode, I am rated the higher: in Guienne I pay the printers, elsewhere they pay me. Those who hide themselves when alive and here, rely on this fortune to bring themselves into repute when dead and gone. I would rather have less of it; and I fling myself into the world only for what I wrest from it. When I leave it, I quit it all.

The crowd escorts him in public state, with admiration, to his door; he puts off, with his gown, the part he plays, and falls as much the lower as he had been uplifted; within, in

1094

Of Repenting

himself, all is commotion and of no account. Even if discipline existed there, it would need a keen and special judgement to perceive it in these mean and secret acts. Moreover, regularity is a dull and dismal virtue. To enter a breach, to conduct an embassy, to govern a people—these are brilliant actions. To chide, to laugh, to sell, to pay, to love, to hate, and to hold intercourse with one's family and with oneself, gently and justly, not to give way, never to derogate from oneself—that is something more rare, more difficult, and less observable. Retired lives, whatever may be said, maintain in these ways duties as severe and exacting as do other lives, or more so. And private persons, says Aristotle, observe a more difficult and higher virtue than they who are in authority.[22] We prepare ourselves for great occasions more for the sake of glory than for the sake of conscience. The shortest way to attain glory would be to do for conscience what we do for glory. And the virtue of Alexander seems to me to exhibit somewhat less strength in its scene of action than does that of Socrates in its humble and obscure exercise. I can easily imagine Socrates in Alexander's place, but Alexander in that of Socrates, I can not. To him who shall ask Alexander what he knows how to do, he will reply: "Subjugate the world"; he who shall ask this of the other will be answered that he knows how "to lead human life in conformity with its natural condition"—a knowledge much more general in its scope, more important, and more legitimate.

The worth of the soul does not consist in moving at a height, but fittingly. Its grandeur is not brought into play in grandeur, but in mediocrity. Thus those who judge and examine us within make no great account of the lustre of our public acts, and see that they are but threads and drops of

Of Repenting

clear water springing from a source otherwise slimy and thick; even so, those who judge us by this brave outward show equally come to conclusions about our internal character, and can not yoke together faculties that are common and like their own and those other faculties, so far from their scope, which astound them. Thus we ascribe to demons monstrous shapes; and who does not endow Tamburlane with lifted eyebrows, open nostrils, a grim visage, and a stature as huge as the stature of the idea conceived of him from the report of his fame? Had I been taken in former times to see Erasmus, it would have been hard for me not to find adages and apothegms in every thing he might say to his servant or the hostess of his inn. We can much more fitly imagine an artisan upon his stool or on his wife than a great President, of venerable demeanour and sufficiency. We imagine that from those lofty thrones they will not even condescend to live. As vicious souls are often incited to do well by some foreign impulsion, so are virtuous souls to do ill. We must therefore judge them by their settled condition, when they are alone with themselves, if sometimes they are so; or, at least, when they are nearest repose and in their true position. Natural inclinations are assisted and strengthened by education; but they are rarely altered and overcome. A thousand characters, in my time, have slipped away toward virtue or toward vice, despite contrary instruction.

So when wild beasts become unhabituated to the forest, and tamed by captivity, and, having lost their fierce look and learned to endure control by men, if a little blood touches their hot lips, their madness and fury return, their throat swells, excited by the taste of

blood; they burn with anger, and hardly refrain from
attacking their frightened master.[23]

These original qualities are not extirpated: they are covered
up, they are hidden. The Latin language is to me as my
own;[24] I understand it better than French, but for forty
years past I have not used it at all in speaking and scarcely
in writing; none the less, in the extreme and sudden emotions into which I have fallen two or three times in my life,
—one was when I saw my father, who was in perfect health,
fall over upon me in a swoon,—my first ejaculations, from
the bottom of my heart, have always been Latin words, Nature coming to the surface and expressing herself forcibly
in spite of such long habits; and this same thing is told of
many others.

They who have tried to correct the morals of the world in
my time, by new ideas, reform the manifest vices; the essential ones they let alone if they do not increase them; and increase in these is to be feared; we readily linger from all
other well-doing on these arbitrary external reforms, of less
cost and greater honour, and thus we cheaply provide for the
other natural vices, consubstantial and intestinal. Consider
a little what our experience warrants: no one, if he listens
to himself, does not discover in himself a personal nature,[25]
a dominant nature, which is at strife with rules of life[26] and
with the storm of passions opposed to it. For my own part, I
feel myself hardly aroused by sudden impulses; I am, as
it were, always in my place, as unwieldy and heavy bodies
are. When I am not entirely myself,[27] I am never far from
being so; my wanderings do not carry me very far; there is
nothing extreme and strange in them; and, besides, my

Of Repenting

second thoughts are sound and vigorous. The real condemnation, and that which concerns the common manner of men of our day, is that their very retirement is full of corruption and filth; their idea of amendment blurred; their repentance diseased, and almost as much at fault as their sin. Some, either because they are fast bound to vice by a natural tie, or from long familiarity, do not perceive its ugliness. To others, in whose ranks I am, vice is a burden; but they counterbalance it with pleasure or other circumstance, and suffer it, and lend themselves to it for a certain reward, albeit viciously and basely. Yet it might be possible, perhaps, to conceive so great a disproportion of degree that the pleasure would justly excuse the sin, as we say of utility; not only if it[28] were accidental and apart from the sin itself, as in theft, but if it existed in the very act of committing the sin, as in intercourse with women, where the provocation is violent, and, they say, sometimes invincible.

The other day, when I was in Armaignac, I saw, on the estate of a kinsman of mine, a peasant whom every one calls "the thief." He told the story of his life thus: being born in poverty, and finding that, gaining his bread by the work of his hands, he would never succeed in sufficiently protecting himself against want, he resolved to become a thief; and by means of his bodily strength, he had safely given his whole youth to that occupation; for he made his harvest and vintage in other men's fields; but it was at a distance, and in such huge bundles that it was inconceivable that any man could carry away so much on his shoulders in one night; and he had taken pains, moreover, to equalise and distribute the loss he caused, so that the burden was less intolerable to each individual. He is now, in his old age, rich for a man of

Of Repenting

his condition, thanks to this business, of which he makes open confession; and to reconcile God to his gettings, he says that he is daily in the way of giving satisfaction by benefits to the successors of those whom he robbed; and that, if he does not finish the task,—for accomplish it all at once he can not,—he will leave it in charge to his heirs, according to the knowledge that he alone has of the injury he has done to each one. This statement, be it true or false, shows that he regards theft as a shameful act and loathes it, but less than poverty; he repents of it in itself, but, in so far as it is thus counterbalanced and compensated, he does not repent of it. This is not that habit which makes us of one body with vice and conforms to it our very understanding; nor is it that impetuous blast which by gusts confuses and blinds our soul and casts us headlong for the time, judgement and all, into the power of vice.

I do ordinarily with my whole being what I do, and all of me is in the action;[29] I have few movements which are hidden and secret from my reason, and which are not guided almost entirely by the concurrence of all my faculties, without division, without intestinal dissension; my judgement has the whole blame or praise for them; and the blame which once it has, it has always; for almost from its birth it is unchanged: the same character, the same course, the same strength. And in the matter of general beliefs, I established myself in my youth at the point where I was to remain.

There are impetuous, hasty, and sudden sins: let us leave them at one side; but in those other sins, so often repeated, meditated, and considered, whether they be sins belonging to the temperament or to the profession and vocation, I can not conceive that they should be so long rooted in the same heart, unless the reason and the conscience of him who has them constantly so wills and so knows; and the repentance of them that he boasts of as coming to him at a certain appointed moment is somewhat hard for me to imagine and shape. I do not follow the school of Pythagoras, which believes that men take on a new soul when they approach the images of the gods to receive their oracles,[30] unless he meant just this—that it must needs be a soul unfamiliar, new, and possessed only for the occasion, since our own shows so little sign of purification and cleanliness suitable for that office. They[31] do just contrary to the precepts of the Stoics, which bid us, indeed, to correct the imperfections and vices which we recognise in ourselves, but order us not to disturb the quiet of our souls therewith.[32] They give us to believe that they have great inward grief and remorse for their vices; but of amendment and correction, or of discontinuance, they show us nothing. Yet it is not a cure if the malady is not got rid of. If repentance were laid in the scale, it would outweigh the sin. I find no quality so easy to counterfeit as godliness, where one's morals and life do not conform to it; its essence is abstruse and hidden; the externals easy and ostentatious.

As for me, I may desire, in general, to be other than I am; I may condemn, and be displeased by, my character as a whole,[33] and beseech God to change me completely, and to excuse my natural weakness; but that, it seems to me, I ought not to call repentance, any more than my discontent in being neither an angel nor Cato. My actions are controlled and fashioned by what I am and by my condition of life. I can do no better; and repentance does not properly concern things that are not in our power, but regret, in truth, does. I can imagine numberless loftier and better ordered

Of Repenting

natures than mine; but I do not thereby amend by faculties; just as neither my arm nor my mind can become more vigorous by conceiving another that is so. If to imagine and to desire a conduct nobler than our own caused repentance for our own, we should have to repent of our most innocent doings, inasmuch as we rightly judge that in a more excellent nature they would have been performed with greater perfection and nobility; and we should wish to do the like. When I take counsel with my old age concerning my conduct in my youth, I find that I usually behaved myself fittingly, in my opinion; that is all that my power to withstand the facts[34] can do. I do not flatter myself: under like circumstances I should be always the same man. It is not being smutched; it is rather a general stain that blackens me. I have no knowledge of a superficial, half-way, formal repentance: it must touch me in every part before I call it so, and must wring my heart and afflict it as deeply as God sees me, and as thoroughly.

As for business affairs, many good chances have escaped me for lack of fortunate management; yet my judgement made an excellent choice according to the matters presented to it; its habit is to take always the easiest and safest course. I find that in my past deliberations I have, in my way, proceeded wisely in respect to the state of the subject that was brought before me; and I should do the same a thousand years hence under like circumstances. I do not regard what its state is now, but what it was when I was considering it. The weight of all opinions depends upon the hour; circumstances and matters change and revolve constantly. I have made some foolish and important mistakes in my life, not for lack of good judgement, but for lack of good-fortune.

Of Repenting

There are, in the matters we deal with, hidden paths, not discoverable, notably in the nature of man; mute conditions that make no show, unknown sometimes even to their possessor, which are produced and aroused by supervening circumstances. If my foresight has been unable to fathom and predict them, I bear it no ill-will therefor; its function is limited to its compass. If the event goes against me, and if it approves the determination that I have rejected, there is no remedy; I do not blame myself for this; I blame my fortune, not what I have done; this is not to be called repentance.

Phocion had given the Athenians certain advice which was not followed. The affair, however, having been carried on prosperously, in opposition to his opinion, some one said to him: "Well, Phocion, are you glad that things are going so well?" "Indeed I am glad," he replied, "that this has happened, but I do not repent having advised the other."[35] When my friends come to me for counsel, I give it freely and clearly, without hesitating as almost every one does because, the thing being a matter of chance, it may turn out contrary to my thought, whereby they may have reason to reproach me for my advice; for which I care not. For they will be in the wrong, since it was not for me to refuse them that service.

I seldom have ground to blame any one but myself for my errors or mishaps; for, in truth, I rarely avail myself of others' advice,—unless it be by way of courtesy,—save when I have need of information, of learning, or of knowledge of the facts; but, in matters in which I have to employ only judgement, outside arguments may serve to confirm me, but rarely to dissuade. I listen graciously and beseemingly to all their reasonings; but, so far as I remember, I have never

Of Repenting

to this hour trusted any but my own. For me, these others are but flitting trifles that buzz about my will.[36] I value little my own opinion, but I value as little those of others. Fortune requires me fittingly: if I do not accept advice, I give it still less. I am seldom asked for it, but I am still more seldom believed; and I know of no undertaking, public or private, which my advice has bettered or hindered. Even they whom fortune has in some sort bound to follow it have allowed themselves more readily to be guided by any other brain than mine. As one who is quite as jealous of the rights of his ease as of the rights of his authority, I prefer it to be so; in putting me aside, they act according to my open profession, which is, to be wholly set forth and comprehended in myself; it is agreeable to me to forgo all interest in the affairs of others, and to be freed from responsibility about them.

About all matters that are gone by, in whatsoever fashion, I have little regret; for this reflection prevents vexation, namely, that they must needs so pass; I see them as in the great movement of the universe, and in the chain of the Stoic causes.[37] The mind can not, in desire and imagination, do away with the smallest part without subverting the whole order of things, both the past and the future. Furthermore, I hate that chance repentance which old age brings. The man who said of old that he was obliged to his years for having rid him of sensuality was not of my opinion; I can never be beholden to impotence for any good it can do me. *Providence will never be seen so hostile to its own work that weakness will rank among the best things.*[38] Our passions are seldom excited in old age; we are seized with an extreme satiety after the act. In that I can see no sign of conscience; vexation and weakness imprint upon us a mean-spirited,

Of Repenting

rheumatic virtue. We must not allow ourselves to be so wholly carried away by our natural alterations as to warp our judgement. Youth and pleasure did not in former years so overpower me that I did not recognize the face of vice in sensual pleasure; nor does the distaste that years bring with it so overpower me now, that I do not recognize the face of sensual pleasure in vice. Now that I am no longer in it I judge as if I were still in it.

If I rudely shake up my reason and examine it attentively, I find it to be the same as in my most licentious years, except perhaps in so far as it has become enfeebled and impaired by age. And I find that the pleasure it refuses me in the interest of my bodily health, it would not refuse me, any more than formerly, for my spiritual health. I do not esteem her to be any more valiant for being *hors de combat*. My temptations are so broken and mortified that they are not worth being resisted by her. I exorcize them by merely spreading out my hands in front of me. Should she be face to face with that old lust, I fear she would have less power to resist it than she once had. I cannot see that she thinks any differently about it than she did then, or that she has acquired any new light. Wherefore if there is any convalescence, it is a broken-down convalescence.

A miserable kind of cure to owe one's health to disease! It is not the part of our misfortune, but of the good fortune of our judgement, to do this office.

No one can make me do any thing by insults and grievances, except curse them; that is for those who rouse themselves only under the lash. My judgement pursues its course more freely in prosperity; it is much more distraught and absorbed when digesting ills than pleasures. I am much

Of Repenting

more clear-sighted in pleasant weather; health admonishes
me not only more gaily, but more effectively, than sickness.
I progressed as far as I was able toward reformation and
discipline when I was in a position to enjoy them. I should
be ashamed and despiteful if I should have reason to prefer
the wretchedness and ill-fortune of my old age to my happy,
healthy, lusty, and vigorous youth; and if men should have
to value me, not by what I have been, but by what I have
ceased to be. In my opinion, it is the living happily, not, as
Antisthenes said, the dying happily,[39] which makes human
felicity. I have not proposed to append, contrary to nature,
the tail of a philosopher to the head and body of a graceless
man; nor that a base ending should renounce and belie the
best, most complete, and longest part of my life. I propose
to present and exhibit myself uniformly, in every part. Had
I to live again, I should live as I have lived; I neither lament the past, nor fear the future; and if I am not mistaken,
it has been with me inwardly about as it has outwardly.
One of my chief obligations to my fortune is that the course
of my bodily existence has been so conducted that every
thing has come in its season. I have seen the leaves and the
flowers and the fruit; and now I see the withering—fortunately, since it has come naturally. I bear much more
easily the ills that I have, because they have come at their
time, and because they make me remember the more
pleasantly the long-continued felicity of my past life. In
like manner, my wisdom may well be of the same degree in
one and the other period; but it was greater in performance,
and of better grace, when lusty, joyous, ingenuous, than it
is now—broken, peevish, toilsome. I renounce, therefore,
these fortuitous and painful reformations.

Of Repenting

It needs be that God touches our hearts; it needs be that our conscience be reformed by the enforcement of our reason, not by the enfeeblement of our appetites. Bodily pleasure is not in itself either pale or colourless because it is viewed by dull and dim eyes. Temperance should be loved for itself and from respect to God, who has enjoined it and chastity upon us; that which fevers bring us, and which I owe to the good offices of my colic,[40] is neither chastity nor temperance. No man can pride himself upon despising and combatting sensuality, if he has no perception of it; if he knows nothing of it, either its charm, or its power, or its most alluring beauty. I know them all; it is I who can say this; but it seems to me that in old age our souls are subject to more troublesome maladies and weaknesses than in youth. I said this when I was young, when my beardlessness was looked down upon;[41] I say it still at this hour, when my gray hair gives me authority. We call the fastidiousness of our tastes, our disrelish for things at hand, wisdom; but the truth is that we do not so much depart from vices as change them, and, in my opinion, for the worse. Besides a foolish and perishable pride, a tiresome love of talk, fault-finding and unsociable humours and superstition, and an absurd care about wealth when the use of it is lost, I find in old age more envy, injustice, and malignity. It imprints more wrinkles in our mind than on our face; and there are to be seen few souls which, as they grow old, do not become sour and peevish.[42] Man in completeness moves toward his increase and toward his decrease.

In considering the wisdom of Socrates and many circumstances of his condemnation, I could venture to believe that he lent himself to it, in some degree, by prevarication,

Of Repenting

designedly, having so soon—he was seventy years of age—
to suffer the benumbing of the rich activity of his mind
and the bedimming of its wonted clearness. What metamorphoses do I daily see old age cause in many of my acquaintances! It is a potent malady and one that comes upon
us naturally and imperceptibly; there is need of a great
store of study and great precaution, to avoid the imperfections which it burdens us with, or at least to retard their
progress. I feel that, in spite of all I can do to diminish its
power, it is gaining upon me step by step; I resist as much
as I can, but I know not where, at last, it will take me.
Whatever may happen, I am glad that it should be known
from what height I have fallen.

Chapter III

OF THREE SORTS

OF INTERCOURSE

A MAN should not rivet himself too tightly to his humours and temperament. Our chief ability is in knowing how to adapt ourselves to various habits. To be bound and compelled by necessity to one sole course is to exist, but not to live. The noblest souls are those which have more variety and suppleness. This is an honourable testimony to the elder Cato: *His versatile genius was so equal to all things that, whatever he did, you would have said that he was born to do that one thing.*[1] Had I the power to fashion myself as I would, there is no way of living so good that I should wish to be so fixed in it that I could not depart from it. Life is an unequal, irregular, and multiform motion. It is not to be a friend to oneself, and still less one's own master—it is to be one's slave, to follow oneself constantly and to be so fast held by one's inclinations that one can not wander away from them, that one can not bend them.

I say this now,[2] because I can not easily free myself from the importunity of my soul, since she can not ordinarily amuse herself except where she is busied, nor employ herself otherwise than intently and entirely. However trivial the subject put before her, she easily magnifies it, and

Of Three Sorts of Intercourse

stretches it to the point where she has to apply herself to it
with all her strength. Her idleness, consequently, is to me
a disagreeable condition,[3] and one that injures my health.
Most minds require an unfamiliar subject to rouse and exercise them; mine requires such rather to rest itself and pause
a while—*the vice of idleness must be avoided by occupation;*[4] for its most laborious and principal study is the study
of itself. Books are for it one of the employments which
draw it away from its study. At the first ideas which occur
to it, it bestirs itself and gives proof of its vigour in all ways,
exercises its control sometimes toward force, sometimes
toward regularity and grace; it adjusts, moderates, and
strengthens itself. It has the wherewithal to arouse its faculties by itself; Nature has given to it, as to all, enough
material of its own to make use of and sufficient subjects
to investigate and to judge. Meditation is a puissant and
ample form of study to one who knows how to examine
himself and set himself about it vigorously; I like better to
shape my mind than to furnish it. There is no occupation
weaker or stronger, according to the mind one has, than that
of conversing with one's thoughts; the greatest men make
it their vocation, *for whom to live is to think;*[5] and Nature
has favoured it with this privilege, that there is nothing that
we are able to do for so long a time, nor any action to which
we devote ourselves more commonly and easily. It is the
occupation of the gods, says Aristotle, from which spring
their beatitude and our own.[6] Reading serves me especially
by arousing my reasoning power[7] in different ways, by setting my judgement to work, not my memory. In comparison with the essential profit and improvement at which my
mind aims, it values little the labour that is employed in

burdening and storing the memory with other men's learning.[8] Consequently few conversations which are not vigorous and forcible hold my attention; it is true that charm and
beauty of speech give me as much satisfaction and enjoyment as weight and profundity, or even more. And since I
nod in every other sort of conversation, and lend it only the
surface of my attention, it often happens to me in such pitiful and feeble talk—talk for the sake of talking[9] to utter in
answer fancies and follies unworthy of a child, or else to be
obstinately silent, even more unseasonably and discour-
teously. I have a way of musing, which withdraws me into
myself,[10] and also stupid and puerile ignorance about many
common things; by these two qualities I have brought it
about that people can truthfully tell five or six stories of me
as foolish as of any man, whoever he be.

Now, to proceed with my discourse, this fastidious disposition makes me squeamish in dealing with men, it causes
me to select carefully,[11] and renders me unfit for acting with
them. We live and deal with the common people; if intercourse with them annoys us, if we disdain to associate with
humble and ordinary souls,—and the humble and ordinary
are often as well disciplined as those of the finest fibre,[12]
(and all wisdom is ignorant which does not adapt itself to
ourselves with our own affairs or with those of others; both
the common ignorance),[13]—we ought to cease to concern
public and private affairs are transacted with such people.[14]
The least strained and most natural motions of our soul
are the most beautiful; the best occupations, the least laborious. Good God! What a great service wisdom does those
whose desires it limits to their power! there is no more useful art. "According to one's ability," was the frequent and

Of Three Sorts of Intercourse

favourite saying of Socrates,[15] a saying of great weight. We should direct and confine our desires to the easiest and nearest things. Is it not a foolish humour in me to dissent from a thousand people with whom my destiny connects me, whom I can not do without, and to attach myself to one or two who are outside my range, or, rather, to a fanciful desire for things that I can not obtain? My easy nature, opposed to all sharpness and bitterness, may well have freed me from envies and enmities. No man ever gave more occasion, I do not say to be loved, but not to be hated; but the coldness of my manner has rightfully prevented me from being liked by many persons, who are excusable for interpreting it in another and worse sense.

I am exceedingly capable of acquiring and retaining rare and admirable friendships, inasmuch as I grasp very eagerly the acquaintances which suit my taste; I make such advances, I throw myself upon them so eagerly, that I rarely fail to fasten myself to them and to make the impression I desire. I have often had happy proof of this. In ordinary friendships I am somewhat sterile and cold, for going forward is not natural to me unless under full sail; besides that my fortune, having led and sweetly allured me in my youth to a sole and perfect friendship, did in some sort give me a distaste for others, and impressed too deeply in my imagination that friendship is a creature for companionship, but not of a herd, as that ancient writer says;[16] also that I have an inborn difficulty in giving myself by half and with reservations, and with that servile and suspicious prudence that is enjoined upon us in the maintenance of numerous imperfect friendships. And it is especially enjoined upon us in these days, when we can not speak of what passes in the world[17]

IIII

except at our peril or falsely. Nevertheless, I see clearly that he who, like myself, aims at the comforts of life (I mean the essential comforts) should avoid like the plague this fastidiousness and sensitiveness of humour. I should praise a soul of divers levels, which can both ascend and descend,[18] which is well off wherever its fortune bears it, which can talk with its neighbour of his building, of his hunting, and of his quarrels, and converse with pleasure with a carpenter and a gardener. I envy those who know how to be familiar with the humblest of their suite and to carry on conversation with those of their train.

And Plato's advice does not please me, to speak always in the tone of a master to one's servant, without jesting, without familiarity, whether they be men or whether they be women;[19] for, besides my previous reason, it is inhuman and unjust to give so much weight to this accidental prerogative of fortune, and the forms of government in which least disparity is permitted between servants and masters seems to me the most equitable.

Others study to push forward and lift up their minds, I to lower mine and draw it in;[20] it is unsound only when stretched too far.

> You talk of the genealogy of Æacus, and of the battles waged under the walls of sacred Ilion; but you are silent about the price at which we are to buy a cask of Chian wine, or who shall heat water for my bath, or who shall offer me, and when, shelter from Peligian cold.[21]

Thus, as Lacedæmonian valour had need of being moderated, and being soothed in battle by the sweet and gentle notes of flutes, for fear that it should be precipitated into rashness and madness,[22] whereas all other nations ordinarily make use of shrill, loud sounds and voices which excite and inflame to the utmost degree the courage of the soldiers, in the same way, it seems to me, contrary to the common idea, that in the use of our mind we for the most part have more need of lead than of wings, of coolness and of quietness than of ardour and of action. Above all, it is to my thinking playing the part of a fool to play the part of a man of wide information[23] among those who are not so; to speak always formally, *favellar in punta di forchetta*.[24] You should descend to the level of those with whom you are, and sometimes affect ignorance. Lay aside strength and cunning; for ordinary usage it is enough to retain coherence; for the rest, keep as close to the ground as they like.[25]

Men of learning easily stumble over this stone; they are always making a parade of their authority and strew their books everywhere. In these days their voices have so resounded in the rooms and the ears of ladies, that if they[26] have not retained their substance, they have at least the air of having done so; in every sort of talk and matter, however mean and commonplace it be, they make use of a new and learned fashion of speaking and writing,—

> In this style they express their fear, anger, joy, anxiety, and all the secrets of their mind. Can I say more? Learnedly they pass away,[27]—

and produce Plato and St. Thomas as authority about things for which the first comer would serve as well for witness; the instruction that has hardly reached their soul has remained on their tongues. If the well-bred ladies will credit me, they will be content to show the value of their own natural pleasures. They conceal and cover their beauties under the beauties of another; it is great folly to stifle one's own brilliancy in order to shine with a borrowed light; they are interred and entombed under art, *quite as if from the bandbox*.[28] It shows that they do not know themselves well enough; the world has nothing more beauteous; it is their part to give glory to the arts and to embellish embellishments.[29]

What do they need but to live beloved and honoured? They possess and know only too much for that. There is need only of a little rousing and kindling of the faculties that are in them. When I see them dealing with rhetoric, judicature, and logic, and the like trash, so vain and useless for their concerns, I begin to fear that the men who advise them to do it have authority to rule them on that ground. For what other excuse could I find for them? It is enough that women can without our aid dispose the charm of their eyes to gaiety, to severity, and to gentleness, tempering a "nay" with harshness, with hesitation, and with kindness; and they seek no interpreter for the discourses delivered in their service. With this art they command absolutely and rule both rulers and the school.[30] If, nevertheless, it vexes them to yield to us in any thing whatsoever, and if they wish from curiosity to have a share in books, poetry is an entertainment suited to their need; it is a trifling and sophisticated art, disguised, a matter of words,[31] all pleasure, all show, like themselves. They will also draw divers advantages from history. In philosophy, from the part that is helpful to life, they may receive the teachings which train them to judge of our dispositions and conditions, to defend themselves from our treacheries, to restrain the rashness of their own desires, to use rightly their liberty, to lengthen the pleasures of life, and to bear quietly the inconstancy of a lover, the surliness of a husband, and the pertinacity of age, of wrinkles, and similar matters. Such at the most is the share I would allot to them in the matter of learning.

There are some natures prone to privacy, withdrawal, and introspection. My essential disposition is adapted to communication and production. I am all outward and in sight, born for social life and for friendship. The solitude that I love and that I preach is chiefly for the purpose of drawing back to myself my interests and my thoughts, of restraining and confining, not my steps, but my desires and my cares, giving over all outside solicitude and shunning servitude and bonds, and not so much the crowding of men as the crowding of affairs. Solitude of place, in truth, tends to give my thoughts a more extensive outlook; I throw myself more freely into affairs of state and into the universe when I am alone. At the Louvre and in the throng I shrink and draw back into my shell. The crowd thrusts me back on myself, and I never converse with myself so rashly, so unrestrainedly, and so privately as in places of respect and ceremonious discretion. It is not our folly that makes me laugh; it is our sapience. By nature I am no enemy to the turmoil of courts; I have passed a part of my life there, and easily carry myself gaily in large assemblies, provided that it is at intervals and when I am in the mood; but the fastidiousness of judgement whereof I have spoken perforce binds me to solitude. Verily, in my own house, with a numerous household, and one of the most frequented of mansions, I see persons enough, but rarely those with whom I care to hold intercourse; and there I preserve, both for myself and for others, unwonted liberty. There is there a truce to ceremony, to ushering guests on their arrival and accompanying them on their departure,[32] and other such tiresome behests of our courtesy (O servile and annoying custom!). Every one conducts himself there as he pleases; whosoever will, talks freely:[33] I remain dumb, meditative, and withdrawn, without offending my guests.

The men whose society and intimacy I seek are those who may be styled upright and clever men; the figure of these gives me a distaste for others. This is, rightly considered, the rarest of all types, and a type that is due chiefly to nature. The scope of such intercourse is simply familiarity, frequent companionship, and talk: action for our souls, without other gain. In our discourse all subjects are alike to me; it does not matter to me that there is neither weight nor depth in them; charm and pertinence are always present; it is all tinged with ripe and firm judgement, and blended with kindliness, frankness, cheerfulness, and friendship. It is not on questions of law and politics[34] only that our mind shews its beauty and its strength, or in the affairs of kings; it shews it no less in private confabulations. I know my friends even by their silence and their smile, and discern them better, it may be, at table than in the council room. Hippomachus well said that he recognised skilful wrestlers merely by seeing them walk in the street.[35] If learning be pleased to join in our talk, her company will not be refused —not as she usually is, magisterial, imperious, and importunate, but subordinate and docile. We are seeking only pastime; when the hour comes to be instructed and preached to, we will go to find her on her throne. Let her descend to our level for the moment if she please; for, most profitable and desirable as she is, I take it for granted that at need we could well dispense with her altogether and do our work without her. A soul well endowed and accustomed to dealing with men becomes of itself agreeable. Art is nothing else than the examination and record of what such souls bring forth.

Intercourse with virtuous women, too, is pleasant to me; *for we too have experienced eyes*.[36] If the spiritual nature has not so much enjoyment therein as in the other, the corporeal senses, which participate in this, bring it to a degree approaching that, although in my opinion not equal to it. But it is an intercourse in which we must be somewhat on our guard, especially those in whom the body counts for much, as with me. I was over-hot in my youth, and suffered all the madness that poets say comes upon those who let themselves go in that direction without discipline and without judgement. It is true that that scourging has since served me as instruction:

> Whoever in the Greek fleet has escaped from the Capharean rocks always turns his sails away from the waters of Euboea.[37]

It is folly to fix all one's thoughts on this, and to involve oneself in it with a frantic and ill-judged emotion; but, on the other hand, to enter into it without love and without a binding attraction,[38] like comedians; to play a part belonging to one's age and to custom, and to put into it nothing of oneself but the words—that is truly to provide for one's security, but in very cowardly fashion, like him who should forgo his honour or his profit or his pleasure for fear of

Of Three Sorts of Intercourse

danger; for it is certain that, from such a course, they who practise it can not hope for any result which concerns or satisfies a noble soul. What one would in good earnest take pleasure in enjoying must have been in good earnest desired; I mean when fortune unjustly has favoured their dissimulation, which often happens because of the fact that there is not a single woman, however ill-favoured she may be, who does not deem herself attractive, who does not think well of herself as to her age, or her hair, or her carriage (for there is none absolutely ugly any more than absolutely beautiful); and the Brahmin maids who lack other attractions—the people being called together by public announcement for this purpose—go to the public square and exhibit themselves, to see if thereby at least they are not worthy to win a husband. Consequently there is not one of them who does not allow herself to be easily persuaded by the first man who swears to be her slave.

Now from the common and every-day treachery of the men of to-day, that must needs happen which experience has shown us, namely, that they rally together and fall back on themselves, or among themselves, to avoid us; or else they dispose themselves on their side after the example that we set them, and play their part in the farce and lend themselves to this traffic, without passion, without heed, and without love; *without affection himself and insensible to that of others;*[39] thinking, according to the persuasion of Lysias in Plato,[40] that they can abandon themselves to us the more profitably and advantageously, the less we love them. It will be with them as with play-actors: the audience will have as much pleasure as themselves, or more. For my own part, I no more recognise Venus without Cupid than motherhood without offspring; these are things which mutually give and owe to each other their essential character. So this imposture reacts on him who is guilty of it; it costs him little, but he gains by it nothing of value. They who made Venus a goddess perceived that her chief beauty was incorporeal and spiritual; but the Venus that such men seek is not merely human, or even bestial. The beasts do not accept her so gross and earthy; we see that imagination and desire often inflame them and urge them, before the body; we see in both the one and the other sex that they have choice and selection among the throng in their inclinations, and that there are between them friendly relations of long liking.[41] Even those to whom old age denies bodily strength will still tremble, neigh, and thrill with love. We may see them, before the deed, filled with hope and ardour, and when the body has played its part, still gratified by the sweetness of the remembrance; and some there are that are afterwards puffed up with pride and, though weary and sated, crow with triumph and glee.

He who has but to relieve his body of a natural necessity, has no need to trouble others with such careful preparations; it is no meat for a coarse and gross appetite.

As I have no expectation of being thought better than I am, I will tell this of the errors of my youth. Not only on account of the danger to health (and yet I did not manage so well but I have had two touches, slight, however, and transitory), but also out of contempt, I have seldom had recourse to venal and public connections. I preferred to whet the pleasure by difficulty, by desire, and by some vainglory. I shared the tastes of the Emperor Tiberius, who in his amours was as much taken with modesty and noble birth

as with any other quality; and the inclination of the courtezan Flora, who gave herself to no man below the rank of
a Dictator, a Consul, or a Censor, and found her delight in
the dignity of her lovers. No doubt pearls and brocades,
titles and retinues, contribute their part to the pleasure.

Furthermore, I set great store by the intelligence, but on
condition that the body was not to seek; for, to speak in
good conscience, if one or the other of those two charms
must necessarily be lacking, I should have chosen to let the
intellectual go; it has its employment in better things; but,
in the matter of love, which has to do principally with the
sight and the touch, one can do something without the
charms of the mind, but nothing without bodily charms.
That is the true advantage of women, is beauty: it is so
wholly theirs that our beauty, although it requires some
features a little different, is, at its best, simply indistinguish-
able from theirs when boyish and beardless. They say that
in the Grand Turk's establishment those who are in his
service because of their beauty, of whom there is an infinite
number, are dismissed at the age of twenty-one at the lat-
est.[42] Good sense, wisdom, and the duties of friendship are
found more generally among men; therefore they rule the
affairs of the world.

These two sorts of intercourse[43] are fortuitous and depend
upon others; one is vexatious because of its rarity, the other
flags with advancing years; so that they could not have
adequately sufficed for the occupation of my life. Intercourse with books, which is the third sort, is much more
sure and more ours. It yields to the first two all other advantages, but it has for its share the steadiness and facility of
its employ. This is at my side the whole way and assists me

everywhere; it comforts me in old age and in solitude; it re-
lieves me from the burden of a wearisome idleness, and rids
me at any moment of annoying society; it dulls the sharpness of suffering unless it be extreme and overmastering.
To divert me from an unseasonable imagination I need only
have recourse to books; they easily turn my thoughts to
them, and steal my unwelcome thoughts from me;[44] and
they never rebel though they see that I seek them only in
default of those other pleasures more real, vivid, and natural; they welcome me always with the same cheer.

It is very well, as the saying is, to go on foot, for one who
leads his horse by the bridle; and our James, King of Naples
and Sicily, who, handsome, young, and healthy, had himself carried about the country in a barrow, resting on a
miserable feather-bed, dressed in a garment of gray cloth
and a cap of the same, yet attended by a great regal train,—
litters, led horses of all sorts, gentlemen and officials,[45]—
exhibited an austerity as yet fickle and tottering; the sick
man is not to be pitied who has his cure in his sleeve. In the
experience and practice of this very true saying lies all the
profit that I derive from books. I use them, in fact, hardly
more than they do who do not know them. I enjoy them, as
misers their treasures, in knowing that I shall enjoy them
whenever I please; my soul is satisfied and content with
this right of possession. I do not travel without books in time
either of peace or of war. Sometimes several days will pass,
and months, without my making use of them. "The time
will come," I say, "to-morrow, perhaps, or whenever I
please." Meanwhile time flies and is gone without harming
me; and it can not be said how much I repose and refresh
myself in the reflection that they are at my side to give me

pleasure when I will, and in recognising what succour they bring to my life. It is the best provision I have found for this human journey, and I very greatly pity those men of intelligence who lack it. I rather accept any other sort of occupation, however trivial it may be, inasmuch as this can not fail me.

At home I betake myself a little oftener than elsewhere to my library, where I can observe all the affairs of my household. It is above the gateway, and I see below me my garden, my base-court, my courtyard, and look into most of the parts of my house. There I turn the leaves, now of one book, now of another, without order and without plan, in disconnected snatches; sometimes I muse, sometimes I record and dictate my reflections while walking about, as now. It[46] is on the third floor of a turret. The first floor is my chapel, the second a bedroom and its appurtenances, where I often sleep, to be alone. Above, it has a large dressing-room; it was in bygone times the most useless part of my house. There I pass both the greater number of the days of my life and most of the hours of the day; I am never there at night. Adjoining is a well-finished small room, where there can be a fire in winter, and it is very agreeably lighted; and if I did not dread the trouble more than the cost,—the trouble that repels me from all labour,—I could easily have added on each side a gallery a hundred paces long and twelve wide, on the same level, having found all the walls built for another purpose to the requisite height. Every place for retirement demands a place for walking; my thoughts fall asleep if I seat them; my mind does not go by itself as well as when the legs keep it in motion. They who study without books are all in the same plight.

Of Three Sorts of Intercourse

In shape it[47] is round, and there is no flat wall except what is occupied by my table and my chair; and it presents me, as it curves, all my books at once, arranged on every side in cases with five shelves. It has three prospects, with fine and open views, and it has sixteen paces of vacant space in diameter. In winter I am less continually there; for my house is perched on a little hill, as its name implies, and no part is more exposed to the wind than this. I like the situation, its being a little difficult of access and out of the way, both because of the benefit of the exercise and also as keeping the throng away from me. There is my domain.[48] I endeavour to make my sway there absolute, and to detach this one corner from all community, whether conjugal, filial, or social; everywhere else I have but a verbal authority, immaterial, vague. Miserable is the man, in my opinion, who has in his house no place where he can be alone, where he can especially pay court to himself, where he can hide himself! Ambition fitly requites her followers by keeping them always on exhibition, like a statue in the market-place; *a great fortune is a great bondage;*[49] they can have no privacy even in their closet.[50] I have judged nothing else to be so severe in the austerity of life that our monks affect as what I see in some of their communities, where the rules require constant companionship and numerous persons present at whatever they do; and I find it somewhat more tolerable to be always alone than never to be able to be so.

If some one tells me that it is degrading the Muses to use them only for play and pastime, he knows not as I do how great is the value of pleasure, of sport and pastime; I am very near saying that every other object is ridiculous. I live from day to day, and, speaking with reverence, I live

Of Three Sorts of Intercourse

only for myself; my purposes end there. In youth I studied for ostentation; afterward, a little for wisdom; now, for pleasure; never merely for the pursuit of learning.[51] An idle and extravagant inclination that I once had for that sort of furnishing, not to provide merely for my necessities, but, beyond that, therewith to torment and adorn myself, I long ago gave over. Books have many agreeable qualities for those who know how to choose them; but no good thing is without ill; it is a pleasure that is not unalloyed and pure any more than other pleasures; it has its disadvantages, and very weighty ones; the mind is exercised therein, but the body, which likewise I have not forgotten to heed, remains meanwhile inactive, is cast down and aggrieved. I know of no excess more injurious for me, or more to be avoided in these declining years.

I note here my three favourite and especial occupations; I say nothing of those which I owe to the world by civic obligation.

Chapter IV

OF DISTRACTION [1]

I WAS once employed to console a lady who was truly afflicted; their mourning is usually artificial.

A woman always has in reserve abundant tears, awaiting a signal from her to flow.[2]

It is an ill-advised course to oppose this emotion, for opposition spurs them on and involves them more deeply in melancholy; the grief is aggravated by anger at the contention. We see in common conversation that if any one ventures to controvert what I may have carelessly said, I take it in dudgeon; I defend it—much more if it be a matter about which I am interested. And also, thus doing, you make a rough beginning of your work; whereas the first addresses of the physician to his patient should be gracious, affable, and agreeable; never did an ill-favoured and sour-looking physician effect any good. Far otherwise, therefore, we must give help at first and countenance their lamentation, and testify to some approbation, and justification for it. By such sagacity you gain ground to go further, and by an easy and imperceptible transition you glide into more stable discourse proper for their cure.

Of Distraction

I, whose chief desire was only to beguile the bystanders, who had their eyes upon me, thought it best to apply a plaster. For I find by experience that I have an unskilful and ineffective hand in persuading. Either my reasonings are too sharp and too dry, or I present them too abruptly or too carelessly. After I had for a time followed the humour of her suffering, I did not attempt to cure her by strong and keen reasonings, because I lacked such, or because I thought to produce a better effect by other means; nor did I choose the various methods of consolation that philosophy prescribes: that the thing lamented about is not an ill, like Cleanthes;[3] that it is a slight ill, like the Peripatetics; that to lament is neither a lawful nor a praiseworthy action, like Chrysippus; nor this precept of Epicurus,—which is nearer my way of thinking,—to transport the thought from disagreeable to delightful things; nor to make a collection of all these together, employing such as occasion offers, like Cicero; but all gently turning our talk, and gradually leading it to subjects near at hand, and then to a little more distant ones, according as she followed me, I imperceptibly took away from her that grievous thought and left her cheerful and altogether tranquillised as long as I was there. I made use of distraction. They who followed me in this same office found no amendment in her, for I had not laid the axe to the root.

I have by chance treated elsewhere[4] of some ways of diverting the course of public affairs. And the military methods of which Pericles availed himself in the Peloponesian War,[5] and a thousand others at other times, to cause hostile forces to withdraw from their country, are frequent enough in histories.

Of Distraction

That was a crafty avoidance of disaster by which the sieur de Himbercourt saved himself and others in the city of Liége, whither the Duke of Burgundy, who held it besieged, had sent him to sign the conditions of the capitulation agreed upon. The people, having assembled at night to arrange for this, began to rebel against the agreed terms; and many of them proposed to fall upon the negotiators whom they had in their power. He, feeling the wind of the first wave of those men who had rushed to his quarters, immediately sent out to them two of the inhabitants of the city (for there were some of them with him) entrusted with milder new offers to propose to their council, which he had invented on the instant to meet his need. These two arrested the oncoming tempest, leading the excited mob to the city hall, to hear what was to be said and deliberate thereon. The deliberation was short: behold, there broke a second storm as violent as the first; upon which he despatched to meet them four new intercessors with like instructions, declaring that this time they had it in charge to lay before them yet more fruitful terms, altogether for their contentment and satisfaction; whereby the people were again sent to consult together. The result was that, by so disposing these delays, diverting their rage and dissipating it in idle consultations, he lulled it to sleep at last and gained the twenty-four hours,[6] which was his main object.

This other tale is also in this category.[7] Atalanta, a maiden of surpassing beauty and of wonderful activity, to rid herself of the throng of a thousand suitors who sought her in marriage, pronounced this decree: that she would accept him who should equal her in a foot-race, on condition that they who failed to do so should lose their lives. There proved to be enough who regarded the prize as worthy of such a risk, and who incurred the penalty of that cruel bargain. Hippomenes, having to make his attempt after the others, appealed to the tutelary goddess of lovers,[8] calling her to his aid; and she, lending a favourable ear to his prayer, supplied him with three golden apples and instructed him how to use them. The race having begun, as Hippomenes feels his mistress close on his heels, he lets fall one of the apples, as if inadvertently. The maiden, attracted by its golden beauty, fails not to turn aside from her way to pick it up;

> The maiden was astonished, and in her desire for the shining apple swerved from her course, and picked up the rolling gold.[9]

He did the like at the right moment with the second and the third, until, by dint of her straying and turning aside,[10] the victory in the race remained with him.[11] When the physicians can not clear away an affection of the brain,[12] they divert it and turn it aside to some less dangerous part. I observe that this is also the most common prescription for diseases of the mind. *The mind should sometimes be distracted by other interests, affairs, pursuits, and occupations; it may often be cured, like sick men not yet convalescent, by a change of place.*[13] We can with difficulty make it confront ills directly. We can make it neither support nor repel the blow; we make it shun it and turn aside.

The other lesson[14] is too lofty and too difficult. It is for those of the first order of mind to pause steadfastly on the thing, to consider it, to judge it. It belongs to a Socrates alone to meet death with an every-day countenance, to be

1128

Of Distraction

familiar with it and to play with it. He seeks no consolation outside the thing; dying seems to him a natural and indifferent occurrence; he fastens his eyes directly upon it and deliberates upon it without looking elsewhere. The disciples of Hegesias, who starved themselves to death, inflamed by the noble teachings of his lessons,—and in such numbers that King Ptolemy forbade him to occupy his school further with those homicidal discourses,[15]—these did not consider death in itself, they passed no judgement upon it; it is not on it that their thought rested; they ran toward a new existence, on which their eyes were fixed.[16] Those poor men whom we see on the scaffold, filled with ardent devotion, and there employing, as much as in them lies, all their senses,—their ears in attention to the instructions given them, their eyes and hands upraised to heaven, their voices in loud prayers with vehement and unceasing emotion,—do what is certainly praiseworthy and suitable in such a hard strait. We should praise them for piety, but not properly for resolution. They shun the struggle, they turn their thoughts away from death, just as we keep children amused when the lancet is to be used on them. I have seen some men whose heart failed them, if for a moment their sight fell upon the horrible preparations for death that surrounded them, and who, in a frenzy, turned their thoughts elsewhere. We bid those who are crossing a terrifying abyss to close their eyes or turn them away.

Subrius Flavius, being about to be put to death by order of Nero, and at the hands of Niger,[17]—both being army commanders,—when they led him to the field where the execution was to take place, and he saw that the hole that Niger had dug to put him in was irregular and ill-shaped,

Of Distraction

"Even this," he said, turning to the soldiers who were present, "is not according to military regulations." And to Niger, who exhorted him to hold his head firmly, "Do you but strike as firmly"; and he divined rightly, for Niger's arm, trembling, had to give several strokes. This man seems to have had his thoughts wholly and fixedly on the subject. The man who dies in the mellay, sword in hand, does not at that moment give his mind to death; he neither is conscious of it nor considers it; the ardour of the combat carries the day. A gentleman[18] of my acquaintance having fallen as he was fighting in an enclosure, and conscious of being stabbed nine or ten times by his opponent while prostrate, every one present called to him that he should think of his conscience; but he told me afterward that, although these words reached his ears, they in no wise affected him, and that he never thought of any thing save disengaging himself and being revenged; he killed his man in this same combat. He who brought the sentence of death to L. Sillanus did him a great service; for, having heard his reply, that he was quite ready to die, but not by a villainous hand, he, to force him, attacked him with his soldiers; and as Sillanus, wholly unarmed, defended himself obstinately with fists and feet, the other put him to death in that contest, changing into sudden tumultuous anger the painful thoughts of the prolonged and prearranged death to which he was destined. We think always of something else: the hope of a better life stays and supports us, or the hope of our children's worth, or the future renown of our name, or the escape from the ills of this life, or the vengeance which menaces those who cause our death.

I hope truly that, if kind gods have any power,

Of Distraction

you will be punished by shipwreck, and will call often
on the name of Dido. . . . I shall hear, and the report
of your death will come to me among the shades.[19]

Xenophon, wreath on head, was offering sacrifice, when
they came to tell him of the death of his son Gryllus at the
battle of Mantinea. On first hearing the news, he threw
his wreath to the ground; but, so the tale continues, learning the nature of a most valiant death, he picked it up and
replaced it on his head.[20] Even Epicurus finds consolation
in his last hours in the immortality and usefulness of his
writings.[21] *All toils that bring fame and glory can be endured.*[22] And Xenophon says that the same wound, the
same toil, does not weigh so heavily on a general as on a
common soldier.[23] Epaminondas accepted his death far
more cheerfully when he was informed that the victory remained on his side.[24] *These are the consolations, the allevia-
tions, of the greatest sufferings.*[25] And other like circumstances occupy us and divert us and turn our thoughts away
from consideration of the thing in itself.

Verily the arguments of philosophy continually skirt
and avoid this subject and scarcely break its crust. The greatest man of the greatest school of philosophy, which was the
guiding influence[26] of the others, the great Zeno, said
about death: "No bad thing is honourable; death is honourable; therefore it is not a bad thing";[27] and about drunkenness: "No man entrusts his secret to the drunkard; every
one entrusts it to the wise man; therefore the wise man is
not a drunkard."[28] Is this hitting the mark? I like to see
these lofty souls unable to free themselves from our fellowship; perfect men as they may be, they are still very unintelligently men.[29]

1131

Of Distraction

Vengeance is a pleasant passion, of great and natural influence; this I see plainly, although I have no experience of it. To divert a young prince therefrom, not long ago, I did not tell him that to him who has struck one cheek we must turn the other, from the duty of charity; nor did I set before him the tragic results that poetry attributes to that passion. I left all that on one side and busied myself in making him savour the beauty of a contrary image: the honour, the favour, the good-will which he would acquire by clemency and kindness; I turned him aside to ambition. That is the way to do. If your emotion in love be too powerful, disperse it, they say; and they say well, for I have often tried this with profit; break it up into various desires, of which let one be the chief and master, if you will; but for fear that this one may domineer and tyrannise over you, weaken it, intermit it, by dividing and diverting it;

> When your wayward heart throbs with violent desires,[30]

> Discharge your passion elsewhere;[31]

and look to this in good time, for fear that you may be in serious trouble from it, if it have once taken possesion of you;

> Unless you combine with the first wounds new blows, and efface the first impressions by unrestrained vagrancy.[32]

I was in other days touched by a sorrow overpowering for one of my temperament, and even more legitimate than overpowering; I should perchance have been lost had I trusted solely to my strength. Having need of something

violently different to distract my thoughts, I became by
design and by effort a lover, wherein my age assisted me.
Love solaced and relieved the pain that had been caused me
by friendship. In all things else it is the same: a bitter
thought holds me; I find it shorter to change it than to overcome it; I substitute another for it—if I can not a contrary
one, at least a different one; the variation always solaces,
dissolves, and dissipates it. If I can not combat it, I escape
from it, and in flying from it I turn one way and another.[33]
I use stratagems; changing place and occupation and companionship, I take refuge in the throng of other employments and thoughts, where it loses my traces and goes
astray.

This is the course of Nature by the good offices of varia-
bility; for time, which she has given us as the chief physician
for our troubles, produces its effect principally thus, that by
presenting other and still other subjects to our mind, it
clears away and destroys that first conception, however
strong it may be. A thoughtful man[34] sees his dying friend
but little less at the end of five and twenty years than in the
first year, and, according to Epicurus, not at all less, for he
attributed no alleviation of afflictions either to the anticipation of them or to their ancientness;[35] but so many other
thoughts come in the way of this one that at last it lan-
guishes and fades away. To divert the tendency of common
rumours, Alcibiades cut off the ears and tail of his beautiful
dog, and drove him into the public square, so that, on his
giving this subject to the populace to gossip about, they
would leave his other actions in peace.[36] I have likewise seen
women with this same purpose cloak their real emotions.
with counterfeit emotions, to divert people's opinions and

1133

Of Distraction

conjectures and to mislead the tattlers. But I have known one of them who, thus counterfeiting, suffered herself to take it in earnest and forsook the true and original feeling for the pretended one; and I learned by her that those[37] who find themselves well lodged are fools to consent to this disguise. Public welcomes and interviews being reserved for the visible suitor,[38] be sure that he is far from clever if he does not in the end put himself into your place and send you into his. This is in effect to cut and sew a shoe for another to wear.

Trifles distract and divert us, for trifles restrain us. We scarcely regard any subjects in their whole extent and by themselves; it is their surroundings, or trivial and superficial images of them, that strike us, and meaningless externals that are shaped by all subjects,—

Like the smooth coats that crickets shed in summer.[39]

Even Plutarch lamenting for his daughter thinks of the pretty ways of her childhood.[40] The memory of a farewell, of an act, of a special charm, of a last injunction, afflicts us. Cæsar's mantle disquieted all Rome, which his death had not done.[41] Even the sound of names, entering into our ears: My poor master! or, My great friend! Alas, my dear father! or, My sweet daughter!—when these repeated utterances pain me, and I regard them closely, I find that they are verbal lamentations; I am bruised by the words and the tone, as the exclamations of preachers often move their auditors more than their reasonings do; and as we are struck by the piteous cries of a beast that is being killed for our use; [I am pained] without, meanwhile, weighing or fathoming the true essence and validity of my subject;

Of Distraction

It is by these incitements that grief is aroused;[42]

these are the bases of our sorrow.

The obstinacy of my stones, especially in the male member, has sometimes caused me long suppression of urine,—for three or four days,—and brought me so near death that it had been folly to hope to escape it, indeed to wish to do so, considering the cruel assaults this state exposes me to. Oh, what a past master in the science of torture was that excellent emperor[43] who caused the members of his criminals to be bound, in order to cause their death because they could not pass water! Finding myself in this condition, I reflected by what trivial causes and objects my imagination nourished in me regret for life; of what atoms the burden and difficulty of this dislodging was composed in my soul; how many frivolous thoughts we give place to about so great a matter: a dog, a horse, a book, a glass—and what not?—counted for something in my loss; with others, no less foolishly in my opinion, their ambitious hopes, their purse, their learning. I view death carelessly when I view it universally as the end of life. I domineer over it as a whole; in its details, it preys upon me; the tears of a servant, the distribution of my cast-off clothes, the touch of a familiar hand, a commonplace consolation, discomfort me and weaken me.

In like manner the lamentations in fictions agitate our souls; and the sorrows of Dido and Ariadne afflict even those who do not believe the narratives of Virgil and Catullus.[44] It is a sign of an unyielding and hard nature to feel no emotion about such things as are told of Polemo as something wonderful; but also he did not even turn pale at the bite of a mad dog which tore away the calf of his leg.[45] And no intelligence so completely conceives by its insight the occasion of sadness so keen and unbroken that the apprehension of it is not increased by being present, when the eyes and the ears have their share in its recognition—organs which are not called into play by merely idle incidents.[46]

Is it reasonable that even the arts should make use of and profit by our natural weakness and stupidity? The orator, the art of rhetoric declares, will in the play of his pleading be moved by the sound of his own voice and by his feigned agitation, and himself will be imposed upon by the passion he represents; he will himself be impressed with real and sincere grief, by means of the jugglery that he is performing, to transmit it to the judges, whom it concerns even less; like those persons who are hired for funerals to assist in ceremonial of mourning; who sell their tears by weight and measure, and their sadness; and although they assume a borrowed manner,[47] yet by dint of practising and arranging their expression, it is certain that they are often completely carried away and are affected with genuine melancholy.

I, with several other friends of his, escorted the body of Monsieur de Grammont to Soissons from the siege of La Fère, where he was killed.[48] I observed that, wherever we passed, the inhabitants we met overflowed with lamentations and tears, at the sight of the character of our convoy; for even the name of the dead man was not known to them. Quintilian says that he had seen actors who had so deeply entered into a mourning part that they continued to weep at home; and of himself he says that, having undertaken to arouse some passion in others, he had espoused it to the

Of Distraction

point of finding himself surprised not only by tears but by the pallor and bearing of a man overwhelmed by grief.[49]

In a region near our mountains the women play priest Martin;[50] for while they augment their regret for the husband they have lost by recalling the good and attractive qualities he had, with the same breath they gather up and publish his imperfections; as if to find some compensation for themselves and to pass from tenderness to contempt. With much better grace, indeed, than we, who, at the loss of any one we know, pride ourselves on bestowing upon him new and false laudations, and on making him quite other when we have lost him from sight than he seemed to us to be when we saw him; as if regret brought information, or as if tears, by washing our understanding, enlightened it. I now renounce the favourable testimony people would give me, not because I am worthy of it, but because I am dead.

If some one is asked: "What interest have you in this siege?" he will reply: "The interest of example and of general obedience to the prince; I look for no profit whatever from it, and as for glory, I know how small a portion falls to a common soldier like me; I have here no personal trouble or quarrel." But see him on the morrow, in his post for the assault, transformed, chafing, and crimson with wrath; it is the glittering of all that steel and the flashing and the rattling of our cannon and our drums that have infused this new sternness and hate into his veins. A frivolous cause! you will say. How a cause? There is none needed to excite our soul; a mere thought, without substance and without object, sways it and excites it. If I set about building castles in Spain, my imagination devises for me agreeable ideas and

Of Distraction

pleasures by which my soul is really touched with enjoyment, and gladdened. How often do we encumber our minds with anger or sadness by such shadows, and involve ourselves in imaginary passions which change both the soul and the body! What amazed, amused, confused expressions pass over our faces when dreaming awake! What sudden starts and agitations are there of limbs and voice! Does it not seem as if this man, quite alone, has false visions of a throng of other men with whom he is doing business, or of some internal demon that is persecuting him? Enquire of yourself where is the occasion of this change: is there any thing in nature but ourselves that feeds on nothingness, over which nothingness has any power?

Cambyses, because he dreamed while sleeping that his brother was to become King of Persia, had him put to death—a brother whom he loved and in whom he had always had confidence.[51] Aristodemus, King of the Messenians, killed himself because of a fanciful idea that he conceived of evil augury from I know not what howling of his dogs;[52] and King Midas did the same, being disturbed and angered by some unpleasant dream that he had dreamed.[53] To abandon one's life for a dream is to value it for just what it is. But here our soul triumphs at the wretchedness of the body and its weakness and its being exposed to all sorts of injuries; in truth, it has good reason so to speak!

O unfortunate primal clay fashioned by Prometheus! He shewed little wisdom in the execution of his work. Framing the body only, he did not see the mind in his art; he ought to have begun with the mind.[54]

1138

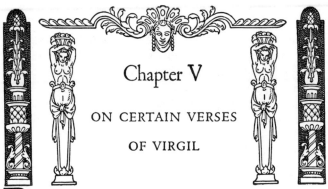

Chapter V

ON CERTAIN VERSES

OF VIRGIL

PROFITABLE thoughts, the more pithy and solid they are, are also the more troublesome and burdensome. Vice, death, poverty, maladies are grave and grievous matters. The soul must needs be instructed as to the means of supporting and combatting ills, and instructed as to the rule for right living and right thinking, and must often be aroused and exercised in this noble study; but with a common sort of soul this must needs be with intervals and moderation: such a one is weakened by being kept too continually strained.

In my youth I had need to admonish myself and look carefully after myself, to keep me to my duty; good spirits and health do not consist so well, they say, with serious and wise reflections. I am now in a different condition; the accompaniments of old age admonish me only too much, teach me wisdom, and preach to me. From excess of gaiety I have fallen into the more irksome excess of gravity; therefore, I now allow myself designedly to indulge a little in disorderly ways, and sometimes employ my soul in lively and youthful thoughts, where it makes holiday. I am at present only too sober, too pondering, and too mature: my

On Certain Verses of Virgil

years daily instruct me in insensibility and temperance. This body shuns and fears irregularity; it is taking its turn to lead the mind toward reformation; in its turn it holds sway, and more harshly and imperiously; not for a single hour, sleeping or waking, does it leave me at rest from teaching about death, endurance, and repentance. I guard myself from temperance as I used to do from enjoyment; it draws me too far back, even to dulness; now I desire to be master of myself in all ways. Wisdom has her excesses, and has no less need than folly of moderation. And so, for fear lest I dry up, wither, and wax mouldy from prudence, I quietly turn aside in the intervals of my bodily ills,—

Lest my mind be intent on its own troubles,[1]—

and avert my eyes from that stormy and cloudy sky which I have before me, and which, God be praised! I regard quite without fear but not without debate and meditation; and I set about to amusing myself with the remembrance of past follies.

The mind longs for what it has lost, and in imagination throws itself altogether into the past.[2]

Let childhood look forward, old age backward; was not that the significance of the double face of Janus? The years drag me along if they will, but with backward steps. So long as my eyes can discern that pleasant lost season, I now and then turn them thither. Though it escapes from my blood and my veins, at least I will not uproot its image from my memory;

To be able to enjoy one's past life is to live twice.[3]

1140

On Certain Verses of Virgil

Plato advises old men to be present at the exercises, dances, and games of the young, in order to be gladdened by the agility and beauty of the body in others which is theirs no longer, and to recall to their memory the charms and comeliness of that blooming age; and desires that in those sports they should attribute the honour of victory to the youth who shall have most exhilarated and gladdened the greater number of them.[4] Formerly I used to mark dull and gloomy days as unusual; these are now the usual ones for me, the unusual are those that are fine and cloudless. I am ready to jump for joy as for an unwonted blessing when nothing pains me. If I try to please,[5] I can scarcely now draw a poor smile from this wretched body. I make merry merely in fancy and in waking dreams, to drive away by cunning the pensiveness of old age; but it is certain that this needs another remedy than such dreams; this is a feeble struggle of art against nature. It is great foolishness to prolong and anticipate human disadvantages as every one does; I like better to be old less long than to be old before I am so;[6] I seize upon the slightest opportunities for enjoyment that I can meet with. I know well by hearsay many kinds of wise pleasures, strong and highly praised; but belief in these has not enough power over me to give me an appetite for them. I do not so much want them to be lofty and magnificent and proud, as delicious and easy and near at hand; *we forsake nature; we give ourselves to the people, who are in no wise good guides*.[7] My philosophy is of action, or natural and immediate practice, little of conceptions; would I could take pleasure in playing with nuts or with a top!

He never set rumours before the safety of the State.[8]

On Certain Verses of Virgil

Pleasure is a quality of little ambition; it thinks itself rich enough in itself without the prize of fame being added, and prefers to be in the shade. A young man ought to be whipped who should occupy himself in discovering the taste of wines and sauces; there is nothing that I have less known and less value; to-day I am learning it. I am greatly ashamed of this, but what can I do about it? I am even more ashamed and troubled by the occasions that drive me to it.

It is for us to dream and idle, and for the youthful to make themselves of repute and value; they are advancing toward the world, toward authority; we are leaving it; *for them let there be arms, and for them horses and spears and foils and balls and swimming and races; and of all the many games let them leave us old men the knuckle-bones and the dice;*[9] the very laws send us into retirement.[10]

I can do no less in favour of this forlorn state into which my years force me than supply it with playthings and amusements, as it were childhood; indeed, we fall back into that condition. Both wisdom and folly will have hard work[11] to support and succour me by alternating services in this calamity of age.

Mingle a little folly with your wisdom.[12]

I avoid even the slightest pricks, and those which in other days would not have scratched me now pierce me; my bodily habit begins to incline so easily to all conditions! *To a feeble body every mishap is hateful.*[13]

A sick mind cannot endure anything disagreeable.[14]

I have always been susceptible and sensitive to harmful

things; I am now more thin-skinned and everywhere exposed,

> And the least effort is enough to break what is already cracked.[15]

My judgement prevents me, indeed, from kicking and grumbling at the discomforts that Nature ordains me to suffer, but not from feeling them. I would go from one end of the world to the other in quest of a gracious year of agreeable and blithe tranquillity, for I have no other aim than to live cheerfully. Of sombre and dull tranquillity there is enough for me, but it puts me to sleep and makes me heavy-headed; I am not pleased with it. If there be any one, any pleasant party, in country, in city, in France, or elsewhere, resident or travelling, to whom my temperament may be agreeable and whose temperaments may be agreeable to me, they have but to whistle and I will go to them and supply them with essays in flesh and bone.

Since it is the privilege of the mind to hold his[16] own in old age, I advise him most earnestly to do so; let him grow green and flourish the while, if he can, like mistletoe on a dead tree. I fear that he is a traitor; he is so closely united to the body that he abandons me continually to follow that in its need. I privately flatter him, I frequent him, to no purpose; in vain do I try to withdraw him from this association and offer to his view Seneca and Catullus, and ladies, and royal dances; if his companion has the stone, it seems as if he had it also. Even the powers which are peculiar to him and especially his own can not then be roused; they are evidently chilled. There is no animation in his doings if at the time there is none in the body.

On Certain Verses of Virgil

Our masters mistake in this, when seeking the causes of the unusual sudden movements of the mind, that besides what they attribute of these to a divine transport, to love, to martial vehemence, to poesy, to wine, they have not assigned to health its share in them—to ebullient, lusty, solid, unbusied health, such as in other days the springtime of life and absence of care supplied me with uninterruptedly.[17] This fire of gaiety kindles in the mind flashes vivid and bright beyond our natural brightness, and the most lively, if not the most wide-reaching,[18] of our inspirations. Now truly, it is no wonder if a contrary condition weighs down my mind, fetters it, and draws from it a contrary effect.

It rises to no task when the body is faint.[19]

And yet the mind insists that I am beholden to him for yielding, he says, much less to this connection than is the ordinary habit of men. At all events, while we are at truce, let us banish evils and difficulties from our intercourse;

While we may, let clouded old age put away its frown;[20]

we ought to make gloomy experiences pleasant by jesting.[21] I love a cheerful and courteous wisdom, and shun harshness of manners and austerity, being suspicious of all grimness of aspect,

And the mournful arrogance of a crabbed countenance;[22]

And this sad-faced band also has its wantons.[23]

I heartily agree with Plato, who says that an easy or dif-

1144

ficult disposition has great influence on the goodness or badness of the soul.[24] Socrates had a uniform countenance, but serene and smiling;[25] not disagreeably uniform, like the elder Crassus, who was never seen to smile.[26] Virtue is a charming and gay quality.

I am quite sure that very few persons will frown at the freedom of my writings who have not more reason to frown at the freedom of their thoughts. I fit well enough with their humour, but I offend their eyes. It is a fine way to do, to be familiar with Plato's writings,[27] and to glide over his alleged relations with Phædo, Dion, Stella, and Archeanassa.[28] *One need not be ashamed to say what one is not ashamed to think.*[29] I detest an ever-complaining and melancholy mind, which glides over the joys of life and seizes and feeds upon its woes; like flies, which can not hold their footing on a very smooth and very slippery body, and cling to and rest on rough and uneven surfaces; and like cupping-glasses, too, which draw up and suck only bad blood.[30] I have determined to dare to say every thing that I dare do, and I dislike thoughts even that are not fit to publish. The worst of my actions and conditions does not seem to me so vile as I find vile and cowardly the not daring to avow it. Every one is discreet in confession; one should be so in action; boldness in doing wrong is in some sort atoned for and held in check by boldness in confession. He who should oblige himself to tell every thing would oblige himself to do nothing about which we are forced to be silent. God grant that the excess of my free-speaking may lead our men toward liberty, rising above these dastardly and hypocritical virtues born of our imperfections, that at the expense of my extravagance I may lead them on even to the point of good sense! To tell of one's vice, it must be seen and studied. They who conceal it from others usuallly conceal it from themselves, and do not deem it sufficiently hidden if they see it; they withdraw it, and disguise it to their own consciousness. *Why is it that no one confesses his own faults? Because he is still subject to them; it is only a waking man who can tell his dream.*[31] The ills of the body are revealed by growing worse; we find that what we call a cold or a sprain is gout. The ills of the soul are obscured by their strength; the most diseased man is least aware of them.[32] It is because of this that they must often be brought to life with a pitiless hand, laid bare, and torn from the depths of our bosom. As in the matter of good deeds, so likewise in the matter of evil deeds, there is sometimes satisfaction in confession. Is there any repulsiveness in misdoing which dispenses us from confession? It pains me to dissemble, so that I avoid taking another's man's secret into my keeping, not having the courage to disavow my knowledge; I can be silent about it, but deny it I can not without an effort and discomfort. To be very secret, one must be so by nature, not by obligation. It is little, in the service of princes, to be secret if one be not also a liar. If the man who asked Thales of Miletus whether he should solemnly deny having committed adultery had referred to me I should have told him not to do so. For lying appears to me still worse than adultery. Thales advised him quite otherwise, that he should swear in order to shield the greater by the lesser sin. Yet he advised him not so much a choice as a multiplication of sins.

Whereupon let us say this by the way, that we make it easy to a conscientious man when we offer him some difficulty to counterbalance a sin; but when we hem him in between two sins, we put him to a rude choice, as in the case of Origen. He was given the alternative of either practising idolatry or suffering himself to be carnally enjoyed by a big ruffian of an Ethiopian who was brought before him. He submitted to the former condition; and sinfully, according to one writer. On this assumption, those ladies would not be in the wrong, according to their erroneous views, who *protest* to us in these days that they would rather charge their conscience with ten men than one mass.

Whether it be indiscreet or not thus to publish one's errors, there is no great danger that it will become a precedent and custom; for Aristo said that the winds that men most fear are those that uncover them.[33] We must tuck away this absurd old mantle that hides our nature.[34] Men send their conscience to the brothel and keep their demeanour in good order. Even traitors and assassins bind themselves by conventional laws and connect with them what they are doing;[35] nevertheless, it is not for what is unlawful to blame what is anti-social, nor for deceit to find fault with indiscretion. It is a pity that a sinful man is not a fool as well and that decency palliates his vice. Such facings[36] befit only a good sound wall, which deserves to be preserved and to be whitened.

In support of the Huguenots, who denounce our auricular and private confession, I confess in public, solemnly and sincerely. St. Augustine, Origen, and Hippocrates have made known the errors of their opinions, and I of my character. I am eager to make myself known, and I care not how fully,[37] so that it be truly; or, to put it better, I have no eagerness at all, but I mortally shun the being mistaken for a different man by those who chance to know my name.[38]

1147

On Certain Verses of Virgil

He who does all things for honour and for renown, what does he think to gain by showing himself to the world masked, concealing his real self from the knowledge of the crowd? Praise a hunchback for his fine figure—he has reason to receive it as an insult; if you are a coward and men honour you as a brave man, is it you who are talked of? They take you for another. I had as lief a fellow who is one of the least of the train should take pleasure in the cap-doffings of those who think that he is the head of the troop. As Archelaus, King of Macedonia, was passing through the streets, some one poured water on him. The bystanders said that he ought to punish the man. "But, indeed," he declared, "he did not pour the water on me, but on him whom he thought I was."[39] Socrates replied to him who informed him that he was spoken ill of, "Not at all; there is nothing of me in what they say."[40] For my part, if any one should praise me for being a good pilot, for being very modest, or for being very chaste, I should owe him no thanks; and likewise, if one should call me a traitor, a robber, or a drunkard, I should deem myself as little insulted. They who do not know themselves may feed upon undeserved approbation; not I, who see myself and scrutinise myself even to my bowels, and who know well what appertains to me. I am pleased to be less praised, provided that I am better known. I might be considered a wise man for wisdom of such sort as I consider to be folly.

It annoys me that the ladies use my Essays merely as a common piece of furniture, furniture for the reception-room. This chapter will make me suitable for the boudoir. I love their society when it is a little private; in public it is without favour or savour.

1148

On Certain Verses of Virgil

In taking farewell we warm up, more than ordinarily, our affection for the things we are leaving. I am taking my last leave of the sports of the world. These are our last embraces. But let us come to my theme.

What harm has the genital act, so natural, so necessary, and so lawful, done to humanity, that we dare not speak of it without shame, and exclude it from serious and orderly conversation? We boldly utter the words, *kill, rob, betray;* and the other we only dare to utter under our breath. Does this mean that the less of it we breathe in words, the more are we at liberty to swell our thoughts with it? For it is amusing that the words which are least used, least written, and most hushed up, should be the best known and the most generally understood. There is no person of any age or morals but knows them as well as he knows the word *bread.* They are impressed upon each of us, without being expressed, without voice and without form. [And the sex that does it most is charged to hush it up.]

It is also amusing that it is an action we have placed in the sanctuary of silence, from which to tear it by force is a crime, even for the purpose of accusing it and bringing it to justice. And we do not dare to scourge it but in roundabout and figurative terms. A great favour indeed for a criminal to be so execrable that justice thinks it wrong to touch and see him; free and saved by the favour of the severity of his sentence! Is it not the same as with books, that sell better and become more public for being suppressed? For my part I will gladly take the word of Aristotle for it, who says, "To be shamefaced is an ornament of youth, but a reproach to old age."

These lines are preached in the old school, a school with

which I hold much more than with the modern; its virtues appear to me greater, its vices less:

> Those who strive too much to flee
> Sin equally with those who follow too closely.[41]

> Thou, Goddess, dost rule the world alone
> Without thee naught rises to the shores of light
> Nor aught of joyful nor of lovely is born.[42]

I know not who could have set Pallas and the Muses at variance with Venus, and made them cool towards Cupid; but I know of no deities that agree so well together, and are more indebted to one another. Take from the Muses their amorous fancies and you will rob them of the best entertainment they have, and of the noblest matter of their work. And if you deprive Cupid of the society and service of Poetry you will blunt his best weapons. In this way you charge the god of sweet intimacy and amity, and the patron goddesses of humanity and justice, with the sin of ingratitude and forgetfulness.

I have not been so long cashiered from the staff of this god but that I still retain a memory of his worth:

> I know the traces of ancient flame.[43]

There is still some heat and emotion after the fever:

> In wintry age let not this love grow cool.[44]

Withered and drooping though I be, I still feel a few tepid remains of that past ardour:

> As the deep Aegean, when no more blow the winds
> That rolled its waves with troublous blast,

1150

On Certain Verses of Virgil

Doth yet of tempests past some show retain,
And here and there its billows cast.[45]

But, if I understand the matter, the power and importance of this god, as portrayed in poetry, are much greater and more alive than they are in reality:

And poetry has fingers too.[46]

Her pictures are somehow more amorous than Amor himself. Venus is not so beautiful, quite naked and alive and panting, as she is in these lines of Virgil:

The Goddess ceased, and with the soft embrace
Of snowy arms about him wound. Quick he caught
The wonted fire; the old heat pierced his heart;
Ran through his melting frame; as oftentimes
A fiery rift, burst by the thunder-clap,
Runs quivering down the cloud, with flash of light.
. . . So saying, he gave
The embrace she longed for, on her bosom sank,
And wooed calm slumber to o'erglide his limbs.[47]

What strikes me is that he depicts her a little too passionate for a married Venus. In this sober contract the desires are not generally so wanton; they are dull and more blunted. Love hates to be held by any tie but himself, and goes feebly to work in intimacies formed and continued under a different name, such as marriage. Family and fortune are there rightly accounted as important, or more so, than charm and beauty. We do not marry for ourselves, whatever they may say; we marry as much, or more, for posterity, for the family. The custom and interest of marriage concern our stock, long after we are dead.

On Certain Verses of Virgil

For this reason I approve of its being arranged by a third hand rather than by our own, by others' good sense rather than our own. How totally different is all this to a love compact! Besides, it is a kind of incest in this sacred and time-honoured alliance to employ the extravagant actions of amorous license, as I think I have said elsewhere. We should, says Aristotle, approach our wives discreetly and soberly, lest the pleasure of being touched too lasciviously should transport them beyond the bounds of reason. What he says upon the account of conscience the physicians say upon the account of health, "that an over-heated, voluptuous and assidious pleasure corrupts the seed and hinders conception." They say, on the other hand, "that in a languid intercourse, as this is by its nature, the man should offer himself rarely and at considerable intervals, in order that a proper and fertile heat may be stored up":

To absorb their fill of love, and entertain.[48]

I know of no marriages that are so soon troubled and that so soon come to grief as those which are contracted on account of beauty and amorous desires. It needs more solid and permanent foundations, and we should proceed circumspectly; such an exuberant vivacity can never serve any lasting purpose.

They who think to honour marriage by joining love with it proceed, it seems to me, like those who, to favour virtue, maintain that nobility is nothing else than virtue.[49] They are things which have some affinity; but therewith great diversity; we should not confound their names and their titles; we wrong both the one and the other by confusing them. Nobility is an admirable function, and invented with

1152

good reason; but inasmuch as it is a function that is dependent upon others and that may belong to a man who is vicious and worthless, it is of a value very far below that of virtue; if it be a virtue,[50] it is an artificial and visible one, dependent upon time and fortune; different in form in different countries; belonging to this life[51] and mortal; as much without origin as the river Nile; a thing of genealogy and generality; that passes from one man to another with no change; that is derived from the force of preceding conditions—a very feeble force.[52] Knowledge, strength, goodness, beauty, wealth, all other qualities have relation to communication and intercourse; this one is fulfilled in itself, of no commerce in the service of others. There was offered to one of our kings the choice between two competitors for the same post, of whom one was of good birth, the other not at all so. He ordered that, without regard to this difference, the one who had the most merit should be chosen; but if their worth were exactly the same, then the point of birth should be regarded; this was giving it its just rank. Antigonus, when an untried youth[53] asked him for the post of his father, a man of worth who had recently died, "My friend," he said, "in such favours I do not so much consider the rank of my soldiers as I do their prowess." In truth, it should not be as with the officials of the kings of Sparta,—trumpeters, minstrels, cooks,—who were succeeded by their children in their offices, however ignorant they might be, in preference to the most experienced in the occupation.[54] The people of Calicut treat their nobles as more than human. Marriage is forbidden them and all other vocations than war. Of concubines they can have their fill, and the woman as many lovers, without jealousy of one another; but it is a capital and irremissible crime to mate with a person of another rank than their own, and they deem themselves polluted if they are merely touched by such a one in passing; and as their nobility is wondrously wronged and dishonoured by this, they kill those who have merely come a little too near them; so that those of low birth[55] are required to cry aloud as they walk,—as the gondoliers in Venice do at street corners,—in order not to hit against one another; and the nobles order them to turn to this side or that, as they[56] choose. Thus they avoid the ignominy which they regard as lasting; the others, certain death. No length of time, no princely favour, no office or virtue or wealth can transform a plebian into a noble. These conditions are favoured by this custom, that marriages between persons of different trades are forbidden: a woman of a shoemaking family may not marry a carpenter; and parents are compelled to train their children to the father's precise occupation and to no other, whereby the distinction and continuance of their lot is maintained.[57]

A good marriage, if there are such, rejects the company and conditions of love; it strives to show forth those of friendship. It is a calm fellowship of life, full of fidelity, of trust, and of an endless number of useful and substantial mutual duties and obligations; no woman who rightly perceives its savour,—

Whom the marriage torch has joined on the desired day,[58]—

would desire to be in the place of mistress to her husband. If she be established in his affection as a wife, she is therein much more honourably and securely established. If he be

1154

elsewhere excited and eager, let him none the less be asked which he would prefer should be put to shame, his wife or his mistress; whose misfortune would grieve him most; for which he desires a higher position; these questions[59] admit no doubt in a sound marriage. That we see so few good marriages is a sign of its price and its value. If well formed and well regarded,[60] there is no more admirable feature of our social life. We can not do without it, and yet we express contempt for it. The same thing happens that we see about cages: the birds outside are in despair at not getting in, and those within feel equal discomfort at not getting out. Socrates, being asked which was more advantageous, to take or not to take a wife, replied: "Whichever a man does, he will repent it."[61] It is a covenant to which the saying, *Man is to man either a god or a wolf*,[62] aptly applies; the meeting of many qualities is needed to frame it. It is in these days apparently best fitted for simple and common souls, with whom pleasures, curiosity, and idleness do not so much disturb it. Natures such as mine, of irregular humours, which detest every sort of bondage and obligation, are not so well adapted to it:

And it is sweeter to me to live with my neck unyoked.[63]

According to my own purpose I should have shunned marrying Wisdom herself, if she would have had me; but say what we may, custom and the usage of ordinary life carry us along. Most of my acts are guided by example, not by choice. As it was, I did not enter into it exactly by my own invitation: I was led to it by others and carried to it by external opportunities; for not only merely desirable things, but things most ill-favoured and imperfect and to be avoided, may become acceptable from some condition or circumstance, so feeble is man's attitude. And I came certainly more ill-prepared at that time, and more reluctant than I am now, after I have tested it; and, libertine as I am thought to be, I have in fact observed the laws of marriage more strictly than I have either promised or hoped to do. It is no longer the time to kick when a man has allowed himself to be hobbled; one should prudently care for his liberty; but when he has submitted to bondage, he must obey the laws of common duty—or at least strive to do so. They who enter into this bargain only to bear themselves therein with hatred and contempt act unjustly and unsuitably; and this fine precept which I see passing from hand to hand among women, like a sacred oracle,—"Treat thy husband as thy master and beware of him as of a traitor,"—which means, bear yourself toward him with a constrained, hostile, and distrustful deference, a war-cry of defiance,—is equally insulting and impossible. I am of too mild a nature for such thorny intentions. To tell the truth, I have not yet attained such perfection of mental ability and agility as to confound reasonableness with injustice, and to turn into ridicule all order and rule that does not please my appetite; because I detest superstition, I do not forthwith fling myself into irreligion. If a man does not always do his duty, he should at least always love it and recognise it. It is treachery to marry without wedding. Let us continue.

Our poet depicts a marriage in which there is perfect harmony and propriety, in which there is, however, not much loyalty. Did he mean to imply that it is not impossible

On Certain Verses of Virgil

to yield to the power of love, and yet reserve some duty towards marriage; and that it may be bruised without being altogether broken? Many a serving man shoes his master's mule without necessarily hating him. Beauty, opportunity, fate (for Fate also has a hand in it).

> There is a Fate that rules our hidden parts;
> For if the stars be not propitious,
> Virility will not avail thee aught,[64]

have attached her to a stranger; not so wholly perhaps but that there remains some tie by which she is still held to her husband. It is like two plans, with distinct routes, not to be confounded with one another. A woman may surrender to a certain man whom she would in no case have married; I do not mean on account of the state of his fortune, but for his personal qualities. Few men have married their mistresses without repenting it.

And even in the other world, what a poor match Jupiter made of it with the wife whom he had first seduced and enjoyed in love's dalliance! That is, as the proverb puts it, "to cack in the basket, and then put it on your head."

I have seen in my time, in a good family, love shamefully and indecently cured by marriage; the considerations are too different. We love, without pledging ourselves, two different and contradictory things.

Isocrates said that the city of Athens pleased after the manner of the ladies we serve for love. Every man loved to go there, to saunter and pass the time; but no one loved it so well as to marry it, that is to say, to reside and settle there.

I have been annoyed to see husbands hate their wives

merely because they themselves have wronged them. We should at all events not love them less for our own faults; pity and repentance should at least make them more dear to us.

They are different ends, he says, and yet in some sort compatible. Marriage has, for its share, usefulness, justice, honour and constancy; a stale but more durable pleasure. Love is grounded on pleasure alone, and it is indeed more gratifying to the senses, keener and more acute; a pleasure stirred and kept alive by difficulties. There must be a sting and a smart in it. It ceases to be love if it have no shafts and no fire. The liberality of the ladies is too profuse in marriage, and blunts the edge of affection and desire. Observe what pains Lycurgus and Plato take, in their Laws, to avoid that disadvantage.

Women are not by any means to blame when they reject the rules of life which have been introduced into the world, seeing that it is the men who made them without their consent. Intrigues and wranglings between them and ourselves are only natural; the closest agreement we enjoy with them is still attended with tumults and storms.

In the opinion of our author we treat them without consideration in this respect: After knowing that they are incomparably more capable and ardent in the sexual act than we, of which that priest of antiquity was a witness, who was first a man and then a woman:

Venus was known to him in both disguises;[65]

after hearing moreover from their own lips the proof that was given, in different centuries, by an Emperor and an Empress of Rome, both famous master-workers in the art

On Certain Verses of Virgil

(he indeed deflowered in one night ten Sarmatian virgins, his captives, but she actually suffered in one night twenty-five assaults, changing her company according to need and liking:

> Still burning with unconquerable lust
> Weary she gave up, but still unsatisfied;[66])

and after the dispute which took place in Catalonia, when a woman complaining of her husband's too unremitting attentions, not so much, I take it, because she was inconvenienced by them (for I believe in no miracles, except in matters of faith), as, under this pretext, to restrict and curb, in this the most fundamental act of marriage, the authority of husbands over their wives, and to show that their perverseness and ill-will extend beyond the nuptial couch and tread under foot even the sweets and delights of Venus; and the husband, certainly an unnatural brute, replying that even on fast-days he could not do with less than ten, the Queen of Aragon interposed with that notable sentence, by which, after mature deliberation with her Council, that good Queen, to establish for all times a rule and example of the moderation and modesty required in a rightful marriage, prescribed as a lawful and necessary limit the number of six per diem; thus renouncing and surrendering a great part of her sex's needs and desires, to set up, as she said, "an easy and consequently permanent and immutable formula;" against which the doctors exclaim, "what must be the appetite and lust of women, when their reason, their amendment and virtue are taxed at such a rate!"

Considering these varying estimates of our sexual needs, and seeing that Solon, head of the school of lawgivers, assesses this conjugal intercourse, if we are not to be found wanting, at no more than three times a month; after believing and preaching all this, we have gone and allotted them continence for their particular portion, at the risk of the last and extreme penalties.

There is no passion more exacting than this, which we expect them alone to resist, as being not simply an ordinary vice, but an abominable and accursed thing, and worse than irreligion and parricide; whilst we men at the same time yield to it without blame or reproach. Even those of us who have tried to master it have often enough had to admit how difficult, or rather how impossible it was, by the use of material remedies, to deaden, to weaken and cool the body.

On the other hand, we expect them to be healthy, robust, plump, well nourished and chaste at the same time; that is to say, both hot and cold. For marriage, whose function we say it is to keep them from burning, brings them but little relief, as we live nowadays. If they take a husband who is still exuberant with the vigour of youth, he will make a boast of expending it on others:

> If you don't mend your ways, we'll go to law.
> Your vigour, bought with a thousand crowns
> Is no more yours, my Bassus; you have sold it.[67]

The philosopher Polemon was rightly haled before justice by his wife, for sowing in a barren field the fruit that was meant for the genital field.

If on the other hand, they take one of the worn-out kind, behold them in full wedlock worse off than virgins and widows! We think they are well provided for because they have a man at their side. By the same reasoning the Romans held Clodia Laeta, a Vestal virgin, to have been violated because Caligula had approached her, although it was averred that he had no more than approached her. Their need is, on the contrary, thereby redoubled, since the contact and company of any male whatever excites their heat, which in solitude would remain more dormant.

And, in order, in all probability, to render their chastity the more meritorious by this circumstance and consideration, Boleslas and Kinge, his wife, King and Queen of Poland, by mutual agreement consecrated it by a vow, while lying together on their very wedding-night, and kept it in the teeth of conjugal opportunities.

We train them from childhood in the service of love; their charm, their dressing up, their knowledge, their language, all their instruction, have only this end in view. Their governesses keep suggesting amorous ideas to them, though always with the intention of exciting their disgust. My daughter (who is the only child I have) is at an age when the most precocious of them are allowed by the laws to marry; she is constitutionally backward, thin and delicate, and has accordingly been brought up by her mother in a retired and particular manner, so that she is only now beginning to put off her childish naïveté.

She was reading a French book when I was present, and came across the word *fouteau*, the name of a well-known tree (beech). The woman to whose care she was entrusted rather rudely stopped her short and made her pass over the danger spot. I let her have her way in order not to disturb their rules, for I never meddle with that government; feminine policy has a mysterious procedure, and we must leave it to them. But, if I am not mistaken, the conversation of

On Certain Verses of Virgil

twenty lackeys could not, in six months, have implanted in her imagination, the meaning and use and all the consequences of the sound of those criminating syllables, as this good old lady did by her reprimand and interdict.

> The virgin joys to learn the Ionic dance
> And bend with plastic limb, still but a child
> Until incestuous love's unhallowed dreams
> Before her fancy swim.[68]

Let them but drop their formal modesty a little, give them occasion to talk freely; compared with them we are but children in that science. Only hear them describing our pursuits and our conversation; they will very soon let you know that we can bring them nothing they have not known and digested without our help. Can it be, as Plato says, that they have once been dissolute boys?

My ear once happened to be in a place where it was able, without being suspected, to snatch a little of their talk. Why cannot I repeat it? By our Lady, said I, what need is there to study the phrases of Amadis and the books of Boccaccio and Aretino, and think ourselves so knowing? It is a mere waste of time. There is no word, no example, no proceeding, that they know not better than our books; it is an instruction that is born in the veins.

> By Venus herself inspired of old,[69]

which those good schoolmasters, Nature, Youth and Health, continually breathe into their souls. They have no need to learn it; they breed it:

> Not more delighted is the snow-white dove,

1162

On Certain Verses of Virgil

> Or if there be a thing more prone to love,
> Still to be billing with her male than is
> Woman with every man she meets to kiss.[70]

If the natural violence of their desire were not held a little in check by the fear and honour with which they have been provided, we should be shamed. The whole movement of the world resolves itself into and leads to this pairing; it is a matter infused throughout; it is a centre to which all things are directed. We may still see some of the laws of old and wise Rome, drawn up for the service of Love; and Socrates' precepts for the instruction of courtezans:

> On silken cushions they love to lie,
> Those little books the Stoics write.[71]

Zeno, amongst his laws, gives rules for the spreading and the attack in deflowering. What was the drift of the philosopher Strato's book, Of Carnal Conjunction? Of what did Theophrastus ·treat in those he called, one The Lover, the other Of Love? Of what Aristippus, in his work Of Ancient Delights? What was the aim of Plato's so lengthy and lively descriptions of the boldest amours of his time? And of the book Of the Lover, by Demetrius of Phalera? And Clinias, or the Ravished Lover, of Heraclides of Pontus? And Antisthenes' Of Begetting Children, or Of Weddings, or his other, Of the Master or the Lover? And Aristo's Of Amorous Exercises? Those of Cleanthes, one Of Love, the other Of the Art of Loving? The Amorous Dialogues of Sphaerus? And the Fable of Jupiter and Juno, by Chrysippus, which is shameless beyond all bearing, and of his fifty so lascivious Epistles? For I must omit the writings of the philosophers who followed the Epicurean school [the protectors of sensuality].

In ancient times fifty deities were subservient to this business. And there were countries where, to assuage the lust of those who came to pay their devotions, they kept girls and boys in the churches for enjoyment, and it was a ceremonious act to use them before going to service. *Doubtless incontinence is necessary for continence, as a fire is extinguished by fire.*[72]

In most parts of the world that part of the body was deified. In one and the same province some flayed off the skin to offer and consecrate a piece of it, and others offered and consecrated their semen. In another province the young men publicly pierced and opened it in several places between the flesh and skin, and through the openings thrust skewers, as long and thick as they could bear them; and of these skewers they afterwards made a fire, as an offering to the gods. They were reputed weak and unchaste if they were dismayed by the force of this cruel pain. In another place the most sacred magistrate was revered and known by that member; and in some ceremonies an effigy of it was carried about in state, to the honour of various divinities.

At the festival of the Bacchanals the Egyptian ladies carried about their necks a wooden effigy of it, exquisitely carved, big and heavy according to their capacity; besides which the statue of their god exhibited one which exceeded in size the rest of the body.

In my neighbourhood the married women twist their kerchief over their forehead into the shape of one, to boast of the enjoyment they have out of it; and when they become widows they turn it behind and hide it under their coif.

On Certain Verses of Virgil

The most sedate of Roman matrons thought it an honour to offer flowers and garlands to the god Priapus; and the virgins at the time of their nuptials were made to sit upon his least seemly parts. And I know not but that I have seen something of the like devotion in my time.

What was the meaning of that ridiculous part of the hose our fathers wore, and which is still seen on our Swiss? What is the idea of the show we still make of our pieces, in effigy under our galligaskins; and what is worse, often, by falsehood and imposture, above their natural size?

I am inclined to think that a dress of this kind was invented in the best and most conscientious ages in order not to deceive the world, and that every man might, publicly and boldly, render an account of his capacity. The most simple nations still have it, nearly corresponding to the real thing. In those days the workman was taught the art, as it is practised in taking the measure of an arm or a foot.

That good man who, when I was young, castrated so many beautiful and antique statues in his great city, that the eye might not be offended, following the advice of that other ancient worthy:

Shame to those who expose the naked body.[73]

should have considered that, as in the mysteries of the Good Goddess all male semblance was precluded, nothing would be gained unless he also had horses and asses, and in short nature, castrated:

> All things on earth, man and brute,
> The ocean tribes, beasts, gaudy birds,
> Rush to passion's pyre.[74]

On Certain Verses of Virgil

The Gods, says Plato, have furnished us with a dis-
obedient and tyrannical member, which, like an animal in
its fury, attempts, in the violence of its desire, to subdue
everything to its power. So also to the women they have
given a greedy and voracious animal which, if denied its
food in due season, goes mad in its impatience of delay;
and, breathing its rage into their bodies, stops up the con-
duits, arrests breathing, and causes a thousand kinds of ills,
till, having imbibed the fruit of the thirst common to all
women, it has copiously bedewed and sown the ground of
their matrix.

Now my legislator should also have considered that it is
perhaps a more chaste and salutary practice to let them
know betimes the living reality, than to leave them to guess
it according to the licence and heat of their imagination.
In place of the real parts their desire and hope substitute
others triply magnified. And a certain man of my acquaintance ruined his chances by openly disclosing his in a place
where he was not yet enabled to put them to their proper
and more serious use.

What mischief is not done by these pictures of enormous
size that the boys scatter all over the galleries and staircases
of the royal houses! From them they derive a cruel contempt
for our natural capacity.

How do we know that Plato had not an eye to this when
he ordained, following other well-established republics, that
men and women, young and old, should appear naked in
view of one another in his gymnasiums?

The Indian women, who see their men undressed, have
at least cooled their sense of sight. And, although the women of that great kingdom of Pegu, who have nothing to

cover them below the waist but a cloth slit in front, and so skimp that, however much modesty they may try to observe, they reveal themselves at every step they take, may tell us that is a device for attracting the men to their sides and wean them from intercourse with their own sex, a practice to which that nation is universally addicted, we might reply that they lose thereby more than they gain, and that a complete hunger is sharper than one that has been satisfied at least by the eyes.

Besides, Livia said, "that to an honest woman a naked man is no more than a statue."

The Lacedemonian women, more virginal as wives than our maidens are, every day saw the young men of their city stripped for their exercises, and were not very particular themselves, as Plato says, sufficiently covered by their virtue without a farthingale.

But those men, mentioned by Saint Augustine, who raised a doubt whether the women, at the universal judgement, will rise again in their own sex, and not rather in ours, lest they should tempt us in that holy state, have ascribed a wonderful power of temptation to nudity.

In short we lure and flesh them by every means; we incessantly heat and excite their imagination, and then we shout when we are hurt. Let us confess the truth: there is hardly one of us who does not fear the disgrace his wife's misdeeds may bring upon him more than his own; who does not look more tenderly after his good spouse's conscience than his own (wonderful charity!); who would not rather be a thief and guilty of sacrilege, and that his wife were a heretic and murderess, than that she should be less chaste than her husband.

On Certain Verses of Virgil

And they would willingly offer to seek a livelihood in the law-courts, or a reputation in war, rather than be obliged, in the midst of pleasures and idleness, to keep so difficult a guard. Do you think they do not see that there is not a tradesman, or an attorney, or a soldier, who will not leave his business to run after this other; nor even a streetporter or cobbler, weary and jaded as they are with labour and hunger?

> For all that did Achaemenes possess,
> Or wealth Mygdonian of rich Phrygia
> Or Arab treasure-house, wouldst give one tress
>   Of thy Licymnia,
>
> While to thy burning kiss her neck she bends,
> Or with feigned cruelty that kiss denies
> Which ravished then the thief she more commends
>   Sometimes to ravish tries?[75]

What an iniquitous balancing of sins! Both we and they are capable of a thousand more mischievous and unnatural depravities than lasciviousness. But we create and weigh sins not according to Nature, but according to our interest; wherefore they assume such unequal shapes. The harshness of our decree makes the addiction of the women to that sin more serious and sinful than its nature admits of, and involves it in consequences which are worse than their cause.

I doubt if the achievements of an Alexander or a Cæsar surpass in difficulty the steadfastness of a handsome young woman, brought up after our fashion, in the open view and in contact with the world, assailed by so many contrary examples, keeping herself entire in the midst of a thousand powerful and persistent solicitations. There is no activity more abounding in thorny difficulties, nor more active, than this inactivity. I should think it easier to wear a suit of armour all one's life than a virginity. And the vow of chastity is the most noble of all vows, as being the hardest. *The power of the Devil is in the loins,* says Saint Jerome.

Certainly the most arduous and rigorous of human duties is that we have resigned to the ladies, and we leave them the glory of it. That should serve them as a particular spur to persist in it; it offers them a fine occasion to challenge us, and to tread under foot that vain pre-eminence in courage and valour that we claim over them. They will find, if they take notice, that they will be not only very highly esteemed for it, but also better loved.

A gallant man does not give up his pursuit for a refusal, provided it be a refusal of chastity, not of choice. Though we swear and threaten and complain ever so much, we lie; we love them the better for it. There is no greater allurement than a chastity that is not hard and forbidding. It is stupid and vulgar to persist obstinately in the face of hatred and contempt; but to do so against a virtuous and constant resolution, accompanied by a grateful disposition, is the action of a noble and generous spirit. They may gratefully accept our services to a certain degree, and with due modesty make us feel that they do not disdain us.

For it is indeed a cruel law, if only for its difficulty, which commands them to abhor us because we adore them, and hate us because we love them. Why should they not listen to our offers and requests, so long as they keep within the bounds of modesty? Why should they try to detect the note of some more licentious meaning under our words? A Queen of our time wittily said that "to repel these approaches was a testimony of weakness, and an accusation of her own facility; and that a lady who had not been tempted could not vaunt her chastity."

The bounds of honour are not by any means cut so closely; it is quite able, without transgressing, to relax its severity, and give itself a freer rein. Beyond its frontier there is some expanse of land, free, indifferent and neuter. He who has hunted and forcibly run it home, even into its corner and stronghold, is wanting in tact if he is not satisfied with his fortune. The prize of victory is ever estimated by its difficulty.

Would you know what impression your assiduity and your merit have made on her heart? Judge of it by her character. Many a woman may give more without giving so much. The obligation of a benefit is entirely in proportion to the will of him who gives. Other circumstances which accompany the conferring of a benefit are dumb, dead and fortuitous. This little may cost her dearer to give than it may cost her companion to give her all. If ever rarity was a sign of esteem it must be so in this case; do not consider how little it is, but how few have it. The value of a coin changes according to the stamp and the place where it is minted.

Whatever the spite and indiscretion of some men, at the height of their discontent, may drive them to say, virtue and truth always recover their ground. I have known women, whose reputation had long been unjustly compromised, to recover their good name in the eyes of the world by their constancy alone, without any effort or cunning. All did penance and took back what they had once believed. From being a little under suspicion as girls they have risen to the first rank among good and honourable ladies.

Somebody said to Plato, "All the world is maligning you." "Let them say," he said, "I will live in such a way that they shall change their tone."

Besides the fear of God and the reward of so rare a fame, which should incite them to keep themselves unspotted, the corruption of the world we live in compels them to do so; and if I were in their place, there is nothing I would not rather do than entrust my reputation in such hands.

In my time the pleasure of telling (a pleasure which in sweetness falls little short of that of doing) was only permitted to those who had some trusty and unique friend. Nowadays, when men come together at table or elsewhere, their ordinary talk consists of boasts of favours received and the secret liberality of the ladies. Truly it shows too mean and vulgar a spirit to allow those tender charms to be so cruelly followed up, pounded and tumbled about by ungrateful, indiscreet, and empty-headed fops.

This our intemperate and unjustifiable exasperation against that sin is born of the most futile and turbulent disease that afflicts the mind of man, which is Jealousy.

> Who'd shrink from torch to take a light?[76]
> Whate'er they give, they nothing lose.[77]

She and her sister Envy appear to me the most foolish of the tribe. Of the latter I can say little; though described as a strong and powerful passion, she has had the good grace never to come my way. As to the other, I know her, at least by sight. The animals have a sense of it: the shepherd Crastis, having become enamoured of a goat, her ram, in a fit of jealousy, came and butted his head as he was asleep, and crushed it.

We have exceeded in this passion, after the example of some barbarian nations; the best disciplined have not escaped, which is reasonable, but they have not been driven to extremes by it:

> Ne'er did adulterer by husband slain
> The purple Stygian waters stain.[78]

Lucullus, Cæsar, Pompey, Antony, Cato, and other brave men were cuckolds and knew it without making a fuss about it. In those times there was only a fool of a Lepidus who died of grief for that reason:

> Ah wretch, if you're taken in the act
> They'll drag you feet first through the door,
> And feed you to turnips and red mullets.[79]

And the god of our poet, when he surprised one of his fellow-gods with his wife, was satisfied with putting them to shame;

> And one of the gods, not most austere,
> Wished to share the blame;[80]

yet none the less is he warmed by the sweet caresses she offers him, and complains that for such a trifle she should distrust his affection:

> Why Goddess mine, invent such pleas?
> And take thy trust from me?[81]

Nay, she asks a favour of him for a bastard of hers,

1172

On Certain Verses of Virgil

As mother I do ask thy arms,[82]

which is generously granted by him; and Vulcan speaks honourably of Æneas:

Arms for a hero must be made.[83]

Truly a superhuman humanity! And I am willing to leave this excess of kindness to the gods:

Nor is it meet to equal men with gods.[84]

With respect to the confusion of children, besides that the most thoughtful legislators consider it desirable and ordain it in their republics, it does not trouble the women, in whom, however, that feeling is, for some reason or other, still more justified:

Often Juno, queen of heaven
Was maddened by her spouse's faults.[85]

When jealousy seizes those poor weak and unresisting souls, it is pitiful to see how cruelly it catches them in its toils and masters them. It worms itself into them under the cloak of affection, but when it once possesses them, the same causes which served as the foundation of kindness, serve as the foundation of a deadly hatred. Of all mental diseases it is the most easily fed and the most difficult to cure. The virtue, the health, the merit, the reputation of the husband are the firebrands of their fury and malevolence:

No hate implacable, save the hate of love.[86]

This feverish passion disfigures and corrupts all that is otherwise good and beautiful in them; and there is no act of

On Certain Verses of Virgil

a jealous woman, however chaste and however good a house-wife she may be, that does not reveal a bitter and nagging spirit. It is a furious perturbation of mind, which will drive them to an extreme the very opposite to its cause.

This was absurdly exemplified by one Octavius in Rome: Having lain with Pontia Posthumia, his affection was so much increased by enjoyment, that he pestered her with entreaties to marry him. Being unable to persuade her, his excessive love hurled him to the opposite extreme of the most cruel and deadly hatred, and he killed her.

In like manner the ordinary symptoms of that other love-malady are intestine hatreds, plots, and conspiracies:

We know what woman scorned can do,[87]

and a rage which eats into itself the more it is obliged to shield itself under the cloak of kindness.

Now the duty of chastity is far-reaching. Is it their will that we would have them curb? That is a very supple and active thing. It is too nimble to be stayed. What if dreams sometimes carry them so far that they cannot deny them? It is not in them, nor perhaps in Chastity herself, since she is a female, to guard against lust and desire. If their will alone had the power of injuring us, where should we be? Imagine the great scramble, supposing any man had the privilege of being borne, fully equipped, without eyes to see or tongue to tell, to every one who had the opportunity to receive him!

The Scythian women put out the eyes of all their slaves and prisoners of war, to make use of them more freely and more secretly.

O what a tremendous advantage is opportunity! Should

1174

any one ask me what is the first advantage in love, I should reply that it is to be able to make one's opportunity; likewise the second, and the third as well. There you have the key to everything.

I have often wanted luck, but sometimes I have also wanted enterprise; God shield him from harm who can laugh at this! It needs greater temerity in these days, which our young men excuse under the name of ardour; but if the ladies looked closely into it, they would find that it rather proceeds from contempt. I used to be scrupulously afraid of giving offence, and am inclined to respect where I love. Besides, in this traffic, if you leave out the esteem, you will destroy the glamour. I like the lover to be something of a boy, timid, and a slave. If not quite in this, I have in other situations something of the foolish bashfulness that Plutarch speaks of, and which at various times in the course of my life has been to me a blemish and a source of harm. It is a quality that is not in keeping with my nature as a whole.

But what are we if not a bundle of rebellions and discrepancies? My eyes are as sensitive to suffer a refusal as they are to refuse; and it troubles me so much to be troublesome to others, that, on occasions where duty compels me to ask a favour of another when the granting of it is doubtful and would put him to any cost, I do so sparingly and reluctantly. But if it is for my own particular benefit (although Homer truly says, "that in a poor man bashfulness is a foolish virtue") I usually commission a third person to blush for me. And if another requests a favour of me, I find it equally difficult to show him the door; so that I have sometimes had the inclination, but not the strength of will, to deny.

On Certain Verses of Virgil

It is folly therefore to try to curb in women a desire that is so acute and so natural to them. And when I hear them boast of having so cold and virginal a disposition, I laugh at them; I tell them they are too backward. If she is a toothless and decrepit old woman, or, if young, sapless and consumptive, though it is not altogether credible, there may at least be a semblance of truth in it. But those who still move and breathe only make the matter worse, seeing that he who excuses himself incautiously accuses himself. Like a gentleman of my neighbourhood who was suspected of impotence,

> Whose dagger, hanging limp as beet
> Could never rise to middle height.[88]

Three or four days after his wedding, to vindicate his reputation, he went about boldly declaring that he had ridden twenty stages the night before. His own words were used to convict him of ignorance, and to unmarry him.

Besides, when the women make the aforesaid boast they prove nothing; for there can be neither continence nor virtue where there is no temptation to resist. "That is true, they should say, but I am not one to make an easy surrender." Even the saints say the same. I am speaking of those who boast in good earnest of their coldness and insensibility, and expect to be believed with a serious countenance. For when they say it with an affected air, when their eyes belie their words, when they talk the cant of the profession, which must be taken against the grain, I find it amusing. I am a great admirer of naturalness and plainness of speech; but there is no hope for them. If it is not wholly simple and childish, it is improper for ladies, and out of place in that kind of intercourse; it very soon inclines to effrontery.

On Certain Verses of Virgil

Only fools are taken in by their masks and faces. Lying is there in the seat of honour; it is a roundabout way, and leads to the truth by the postern-gate. If we cannot curb their imagination, what do we expect of them? Deeds? There are enough of these that avoid all outside communication, by which chastity may be corrupted:

That's often done that's done in secret.[89]

And the people we fear least are perhaps the most to be feared; their silent sins are the worst:

A simple prostitute offends me less.[90]

There are acts which, without immodesty on their part, may cost them their virginity, and, what is more, without their intention. *Sometimes a midwife, examining a virgin's chasitity, by evil-mindedness, unskilfulness, or accident, has destroyed it.*[91] Many a one, in seeking her maidenhead, has lost it; and many a one has killed it in sport.

We cannot precisely circumscribe the actions we would forbid them. Our rules must be worded in general and ambiguous terms. The very idea we create of their chastity is ridiculous; for, among the extreme patterns I have are Fatua, wife of Faunus, who never allowed any man to see her after her wedding, and the wife of Hiero, who did not realize the fact that her husband had a stinking breath, thinking it was a characteristic of all men. To satisfy us, they must become invisible and devoid of senses.

Now we must confess that our difficulty in estimating this duty lies chiefly in the disposition. There have been husbands who have suffered that mishap, not only without blaming their wives or feeling injured by them, but under a sense of singular obligation and acknowledgement of their virtue. Many a woman there has been who, though she loved honour more than life, has prostituted herself to the furious appetite of a deadly enemy, to save her husband's life; doing for him what she would never have done for herself. This is not the place to enlarge upon these examples: they are too sublime and too precious to be set off by this foil: let us reserve them for a nobler setting.

But for examples of more commonplace distinction, are there not women amongst us who every day lend themselves out for their husbands' sole benefit, and by their express command and mediation? And, in ancient times, Phaulius of Argos offered his wife to King Philip out of ambition. The same was done out of civility by that Galbus, who, entertaining Maecenas to supper, and seeing his wife and him beginning to conspire together by signs and oglings, sank down upon his couch, pretending to be overcome with sleep, in order to help on their understanding. And he very graciously gave himself away; for when, at this point, one of his slaves made bold to lay hands on the plate which was on the table, he called out, "Don't you see, you rascal, that I am only asleep for Maecenas?"

This woman may be of loose conduct, and yet of a more moral disposition than that other whose behaviour appears more correct. As we hear some lamenting the fact that they had made a vow of chastity before the age of discretion, I have also heard others truly complain of having been given over to a dissolute life before the age of discretion. This may be due to the sin of the parents, or to the force of necessity, who is a rude counsellor. In the East Indies, although chastity was there held in singular esteem, yet custom permitted a married woman to abandon herself to any man who presented her with an elephant; and it reflected a certain glory to have been valued at so high a price.

Phaedo the philosopher, a man of good family, after the capture of his country Elis, made it his trade to prostitute his youthful beauty, as long as it endured, to any man who would pay the price, and thereby gained a livelihood.

And Solon is said to have been the first in Greece who by his laws gave women the liberty, at the cost of their chastity, to provide for the necessities of life; a custom which Herodotus asserts to have been usual, before his time, in several states.

And then, what do we gain by this painful anxiety? For, however justified this feeling may be, it still remains to be considered whether it carries us very far. Does any man think he can confine them, with all his ingenuity?

> Confine her, but who will watch the guards?
> The crafty wife begins with them.[92]

Will they ever lack opportunities in so knowing an age?

Curiosity is mischievous in all things; but here it is fatal. It is madness to seek enlightenment on a disease for which there is no physic that does not aggravate it and make it worse, the disgrace of which grows greater and becomes public chiefly through jealousy; revenge for which wounds our children more than it heals us. You will pine away and die whilst searching in the dark for proofs.

How pitifully they have fared who in my time have succeeded in this quest! If the informer does not offer a remedy and relief together with the information, he will only make mischief, and deserves the poniard more than if he kept back the truth. The man who is at pains to prevent it is laughed at no less than the man who is in ignorance. The mark of cuckoldry is indelible; the man who is once stamped with it will always carry it; the punishment makes it more visible than the guilt. It is a fine thing to see our private misfortunes dragged out of doubt and obscurity, to be trumpeted on the tragic boards; and especially misfortunes that only pinch us by being told. For we say, "Good wife" and "Happy marriage" not of those that are so, but of those no man speaks of.

We must exercise our ingenuity to prevent that awkward and useless knowledge from reaching us. It was customary with the Romans, when returning from a journey, to send a messenger before them to the house, to give their wives notice of their coming, in order not to surprise them. And for the same reason a certain nation arranged that the priest should "open the ball" with the bride on the wedding night, to relieve the bridegroom of doubt and curiosity, on his first trial, as to whether she comes to him a virgin, or bruised by another's love.

But the world will be talking. I know a hundred respectable men who are cuckolded, respectably and not discreditably. A gentleman is pitied for it, but not held in less esteem. See to it that your worth drowns your misfortune, that good men curse the occasion; and that he who wrongs you trembles at the mere thought of it. And besides, does any one escape being talked of in that sense, from the little man to the greatest?

One who ruled mighty empires

On Certain Verses of Virgil

Was a better man than you, wretch![93]

When you hear so many decent men involved in this reproach in your presence, remember that neither will you be spared in other quarters. But even the ladies will laugh at it; and what are they more ready to laugh at in these days than a tranquil and well-settled married life?

There is not a man of you who has not made some one a cuckold; now, Nature runs quite on parallel lines, in compensation, and turn for turn.

The frequency of this mishap must by this time have tempered the bitterness of it; it will soon have become the rule.

A miserable passion! which has this also, that it is incommunicable:

Fortune denies an ear to our laments;[94]

For where will you find a friend to whom you dare confide your doleful complaints, who, if he does not laugh at them, may not use them as a stepping-stone and an instruction to take his share in the quarry? Both the bitter and the sweet of marriage the wise man keeps to himself. And among its other awkward conditions one of the chief, to a communicative man like myself, is this, that custom makes it improper and prejudicial to confide to anybody all we know and feel about it.

To give the women the same advice, in order to disgust them with jealousy, would be a waste of time; their nature is so steeped in suspicion, vanity, and curiosity, that to cure them by legitimate means is not to be expected. They often recover from this infirmity by a form of health much more to be feared than the malady itself. For, as there are spells which cannot remove a disease except by laying it upon another, so they are apt, when they lose this fever, to transfer it to their husbands.

Yet I know not, to tell the truth, that a man can suffer worse at their hands than jealousy; it is the most dangerous of their conditions, as the head is of their members. Pittacus said, "that every man had his trouble, and that his was his wife's jealous temper, but for which he would be perfectly happy." It must be very hard to bear, when a man so just, so wise, so valiant, felt his whole life poisoned by it; what are we other little fellows to do?

The Senate of Marseilles was right to grant the request of the man who asked permission to kill himself, that he might be delivered from his wife's tempestuous temper; for it is a disease which is only removed by removing the whole piece, and has no effectual remedy but flight or suffering, both, however, very difficult.

That man, I think, knew something about it who said "that a happy marriage might be arranged between a blind wife and a deaf husband."

We must also see to it that that great and violent strictness of obligation we lay upon them does not produce two results that may run counter to our purpose; to wit, that it may spur on the followers, and make the women more ready to surrender. For, as to the first point, by enhancing the value of the fortress, we enhance the value and desire of conquest. Might not Venus herself have thus cunningly raised the price of her wares by making the laws her brokers; knowing how insipid a pastime it would be, if not heightened by the imagination and by its dearness? In short, it is

1182

all swine's flesh, varied by sauces, as Flaminius' host said.
Cupid is a rogue of a god, who makes it his sport to wrestle
with religion and justice; it is his glory that his power battles with every other power, and that all other laws give
way to his:

> He ever seeks victims for his guilt.[95]

And with regard to the second point: Should we not be
less often cuckolded if we were less afraid of it, considering
the nature of woman? For prohibition incites and invites
them:

> You will, they won't; you won't, they will;[96]
> They are shamed to go as allowed.[97]

How could we better interpret Messalina's behaviour? At
first she conceals her amours from her husband, as they
commonly do; but finding that, by reason of his dullness,
she could carry on her intrigues too easily, she soon disdained
that customary way. Behold her then making love openly,
owning her admirers, entertaining and favouring them in
the sight of all. She wished to make him resent it. When
that animal was not to be roused by all this; when her
pleasure was rendered flat and tasteless by his weak and
easy-going nature, which appeared to authorize and legalize
her conduct, what did she do? Wife of an Emperor still
living and in good health, and at Rome, the theatre of the
world, at full noon, with public pomp and ceremony, and
to Silius, whom she had already long enjoyed, she is married
on a day when her husband was outside the city.

Does it not appear as if she were on the way to becoming
chaste through her husband's nonchalance, or as if she were

seeking another husband who might whet her appetite with his jealousy and rouse her by opposition? But the first difficulty she encountered was also the last. The beast woke up with a start. We often drive the worst bargain with those who appear to be deaf or asleep. I have found by experience that this extreme long-suffering, when once dissolved, will vent itself in the most cruel acts of revenge; for anger and fury, being heaped up in a mass and suddenly taking fire, discharge all their energy at the first attack:

and so let loose the reins of wrath.[98]

He put her to death, together with a large number of those who were intimate with her; even some who had been guilty against their will, having been invited to her bed with scourges.

What Virgil says of Venus and Vulcan, Lucretius had said more fittingly of a stolen meeting between her and Mars:

Mars, lord of arms, who rules over the cruel works of warfare, often throws himself upon thy bosom, vanquished by the everlasting wound of love. . . . He feasts his eager looks with love, gazing at thee, goddess; and as he reclines, his breath hangs on thy lips; and do thou, goddess, as he reposes in the embrace of thy sacred body, pour forth sweet sayings from thy mouth.[99]

When I ponder upon this *rejicit, pascit, inhians, molli, fovet, medullas, labefacta, pendit, percurrit*, and this noble *circumfusa*, mother of the dainty *infusus*,[100] I hold in contempt these unmeaning glitterings and verbal artifices[101]

1184

that have come into the world since. For those worthy
writers there was no need of keen and subtle conceits; their
language is full and forcible, with natural and unfailing
vigour; they are all epigrams—not the tail only, but the
head, stomach, and feet. There is nothing that signifies
effort, nothing that drags; every part moves on at the same
pace. *Their writing is of a manly texture; they were not concerned about florid ornaments.*[102] It is not an effeminate
eloquence and merely faultless: it is sinewy and solid, and
does not so much please as it fills full and entrances the
mind, and entrances most the strongest minds. When I behold those noble modes of expression, so vivid, so profound,
I do not say this is speaking rightly, I say it is thinking
rightly. It is the vivacity of the imagination which exalts
and inflates the words. *It is the understanding that makes a
man eloquent.*[103] To these, mere insight was one with language, and large conceptions with appropriate words.[104]
Their painting is guided not so much by manual dexterity
as by having the object more vividly imprinted on the soul.
Gallus[105] speaks simply because he thinks simply. Horace is
not satisfied with a superficial expression: it would wrong
him; he looks more clearly and further into things; his
mind breaks into and ransacks the whole storehouse of words
and figures of speech to express itself; and he must have
them out of the ordinary, as his conception is out of the ordinary. Plutarch says that he discerned the Latin language
by means of things;[106] here it is the same: the meaning il-
luminates and creates the words; they are not of wind but
of flesh and bone. They express more than they utter.
Weak wits also feel something resembling this; for in Italy,
in common talk I said what I wished to say; but in serious

conversation I should not have dared to trust myself to a form of speech which I could not turn or twist out of its usual course. I wish to do with it something personal.

Language gains in value not so much by being handled and used by vigorous minds, not so much from innovations, as by being put to more forcible and various service, stretching it and bending it; they do not bring words to it but they enrich those they use; they give weight and force to their signification and their use, teaching the language unwonted action, but discreetly and dexterously. But how little this agility is given to all men is seen in so many French writers of this age. They are bold enough and scornful enough not to follow the common path; but lack of invention and discretion is their undoing. There is seen in them only a miserable affectation of singularity, feeble and absurd dissimulations which, instead of uplifting, debase the subject. Provided they can pride themselves on novelty, they care nothing for its effectiveness; to lay hold of a new word, they forsake the usual one, often stronger and more pithy.

I find material enough in our language, but some failure in fashioning it, for there is nothing that might not be done with the terms of hunting and of war, which is a fruitful soil to borrow from; and forms of speech, like plants, are improved and strengthened by transplanting. I find it sufficiently copious, but not sufficiently pliable and vigorous; it usually succumbs under a powerful conception. If you are hard pressed,[107] you often perceive that it weakens and bends beneath you, and that in its default the Latin comes to your aid, and to others Greek. Of some of these words which I have just selected we perceive the force with greater difficulty because usage and familiarity have in some sort cheapened their charm to us and made it commonplace; as in our ordinary speech, there are to be found excellent phrases and metaphors of which the beauty withers with age and the colour is tarnished by too general handling. But this takes nothing from their relish for those who have good perceptions,[108] nor does it lessen the glory of those ancient authors who, it is probable, first used these words with brilliancy.

Men of learning[109] treat these things with too great refinement, in an artificial manner, different from the common and natural one. My page makes love and understands it; read him Leon Hebreu and Ficino;[110] they speak of him, of his thoughts and his acts, and yet he understands nothing of what they say. I do not recognise in Aristotle the greater part of my ordinary emotions; they have been covered and clothed in a different garment, to be worn by his school. God help them![111] Were I of the profession, I would naturalise art as much as they artificialise nature.

Let us put aside Bembo and Equicola.[112] When I write, I readily do without the company and remembrance of books, for fear lest they interfere with my manner; and also because, in truth, the good authors humble me too much and break down my courage. I freely imitate the shift of that painter who, having wretchedly pictured some cocks, forbade his assistants to let any real cocks come into his shop.[113] And I should rather need, to give me a little lustre, the device of the musician Antinonydes[114] who, when he was to give a musical performance, arranged that, before or after him, his audience should listen to other poor singers. But it is less easy for me to do without Plutarch; he touches so many subjects[115] and is so full of matter, that on all oc-

On Certain Verses of Virgil

casions, and however out of the common the subject you have in hand, he offers himself to your need and extends to you a liberal hand, inexhaustible in treasures and embellishments. It vexes me to be so greatly exposed to the accusation of pillage by those who are familiar with him. I can not be with him so casually that I do not steal a leg or a wing from him.

To carry out this purpose of mine, it also suits well that I should write in my own house, in an uncivilised region, where no one assists me or stimulates me, where I seldom meet a man who understands the Latin of his Pater Noster and who does not know French even less. I should have done it better elsewhere, but the work would have been less mine; and its chief aim and perfection is to be precisely mine. I should rightly correct an accidental error, of which, since I hasten on heedlessly, I am full; but the imperfections which are common and constant in me it would be disloyal to remove. When some one has said to me, or I have said to myself: "You make too much use of figures of speech; there you have a word of Gascon growth; there you have a hazardous expression" (I eschew none of those that are used on the French streets; they who think to combat usage with grammar make fools of themselves); "there you have an ignorant remark; there a paradoxical one; this other is too simple"; "you often play a part; it will be thought that you say in earnest what you say in an assumed character."[116] "Yes," I answer, "but I correct heedless errors, not those of habit. Do I not commonly talk thus? Does not this represent me to the life? Enough. I have done what I desired to do: every one recognises me in my book and my book in me."

1188

On Certain Verses of Virgil

I have an aping and imitative tendency; when I under-took to write verses,—and I never wrote any but Latin ones, —they clearly betrayed what poet I had lately read; and of my first Essays some have a slightly extraneous flavour. At Paris I speak a somewhat different language from that I speak at Montaigne. Whoever I regard attentively quickly stamps me with something belonging to him. What I examine I make my own: an ungainly bearing, a disagreeable grimacing, a ridiculous way of speaking; vices even more; in proportion as they fret me, they attach themselves to me and will not let go without being shaken off. I have been heard to swear more by contagion than by nature:[117] fatal imitation, like that of the monkeys of horrible size and strength which King Alexander found in a certain region of the Indies, creatures which, except for this, it would have been very difficult to master; but they afforded them the means to do so by their fondness for mimicking every thing they saw done; for thereby the hunters learned to put on their shoes in their sight with many knots of the strings, to muffle their heads with wrappings that were nooses, and to seem to anoint their eyes with birdlime. So those poor beasts unwisely employed to an ill end their imitative propensity: they limed and shackled and strangled themselves.[118] The different faculty of wittily imitating by design the gestures and words of another person, which often causes pleasure and admiration, is no more in me than in a log. When I swear after my own fashion, it is simply by God, which is the most straightforward of all oaths. They say that Socrates swore by the dog; that Zeno used the same exclamation that the Italians use to this day—*Cappari!*[119] that Pythagoras swore by water and air.[120]

On Certain Verses of Virgil

I am so thoughtlessly apt to receive these superficial impressions that, if I have had on my lips, "Your Grace," or "Your Highness," three days in succession, a week later they escape me instead of "Your Excellency," or "Your Lordship." And what I may have said jestingly and mockingly, I may say the next day seriously. Because of this, I make use in writing somewhat unwillingly of much beaten subjects, for fear of treating them with borrowed ones.[121] Every subject is equally fertile for me. I can find them in any trifle, and may it please God that this I have now in hand was not taken up at the bidding of a merely flighty will! I may be allowed to begin with any one that may please me, for all matters are linked together.

But my wits annoy me because they usually bring forth their most copious and widely floating thoughts,[122] which best please me, unexpectedly and when I am least seeking them; and they quickly vanish, I not having at the moment any means of retaining them: they come when I am on horseback, at the table, in bed, but mostly when on horseback, where I have the most abundant converse with myself. When speaking, I am somewhat sensitively demanding attention and silence, if I am speaking earnestly; whoever interrupts me, stops me. In travelling, the necessary attention to the road cuts into conversation; besides this, I oftenest travel without company suited to continuous talk; wherefore I have leisure enough to talk to myself. It often happens as in my dreams; when dreaming, I entrust them to my memory (for I am apt to dream that I am dreaming); but the next day I well remember of what colour they were, whether merry or sad or strange; but what they were besides, the more I labour to recall, the deeper I thrust it into oblivion. In like manner, of the fortuitous conceptions that come into my imagination there remains in my memory only a vague outline—only so much as is needed to make me fret and fume to no purpose in quest of one.

Well then, setting books aside and speaking more materially and simply, I find after all that Love is nothing else but the thirst for enjoying the desired object, and that Venus is but the pleasure of discharging one's vessels (like the pleasure Nature gives us in discharging other parts), which becomes vicious by immoderation or indiscretion. For Socrates Love is the appetite for generation, by the mediation of beauty.

And when I think, as I have done many a time, of the ridiculous titillation of this pleasure, the absurd, giddy, crack-brained emotions which it stirs up in Zeno and Cratippus, of that unreasonable rage, that countenance inflamed with fury and cruelty at the most delightful moment of love, and then that solemn, stern, ecstatic mien in so extravagant an action; when I consider besides that our joys and excrements are lodged together pell-mell, and that sensual pleasure at its height is attended, like pain, with faintness and moaning, I believe it is true what Plato says, that man is the plaything of the gods:

> truly a cruel way
> To sport with us![123]

and that Nature was in a mocking mood when she left us that most common and most disturbing of our actions to make us all alike and put us on the same level, wise men and fools, men and beasts. The most contemplative and wisest of men, when I picture him in that attitude, appears to me a humbug with his wise and contemplative airs; it is the peacock's feet that humble his pride:

> Why may not truth
> In laughing guise be dressed?[124]

Those who refuse to discuss serious matters playfully act, as somebody says, like the man who fears to worship the statue of a saint unless it has an apron.

We eat indeed, and drink like the animals; but these are not actions that hinder the workings of the mind. In these we maintain an advantage over them; the other brings every other thought under its yoke, brutifies and bestializes, by its imperious authority, all the theology and philosophy that is in Plato; and yet he does not lament it. In all other things you may observe some decorum. All other operations may be subjected to the rules of decency; this one cannot even be imagined other than vicious and ridiculous. Try to find, if you can, some modest and sober way of doing it.

Alexander said that he knew himself to be mortal chiefly by this action, and by sleeping. Sleep stifles and suppresses the faculties of our mind. The sexual act similarly absorbs and dissipates them. Truly it is a mark, not only of our original corruption, but also of our inanity and deformity.

On the one hand Nature pushes us on to it, having connected with this desire the noblest, most useful, and pleasant of all her operations; and on the other hand she allows us to condemn and fly from it as from a shameless and immodest action, to blush at it and recommend abstinence.

Are we not indeed brutes to call brutish the operation that makes us?

The nations, in their religions, have met together in a

On Certain Verses of Virgil

number of conventions, as sacrifices, candles, incense, fasts, offerings and, among other things, in their condemnation of this action. All opinions tend that way, as well as to the widespread custom of cutting off the foreskin, which is a punishment of it.

We are perhaps right in blaming ourselves for producing so foolish a thing as man; in calling the action shameful, and shameful the parts that serve that purpose. (At present mine are really shameful and shamefaced.)

The Essenians, of whom Pliny speaks, kept up their numbers for several centuries without nurses or baby-clothes, through the influx of foreigners who, following that pretty humour, continually joined them: a whole nation risking extermination rather than become entangled in a woman's embrace, and breaking the continuity of men rather than create one.

It is said that Zeno never had to do with a woman but once in his life, and then only out of civility, that he might not seem too obstinately to disdain the sex.

Every one avoids seeing a man born; every one runs to see him die. For his destruction they seek out a spacious field, in the full light of day; for his construction they creep into some dark little corner. It is a duty to hide and blush when making him; and it is a glory, and the source of many virtues, to be able to unmake him. The one is offence, the other is grace; for Aristotle says that in a certain phrase of his country, to benefit some one is to kill him. The Athenians, to equalize the disgrace of these two actions, having to purify the island of Delos and justify themselves to Apollo, forbade at once all burials and births within its territory. *We are ashamed of ourselves;*[125] we regard our being as a sin.

On Certain Verses of Virgil

There are some nations that conceal themselves while eating.[126] I know a lady, and one of the greatest,[127] who is of the same opinion, that chewing is unseemly in appearance and much lessens woman's charm and beauty; and she does not willingly take food in public.[128] And I know a man who can not endure to see others eat, or to have any one see him and who shuns all bystanders more when he is filling himself than when he is emptying himself. In the Turkish Empire there are many who, to excel others, never allow themselves to be seen at meal-time; who have but one meal a week; who slash and slit their faces and limbs; who never speak to any one;[129] fanatics all, who think that they honour their nation by denaturing themselves; who prize themselves for their misprision;[130] and think to better themselves by becoming worse. What an unnatural creature is he who horrifies himself! whose very pleasures burden him; who clings to unhappiness!

There are those who hide their life,—

> Who leave their homes and their dear thresholds
> for exile,[131]

and withdraw it from the sight of other men; who shun health and cheerfulness as hostile and harmful qualities. Not many sects only, but many peoples, curse their birth and bless their death. There are some peoples by whom the sun is abhorred,[132] darkness adored. We are quickwitted only in misusing ourselves; that is the real pursuit of the power of our mind, which is a dangerous tool when out of order.

> Poor creatures! who think their joy a sin.[133]

On Certain Verses of Virgil

Ah! poor man, thou hast enough inevitable disadvantages without adding to them thine invention; and art wretched enough by nature without being so by art; thou hast real and essential deformities in sufficiency without creating imaginary ones. Dost thou find thyself too much at ease unless thine ease molest thee? Dost thou find that thou hast to perform all the needful duties to which Nature pledges thee, and that she will be remiss and idle in thee unless thou dost impose on thyself new duties? Thou dost not fear to offend against her universal and indubitable laws, and dost spur thyself to obey thine own one-sided and imaginary ones; and the more special, uncertain, and the more gainsaid they are, the more effort dost thou make about them. The prescribed rules of thy parish bind thee, those of God and of the world do not touch thee. Ponder a little the examples of this thought; thy life is all there.

The lines of these two poets, treating lasciviousness as they do with so much reserve and discretion, appear to me to disclose it more fully and cast a strong light upon it. The ladies cover their bosoms with open-work lace, the priests keep many sacred things hidden, painters put shadows into their work to set off the light, and they say that the sun's rays and the wind are harder to bear when reflected than direct. The Egyptian who was asked, "What are you hiding under your cloak?" answered discreetly, "I am hiding it under my cloak that you may not know what it is." But there are certain other things that are hidden to be shown. Listen to this man, who is more unreserved:

And pressed her naked body to mine.[134]

I feel as if he were caponizing me. Let Martial gather up

On Certain Verses of Virgil

Venus's skirts as high as he pleases, he will not succeed in making her appear so entire. He who says all sates and disgusts us. He who fears to be explicit leads us on to thinking more than is meant. There is treachery in this kind of modesty, and especially when they half open, as these do, so fair a path to imagination. And the action and the painting should smack of theft.

I like the Spanish and Italian methods of making love, which are more respectful, more timid, more affected and discreet. Somebody in ancient times, I forget who, wished for a gullet as long as a crane's neck, that he might the longer relish what he was gulping down. This wish is more appropriate to this quick and hasty pleasure, especially in a nature like mine, whose failing it is to be too sudden. To arrest its flight and lengthen out the preliminaries, everything serves as a favour and recompense between them: a look, a nod, a word, a sign. If we could dine off the steam of a roast joint, what an expense we could save!

It is a passion in which very little solid reality is mingled with much more unreality and feverish imagination; it should be paid and served accordingly. Let us teach the ladies to make the most of themselves, to observe self-respect, to keep us in suspense and fool us. We begin with the final attack, and always show our French impetuosity. When they spin out their favours and spread them out in small portions, each of us, even miserable old age, will find a little to glean, according to his substance and merit.

He who finds no enjoyment except in enjoyment, who wins nothing unless he sweeps the stakes, who loves the chase only for the sake of the quarry, has no business to intrude into our school. The more steps and degrees there are, so much higher is the uppermost seat, and so much more honourable it is to reach it. We should take a pleasure in being led to it, as into a magnificent palace, through divers porticoes and passages, long and pleasant galleries and many turnings. This dispensation would turn to our advantage; we should dwell there the longer, and love the longer. Without hope and without desire we can make no progress worth a rap.

They should infinitely dread our mastery and entire possession of them. As soon as they have wholly surrendered to the mercy of our fidelity and constancy, their position is a little too risky; for those virtues are rare and hard to find. No sooner are they ours than we are no more theirs.

> The lust of greedy soul once satisfied
> Nor oaths nor promises they reck.[135]

And Thrasonides, a young Greek, was so much in love with his love that, having won his mistress's heart, he refused to enjoy her, that he might not thereby deaden, sate, and weaken that restless ardour on which he fed and so prided himself.

Dearness gives relish to the meat. See how the form of salutation, which is peculiar to our nation, spoils by its cheapness the charms of the kiss which, as Socrates says, is so powerful and dangerous a stealer of hearts. It is a disagreeable and offensive custom for a lady to have to lend her lips to any man, however disgusting, who has three lackeys at his heels:

> From his snout, like a dog's
> Hoarfrost hangs and clogs his beard
> I'd rather kiss his rump.[136]

On Certain Verses of Virgil

And we ourselves do not gain much by it; for the world is so divided that for three pretty women we must kiss fifty plain ones. And for a tender stomach, such as we have at my age, a bad kiss is too high a price to pay for a good one.

In Italy they act the part of the languishing suitor even with the ladies who are for sale, and defend this practice as follows: "that there are degrees in enjoyment, and that by paying them homage we try to produce for ourselves the most complete. For these ladies sell only their bodies; their good-will cannot be on sale, it is too free and too much at its own disposal." Hence they say that it is the will they lay siege to; and they are right. It is the will we must serve and win by our attentions. To me it is a horrible idea that a body void of affection should belong to me. It can only be compared to the mania of that youth who defiled by his love the beautiful statue of Venus that Praxiteles made; or of that raving Egyptian whose lust was kindled by a dead body he was embalming and shrouding, which was the occasion of the law since made in Egypt, which ordained that the bodies of beautiful young women and those of good family should be kept for three days before being delivered into the hands of the undertakers. Periander acted still more unnaturally by carrying his conjugal affection (although more regular and lawful) to the point of enjoying his wife Melissa after she was dead.

Does it not appear a lunatic humour in Luna, when she could not otherwise enjoy her darling Endymion, to put him to sleep for several months, and browse in the enjoyment of a youth who stirred only in his dreams?

So I say that we love a body without a soul, or without feeling, when we love a body without its consent and desire.

1198

On Certain Verses of Virgil

All enjoyments are not alike; some are hectic and some languid. A thousand other causes besides good-will may win us this favour of the ladies; it is not a sufficient evidence of affection. Treachery may lurk there, as elsewhere; sometimes they respond with only one buttock:

> As cool as at a sacrifice;
> You'd think her marble or absent.[137]

I know some who would rather lend that than their coach, and who have nothing else to communicate. You must observe whether she enjoys your company on any other account, or on that alone, as if you were some burly stableboy; in what degree of favour or esteem you are housed:

> If she comes to thee alone,
> And marks thy day with whiter stone.[138]

What if she eats your bread with the sauce of a more pleasing imagination:

> She holds you, and sighs for absent loves.[139]

What! Have we not heard of some one, in our time, who turned this action to a horrible revenge, to poison and kill, as he did, an honest woman?

They who know Italy will never find it strange if on this subject I seek examples nowhere else; for that nation may be called the mistress of the world in this respect. They have a greater abundance of beautiful women and fewer ugly ones than we; but in rare and surpassing beauties I consider that we are equal. And I judge the same about their minds:[140] of those of the ordinary sort they have many more, and manifestly an animal-like want of intelligence[141] is incomparably more infrequent there; in exceptional souls, and of the highest rank, we are in no wise inferior to them. Were I to extend this comparison, it would seem to me that I might say in respect to valour that it is, on the other hand, as compared with them, universal among us, and inborn;[142] but sometimes we find them possessed with it so complete and so vigorous that it surpasses all the sturdiest examples that we have of it. Marriages in that country go amiss in a certain respect: custom there habitually makes the authority over women so harsh and slavish that the most distant acquaintance with a stranger is as capital as the closest. As a result of this authority, any drawing together is rendered necessarily a reality;[143] and since it all comes to the same thing for them, they have a very easy choice. And when they have broken down the barriers, be assured that they are on fire: *wantonness, like a wild beast, is maddened by the very bonds that imprison it, and then bursts forth.*[144] They must be given the rein a little;

> I saw of late a horse, rebellious against his bit, tug with his mouth and plunge like a thunderbolt.[145]

The desire for companionship is weakened by giving it some liberty.[146] We experience almost the same fortune. They are too extreme in restraint, we in license.

It is an excellent custom of our nation that our children are entertained in households of the great, there to be nurtured and bred up as pages, as in a school of nobility; and it is a discourtesy, they say, and an affront to refuse this to a gentleman.[147] I have observed (for there are as many different ways and methods as there are households) that the ladies who have chosen to give waiting-maids the sternest rules have not had better luck in consequence. There must be moderation about this; a large part of their conduct must be left to their own discretion; for at the best there is no schooling that could check them on all sides. And the truth is that she who has come out scot free from an unrestraining tutelage is much more to be relied on than she who comes forth in good plight from a severe and prison-like school. Our fathers trained the demeanour of their daughters to shyness and timidity (hearts and desires being ever the same); we train ours to boldness; we understand this matter not at all. That is all very well for the Sarmatian women, who are not allowed to lie with a man until they have with their own hands killed another in war.

For me, who have no authority over them except through the ears, it is enough if they retain me for their counsel, in accordance with the privilege of my age. So I counsel them, as well as ourselves, abstinence; but, if this generation is too hostile to it, at least discretion and modesty. For, as Aristippus, according to the tale, said to some young men who blushed to see him enter the house of a courtesan, "The sin is not in entering, but in not coming out again." If she has no care for her conscience, let her have some regard to her good name. Though the substance be not worth much, let the appearance hold good.

I commend gradation and delay in the dispensation of their favours. Plato points out that in every kind of love an easy and prompt surrender is forbidden in those who hold the fort. It is a sign of gluttony, which they should conceal with all their cunning, to surrender so heedlessly and impetuously all they have. By observing order and

1201

measure in granting their favours, they fool our desire the better, and conceal their own. Let them ever flee before us. I mean even if they wish to be caught. They will conquer us the better in flight, like the Scythians. Indeed, according to the law that Nature has given them, it is not properly their part to will and desire; their part is to suffer, obey, and consent. That is why Nature has given them a perpetual capacity; to us a rare and uncertain one. They always have their hour, that they may always be ready for ours; *born to suffer*.[148] And, whilst she has decreed that our appetites should show and declare themselves prominently, she has arranged for theirs to be hidden away and inward, and has provided them with parts fitted simply for the defensive, and not for show.

They must leave pranks like the following to Amazonian licence: when Alexander was marching through Hyrcania, Thalestris, Queen of the Amazons, came to see him with three hundred troopers of her own sex, well mounted and well armed, having left the remainder of a large army that was following her beyond the neighbouring mountains, and said to him aloud and publicly, "that the reports of his victories and his valour had brought her thither to see him and offer her power and resources to help him in his enterprise; and that, seeing he was so handsome, young and strong, she, who was perfect in all his qualities, proposed to him that they should cohabit, that there might be born, of the most valiant woman in the world and the most valiant man then living, something great and rare for the time to come." Alexander thanked her for the rest; but to gain time for the accomplishment of her last request, he stayed thirteen days at that place, which he spent in feasting and jollity to the best of his powers, to welcome so courageous a princess.

We are, in almost all things, unjust judges of their actions, as they are of ours. I confess the truth when it tells against me as when it is on my side. It is an infamous and badly ordered state of things that so often drives them to change, and prevents them from fixing their affections on any object whatever; as we see in that goddess to whom we attribute so much fickleness and so many lovers. Yet it is true that it is contrary to the nature of love not to be violent, and contrary to the nature of violence to be constant. And they who wonder at it, who exclaim against it and look for the causes of this frailty in them, as if it were unnatural and incredible, why can they not see how often they themselves share it, without being amazed and crying "miracle"? It would perhaps be more strange to see them attached to one object. It is not a merely bodily passion. If there is no end to avarice and ambition, neither is there to lechery. It still lives after satiety; and neither constant satisfaction nor limit can be set to it; it ever outlives possession.

And besides, inconstancy is perhaps rather more pardonable in them than in us. They may plead, as we do, the inclination to variety and novelty common to both sexes; and secondly they may plead, as we do not, that they buy a cat in a poke.

Joan, Queen of Naples, had her first husband Andreasso hanged at the bars of her window with a cord of silk and gold thread twisted with her own hands, because in the matrimonial fatigue-duties she found that neither his parts nor his performances answered the expectations she had formed of him when she saw his stature, his youth and activity, by which she had been caught and deceived.

On Certain Verses of Virgil

They may plead that the active part needs more effort than the passive, so that on their part the effort is always equal to the occasion, whilst on our part it may fall out otherwise. For this reason it was that Plato wisely made a law that, in order to decide upon the expediency of a marriage, the judges should see the youths who contemplated it stark naked, and the girls nude only as far down as the girdle.

When they come to try us they do not perhaps find us worthy of their choice:

> All efforts vain to excite his vigour dead
>> The married virgin flies
> The unjoyous bed.[149]

It is not enough that the will should drive straight. Weakness and incapacity lawfully dissolve a marriage:

> A lover much more vigourous she needs
>> To undo her virgin zone.[150]

Why not? and, according to her standard, a more licentious and more active capacity for love:

> Lest to his pleasant toil he prove unequal.[151]

But is it not a great impudence to bring our imperfections and weaknesses where we desire to please and leave a good opinion and recommendation of ourselves? For the little that I now need,

> for one encounter only
> Am I fit,[152]

I would not trouble a person I have to respect and fear:

1204

On Certain Verses of Virgil

> Let me not
> Suspicion rouse, who now, alas,
>   Have passed my fiftieth year.[153]

Nature should be satisfied with making this age miserable, without also making it ridiculous. I should hate to see it, for one inch of pitiful vigour that inflames it three times a week, strutting and swaggering as fiercely as if it had some big and lawful day's work in its belly: a regular strawfire. What wonder if, after leaping up into a sudden and crackling flame, it dies down in a moment and becomes cold and lifeless!

That desire should only be found in the prime of youth and beauty. Trust your age, if you would be convinced, to back up that indefatigable, full, constant and courageous ardour you feel in yourself; it will leave you nicely in the lurch. Better to boldly hand on your experience to some nerveless, wide-eyed, ignorant boy, who still trembles under the rod, and will blush at it:

> A crimson blush her face o'erspread
> As Indian ivory, stained with red,
> Or lilies mixed with roses.[154]

He who can await, in the morning, without dying of shame, the contempt of those beautiful eyes that have witnessed his slackness and impertinence,

> And eloquent with dumb reproof,[155]

has never felt the satisfaction and pride of wearying them and setting dark rims around them by the vigorous exercise of an active and busy night.

When I have seen one dissatisfied with me, I did not at

once accuse her of fickleness; I began to wonder whether I should not rather blame Nature, who has certainly treated me unfairly and unkindly:

> He is not very tall, nor very stout.[156]

> The matrons look with much disfavor
> Upon a man with little parts,—[157]

and done me a most enormous hurt. Every part of me makes me what I am, as much as any other. And no other makes me more properly a man than this.

I owe it to the public to give them my full-length portrait. The wisdom I have learned lies wholly in truth, freedom of speech, reality. It disdains to include in the catalogue of its real duties those petty, invented, customary provincial rules. It is entirely natural, constant, universal. Its daughters, but bastard daughters, are civility and conventionality.

We shall easily get the better of the sins of appearance when we have conquered those of reality. When we have done with the latter, we may run full tilt at the others, if we find it necessary to run at them. For there is danger of our setting up new duties in our imagination, to excuse our neglect of our natural duties, and to obscure them. As a proof of this we may see that in places where faults are crimes, crimes are no more than faults; that with the nations where the laws of propriety are more uncommon and more laxly kept, the primitive and common laws are better observed; since the innumerable crowd of so many duties stifles, deadens, and scatters our attention. Our application to little things withdraws us from more urgent ones.

O what an easy and pleasant path do those superficial

men take, in comparison with ours! They are shadowy things wherewith we plaster our conscience and pay one another's debts. But we do not pay, but rather pile up, our debts to that great judge, who pulls up our rags and tatters around our shameful parts, and does not pretend not to see through us, even to our inmost and most secret impurities. Our virginal modesty would be usefully covered if it could keep this discovery from him.

In short, whoever could sharpen the wits of man and rid him of these over-nice verbal superstitions would do the world no great harm. Our life is part folly, part wisdom. He who only treats of it reverently and canonically will leave more than half unsaid. I do not indulge in self-excuses, and if I did, I should rather excuse myself for my excuses than for any other fault. I excuse myself to those of a certain way of thinking, whom I hold to be more numerous than those on my side. For their consideration I will say this besides—for I wish to please every one; though it is a difficult thing *for a single man to conform to that great variety of manners, discourses and wills,*[158] that they ought not strictly to blame me for the things I quote from authorities accepted and approved by many centuries; and that there is no reason why, because I do not write in verse, they should deny me the freedom that is enjoyed, in our days, even by church dignitaries, and those of our nation and the most tufted. Here are two speciments:

Rimula, dispeream, ni monogramma tua est.[159]

Un vit d'ami la contente et bien traicte.[160]

And what about so many others? I love modesty, and it

is not judgement that prompts me to choose this scandalous way of speaking. It is Nature who has chosen for me. I do not commend it any more than I do all methods that are contrary to accepted custom; but I excuse it, and, by particular and general circumstances, lighten the accusation.

But to proceed. Whence too comes that sovereign authority you usurp over one who grants you favours at her own cost,

Who gives you little present in the night;[161]

and whom you immediately treat with the self-interest, coolness, and authority of a husband? It is a free compact; why do you not keep it as you would hold her by it? There is no law to bind voluntary actions.

It is contrary to custom, but it is true none the less that in my time I have carried out this bargain, as far as the nature of it would permit, as conscientiously as any other bargain, and with some appearance of justice; that I never pretended more affection than I felt; and that I gave simple expression to its decline, its vigour and birth, its outbursts and slack periods. One does not always go at the same pace. I was so sparing of promises that I think I did more than I promised or owed. They found me faithful to the point of serving their interest when they were inconstant to me, I mean avowedly and sometimes repeatedly inconstant. I never broke with them as long as I was attached to them even by a thread; and whatever cause they may have given me I never broke with them so far as to hate and despise them. For those intimacies, even when gained on the most shameful terms, still oblige me to have some kindly feeling for them.

On Certain Verses of Virgil

At times I have given way to anger and somewhat unwise impatience on detecting their tricks and shifts, and in our quarrels; for I am naturally liable to sudden fits of temper which, though fleeting and soon over, are often prejudicial to my interest. If they were minded to test the freedom of my judgement, I did not shirk giving them some sharp paternal advice, and pinching them where they smarted. If I gave them any cause for complaint, it was rather because they found me too foolishly conscientious in my love, compared with modern ways. I have kept my word when I might easily have been excused from doing so; they would then sometimes surrender with credit to themselves, and on conditions which they would readily have allowed the victor to break.

More than once I have made the pleasure at its highest point to yield to the interest of their honour. And when urged by reason I have armed them against myself, so that they acted more securely and decorously by my rules, when they freely submitted to them, than they would have done by their own.

As often as I could I took upon myself all the risks of our rendezvous, to relieve them of responsibility; and always contrived our meetings at the most difficult and unexpected times and places, because they arouse less suspicion and are besides, I think, more accessible. A place is chiefly open at a spot which is supposed to be of itself covered. The less we fear a thing the less are we on the defensive and on the watch for it. You may more easily dare a thing that nobody thinks you will dare, so that it becomes easy through its difficulty.

No man ever acted with more regard to consequences.

On Certain Verses of Virgil

This way of loving is more correct; but who knows better than I how ridiculous it appears nowadays, and how little it is practised? Yet I shall not repent of it; I have nothing more to lose there:

> My votive tablet
> Proclaims that I to Ocean's God
> Have hung the garments
> From my latest shipwreck wet.[162]

I can now speak openly about it. But, just as I might perhaps say to another, "My friend, you are dreaming; love, these days, has little to do with faith and honesty":

> If you try to make unstable counsel
> Stable by reason's rules, you only add
> To madness, and are reasonably mad;[163]

so, on the contrary, if I had to begin anew I should certainly pursue the same path and the same course of proceeding, however fruitless it might be to me.

Incapacity and folly are praiseworthy in an unpraiseworthy action. The further I depart from their point of view in this, the nearer I keep to my own.

For the rest, in this traffic, I did not let myself go entirely; I took pleasure, but I did not forget myself, in it; I kept entire the little sense and judgement that Nature has given me, for their sake as well as for my own; a little excitement, but no delirium. My conscience was also involved to the point of making me licentious and dissolute; but ungrateful, treacherous, malicious or cruel, never. I was not reckless in pursuing the pleasure of this vice, but bought it for what it cost and nothing more. *No vice is self-contained.*[164]

On Certain Verses of Virgil

I hate a stagnant and sleepy idleness almost as much as a toilsome and thorny activity; the latter pinches me, the other makes me drowsy. I like a wound as well as a bruise, a cut as well as a dry blow. I found in this traffic, when I was fitter for it, a right moderation between those two extremes. Love is an excitement, widewake, lively and gay; it did not disturb or afflict me, but it made me warm and thirsty for more. One should stop there; it is hurtful only to fools.

A young man asked the philosopher Panaetius whether it was becoming in a wise man to be in love. "Let us leave the wise man out of the question," he replied; "but you and I, who are far from being wise, must not become entangled in so violent and exciting a business, which enslaves us to another and makes us contemptible to ourselves." He spoke truth, that a soul is not to be trusted that has not the strength to withstand the attack of a thing that comes so suddenly, and that is not able practically to disprove the saying of Agesilaus "that wisdom and love cannot go abreast."

True, it is a vain pastime, unbecoming, shameful and unlawful; but, conducted in this fashion, I regard it as salubrious, proper to enliven a dull body and soul. And, as a physician I would prescribe it for a man of my temperament and condition as readily as any other remedy, to stir him up and keep him robust till well on in years, and to ward off the attacks of senility. Whilst we are yet but in the suburbs and the pulse still beats;

> While hair is gray and age stands upright,
> While still are threads for Lachesis to spin,
> While on my feet I walk and need no staff,—[165]

we need to be solicited and tickled by some such biting
excitation as this. See what youth, vigour and sprightliness
it put into the wise Anacreon. And Socrates, when older
than I now am, said, speaking of a girl he fell in love with,
"With her shoulder touching mine, and my head near to
hers, as we were looking together into a book, I suddenly
felt a pricking in the shoulder, if you will believe me, like
the bite of an insect; and for more than five days it tingled,
and through my heart ran a continual itching pain." What!
a touch, and that an accidental one, and of a shoulder, disturb and kindle a soul cooled and weakened by age, and of
all human souls the most chastened! Why not, in heaven's
name? Socrates was a man, and desired neither to be nor
seem anything else.

Philosophy does not at all contend against natural pleasures, provided due measure be kept; and it preaches moderation in them, not avoidance; the force of its resistance
is exerted against unwonted and counterfeit ones. It says
that the appetites of the body ought not to be augmented by
the mind, and wisely warns us to avoid arousing our hunger
by gluttony; not to desire to stuff instead of filling the stomach; to shun all enjoyment that brings us to want, and all
food and drink that makes us thirsty and hungry;[166] as, in
the service of love, it[167] bids us take an object which simply
satisfies the needs of the body, and does not arouse the
mind, which should not attend to its own duty, but merely
follow the body and assist it. But am I not right in thinking
that these precepts, which by the way are in my opinion a
little too rigorous, concern a body that is equal to its functions; and that when a body is in a low condition, like a
disordered stomach, it is excusable to warm and sustain it

artificially, and by means of the imagination to restore the appetite and cheerfulness which it loses when left to itself?

May we not say that there is nothing in us while we are in this earthly prison that is either purely corporeal or purely spiritual, and that we wrongfully dismember a living man? and that it seems to be reasonable that we should conduct ourselves toward the enjoyment of pleasure as favourably as we do toward pain? Pain, for example, was violent to the point of perfection in the soul of the saints by the practice of penance; the body naturally had a share therein by virtue of their connection, and yet could have small share in the cause; still, they were not content that it should barely follow and assist the afflicted soul; they afflicted the body itself with atrocious and suitable torments, to the end that the soul and the body should die with each other in plunging men into suffering, the more severe, the more salutary. In like manner is it not unjust in respect to the pleasures of the body to chill the soul regarding them, and to say that she must be dragged to them as to some enforced and slavish obligation and necessity? It is her part rather to brood over them and cherish them, to go to meet them and welcome them, since the office of controlling them belongs to her; as it is also in my opinion for her, in respect to the pleasures which are peculiar to her, to inspire and infuse in the body all sense of them that comports with its nature, and to study that they be agreeable and salutary for it; if it be quite right, as they say, that the body should not follow its appetites to the prejudice of the mind, why is it not also right that the mind should not follow its appetites to the prejudice of the body?

I have no other passion to keep me in breath. What

On Certain Verses of Virgil

avarice, ambition, quarrels, lawsuits, do for other men who, like myself, have no fixed occupation, love would do more beneficially. It would wake me up again, make me more sober, pleasing and careful of my person; it would recompose my countenance and prevent the grimaces of old age, those ugly and pitiful grimaces, from spoiling it; it would bring me back to wise and healthy studies, whereby I might become more delicate and fastidious. We demand more its hopelessness in itself and its employment, and restoring it to itself; it would divert me from a thousand troublesome thoughts, a thousand melancholy humours, which idleness and the poor state of health impose upon us at this age; would warm up, at least in dreams, this blood that Nature forsakes, would raise the chin and stretch out a little the nerves and the vigour and the gaiety in the soul of this poor man who is moving full speed towards disintegration.

But I know well that it is a blessing very hard to recover. Through failing strength and long experience our taste has become more delicate and fastidious. We demand more when we can bring less; we are more anxious to choose when we least deserve to be accepted. Knowing ourselves for what we are, we are less confident and more distrustful of our powers; nothing can make us sure of being loved, knowing our condition and theirs.

I am ashamed of being found in the midst of these green and exuberant young people,

> In whom their hardy vigour is more firm
> Than sapling on the mountainside.[168]

Why should we go and intrude our misery into that gay throng,

1214

On Certain Verses of Virgil

That fervid youngsters may behold
   With laughter long
The burned-out torch in ashes flung?[169]

They have strength and reason on their side; let us give place to them; we can only look on.

And that germ of budding beauty will not be touched by such stiff old hands, nor won by mere material means. For, as the old philosopher replied to the man who jeered at him for being unable to win the good graces of a tender lass he was pursuing, "My friend, the hook will not bite in such fresh cheese."

Now, it is an intercourse that needs reciprocity and mutual exchange. The other pleasures we receive may be acknowledged by returns of a different nature; but this can only be paid for in the same kind of coin. Indeed in this pastime the pleasure I give tickles my imagination more agreeably than that which I feel. Now there is no generosity in the man who can receive pleasure where he confers none; it is a mean soul that would be beholden for everything, and is content to keep up relations with a person to whom he is a charge. There is no beauty, favour or intimacy so exquisite that a gentleman should desire it at that price. If they can be kind to us only out of pity, I would much rather not live, than live on alms. I would like to have the right to ask it of them in the way in which I heard them beg in Italy: *Fate ben per voi;*[170] or after the manner of Cyrus exhorting his troops: "Who loves himself, follow me!"

You may tell me to consort with persons in my own state, who, sharing the same fortune, will be more easy of access. O foolish and insipid compromise!

On Certain Verses of Virgil

> I will not pluck
> The beard of lion dead.[171]

Xenophon makes it the ground of his objection and accusation against Menon, that in his amours he set to work on faded flowers.

I find more sensual pleasure in merely witnessing, or even in only imagining, the sweet and honest pairing of two fair young people, than in myself making a second in a pitiful and imperfect conjunction. I leave that fantastic appetite to the Emperor Galba, who preferred his meat when it was old and tough; and to this poor wretch:

> Oh that the Gods would grant to me
> To kiss thyself with changed locks
> And clasp thy withered body close![172]

And among the chief disfigurements I count a forced and artificial beauty. Emonez, a young boy of Chios, thinking by pretty ornaments to acquire the beauty that Nature had denied him, appeared before the philosopher Archesilaus and asked him whether a wise man might fall in love. "Yes, by heaven," he replied, "as long as it is not with a dressed up and sophisticated beauty like yours." The confessed ugliness of old age is less old and less ugly, to my mind, than when it is painted and polished.

Shall I say it? Provided you do not seize me by the throat. Love, in my opinion, is not properly and naturally in season except in the age next to childhood:

> Should you among the pretty girls
> Dishevelled hair and ambiguous face bring in,
>   He would receive the wisest there,

On Certain Verses of Virgil

So smooth and rosy is his skin.[173]

Nor beauty either. For while Homer extends it until the chin begins to be shaded, Plato himself remarked that that was rare. And the reason is notorious why the Sophist Bion so wittily called the downy hairs of adolescence Aristogeitons and Harmodians'. In manhood I think it already out of date; not to speak of old age.

> Ruthless Love, for past the withered oak
> He flies.[174]

And Margaret, Queen of Navarre, being a woman, greatly extends the privileges of her sex, ordaining that thirty is the season for them to exchange the name of "beautiful" for that of "good".

The shorter the possession we grant Cupid over our lives, the better we are for it. Look at his bearing, and his boyish chin! Who knows not how, in his school, all goes backward, against all rule? Study, exercise, use, are the ways that lead to inefficiency; there the novices are the teachers. *Love knows no order.*[175] Truly his conduct is much more charming when blended with heedlessness and irregularities; mistakes and checks give point and grace to it. Provided it be eager and hungry, it matters little whether it be prudent. See how he goes reeling, tripping and wantoning; you put him in the stocks when you guide him by art and discretion, and he is restrained in his divine freedom when put under those hirsute and callous hands.

For the rest, I have often heard the ladies describing this intercourse as entirely spiritual, and disdaining to consider the part the senses play in it. Everything serves, and I may say that I have often observed that we pardon their intellectual shortcomings in consideration of their bodily charms; but I have not yet observed any of them to be willing to favour intellectual beauty in us, however wise and mature, when joined to a body that shows the least signs of decay. Why does not one of them feel a desire to make that noble Socratic exchange of body for soul, purchasing a spiritual and philosophical generation and intelligence at the price of her thighs, the highest rate at which she can value them?

Plato, in his Laws, ordains that one who has performed a signal and useful exploit in war shall, as long as it is being waged, not be denied, however old or ill-favoured he may be, a kiss or any other amorous favour from any woman he may choose. Can that which he thinks so fair in consideration of military worth not also be fair consideration of some other kind of worth? And why does not one of them seek to forestall her sisters and win the glory of so chaste a love? I may well say chaste:

> for if an ancient horse is come to love,
> As fire in stubble blusters without strength,
> He rages idly.[176]

The vices that are confined to thought are not the worst.

To conclude this remarkable commentary, which has slipped from me in a torrent of babble, a torrent sometimes impetuous and hurtful:

> Like the apple, her lover's secret gift,
>   In the chaste bosom of the maiden fair,
> Where hidden it lies in silken tunic;
>   As she hears her mother's step she starts;
> Away it rolls, and conscious of her crime

On Certain Verses of Virgil

Her cheeks are steeped in red.[177]

I say that male and female are cast in the same mould; saving education and habits, the difference is not great. Plato, in his Republic, invites all indiscriminately to share all studies, exercises, charges and occupations, in peace and war; and the philosopher Antisthenes rejected all distinction between their virtue and ours. It is much easier to accuse one sex than to excuse the other; it is, in the words of the proverb, "the poker calling the shovel black."

Chapter VI

OF COACHES

IT is very easy to verify that the great authors, when writing of causes, take account not only of those which they think are true causes, but also of those which they do not believe, provided that these have some novelty or some beauty. They speak truly and profitably enough if they speak sagaciously. We can not make sure of the sovereign cause; we pile up many causes, to see if by chance it will be found among the number,

> For it is not enough to mention one cause; but we should mention many, of which one may prove to be the true one.[1]

Do you ask me whence comes the custom of blessing those who sneeze? We produce three sorts of wind; that which comes from below is too foul; that which comes through the mouth implies some reproach of gluttony; the third is sneezing, and, because it comes from the head and is blameless, we give it this honourable greeting. Do not laugh at this conceit; it is, they say, Aristotle's.[2] It seems to me that I have seen that Plutarch (who is, of all the authors I know, the one who most successfully commingled art with

nature and insight with knowledge[3]), when considering
the cause of sickness of the stomach that befalls those who
travel by sea, says that it is due to fear, he having found
some reason by which he proved that fear may produce such
an effect.[4] I, who am very subject to it, know well that this
cause does not touch me, and I know it, not by argument,
but by actual experience; without bringing forward what I
have been told, that the same thing happens often to beasts,
especially to swine, which are without any apprehension of
danger; and what an acquaintance of mine testified to me
about himself, that being very subject to it, the desire to
vomit had two or three times passed away when he was
much frightened in a great storm; as with this ancient
writer: *I was in too great distress to think of danger.*[5] I have
never felt fear on the water,—nor have I elsewhere (and just
occasion for it has often enough presented itself, if death be
one),—which has disturbed or bewildered me. Fear proceeds sometimes from lack of judgement as well as from lack
of courage. All the dangers that I have seen I have seen
with my eyes wide open, with clear vision, sound and perfect; indeed, it needs courage to fear.[6] Fear served me on one
occasion, more than any thing else, to guide and order my
escape so that it was if not without fear, at all events without terror and without confusion; it was excited, but not
heedless or dismayed. Great souls go much further and show
us escapes not only composed and steady,[7] but audacious.
To mention that which Alcibiades tells of Socrates, his
companion in arms: "I found him," he says, "after the rout
of our army, him and Laches, among the last of the fugitives,
and I watched him at my leisure and in safety, for I was on
a good horse and he on foot, and thus we had fought. I

Of Coaches

observed specially how much discretion and resolution he showed in comparison with Laches; and then the gallantry of his step, in nowise different from his usual pace, his steady and well-directed glance, regarding and judging what was taking place about him, looking sometimes at these, sometimes at those,—friends and foes,—in a way that encouraged the former and signified to the latter that he would sell his blood and his life dear to whosoever should try to take it from him; and thus saved himself and Laches. For such men are not readily attacked; it is the terrified who are pursued."[8] Such is the testimony of this great captain which teaches us, what we experience every day, that nothing so casts us into danger as an inconsiderate eagerness to avoid it. *Usually the less fear there is, the less is the danger.*[9] Our common people are mistaken when they say that such a man fears death because they recognise that he is thinking about it, and that he foresees it. Foresight belongs equally to what touches us for good and for ill. To consider and estimate our danger is to some extent the opposite of being daunted by it.

I do not feel myself to be strong enough to withstand the onset and impetuosity of this passion of fear or of any other vehement passion.[10] If I were once vanquished and prostrated by it I should never quite wholly recover myself. What had caused my soul to lose her footing would never permit her to stand upright again as before; she examines and searches herself too keenly and profoundly, and therefore would never allow the wound she had received to close and heal. It has been well for me that no illness has ever yet upset her; every attack that is made upon me I meet and resist armed from head to foot;[11] so the first one who should

Of Coaches

prevail over me would leave me without resource. There is no need of a second;[12] at whatever point the flood breaks through my embankment, there I find myself irremediably open and submerged. Epicurus says that the wise man can never pass from that state to its contrary.[13] I have some belief, on the other hand, that he who has once been very foolish will never at any other time be very wise. God sends the cold according to the garment, and sends me afflictions[14] according to the power that I have to withstand them. Nature, having uncovered me on one side, has covered me on the other; having sparingly supplied me with strength, she has supplied me with insensibility and with a limited or dull power of apprehension.[15]

Now, I can not endure for long (and I found it in my youth more difficult to endure) either coach, or litter, or boat, and I detest every other conveyance than a horse whether in a city or in the country; but I can endure a litter less well than a coach, and I can more easily endure, for the same reason, a rough agitation of the water, enough to give rise to fear, than the motion that is felt in calm weather. By the slight shock that the oars give in pushing the boat under us, I feel my head and stomach disordered, I know not how; just as I can not endure an unsteady seat beneath me. When a sail or a current carries us along smoothly, or when we are towed, that unbroken movement does not disturb me at all; it is intermittent motion that harms me, and especially when it is gentle. I can not otherwise describe it. Physicians have ordered me to compress and gird my abdomen with a bandage, to provide for this mishap, but I have not tried it, being wont to wrestle with the defects of my nature and to overcome them by myself.

Of Coaches

Were my memory sufficiently instructed, I would not grudge the time to speak here of the infinite variety that history presents of the use, varying in different nations and in different periods, of chariots for service in war; of great effect, it seems to me, and of urgent necessity; so that it is a wonder that we have lost all knowledge thereof. I will say about this only that just recently, in the time of our fathers, the Hungarians made very profitable use of them against the Turks, each of them carrying a soldier with a buckler[16] and a musketeer and a number of harquebuses side by side, ready loaded, the whole protected by a screen of shields[17] after the fashion of a galley. Their battle-front was formed by three thousand such chariots, and, after the cannon had given the signal, they sent them forward and made the enemy swallow that volley before tasting the rest; or else they drove the chariots into the enemy's ranks, to break them and open the way—not to speak of the assistance derived from them in flanking, in a dangerous spot, troops marching from place to place, or in quickly protecting and fortifying a post. In my time a gentleman living on one of our frontiers, who was of unwieldly size and could find no horse able to carry his weight, being engaged in hostilities,[18] travelled through the country in a chariot of this description and found himself well suited by it. But let us leave these war-chariots. The kings of our first race,[19] as if their indolence were not well enough known by stronger tokens,[20] drove through the country in a coach drawn by four oxen. Mark Antony was the first who had himself drawn through Rome, and a minstrel wench with him, by lions harnessed to a coach. Heliogabalus afterward did the same, calling himself Cybele, mother of the Gods; and was also drawn by tigers, counterfeiting the god Bacchus; sometimes, too, he harnessed two stags to his coach, and at another time four dogs, and again four naked wenches, being drawn by them in state, himself stark naked. The Emperor Firmus had his coach drawn by ostriches of marvellous size, so that he seemed to fly rather than to roll along.[21]

The strangeness of these manners puts into my head this different thought: that it is a kind of pusillanimity in monarchs and a proof that they do not sufficiently recognise what they are, when they labour to make themselves honoured and conspicuous by excessive expenditure. It would be excusable in a foreign land; but among his own subjects, where he is all-powerful, he derives from his high position the most extreme degree of honour to which he can attain; as likewise in the case of a gentleman, it seems to me that it is superfluous to dress handsomely at home: his house, his retinue, his table sufficiently answer for him. The advice that Isocrates gives his king does not seem to me unreasonable: that he should be splendid in furniture and household articles, since that is a permanent outlay which descends to his successors; and that he should avoid all kinds of magnificence that shortly pass out of use and out of remembrance.[22] I liked when I was young to dress handsomely, lacking other handsomeness, and it became me well; there are those on whom fine clothes are wasted.[23]

We have wonderful accounts of the frugality of our kings in regard to their persons and their gifts—great kings in reputation, in valour, and in fortune. Demosthenes opposed valiantly the law of his city which allotted the public funds for the stately conduct of games and of their festivals; he would have their greatness shew itself in a number of well-equipped ships and of good, well-furnished armies.[24] And there is reason to blame Theophrastus, who sets forth a contrary opinion in his book on riches, and maintains that kind of outlay to be the proper fruit of opulence.[25] These are pleasures, says Aristotle,[26] which concern only the lowest commonalty, which vanish from the memory as soon as one is sated with them, and which no judicious and sober-minded man can value. It would seem to me much more royal as well as more useful, just, and durable, that such funds should be used for ports, harbours, fortifications, and walls, stately buildings, churches, hospitals, schools, and the improvement of streets and roads;[27] wherein Pope Gregory XIII left a memory long to be praised; and wherein our Queen Catherine would testify for long years to come her natural liberality and munificence, if her means were sufficient for her desires. Fortune has greatly pained me by interrupting the fine structure of the new bridge of our great city and depriving me of the hope of seeing it in use before I die.

Moreover, it seems to the subjects who are spectators of these triumphal shows that their own riches are displayed to them and that they are feasted at their own expense; for the people generally presume with their kings, as we do with our servants, that they are to take care to supply us in abundance with all that we need, but that they are in no wise to have any part in it. And therefore the Emperor Galba, having received pleasure from a musician during his supper, had his money-box brought and gave him a handful of crowns, which he took from it, with these words; "This is not public money, it is my own."[28] But it most often happens that the people are right, and that their eyes are fed

1226

with what should feed their stomachs. Liberality itself has not its full lustre in the hands of a sovereign; private persons have more claim; for, to take it as things are, a king has nothing really his own: he owes himself to others. The power of administering justice is conferred not for the benefit of him who judges, but for the benefit of him who is judged. One man is made superior to another, never for his own benefit, but for the benefit of the inferior; and a physician is a physician for the sick man's sake, not for his own. The purpose of all authority,[29] as of all art, lies outside of itself: *No art is concerned with itself.*[30] For this reason they who have charge of the childhood of princes, when they pride themselves upon inculcating in them this virtue of open-handedness, and teach them never to deny any thing and to regard nothing so well employed as what they give (instruction which I have seen to be much in favour in my day) either look more to their own profit than to the profit of their master, or ill understand to whom they speak. It is too easy to instill liberality in him who has the wherewithal to indulge it as much as he will at the expense of others. And as the esteem in which he is held is governed, not by the measure of the present, but by the measure of the means of him who practises liberality, it becomes a vain thing in hands so powerful. They find that they are prodigal before they are liberal. Hence, it[31] is of little worth in comparison with other kingly virtues, and is, as the tyrant Dionysius said, the only one that suits well with tyranny itself.[32] I would teach them rather this verse of the husbandman of old,—

Τῇ χειρὶ δεῖ σπείρειν, ἀλλὰ μὴ ὅλῳ τῷ θυλάκω,[33]—

1227

that he who would have a good crop must sow with the
hand, not pour from a bag; the seed must be scattered, not
spilt; and that, having to give, or, to say better, to pay and
return to so many people according to what they have deserved, he must be a loyal and discreet dispenser. If a prince's
liberality lacks prudence and moderation, I like better that
he should be avaricious.

Kingly virtue seems to consist chiefly in justice; and of all
the parts of justice, that which is in company with liberality
best stamps kings; for that they have reserved for their special office, while all other forms of justice they administer
through the instrumentality of others. Unmeasured bounty
is a feeble means for them to acquire good-will; for it repels
more people than it attracts. *The more you use it for the
good of many, the less you can use it for the good of many.
Now what is more foolish than to make it impossible for
you to continue to shew your good-will?*[34] And if it be
employed without respect to merit, it puts to shame him
who receives it, and it is received without gratitude. Tyrants
have been sacrificed to the hatred of the people by the
hands of the very men whom they have wrongfully advanced,—buffoons, panders, minstrels, and other such riff-
raff,[35]—these thinking to make secure their possession of advantages improperly received, by shewing that they hold in
contempt and hatred him from whom they came, and that
therein they agree with the popular judgement and opinion.
The subjects of a prince immoderate in gifts become immoderate in demands; they carve for themselves[36], not with
reason, but by example. Surely there is often cause for blushing at our impudence; we are overpaid from the standpoint
of justice, when the recompense equals our service; for do

we owe to our prince nothing by natural obligation? If he makes good all we have expended, he does too much; it is enough if he helps with it; more than that is to be called beneficence, which can not be exacted, for the very word liberality suggests liberty. With our way of doing, this has no end; what has been received is not taken into account; only future liberality gives pleasure; wherefore the more a prince exhausts himself in giving, the more he impoverishes himself in friends. How should he satisfy desires which increase in proportion as they are replenished?[37] He whose thoughts are of taking no longer thinks of what he has taken; greed has nothing so much its own as being ungrateful.

The example of Cyrus will not ill fit this place, to serve the kings of to-day as a touchstone to recognise whether their gifts are well or ill bestowed, and to show them how much more fortunately that emperor aimed his gifts than they do; since they are reduced to make their subsequent borrowings from subjects unknown to them, and rather from those whom they have treated ill than from those whom they have treated well, and they receive assistance in which there is nothing gratuitous save the name. Crœsus reproved him[38] for his bounty and reckoned up what his wealth would have amounted to if he had kept his hands more tightly closed. He desired to justify his liberality, and, sending messengers on all sides to the grandees of his realm whom he had especially favoured, requested each of them to assist him with as much money as he could, to meet an urgent call upon him, and to send it to him with a statement.[39] When all the notes were brought to him, each of his friends, thinking that it was not enough to do for him to offer him only as much as he himself had received from his munificence, adding thereto much of his own wealth, it was found that the total amounted to much more than what was claimed by the thrift of Crœsus. Whereupon Cyrus remarked: "I am no less enamoured of wealth than other princes and am rather a better manager of it. You see at how little cost I have acquired the inestimable treasure of so many friends, and how much more loyal treasurers they are for me than would be mercenary men, without obligation or affection; and that my substance is better placed than in strong boxes calling down upon me the hatred, envy, and contempt of other princes."[40]

The emperors found an excuse for the extravagant cost of their games and public shows in that their authority some-what depended (at least in appearance) on the humour of the Roman people, who had been accustomed time out of mind to be courted by spectacles and excessive expenditure of this sort. But originally it had been private persons who had fostered this custom of conferring pleasure on their fellow citizens and friends, chiefly from their own purse, by such profusion, and magnificence; it had quite a different savour when the masters came to copy it. *The transference of money from its rightful owners to strangers should not be regarded as generous.*[41] Philip, because his son tried by gifts to gain the good-will of the Macedonians, thus rebuked him in a letter: "What! dost thou desire that thy subjects should regard thee as their purse-bearer, not as their king? Wouldst thou bribe them? Bribe them with the benefits of thy virtue, not with the benefits of thy strong-box."[42]

It was, however, a fine thing to have brought and planted in the amphitheatre a large number of big trees, all growing

Of Coaches

and flourishing, disposed in a beautiful arrangement to represent a great shady forest; and the first day to turn therein a thousand ostriches, a thousand stags, a thousand wild boars, and a thousand fallow deer, abandoning them to the populace to destroy; the next day, to have slaughtered in its presence a hundred great lions, a hundred leopards, and three hundred bears; and the third day to have three hundred pairs of gladiators fight to the death—and this was done by the Emperor Probus.[43] It was also a fine thing to see those vast amphitheatres, the outside faced with marble, wrought with carvings and statues, the interior gleaming with rare enrichment,—

> The circuit of the theatre bestudded with gems, the
> portico overlaid with gold,[44]—

all the sides of this great open space filled and environed from the bottom to the top with sixty or eighty rows of seats, also of marble, covered with cushions,—

> "Let him depart," he says, "if he is ashamed, and
> let him rise from the cushioned seat of a knight, if his
> property is not enough for the law,"[45]—

on which a hundred thousand men could sit comfortably, and [when the sports began] the space in the centre, where the games were played, was made, first by artificial means, to gape and split into chasms, representing caves which vomited forth the beasts appointed for the spectacle; and then it was inundated with deep water in which swam many sea monsters and on which floated armed ships, to represent a naval battle; and after that it was drained and dried up anew for the combats of the gladiators; and finally it was strewn with cinnabar and storax, instead of sand, to prepare for an accustomed festival for that whole infinite number of people—the last act of a single day;

> How often we have seen part of the arena sink, and wild beasts come forth upon it from a cavern forced open in the earth; and often then, from the same dark place, a grove of gilded trees with saffron bark grow up. Nor was it only the monsters of the forest that we saw: I have beheld sea-calves fighting with bears, and beasts like horses, but for their hideous form.[46]

Sometimes there was constructed there a high hill covered with fruit trees and trees in full leaf, and at its summit gushed a stream of water as from the mouth of a living spring. Sometimes a great ship was sailing along, which opened and divided of itself, and having brought forth from its womb four or five hundred beasts to be fought with, closed again and vanished without help. At other times, from the floor of the arena they made springs and streams of water shoot out, which mounted aloft to that measureless height, and sprinkled and perfumed that great multitude. To protect themselves from the inclemency of the weather, they covered that vast space sometimes with embroidered purple curtains, sometimes with silk of this or that colour, and spread them and drew them back in a moment as they chose:

> Though the amphitheatre is hot under an intemperate sun, the awnings are taken in when Hermogenes comes.[47]

The screens, too, which were placed in front of the spectators, to protect them from the fury of those unchained beasts, were woven of gold:

The screens, too, gleam, wrought with gold.[48]

If there is any thing excusable in such extravagance, it is where the conception and the novelty, not the expense, are the source of admiration.

Even in these vanities we perceive how fertile those past ages were in other wits than ours. It is with this kind of fertility as with all other productions of Nature. This is not to say that she then put forth her supreme effort. We do not advance at all, rather we wander and turn about in circles here and there; we retrace our steps. I fear that our knowledge is weak in all directions; we see neither far forward nor far backward; it embraces little and lives little, being short both in extent of time and in extent of matter.

There lived many brave men before Agamemnon, but they all lie forgotten in darkness, where none can weep for them.[49]

And before the Theban war and the calamity of Troy, many other poets sang of other deeds.[50]

And Solon's narrative of what he had learned from the priests of Egypt of the long continuance of their method and manner of learning and preserving the histories of other nations,[51] seems to me a testimony not to be rejected in this regard. *If we could see the boundless extent of space and of time into which the mind casts itself, and which in its contemplation it traverses far and wide, without finding an ultimate limit on which to rest, in this infinite immensity there would appear an innumerable multitude of forms.*[52]

1233

Of Coaches

If all that has come down to us from the past were true and were known to any one, it would be less than nothing compared with what is unknown. And of the present state of the world that is slipping on while we are in it, how trivial and restricted is the knowledge of the most studious! Not only regarding special occurrences, which chance often renders characteristic[53] and important, but regarding the condition of great governments and nations, a hundred-fold more about them escapes us than comes to our knowledge. We exclaim at the miracles of the invention of our artillery, of our printing; other men, at the other side of the world, in China, enjoyed them a thousand years earlier. If we saw as much of the world as we do not see, we should discern, so it is to be believed, a perpetual multiplication and vicissitude of forms. There is nothing single and rare in respect to nature, but there is in respect to our knowledge, which is a wretched foundation for our rules, and which easily offers us an exceeding false image of things. As we to-day idly conclude the downward tendency and decrepitude of the world by arguments which we derive from our own weakness and decadence,—

So now our age is corrupted, and the earth is less productive,[54]—

so idly did this poet[55] conclude its recent birth and youth from the vigour that he saw in the minds of his time, abounding in various thoughts and inventions of various arts:

Nay, the universe, I think, is new, and the world is fresh, and did not come into being long ago; so some arts are now being perfected, or are now even becoming greater, and many things are now discovered in the art of navigation.[56]

Our world has lately discovered another (and who can assure us that it is the last of its brethren, since the spirits, the sibyls, and we ourselves have known nothing of this one until now?[57]), no less large, as fully peopled and fruitful as our world,[58] but so new and so infantine that it is still taught its A B C; it is not fifty years since it knew neither letters nor weights nor measures nor garments nor corn nor vines; it was still a naked baby in arms, and lived solely on what it received from its mother-nurse. If we judge aright of our end, and this poet[59] of the youth of his period, this other world will come into full light when ours is departing therefrom; the universe will be paralysed; one member will be useless, the other in full vigour. I much fear that we shall have greatly hastened its decline and ruin by our contagion, and that we shall have sold our beliefs and our arts to it very dear. It was an infant world, yet we have not whipped and subdued it to our teaching by the advantage of our worth and native strength, or won its favour by our justice and kindness, or subjugated it by our magnanimity. The greater part of the answers and of the negotiations entered into with them witness that they are in no wise inferior to us in native clearness of mind and pertinence. The startling magnificence of the cities of Cuzco and of Mexico and, among other like matters, the king's garden in which all the trees and fruits and all the plants, in the same arrangement and size that they have in a garden, were wonderfully fashioned of gold,—as, in his cabinet, were all the animals native to his land and his waters,—and the beauty of their

Of Coaches

work in precious stones, in feathers, in cotton, and in painting,[60] shew that in craftsmanship also they are in no wise inferior to us.

But as for piety, observance of the laws, kindliness, liberality, loyalty, frankness, it has served us well to have less
than they; they were lost by this advantage over us, and sold
and betrayed themselves. As for hardiness and courage, as
for staunchness, constancy, resolute endurance of pain and
of hunger and of death, I should not fear to oppose examples
that I could find among them to the most famous ancient
examples that we have in the traditions of our world on this
side of the ocean.[61] For, as to those who have subjugated
them, take away the strategems and trickery which they
made use of to deceive them, and the natural amazement
which it brought to the latter nations—to see so unexpectedly the arrival of bearded men different from themselves in language, in religion, in bearing, and in aspect,
coming from so distant a part of the world which they had
never known to be inhabited at all, mounted on great unfamiliar monsters, opposed to those who had never seen, not
only a horse, but any beast whatever trained to carry and
support a man or any other burden; furnished with a shin-
ing and hard skin and armed with a sharp and glittering
weapon, opposed to those who bartered great wealth of gold
and pearls for the marvel of the gleam of a mirror or a knife,
and who had neither knowledge nor substance by which
they could in any length of time pierce our steel; and
furthermore to the lightning and thunder of our cannon
and harquebuses, capable of dismaying even Cæsar, had he
been surprised by them as unprepared as were these, opposed
to peoples that were naked except where some weaving of

1236

Of Coaches

cotton had been invented, without other weapons, for the most part, than bows, stones, clubs, and wooden shields, peoples taken by surprise under colour of friendliness and good faith and by curiosity to see strange and unfamiliar things—take away, I say, from the conquerors this disparity and you take from them the whole occasion of so many victories. When I consider the indomitable ardour with which so many thousands of men, women and children so often come forward and fling themselves upon inevitable dangers in defence of their gods and of their liberty—this generous obstinacy in enduring all extremities and difficulties, and death, rather than submit to the domination of those by whom they have been so shamefully deceived, some choosing rather, when captured, to pine away from hunger and fasting than to accept food from the hands of their enemies, so basely victorious—I perceive that whosoever should have attacked them on equal terms, of weapons and of experience and of numbers, would have been as much in peril as in any war that we know, and even more so.

Would that so noble a conquest had occurred under Alexander, or under the old Greeks and Romans; and that such a vast change and transformation of so many empires and peoples had fallen into hands which would have gently trimmed and done away with what there was of barbarism and would have encouraged and strengthened the good roots that nature had there implanted, not only introducing in the cultivation of the soil and the adornment of the cities the arts of this part of the world so far as they might have been necessary, but also adding the Greek and Roman virtues to those native to the country! What a reparation to them it would have been, and what an improvement for the whole

world, if the first examples of our conduct that we offered to
view in those parts had inspired those nations with admiration and imitation of virtue, and had brought about between them and us a fraternal intercourse and understanding. How easy it would have been to make a helpful use[62] of
souls so pure, so eager to be taught, having for the most part
such admirable inclinations! On the contrary, we made use
of their ignorance and inexperience to bend them more easily
toward treachery, lust, covetousness, and toward every sort
of inhumanity and cruelty, by the example and pattern of
our conduct. When was so high a price ever set on the course
of trade and traffic? So many cities destroyed, so many nations exterminated, so many millions put to the sword, and
the richest and fairest portion of the world turned topsy-
turvy to obtain pearls and pepper—victories of commerce![63]
Never did ambition, never did national enmities, impel men
to such horrible hostility toward others.

Some Spaniards, coasting the sea in quest of mines,
landed in a fertile and attractive region, thickly inhabited,
and made their wonted representations to the people: that
they were peaceable folk, coming from far countries, sent by
the King of Castile, the greatest prince of the habitable
world, to whom the Pope, the representative of God on
earth, had given the sovereignty of all the Indies; that, if
the people chose to be his tributaries, they would be most
benignantly treated. They[64] asked for provisions for their
sustenance, and gold to use for a certain medicine; furthermore, they urged upon them belief in one God and the truth
of our religion, which they advised them to accept, adding
to their advice some threats. The reply was this: that, as for
being peaceably inclined, they had not the look of it, if they

were so; as for their king, since he asked alms, he must be poor and necessitous; and he[65] who had made this allotment to him must be a man who loved dissension, giving to a third person something that was not his to give, thus placing him at odds with the former possessors; as for provisions, those they would supply; as for gold, they had little of it and it was a thing they held in little esteem, inasmuch as it was useless in the service of their life, about which all their care looked solely to passing it happily and pleasantly, but whatever they[66] could find of it, save that which was used in the service of their gods, they might freely take; as for a single God, what had been said had pleased them, but they did not wish to change their religion, having been for so long a time so beneficially helped by it, and that they were wont to take counsel only of their friends and acquaintance; as for the threats, it was a sign of lack of judgement to threaten those whose character and resources were unknown; therefore, let them make haste to vacate the territory forthwith; for they[67] were not accustomed to take in good part the familiarities[68] and admonitions of armed men who were strangers; otherwise (exhibiting to them, without their city, the heads of several men who had been executed), they would treat them as they had these others. This is an example of the childish speech of this infant people. But it is to be observed that neither in this place nor in several others where the Spaniards did not find the articles of value they sought, did they make any stay or enter into any relations, whatever other conveniences there were there; witness my cannibals.[69]

Of the two most powerful kings in that part of the world (and perchance in the whole world), kings of so many kings, the last two whom they[70] expelled from this land, one was the King of Peru, who was taken in battle and held for ransom in so exorbitant a sum that it passes all belief; and when this had been loyally paid, and when in intercourse he had given proof of a frank, free, and faithful nature and of a clear and well-ordered understanding, the conquerors (after they had extorted from him one million, three hundred and twenty-five thousand, five hundred weight of gold, besides silver and other things which amounted to no less a sum, so that their horses were thenceforth shod only with solid gold) were desirous still to find out, at whatever cost of faithlessness, what might be the rest of the king's treasures, and freely to possess themselves of what he had locked up. They brought a false charge and witness against him: that he intended to induce his provinces to rise and restore him to liberty. Whereupon, by the admirable sentence decreed by the very men who had plotted this treachery against him, he was condemned to be publicly hanged and strangled, having been forced to purchase remission from the torture of being burned alive, by the baptism which they gave him in his last hour: a shocking and unheard of irregularity, which he none the less endured without derogating from himself either in bearing or in speech, with a truly royal demeanour and stateliness. And then, to calm the people, stunned and bewildered by so strange a spectacle, they feigned great grief at his death and appointed a magnificent funeral ceremony.[71]

The other, the King of Mexico,[72] having for a long time defended his besieged city, and having shewn during the siege all that both endurance and perseverance can do, if ever it was shewn by prince and people, and his ill-fortune

Of Coaches

having delivered him alive into the hands of his enemies on condition that he should be treated as a king,—and nothing was seen in him whilst in prison unbefitting that title,—they,[73] not having found after this victory all the gold that they had promised themselves, when they had ransacked and rifled everywhere, began to seek information about it by inflicting upon the prisoners whom they held the severest tortures they could devise. But as they gained nothing by this, finding their victims' hearts stronger than their tortures, they at last became so enraged that, contrary to their faith and to every law of nations, they condemned the king himself and one of the chief nobles of his court to be put to the torture in each other's presence. This noble, finding himself overcome by the pain, being surrounded with hot coals, turned his face piteously at last to his master, as if to ask for mercy because he could endure no more. The king, fixing his eyes haughtily and sternly upon him, as in reproof of his cowardice and pusillanimity, said these words only, in a harsh and unfaltering voice: "And I, am I in a cold bath? Am I more comfortable than you?" The other immediately succumbed to the suffering, and so died. The king, half-roasted, was taken thence, not so much from pity (for what pity ever touched souls so inhuman that, for the sake of uncertain information about some vessel of gold to steal, they would have a man broiled before their eyes, to say nothing of his being a king so great both in fortune and in merit), but because his firmness made their cruelty more and more shameful. They hanged him afterward, he having courageously attempted to free himself by his own hand[74] from the long captivity and subjection; and even thus he rendered his end worthy of a high-minded prince.

Of Coaches

At another time they caused to be burned, in one and the same fire, four hundred and sixty living men; four hundred of the common people, sixty of the chief nobles of the province, mere prisoners of war.[75] We have these narrations from themselves,[76] for not only do they admit them, they boast of them and proclaim them. Is it as testimony of their justice or of religious zeal? Unquestionably these are methods too contrary and inimical to so holy an end. Had they proposed to themselves to extend our faith, they would have considered that it is not by the possession of territory that it increases in power, but by the possession of men, and would have been only too well satisfied with the slaughter made necessary by war, without adding thereto likewise a butchery as of wild beasts, as nearly universal as sword and fire could bring to pass, having intentionally preserved from it only so many as they wished to use as unhappy slaves for labour and service in their mines. Consequently, many of the leaders[77] were put to death in the locality that they had conquered, by order of the kings of Castile, justly outraged by the horror of their conduct; and almost all were held in contempt, and hated. God deservedly ordained that this vast booty should be swallowed up by the sea, in transport, or by the intestine wars in which they consumed one another; and the greater number were buried where they died[78] and had no fruit from their victory.

As for the revenue,—even in the hands of a thrifty and prudent prince,[79]—it answers very little to the hopes that were held out about it to his predecessors, and to the first abundant supply of riches which were found in the beginning in these newly discovered lands (for, although much is being drawn therefrom, we see that it is nothing in comparison with what might be expected); this is because the use of coin was entirely unknown there, and consequently their gold was found all in masses, serving no other purpose than for show and parade, as an heirloom descending[80] from father to son through many powerful kings, who were always working their mines to the utmost, in order to make that vast quantity of vessels and statues for the adornment of their palaces and temples; whereas our gold is all used in business and in commerce. We cut it up and change it, circulate it, and disperse it in a thousand ways. Imagine if our kings should thus hoard up for several centuries all the gold that they could lay their hands on and let it lie idle!

The people of the Kingdom of Mexico were somewhat more civilised and more well-informed than the other nations of those lands; so they judged, as we do, that the universe was near its end, and took as a sign of this the desolation that we brought upon them. They believed that the existence of the world is divided into five ages and into the life of five consecutive suns, of which four had already completed their time; and that the one which then shone upon them was the fifth. The first perished with all the other creatures by a universal flood. The second by the fall of the heavens upon the earth, which stifled every living thing; to which age they assigned the giants, and they shewed the Spaniards bones, according to the proportion of which the stature of men reached twenty palms. The third, by fire, which burned and consumed all things. The fourth, by a tumult of air and wind which cast down even many mountains; human beings did not die, but men were changed to apes (what impressions does not the foolishness of human belief receive!). After the death of this fourth sun the world was in unbroken darkness for twenty-five years, in the fifteenth year of which were created a man and a woman who renewed the human race. Ten years later, on a certain day, the sun appeared, newly created, and since then the numbering of their years begins from that day. On the third day after the creation of the sun, the ancient gods died; the new ones were born after that, from day to day.[81] My authority learned nothing of what they think of the manner in which this last sun will perish; but their reckoning of this fourth change falls in with that great conjunction of the planets which caused, some eight hundred and odd years ago, as the astrologers calculate, many great alterations and new conditions in the world.

As to pomp and magnificence, by which path I entered into this subject, neither Greece, nor Rome, nor Egypt can compare, whether in usefulness or difficulty or nobleness, any of its public works to the road which is seen in Peru, built by the kings of the country, from the City of Quito to that of Cusco,—three hundred leagues,—straight, level, twenty-five paces wide, paved, enclosed on one and the other side by beautiful and high walls; and all along these walls, on the inner side, two never-failing streams bordered by fine trees which they call *molly*. Where they met with mountains and rocks, they cut and levelled them, and filled the hollows with stone and lime. At every limit of a day's journey there are fine palaces supplied with provisions, garments, and weapons, as well for travellers as for the armies which have to pass that way. In estimating this work I have taken into account the difficulty of it, which is especially considerable in that region. They did not build with stones smaller than ten feet square; they had no other means of

Of Coaches

transportation than dragging their load by strength of arm; and had not even the art of scaffolding, knowing in its stead no other way than to pile earth against the building as it rose, and take it away afterward.[82]

Let us return to our coaches. In place of them and of any other vehicle, these people had themselves carried on men's shoulders. The last King of Peru, the day he was captured, was thus borne among his troops, seated in a chair of gold. As fast as they killed his bearers in order to make him fall to the ground (for they wished to take him alive), as many others immediately took the places of the dead, so that he could not be cast down, whatever the slaughter of those men, until a horseman seized hold of his body and threw him to the earth.[83]

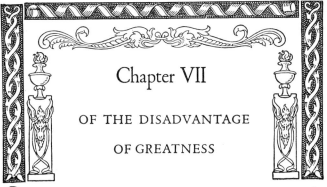

Chapter VII

OF THE DISADVANTAGE

OF GREATNESS

SINCE we can not attain it, let us avenge ourselves by speaking ill of it. Yet it is not altogether speaking ill of a thing to discover defects in it; there are some in all things, however admirable and desirable they may be. Generally speaking, greatness has this manifest advantage, that she can descend from her heights when she pleases; and she well-nigh has her choice between the two conditions: for it is not from all heights that a man falls; from most he can descend without falling.[1] It seems to me in truth that we place too high a value on greatness, and that we also overvalue the determination of those whom we have seen or heard of as having despised it or as having renounced it intentionally. Its essential quality is not so distinctly of value that we can not without a miracle refuse it. I hold the endurance of ills to be a very difficult effort, but I hold that contentment with a moderate degree of fortune and the absence[2] of greatness is a small matter. That is a virtue, it seems to me, to which I, who am but a green goose, might attain without much struggle. What is to be said of those[3] who might also take into consideration the glory that accompanied this rejection, in which perchance there may be more

Of the Disadvantage of Greatness

ambition than in the desire itself and the enjoyment of greatness; inasmuch as ambition never conducts itself more in
accordance with nature than by an out-of-the-way and un-
frequented path?

I strengthen my heart in respect to patience, I weaken it
in respect to desire. I have as much to wish for as another,
and I allow my wishes as much liberty and indiscretion; but
yet it has never happened to me to desire either imperial or
royal power,[4] or the preëminence of high and commanding
station. I do not aim thereat; I love myself too much. When
I think of becoming greater, it would be in a humble way,
by an increase in resolution, in good sense, in health, in
beauty, and in wealth also—an involuntary and unpretend-
ing growth suitable for me. But a great reputation, a powerful authority, oppresses my imagination; and, just the opposite of that other,[5] I should peradventure like better to be
second or third in Périgueux than first at Paris;[6] or at least,
quite truly third rather than first in office at Paris. I do not
desire either to wrangle with an usher as an unrecognised
nobody, or have the throng through which I may pass open
to do me honour. I am adapted to a middle station, as by my
fate, so by my taste; and I have shown in the conduct of my
life and of my undertakings that I have rather avoided than
otherwise climbing higher than the degree of fortune in
which God placed my birth. All natural appointment[7] is
equally just and easy.

I have so indolent a soul that I do not measure good-fortune by its height, I measure it by its facility. But if my
heart is not great enough, it is proportionably a frank one,
and bids me boldly publish its weakness. Should some one
propose to me to compare the life of L. Thorius Balbus,—a

Of the Disadvantage of Greatness

brave, handsome, learned and healthy man, who was familiar with, and abounding in, all kinds of advantages and pleasures, passing tranquil days of which he was absolute master,[8] his soul well fortified against death, superstition, sufferings, and other afflictions incident to humanity; dying finally in battle, arms in hand, in defence of his country,— if, I say, it were proposed to compare his life with the life of M. Regulus, great and lofty, as every one knows, and his admirable end, the one life nameless and unhonoured, the other extraordinarily conspicuous and glorious, I should certainly say of them what Cicero says of them,[9] could I express myself as well as he. But were I obliged to write of them in relation to my own life,[10] I should add that the first is as much according to my scope, and my desire, which I conform to my scope, as the second is far beyond it; that I can touch the one only through veneration, while I would willingly touch the other through familiarity.

Let us return to our temporal greatness, from which we have digressed.

I greatly dislike control, whether active or passive. Otanez, one of the seven who had a lawful claim to the kingdom of Persia, took a course which I would readily have taken: he relinquished in favour of his competitors his right to be raised to the throne by election or by lot, provided that he and his might live in that realm free from all subjection and control save that of the ancient laws, and might enjoy all liberty that would not be prejudicial to those laws, being as intolerant of ruling as of being ruled.[11]

The most unpleasant and the most difficult profession in the world, in my opinion, is to act worthily the part of king. I excuse more of their shortcomings than people commonly

Of the Disadvantage of Greatness

do, in consideration of the terrible burden of their office, which astounds me. It is difficult to keep within bounds, with such unbounded power; yet the fact is that, even for those who are least excellent by nature, there is a special incitement to virtue in being placed in a position where your every good act is registered and reported, and where the least well-doing affects so many persons, and where your faculties, like those of preachers, are used chiefly for the common people, a judge far from exacting, easily deceived, easily satisfied. There are few things about which we could give a sincere judgement, because there are few in which we have not, in one way or another, a private interest. Superiority and inferiority, control and subjection, are bound to innate rivalry and contestation; they must needs perpetually encroach on one another.[12] I believe neither the one nor the other concerning the rights of his associate; let us leave it to reason, which is inflexible and impassive, to pronounce upon this when we can have recourse to it. Not a month ago I was turning the leaves of two Scotch books[13] which are at odds on this subject: the one[14] on the side of the people makes the king to be of lower station than a carter; the one on the side of monarchy sets him some degrees above God in power and sovereignty.

Now the disadvantage of greatness, which I have undertaken to comment on here because of a certain occurrence which lately brought it to my mind, is this: there is, peradventure, nothing more delightful in human intercourse than the contests that we engage in against one another, from rivalry in honour and prowess, whether in exercises of the body or of the mind, in which sovereign greatness has no part. In truth, it has often seemed to me that by force of re-

Of the Disadvantage of Greatness

spect we treat princes scornfully and insultingly; for the thing which infinitely offended me in my youth—that they who competed with me forbore exerting themselves in good earnest, because they found me unworthy of their full strength—that is what we see happen to them[15] every day, every one finding himself unworthy to put forth his full strength against them. If it is perceived that they have ever so little desire for victory, there is no man who does not labour to give it to them, and who does not prefer to be faithless to his own fame rather than to injure theirs; only so much effort is used as is necessary for their honour. What share have they in the mellay when every one is on their side? I seem to see those paladins of old days appearing in tournaments and combats, with their bodies and armour protected by enchantments. Brisson, running a race against Alexander, hung behind;[16] Alexander reproved him for it, but he should have had him whipped. In this connection Carneades said that the children of princes learn nothing rightly except to manage horses, inasmuch as in all other doings every one yields to them and owns himself beaten; but a horse, which is neither a flatterer nor a courtier, throws the king's son to the ground as he would the son of a porter.[17]

Homer was forced to agree that Venus, a divinity so gentle and so delicate, should be wounded at the siege of Troy, in order to show her courage and daring, qualities which in no wise belong to those who are exempt from danger. The gods are represented as angry, afraid, running away, jealous of one another, grieving, impatient, in order to do them honour by endowing them with the virtues which for us are founded upon these imperfections. He who does not partici-

1250

Of the Disadvantage of Greatness

pate in the hazard and difficulty can claim no share of the honour and pleasure that follow hazardous deeds. It is a misfortune to be so powerful that all things must needs give way to you. Your high fortune puts society and companionship too far from you; it places you in solitude.[18] This ease and meaningless facility in making every thing bend beneath one is a foe to every sort of pleasure; this is sliding, not walking; sleeping, not living. Conceive man invested with omnipotence—you cast him into unknown depths; he must beg you, as alms, for opposition and resistance; his very being and his welfare depend upon indigence.

The good qualities[19] are as if dead and hidden, for these are perceived only by comparison and they are outside that; they have little knowledge of true praise, being exposed to such continuous and uniform approbation. If they have to deal with the dullest of their subjects, they have no means of gaining an advantage over him; by saying, "It is because he is my king," it seems to him[20] that he has said clearly enough that he has lent a helping hand in being overmastered. This quality[21] stifles and swallows up all the other real and essential qualities; those are buried in the royalty, and it allows them[22] to show their worth only by the actions which are immediately connected with their rank and which are of avail in it—the duties of their office; it is so much to be king that they can be nothing else.[23] The peculiar glamour that surrounds a king conceals him and secretes him from us; our sight is dimmed and bewildered by it, being dazzled and stayed[24] by that strong light. The Senate awarded the prize for eloquence to Tiberius; he declined it, thinking that he could not be benefitted by a judgement so far from free, even were it sincere.[25]

Of the Disadvantage of Greatness

As we concede to them all advantages of honour, so do we encourage and justify their defects and vices, not only by approval but also by imitation. All Alexander's courtiers carried their heads on one side as he did; and the sycophants of Dionysius knocked against each other in his presence, and stumbled over and upset what came under their feet, to imply that they were as short-sighted as he.[26] Ruptures also have sometimes served as recommendation to favour. I have seen deafness affected; and Plutarch saw courtiers, because their master hated his wife, repudiate theirs whom they loved.[27] What is more, lechery has been known to be thought well of, and all sorts of dissoluteness, as well as disloyalty, blasphemy, cruelty, and heresy, and superstition, irreligion, laxity, and worse, if worse there be; following a course even much more dangerous than that of the sycophants of Mithridates, who, because their master laid claim to the distinction of being a good physician, allowed him to cut and cauterise their limbs;[28] for these others allow their souls, a more delicate and more noble part, to be cauterised.

But, to the end where I began, the Emperor Hadrian discussing with Favorinus the philosopher about the meaning of some word, Favorinus very soon gave him the victory. When his friends remonstrated with him, "You are jesting," he said; "would you have it that he, who commands thirty legions, does not know more than I do?"[29] Augustus wrote verses against Asinius Pollio; "And I," said Pollio, "am silent; it is not wise to write in competition with him who can prescribe." And they were right; for Dionysius, because he could not equal Philoxenus in poetry and Plato in argument, condemned one of them to the quarries and sent the other to be sold as a slave in the island of Ægina.[30]

1252

Chapter VIII

OF THE

ART OF CONVERSATION [1]

I T is a habit of our jurisdiction to condemn some persons for wrong-doing only as a warning to others. To condemn them because they have erred would be folly, as Plato says;[2] for what is done can not be undone; it is, therefore, to the end that they may not again err in the same way, or that the example of their offence may be shunned. We do not reform the man whom we hang: we reform others through him. What I do is of like character. My errors have become a part of my nature and incorrigible; but the public good that excellent men do by causing themselves to be imitated I shall do, perchance, by causing my example to be avoided.

> Do you not see what an evil life the son of Albus lives, and how needy Barrus is? They are a great lesson, to warn us against squandering a patrimony.[3]

As I publish and disclose my imperfections, some one may learn to fear them.[4] The qualities in myself which I value most derive more honour from my informing against myself than from my speaking well of myself; that is why I so frequently fall into this strain and remain in it. But when all is said, a man never talks of himself without loss: his own

Of the Art of Conversation

blame is always credited, his praise discredited. There may be some persons of my nature who learn more by contrariety than by conformity, and by avoidance than by following.[5] It was this sort of teaching that the elder Cato had in mind when he said that wise men have more to learn from fools than fools from wise men;[6] and that ancient player on the lyre, who, Pausanias reported, was in the habit of compelling his pupils to go to hear a bad player who lived opposite him, where they learned to detest his discords and false modulations. Horror of cruelty impels me more toward clemency than any pattern of clemency could attract me. A skilful horseman does not correct my seat so much as does an attorney or a Venetian on horseback; and a bad fashion of language improves mine more than a good one. Every day another's foolish behaviour admonishes me and counsels me; what stings touches and arouses better than what pleases. In these days it would be well for us to amend our ways by going backward, by disagreement rather than by agreement, by difference rather than by accord. Having learned little of what is good by examples, I make use of examples of what is bad, which lesson is common enough; the common spectacle of theft and perfidy has regulated and restrained my morals. I have endeavoured to make myself as agreeable as I saw others to be tedious; as firm as I saw others to be weak; as gentle as I saw others to be hard; as kind as I saw others to be unkind; but I proposed to myself unattainable standards.

The most fruitful and natural exercise of our minds is, in my opinion, conversation. I find the habit of it pleasanter than any other action of our lives; and that is why, if I were at this hour compelled to choose, I would consent, I do be-

Of the Art of Conversation

lieve, to lose my sight rather than hearing or speech. The Athenians and the Romans also held the practice of this art in high esteem in their academies. In our day the Italians retained some traces of this, to their great advantage, as may be seen by comparing our wits with theirs. The study of books is a languid and feeble process, which has no warmth; whereas conversation teaches and exercises at one stroke. If I converse with a powerful thinker and a sturdy fighter, he presses me close, touches me to the quick on the left and the right; his conceptions stimulate mine. Rivalry, vanity, the struggle, urge me on and raise me above myself; and accordance is an altogether irksome quality in conversation.

But just as our mind is strengthened by communication with vigorous and well-regulated minds, it is not to be said how much it loses and is debased by the constant intercourse and association that we have with low and weak minds. There is no contagion which spreads as that does; I know by ample experience what its price is by the ell. I like to dispute and to discuss, but with few men at a time, and for my own pleasure; for to serve in emulation as a spectacle for the great and to make a show of one's wit and one's prating,[7] I consider that to be an affair very unbeseeming a man of honour. Stupidity is a poor quality; but to be unable to endure it and to be wroth with it and chafe at it, as happens to me, is another sort of weakness, which is not far behind stupidity in unsuitableness;[8] and it is of that I am ready now to accuse myself.

I enter into conversation and discussion with great freedom and facility, forasmuch as dogmatic opinion finds in me a soil ill suited for it to penetrate and send forth deep roots; no propositions astound me, no belief offends me, however

Of the Art of Conversation

contrary it may be to my own. There is no fantastic idea so idle and extravagant that it does not seem to me a fitting production of the human mind. Those of us who deny to our own judgement the right of final decisions look leniently on differing beliefs, and if we do not give acceptance to them, we readily give them hearing. Where one scale of the balance is altogether empty, I let the other vacillate under an old woman's dreams; and it seems to me excusable if I accept an odd number by preference; Thursday rather than Friday; if I like better to be the twelfth or fourteenth at table than the thirteenth; if I more willingly see a hare running beside my path than crossing it when I travel, and put out my left foot before my right to be shod. All such idle fancies which have standing among us deserve at least to be listened to; for my part, they outbalance only emptiness, but they do outbalance that. Also, common and uncertain beliefs are in their nature of more weight than nonentity; and he who does not let himself go so far in regard to them falls perchance into the fault of opinionativeness while avoiding that of superstition. Opposing opinions consequently neither offend me nor change me; they merely arouse and exercise my mind. We evade correction; we ought to offer and present ourselves to it, especially when it comes in the shape of discussion, not of instruction.[9] At any opposition, we do not consider whether it is just, but how, wrongly or rightly, we can extricate ourselves from it; instead of opening our arms to it, we open our claws. I could well endure being roughly handled by my friends: "You're a fool, you're dreaming." Among men of worth I like to have every one express himself fearlessly, to have the words keep company with the thought. We should strengthen our hearing and harden it

1256

Of the Art of Conversation

against this pleasure in the punctilious sound of words.[10] I like a strong and virile companionship and intimacy, a friendship which takes pride in the asperity and vigour of its intercourse, as love does in bites and scratches that draw blood. It is not vigorous and free enough if it is not quarrelsome, if it is tame and artificial, if it fears conflict and is constrained in its ways; *for there can be no discussion without contradiction.*[11]

When I am opposed, my attention is aroused, not my anger; I go to meet him who contradicts me, who instructs me. The cause of truth should be the common cause for him and for me. How does he reply? The passion of anger has already overmastered his judgement; confusion has taken possession of it in advance of reason. It would be of use if the decision of our disputes were settled by wager; if there were a material note of our losses, so that we could keep a record of them, and that my secretary could say to me, "You paid last year a hundred pounds for being a score of times ignorant and opinionated."

I do honour to truth, and embrace it, in whosesoever hand I find it, and cheerfully surrender myself to it, and hold out to it my vanquished weapons from afar, as I see it approaching. And provided it be not done with a too imperiously authoritative air, I take pleasure in being reprehended; and I often agree with my accusers, more because of courtesy than because of reformation, liking to gratify and foster freedom in warning me by facility in yielding, even at my own expense. It is, however, difficult to lead men of my time to this. They have not the courage to correct, because they have not the courage to bear being corrected; and in each other's presence they never speak openly. I take such great pleasure

Of the Art of Conversation

in being judged and known that it is, as it were, indifferent to me in which of the two ways it may be. My intelligence[12] so frequently contradicts and condemns itself that it is all one to me that another does it, especially seeing that I give his reprehension only what authority I like; but I fall out[13] with him who carries himself in so surly a fashion as some one whom I know, who grudges his warning if it be not believed and takes it as an affront if you hesitate about following it. That Socrates always smilingly welcomed the contradictions opposed to his reasoning was due, it might be said, to his strength, and that, since the advantage was certain to be on his side, he accepted them as matter for a new victory. Still we see, on the other hand, that there is nothing which makes our perception so sensitive as a belief in the preeminence of our adversary and of his scorn for us; and that consequently it is for the weaker to accept thankfully these oppositions, which set him right and correct him. And truly I seek rather the company of those who buffet me than of those who are afraid of me. It is an insipid and harmful pleasure to have to do with people who admire us and give place to us. Antisthenes bade his children never to regard with gratitude or favour the man who praised them.[14] I feel much prouder of the victory that I gain over myself when, in the very heat of the conflict, I make myself bow to the strength of my adversary's argument, than I am pleased with myself for the victory I gain over him from his weakness.

Finally, I receive and acknowledge all sorts of attacks that are well aimed, however feeble they may be; but I am much too intolerant of those that are given at random.[15] I care little what the subject is, and to me all opinions are the same; and victory in the manner is almost unimportant to me. I

1258

Of the Art of Conversation

can argue peaceably a whole day, if the discussion is conducted in orderly fashion. It is not so much force and subtlety that I demand as order, the order that may be seen any day in the wranglings of shepherds and 'prentices,[16] never among ourselves. If they leave the straight path, they do it to be rude, and so indeed do we; but their brawling and impatience does not make them forgo their subject: their argument follows its course. If they interrupt each other, if they do not stay for each other, at least they understand each other. He always answers more than he needs for me who answers what I say. But when the discussion is confused and disorderly, I forsake the matter and fasten upon the manner, with vexation and rashness, and throw myself into a testy, malicious, and domineering style of disputation for which I have later to blush.

It is impossible to deal in good faith with a fool. Not my judgement alone is vitiated by the control of so impetuous a master, but my conscience likewise. Our disputes should be prohibited and punished like other verbal crimes. What vice do they not arouse and multiply, they being always ruled and directed by anger! We quarrel, first with the reasonings, then with the men. We learn in discussing only to contradict, and, every one contradicting and being contradicted, it comes about that the result of the discussion is to destroy and annihilate truth. Therefore Plato, in his *Republic*, forbids this exercise of unskilful and ill-bred minds.[17]

To what purpose do you set about seeking that which is,[18] from him who has neither pace nor procedure that is of worth? One does not wrong the subject when one forsakes it to find the method of treating; I do not mean the scholastic and artificial method, I mean the natural method of a

Of the Art of Conversation

sound intelligence. What will be the end of this? One goes east, the other west; they lose the chief thing and disperse it in the throng of by-matters. After an hour's storming, they know not what they are seeking; one is below, another above, another at the side; this one fastens on a word or a simile; that one no longer hears the objections made to him, so intent is he upon his course, and thinking of following himself, not of you; another, finding himself lacking in strength,[19] fears every thing, refuses every thing, and from the beginning mixes up and confuses the subject; or at the height of the discussion, becomes sulkily silent,[20] from peevish ignorance, affecting a proud contempt or a foolishly modest avoidance of disputation. For another man, provided he gives a blow, it matters not to him how much he exposes himself. This other counts his words and weighs them as arguments; that one makes use only of his advantage in the matter of voice and lungs. Here is one who decides against himself, and another who deafens you with useless prefaces and digressions. This other arms himself with undisguised insults and seeks an idle altercation[21] to rid himself of the society and conversation of a mind that presses him hard. This last one sees nothing in argument, but holds you beleaguered with the logical enclosure of his propositions[22] and the formulas of his art.

Now, who does not distrust the sciences, and who is not in doubt whether he can derive from them any substantial profits for the needs of life, in view of the use that we make of them, *of the learning that cures nothing?*[23] Who has acquired intelligence by logic? Where are its fine promises? *Neither for living better, nor for arguing more profitably.*[24] Do we find more confused jumbling of things in the gab-

Of the Art of Conversation

bling of fish wives[25] than in the public debate of men of this profession? I had rather that my son should learn to talk in taverns than in the school of elocution. Take a master of arts, converse with him; why does he not make us feel this excellence of art, and why does he not enrapture women and such ignorant folk as we are with admiration of the solidity of his reasoning, of the beauty of his method? Why does he not sway us and persuade us as he will? Why does a man so advantaged in matter and in management mingle with his fencing, insults and indiscretion and passion? If he drops off his cap, his gown, and his Latin; if he does not batter our ears with Aristotle pure and crude, you will take him for one of us, or worse. It seems to me that by this complication and entanglement of language with which they press upon us it is as with jugglers: their dexterity contends with our senses and masters them; but it in no wise shakes our faith; beyond this legerdemain they do nothing that is not commonplace and worthless. For, being more learned, they are no less foolish.

I love and honour knowledge as much as they do who possess it; and properly used it is the noblest and most potent acquisition of man. But in those (and their number is infinite) who base thereon their fundamental competence and worth, who rely for their intelligence upon their memory, *hiding under the protection of others*,[26] and can do nothing but out of a book, I hate it, if I dare say so, a little more than stupidity. In my country and in my day scholarship fills purses enough, but minds not at all. If it finds them dull, it oppresses and suffocates them, a crude, undigested mass; if it finds them easily acted upon,[27] it purges and refines and subtilises them, even to exinanition.

Of the Art of Conversation

It is a thing of one and another quality almost indifferently; a very useful accessory to a well-endowed mind, pernicious and harmful to another mind; or, it may be said, a thing of very valuable use which does not allow itself to be acquired at a low price;[28] in some hands it is a sceptre, in others a fool's bauble.

But let us proceed. What greater victory do you expect than to teach your enemy that he can not withstand you? When you gain the advantage by that which you propound, it is truth that gains it; when you gain the advantage by method and handling, it is you who gain it. It is my opinion that Socrates, in Plato and in Xenophon, debates more for the sake of the disputants than for the sake of the debate, and to teach Euthydemus and Protagoras[29] to perceive their own irrelevancy rather than the irrelevancy of their art. He takes hold of the first matter at hand, as one who has a more useful purpose than to make it clear—to wit, to clear the minds that he undertakes to train and exercise. The real object of our hunting is excitement and the hunt itself; we have no excuse for conducting it badly and irrelevantly. To fail in capturing any thing is another matter, for we are destined from birth to quest the truth; to possess it belongs to a greater power. It is not, as Democritus said, hidden in the depths of abysses, but rather elevated to an infinite height in the divine knowledge.[30] The world is but a school of inquisition. It matters not who hits the ring,[31] but who makes the best running. He who says what is true can be as foolish as he who says what is false; for we are upon the manner, not the matter, of what is said. My inclination is to consider the form as much as the substance, the advocate as much as the cause, as Alcibiades declared should be

Of the Art of Conversation

done. And every day I entertain myself by reading authors, without thought about their learning, enquiring after their style, not their subject. Just as I seek intercourse with some famous wit, not to the end that he may teach me, but to the end that I may know him, and that, knowing him, I may, if he be worth it, imitate him. Every man can speak truthfully; but to speak methodically, prudently, and ably— that few men can do. Therefore it is not the mistake that comes from ignorance that offends me, but ineptitude. I have broken off many bargains which were profitable to me because of the irrelevancy of the haggling of those with whom I was bargaining. I am not irritated once in a year by the shortcomings of those over whom I have authority; but from the stupidity and obstinacy of their asinine and clumsy assertions, excuses, and justifications we are by the ears together[32] every day. They understand neither what is said nor why it is said, and reply in that fashion; it is a hopeless business. I do not feel my head hit hard except by another head, and I compromise with the vices of my servants more readily than with their hastiness and importunity and their folly. Let them be less active, provided they are capable of activity; you live in hopes of kindling their will, but from a log there is nothing either to hope for or to be had that is worth any thing. But now, suppose I take things as other than they are? This may be; and therefore I find fault with my impatience and I consider, in the first place, that this is equally erroneous in him who is in the right and in him who is in the wrong; for it is always a tyrannical sourness of spirit to be unable to endure a way of thinking different from one's own; and further, that there is in truth no greater and more persistent folly than to be disturbed and nettled by follies of the world, or one more anomalous, for it irritates us chiefly against ourselves. And that philosopher of ancient time[33] would never have lacked occasion for his tears whenever he considered himself. Miso, one of the seven sages, of a Timonian and Democritian humor, being asked why he laughed when alone, replied, "because I alone laugh."[34]

How many foolish things, in my own opinion, I say and reply every day, and naturally[35] how many more in the opinion of others! If I bite my lips because of them, what may not others do? In short, we must live with the living, and let water flow under the bridge without paying heed to it, or at least without discomposure. But truly, why without being stirred up do we meet one who has a crooked and misshapen body, yet can not endure the meeting with an ill-framed mind without being angry? This mistaken asperity arises more from the judge than from the offence. Let us have always on our lips this saying of Plato: "What seems to me unhealthy, is it not because I am healthy myself? Am I not in fault myself? May not my admonition turn against myself?"[36] Oh, wise and divine saying, which lashes the most universal and common error of mankind! Not only the reproofs we give one another, but also our reasons and our arguments and matters of controversy, can commonly be turned back upon us, and we wound ourselves with our own weapons; whereof antiquity affords me many important examples. It was wittily said, and very aptly, by him who forged the phrase,

Every man's filth smells sweet to himself.[37]

Our eyes see nothing behind us. A hundred times a day

Of the Art of Conversation

we laugh at ourselves when laughing at our neighbours, and detest in other men the defects which are more visible in ourselves, and wonder at them with marvellous shamelessness and inadvertence. It was but yesterday that I was so placed as to observe a man of intelligence making fun, as amusingly as justly, of the foolish habit of another who wearies every one with the record of his genealogy and alliances, more than half false (those people enter most readily into such ridiculous talk whose titles are most doubtful and least assured); and he, had he retired into himself, would have found himself scarcely less immoderate and wearisome in spreading abroad and setting forth the preëminence of his wife's family. Oh, unmannerly presumption, with which his wife finds herself armed by the hands of her husband himself! If he understood Latin, he should be told,—

Come! if she is not mad enough of her own accord, provoke her.[38]

I do not say that no one should find fault who is himself to be blamed (yes, and even blamed for the same sort of blemish), for then no one would find fault; but I mean that our judgement, lying heavy upon another of whom at the time there is question, does not exempt us from an inward and stern jurisdiction. It is a duty of charity that he who can not do away a vice in himself should none the less seek to do it away in another person in whom it may have a less poisonous and less obstinate root; nor does it seem to me answering to the purpose to say to him who warns me of my failing that it is also in him. What matters that? The warning is still true and useful. If we had a keen scent, our ordure would stink to us the more for as much as it is our

Of the Art of Conversation

own; and Socrates is of the opinion that whosoever should find himself and his son and a stranger guilty of any violence and injury should first accuse himself and present himself for the condemnation of the law, and implore for his expiation the aid of the excutioner's hand; in the second place, for his son's, and lastly for the stranger's.[39] If this precept takes somewhat too lofty a tone, at least he should present himself the first for punishment by his own conscience.

The senses are our peculiar and principal judges, which perceive things only by external circumstances; and it is no wonder if in all the parts of the action of our social life there is such a perpetual and universal composition of ceremonies and superficial happenings that the best and most effective part of governments consists therein. It is always with man that we have to do, whose condition is marvellously corporeal. Let not those be surprised who have thought of late years to build up for us so contemplative and immaterial a practice of religion, if there may be found some who think that it would have slipped through their fingers and melted away if it did not remain among us, more as a mark, title, and instrument of division and faction, than for its own sake. So in conversation: the gravity, the gown, and the luck of the speaker often give weight to idle and inept discourse; it is not to be presumed that a gentleman so followed after, so redoubtable, has not in him more than common ability, and that a man to whom are given so many charges and offices, a man so disdainful and of such severe countenance, is not more able than that other who salutes him from a distance and whom no one employs. Not only the words, but also the expression of countenance, of such men are considered and taken into account, every one striving to give them some pleasing and trustworthy interpretation. If they stoop to common talk, and you shew them any thing save approbation and respect, they fell you with the authority of their experience: they have heard, they have seen, they have done; you are overwhelmed with proofs. I could readily say to them that the fruit of a surgeon's experience is not the tale of his patients and the calling to mind that he has cured four persons of the plague and three of the gout, if he does not derive from that success the wherewithal to form his judgement and does not make us perceive that he is the wiser for the practice of his art; just as in a concert of instruments we do not hear a lute, a spinet, and a flute—we hear a full harmony, the union and result of them altogether. If travels and official positions have improved them, it is for the product of their intelligence to make this appear. It is not enough to number experiences—they must be weighed and sorted, and they must have been digested and analysed to extract from them the information and conclusion which they contain. There were never so many historians. It is always well and profitable to listen to them, for they supply us abundantly with excellent and praiseworthy instruction from the storehouse of their memory—a large item, assuredly, of assistance in life; but we are not at this moment enquiring as to that; we are enquiring whether these narrators and collectors are themselves worthy of praise.

I hate every sort of tyranny, both of words and of deeds.[40] I readily resist to the utmost the power of these idle circumstances which delude our judgement through the senses; and, carefully watching these unusual greatnesses, I have found that they are for the most part men like other men.

> For common sense is seldom found among those of such fortune.[41]

Perchance we judge them and perceive them to be less than they are because they assume to be more and display themselves as being more; they do not correspond to the burden they have taken on themselves. There must needs be more strength and power in the bearer than in the burden; he whose strength has not been exhausted leaves it to you to divine whether he has still more strength, and whether he has been tested to the utmost; he who succumbs to his burden reveals the measure of his power and the weakness of his shoulders. This is why we find so many inept minds among scholars, and more than of other kinds; they would have made good heads of a household, good tradesmen, good artisans; their natural vigour was cut to that measure. Learning is a thing of great weight; they sink under it; their understanding is not powerful enough or manageable enough to exhibit and deal out that rich and potent material, to make use of it for others and to assist themselves by it; learning can accomplish this only in a strong nature; now, such natures are very rare. And the weak, says Socrates, impair the dignity of philosophy by meddling with it; it appears both useless and harmful when it is in a poor receptacle.[42] See how they injure and befool themselves,

> Like a monkey, whose face is like a man's, which a boy has laughingly covered with a costly garment of silk, but whose buttocks and back he has left bare, the laughing-stock of the guests.[43]

1268

Of the Art of Conversation

In like manner, for those who rule over us and command us, who hold the world in their hands, it is not enough for them to have an ordinary intelligence, to be able to do what we can do; they are very far beneath us if they are not very far above us. As they promise more, so they owe us more; and therefore silence is in them not only an attitude of discretion and seriousness, but often of advantage and policy as well; as when Megabysus, having gone to see Apelles in his working-room, was a long while without saying a word, and then began to talk about the painter's works; he thereupon received this sharp rebuke: "Whilst you kept silent, you seemed to be something great because of your gold chain and your splendour; but now that you have been heard talking, there is no one, even to the boys in my shop, who does not despise you."[44] His magnificent apparel, his great state, made it not permissible for him to be ignorant with a vulgar ignorance and to speak unintelligently of painting; he should have maintained, by remaining mute, that external and presumptive competence. For how many feeble minds in my day has a cold and taciturn bearing served as a proof of good sense and capacity!

Dignities, offices are necessarily bestowed rather by fortune than by merit; and it is often a mistake to lay the blame on kings. On the contrary it is a marvel that they have so much luck, having so little skill;

> The greatest virtue of a prince is to know his own subjects;[45]

for nature has not given them the vision that can extend its sight over so many folk to discover preëminence amongst them, and to enter into our breasts, where may be recog-

nised our will and our best worth. They must needs choose
us by conjecture and gropingly, by family, wealth, learning, and the popular voice: very weak evidence. He who
could find a way to judge of men justly and to select them
reasonably would establish by that sole proceeding a perfect form of government. "But truly he fitly conducted
this great business." That says something, but it does not
say enough; for this opinion is justly approved, that we
must not judge of counsels by results.[46] The Carthaginians
punished the ill-advised plans of their commanders even
though they were redressed by a fortunate issue;[47] and the
Roman people often denied a triumph to great and very
useful victories, because the general's management did not
correspond to his good-fortune. It is usually seen in the affairs of the world that Fortune, who takes pleasure in humbling our presumption, to teach us how great her power is
over all things, being unable to make the incompetent wise,
makes them lucky, as if to despite virtue, and lends herself
readily to favour performances of which the framework
is most purely her own. Whence it is seen every day that
the most unskilful of us carry to an end very important
affairs, both public and private; and, as Sirannes the Persian replied to those who were surprised that his affairs
prospered so ill, seeing that his words were so wise, that he
was the sole master of his words but that the success of his
affairs was in the hands of Fortune,[48] so these persons can
reply to the same effect, but from an opposite standpoint.
The greater number of things in the world are shaped by
themselves,—

The Fates find a way.[49]

1270

Of the Art of Conversation

The issue often gives authority to very incapable guidance. Our interposition is scarcely more than following a beaten path, and is commonly an advisement of custom and example rather than of reason. Some time ago, when I was amazed by the greatness of an affair, I learned, from those who had carried it through, their motive and their methods; I found therein only commonplace counsels; and the most commonplace and threadbare are, perchance, also the surest and best adapted for practice, if not for show. What if the simplest reasons are the best based, if the humblest and loosest ones and those most threshed out are best applied to public affairs?[50] To preserve the authority of the council chamber of kings there is no need that worldlings[51] should enter it and see further into it than the first barrier; it must be reverenced on credit and as a whole, if it is desired to sustain its reputation. My examination rough-hews the matter a little, and lightly regards it in its first aspect; the stress and chief part of the business I am wont to resign to heaven:

Leave the rest to the gods.[52]

Good-fortune and ill-fortune are to my mind two sovereign powers. It is ignorance to deem that human knowledge can play the part of fortune; and vain is the undertaking of him who presumes to embrace both causes and consequences and to lead by the hand the course of his action—especially vain in the deliberations of war.[53] There was never more military circumspection and prudence than is seen sometimes amongst us; can it be that, reserving themselves for the final act of the play, men fear to lose their way? I say further that our very wisdom and deliberation follow for the most part the guidance of chance. My will and my judgement are moved, now in one direction, now in another; and there are many of these motions that are governed without me; my reason has uncertain and transitory impulses and revolutions.

> The dispositions of minds are changed; and hearts feel some emotions now, others when the wind drives the clouds away.[54]

If one observes who in cities have the most power and who best do their business, it will commonly be found that they are the least skilled. It has happened that feeble women and children and witless men have ruled over great states equally well with the most capable princes. And Thucydides says that dull minds more commonly succeed[55] in this than cunning ones.[56] We attribute the effects of their good-fortune to their discretion.

> Only by favour of fortune does a man rise, and fortune is the touchstone by which we all judge of his skill.[57]

Wherefore I say distinctly that occurrences are weak testimonies to our value and capacity.

I was just now treating here of this point, that it needs but to see a man raised in rank: if we knew him three days before as a man of little consequence, there glides insensibly into our minds a conception of great ability; and we are persuaded that, as his retinue and influence are larger, his merit has increased. We judge him not according to his work but as with counters,[58] according to the preëminence of his rank. Let chance change again, let him fall and be

Of the Art of Conversation

lost in the crowd, every one asks himself wonderingly what cause hoisted him so high. "Is this the same man?" they say. "Did he know nothing more when he was there placed? Are princes contented with so little? Verily we were in good hands!" This is a thing that I have often seen in my time, aye, and the semblance of grandeur that is represented in plays somewhat touches us and gulls us. What I myself adore in kings is the crowd of their adorers. All deference to them and bowing before them is their due, except with the understanding; my reason is not framed to bend and stoop—that is for my knees.

Melanthius, being asked what he thought of the tragedy of Dionysius, "I did not see it," he replied, "it is so obscured with language."[59] So most of those who judge the utterances of the great might say, "I did not hear what he said, it was so obscured by solemnity, grandeur, and magnificence." Antisthenes one day advised the Athenians to order their asses to be as much used in tilling the ground as were horses; upon which he was answered that that animal was not made for such work. "It is all the same," he rejoined, "for the most ignorant and incapable men whom you employ to direct your wars do not fail immediately to become most worthy of the task because you thus employ them."[60] To which is akin the custom of so many nations of canonising the king they have chosen from among themselves, not being contented with honouring him if they do not adore him. The Mexicans, after the ceremony of his consecration is consummated, no longer dare to look him in the face; but, as if they had deified him by his royalty, amongst the oaths which they make him swear, to maintain their religion, their laws, their liberties, and to be

brave, just, and affable, he swears also to make the sun roll
on with its wonted light, to drain the clouds at timely seasons, to make rivers run their course, and the earth bring
forth all things necessary for his people.[61]

I differ from the common fashion, and distrust ability
the more when I find it accompanied by greatness of fortune and popular commendation. We must needs be on our
guard against the advantage it is for a man to speak when
he will, to choose his own time, to break off talk or to change
it with a master's authority, to defend himself from the objections of others by a shake of the head, a smile, or silence,
before an assembly tremulous with reverence and respect.
A man of prodigious fortune, bringing forward his opinion
about some slight matter which was being carelessly tossed
to and fro at his table, began in just this way: "It can be
only a liar or a fool who says otherwise than," and so forth.
Follow up this wise proposition with a poniard in your hand.

Consider here another admonition from which I derive
much profit: that in altercations and formal discourse all
sayings which seem to us to be sound should not be hastily
accepted. Most men are rich with borrowed ability. It may
well happen to such a one to use an admirable expression,
make an apt response and remark, and put it forth without
perceiving its force. That one does not possess all that one
borrows may perchance be verified in my own case. We
must not always give way to this faculty, whatever truth
or beauty it may have. We must combat it in good faith,
or draw back under colour of not understanding it, to examine in every way how it has entered the speaker's mind. It
may happen that we aid the word-stroke of our adversary to
carry it beyond its own reach.[62] I have in other days, in the

Of the Art of Conversation

necessity and stress of combat, made use of back-thrusts which pierced beyond my purpose and my hope; I dealt them only by number, their effect was by weight.[63] Exactly as, when I am debating with a vigorous man, I please myself by anticipating his conclusions, I relieve him of the trouble of interpreting himself, I try to anticipate his still imperfect and unformed thoughts (the regularity and the pertinency of his intelligence admonishing and menacing me from afar), so with those others I follow just the contrary course; we must understand nothing except through them, nor pre-suppose any thing. If they give judgement in general terms, "This is good, that is not so"; and if they hit the mark,[64] see whether it be chance that does it for them.

Let them circumscribe and limit their remark a little: why it is so; how it is so. These sweeping judgements which I find to be so common mean nothing; they are like persons who salute a large body of people in a crowd and in a body; they who have real knowledge of them salute them and take note of them by name and individually.[65] But it is a dangerous undertaking. Whence I have seen it happen—and oftener than every day—that ill-grounded minds, wishing, when reading some work, to appear well skilled by remarking on some special beauty, fix their admiration with so bad a choice that instead of shewing us the excellence of the author, they show their own ignorance. It is a safe exclamation: "How fine that is!" after listening to a full page of Virgil. In that way the wily ones save themselves. But to undertake to follow him step by step[66] and with peculiar and considered judgement; to try to point out where a good author rises above himself, weighing his

words, his phrases, his conceits, and his various excellences
one after another—beware of attempting that! *We must
scrutinise not only men's words, but also their opinions,
and even the bases of those opinions.*[67] I daily hear fools say
things that are not foolish.

They[68] say a good thing; let us find out how far they
understand it, let us see whence they obtained it. We help
them to make use of this fine expression, and this fine argument which is not their own; they simply have it in keeping;
they have brought it out at a venture, and feeling their way;
we place it for them in credit and esteem. You lend them a
hand—for what? They are in no wise grateful to you for
it and become thereby the more stupid. Do not aid them,
let them go on; they will handle the matter like people
who are afraid of burning themselves; they dare not change
its position or the light it is in, or go deep into it. Give it
ever so little a shake, it slips from their hands; they abandon
it to you, however strong and fine it may be; the weapons
are excellent, but are poorly helved. How many times have
I had experience of this! Now if you set about enlightening
them and confirming them, they seize upon you and immediately steal from you the advantage of your interpretation. "That is what I meant to say, that is exactly my
idea; if I didn't so express it, it was merely for lack of
language." Nonsense![69] Even guile must be employed to
correct this arrogant ignorance. The dogma of Hegesias,
that we must neither hate nor blame, but instruct,[70] is reasonable elsewhere; but here it is unjust and inhuman to
succour and make right him who cares not and who is worth
the less. I like to let them sink deeper into the mire and
involve themselves even more than they now are involved,

and so deep, if it be possible, that they will at last recognise themselves for what they are.

Stupidity and confusion of thought is not a matter that can be cured by a single word of warning. And we may fitly say of such correction[71] what Cyrus said in reply to him who urged him to exhort his army on the eve of a battle: that men are not made suddenly brave and warlike by a fine harangue, any more than one becomes a musician immediately from hearing a fine song.[72] There are apprenticeships that must be served beforehand, with long and constant education. We owe this attention to those under our care, and this assiduity in correction and instruction; but to go preaching to the first passer-by and tutoring the ignorance or stupidity of the first man you meet is a habit I can not endure.[73] I rarely do this, even in talks with myself alone; and I give up everything rather than proceed to these out-of-the-way and schoolmasterlike instructions. My nature is as little adapted to speak as to write for beginners.[74] But as to the things that are said by every one or in the presence of other persons, however false and absurd I consider them, I never put myself in opposition to them either by word or by sign. As to the rest, nothing vexes me so much in stupidity as that it is more pleased with itself than any intelligence can reasonably be with itself. It is ill-luck that discretion forbids you to be satisfied with yourself, and to trust in yourself, and always dismisses you ill content and faint-hearted, whereas opinionativeness and rashness fill their possessors with rejoicing and assurance. It is those who most lack ability who look at other men over the shoulder, always returning from the fray full of pride and gladness. And most frequently, too, this arrogance of speech and cheerful aspect give them the better of it in the opinion of bystanders, who are ordinarily of weak intelligence and incapable of judging well and discerning the real advantage. Obstinacy and heat of opinion are the surest signs of dulness: is there any thing so firm, resolute, disdainful, meditative, serious, and solemn as the ass?

May we not include under the name of conversation and exchange of thoughts[75] the brief and pointed remarks which vivacity and intimacy introduce among friends jesting and jibing at one another merrily and wittily? a practice for which my natural gaiety makes me well suited; and if it be not as forcible and serious as the other I have been speaking of, it is not less penetrating and able, nor less profitable, as it seemed to Lycurgus.[76] For my part, I bring to it more freedom of speech than wit, and I have more luck in it than originality; but I am perfect in toleration, for I endure a retort not only sharp, but inconsiderate, without wincing. And when I am attacked, if I have not the wherewithal to reply instantly with vivacity, I do not stay to follow up the point with a tedious and flagging contest verging on obstinacy; I let it pass, and, cheerfully humbling myself,[77] I postpone getting my dues to some more fortunate hour; there is no merchant who always gains. Most men change in face and voice when strength fails them and, by unseasonable anger, instead of revenging themselves, betray their weakness together with their discomfort. In this jollity we sometimes twitch the secret strings of our imperfections (which in soberness we can not touch without giving pain) and warn one another profitably of our defects.

There are also bodily pastimes,[78] reckless and rough after the French manner, which I mortally hate; my skin

Of the Art of Conversation

is tender and sensitive;[79] in my lifetime I have seen two princes of our blood royal[80] laid in their graves by them. It looks ill to slay in sport.[81]

For the rest, when I wish to form a judgement of a man, I ask him how well content he is with himself, how much what he says or what he does pleases him. I wish to avoid such fine excuses as, "I did it without effort;

This work was taken unfinished from the loom;[82]

I was not an hour about it; I have not looked at it since." To this I say: "Let us then lay aside these things; give me one which represents the whole of you, by which it may please you to be measured." And again: "What do you consider most excellent in your work? Is it this part, or this? its beauty, or its matter, or its conception, or its insight, or its learning?" For usually I observe that a man errs as much in judging his own work as that of another, not only from the good-will he bears it but from not having the ability to recognise and distinguish what it is. The work, by its own force and fortune, can assist the workman and anticipate him beyond his conception and knowledge. For my part, I do not judge of the worth of other work more vaguely than of my own, and I place the Essays now low, now high, very hesitatingly and doubtfully.

There are many books, useful by virtue of their subjects, from which the author derives no commendation, and good books, like good works, which shame the workman. I may write of the style of our banquets and our clothes, and I shall write with an ill grace; I may publish the edicts of my time and the letters of princes which come into the hands of the public; I may make an abridgement of a good

Of the Art of Conversation

book (and every abridgement of a good book is a foolish abridgement), which book may be lost—and like matters. Posterity may derive singular benefit from such compositions; I, what honour unless it be by my good-fortune? A goodly number of famous books are of this nature.

When, many years ago, I read Philippe de Commines, certainly a most excellent author, I noticed this saying as not commonplace, that a man must beware of doing so much for his master as to prevent him from finding a just recompense therefrom.[83] I should have praised the thought, not him. I found it not long ago in Tacitus: *Benefactions are welcome so long as we know that we are able to return them; but if they far surpass our means of requiting them, they become hateful to us.*[84] And Seneca vigorously says: *For he who deems it disgraceful not to return a favour would like to have nobody to whom he is indebted.*[85] Quintus Cicero, in weaker phrase: *The man who thinks he has not discharged his debt to you can by no means be a friend.*[86]

The subject in itself may make a man appear learned and possessed of a good memory; but to judge in him those parts most his own and of most worth, the strength and beauty of his soul, we must know what is his own and what is not so, and in that which is not his, how much is due to him in respect to the choice, arrangement, adornment, and language which he has therein supplied. What if he has borrowed the substance and impaired the form, as often happens?

We who have little dealing with books are in this difficulty, that, when we see some fine fancy in a new poet, some forcible argument in a preacher, we do not dare to praise them for it until we have learned from some scholar

Of the Art of Conversation

whether this is their own or whether it is borrowed. Until then I always stand on my guard.

I have lately been reading without a break the history of Tacitus (which seldom happens to me; it is twenty years since I gave an entire hour to a book);[87] and I did it at the suggestion of a gentleman whom France greatly esteems, both for his own worth and for an unfailing sort of ability and goodness which is seen in the many brothers there are. I know no author who connects with a public chronicle so much consideration of private manners and tendencies. He is in this no less careful and diligent than Plutarch, who made express profession of it.[88] And it seems to me the opposite of what it seemed to him: that, having especially to follow the lives of the emperors of his time, so diverse and so extreme in all sorts of ways, and so many noteworthy deeds that their cruelty expressly produced in their subjects, he had matter more solid and attractive to discourse of and to narrate than if he had had to tell of universal battles and commotions;[89] so that I often find him unprofitable, hurrying over those noble deaths[90] as if he feared to annoy us with their multitude and wearisomeness.

This sort of history is much the most useful; public movements depend chiefly on the guidance of fortune, private ones on our own; and yet he has not forgotten what he owed to the other side.[91] He gives us personal judgement rather than a deduction from history; there are more precepts in it than narratives. It is not a book to read, it is a book to study and learn; it is so full of opinions that there are both wrong and right ones; it is a nursery of ethical and political discourses for the purveying and garnishment of those who have some prominence in managing the world. He argues

Of the Art of Conversation

always with solid and vigorous reasons, in a keen and subtle manner, following the style belonging to the time, when men so greatly liked to rise above the common[92] that when they did not find point and subtlety in things, they borrowed it from words. His style is not unlike that of Seneca: it seems to me more full in words, Seneca's the more concise.[93] He is more adapted to be of service to a disturbed and disordered state like our present one; you would often say that he is painting us and pinching us. Those who question whether he is to be trusted betray plainly that they bear him ill-will on some other ground. He has sound opinions and inclines to the right side in Roman affairs. I regret a little, however, that he judged Pompeius more severely than comports with the opinion of men of worth who lived in his day and had dealings with him; that he estimated him as entirely on a par with Marius and Sylla save inasmuch as he had more dissimulation.[94] His intention in the government of affairs has not been acquitted of ambition or of vengeance; and even his friends feared that success would have swept him beyond the bound of reason but not to so reckless an extent.[95] There is nothing in his life which threatened such manifest cruelty and tyranny. Besides, suspicion must not be allowed to balance evidence; so I do not believe Tacitus in this. That his narratives are honest and sincere might perhaps be argued from just this, that they are not always exactly in conformity with the conclusions of his judgements, which follow the bias he has taken often outside the matter he puts before us, which he has not deigned to distort by a hair's breadth. He needs no excuse for having avowed the religion of his time and for having ignored the true religion; that is his misfortune, not his fault.

Of the Art of Conversation

I have considered chiefly his judgement, and I am not everywhere clearly enlightened by it. For instance, these words in the letter that Tiberius, old and sick, sent to the Senate: "What shall I write to you, sirs,[96] or how shall I write to you, or what shall I not write to you at this time? May the gods and goddesses destroy me more cruelly than I every day feel myself to be perishing, if I know!"[97] I do not perceive why he ascribes them so surely to a poignant remorse that torments the conscience of Tiberius; and in other days, when I was more competent than now, I did not see it. This also seems to me a little unmanly, that, having had occasion to mention that he had held a certain honourable office at Rome, he says in excuse that it was not from ostentation that he spoke of it.[98] This trait seems to me poor-spirited[99] for a soul like his, since there is some lack of courage in not daring to speak freely of oneself; a firm and lofty judgement, which judges sanely and surely, makes use unhesitatingly of personal examples as well as of other things, and bears witness as frankly about itself as about a third person. The ordinary rules of modesty must be overlooked in favour of truth and freedom.

I dare not only to speak about myself, but to speak only about myself. I go astray when I write of anything else, and wander from my subject. I do not so unreasonably love myself and am not so united and blended with myself that I can not distinguish and consider myself apart, like a neighbour, like a tree. It is equally a mistake not to see what one is worth, or to say more of it than one sees. We owe more love to God than to ourselves and we know him less, and yet we talk our fill of him.

If his writings[100] reveal any thing of his qualities, he

1283

was a man of great distinction, upright and fearless, of a virtue not superstitious but philosophical and of the right stamp.[101] He may be found over-bold in his statements: as when he believes that, as a soldier was carrying a load of wood, his hands were stiffened by the cold and were fast joined to his burden, so that they remained attached to it and dead, having separated from his arms.[102] I am wont in matters like this to bow to the authority of such great witnesses. When he says also that Vespasian, by the grace of the god Serapis, cured a blind woman[103] in Alexandria by anointing her eyes with his saliva, and I know not what other miracle, he does so according to the example and duty of all good historians. They keep a record of important events; amongst the public happenings are comprised common rumours and opinions. It is their business to set down popular beliefs, not to square them. That part concerns theologians and philosophers, directors of consciences. Wherefore this friend of his, and like him a great man, says very wisely: *Indeed, I set down more than I believe; for I undertake neither to affirm matters about which I am in doubt nor to withdraw what I have accepted as true;*[104] this is very well said. And this other: *It is not worth the trouble either to affirm or to disprove these matters . . . we must abide by the tradition.*[105] And, writing in an age when belief in miracles was beginning to diminish, he says that none the less he does not choose to fail to insert in his annals, and give standing to, any thing accepted by so many men of worth and regarded with such reverence in ancient times.[106] Let them give us history more according to what they receive than to what they believe. I, who have unlimited power over the subjects that I treat,[107] and am accountable for it to no one, do not, nevertheless, altogether believe myself about it; I often hazard sudden bursts of my mind, which I distrust, and certain verbal refinements which I am inclined to shake off.[108] But I let them pass at a venture. I see that some persons take pride in such things; it is not for me alone to judge of them. I present myself standing up and lying down, front and back, right and left, and in all my natural attitudes. Men's minds, even if alike in strength, are not always alike in conformity[109] and in taste.

This is what my memory of Tacitus presents to me in gross and with much uncertainty. All general judgements are weak and imperfect.

Chapter IX

OF VANITY [1]

THERE is perchance no more express vanity than to write of it so vainly. That which the Deity has thereon so divinely said to us should be carefully and constantly thought of by men of understanding. Who does not see that I have entered on a road by which without pause and without toil I may travel, as long as there are ink and paper in the world? I can not keep a record of my life by my actions; fortune makes them too humble; I keep it by my thoughts. In like manner I once saw a gentleman who made known his life only by the operation of his bowels; you might see at his house, on exhibition, a row of pots of seven or eight days' use; it was his study, his conversation; every other subject had a bad smell to him. In these pages are found, a little more decently, the voidings of an old mind, now hard, now lax, and always undigested. And when shall I have done setting forth the continual motion and mutation of my thoughts, whatever matter they fall upon, since Diomedes wrote six thousand books on the sole subject of grammar? [2] What may not careless talk give birth to, when the stammering and imperfect speech of early ages stuffed the world with such a horrible mass of volumes! So many words about

Of Vanity

mere words! O Pythagoras, would that thou couldst have conjured to silence this tempest![3] One Galba in ancient times was blamed because he lived in idleness; he answered that every man should render an account of his actions, not of his inaction.[4] He was mistaken; for justice takes cognisance of, and censures, those who work not.

But there should be some legal restraint of stupid and useless writers, as there is of vagabonds and loiterers; I and a hundred other writers would then be cast out from the hands of our people. I am not jesting: scribbling seems to be a symptom of an age of excess; when did we ever write so much as since our public disturbances? And when did the Romans write so much as at the time of their downfall? Moreover, the bettering of men's minds is not one with the bettering of the government;[5] this idle kind of working is due to this, that every one goes laxly about the business of his calling and wanders away from it. The corruption of the age is made up by the special contribution of each one of us; some furnish treachery, others injustice, irreligion, tyranny, avarice, cruelty, according to the degree of their power; the weaker bring to it dulness, trifling,[6] idleness— of whom I am one. It would seem as if it were the season for trifling things when harmful ones press upon us. At a time when to do evil is so common, to do only what is useless is, as it were, praiseworthy. I am of good cheer because I shall be amongst the last upon whom there will be occasion to lay hands. While the more prominent [sinners] are being attended to, I shall have time to mend my ways; for it seems to me that it would be contrary to reason to proceed against petty unsuitablenesses when we are infested by great ones. And the physician Philotimus said, when a man presented him his finger to dress, who, by his face and his breath, he perceived had an ulcer on the lung, "My friend, now is not the time to concern yourself about your nails."[7] However, I saw some years ago—I may say here—that a person whose memory I hold in peculiar regard thought well to publish at the height of our great disasters,—when neither law, nor justice, nor magistracy performed its functions any more than to-day,—certain trivial reforms concerning apparel, cookery, and legal pettifogging. Such are matters with which a misguided people is occupied and fed, to show that it is not entirely forgotten. These others do likewise, who insist on urgently prohibiting certain forms of speech, dances, and games, to a people given over to all sorts of execrable vices; it is no time to bathe and cleanse oneself when one is attacked by a violent fever. It is for the Spartans alone to comb and curl their hair at the moment that they are about to throw themselves headlong into some extreme risk of life.[8]

As for myself, I have this other worse habit: if I have a slipper carelessly put on, I am careless also about my shirt and my cloak;[9] I scorn to amend myself by halves. When I am in a bad plight, I desperately aid the evil; I give myself up, from despair, and let myself go toward my overthrow, and, as they say, cast the helve after the hatchet. I insist that things are getting worse and worse, and think myself no longer worth my care; either all well or all ill. It is favourable for me that the ruin of this kingdom comes at the same time with the ruin of my years; I more willingly suffer the increase of my ills thereby, than if my former good estate had been disturbed. The language that I use toward misfortune is the language of anger;[10] my courage bristles instead of sinking; and, unlike other men, I find myself more devout in good- than in ill-fortune, in conformity with Xenophon's precept, but not in conformity with his reason,[11] and I more readily do homage to heaven[12] in thanksgiving than in supplication. I take more pains to improve my health when it smiles upon me than I do to bring it back when I have driven it away; prosperity serves me as discipline and instruction, as adversity and scourgings serve others. As if good-fortune were incompatible with a good conscience, men become of worth only in ill-fortune.[13] Good-fortune is for me a peculiar spur to temperance and self-control; entreaties avail with me, menaces drive me the wrong way. Kindness makes me kind; fear stiffens me.

Amongst human states of mind this is rather common: to take more pleasure in unfamiliar than in habitual conditions, and to love movement and change:

> The light of day so rejoices us as it bathes us in its waves, because each hour comes with changed horses.[14]

I have my share of this. They who go to the other extreme of being satisfied with themselves, of thinking of what they have as above the rest, and of recognising nothing as more beautiful than what they see—if they are not more well-advised than we, they are certainly happier; I do not envy their wisdom, but their good-fortune I do. This eager liking of new and unknown things greatly helps to foster in me the desire to travel, but many other circumstances contribute to it; I gladly withdraw from the management of my household. There is some advantage in being in command, were it only in a barn, and in being obeyed by

Of Vanity

those about you; but it is too monotonous and languid a pleasure. And then it is necessarily commingled with many disturbing thoughts: sometimes the poverty and oppression of your people, sometimes quarrels among your neighbours, sometimes their encroachments upon you, afflict you,

> Or the vines are lashed by hail, and the farm proves false to its promise—the trees blaming now the rains, now the stars that parch the fields, now the harsh winters;[15]

and that hardly once in six months shall God send you a season by which the keeper of your purse will be fully contented; and which, if it be beneficial to the vineyards, will not injure the meadows;

> Either the sun in the sky parches your fields with too great heat, or sudden storms and cold frosts destroy them, and blasts of wind shake them in a violent storm;[16]

and there may be added the new and well-made shoe of that man of old days, which hurts your foot;[17] and that no stranger understands how much it costs you, and how much you contribute to maintain that show of order which is seen in your household and which perchance you buy too dear.

I came late to the management of my property. They whom Nature caused to be born before me relieved me of it for a long time. I had already taken another bent, more in accordance with my temperament. However, as I see it, it is an occupation more troublesome than difficult; he who has capacity for any thing will easily master this. If I sought to enrich myself, this road would seem to me too long; I

Of Vanity

should have taken service under our kings—a more fruitful commerce than any other. Since I aim to acquire only the reputation of having not gained and not wasted, conformably to the rest of my life, which is unfitted to do good or to do evil of consequence, and since I seek only to pass my days,[18] I can do that, thank God, without taking much thought. At the worst, one must always hasten to be in advance of poverty by retrenchment of expenses; that is what I depend upon, and to change my ways before it[19] compels me to do so. Meanwhile I have fixed in my mind several steps by which to get on with less than I have; I mean, to get on contentedly. *The measure of one's fortune is reckoned, not by the estimate of the census, but by one's manner of life.*[20] My real needs do not use up so entirely all my means that Fortune could not take a bite without going to the quick. My presence, ignorant and disregardful as it is, is a great assistance[21] to my domestic affairs; I busy myself about them, but against the grain;[22] moreover, I have this state of things in my house, that because I on my side burn the candle at my end, the other end is in no wise spared.

Journeys harm me only by the expense, which is great and beyond my means, as I am wont to take with me not merely essential, but also well-befitting, attendance. I must needs make them shorter and less frequent, and use for them only my superfluity,[23] and my reserve supply, delaying and deferring according as this increases. I will not have the pleasure of wandering spoil the pleasure of being at home. On the contrary, I propose that they shall nourish and assist one another. Fortune has aided me in this, that, since my principal vocation in this life was to live it easily, and rather negligently than busily, she has taken from me the

Of Vanity

need of increasing my wealth in order to provide for the multitude of my heirs. If that is not enough for one which has been so plentifully enough for me, the worse for him; his imprudence will not deserve that I should desire more for him. And every man, according to Phocion's example,[24] provides sufficiently for his children who provides for them to such extent that their condition is not unlike his. I should never be in sympathy with the doings of Crates. He left his money in the hands of a banker with this condition; that if his children were ignorant, he should give it to them; that if they had ability, he should distribute it among the more ignorant of the common people,[25] as if the ignorant, while less capable of doing without riches, were more capable in the use of them. However this may be, the loss that comes from my absence does not seem to me to demand, whilst I have the wherewithal to support it, that I should refuse to accept such opportunities as present themselves to withdraw from my toilsome presence.

There is always something askew. The business dealings, now with one house, now with another, harry you. You look into every thing too closely. Your clearsightedness, here as elsewhere, is harmful for you. I shun occasions for being vexed, and turn away from the knowledge of things that are going wrong, and yet I can not so manage that I do not constantly meet at home with something that I dislike. And the tricky expedients that are most carefully hidden from me are those that I best know. There are some which, that the less harm may come, one must assist oneself in hiding: trivial vexations—trivial sometimes, but always vexations. The smallest and slightest troubles are the sharpest; and as little letters tire the eyes most, so do little mat-

Of Vanity

ters harass us most.[26] The throng of petty ills is more disagreeable than the violence of one, however great that may
be. In proportion as these domestic thorns are thicker and
looser, they prick more sharply and without warning, easily
taking us by surprise and unprepared.[27] I am no philosopher;
ills press upon me according to their weight, and their
weight comes from their form as much as from their substance, and often more. I feel them more keenly than is
common, even if I have more endurance; in short, if they
do not wound me, they weigh upon me.

Life is a delicate thing and easily disquieted. When my
face is turned toward depression,—*for no man resists himself when he has begun to be moved,*[28]—however foolish
the cause that may lead me to it, I excite my disposition in
that direction, which is afterward fostered and aggravated
by its own motion, attracting and heaping up one matter
upon another, whereon to feed,—

The fall of water, drop by drop, hollows out stone.[29]

I become raw and festering with these every-day gutter-
droppings.[30] Every-day mishaps are never slight; they are
continuous and irreparable; when they arise from the details
of household cares, they are continuous and inseparable.
When I consider my affairs at a distance and as a whole, I
find, perhaps because my memory of them is not very exact,
that they have prospered beyond my reckoning and my
calculation. I draw from them, it seems to me, more than
there is in them; their good success betrays me. But if I am
inside the work, if I see how all the parts of it are going,—

Then we divide our minds amongst all these cares,[31]—

Of Vanity

I find there a thousand things to desire and to fear. To pay no attention to them is very easy to me; very difficult, to take hold of them and not be harassed by them. It is a miserable thing to be in a place where all that you see gives you work to do and concerns you; and it seems to me that I enjoy more blithely the pleasures of a strange house, and that I bring to them a freer and purer appreciation. Diogenes replied, in accordance with my feeling, to him who asked what kind of wine he found best, "the unfamiliar."[32]

My father took pleasure in building at Montaigne, where he was born; and in all this government of domestic affairs I like to make use of his example and his rule, and I shall bind my successors to them so far as I can. If I could do better for him, I would do so. I am proud that his will is still being carried out and acting through me. God forbid that I should allow to slip through my hands any appearance of continued life which I can give to so good a father. If I have undertaken to finish some old section of wall and to restore some ill-constructed building, it has certainly been more out of regard for his intention than for my own pleasure. And I blame my indolence in not having gone further to complete the things that he left unfinished in his house, because there is great likelihood that I am to be its last possessor of my family, and to give the last hand to it. For as to my personal inclination, neither the pleasure in building which is said to be so attractive, nor hunting, nor gardens, nor the other pleasures of a secluded life, have the power to interest me much. This is something in which I displease myself, as in all other opinions which are disadvantageous to me. I do not desire so much that they should be vigorous and learned as I desire that they should be pleasurable and

Of Vanity

adapted to life. They are, indeed, true and sound enough, if they are useful and agreeable.

Those who, hearing me declare my incompetence in the things pertaining to husbandry, whisper in my ear that it is disdain, and that it is because I have at heart some higher kind of knowledge that I fail to learn about the implements of tillage, its seasons, its methods, how my wines are made, how grafting is done, and to know the names and appearance of the herbs and fruits, and what is the mode of preparation of the meats on which I live, and the names and prices of the stuff with which I clothe myself—they vex me beyond words; it is due to dulness and is rather stupidity than pride. I should like better to be a good horseman than a good logician.

> Why do you not rather prepare to weave of osiers
> and pliant rushes something which daily need re-
> quires?[33]

We busy our thoughts with matters of general interest, and with universal causes and conduct which are conducted very well without us, and lose sight of our own doings,[34] and of Michel, who is nearer to us than man.

Now I am, for the most part, content to stay at home, but I would like to enjoy myself there more than elsewhere.

> Oh, that I may find a place of repose for my old
> age! May my weariness find an end of voyaging and
> war![35]

I do not know whether I shall succeed in this. I could wish that, instead of some other part of what I inherit from him, my father had bequeathed to me that passionate interest

Of Vanity

which, in his last years, he felt for his domestic affairs. He was very fortunate in conforming his desires to his fortune and in pleasing himself with what he had. The philosophy of state government[36] may do its best to blame the meanness and fruitlessness of my occupation if I can once acquire the taste for it that he had. I am of this opinion, that the most honourable employment is to serve the public, and to be useful to many. *For the fruit of genius and valour and all excellence is most abundantly garnered when it is bestowed on our neighbours.*[37] As for myself, I take no part in it; partly from conscience,—for when I see the weight that belongs to such employments I see how little means I have to supply it; and Plato, a master workman in all state government, did not fail to abstain from it,[38]—partly from laziness; I am content to enjoy the world without eagerness, to live a life simply excusable, and one which simply burdens neither myself nor others.

Never did man abandon himself more entirely and more negligently to the care and management of another than I would do if I knew to whom to commit myself. One of my wishes for these days would be to find a son-in-law who could fitly feed my old age and lull it to sleep; to whose keeping I might entrust the complete conduct and employment of my property, that he might do with it what I do with it, and gain from me what I gain by it, provided that he bring to the work a truly grateful and friendly heart. But what am I saying! We live in a world where loyalty in one's own children is unknown.

He who has charge of my purse in travelling has it absolutely and without oversight; he could easily deceive me in his accounts; and if he be not a devil, I compel him to

Of Vanity

do rightly by such utter confidence. *Many have taught deception through fear of being deceived, and by their suspicion have justified others in doing evil.*[39] My habitual security about my people is an absence of knowledge. I do not
presume vices until I have seen them, and I put the most
confidence in the young, whom I think the least spoiled by
bad examples. I am more ready to be told at the end of two
months that I have spent four hundred crowns, than to have
my ears assailed every evening with three, five, seven; yet
I have been robbed as little as another by that sort of theft.
It is true that I lend a helping hand to ignorance; I purposely
keep my knowledge of my money somewhat confused and
vague; up to a certain point I am glad to be able to doubt
about it. A little margin must be left for the disloyalty or
imprudence of your servant; if we have enough left to do
what we propose to do,[40] let us let this surplus of the liberality of Fortune pass a little the more at her mercy, as the
gleaner's portion. After all, I do not value the fidelity of my
people so much as I despise their harmfulness. Oh, it is a
mean and foolish study, the study of one's money, the pleasure of handling it and counting it over and over! It is thus
that avarice draws nigh.

In the eighteen years[41] that I have had property in charge,
I have never been able to prevail upon myself to examine
either my title-deeds or my principal affairs, which should
necessarily pass under my knowledge and attention. This
is not from a philosophic scorn of transitory and mundane
things; my taste is not so refined, and I value them at least
as much as they are worth; but it certainly is inexcusable
and puerile sloth and negligence. What would I not do
rather than read a contract; and rather than, the slave of my

affairs,—or, still worse, of those of another,— disturb those dusty old papers, as there are many who do for money? I hold nothing costly save care and labour, and I seek only to become indifferent and inactive. I was, I think, better adapted to live on somebody else's fortune, if it could be done without obligation and without servitude; and indeed I am not sure, on close scrutiny, whether, considering my disposition and my lot, what I have to endure with affairs, servants, and the household has not in it more that is abject, importunate, and bitter than to be in the service of a man born to higher station than I, who, would guide me somewhat at my ease. *Servitude is the obedience of a broken and abject spirit that has no will of its own.*[42] Crates did worse, who cast himself into the freedom of poverty, to be rid of the indignities and burdens of a house. That I would not do; I hate poverty not less than pain; but indeed I would change this kind of life for a humbler and less busied one. When I am away from home, I cast off all thoughts of such things; and I should then feel less the ruin of a tower than I feel, when on the spot, the fall of a tile. My mind is easily managed when I am absent, but, when I am at home, it suffers like that of a peasant; a rein twisted on my horse, an end of a stirrup-leather striking against my leg, will spoil my pleasure all day; I can raise my courage well enough to meet discomforts; my eyes, I can not.

The senses! O ye gods, the senses![43]

I am answerable in my own house for every thing that goes ill. Few masters—I speak of those of medium condition like myself, and if there are any, they are more fortunate than I —can so depend upon another that a large part of the burden

Of Vanity

does not remain on their shoulders. This easily impairs somewhat my behaviour in entertaining unexpected guests; and I have been able, perchance, like a tiresome host, to detain some of them more by my table than by my charms. And this household care detracts much from the pleasure which I ought to take in the visiting and assembling of any friends at my house. The most unsuitable bearing of a gentleman in his own house is to see him occupied about the carrying out of his orders,[44] whispering in the ear of one servant, threatening another with his eye; the service should glide on insensibly, and present an every-day course; and I think it unbecoming for a man to hold talk with his guests, whether in a way of excuse or of boasting, about the entertainment that is offered them. I love orderliness and neatness,—

My tankard and my dish shew me my face,[45]—

rather than abundance, and at home I pay careful attention to what is necessary, very little to outward show. If in another man's house a servant begins a quarrel, if a dish is upset, you merely laugh about it; you sleep while my lord arranges matters with his steward for your next day's entertainment. I speak of these things as they seem to me, not failing to recognise in general how agreeable a pleasure to certain natures is a peaceable, prosperous household, directed according to a well-ordered system; for I do not wish to attach to this matter my own mistakes and mishaps, or to gainsay Plato, who considers it to be the most fortunate occupation for every man "to carry on his private affairs without injustice."[46]

When I travel, I have to think only of myself and of the

spending of my money, which is disposed of by a single precept. Too many elements are required in amassing it; I understand nothing at all about that. About spending it I understand a little, and how to display my expenditure, which is in truth its principal use; but I look after it too ambitiously, which renders it irregular and disproportionate, and, besides, extravagant on both sides. If the occasion makes a show, if it serves the purpose, I indiscreetly let myself go, and I draw back no less indiscreetly if it is not brilliant and does not shine upon me.

Whether it be an acquired tendency, or nature,[47] which imprints in us this condition of living in relation to others, it does us more harm than good. We defraud ourselves of what is useful to ourselves in creating appearances in accordance with common opinion. We are not so much concerned as to what our existence is in ourselves and in fact, as we are as to what it is in public observation. Even the goods of the mind, and wisdom itself, seem to us fruitless if it[48] be enjoyed only by ourselves, if it be not brought forward to the eyes and approbation of others. There are men in whom gold flows in great streams through underground passages, imperceptibly; others stretch it all out into plates and sheets; so that, with these, farthings count for crowns; with those, the opposite, the world esteeming the usefulness and value according to the display. All overcareful attention to riches savours of avarice; even their distribution and a too systematic and artificial liberality are not worth a laborious watchfulness and solicitude. He who chooses to make his outlay accurate makes it narrow and limited. Keeping and spending are paltry matters, and take on the colour of good or evil only according to their relation to our will.

Of Vanity

The other cause that invites me to these excursions is my disagreement with the present conditions of our State. I could easily console myself for its corruption, so far as regards the public interest, —

An age worse than the age of iron, for whose crimes Nature herself can find no name, and has taken none from any metal,[49]—

but as regards my own, I can not. I am especially preoccupied by it because in my neighbourhood, in consequence of the long-continued license of these civil wars, we have now become familiar[50] with so disordered a form of government,

In which right and wrong have changed places,[51]

that in truth it is a marvel that it can be maintained;

All armed they till the ground, and they take delight always in collecting fresh plunder, and in living on booty.[52]

In fine, I see by our example that human society holds together and becomes united under all conditions; however men may for a time be situated, they form masses and come into order by stirring about and gathering themselves together, just as ill-fitting bodies which are packed up together without arrangement find of themselves a way to unite and settle into their proper places, often better than art could have arranged them. King Philip made an assemblage of the most wicked and incorrigible men he could find, and placed them all in a city which he had built for them and which bore their name.[53] It is my belief that they

Of Vanity

fashioned among themselves from their very vices a political framework and a congruous and regular society. I see not one action, or three, or a hundred, but customs in common and received usage, so savage especially in inhumanity and in treachery (which is to me the worst of vices), that I have not the courage to conceive them without horror, and I marvel at them almost as much as I detest them. The practice of these signal crimes marks mental vigour and force as much as error and disorder. Necessity accords them and brings them together. This fortuitous union takes shape later in laws; for there have been some as barbarous as any human thought can conceive, which nevertheless have maintained their faith with as much soundness and length of life as those of Plato and Aristotle could have done. And in truth all such picturings, artificially devised, of forms of government are absurd and unfit to be put into practice.

These intense and long-continued altercations concerning the best form of society and the rules best adapted to bind us are altercations suitable only to exercise our wits; just as in the learning of the schools[54] many subjects have their being in excitement and in discussion and have no life outside that. Such ideas about government[55] would be acceptable in a new world; but we have to deal with one already fitted and shaped to certain customs; we do not engender them as did Pyrrha or Cadmus. By whatever means we have the power to amend it and dispose it anew, we can hardly wrench it from its accustomed bent without altogether shattering it. Solon was asked whether he had established for the Athenians the best laws that he could. "Yes, truly," he answered, "of those that they would have accepted."[56] Varro excuses himself in the same tone: that, if he had to

write of religion as something wholly new, he would say
what he thought about it; but, it being already accepted, he
will speak rather of its practice than of its nature.[57]

Not in theory merely, but in truth, the most excellent
and best form of government for each nation is that under
which it has been maintained. Its form and essential utility
depend upon customs. We are apt to be dissatisfied with
present conditions; but none the less I hold that to desire
in a democracy the supreme control of a few, or in a monarchy another kind of government, is wrong and foolish.

> Love the State as you find it existing: if it be a mon-
> archy, love royalty; if it be an oligarchy, or a com-
> monwealth, love that no less, for God caused you to be
> born in it.[58]

Thus wrote the excellent monsieur de Pibrac, whom we
have just lost—of an intelligence so agreeable, opinions so
sound, a character so delightful. This loss, and that which
we suffered at the same time in the death of monsieur de
Foix,[59] are important losses to our crown. I do not know if
there is left in France another pair to take the place of these
two Gascons in the council of our kings, equal to them in
integrity and ability. They were souls admirable in different ways, and assuredly, considering the times, each rare
and admirable in his kind. But what housed them in this
age, so unsuited and out of keeping as they were with our
corruptions and our tumults?

Nothing so weighs upon a state as does innovation; mere
change gives shape to injustice and tyranny. When a structure is weakened, we can prop it; we can prevent the impairment and decay natural to all things from removing us too

far from our beginnings and our principles; but to undertake
to remould so great a mass and to change the foundation of
so great a structure is to do like those who, to cleanse, efface;
who propose to reform special defects by a universal confusion, and to cure maladies by death, *desiring not so much
to change things as to overturn them.*[60] The world is ill
adapted to cure itself; it is so impatient of what constrains
it that it aims only at ridding itself of it, without considering
at what price. We see by a thousand examples that it is
generally cured at its own expense. Relief from immediate
illness is no cure, if there be not a general amendment of
conditions. The surgeon's object is not to kill the diseased
flesh; that is but the means for its healing; he looks further,
to making the natural soundness exist again and to restoring
the organ to its proper state. Whoever proposes merely to
get rid of what is preying upon him falls short; for good
does not necessarily succeed ill; another and a worse ill may
follow; as happened to the slayers of Cæsar, who brought
the commonwealth to such a pass that they had to repent
of having intermeddled. To many men since, even in our
own time, it has happened in like manner; Frenchmen of
my age know well what to say about this. All great mutations shake a state and disorder it.

He who should aim straight at a cure and should consider carefully about it before doing any thing would be
likely to grow cool about putting his hand to it. Pacuvius
Calavius corrected the imperfection of such a course by a
notable example.[61] His fellow citizens had rebelled against
their magistrates; he, being a personage of great influence
in the city of Capus, found means one day to confine the
Senate in the palace;[62] and, calling the people together on

Of Vanity

the public square, he said to them that the day had come when with perfect freedom they could take vengeance on the tyrants who had for so long a time oppressed them, whom he held at his mercy, alone and unarmed; he was of opinion that they should be drawn by lot, one after another, and that each one should be specially dealt with, whatever might be decreed being carried out immediately; provided also that at the same time they should take thought to establish in the place of the condemned some worthy man, so that the office should not be left vacant. They had no sooner heard the name of a senator than there arose an outcry of general dissatisfaction with him. "I see clearly," said Pacuvius, "that we must remove this one; he is a bad man; let us have a good man instead of him." There was immediate silence, every one being much embarrassed about the selection. When one bolder than the others first named his choice, there was heard an even greater unanimity of voices for rejecting this one, proclaiming a hundred imperfections and just reasonings for repelling him. This opposing temper becoming inflamed, it was even worse for the second senator and the third; as great discord about the election as agreement about the dismissal. Having uselessly wearied themselves in this confusion, they began, one here, one there, to steal away little by little from the assembly, each carrying away in his mind this conviction, that the oldest and best-known evil is always more endurable than one new and untried.[63]

Although I see that we are pitiably perturbed—for what have we not done!—

Alas, for the shame of our scars and our crimes and our fratricidal wars! What has our cruel age shunned?

Of Vanity

What sin have we left undone? From what guilt have our youths, restrained by fear of the gods, withheld their hands? What altars have they spared?[64]

I do not instantly make up my mind;

If the goddess Safety herself wished to save this family, she could not do it;[65]

we are not perchance at our last stage.

The conservation of states is a thing which seemingly exceeds our intelligence. A civil government, as Plato says, is a puissant thing and one difficult of dissolution;[66] it often endures, notwithstanding deadly internal diseases, notwithstanding the injury of unjust laws, notwithstanding tyranny, nothwithstanding the excesses and ignorance of magistrates, the license and sedition of the populace. In all our fortunes we compare ourselves with what is above us and look toward those that are better than ours; let us measure ourselves by what is below us; there is no one so forlornly wretched[67] that he may not find a thousand examples with which to console himself. It is an imperfection in us that we see more unreadily what is above us than readily what is below us.[68] Yet Solon said, "Were all ills heaped together, there is no one who would not choose rather to bear with him the ills that he has than to have an equitable division with all other men of this heap of ills, and to take his several portion of them."[69] Our state is in ill health, but there have been others sicker that have not died. The gods use us like tennis balls and toss us hither and yon.

The gods treat us men like balls.[70]

The stars have fatally destined the Roman state as an

1306

example of what they can accomplish in this kind; it comprises in itself all the conditions and chances that befall a state, all that established usage can effect in it, and disturbance, and good-fortune and ill-fortune. What state should despair of its condition, seeing the shocks and commotions wherewith that one was agitated, and which it withstood? If extent of dominion be the health of a state (of which I am in no wise assured,—and Isocrates gives me pleasure when he instructs Nicocles not to envy princes who have great dominions but such as know how to maintain those which have fallen to them),[71]—that one was never so healthy as when it was most sick. The worst period of its government was for it the most fortunate one. We can scarcely recognise the image of any government under the first emperors; it is the most horrible and the most dense confusion that can be imagined. Nevertheless, the state endured it and continued to exist, maintaining not a monarchy restricted to its limits, but one composed of many nations very different from one another, very distant, very ill-disposed, very irregularly ruled and unjustly conquered.

> And Fortune does not allow any nation to nourish
> its hatred against a people that rules land and sea.[72]

Every thing that totters does not fall. The frame of so great a body holds by more than one nail; it holds even by its antiquity, like old buildings without plastering and without mortar whose foundations time has purloined, which yet, for all that, exist and are upheld by their own weight;

> Clinging by roots no longer strong, it is made safe
> by its own weight.[73]

Of Vanity

Moreover, it is not a wise proceeding to inspect only the flanking fortification and the moat in order to judge of the strength of a place; we must observe how it can be reached and in what condition the assailant is. Few vessels sink of their own weight and without outside violence. Now, if we turn our eyes on all sides, every thing around us is crumbling; look at all the great states, whether of Christendom or elsewhere, which we know about; you will find a manifest menace of change and ruin;

> They have their own misfortunes, and the same storm awaits them all.[74]

Astrologers run no chances in warning us, as they do, of great impending alterations and mutations; their presages are in view and palpable—there is no need of going for them to the skies. We have reason to derive not only consolation from this universal companionship in ills and menaces, but also some hope for the duration of our state, forasmuch as naturally nothing falls where every thing falls; universal sickness is individual health; conformity is a quality hostile to dissolution. For my own part, I do not at all yield to despair, and it seems to me that I see paths by which we can be saved.

> Perhaps some god will restore these things to their place by a propitious change.[75]

Who knows but that God may have it happen that it shall be as with our bodies, which are purged and brought to a better condition by long and grievous sicknesses, which give back to them a more entire and purer health than that of which they deprive them? What depresses me most is that,

1308

in reckoning the symptoms of our malady, I see amongst them as many natural ones and of those which heaven sends us and which evidently came thence,[76] as of those which our unreasonableness and human unwisdom contribute to it. It seems as if the stars themselves ordain that we have lasted long enough, and beyond the ordinary term; and this also depresses me, that the nearest ill that threatens us is not an alteration of the whole and solid mass, but its dispersion and disintegration, the extremest of our fears.

And in these very musings I fear the treachery of my memory, that inadvertently it may have caused me to record the same thing twice. I hate to scrutinise my work, and never but with reluctance review what has once escaped me. Now I bring hither nothing of new attainment; these are familiar ideas; since I have conceived them perchance a hundred times, I am afraid that I have already set them down. Repetition is tiresome everywhere, though it were in Homer; but it is fatal in subjects that have only a superficial and passing exhibition. I am annoyed by inculcation, even in profitable matters, as in Seneca; and I am annoyed by the custom of the Stoic school, of repeating in all their length and breadth, on every subject, the principles and presuppositions which are of general application, and of constantly alleging anew common and universal arguments and reasonings. My memory becomes cruelly worse every day.

As if I had drained with parched throat the cups that bring the slumber of Lethe.[77]

It will be necessary henceforth (God be praised, down to this moment there has been no mishap!) that, whereas others seek time and occasion to think what they have to

Of Vanity

say, I avoid preparation, for fear of binding myself to some obligation on which I may have to depend. To be bound and obliged, and to depend upon so weak an instrument as my memory, makes me miss the way. I never read the following narrative that I do not feel a personal and natural emotion. Lyncestes, accused of conspiring against Alexander, on the day when he was brought before the army, according to custom, to be heard in his own defence, had in his head a studied harangue, of which, very hesitatingly and stammeringly, he pronounced a few words. As he grew more and more confused, whilst he struggled gropingly with his memory, lo, he was attacked and killed with their pikes by the soldiers nearest to him, who regarded him as convicted; his agitation and his silence were to them confession.[78] Having had in prison so much leisure to prepare himself, it is not in their opinion memory that fails him; his conscience ties his tongue and deprives him of strength. Truly this is evident—that the place, the bystanders, the suspense, are agitating, even when it is only a matter of ambition to speak well; what becomes of a man when it is a public speech on which his life depends?

For my part, the very fact that I am fettered to what I have to say serves to loose me from it. When I commit and entrust myself wholly to my memory, I lean so heavily upon her that I oppress her; the burden affrights her. In proportion as I rely upon her, I become so out of myself as to test my composure, and I have found it difficult sometimes to conceal the servitude in which I was immured; whereas my purpose is to exhibit in speaking great carelessness in tone and visage, and fortuitous and unpremeditated gestures, as if born of the immediate occasion; liking better to say nothing worth while than to seem to have come prepared to speak well—a misbecoming thing, especially in men of my profession,[79] and one that imposes too great constraint on him who can not retain much. Preparation gives more to be hoped for than it brings forth; often a man foolishly strips to his doublet, to leap no better than in his long coat;[80] *he who wishes to please has no enemy so potent as tardiness.*[81] It is recorded of the orator Curio that when he undertook to divide his oration into three parts, or four, or into the number equal to that of his arguments and reasonings, it easily happened to him to forget some one of them or to add one or two more to them.[82] I have always carefully avoided falling into this mishap, detesting such earnests and prescriptions; not only from distrust of my memory, but also because that method is too much like artifice. *Simplicity becomes soldiers.*[83] Suffice it that I have now promised myself never again to assume the burden of speaking in public;[84] since, as for speaking by reading one's manuscript, besides its being very unsuitable, it is a great disadvantage to those who can by nature produce some effect by gestures; and still less would I throw myself on the mercy of my ability to speak extemporaneously;[85] that is in me a heavy and obscure quality, which can not give aid in sudden and important necessities.

Reader, let this apprentice work[86] run on, and this third prolongation of the remaining portions of my picture. I add, but I do not correct.[87] In the first place, because he who has hypothecated his work to the world seems to me to have no longer any rights in it; let him, if he can, utter himself better elsewhere, and not vitiate the work that he has sold to us. Nothing of the work of such men should be bought

Of Vanity

until after their death. Let them consider it carefully before publishing it; what hurries them? My book is always the same, save that, when they set about dressing it up again in order that the purchaser may not go away with hands quite empty, I permit myself to attach to it (as it is only ill-laid mosaic) some supernumerary bits. They are mere overweight trifles, which do not damn the first form, but give some value to each of the following ones by a little, sought-for detail.[88] Thence, however, it may easily happen that some transposition of chronology is involved, my narrations taking their places according to their occasion, not always according to their age.

In the second place, because as regards myself I fear to lose by change, my intelligence does not always go forward: sometimes it goes backward too. I distrust my ideas scarcely less when they are the second or third than the first, or today's, not yesterday's. We oftentimes correct ourselves as foolishly as we correct others.

I have grown older by a number of years since my first publication, which was in the year one thousand five hundred and eighty; but I doubt whether I am one whit wiser. Myself now and myself then are two persons; which the better? I do not at all know. It would be a fine thing to be old if we progressed only toward improvement; it is the motion of a drunken man, staggering, dizzy, tortuous, or of reeds which the wind sways casually as it lists. Antiochus had written vigorously in favor of the Academy; in his old age he took the opposite side;[89] whichever of the two I should follow, would it not always be following Antiochus? After having established the doubtfulness of human opinions, to seek to establish their certainty—was it not to estab-

lish doubt, not certainty, and to promise that, were another
term of life given him, he would always be on the point of
fresh changes, not so much better as different?

Public favour has given me a little more courage than
I could hope for; but what I dread most is to be wearisome;
I should like better to spur than to fatigue, as a learned man
of my time has done; praise is always agreeable, no matter
from whom or why it comes; yet, would we be rightly
pleased by it, it is needful to be informed of its cause. Imperfections even have a way of being commended. Public
and general esteem is seen to be lucky in hitting its mark;
and I am mistaken if in my day the worst writings are not
those which have won the most popular favour. Assuredly
I return thanks to the estimable men who deign to take my
feeble efforts in good part; nowhere are faults in execution
so apparent as in a matter that in itself has nothing to recommend it. Do not, reader, blame me for those which slip
in here through the whim or carelessness of others; each
hand, each workman, contributes his share. I do not meddle with orthography, but simply bid them follow the old
forms; nor with punctuation; I am far from expert with
either. When they[90] wholly spoil the sense, I give myself
little concern about it, for at least they exonerate me; but
when they substitute a false meaning, as they so often do,
and alter me according to their understanding, they ruin
me. Howbeit, whenever the sentence does not measure up
to my strength, an estimable man should deny it to be
mine. Whoever knows how indiligent I am, how I am made
after my own fashion, will easily believe that I would more
willingly indite anew as many more Essays than subject
myself to going over these again for such trivial corrections.

Of Vanity

I was saying then, just now, that, being fixed in the deep-
est mine of this new metal,[91] not only am I debarred from
much familiarity with persons of other natures and of other
opinions than mine, by which they are held together as by
a tie which governs every other tie, but also I am not without risk among those to whom every thing is equally permissible and of whom the greater part can not now render
worse their dealings with our laws, whence arises the last
degree of license. Considering all the special circumstances
that concern me, I find no man of our party to whom ad-
herence to the laws costs more than to me, both in cessa-
tion of profit and the emergence of loss,[92] as the lawyers say.
And some there be who make a show of their worth with
their ardour and eagerness, who, fairly weighed, do much
less than I. My house, being a house which is at all times
open, much frequented, and friendly,—for I have never
allowed myself to be led into making it an instrument of
war, which I go in search of most readily[93] when it is far-
thest from my neighbourhood,—has well deserved general
good-will, and it would be very difficult to crow over me on
my own dung-heap; and I consider it a wonderful and exemplary achievement that it is still unstained by blood and
pillage during so long-continued a tempest and so many
near-by changes and commotions. For, to say truth, it was
possible for a man of my disposition to evade a uniform and
continuous condition of things, whatever it might be; but
the mutually opposing invasions and incursions, and the
alternations and vicissitudes of fortune round about me,
have to the present time rather exasperated than pacified
the temper of the country and surcharged me with invincible difficulties and dangers. I escape, but it does not please

1314

me that it should be by good luck, and indeed by my own prudence, rather than by justice; and it does not please me to be outside the protection of the laws and under other safeguard than theirs. As things are, I live more than half by the favour of others, which is a harsh indebtedness. I do not like to owe my safety either to the good-will and benignity of the great, to whom my loyalty and my liberty are acceptable, or to the liberal character of my predecessors and of myself; for what if I were different? If my demeanour and the frankness of my intercourse are of service to my neighbours or my kindred, it is a cruel thing that they can acquit themselves by letting me live, and that they can say: "We allow him freely to continue divine service in the chapel of his house, all the churches hereabout being ruined by us; and we permit him the use of his property and his life, as he safeguards our women and our cattle in case of need."

For successive generations[94] my house has shared the honour of Lycurgus the Athenian, who was the general depositary and keeper of the purses of his fellow citizens.[95] Now I hold that a man's life should depend on law and public authority, not be a matter of recompense or of favour. How many gallant men have chosen rather to lose life than to be indebted for it! I shrink from subjecting myself to any kind of obligation, but especially to such as binds me by the claims of honour. I find nothing so costly as that which is given to me, and this is because my will remains pledged under the name of gratitude; and I am the more willing to accept services that are for sale. That is not surprising:[96] for these I give only money; for the others I give myself.

The tie that holds me by the law of courtesy seems to me

Of Vanity

much tighter and stronger than that of legal compulsion. I am more agreeably tied up by a notary than by myself. Is it not reasonable that my conscience should be much more pledged by that which has been simply entrusted to it? In other cases, my loyalty owes nothing, for nothing has been lent to it; let support be had from the confidence and security derived from outside sources. I should find it much easier[97] to break from the prison of a stone wall and of the laws than from my word. I am punctilious even to superstition in keeping my promises, and on all subjects I preferably make them vague and conditional. To those which are of no weight I give weight by devotion to my discipline;[98] it torments and burdens me with its own importance. Indeed, in any undertaking wholly my own and free, if I tell its object it seems to me that I prescribe it to myself, and that making it known to others is to impose it upon myself; it seems to me that I promise it when I tell it, and so I air my plans but little. My condemnation of myself is sharper and more severe than that of those who judge me, who deal with me only according to the aspect of common obligation; the constraint of my conscience is closer and more strict; I follow laggingly those duties to which I should be driven if I did not go to them. *Even an act that is rightly done is just only if it is voluntary*.[99] If the action has not some glamour of freedom, it has neither grace nor honour.

What duty compels me to do, I can hardly be induced to do voluntarily;[100]

Where necessity draws me I like to relax my will, *because whatever is required by authority is credited to him who*

requires rather than to him who obeys.[101] I know some who
carry this attitude even to injustice, who give sooner than
restore, lend sooner than pay, do good in niggardly fashion
to him to whom they are beholden. I do not go so far, but
I come near it. I so desire to disburden and relieve myself
of obligation that I have sometimes counted as gain the ingratitude, wrongs, and affronts that I have received from
those toward whom, either by nature or by accident, I had
some indebtedness of friendship, seizing this occasion of
their fault as so much acquittal and discharge of my debt.
Although I continue to pay them the manifest duties of
common reason, I find nevertheless a great saving in doing
from justice what I had been doing from good-will, and in
being a little relieved from attention and solicitude in my
inward mind, and from the inner binding force of my good-
will,[102]—*it is the part of a wise man, just as he holds back a
horse in a race, to restrain the first impulse of friendship,*[103]
which is too urgent and pressing when I yield to it, at least
for a man who does not wish to be at all pledged; and this
thriftiness[104] serves as some consolation for the imperfections of those who approach me. I regret that they are less
worthy of my attention and engagements to them; but,
however that may be, I thereby am saved some part of it.
I regard as reasonable the man who is less fond of his child
if he be scrofulous or misshapen, and not only when he is
knavish, but also when he is unlucky and ill-begotten (God
himself has diminished by so much his value and natural
worth), provided that in this lack of affection he carries
himself with moderation and with exact justice. For me,
proximity does not lessen impertections, but rather makes
them worse.

Of Vanity

All things considered, according to my apprehension of the art of good deeds and gratitude, which is a subtle art and of constant employ, I see no man more free and less indebted than I am at this hour.[105] What I owe, I owe simply because of common and natural obligations; there is no man who is otherwise more entirely free;

> Nor are gifts of the mighty known to me.[106]

Princes give me much if they take nothing from me, and do me enough good when they do me no harm; that is all that I ask of them. Oh, how beholden I am to God that it has pleased him that I should receive directly by his favour all I have! That he has specially kept in his own possession all my debts! How earnestly I implore his sacred compassion that I may never owe essential things[107] to any one! Most fortunate freedom that has accompanied me so far—may it continue to the end! I endeavour to have no special need of any one; *all my hope is in myself;*[108] this is something that every man can effect for himself, but those more easily whom God has placed beyond the reach of natural and urgent necessities. It is very pitiful and hazardous to depend on another. We ourselves, to whom we can address ourselves for and with the most reason and sureness, are not sufficiently secure.[109] I have nothing of mine but myself, and indeed my possession of myself is partly defective and borrowed. I strive to improve myself in spirit, which is the most important, and also in fortune, that I may find thus the means to content myself should all else abandon me. Eleus Hippias provided himself, not only with learning, that in time of need he might be able happily to withdraw, in the lap of the Muses, from all other companionship; nor only with a knowledge of philosophy, to teach his soul to be content with itself and, when faith so ordains, manfully to do without the pleasures that come to it from outside. He was so careful as also to learn to cook for himself, to cut his hair, to make his garments, his shoes, his breeches, that he might depend on himself as far as possible, and be free of assistance from others.[110] We enjoy borrowed satisfaction[111] much more freely and gladly when our enjoyment is not forced and compelled by need, and when we have both in our will and in our fortune the strength and the means to do without them.

I know myself well; and it is difficult for me to imagine any such pure liberality toward me in any one, any hospitality so bountiful and gratuitous that it would not seem to me disastrous, cruel, and tainted with disgrace, if necessity had fettered me in it. As giving is of an ostentatious nature and a mark of superiority, so accepting is of the nature of submission; witness the insulting and contentious refusal that Bajazet made of the gift that Temir sent him;[112] and those that were offered by the Emperor Solyman to the Emperor of Calicut so angered him that he not only rudely refused them, saying that neither he nor his predecessors were accustomed to receive and that it was their office to give, but, moreover, had the ambassadors sent for this purpose cast into a dungeon.[113] When Thetis, Aristotle says, flatters Jupiter,[114] when the Lacedæmonians flatter the Athenians, they do not undertake to refresh their memory of the benefits they have done them, which is always odious, but their memory of the benefits they themselves have received from them. Those persons whom I see employ every one in such friendly fashion, and thereby bind themselves, would not

Of Vanity

so do if they relished as I do the sweetness of unalloyed
liberty, and if they weighed, as much as a wise man should
weigh, the burden of an obligation. It is sometimes, perchance, requited, but it is never done away with—a cruel
fetter for one who likes to have completely free elbow-room.
Those who are acquainted with me, both above and below
me in rank, know whether they have ever seen any one less
given to soliciting, demanding, begging, or less burdensome
to others. If I am so beyond all modern example, it is no
great wonder, so many parts of my character contribute
thereto. A little natural pride, intolerance of refusal, moderation in my desires and plans, unfitness for every sort of
affairs, and my most favourite qualities,—laziness, freedom,
—from all these sources I hold in mortal hatred the being
beholden to another or having another beholden to me.[115]
I eagerly make use of every means in my power to do without the kindness of another before making use of it on any
occasion or need, whether trivial or important. My friends
annoy me amazingly when they request me to request something of a third person; and it seems to me to cost scarcely
less to free myself from some one who is indebted to me, by
making use of him, than to become indebted myself to one
who owes me nothing. This condition being removed, and
this other, that they do not desire of me a matter of business
perplexity (for I have declared mortal war against all care),
I am readily compliant and prepared for the need of any
one. I have very gladly sought opportunities to benefit
others and attach them to me, and it seems to me that there
is no more agreeable use of our means;[116] but I have even
more avoided receiving than I have sought to give. And
according to Aristotle this is much more easy.[117] My for-

Of Vanity

tune has allowed me to benefit others but little, and the little
that it has allowed me to do of this sort has been rather
poorly placed. Had I been born to high position among
men, I should have been ambitious to make myself beloved,
not to make myself feared or admired. Shall I express it
more arrogantly? I should have considered giving pleasure
as much as doing good. Cyrus very wisely—as reported by a
most excellent captain and still better philosopher[118]—ranks
his own kindness at heart and his good deeds far above his
valour and his conquests in war; and the elder Scipio,
whenever he wishes to set forth his own worth, rates his own
mildness and humanity above his prowess and his victories,
and has always on his lips this praiseworthy saying, that he
gave his enemies as much occasion to love him as he gave
his friends.[119]

I mean to say then that, if we must needs owe something,
it should be by a more legitimate title than that of which I
speak, to which the authority of this miserable war binds
me, and not for so great a debt as that of my total preservation;[120] this overwhelms me. I have gone to bed in my
house a thousand times imagining that I should be betrayed and done to death that night, compounding with
fortune that it might be without terror and not lingering;
and I have exclaimed, after my Pater Noster:

Shall an impious soldier possess these well-tilled
fields?[121]

What remedy is there? This is the place of my birth and
of most of my ancestors'; they set their affections and their
name upon it.[122] We become enured to all to which we become accustomed, and, in so miserable a condition as ours

1321

Of Vanity

is, accustomedness has been a very friendly gift from nature;
it benumbs our sensitiveness to the sufferance of many ills.
Civil wars have this worse effect than other wars: they turn
every man into a sentinel in his own house.

> How sad to protect one's life with a gate and a wall,
> and scarcely to be safe in the strength of one's own
> house![123]

It is a dire extremity to be under constraint even in one's
household and domestic repose. This misfortune concerns
me more than any one else because of the situation of the
place where I am, which is always the foremost and the
hindmost in the battery of our disturbances, and peace has
never its full aspect there;

> Even in peace, they tremble in fear of war.[124]

> As often as Fortune overthrows peace, war enters
> in. You would have done better, Fortune, to give us
> a place in the East, or wandering homes under the
> cold Bear.[125]

I sometimes derive from indifference and negligence power
to strengthen myself against these considerations; these
conditions also somewhat lead us to a resolute frame of
mind. It often happens to me to imagine with some pleasure mortal dangers, and to expect them; I plunge stupidly
headlong into death, without considering or recognising it,
as into a silent, dark abyss which swallows me in a trice and
smothers me in an instant with a puissant sleep full of
torpor and painlessness.[126] And in such sudden and violent
deaths the result which I foresee from them gives me more
of consolation than does the fact of fear. They say that,

Of Vanity

while life is no better for being long, death is better for not being long. My repugnance to being dead is less than the courage with which I face dying,[127] I wrap myself up and lie close in this storm, which will blind me and whirl me away furiously, with a sudden assault of which I shall be unaware.

Again, if it be true, as some gardeners say,[128] that roses and violets are more odoriferous when they grow near garlic and onions, inasmuch as these suck up and draw into themselves what evil odour there is in the soil, would that thus these depraved natures might breathe in all the venom of my air and region and make it so much the better and purer for me by their proximity that I should not be wholly a loser. This is not the case; but something of it there may be: that goodness is more beautiful and more attractive when it is rare, and that diametrical difference and unlikeness stiffen and confirm well-doing in oneself and fill it with ardour from emulation of what is opposed to it and from desire of renown.

Robbers, many thanks to them, bear me no special ill-will; nor I them. I should have to deal with too large a number. Similar consciences lodge under diverse kinds of gowns—similar cruelty, disloyalty, robbery; and so much the worse since they are most cowardly, most secure, and most hidden under the shadow of the laws. I detest an open insult less than that which is treacherous; that which is contentious less than that which is peaceful and lawful. Our fever has suddenly seized a body which it has little impaired; fire was there, flame has broken out; the noise is greater, the evil but little.

I usually reply to those who ask me the reason of my

Of Vanity

travels, that I well know what I fly from but not what I seek. If I am told that amongst strangers there may be as little health, and that their morals are no purer than ours, I reply in the first place that it is hard,

There are so many forms of crime [amongst us]![129]

secondly, that it is always a gain to change a bad condition for an uncertain one, and that the ills of other peoples can not fret us as do our own.

I would not forget this—that I never am so rebellious against France that I do not regard Paris with admiring eyes. She has ever had my heart from my youth,[130] and it has befallen me as with surpassing things: the more I have seen of other beautiful cities, the more the beauty of this one has power over me, and the more she gains in my affection. I love her for herself, and more in her own being than overlaid with acquired magnificence; I love her tenderly, even to her warts and blemishes. I am a Frenchman only through that great city, great in population, great in the felicity of her situation, but, above all, great and beyond compare in variety and diversity of pleasure; the glory of France and one of the noblest ornaments of the world. May God drive our discords far from her! Undivided and united, I find her protected from all other violence. I warn her that, of all the factions, the worst will be that which shall breed discord in her, and I have no anxiety about her except from herself; and my anxiety for her is as great surely as for any part of this realm. So long as she may endure I shall not lack a refuge in which to stand at bay, one sufficient to make me forget to regret any other refuge.

Not because Socrates said so,[131] but because it is in truth

1324

my own disposition,—and perchance to some excess,—I regard all men as my compatriots and embrace a Pole as a Frenchman, making less account of the national, than of the universal and common, bond. I am not much smitten by the charm of a fellow countryman;[132] acquaintances that are wholly new and wholly of my own making seem to me to outvalue these other every-day, fortuitous, neighbourhood acquaintances; pure friendships acquired by us usually surpass those in which the being of the same region or of the same blood joins us. Nature has put us into the world free and unfettered; we imprison ourselves within certain narrow limits, as did the kings of Persia, who bound themselves to drink no other water than that of the river Choaspes, foolishly renouncing their right of usage over all other streams, and dried up all the rest of the world so far as they were concerned.[133] Socrates, toward the end of his life, regarded a sentence of banishment as worse for him than a sentence of death;[134] I think that I shall never be so enfeebled or so rooted in my country that I shall feel the like. Such divine lives have many conceptions which I accept from respect rather than from sympathy; and there are also some so lofty and extraordinary that I can not accept them even from respect, because I can not understand them. This disposition was somewhat of a weakness[135] in a man who regarded the world as his city; it is true that he disdained peregrinations and had hardly set foot outside the territory of Attica.[136] Consider that he found fault with his friends for offering money to redeem his life,[137] and that he refused to come out of prison through the mediation of others, in order not to disobey the laws at a time when they were so very corrupt.[138] These examples are of the first sort[139] to me.

Of Vanity

Of the second are others which I could find in the same personage; many of these rare examples surpass even my strength of judgement.

In addition to these reasons, travelling seems to me a beneficial occupation. The mind is then constantly busied in observing novel and unknown things; and I know no better school, as I have often said,[140] wherein to fashion life, than to set before it incessantly the diversity of so many other lives, opinions, and customs, and to cause it to have a little knowledge of so perpetual a variety of forms of our nature. The body is then neither idle nor wearied, and this moderate motion keeps it in easy breathing. I stay on horseback, without dismounting and without discomfort, subject to colic[141] as I am, eight and ten hours—

Beyond the strength allotted to old age.[142]

No season is inimical to me, except the parching heat of a scorching sun; for the umbrellas which have been used in Italy from the time of the ancient Romans burden the arms more than they relieve the head. I should like to know what was the skill the Persians had, so long ago, in the early days of luxury, in creating fresh air and shade when they chose, as Xenophon says.[143]

Change of air and climate does not affect me; all skies are the same to me; I am beaten only by the internal changes which I give rise to in myself; and these occur less frequently while travelling. It is difficult to set me in motion, but when I am once started, I go as far as you please. I fuss as much about small undertakings as great ones, and in preparing for a day's ride to visit a neighbour as for a real journey. I have learned to make my daily stages in the Spanish

Of Vanity

fashion, without halting—long and reasonable stages; and in the extreme heat I travel at night, between sunset and sunrise. The other fashion, of baiting on the road, dining in a hurly-burly and in haste, especially on short days, is unprofitable. My horses are the better for it; no horse has ever failed me which was able to make the first day's journey with me. I water them everywhere and only look to it that they still have far enough to go to digest the water. My laziness about getting out of bed gives opportunity for my followers to dine at their leisure before we start. For myself, I never dine too late; my appetite comes with eating, and never otherwise; I am never hungry but at table.

People blame me because I have chosen to continue this practice of travelling when married and old. It is the best time for a man to leave his household, when he has put it in the way to go on without him; when he has so ordered it that it in no wise belies its wonted form. It is much more imprudent to go from home leaving in the house a less faithful guardian, and one who may be less careful to provide what is needed.

The most useful and honourable knowledge and occupation for the mother of a family is the knowledge of housewifery. I see some who are miserly, but very few good managers. This is woman's most important quality, and the one which should be sought before all others, as the only dowry which serves to ruin or to save our houses. No one need tell me about this; in accordance with what experience has taught me, I require of a married woman, above every other virtue, the virtue of domestic economy. I make use of this quality,[144] leaving by my absence the whole management in her hands.[145] I see with indignation, in some

Of Vanity

households, the husband return home at noon tired out and dishevelled from the turmoil of business, while the wife is still in her dressing-room, having her hair dressed and adorning herself; this is behaving like a queen, and yet as to that I question. It is absurd and unfair that the idleness of our wives should be maintained by our sweat and toil. So far as in me lies, it will befall no man to have a more certain, peaceful, and free enjoyment of his property than I.[146] If the husband supplies the substance, Nature herself wills that they[147] supply the form. As for the duties of conjugal friendship, which are thought to be wronged by such absences, I do not believe so; on the contrary, it is an intercourse which easily grows cool with a too continuous companionship and which assiduity injures. Every woman who is a stranger seems to us a worthy woman; and we all know by experience that continually being together can not equal the pleasure that we feel in parting and meeting by turns.[148] These interruptions fill me with fresh love for my family, and make the resumption of my home life the sweeter to me; the alternation quickens my appetite, first for one, then for the other course. I know that friendship has arms long enough to clasp and hold from one end of the world to the other; and especially this,[149] in which there is a constant interchange of services which excite obligation and remembrance thereof.

The Stoics well say that there is so close a connection and relation between wise men that he who dines in France gives nourishment to his companion in Egypt, and that whoever of them but holds out his finger in any place soever, all the wise men on the habitable globe feel that they are assisted.[150] Possession and fruition appertain chiefly to the imagination.

Of Vanity

It embraces more warmly and more persistently that of
which it goes in quest than that which we have at hand.
Take account of your ordinary musings—you will find that
you are most absent from your friend when he is with you;
his presence relaxes your attention and sets your thought
free to absent itself at any time, on any occasion. When in
Rome, I keep hold of my house and rule it, and the possessions that I have left there; I see my walls, my trees, and my
income rise and fall, almost as well as when I am there;

> Before my eyes wanders my house, wanders also the
> image of the places I have left.[151]

If we enjoy only what we have at hand, farewell to the
money in our strong-boxes and to our sons when they are
hunting. We wish them nearer. The garden—is that far
off? how about half a day's journey? And ten leagues—
is that far or near? If that is near, what of eleven, twelve,
thirteen? and so step by step. Truly she who thinks to
prescribe to her husband that "the fortieth step is the end
of the near and the same step begins the far"—I am of
opinion that she should stop him midway,—

> Let an end be made of argument. . . . I make use
> of this concession, and as I pluck the hairs of a
> horse's tail, I take away gradually one, then another,
> till the number falls, hoodwinked on the principle
> of the sorites,[152]—

and that they should boldly call philosophy to their assistance. To whom it might be objected that since she[153]
sees neither one end nor the other of a connection between
the too much and the too little, the long and the short,

the light and the heavy, the near and the far; since she recognises neither their beginning nor their end, she judges very uncertainly of the middle. *Nature has given us no knowledge of the beginnings of things.*[154] Are they not still wives and friends of the departed, who are in another world, not merely in the utmost part of this one? We embrace both those who have existed and those who do not yet exist—not the absent only. We did not make an agreement, in marrying, to keep constantly coupled together, like I know not what little animals that we see; or, like the bewitched folk of Karenty,[155] after the manner of dogs; and a wife should not have her eyes so greedily fastened upon her husband's front that she can not see his back when need is. But would not this saying of that excellent painter of their natures be appropriate in this place, to depict the cause of their lamentations?

> If you loiter, your wife thinks that you are in love, or that some one else loves you, or that you are drinking, or following your inclinations, and that you alone are enjoying yourself, while she suffers;[156]

or may it not be that in themselves opposition and contradiction sustain and nourish him, and that they are accommodated provided they incommode us?

In true friendship, wherein I am well versed, I give myself to my friend more than I draw him to me. I not only prefer to benefit him rather than that he should benefit me, but also that he should benefit himself rather than me; he benefits me most when he benefits himself; and if absence is either agreeable or useful for him, it is much more acceptable to me than his presence; and it is not really absence when there is means of communicating with one another. I have sometimes found our separation useful and agreeable; we better filled our life and extended its possession by being apart; he[157] lived, he enjoyed, he saw, for me, and I for him, as fully as if he had been there; one part remained idle when we were together; we were blended into one; separation as to place made the conjunction of our wills the stronger. This insatiable hunger for the bodily presence denotes a little weakness in the fruition of souls.

As to my being old, which is brought up against me, it is on the contrary for youth to subject itself to commonly held opinions, and to restrain itself because of others. It has the wherewithal to suffice both for people in general and for itself; we have only too much to do for ourselves alone. In proportion as natural enjoyments fail us, let us sustain ourselves by artificial ones. It is injustice to excuse youth for pursuing pleasures and to forbid old age to seek them. When I was young I covered over my jocund dispositions with prudence; being old, I do away with melancholy ones by diverting myself. The Platonic laws, indeed, forbid travelling before the age of forty or fifty, to render it more profitable and instructive. I would agree more readily to the second article of the same laws, which prohibits it after sixty.[158] But at so great an age you may never return from such long wandering." What matters that to me? I undertake it neither to return from it nor to complete it. I undertake it solely to keep in motion while motion is agreeable to me, and I travel for the sake of travelling. Those who pursue a living or a hare run after them, we say; but they do not intentionally run; those

Of Vanity

run who run at barriers or to practise for racing;[159] my design is in portions throughout; it is not based on great hopes; each day's journey is an end, and my journey through life is carried on in the same way. I have, however, seen many distant places where I could have wished that I had been detained. Why not, if Chrysippus, Cleanthes, Diogenes, Zeno, Antipater, so many wise men of the roughest sect,[160] abandon their country without any occasion to complain of it and solely to enjoy a different atmosphere? Truly the greatest unpleasantness in my peregrinations is that I can not carry with me the resolution to establish my abode wherever I please, and that I must needs always propose to return, in order to accommodate myself to ordinary ideas.

If I feared dying in another place than that of my birth, if I thought that I should die less at ease far from my family and friends, I should hardly go out of France; I should not go outside my parish without dread; I should feel death continually twitching at my throat or my loins. But I am of another temper; death is the same to me everywhere. If, however, I had to choose, my choice would be, I think, that it should be on horseback rather than in bed, away from my house and far from my family and friends. There is more heartbreak than consolation in going to take leave of one's friends. I willingly forget this duty of our social conduct; for of all the offices of friendship this is the only unpleasant one; and I should likewise willingly, myself, when dying, forget to say this eternal farewell. If any comfort is derived from this crowd of bystanders, it involves a hundred discomforts. I have seen many persons dying in a very pitiful case, surrounded by all this troop; the

1332

Of Vanity

throng suffocates them. It is contrary to what is due, and testifies to little affection and little consideration, if you are let die in peace; one vexes your eyes, another your ears, another your mouth; there is not one of your senses or your limbs that they do not assail. Your heart is wrung with pity on hearing the lamentations of friends, and with anger, perchance, on hearing other lamentations, feigned and counterfeit. A man who has always been sensitive is still more so when weakened; in such great need he requires a gentle hand, adapted to his sensations, to relieve him just where he suffers; otherwise, let no attempt at all be made to relieve him.[161] If we need a wise woman[162] to bring us into the world, we have indeed need of a still wiser man to lead us out of it. Such a one, and a friend to boot, one might well buy at a very high price for service on such an occasion.

I have not yet attained that disdainful vigour which is fortified in itself, which nothing either assists or disturbs. I am on a lower level; I try to seek a hole to hide my head in, and to steal away from this passage, not with fear, but with skill. It is not my thought to make proof or display of my firmness in this act of dying. Why should I? At that time will cease all my claim and concern for renown. I content myself with a death withdrawn into itself, peaceful and solitary, belonging to me alone, suited to my retired and secluded life; in contrast to the irrational Roman belief, which esteemed unfortunate him who died in silence and who had not his nearest friends to close his eyes.[163] I have enough to do to console myself, without consoling others; thoughts enough in my head, without having surrounding conditions bring me new ones; and enough substance to maintain me without borrowing. This part of our existence is not in the register of social relations;[164] it is the act of a single individual. Let us live and laugh among our friends; let us go among strangers to die and be grim. By paying, you can find some one to turn your pillow and to rub your feet, who urges you only as much as you desire, shewing you an indifferent countenance, allowing you to manage yourself and complain as you list.

I rid myself continually, by reasoning, of that childish and unkind inclination which makes us desire to excite for our ills the compassion and grief of our friends. We make our discomforts weigh beyond their true measure, to draw tears from them; and that constancy in supporting his own ill-fortune which we praise in any one, we blame and reproach in those about us when the ill-fortune is ours. We are not satisfied with their perceiving our ills—they must be grieved by them as well. We must increase joy but diminish sadness as much as we can. He who complains unreasonably is not pitied when there is reason for it; it is a sure way to avoid ever being pitied, to be forever complaining, making yourself out as pitiable so often that you are pitiable to nobody; he who plays that he is dead when living is likely to be regarded as alive when dying. I have seen some persons take it in dudgeon[165] that it was thought that their colour was good and their pulse regular, restrain their smiles because it would betray their recovery, and hate health because it was not to be deplored; what is more, these were not women.

I picture my sicknesses, for the most part, just as they are, and avoid words of evil presage and studied[166] exclamations. If not joyfulness, at least a serene bearing is suitable in those attending on a wise sick man. Because he sees himself in a different condition, he does not pick a quarrel with health; it pleases him to contemplate it in others, strong and sound, and to enjoy at least its companionship. Because he feels himself sinking, he does not reject all thoughts of life or shun common talk. I would study sickness when I am well; when it comes, it makes a sufficiently real impression without the help of my imagination. We prepare beforehand for the journeys we undertake, and are fully determined thereon; the hour at which we must take horse we give to the bystanders and lengthen it for their sake.

I feel this unhoped for benefit from the publication of my habits of mind,[167] that it serves me somewhat as a pattern: I have at times some thought of not being false to the narration of my life.[168] This public declaration compels me to keep to my road and not belie the picture of my conditions, which, for the most part, are less misshapen and contradictory than the malignity and unhealthiness of present-day judgements imply. The uniformity and simplicity of my character gives me an outer appearance of easy interpretation; but because its fashion is a little novel and unusual, it gives a fine opportunity for speaking ill of it. Yet is it true that to him who desires in good faith to abuse me, it seems to me that I offer sufficient surface wherein to set his teeth, in my acknowledged and well-known imperfections, and the wherewithal to have enough of it without idle skirmishing.[169] If by my anticipation of the accusation and the disclosure it seems to him that I frustrate his bite, it is reasonable for him to use his rights of amplification and extension (attack has its rights beyond justice), and that he should enlarge into trees vices of which I show him the roots in myself. Let him make use in this not solely of those vices that possess me, but of those also that only threaten me—harmful both in quality and in number; let him therewith cudgel me.

I would readily adopt the example of the philosopher Bion. Antigonus tried to tease him on the subject of his origin; the philosopher cut him short: "I am," he said, "the son of a slave, a butcher, who was branded, and of a strumpet whom my father married because of the lowliness of his station. Both were punished for some misdeed. An orator bought me when a child, finding me handsome and well-behaved; and at his death left me all his property, which having brought hither to this city of Athens, I have devoted myself to philosophy. Let not historians trouble themselves to seek tales about me: I will tell them all there is to tell."[170] A generous and free confession enfeebles blame and disarms offence.

However that may be, all things considered, it seems to me that I am as often unreasonably praised as disesteemed; as it also seems to me that from my childhood I have been given a station, both in rank and in honour, rather above than below what appertains to me. I should find myself more comfortable in a country where these degrees were either regulated or disregarded; with the male sex, when the altercation as to precedence in walking or sitting goes beyond three rejoinders, it is discourtesy. I never shrink from wrongly giving or taking place, to avoid so troublesome a contestation; and never did any man grudge my precedence that I did not abandon it to him.

Beyond this benefit that I derive from writing of myself, I have hoped for this further one, that, if it happened that my humours should, before my departure, please and harmonise with those of some worthy man, he would seek to bring us together. I have given him much ground, since all that he might have acquired in several years of long acquaintance and intimacy he has seen in three days in this record, and more surely and accurately. An amusing thought! Many things which I would not say in private I say in public, and send my most loyal friends to a bookshop to learn my most secret studies or thoughts;

We give our hearts to be examined.[171]

Had I known by such sure tokens of any one who would have suited me, I surely would have gone very far to find him; for the charm of congenial and pleasant companionship can not be bought too dear, in my opinion. Ah! what is a friend? How true is that ancient saying that a friend is more necessary and more delightful than the elements of water and fire![172]

To return to what I was saying, there is, then, no great ill in dying far from home and by oneself. But we regard it as a duty to retire for natural actions which are less uncomely than this and less grim. But again, they who have come to the point of feebly dragging on a long period of life ought not, perchance, to desire to burden with their wretchedness a large family. Therefore the Indians of a certain province thought it right to kill him who had fallen into such necessitous case; in another of their provinces they forsook him, to save himself alone as he could.[173] To whom do they not at least become wearisome and insupportable? Ordinary kindnesses[174] do not extend so far as that. You teach cruelty perforce to your best friends, hardening wife and children, by long accustomedness, no more to fear and sympathise with your ills. The moans of my colic no longer are considered by any one. And if we derived some pleasure from intercourse with them,[175]—which does not always happen, because of the disparity of conditions readily creating contempt or envy toward any one whatsoever,—is it not too much to misuse thus a great number of their years?[176] The more I saw them bravely constraining themselves out of kindness for me, the more sorry I should be for the trouble they take. We are at liberty to lean on others, not to weigh upon them so heavily and prop ourselves by their ruin; like him who caused little children's throats to be cut in order to make use of their blood for the cure of a disease he had;[177] or that other for whom they provided young delicate bodies to warm his old limbs at night,[178] and to mingle with his rank and heavy breath the sweetness of theirs. I would warmly advise Venice for the place of retirement of such a weak condition of life.[179]

Decrepitude is a condition for solitude. I am sociable even to excess; yet it seems reasonable to me that henceforth I withdraw my unfitness from the sight of the world and cower over it alone; that I draw myself together and retreat into my shell like the tortoises; that I learn to see men without clinging to them. I should do them a wrong in so steeply sloping a path; it is time to turn my back on my companions.

"But in these journeys you may be disastrously caught in some beggarly hole where you will lack every thing." The greater number of essential things I carry with me; and then, besides, we are not able to evade Fortune if she undertakes to set upon us. When I am sick I need nothing out of the ordinary; what Nature can not effect in me, I do

Of Vanity

not choose that a bolus should do. At the outset of my
fevers and sicknesses, when they attack me, being still myself and not far from health, I make my peace with God
by the last Christian offices; and I find myself thereby more
free and unburdened, and it seems to me that I have thus
brought my malady to more equal terms. Of a notary and
of advice I have less need than of physicians. What I shall
not have settled about my affairs when I am in sound health,
let it not be at all expected that I shall do when I am sick.
What I desire to do in preparation for death is always done;
I should not dare delay it a single day. And if there is nothing done, that means either that uncertainty will have re-
tarded my choice,—for sometimes not to choose is really to
choose,—or that I shall have indeed wished to do nothing.

I write my book for few men and for few years; if it had
been a thing to last, it would have been needful to commit
it to a more fixed language. Judging by the constant variation that our own language has undergone to this moment,
who can hope that its present form will be in use fifty years
hence? It slips from our hands every day, and in my lifetime it has altered by half. We say that it is not perfect;
every age says as much of its own. I have no mind to hold
it as such so long as it remains unstable[180] and misshapes
itself as it does; it is for excellent and profitable writings to
rivet it to them, and its favour with the world will be according to the fortune of our State. Therefore I do not hesitate to insert here many personal points which will have
meaning only for men who are living to-day, and which
touch the private knowledge of some who will see further
into them than can the general intelligence. I do not choose,
when my end comes,—as I often see the memory of the

1339

Of Vanity

dead discussed,—that people shall argue: "He thus thought and lived; he desired this; if he had spoken at the end, he would have said this, he would have bestowed that; I knew him better than any one else." Now, so far as decorum permits me, I make my inclinations and affections apparent here; but I do it more freely and readily by word of mouth to whoever desires to be informed about them. However, in these records, if they are considered, it will be found that I have said or indicated every thing; what I can not express, I point at.

But these slight traces are enough for a keen mind; through them you will be able to learn the rest.[181]

I leave nothing to be desired or to be guessed about myself. If I am to be talked about, I desire that it shall be truthfully and justly; I would willingly return from the other world to contradict him who should make me out other than I was, though it were to do me honour. The living even, I feel, are always spoken of as other than they are. And if I had not upheld with might and main a friend whom I had lost, he would have been distorted into a thousand differing aspects.[182] I well know that I shall leave behind me no surety at all approaching in affection and in knowledge of me what mine was of him; nor any one to whom I should be willing to entrust my portraiture; he alone possessed my true likeness, and he carried it away with him. This is the reason I depict myself so carefully.[183]

To finish talking of my weaknesses, I acknowledge that in travelling I scarcely reach any lodging that the thought does not pass through my mind, whether, when sick and dying, I shall be comfortable there. I wish to be lodged in

Of Vanity

a place which can be very private, noiseless, not gloomy or smoky or close. I seek to soothe Death by these trivial surroundings, or, to say better, to relieve myself from all other encumbrances, so that I may have only to count on her, who will easily weigh enough upon me without other burden. I wish that she should have her share in the ease and fitness of my life; this matter of dying is a large and important piece of it, and I hope that, when it comes, it will not belie the past.

Death has some forms more gentle than others, and takes on diverse qualities according to each one's mind. Of natural deaths those that come from weakness and stupour seem to me easy and kind; of violent deaths I dislike more to imagine a fall from a precipice than a ruin falling upon me, and a sword-thrust more than a musket-shot; and I should rather have drunk the draught of Socrates than have stabbed myself like Plato. And though it may be all the same thing, yet my imagination feels a difference, as betwixt death and life, betwixt throwing myself into a red-hot furnace and into the channel of a shallow river; so foolishly do our fears regard more the means than the effect. It is only an instant; but it has such weight that I would readily give many days of my life to pass it after my fashion. Since every man's mind finds something of more or of less bitterness in death, since every one has some choice amongst the ways of dying, let us try a little more deeply if we can find some form free from all unpleasantness. Could it not even be made voluptuous, as the Commorans[184] of Antony and Cleopatra made it? I leave aside the austere and exemplary efforts made by philosophy and religion. But amongst men of little note there are found some, as a Petronius and a Tigellinus at

Rome,[185] bound to inflict death on themselves, who, as it were, have lulled it to sleep by the delicacy of their preparations; they made it flow and glide amidst the worthlessness of their wonted pastimes, amongst wenches and boon companions; no talk of consolation, no mention of a testament, no ambitious affectation of firmness, no discourse about their future condition; amidst games, feasts, jests, common and familiar conversations, and music, and amorous verses. Could we not imitate this resoluteness with a wiser demeanour? Since there are deaths suitable for fools, and others suitable for wise men, let us find some that may be suitable for those who are neither the one nor the other. My imagination suggests to me some of gracious aspect and, since we must die, desirable. The Roman tyrants thought that it was giving life to the criminal when they gave him a choice about his death. But was not Theophrastus, a philosopher so refined, so modest, and so wise, compelled by force of reason to dare to repeat this verse, latinised by Cicero,—

Life is ruled by fortune, not by wisdom?[186]

Fortune assists in making easy the marketing of my life,[187] having placed it in such case that henceforth it is neither a need nor a burden to those nearest me. This is a condition which I would have accepted at all periods of my life; but at this time of preparing for my departure[188] and of packing up my baggage, I more especially take pleasure in that my dying is for them neither a kindness nor an unkindness. By an artistic counterpoise she has arranged that those who can lay claim to some material profit from my death will sustain by it also, conjointly, a material loss. Our death often weighs upon us because it weighs upon others, and

Of Vanity

concerns us for them almost as much as for ourselves, and sometimes even more.

In the comfortable quarters that I seek I do not include sumptuousness and spaciousness,—rather, I detest them,— but a certain simple nicety, which is found more frequently in places where there is less elaborateness and which Nature honours with some charm all her own: *a feast not abundant, but neatly served; where there is more good-fellowship than luxury.*[189] And, moreover, it is for those whose business carries them in midwinter through the Grisons to be surprised on the road in such an extremity. I, who oftenest travel for my pleasure, do not so poorly guide myself; if the road be unattractive on the right hand, I take the left-hand road; if I find myself unfit to ride, I stay where I am. And so doing, I see, in truth, no place that is not as agreeable and convenient as my house. It is true, I find superfluity always superfluous, and even in daintiness and abundance I note some encumbrance. If I have left behind me something to be seen, I return thither; it is always on my way; I mark no fixed line, either straight or circuitous. If I find not where I go what I had been told that I should find, —as it often happens that the judgements of others do not agree with mine and I have found them for the most part to be mistaken,—I do not complain of my trouble; I have learned that what had been told me was not so.

I have a bodily consitution as free, and a palate as unfastidious, as any man in the world; the diversity of modes of living between one nation and another affects me only with pleasure in the variety. Every custom has its reason. Let the dishes be of pewter, of wood, or of clay, boiled meat or roasted, butter, or oil of nuts or olives, hot or cold, it is all

one to me, and so much so that, as I grow old, I find fault
with this liberal faculty, and I shall need to have the indiscretion of my appetite stayed, and sometimes my stomach
eased, by daintiness and selection. When I have been elsewhere than in France, and have been asked out of courtesy
if I wished to be served in the French fashion, I have laughed
at the idea and have always frequented the tables most full
of foreigners. I am ashamed to see my countrymen besotted
by the foolish humour of being exasperated by fashions
contrary to their own; they seem to themselves to be out
of their element when they are out of their village; wherever
they go, they cling to their customs and abhor those that
are strange to them. If they find a compatriot in Hungary,
they make much of this luck; see them join together and
unite in condemning all the barbarous manners that they
behold. Why not barbarous, since they are not French? Yet
it is only the cleverest who have taken sufficient note of them
to speak ill of them. The greater number go from home only
for the coming back; they travel secretly and withdrawn,[190]
protecting themselves with silent and uncommunicative
prudence from the contagion of unknown ways.

What I say of them brings to my mind what I have oc-
casionally observed as a similar thing in some of our young
courtiers: they associate only with men of their own sort,
looking upon us as of another world, with disdain or pity.
Deprive them of talk about the mysteries of the court—
they are out of their element, and as strange and stupid to
us as we are to them. It is very well said that a well-bred man
is a man of many ingredients. I, on the contrary, wander in
unfamiliar countries, thoroughly sated with our ways; not
to seek Gascons in Sicily—I have left enough of them at

Of Vanity

home. I seek Greeks rather, and Persians; I make their acquaintance and observe them; it is to that that I give myself, and there I employ myself. And what is more, it seems to me that I have fallen in with few customs that are not as good as ours; herein I risk little, for I have hardly lost sight of my own weather-vanes.

Besides, the greater part of the chance company you meet on your way causes more annoyance than pleasure. I do not consort with them; less nowadays, when old age severs me from others and somewhat separates me from common social forms. You are discomfitted by others, or others by you; either mischance is burdensome, but the latter seems to me the more painful. It is a rare fortune, but of inestimable solace, to have a worthy man, of sure intelligence and of character concordant with your own, who is glad to accompany you, and who takes pleasure in aiding you.[191] I have sadly lacked such companions in all my travels. But it is essential that they be chosen and acquired before leaving home. No pleasure has any savour for me without imparting it; not even a lively thought comes into my mind that I am not vexed at expressing it when alone and at having no one to offer it. *If wisdom were granted me on this condition, that I keep it shut up and do not impart it, I would refuse it.*[192] This other carried it a step further: *If it were to happen to a wise man that amidst great abundance of all things he had leisure to contemplate and reflect on all that is worthy to be known, but if his solitude were so great that he could see no other person, he would quit this life.*[193] The opinion of Archytas is acceptable to me, that this would be unpleasant in heaven itself, and to wander among those great and divine celestial bodies without the presence of a companion.[194] But yet it is better to be alone than in tiresome and stupid company. Aristippus liked to live as a stranger everywhere.[195]

> If the fates allowed me to lead my life in my own way,[196]

I would choose to pass it in the saddle,—

> Longing to go to see in what quarter the fiery heat revels furiously, in what quarter are the clouds and the showers of rain.[197]

[198]"Have you not easier pastimes? What do you lack? Is not your house in a pleasant and healthy air, sufficiently furnished and more than sufficiently large? The royal majesty has been there more than once in state.[199] Has not your family, as regards rank, more beneath it than above it in eminence? Is there any fixed thought, unusual, not to be digested, which causes you suffering, —

> Which now, fixed in your breast, torments and distresses you?[200]

Where do you imagine that you can exist free from hindrance and disturbance? *Fortune never bestows her favours without reserve.*[201] Observe that it is only you yourself who hinders you; and you will follow yourself everywhere, and you will repine everywhere; for there is no satisfaction here below, save for brutish or divine souls. He who finds not contentment on so just an occasion, where does he think to find it? For how many thousands of men is not such a condition as yours the limit of their desires? Reform only yourself, for there you have full power, whereas you have no title to aught save patience toward fortune. *There is no tranquil peace save that which reason has made.*[202]

I see the reasonableness of this advice, and see it very clearly; but it would have been shorter and more to the point to say to me in one word, "Be wise." Such a determination is beyond wisdom; it is its work and its creation. It is like the physician who urges a poor feeble sick man to be cheerful; he would counsel him a little less foolishly if he said, "Be well." As for me, I am only a man of the ordinary sort. There is a salutary, definite precept, and of easy understanding: "Be content with what you have"; that is common sense; its execution, however, is no more possible for the wisest men than for me. It is a familiar saying, but it is terribly far-reaching; for what does it not include? All things are subject to discrimination and qualification. I am well aware that, looked at from the outside,[203] this enjoyment of travel gives evidence of restlessness and unsteadiness, and in sooth these are our controlling and predominant qualities.

Yes, I confess that I can see nothing, even in imagination and in desire, which I could hold fast to; variety alone satisfies me, and the enjoyment of diversity; at least, if any thing satisfies me. In travelling I am at ease,[204] in that I can stop without loss and that I can alter my course as I see fit.[205]

I enjoy private life, because it is by my choice that I enjoy it, not from unfitness for public life, which is perchance not less suited to my temperament. I serve my prince in it the more cheerfully because I do it by the free preference of my judgement and my reason, without special obligation, and because I am neither hindered nor compelled about this

Of Vanity

by being unwelcome to any other party, and disliked; and so in other matters. I hate the morsels that necessity carves out for me; any thing advantageous upon which alone I should have to depend would strangle me.

> Let one of my oars graze the water, the other the shore.[206]

A single bowstring never suffices me comfortably. "There is vanity," you say, "in this amusement." But where is there none? these fine precepts are vanity, and all wisdom is vanity. *The Lord knoweth the thoughts of man, that they are vanity.*[207] Such refined subtleties are suited only for sermons; they are arguments which aim at sending us ready-prepared into the other world. Life is a material and corporeal movement; an action imperfect in its very essence, and irregular; I make it my business to wait on it in accordance with its nature.

> Each of us suffers his own spirit's doom.[208]

We must so act as not at all to contend against universal nature; but that being safeguarded, let us follow our own.[209] To what end are these lofty points of philosophy, to which no human being can adjust himself, and these rules, which exceed our usage and our strength?

I often see that conceptions of life are proposed to us, which neither he who proposes them nor his auditors have any hope of following; or, what is more, any desire to do so. From the same paper on which he has just written the decree of condemnation of an adulterer, the judge steals a page on which to write a love letter to the wife of his fellow judge. The woman whom you have just unlawfully embraced will soon after, in your very presence, on hearing of a similar fault in her friend, cry out more loudly than Portia herself[210] would do; and men there are who condemn others to death for crimes which in themselves they do not regard as faults.

In my youth I saw a man of note[211] offer to the people with one hand verses excelling in beauty and in licentiousness, and with the other hand, at the same moment, the most contentious argument dealing with divine matters on which the world has broken fast for a long time. Thus go men; we leave the laws and the precepts to follow their course; we take another course, not from irregularity of morals only, but often from judgement and diverse opinion. Listen to a philosophical discourse: its originality, eloquence, pertinence immediately strike your mind and move you; there is nothing which tickles or prickles your conscience; it is not to it that the discourse speaks. Is not this true? Yet Aristo said that neither a hot bath nor a lecture is of any worth if it does not purify and cleanse.[212] We can linger over the bark, but we do so after we have removed the pith; as, after we have drunk good wine from a beautiful cup, we examine its carvings and workmanship.[213] In all the schools of ancient philosophy this will be found, that the same teacher publishes rules of temperance and at the same time publishes writings of love and wantonness. And Xenophon, in the bosom of Clinias, wrote against the Aristippic virtue.[214] It is not that there is a miraculous conversion that moves them in waves, but that Solon presents himself, now in his own person, now in the guise of a legislator; now he speaks for the multitude, now for himself; and adopts for himself free and natural laws, feeling assured of perfect health.

Of Vanity

Let sick men who are in danger be treated by the greatest physicians.[215]

Antisthenes allows the wise man to love, and to do in his own way what he finds to be opportune, without regard to the laws, forasmuch as he has better judgement than they and more knowledge of virtue.[216] Diogenes, his disciple, said that to unquietness of mind should be opposed reason; to fortune, confidence, and to the laws, nature.[217] For delicate stomachs, compulsory and artificial rules are necessary; good stomachs use simply the prescriptions of their natural appetite. Thus our physicians eat melons and drink new wine whilst they keep their patient limited to syrup and panada. "I know nothing of their books," said the courtesan Laïs, "nor of their wisdom or their philosophy, but those people knock at my door as often as any others."[218] Inasmuch as our freedom is always carrying us beyond what is lawful and permissible for us, the precepts and laws of our life have often been narrowed beyond general reason.

No one thinks that such measure of transgression as you allow him is enough.[219]

It could be desired that there were more proportion between the command and the obedience, and the mark seems unreasonable which can not be hit. There does not exist a man of such worth that, were he to lay open to the scrutiny of the laws all his actions and thoughts, he would not deserve hanging ten times in his life—in truth, such a man as it would be very harmful and very unjust to punish and to cast away.

What is it to you, Ollus, what this man or this woman does with his skin?[220]

1350

Of Vanity

And a man might be such as never to offend the laws, who would not for that deserve the praise of being a virtuous man, and whom philosophy would very justly order to be whipped, so confused and irregular is the relation of these conditions. We take no heed to being good men in the opinion of God; we could not be so in our own. Human wisdom never attained to the duties which she had prescribed for herself; and if she had attained to them, she would have prescribed for herself other duties higher still, which she would always aspire to and aim at, so great an enemy to consistency is our existence.

Man commands himself to be necessarily in fault. It is not very crafty to measure one's bounden duty by the consideration of another existence than one's own. To whom does he prescribe what he expects no one to do? Is it wrong for him not to do what it is impossible for him to do? The laws which condemn us to be powerless condemn us for being powerless.[221]

At the worst, this misshapen liberty to offer oneself on two sides, our actions in one fashion, our reasoning in another, may be permissible for those who discourse of things; but it can not be permissible for those who discourse of themselves, as I do. My pen must accompany my feet. Life in common must have relation to other lives. Cato's virtue was vigorous beyond the understanding of his time; and in a man who took part in ruling other men, dedicated to the service of all, it might be said to have had in it a sort of justice which, if not unjust, was at least idle and unseasonable. Even my own character, which differs scarcely an inch from those of common fashion,[222] renders me nevertheless somewhat untractable to the age I live in, and austere. I know not

Of Vanity

whether I find myself unreasonably without relish for the world I am familiar with, but I well know that it would be unreasonable if, since this is the case, I bemoaned myself because it had no relish for me. The virtue that appertains to worldy affairs is a virtue with many twists and turnings and elbowings, that it may be adapted and joined to human weakness; complicated and artful, not upright, pure, firm, or altogether innocent. Our annals even to this day reproach some one of our kings for having too simply followed the godly advice of his confessor. Affairs of state have bolder precepts:

Let him leave the court who would be just.[223]

I formerly attempted to employ in the service of public negotiations ideas and rules of life as blunt, inexperienced, unpolished, and unpolluted as when they were born in me or imprinted on my mind by my education, and of which, if not fitly, at least with safety, I make use for myself; a bookish and unskilful virtue. I have found these ideas to be in such matters unseasonable and dangerous. He who enters into the crowd must wind about, keep his elbows close, go back or go forward—must, in truth, leave the straight path because of what he encounters; he must live not so much according to his own ideas as according to those of others; not according to what he himself proposes, but according to what is proposed to him—according to the times, the men, and the affairs of the moment. Plato says that he who escapes with clean skirts from the handling of the world escapes by a miracle;[224] and he says also that, when he decrees that his philosopher shall be the head of a government, he does not mean to speak of a corrupt government like that

Of Vanity

of Athens;[225] and even much less would it be of one like ours, where wisdom itself would be at a loss. And a healthy plant transplanted into a soil very foreign to its nature much more readily adapts itself to the soil than it changes the character of the soil. I feel that, if I had to train myself thoroughly for such employments, I should need much change and correction. Even if I could expect this in myself (and why could I not with time and pains?), I would not do it. From the little that I have essayed of this vocation I have in due measure felt distaste for it; I sometimes perceive smouldering in my soul some temptings toward ambition, but I stiffen myself and persist obstinately in an opposite course.

But thou, Catullus, be firm and obdurate.[226]

I am seldom summoned thither, and I invite myself there as little. Freedom and laziness, which are my predominant qualities, are diametrically contrary to that profession.

We have not learned to distinguish the facilities of men: they have divisions and limits which are difficult to discern and scarcely perceptible. To infer from ability in private life ability for public employ is a weak inference: a man may guide himself well who does not guide others well, and he may produce essays who could not produce results; a man may direct a siege well who would direct a battle ill, and may discourse well in private who would harangue ill a multitude or a prince. It is in truth, perhaps, rather than otherwise, a proof that he who is capable of the one is not at all capable of the other. I find that great minds are not better fitted for small matters than small minds are for great matters. Is it believable that Socrates could give the Athenians food for laughter at his expense from never having been

Of Vanity

able to reckon up the votes of his tribe and make report thereof to the Council?[227] Truly the veneration in which I hold
the perfections of that great mind deserves that his fortune
should offer such a magnificent example for the excuse of
my principal imperfections. Our ability is cut out in small
parcels; mine has no breadth, and in number it is paltry.
Saturninus said to those who had conferred upon him supreme command: "My friends, you have lost a good captain
by making of him a bad general."[228]

He who boasts, in such ill-conditioned times as these, of
employing in the world's service simple and sincere virtue
either does not know what that is, opinions becoming corrupt with morals (in truth, hear men's description of it,
hear most men glory in their conduct and form their rules:
instead of describing virtue, they describe perfectly pure
injustice and vice, and offer it thus falsified for the education
of princes), or, if he does know what it is, he boasts without warrant, and, whatever he may say, he does a thousand
things for which his conscience blames him. I would readily
believe Seneca as to his experience in similar conditions,
provided he were willing to speak of it to me frankly. The
most honourable indication of sincerity in such necessity is
freely to acknowledge one's own fault and that of others; to
resist and retard with all one's might the tendency toward
evil; to follow this propension only against one's will; to
have better hope and better desire.

In these dismemberments of France and the disagree-
ments we have fallen into, I perceive that every one labours
to defend his own cause; but even the best do so with dissimulation and falsehood. He who should write plainly of
these matters would write of them at haphazard and erro-

neously. The most upright party is still a limb of a rotten
and decayed body; but of such a body the least diseased
limb is called sound, and rightly, forasmuch as our qualities
have no rank but in comparison. Innocence in matters of
government[229] is measured according to places and periods.
I should like well to find in Xenophon[230] praise of Agesilaus
for such an incident as this: that, being entreated by a neighbouring prince, with whom he had formerly been at war,
to allow him to pass through his territory, he assented,
giving him passage through the Peloponnesus; and not only
did not imprison or poison him when at his mercy, but welcomed him courteously in accordance with the obligation of
his promise, doing him no injury. To the disposition of the
minds of those days, this would mean nothing; elsewhere
and in other times the generosity and magnanimity of such
an act will be taken into account; knavish and worthless
men of our day[231] would jeer at it, so little does Spartan innocence resemble the French.

We are not lacking in virtuous men, but they are of our
fashion. He whose character is established by a standard
superior to his time must either bend and blunt his rules or
—which I advise him rather—withdraw apart and mingle
not at all with us. What could he gain thereby?

If I see an honourable and virtuous man, I think
him as great a prodigy as a boy that is half beast, or as
fish found, to our amazement, under the ploughshare,
or as a mule with foal.[232]

We may sigh for better days, but not fly from the present;
we may desire other magistrates, but we must, none the
less, obey those we have; and perchance there is more to be

Of Vanity

commended in obeying the bad than the good. So long as
the semblance of the accepted and long-held laws of this
realm shall shine in any corner of it, there shall I be found
rooted; if by misfortune the laws arrive at contradicting and
hindering one another and create two parties of doubtful
and difficult choice, I shall quickly choose to escape and
steal away from that confusion; meanwhile, nature may perhaps lend me a hand, or the fortunes of war. Between
Cæsar and Pompeius I should have declared myself openly;
but as between those three thieves who came later,[233] it
would have been necessary either to hide or to go with the
current, which I think permissible when reason no longer
shews the way.

> Whither go you, away from the course?[234]

These considerations[235] are a little outside of my subject.
I stray from my path, but rather consciously than carelessly; my ideas follow one another, but sometimes at a
distance, and regard one another, but with a sidelong glance.
I have noticed a certain dialogue of Plato,[236] composed of
two halves of fantastic diversity—the beginning, of love,
all the rest, of rhetoric. They[237] do not shrink from these
changes, and have a wonderful grace in letting themselves
be thus carried along by the wind, or in seeming to be so.
The titles of my chapters do not always describe their content; often they only indicate it by some badge as these
others did: *Andria* and *Eunuchus*;[238] or these: *Sylla, Cicero,
Torquatus.*[239]

I like the skipping and gamboling motions of poetry; it
is, as Plato says, a light, flitting art possessed by a spirit.[240]
There are pieces in Plutarch in which he forgets his theme,

Of Vanity

in which the drift of his argument is found only incidentally, quite stifled under foreign matter; observe his procedure in the *Dæmon of Socrates*. Lord! what beauty there is in those spirited irregularities and that variety; and greatest when the charm seems most careless and fortuitous! It is the inattentive reader who loses sight of my subject, not I; there will always be found in a corner some word which does not fail to be sufficient, although it may be concise. I wander here and there[241] inconsiderately and inadvisedly; my style and my mind go vagabonding alike. A little folly is needful for one who does not desire to be the more foolish—so say the precepts of our masters, and even more their examples.

A thousand poets drag along feebly and prosaically, but the best ancient prose—and I strew it here indifferently with verse—glows in every part with the vigour and boldness of poetry, and offers some image of its impetuosity; there must be granted to it superiority and preëminence in social intercourse.[242] The poet, says Plato, seated on the tripod of the Muses, pours forth impetuously all that comes to his lips, like the spout of a fountain, without reflecting upon it and weighing it; and there escape from him things of divers colours, of contradictory substance, and of irregular flow.[243] Plato himself is poetic throughout, and the learned tell us that the old theology and the earliest philosophy are all poetry; it is the original language of the gods.

I think that the subject appears distinctly of itself; it shews sufficiently where it changes, where it concludes, where it begins, where it is resumed, without interlacing it with words of connection and joining, introduced for the behoof of weak and careless understandings, and without my annotating myself. Who does not prefer not to be read

Of Vanity

rather than to be read drowsily or hurriedly? *There is noth-ing so useful that it is useful in passing.*[244] If to take books in the hand were to learn their contents, and if to look at them were to consider them, and to run through them were to grasp them, I should be mistaken in making myself out quite so ignorant as I say I am. Since I can not arrest the attention of the reader by the weight of what I write, *manco male* if I arrest it by my intricacy. Yea, but he will after-ward be sorry that he was stayed by it. That may be, but all the same he will have been stayed by it. And then there are dispositions of a kind in which understanding produces con-tempt; which will esteem me the more highly because they will not comprehend what I say; they will infer the pro-fundity of my meaning by its obscurity, which to speak in all sincerity, I greatly detest, and I would shun it if I knew how to shun myself. Aristotle somewhere boasts of affecting it.[245] An erroneous affectation! Because the so frequent cut-ting up into chapters which I practised at the beginning has seemed to me to interrupt attention before it was born, and to break it up, making it scorn to apply itself and collect itself for so little, I have betaken myself to making them longer, which demands forethought and allotted leisure. In such an occupation, to him to whom you choose to give a single hour you choose to give nothing; and you do noth-ing for him for whom you do only while doing something else; to which it may be added that perchance I have some special compulsion to express myself only by halves, con-fusedly, and discordantly. I was about to say that I have a grudge against this importunate reason, and these extrava-gant purposes which trouble life; and as for these subtle opinions, if they have any truth, I find it too clearly bought

1358

Of Vanity

and unprofitable. On the contrary, I busy myself in shewing
the value of very trifles and of doltishness, if it affords me
pleasure; and I let myself follow my natural inclinations
without overseeing them so closely.

I have seen in other lands ruined buildings and statues,
and the sky and the earth; men are everywhere. That is
quite true; and yet I could not so often revisit the tomb of
that so great and so powerful city[246] that I should not marvel
at it and revere it. Regard for the dead is enjoined upon us.
Now, I was brought up from my childhood with the dead;
I was familiar with the affairs of Rome long before I was with
those of my own family. I knew the Capitol and its plan before I knew the Louvre, and the Tiber before the Seine. I had
in my head the characters and fortunes of Lucullus, Metul-
lus, and Scipio more than those of any of our fellow countrymen. They have departed; so has my father,—indeed, as
completely as they, and is as distant from me and from life
in eighteen years as these in sixteen hundred,—whose
memory, affection, and companionship I none the less continue to embrace and cherish in a perfect and very vivid
union. Verily, by my nature I give myself more dutifully to
the departed; they can no longer aid themselves; therefore,
it seems to me, they need my aid so much the more. Gratitude there is rightly in its lustre; beneficence is less nobly
bestowed where there is reciprocal action and reflected good-
will.[247] Arcesilaus, visiting Ctesibius who was ill, and finding him in a poor condition, very softly thrust under his pillow some money which he gave him, and by concealing it
from him he gave him also quittance from thanking him.[248]
They who have merited affection and gratitude from me
have never lost it from being no longer here; I pay them the

Of Vanity

more fully and more heedfully when they are absent and unaware. I speak more fondly of my friends when there is no way of their knowing it. Thus I have entered into a hundred disputes in defence of Pompeius and in the cause of Brutus. This commerce still endures between us.

Even things that are present we have hold of only by imagination. Finding myself useless in this age, I throw myself into that other, and am thereby so ravished that the state of that ancient Rome, free, uncorrupt, and flourishing (for I love neither her infancy nor her old age), interests me and impassions me. Consequently I can not see the situation of their streets and their houses and those ruins whose foundations reach to the antipodes, so often that I do not wonder at them. Is it naturally, or through an error of the imagination, that the sight of places that we know to have been frequented and dwelt in by persons whose memory is endeared to us, moves us in some sort more than to listen to the story of their deeds or to read their writings?[249] *So great is the power of evocation that lies in places. . . . And of this there are countless examples in this city: for wherever we go, we set our foot upon history.*[250] I enjoy looking at their faces, their bearing, and their garments; I mumble to myself those great names, and make them echo in my ears. *I reverence them and always rise at such names.*[251] In matters which are in some parts great and admirable I admire even the commonplace parts. I would gladly see these people talk and walk about and sup together. It would be ingratitude to set naught by the relics and representations of so many worthy and brave men whom I have seen living and dying, and who give us so many good lessons by their example, if we but knew how to follow them.

1360

Of Vanity

And then this same Rome that we behold deserves to be beloved, having been allied to our crown for so long a time and by so many titles—the sole common and universal city; the sovereign ruler who commands there is likewise acknowledged elsewhere; it is the metropolitan city of all Christian nations; Spaniard and Frenchmen both are at home there; to be one of the princes of that realm one needs only to be a prince of Christendom, wheresoever it be. There is no place here below that Heaven has embraced with such a flow of favour and such persistency; her very ruin is glorious and grandiose;

> The more precious for her admirable ruins.[252]

She still retains in the tomb the symbol and image of Empire. *So that it is clear that in a single place Nature must rejoice in her work.*[253] Some man might censure himself and rebel inwardly at finding himself delighted by so vain a pleasure. The personal moods[254] which are agreeable to us are not too vain. Of whatever kind those may be which unfailingly give pleasure to a man capable of common intelligence, I could not have the heart to blame him.

I am much beholden to Fortune in that, to this hour, she has done me no excessive unkindness and beyond what I could bear. May it not be her way to leave in peace those by whom she is not importuned?

> The more we renounce, the more we receive from the gods. Stripped of every thing, I seek the tents of those who desire nothing. . . . They who seek much lack much.[255]

If she thus continues, she will dismiss me well satisfied;

Of Vanity

I ask nothing more of the gods.[256]

But look out for accidents![257] There are thousands who founder in port. I console myself easily about what will happen here when I am gone; present things keep me sufficiently busy;

I leave the rest to Fortune.[258]

Furthermore, I have not that strong tie which, they say, binds men to the future by the children who carry on their name and their honour; and I must needs perchance desire these things, if they be desirable, so much the less. I hold too much to the world and to this life by myself; I am best pleased to be in Fortune's clutches with regard to the circumstances personally necessary to my being, without otherwise extending her jurisdiction over me; and I have never thought that to be childless was a lack which must render life less complete and less contented. The vocation of sterility has indeed its advantages. Children are amongst those things which have not in them very much for which to be desired, especially in these days, when it would be so difficult to make them good men; *nothing good can now be born, so corrupt are the seeds;*[259] and yet have they in them exactly that which causes them to be regretted by him who loses them after having had them.

He who left me my establishment in charge prognosticated my ruin, in view of my little interest in the matters of an estate. He was mistaken: here am I, as well off as when I entered into my inheritance, if not a little better, though without any public office or church living. Moreover, if Fortune has done me no violent and unusual injury, neither

1362

Of Vanity

has she done me any particular favour. All there is of her gifts in my family was there before me and more than a hundred years ago. I personally have no essential and solid good that I owe to her liberality; she has done me some airy, honorary, and titular favours, without substance, and has also, in truth, not granted them at my request, but freely presented them, God knows! to me who am all material, who am satisfied only with reality and that very substantial, and who, if I dare confess it, consider avarice hardly less excusable than ambition, or pain less to be avoided than shame, or health less desirable than learning, or wealth than nobility.

Amongst her vain favours I have none that so much gratifies this foolish humour which lives within me, as an authoritative edict of Roman citizenship, which was lately granted me when I was there—magnificent in seals and gold lettering, and granted with most gracious munificence. And because they are couched in divers styles more or less commendatory, and because, before I had seen one, I should have been very glad to be shewn a document of this kind, I think it well, to satisfy some one, if there be any one, who feels a curiosity like my own, to transcribe it here.

On the report made to the Senate by Orazio Massimi, Marzo Cecio, and Alessandro Muti, Conservators of the bountiful city, with regard to endowing with Roman citizenship the most illustrious Michel de Montaigne, knight of the Order of St. Michel and gentleman of the Chamber of the Most Christian King, the Senate and People of Rome have decreed as follows:

Whereas, according to ancient custom and decree those

1363

Of Vanity

have always been eagerly received who have excelled in virtue and nobility, and who have been, or who at any time might be, of great use and ornament to our Republic, We, moved by the example and influence of our forefathers, decree that this famous custom is to be imitated and preserved by us.

Wherefore, since the most illustrious Michel de Montaigne, knight of the Order of St. Michel, and gentleman of the Chamber of the Most Christian King, is filled with zeal for the Roman name, and is, both on account of the splendour of his family and on account of his own merits, most worthy of admission by the special vote and the goodwill of the Roman Senate and People to Roman citizenship, it has pleased the Senate and People of Rome that the most illustrious Michel de Montaigne, distinguished in all things and very dear to this renowned People, be enrolled, he and his heirs, in the Roman citizenship, and be granted all the honours and advantages which those enjoy who were born citizens and patricians of Rome, or who have by full process of law been made such.

And in this they believe that the Senate and People of Rome do not so much bestow on him the right of citizenship as a gift, as discharge a debt, and that they no more confer a favour on him than receive one from him, who, by accepting this gift of the State, has shed on this very citizenship a peculiar distinction and honour.

Which act of the Senate's authority the same Conservators have had recorded by the secretaries of the Senate and People of Rome, and deposited in the archives of the Capitol, and have had the prerogative engrossed and sealed with the ordinary seal of the city. In the year after the foundation of

Of Vanity

Rome 2331, and after the birth of Jesus Christ 1581, March 13.

Orazio Fosco
Secretary of the Sacred Senate and People of Rome.

Vincente Martoli
Secretary of the Sacred Senate and People of Rome.[260]

Being a burgess of no [foreign] city, I was very glad to become so of the noblest city that ever was or ever will be.

If other men scrutinised themselves as I do, they would find themselves, as I do, full of inanity and witlessness. I can not rid myself of these qualities without getting rid of myself. We are all steeped in them, one man as well as another, but they who are conscious of this have thereby a little better bargain; yet I do not know.

This common fashion and custom of looking elsewhere than at ourselves has well served us. It[261] is an object replete with dissatisfaction; we see there only wretchedness and emptiness. To avoid discomforting us, Nature has fitly directed the action of our vision outside ourselves. We are carried forward with the current, but to turn backward toward ourselves is a different movement; so do the waves of the sea break confusedly and dash against one another when they are driven back upon themselves. Regard, every one says, the changes of the sky; regard the public affairs—this man's quarrel, that one's pulse, this other's testament; in fine, regard things above or below, or at one side, or before or behind you. It was a paradoxical command that the god at Delphi gave us in ancient times; look within yourself; know yourself; keep close to yourself; call back to yourself

1365

Of Vanity

your mind and your will, which are wasted elsewhere; you slip away from yourself, you scatter yourself abroad; concentrate yourself, uphold yourself; you are betrayed, you are despoiled, you are stolen from yourself. Dost thou not see that this world demands all vision to be bent within and all eyes opened to self-contemplation? For thee all is vanity, within and without, but less vanity when it is less enlarged. "Except thee, O man," said that god, "every thing first studies itself and according to its need has limits to its labours and desires. There is not another thing so empty and necessitous as thou art, who dost embrace the universe; thou art the seeker without knowledge, the magistrate without jurisdiction, and, when all is said, the clown of the play."

Chapter X

OF THE MANAGEMENT

OF ONE'S WILL [1]

IN comparison with most men, few things touch me, or, to say better, have any hold upon me; for it is reasonable to be touched by them, provided they do not have possession of us. I take great care to increase by study and reflection this quality of insensitiveness which is naturally well developed in me. Consequently, I espouse and am greatly interested by few things. My sight is clear, but I fasten it upon few objects; my perception[2] is delicate and pliant; but I am slow and dull in apprehension and application. I with difficulty bind myself to any thing. So far as I can, I give my whole attention to myself; and even in relation to this subject I would readily somewhat curb and hold back my interest from too completely entering into it, since it is a subject which I possess at the mercy of others and over which Fortune has more rights than I;[3] so that, even in the matter of health,—which I rank so high,—it would be well for me not so intensely to desire it and devote myself to it as to find sickness unbearable. We should moderate equally hatred of pain and love of pleasure, and Plato prescribes an intermediate course betwixt the two.[4] But the interests which draw me away from myself and rivet me elsewhere,

Of the Management of One's Will

those indeed I oppose with all my strength. My opinion is that a man must lend himself to others and give himself only to himself. If my will found it easy to pledge and adapt itself, it would be the end of me; I am too thin-skinned both by nature and by habit,—

> Avoiding affairs, and born for care-free leisure.[5]

The contested and obstinate discussions that would finally give the advantage to my opponent, the result that would make my heated persistence shameful, would perchance chafe me cruelly. If I attacked the source of the matter,[6] as others do, my soul would never have the strength to endure the shocks and emotions which accompany those who undertake so much; it would immediately be unhinged by this inward agitation. If at times I have been forced into the handling of other people's affairs, I have promised to take them in hand, not to be completely engrossed by them;[7] to burden myself with them, not to make them a part of myself; to pay heed to them, yes; to be excited about them, not at all; I consider them, but I do not brood over them. I have enough to do to order and arrange the crowd of domestic concerns that I have at heart,[8] without admitting there, and being overwhelmed by, outside concerns; and I am sufficiently occupied by my own essential affairs, proper and natural to me, without inviting others foreign to me. They who know how much they owe to themselves, and by how many duties they are bound to themselves, find that Nature has given them a mission ample enough and in no wise idle: "You have very much to do at home—do not go far away."

Men hire themselves out; their faculties are not for themselves, but for those to whom they enslave themselves; it is their tenants, not themselves, who occupy the house. This inclination to connect myself with others[9] does not please me. We must be careful about the liberty of our soul and we must pledge it only on rightful occasions, which are very few in number if we judge wisely. Observe those persons who have acquired the habit of letting themselves be seized upon and carried away: it is so with them in all things, in small matters as in great, in what concerns them not as in what does concern them; they throw themselves indifferently into any thing going on, and lack life if they lack irregular excitement. *In negotiis sunt, negotii causa;*[10] they seek business only to be busy. It is not so much that they desire to be moving, as that they can not keep still; exactly like a rolling stone which is not checked until it has come to the bottom.[11] Occupation is to a certain sort of man a mark of ability and of dignity. Their minds seek repose by being swung back and forth, like children in the cradle. They might say that they are serviceable to their friends in proportion as they are irksome to themselves. No one distributes his money amongst others; every one does so distribute his time and his life; there is nothing of which we are so lavish as of things about which alone avarice would be useful and laudable.[12] I am of a wholly different humour; I think only of myself, and usually desire very mildly what I desire, and I desire little; occupying myself and likewise busying myself at intervals and tranquilly. Whatever they determine upon and take in hand, that they do with all their will and earnestness. There are so many dangerous places for our feet that, for greater safety, we must glide through this world rather lightly and superficially, and slide over it, not break through. Even pleasure is painful in its depth;

Of the Management of One's Will

> You pass through fires concealed beneath treacherous ashes.[13]

The high authorities[14] of Bordeaux elected me mayor of their city when I was far from France and still farther from such a thought. I declined; but they shewed me that I was wrong, the king's command also interposing in the matter. It is an office which should seem the more desirable because it brings neither praise nor profit other than the honour of administering it; the term is two years, but it may be prolonged by the second election, which rarely occurs. It was accorded to me, and had been but twice before—to monsieur de Lansac some years earlier, and recently to monsieur de Biron, marshal of France, whom I succeeded; and I left the place to monsieur de Matignon, also marshal of France, proud of such noble fellowship;

> Good administrators both, in peace and in war.[15]

Chance chose to share in my promotion by this special circumstance, not at all unimportant, which she herself gave to it; for Alexander was disdainful of the Corinthian ambassadors who offered him the citizenship of their city; but when they announced to him that Bacchus and Hercules were also on that register, he graciously thanked them.

On taking office, I faithfully and conscientiously depicted myself as just what I feel myself to be: without memory, without vigilance, without experience, and without vigour; also without hatred, without ambition, without avarice, and without violence, that they might be informed and apprised of what they had to expect from my service. And because their knowledge of my late father and honour for his memory had alone incited them to do this, I plainly added

that I should be very sorry that any thing whatever should
so much affect me as their affairs and their city had formerly
affected him while he had the administration of them in the
same post to which they had summoned me. I remembered
that, in my childhood, I had seen him, an old man,[16] cruelly
perturbed by the hurried public activities, neglecting the
pleasant air of his house, where the feebleness of advancing
years had long since confined him, and his household affairs
and his health, and certainly disdaining his life, which he
came near losing in that employment, being compelled in
their behalf to take long and difficult journeys. Such was he;
and this disposition was due to a great natural kindliness;
never was there a more charitable and accessible soul. This
way of proceeding, which I praise in another, I do not like
to follow, and I am not without excuse.

He had heard it said that we must needs forget ourselves
for our neighbour's sake; that the private individual was not
to be considered in comparison with the public interest.
Most of the rules and precepts of the world take the course
of forcing us out of ourselves and driving us into public view
for the use of society as a whole; they have thought to produce a fine effect by diverting and distracting us from ourselves, presupposing that we were attached to ourselves only
too closely and by a too natural tie; and to this end they have
said all that could be said; for it is nothing new for the wise
to preach things that may be of service, not things that may
be true. Truth has for us its embarrassments, disadvantages,
and incompatibilities. We must often deceive that we may
not ourselves be deceived, and shut our eyes and dull our
wits, in order to benefit and amend them: *Ignorant men
pass judgement, and they often have to be deceived, lest*

Of the Management of One's Will

they go astray.[17] When they command us to love, more than ourselves, things of three, four, and fifty different kinds, they imitate the art of archers, who, to hit the mark, aim high above it. To straighten a bent stick we bend it in the contrary way.[18]

I believe that in the temple of Pallas, as we see in all other forms of religion, there were visible mysteries shewn to the people, and other mysteries, more secret and lofty, shewn only to the initiated. It is apparent that in such as these latter is found the true nature of the friendship which every man owes to himself—not a false friendship which leads us to embrace glory, learning, wealth, and such matters with predominant and immoderate affection, as essential parts of our existence, nor a weak and inconsiderate friendship, in which that happens which is seen in the ivy, that it decays and ruins the wall to which it clings; but a salutary and well-ordered friendship, equally beneficial and agreeable. He who knows its duties and fulfills them has truly the familiar companionship of the Muses;[19] he has attained the very summit of human wisdom and of our happiness. Knowing exactly what he owes to himself, he finds in the part he has to play that he must adapt to himself the conditions of other men and of the world, and, to do this, must contribute to society at large the duties and services which belong to it. He who does not live somewhat for others scarcely lives for himself: *Know that he who is a friend to himself is friend to all men.*[20] The chief charge we have is for each one his own conduct. And this is why we are here. As he would be a fool who should forget to live a good and godly life and should think that he had fulfilled his duty by guiding and teaching others so to do, so not less he who abandons, to serve others, a healthy and cheerful life for himself, adopts, in my opinion, a wrong and unnatural course. I would not that a man should deny to the offices that he assumes his attention, his steps, his words, his sweat, and, if need be, his blood,—

> Not afraid to die for his dear friends, or for his fatherland,[21]

but only by way of loan, and, incidentally, the mind maintaining itself always in repose and in health; not without action, but without vexation, without passion. Mere action costs it so little that even when sleeping it acts. But we must set it in motion with due consideration; for whilst the body receives the burdens that are laid on it for just what they are, the mind often enlarges them and weights them at its own expense, giving them such proportions as seems well to it.[22] We effect things that are similar with varying efforts and different exertions of the will. The character of the doing is not dependent on the character of the thing done;[23] for how many men risk their lives every day in wars that matter not to them, and press forward into the dangers of battles the loss of which will not disturb their next night's sleep! Whereas a man in his own house, safe from that danger which he would not have dared to face, is more passionately moved about the results of this war than is the soldier who gives his blood and his life to it, and his soul is more exercised.

I have been able to take part in public affairs, without quitting myself by a hair's breadth, and to give myself to others without losing myself.[24] The vehemence and intensity of desires hinders more than it serves, in carrying on

Of the Management of One's Will

what we undertake;[25] if fills us with impatience when events are unpropitious or tardy, and with bitterness and distrust toward those persons with whom we are dealing. We never guide well the affairs by which we are obsessed and guided.

Passion manages every thing badly.[26]

He who employs in the matter only his judgement and his skill proceeds in it more blithely; he makes believe, he gives way, he procrastinates, quite at his ease, according to the needs of the moment; he misses his stroke without dismay and distress, being ready and prepared for a new attempt; he walks always with the reins in his hands. In him who is intoxicated by violent and tyrannical intentions, we find of necessity much imprudence and injustice; the impetuosity of his desire carries him away. His impulses are reckless, and, unless Fortune lends much aid, they bear little fruit. Philosophy directs that, in chastising offences received, we turn away from anger, not to the end that our vengeance may be less, but, on the contrary, that it may be the better aimed and heavier, which result philosophy considers that impetuosity tends to hinder.[27] Not only is anger disquieting, but in itself it enfeebles the arm of those who chastise; this flame dulls and consumes their strength. As in precipitancy, *haste is slow,*[28] haste trips itself up, fetters and delays itself. *Swiftness entangles itself.*[30] For example, as I see by common experience, avarice has no greater impediment than itself; the more intent on its object and vigorous it is, the less fertile is it. Usually it seizes upon riches more quickly when it is disguised by an appearance of liberality.

A most worthy gentleman, a friend of mine, impaired

1374

Of the Management of One's Will

the soundness of his brain by a too eager attention and devotion to the affairs of a prince, his master,[31] which master thus described himself to me: that he perceives the importance of occurrences as clearly as any other; but that in regard to those for which there is no remedy, he instantly resigns himself to endurance; as for the others, after having arranged the necessary preparations, which he can do promptly from the activity of his mind, he awaits tranquilly what may ensue. In fact, I myself have seen him maintain great indifference and freedom in action and manner whilst concerned with very important and difficult affairs. I find him greater and more able in ill-fortune than in good. His defeats bring him more glory than his victory, and his affliction more than his triumph.

Observe that, even in unimportant and trivial occupations,—in playing chess, tennis, and the like,—the keen and ardent pressure of impetuous desire immediately throws the mind and the limbs into indiscriminate and disorderly action. We are bewildered and embarrassed by ourselves. He who carries himself more moderately about gain and loss is always at his ease;[32] the less pricked and excited he is by the gain, the more advantageously and safely does he conduct it. Furthermore, we hinder the mind's power of seizure and holding fast by giving it so many things to grasp. Some we must simply present to it, others attach to it, and still others incorporate in it. It can see and feel all things, but it should feed only on itself and be instructed as to what properly concerns it and what is properly its possession and its substance. The laws of Nature teach us what is rightly necessary for us. When wise men tell us that by nature no one is indigent, and that by general opinion every

one is so, they herein distinguish between the desires that
come from her and those that come from the unruliness of
our imagination. Those of which we see the end are hers,
those which flee before us and of which we can not overtake
the end are our own.[33] Poverty in worldly goods is easy to
cure; poverty of the soul, impossible.

> For if what is sufficient for man could suffice for
> him, this would be enough; but now, since this is not
> so, how are we to believe that any riches could satisfy
> my desire?[34]

Socrates, on seeing a great quantity of riches, jewels, and
costly stuffs borne in pomp through his city, exclaimed:
"How many things I do not desire!"[35] Metrodorus lived on
twelve ounces in weight a day; Epicurus, on less;[36] Me-
trocles slept in winter with the sheep and in summer in the
cloisters of churches.[37] *Nature provides for what it requires.*[38]
Cleanthes lived by his hands, and boasted that Cleanthes,
if he so wished, could support still another Cleanthes.[39]

If what Nature precisely and from the first demands of
us for the preservation of our existence is too little (as, in
truth, how much it is so and how cheaply our life can be
supported can not be better expressed than by this consideration, that it is so little that it escapes the grasp and shock
of fortune by its littleness), let us allot ourselves something
more; let us give the name of Nature to the customs and
conditions of each of us; let us value ourselves and deal with
ourselves by this measure; let us stretch our belongings and
our reckonings to that extent, for, so far as that, it truly
seems to me that we have some excuse. Accustomedness is
a second nature and no less powerful; what is lacking that I

Of the Management of One's Will

am accustomed to I hold is lacking in myself; and I should like almost as well to have my life taken from me as to have it diminished and retrenched very far below the conditions in which I have lived so long. I am not now in a condition for a great change and plunge into a new and unwonted course, not even a better one; it is too late to become different. And I should deplore any great luck that might fall to my lot at this hour, because it had not come at a time when I could enjoy it.

> To what purpose have I good-fortune, if I may not make use of it?[40]

I should deplore likewise any inward gain. It were almost better never, than so tardily, to become a man of worth and of understanding how to live, when one no longer has life. I, who am about to depart, would readily resign to one who comes later what wisdom I have learned about intercourse with the world—mustard after dinner. I have no use for the well-being with which I can do nothing. What does knowledge avail him who has no longer a head? It is an affront and unkindness of Fortune to offer us gifts which fill us with just vexation that we had them not in their season. Guide me no longer, I can no longer walk. Of all the members that ability possesses, patience is sufficient for us. Shall the talent of an excellent tenor be given to a singer whose lungs are diseased, and eloquence to the hermit relegated to the deserts of Arabia?[41]

To fall requires no skill; the end comes of itself at the conclusion of each piece of work. My world has passed away, my form expired; I am wholly of the past and am bound to give authority to it and to conform my exit to it. I want to say this by way of example: that the recent disappearance, by the Pope's decree, of ten days[42] has taken me so aback that I can not properly adjust myself to it; I belong to the years when we reckoned differently. So old and long a habit claims me and draws me back to it; I am constrained by being something of a heretic in this respect, not acceptant of innovation even when corrective. My imagination, do what I may,[43] is always ten days before or behind, and mumbles in my ear: "This rule concerns those who are yet to exist." If health even, sweet as it is, comes to me by fits and starts, it gives me cause for regret rather than enjoyment of it; I no longer have ground for welcoming it. Time departs from me, without which nothing can be enjoyed. Oh, how little account would I make of those great elective offices which I see in the world, which are given only to men about to go hence, as to whom it is not so much considered how fitly they will be employed as how long they will be employed! From the moment of their entrance, their exit is in view. In short, here am I about to finish this man, not to make from him another. By long habit this form has become substance, and accident nature.[44]

I say, then, that every one of us feeble creatures is excusable for regarding as properly his what is included within this extent; but equally beyond these limits there is naught but confusion; this is the greatest latitude that we should give to our rights. The more we amplify our needs and our possessions, the more we expose ourselves to the blows of fortune and of adversity. The field of our desires would be circumscribed and confined to a brief space of the nearest and contiguous advantages;[45] and, furthermore, their course should be conducted, not in a straight line which ends nowhere,

Of the Management of One's Will

but in a circle of which the two points meet and terminate in ourselves by a brief circuit. Actions which are carried on without this return on oneself—I mean an immediate and essential return,[46] like those of the avaricious and ambitious and so many others who run straight ahead,[47] whose course always carries them forward—these are erroneous and unsound actions.

Most of our performances are like a stage-play; *the whole world performs a play.*[48] We must play our part duly, but as the part of a borrowed personage. We must not make of the mask and outer garb a real being, nor make our own what is foreign to us. We do not know how to distinguish the skin from the shirt. It is enough to disguise the face without disguising the breast. I see those who transform and metamorphose themselves into new shapes and new beings as numerous as the public duties that they assume, and who play the dignitary[49] even to their heart and bowels, and carry their office with them even into their retiring room. It is not for me to teach them to distinguish the cap-doffings[50] which are paid to themselves from those paid to their office, or their retinue, or their mule. *They give themselves over to fortune only so far as to forget nature.*[51] They puff up and distend their minds and their natural talk in accordance with the height of their magisterial position. The mayor and Montaigne have always been two, with a very distinct separation. Because a man is a lawyer or a financier, he must not ignore the knavery there is in such professions. A worthy man is not responsible for the vice or folly of his profession, and ought not because of that to refuse to practise it; it is the custom of his country and it is of profit; we must live in the world and make use of it as we find it. But

Of the Management of One's Will

the judgement of an emperor should be above his empire and should view it and consider it as an external accident; and he should be able to find pleasure in himself apart, and to have companionship at least with himself.

It is not in me to pledge myself very deeply and very completely. When my will connects me with one party, it is not with so binding a tie that my understanding is thereby infected. In the present confusion of this state my personal concern has not made me ignore either the praiseworthy qualities in my adversaries or those that are reprehensible in the leaders whom I have followed. Others adore every thing on their side; as for me, I do not even excuse the greater part of things done by my party; and a good piece of work does not lose its charm in my eyes because it argues against me. Except as regards the knot of the controversy, I have held myself in equanimity and simple indifference; *and I feel no deadly hatred beyond the necessities of war;*[52] for which I am pleased with myself, inasmuch as I see the opposite erroneous course to be common.[53] They who extend their angry hatred beyond public matters, as most men do, shew that it springs from other sources and from a personal cause; just as, when fever persists in one who is cured of an ulcer, it shews that it had another more hidden origin. It is because they have nothing against the cause in general, as it attacks the welfare of all and of the state, but are wroth with it only in so far as it preys upon them in private. That is why they are spurred by private passion, and beyond justice and what concerns the public—*they did not all find fault with every thing, but each one with the things that concerned himself.*[54] I desire the advantage to be on our side, but I am not furious if it is not so.

1380

Of the Management of One's Will

I adhere steadfastly to the sanest of the parties; but I do not seek to be specially noted as inimical to the others and further than the general cause induces. I prodigiously blame this vicious way of judging: "He is of the League, for he admires the charm of monsieur de Guise"; "The activity of the King of Navarre astonishes him—he is a Huguenot"; "He finds this lacking in the king's conduct—he is seditious at heart"; and I did not concede even to a person in authority that he was justified in condemning a book for numbering a heretic among the best poets of this age.[55] Should we not dare to say of a thief that he has a fine leg? And because she is a prostitute, must she also be syphilitic? In wiser times did they revoke the proud title of Capitolinus, which had previously been given to Marcus Manlius as the preserver of religion and public liberty? Did they stifle the memory of his beneficence and feats of arms, and of the military reward granted to his valour, because he afterward aimed at sovereignty to the prejudice of the laws of his country?[56] If they have come to hate an orator, the next day he becomes to them not eloquent. I have touched elsewhere on the zeal which impels men of worth into such error. For my part, I can easily say, "That thing he does wickedly and this thing virtuously"; likewise with regard to prognostics or sinister incidents in affairs, they desire every man of their party to be blind or stupefied; and our conviction and our judgement to subserve, not truth, but an idea proceeding from our desires. I should err rather toward the other extreme, so greatly do I fear that my desire may mislead me. Add to this that I am somewhat sensitively distrustful about things that I desire.

I have seen wonders in my day in the indiscreet and pro-

Of the Management of One's Will

digious facility of the people of a country in letting their belief and their hope be led and governed as it has pleased and served their leaders, overlooking hundreds of shortcomings, one after another, overlooking phantasms and dreams. I am no longer surprised at those whom the absurdities of Apollonius and Mohammed led by the nose.[57] Their sense and understanding are completely smothered by their passion; their judgement no longer has any other choice than what smiles upon them and encourages their cause. I had especially observed this in the first of our feverish troubles. This other, of later birth, whilst resembling it, goes beyond it; whence I conclude that it is an inseparable characteristic of popular errors. Opinions press on after the first that sets off, driven, like the waves, by the wind. A man is not a member of the body if he can dissent from it, if he does not follow along the common course; but certainly wrong is done to the upright parties when we seek to assist them by imposture. I have always been opposed to this. This method is effective only upon weak brains; for the sound ones there are ways more sure, and not simply more honourable, of keeping up their courage and explaining away unfavourable happenings.

The heavens have never again seen, nor ever will see in the future, so mighty an opposition as that of Cæsar and Pompeius. Yet it seems to me that I discern in those noble souls great freedom from ill-will[58] toward each other. It was a rivalry in honour and in power, without malignity and disparagement, which did not carry them to violent and inconsiderate hatred. In their sharpest contests I discover some persisting respect and good-will; and from this I judge that, had it been possible, each of them would have desired

1382

to gain his end without the overthrow of his rival, rather than by his overthrow. How far otherwise it was with Marius and Sylla! Take notice of this.

We must not rush so madly in pursuit of our desires and interests. As in my youth I resisted the progress of love, which I felt to be gaining too fast upon me, and took care that it should not be so agreeable to me that it might end by putting force upon me and holding me captive quite at its mercy, so I do likewise on all other occasions into which my will enters with too much zest: I lean in the direction opposite to her inclination as I see her sink and become drunken with her wine;[59] I avoid nourishing her pleasure to such a degree that I can not take it from her without a bleeding loss. Souls which from stupidity see things only by halves enjoy this good-fortune, that harmful things wound them less; it is a mental leprosy which has some appearance of health, and such health as philosophy does not at all despise; but none the less it is not reasonable to call it wisdom, which we often do. And on this ground some one in ancient times made sport of Diogenes, who in mid-winter, entirely naked embraced a snow-image, as a test of his endurance. This man, meeting him in that posture, said to him: "Are you not very cold now?" "Not the least," replied Diogenes. "Why, then," rejoined the other, "do you think you are doing something that is difficult and exemplary in standing there?"[60] To measure endurance, one must know suffering.

But the souls which are to behold adverse occurrences and the affronts of fortune in their depth and sharpness, which are to weigh and taste them according to the bitterness and burden of their nature—let them employ their skill in saving themselves from entering into their causes and turning back

1383

their approach. What did King Cotys do? He paid liberally for the rich and beautiful dish which had been brought to him; because it was singularly fragile, he immediately broke it himself, to get rid of so easy a matter for wrath against all his servants.[61] For a similar reason, I have gladly avoided having my affairs confused with those of others and have not desired that my lands should touch only those of my kindred and of persons to whom I am united by close friendship; for thence commonly spring subjects of alienation and breaking off of fellowship.

I used to like games of chance of cards and dice; I gave them up long ago, solely because whatever good outward appearance I made when I lost, I did not fail to feel an inward pang. A man of honour who feels keenly being given the lie or an insult, and who is not one to accept a bad excuse as payment and satisfaction, let him avoid the rise of contentious altercations. I shun gloomy temperaments and churlish men as I would the plague-stricken, and I do not, unless my duty compels me to do so, enter into talk which I can not carry on without personal feeling and without excitement. *They will do better not to begin than to stop.*[62] The safest way, consequently, is to be prepared beforehand for the occasion.

I am well aware that some wise men have taken another course, and have not feared to grapple and struggle to the utmost with many subjects. Such men are assured of their strength, by means of which they are under cover from every sort of hostile success, causing, by the vigour of their patience, their foes to do the fighting;[63]

Just as a rock that juts out into the vast sea, meeting

1384

Of the Management of One's Will

the fury of the winds and exposed to the waves, endures all the might and the threats of the sky and the sea, itself remaining immovable.[64]

Let us not undertake to follow these examples; we should never attain to them. They[65] are persistent in beholding with resolution and without perturbation the ruin of their country, which had wholly possessed and commanded their affection. For common souls there is too much effort and too much severity in this. Cato gave up the noblest life that ever was because of this. We meaner natures must fly from the storm at a distance; we must make provision of right feeling, not of endurance,[66] and evade the blows that we can not parry. Zeno, seeing Charemonides, a young man whom he loved, coming to sit beside him, suddenly arose; and upon Cleanthes asking him why he did so, "I understand," he answered, "that physicians especially prescribe rest for all swellings, and forbid excitement."[67] Socrates does not say, "Do not surrender to the charms of beauty; face it; strive against it"; he says, "Shun it; run from the sight of it and from meeting it as from a powerful poison which shoots forth and strikes from afar."[68] He does not hope that youth can succeed in this.[69] And his worthy disciple,[70] imagining or reciting (but to my mind rather reciting than imagining) the rare perfections of the great Cyrus, represents him as distrustful of his strength to withstand the fascination of the divine beauty of the renowned Panthea, his prisoner, and as giving over to another, who had less liberty than himself, the duty of visiting and guarding her. And likewise the Holy Spirit says: "Lead us not into temptation." We do not pray that our reason may not be assailed and overcome

Of the Management of One's Will

by lust, but that it may not be even tried by it; that we may not be led into a condition where we have even to endure the approach, the solicitations, and temptations of sin; and we beseech our Lord to keep our conscience clear, fully and perfectly delivered from intercourse with evil.

They who say that they are justified in their vengeful passion, or in any other sort of painful passion, often say true, as things are, but not as they were; when they speak to us, the causes of their error have been fostered and forwarded by themselves; but go further back, trace these causes to their origin; there you will take them by surprise.[71] Would they have it that their fault is the less from being older, and that the sequel of a wrong beginning can be right? He who desires the welfare of his country, as I do, without being inflamed by passion or pining over it, will be afflicted, but not overwhelmed, to see it threatened either with its downfall or with a not less ruinous continuance. Unhappy bark, which waves, winds, and pilot drive hither and yon with such opposing impulsions!

> Dragged in different ways
> By master, waves and winds.[72]

He who does not eagerly seek for the favour of princes as for something which he can not do without is not much wounded by the coldness of their reception and countenance or by the inconstancy of their good-will. He who does not brood over his children or his honours with slavish engrossment[73] does not fail to live comfortably after he has lost them. He who does right chiefly for his own satisfaction is scarcely discomposed by seeing men judge his deeds not according to his deserts. A quarter of an ounce of patience suf-

1386

fices for such annoyances. I find myself well off with this
receipt, redeeming myself at the beginning as advantageously as I can; and I feel that by means of it I have avoided
many labours and difficulties. With very little effort I stay
the first movement of my emotions, and forsake the subject
that begins to weigh upon me before it carries me away. He
who does not stay the start does not care to stay the race;[74]
he who knows not how to shut a door will not drive out those
who enter in.[75] He who can not be master at the beginning
will never be master at the end; nor will he who was not
able to withstand the first push have the strength not to
fall;[76] *for they drive themselves on when once they have
taken leave of reason, and weakness is self-indulgent and is
heedlessly carried out to sea, nor does it find a place to halt.*[77]
I am conscious betimes of the little winds that murmur and
rustle within me, forerunners of the storm,

> As rising blasts, pent up in a forest, roar and give
> forth dull rumblings that foretell to sailors the coming
> storm.[78]

How many times have I done myself a very manifest injustice to avoid the risk of receiving a still worse one from
the judges, after an age of vexations and of dirty and mean
practices, more repulsive to my disposition than the rack and
the stake! *It is proper to do all that one can, and perhaps
even a little more, to avoid a lawsuit; for it is not only generous, but at times even profitable, to yield a little of one's
right.*[79] If we were really wise, we should be glad and boastful, as I one day heard a boy of good family very naïvely
rejoicing to everybody that his mother had lost her lawsuit,
as if it were her cough, or her fever, or some other thing irk-

some to keep. The very favours which Fortune might have bestowed upon me from kinships and friendly relations with those who have sovereign authority in such matters as these, I have conscientiously taken pains to avoid making use of to the prejudice of others, so as not to set my rights above their just value. In fine, I have effected so much by my labours (happily I can say this), that I am still undefiled by law-suits,—which have not failed to offer themselves many times for my service on very just grounds, had I chosen to listen,—and undefiled by quarrels. I shall soon have lived a long life without having either suffered or committed any injury of moment, and without hearing myself called by a worse word than my own name;[80] which all must admit is a rare favour of heaven!

Our greatest commotions have absurd sources and causes. How great a disaster did our last Duke of Burgundy[81] incur from a dispute about a wagon-load of sheepskins! And the engraving on a seal—was not that the first and controlling cause of the most horrible catastrophe that this world has ever suffered?[82] For Pompeius and Cæsar are but the off-shoots and the sequel of the other two. And I have seen in my time the wisest heads of this kingdom assembled with great ceremony and at public expense to make treaties and agreements of which the real decision depended meanwhile, in full sovereignty, on the talk of the cabinet of ladies, and on the inclination of some little woman. The poets well understood this when they delivered Europe and Asia over to fire and blood about an apple. Enquire why this man ventures to risk his honour and his life on his sword and dagger; let him tell you the origin of his quarrel; he can not do so without blushing, so idle and frivolous is its cause.

1388

Of the Management of One's Will

At the beginning there is need only of a little advisement; but when once involved, all the strings pull. There is need of great preparation, much more difficult and important. How much easier it is not to go in than to come out! Now our proceeding should be the opposite of that of the reed, which produces a long, straight stalk for its first growth, but afterward, as if it had been made weary and out of breath, comes to making frequent thick knots, like pauses, which shew that it no longer has its primitive vigour and persistence.[83] It is needful rather to begin gently and calmly, and keep our breath and our vigorous efforts for the climax and the completion of the business.

We guide affairs at the outset and have them at our mercy; but later, when they are in motion, it is they that guide us and carry us along, and we have to follow them. However, this is not to say that the reasoning has relieved me from all difficulty, and that I have not often had much ado to curb and bridle my passions. They do not always regulate themselves in proportion to the cause, and often are rough and violent even at the beginning. Nevertheless, there may be derived from this counsel good profit and fruit, save for those who in well-doing are satisfied by no fruit if renown be lacking; for in truth such mental action is of no account except for each man within himself. You are more content because of it, but not more esteemed, having amended before you have entered into action, and before the matter was seen by others.

Always, also, not in this matter alone, but in all other duties of life, the path of those who aim at honour is very different from that which those follow who set before themselves order and reason. There are those who enter the lists heedlessly and furiously, and flag in the course. Plutarch says that they who, through the weakness of false shame, are yielding and ready to grant whatever is asked of them, are ready later to fail in their word and to retract it;[84] and in like manner he who lightly enters into a quarrel is likely to abandon it as lightly. The same obstacle that keeps me from beginning it would incite me to hold to it strongly when I was once set in motion and heated. It is a bad business; since you are involved in it, you must go on or be shamefully killed. "Be deliberate in undertaking, but ardent in pursuit," said Bias;[85] for lack of wisdom we fall into a lack of courage which is even less tolerable.

In these days most accommodations of our quarrels are shameful and deceptive; we seek only to save appearances, and meanwhile we are false to our real purposes and disavow them. We salve over the facts; we know how we said it, and in what sense, and the bystanders know, and our friends, whom we have desired to make aware of our superiority. It is at the expense of our frankness and of the honour of our courage that we disavow our thought and seek hiding-places in mendacity, in order to come to an agreement. We belie ourselves, to justify having given the lie to another. Whether your conduct or your words may bear another interpretation is not to be considered; it is the honest and sincere interpretation of them that you must now maintain, whatever it may cost you. Your courage and your conscience are addressed; these are not qualities to be masked; let us leave such base methods and such expedients to the pettifogging of the courts. The excuses and reparations which I hear made every day, to do away with indiscretion, seem to me more improper than the indiscretion itself. It would be better to

Of the Management of One's Will

offend one opponent yet again than to offend oneself by making him such amends. You have defied him when heated with anger, and you set about appeasing and flattering him in your cool and better senses; thus you draw back[86] further than you had advanced. I find nothing that a gentleman can say so faulty in him as recantation seems to me to be disgraceful to him, when it is a recantation extorted from him by authority; inasmuch as stubbornness is more excusable in him than pusillanimity. Passions are as easy for me to avoid as they are difficult to moderate. *They are more easily rooted out of the mind than moderated.*[87] Let him who can not attain to the noble Stoic impassibility take refuge in the bosom of this commonplace insensibility of mine. That which they[88] did through virtue, I am led to do by temperament. The middle region harbours storms;[89] the two extremes—philosophers and rustics—compete in tranquillity and in happiness.

> Fortunate was he who could learn the causes of things, and tread under foot all fears and belief in inexorable destiny, and the din of greedy Acheron! Fortunate, too, who knows the rustic gods, and Pan and old Silvanus and the sister Nymphs![90]

All things are weak and delicate at birth. Consequently, we must at the beginning have our eyes open; for if then, when the thing is small, we do not discover the danger from it, when that has increased we can no longer discover the remedy for it. I should have encountered every day, in the path of ambition, a million crosses more difficult to put up with than it has been difficult for me to check the natural inclination that led me thither;

Of the Management of One's Will

> I have justly feared to raise my head so as to be
> conspicuous at a distance.[91]

All public actions are open to uncertain and differing interpretations, for too many heads pass judgement on them. Some say of my municipal employment[92] (and I am glad to speak of it a little—not that it is worth it, but as serving to shew my way of thinking in such matters) that I bore myself therein like a man who bestirs himself too sluggishly and with a languid interest; and they are not very far from what was visible. I endeavour to keep my mind and my thoughts in quietude; *always calm by nature, and now by reason of old age as well;*[93] and if sometimes they are excited[94] by some violent and penetrating impression, it is, in all honesty, without my consent. From this natural indolence of mine, however, there must not be drawn any inference of weakness (for lack of attention and lack of understanding are two things), and still less of unthankfulness and of ingratitude to those citizens who employed the utmost means that they had in their hands to oblige me, both before they knew me and after; and did much more for me in giving me my office a second time than in giving it to me at first. I wish them all possible good; and surely, if occasion had offered, I would have spared nothing for their service. I bestirred myself for them as I do for myself. They are excellent people, warlike and high-spirited, yet capable of obedience and discipline, and of serving some good purpose if they are well guided therein.

They say also that my administration passed without mark or trace. That is well! They blame my abstinence from action in days when almost all men were convicted of doing too much. I am eager in action[95] where my will carries me; but this vivacity is inimical to perseverance. Whoever shall desire to make use of me in my own way, let him give me matters in which there is need of vigour and freedom of action, which may be handled straightforwardly and directly, but which are at the same time hazardous, and I shall be able to do something about them; if the handling must be lengthy, crafty, laborious, skilful and tortuous, he will do better to address himself to some one else.

Not all important commissions are difficult. I was prepared to busy myself a little more vigorously had there been need of this; for it is in my power to do more than I do or than I like to do. I did not leave undone, so far as I know, any thing which duty actually demanded of me; I readily forgot those things which ambition commingles with duty and covers with her name. They are the ones which oftenest fill the eyes and the ears, and content men. Not the thing but the semblance satisfies them. If they hear no noise it seems to them that every one is asleep. My temperament is inconsistent with loud emotions. I could easily check a disturbance without being disturbed, and I could punish an uproar without mental trouble. Am I in need of angry excitement—I borrow it and wear it as a mask. My deportment is inert, rather dull than sharp. I do not blame a magistrate who sleeps, provided that they who are at his orders sleep at the same time; and the laws likewise sleep. As for me, I commend a smoothly gliding, shadowed, and silent life; *not submissive and abject, and yet not haughty,*[96] my fortune so wills it. I was born of a family that slipped along without show and noiselessly, and ever and always aiming especially at integrity.

Of the Management of One's Will

In these days men are so fashioned to commotion and ostentation that kindness, moderation, equability, stability, and other such quiet and obscure qualities are no longer known. Rough bodies make themselves felt, smooth ones are handled without perception. Sickness makes itself felt; health, little or not at all; nor do the things that soothe us compared with those that sting us.[97] It is acting for the sake of one's reputation and private profit, not for the common good, to wait to do in the market-place what might be done in the council chamber, and till high noon what might have been done the night before; and to be eager to do oneself what one's associate does as well. So did some surgeons in Greece perform the acts of their profession on platforms, in sight of the passers-by, in order to acquire more practice and more custom.[98] Men think that good laws are to be hearkened to only when trumpeted abroad. Ambition is not a vice for petty souls and for such powers as ours. Some one said to Alexander: "Your father will leave a vast empire at ease and at peace." The youth was envious of his father's victories and of the justice of his rule. He would not have desired to enjoy command of the world lazily and peacefully.[99] Alcibiades, in Plato, would prefer to die, young, handsome, rich, noble, learned, all of which he was in high degree, rather than not to advance beyond the state of that condition.[100] This infirmity is perchance excusable in so strong and so large a soul. When these dwarfed and paltry little intelligences deceive themselves and think to spread abroad their name by having judged a cause justly or been on guard at a city-gate, they the more shew their hind-sides where they hope to exalt their heads. Such trivial well-doing has neither body nor life; it vanishes in the first mouth, and

1394

passes only from one street corner to another. Talk boldly of it to your son and your servant, like the man of old who, having no other auditor of his self-praise and witness of his valour, boasted to his housemaid, exclaiming: "O Perrette, what a brave and able man thou hast for a master!"[101] Talk of it to yourselves at the worst; as a councillor of my acquaintance, after disgorging a mass of paragraphs of extreme quarrelsomeness and equal folly, having withdrawn from the council chamber to the closet, was heard mumbling between his teeth most conscientiously: *Not unto us, O Lord, not unto us, but unto thy name, give glory.*[102] He who can not pay himself elsewise does it from his own purse. Fame does not prostitute itself so cheaply. The rare and exemplary actions to which it is due would not endure the companionship of this innumerable multitude of trivial every-day actions. Marble may exalt you as you choose for having repaired a piece of wall or cleansed a public ditch, but not men of sense. All goodness is not followed by renown if difficulty and strangeness be not connected with it; nor, indeed, is bare esteem due to every action that is virtuous, according to the Stoics;[103] and they will not that we should even think well of the man who, from temperance, abstained from a blear-eyed old woman. They who have recognised the admirable qualities of Scipio Africanus deny him the honour which Panætius attributes to him of having been abstinent from gifts, as an honour not so much his as belonging to his time.[104]

We have the pleasures adapted to our lot; let us not encroach upon those of grandeur. Ours are more natural, and the humbler they are, the more solid and sure. If it be not from conscience, let us at least from ambition reject ambition; let us disdain this base and importunate hunger for renown and honour which impels us to beg for it from every sort of people *(what sort of renown can be won in the shambles?*[105]) by despicable methods and at any price, however degrading; it is dishonour to be thus honoured. Let us learn to covet no more glory than we are capable of attaining. To puff oneself up over every useful and innocent action is for those to whom such action is extraordinary and rare; they value it at the price that it cost them. In proportion as a good deed is more striking, I abate its goodness by the suspicion that I conceive, that it was done more because it was striking than because it was good; displayed, it is half sold. Those actions have much more charm which escape carelessly and noiselessly from the hands of him who does them, and which, later, some worthy man selects for their own sake and lifts out of shadow to push them forward into light. *All things seem to me the more commendable when they are done without ostentation and without witnesses,*[106] says the most vain-glorious man who ever lived.

I had only to preserve things as they were and to make them last,[107] which are hidden and imperceptible processes. Innovation makes a great display, but it is forbidden in these times, when we are harassed and can prohibit to ourselves only what is new. To abstain from doing is often as magnanimous as to do, but it is less visible, and the little I am worth is almost all of that sort.

In short, the opportunities in this office of mine were in harmony with my nature, for which I owe them very many thanks. Is there any one who wishes to be sick in order to give work to his physician? And should not the physician be thrashed who should wish us to have the plague that he might exercise his skill? I never had that iniquitous and common-enough disposition to desire that the confusion and evil plight of the affairs of that city should enhance the honour of my government; I heartily lent my aid toward their being easy and facile. He who does not choose to be grateful to me for the good order, the sweet and silent tranquillity, which accompanied my guidance can not at least deprive me of the share therein which belongs to me under the name of my good-fortune. And I am so made that I love as well to be lucky as to be wise, and to owe my successes solely to the grace of God as to owe them to the medium of what I effected. I had proclaimed to the world eloquently enough my incapacity in such public matters; I have something worse than incapacity: it is that this scarcely displeases me, and that I scarcely attempt to cure it, considering the course of life I have planned. Neither did I satisfy myself in this employment, but I almost attained in it what I had promised myself about it; and truly I much surpassed what I had promised about it to those with whom I had to do; for I usually promise a little less than I can do and than I hope to have in my power. I feel assured that I left behind me no resentment or hatred; as for leaving regret and desire for me, I know at least this, that I have not greatly wished to do so.

That I should trust this monster! That I should be unaware of the treachery of this placid sea and the tranquil waves![108]

Chapter XI

OF CRIPPLES

IT is two or three years since in France the year was short-ened by ten days. How many changes must follow this reform! It was really to move heaven and earth at once; nevertheless, nothing is thrown out of place: my neighbors find the time for sowing, for reaping, opportuneness for their business, and lucky and unlucky days, at exactly the same dates which had been assigned to them from time im-memorial; nor had error been perceptible in our habits, nor is there now perceptible improvement in them, so much uncertainty is there everywhere, so stupid and dull is our perception. It is said that this adjustment might have been managed in a less inconvenient way by following the ex-ample of Augustus and dropping for some years the bis-sextile day,[1] which in one way and another is a day of em-barrassment and confusion, until what was lacking had been supplied;[2] which has not been done even by this correction, for we remain still several days in arrears; indeed, by this same means we could provide for the future, decreeing that after the lapse of such or such a number of years this extra day should disappear forever; our miscalculation could not thereafter exceed twenty-four hours. We have no other count

Of Cripples

of time than by years; for many centuries the world has made use of this; nevertheless it is a measurement of which we have not yet decided the extent;[3] and it is of such nature that we daily question what forms other nations have diversely given to it and what custom about it has been. Suppose that, as some say, the heavens, as they grow old, are drawn nearer to us and throw us into uncertainty even of the hours and the days; and consider what Plutarch says about the months—that even in his time astrology[4] had not yet learned how to determine the movements of the moon. Well fitted are we to know the dates of past things!

I was pondering just now, as I often do, on the thought, what a free and roving agent the human reason is. I see that commonly men more readily occupy themselves in seeking the causes of facts laid before them than in seeking whether they be true. They disregard the antecedents, but carefully examine the consequences. Ridiculous chatterers! The knowledge of causes concerns only him who has the guidance of things, not us who have only passive receptivity of them, and who have the perfectly full and complete use of them according to our need, without penetrating into their origin and essence; wine is none the more agreeable to him who knows its primal properties. On the contrary, both the body and the soul interrupt and modify the right that they possess to the use of the world and of themselves by mingling therewith the idea of knowledge; the results concern us, but the means not at all; to pronounce authoritatively and to apportion belong to mastership and authority, as it is the part of deference and ignorance[5] to accept this.

Let us consider again our custom. Usually people begin thus: "How is it that this has happened?" They should

Of Cripples

say: "But has it happened?" Our imagination is capable of filling out a hundred other worlds and discovering their origins and contexture. It has need neither of substance nor of foundation; if it has its way, it builds as well on vacuity as on plenitude,[6] and with nothingness as with substance,—

> Able to give weight to smoke.[7]

I find that almost everywhere it is needful to say, "There is nothing in this";[8] and I should often employ this refutation; but I dare not, for they cry out that it is an evasion resulting from weakness of understanding and ignorance; and I must needs commonly play tricks for company's sake in dealing with trivial matters and tales that I entirely disbelieve; besides that, in truth, it is a little churlish and captious to deny curtly a statement of fact; and few persons fail —notably as to a matter difficult of belief—to affirm that they saw it, or to allege witnesses whose authority checks our contradiction. In conformity with this custom, we know the foundations and the conditions of a thousand things that never existed, and the world bickers over a thousand questions of which both sides are equally false. *The false is so near the true that a wise man ought not to venture on a precipitous spot.*[9]

Truth and falsehood have like aspects: similar bearing, style, and proceedings; we regard them in the same way. I find not only that we are remiss in defending ourselves from deception, but that we seek and desire to fall into its power; we like, as conformable to our being, to confuse our minds with what is of no value.

I have seen the birth of many miracles in my day. Although they are smothered as soon as born, we do not fail to

have a vision of the course they would have run if they had
lived to maturity; for if only the end of the thread is found,
you can wind off as much as you choose; and it is further
from nothing to the smallest thing in the world than it is
from that to the greatest. Now the first who are imbued with
this beginning of strange things,[10] when they come to
scatter abroad their story, find, from the opposition they
encounter, where the difficulty of persuasion lies and proceed
to stop up that crack with some false patch; besides that,
men having a natural desire diligently to spread rumours,[11]
we naturally make it a matter of conscience not to give back
what has been lent us without some interest and some addition from our store. The private error first creates the public
error, and in its turn the public error afterward creates the
private error.[12] Thus the whole structure goes on being built
up and shaped from hand to hand, so that the most distant
witness knows more fully about it than the nearest, and the
last informed is more fully persuaded than the first. It is a
natural progression; for whosoever believes a thing thinks
it a charitable deed to persuade another of its truth, and, to
do this, he does not hesitate to add as much of his own invention to his story as he sees to be necessary to make up for
the opposition and deficiency which he thinks exist in other
men's conceptions. I myself, who am peculiarly scrupulous
about lying,[13] and who care but little to give credibility and
authority to what I say, none the less perceive about the
gossip I take in hand that, being heated either by the opposition of another or by the very warmth of my narration,
I magnify and inflate my theme by voice and gestures, by
energy and force of language, and also by extension and
amplification, not without detriment to the simple truth;

Of Cripples

but yet I do so on these terms, that for the first man who brings me to myself and asks from me the bare and plain truth I immediately abandon my overstraining, and give it to him without exaggeration, without emphasis and amplification. An eager and vehement way of talking, as mine is commonly, is easily carried into hyperbole.

There is nothing upon which men are more usually bent than to make way for their opinions; where ordinary means fail us, we add to them command, force, fire, and sword. It is unfortunate to be at such a pass that the best test of truth is the multitude of believers in a crowd in which fools so largely outnumber wise men. *As if any thing were so exceedingly common as folly.*[14] *The multitude of the insane is the safeguard of the wise.*[15] It is difficult to determine one's judgement against generally held opinion. The first conviction, derived from the subject itself, takes possession of simple minds; from them it spreads to the intelligent under the authority of the number and length of life of the testimonies. For my part, what I would not believe one man about, I would not believe a hundred ones about, and I do not judge of opinions by their long-standing.

A short time ago, one of our princes, in whom gout had ruined a fine nature and a cheerful temperament, allowed himself to be so strongly convinced by reports of the marvellous works of a priest, who, by means of words and gestures, cured all diseases, that he made a long journey to seek him, and by the power of his imagination[16] his legs were affected and quieted for a few hours, so that he obtained from them the service which they had long forgotten how to give him. If chance had allowed five or six similar happenings to accumulate, it had been enough to place this miracle among things belonging to Nature. There was found afterward so much simpleness and so little art in the builder-up of such results,[17] that he was judged undeserving of any punishment; as indeed would be the case with most such matters, were their home discovered.[18] *We wonder at things that deceive us by their distance.*[19] Our vision often thus represents to us strange shapes at a distance, which vanish as we approach them: *never is rumour reduced to certainty.*[20]

It is a wonder from what idle beginnings and trivial causes such much-talked-of beliefs are usually born. That fact itself hinders information about them; for whilst we seek causes and ends worthy of such great fame, we miss the real ones; they escape our sight by reason of their smallness; and in truth there is needed for such investigations a very prudent, careful, and acute enquirer, impartial and unprejudiced. To this hour all these miracles and strange events have hidden themselves from me. I have seen no monster or miracle on earth more evident than myself; we become wonted to all strangeness by habit and time; but the more familiar I am with myself and the better I know myself, the more my misshapenness astonishes me, and the less do I comprehend myself.

The special privilege of bringing forward and producing such incidents is reserved for fortune. As I was passing day before yesterday through a village two leagues from my house, I found the place all excitement about a miracle which had just failed there, by which the neighbourhood had been deceived for many months; and the neighbouring provinces were beginning to be aroused about it and to flock thither in great crowds of all ranks. A young man of the

Of Cripples

village had one night, in his house, in sport, counterfeited
the voice of a spirit, without thought of other purpose than
to enjoy a moment's fooling. As it succeeded a little better
than he had hoped, in order to carry his joke to greater
length he made an associate of a young village girl utterly
stupid and simple; and later there were three of them, of
like age and intelligence; and from domestic preachings
they proceeded to public preachings, concealing themselves
behind the altar of the church, speaking only at night, and
forbidding any light to be brought. From words which
aimed at the conversion of souls, and threats of the day of
judgement,—for these are subjects under whose authority
and reverence imposture most easily stoops for shelter,—
they passed on to certain chimeras and actions so silly and
so absurd that there is hardly any thing so clumsy in the
sports of little children. Yet, if fortune had chosen to favour
it a little, who knows how greatly that juggling might have
increased! Those poor devils are now in prison and will
probably pay the penalty for the universal folly; and I dare
say some judge will avenge himself upon them for his own
share.

In this case, which has been laid bare, we see clearly; but
in many matters of the same nature, which go beyond our
knowledge, I am of the opinion that we should suspend our
judgement as well in rejecting as in accepting them. Many
illusions in the world are engendered, or, to speak more
boldly, all the illusions in the world are engendered, by the
fact that we are taught to be afraid of confessing our ignorance and are constrained to admit whatever we can not
refute. We speak of every thing as by mandate and pre-
determination. The practice at Rome was that even what

Of Cripples

a witness deposed he had seen with his own eyes, and what a judge decreed from his own certain knowledge, were expressed in this form: "It seems to me."[21] I am led to distrust things that are probable when they are set before me as infallibly true. I like those phrases which soften and moderate the extravagance of our assertions: "Perhaps," "In some measure," "Some," "They say," "I think," and the like; and if I had had to train children I should have put so often in their mouths this sort of response, enquiring, not assertive: "What does it mean?" "I don't understand," "It might be," "Is it true?" that they would have retained at sixty years the air of learners, rather than, at ten years, resemble instructors as they do. He who would be cured of ignorance must needs confess it. Iris is the daughter of Thaumantis. Wonder is the basis of all philosophy, inquisition the progress, ignorance the end.[22] In very truth there is a certain sturdy and valiant ignorance which is in no wise inferior in honour and courage to knowledge; an ignorance which to beget needs no less knowledge than to beget knowledge.

I read in my youth a report which Corras, councillor at Toulouse, had printed of an extraordinary incident of two men, each of whom represented himself to be the other.[23] I remember (and I do not remember any thing else about it) that he seemed to me to have made out the imposture of him whom he adjudged guilty to be so wonderful and so beyond our experience and his who was the judge, that I thought that there was much rashness in the sentence which condemned him to be hanged.[24] Let us accept some form of sentence which declares: "The Court understands nothing of this," more freely and openly than did the Areopa-

gites, who, finding themselves in difficulty about a cause
which they could not clear up, ordered that the parties
should return a hundred years later.[25]

The witches of my neighbourhood are in danger of their
lives upon the report of every new authority who gives
body to their dreams. To adapt the examples that Holy
Writ gives us of such things—very certain and irrefragable
examples—and to connect them with our modern incidents, when we perceive neither the causes nor the ground
of these, requires a differerent intelligence from ours; it belongs peradventure to that sole most potent witness to tell
us: "This has true life,[26] and that, and not this other." God
is to be believed—that is, in very truth, altogether reasonable; but not, however, one of ourselves who is astounded
by his own tale (and necessarily astounded by it he is, if
he be not out of his senses), whether his astonishment be
excited by another's, or whether he feels it about his own.[27]

I am dull and hold a little to what is substantial and
probable, avoiding the old-time reproofs: *Men put more
faith in what they do not understand.*[28] *From a natural desire of the human mind, obscure things are most willingly
believed.*[29] I see well that this is a challenge;[30] and I am forbidden to feel doubt on pain of damnable insults—a strange
way of persuasion. Thanks be to God, my belief is not controlled by fisticuffs! Let them be angry with those who
accuse their belief of being false; I accuse it only of difficulty
and rashness, and condemn the contrary affirmation as much
as they do, if not so imperiously. He who establishes his
argument by defiance and by command shews that his
reasoning is weak. In a verbal and scholastic discussion, they
may make as fair a show as their opponents,—*let them be put*

Of Cripples

forward as opinions, but not asserted,[31]—but in the effective consequences they derive from it these latter have much the advantage. To kill, there is need of a luminous and honest clearness; and our life is too real and vital to warrant these supernatural and chimerical chances. As for drugs and poisons, I leave them out of my reckoning; they who use them are murderers and of the worst kind; yet even in this matter it is said that we must not always rely on the confession of such persons, for they have been known sometimes to accuse themselves of killing persons who were found to be living and in health.

In respect to these other extravagant accusations, I should readily say that it is quite enough that a man, however greatly he is esteemed, be believed about what belongs to human nature; about what is beyond his apprehension and is of supernatural manifestation he should be believed only when sanctioned by a supernatural confirmation. This privilege, which it has pleased God to bestow upon some of the things testified to, should not be debased and lightly imparted. I am deafened with a thousand stories like this: "Three men saw him on such a day in the east; three saw him the next day in the west, at such an hour, in such a place, dressed thus and so." Truly, I would not believe myself about this. How much more natural and probable it seems to me that two men lie than that a man should go with the winds, in twelve hours, from east to west! How much more natural that our understanding should be pushed out of place by the agitation of our distraught mind than that one of us, in flesh and blood, should be whisked up on a broomstick through his chimney by an unknown spirit! Let us, who are constantly disturbed by our own

Of Cripples

internal delusions, not seek delusions from without and in-comprehensible. It seems to me that we may be pardoned for not believing a marvel, in so far at least as we can turn it aside and cut off its verification in a way not marvellous; and I follow the opinion of St. Augustine,[32] that it is better to lean toward doubt than toward assurance in matters that are difficult of proof and dangerous of belief.

Some years ago I passed through the territory of a sovereign prince who, as a courtesy and to abate my incredulity, did me the favour to let me see, in his presence and in private, ten or twelve prisoners of this sort, and amongst them an old woman, a true witch in ugliness and deformity, very famous and of great influence for many years in that profession. I heard both testimony and free confessions, and saw I know not what painless mark upon that wretched old woman; and I investigated and talked my fill, giving to this matter the soundest attention I could—and I am not a man who allows his judgement to be strangled by prejudice. In the end, and in all conscience, I should have decreed for them hellebore rather than hemlock. *The case seemed more like a deranged mind than a criminal one.*[33] Justice has its own proper way of treating such maladies.

As for the contradictory opinions and arguments which worthy men have placed before me, both there and often elsewhere, I have not heard any that hold me, or that do not admit of a solution always more probable than their conclusions. To be sure, it is true that those testimonies and arguments which are based on experience and on fact, those I do not unravel—indeed, they have no end to take hold of; I often cut them as Alexander cut his knot. After all, it is placing a very high value on one's conjectures to cause a man to be burned alive because of them. We are told of divers instances resembling what Prestantius says of his father, that, having fallen into a slumber much more profound than a sound sleep, he imagined that he was a mare and served the soldiers as a sumpter beast; and what he imagined, he was.[34] If what witches dream be thus materialised, if dreams can sometimes be thus embodied in facts, still I do not believe that our imagination is therefore in the keeping of men's justice.[35] This I say as one who is neither a judge nor a counsellor of kings, and who deems himself very far from worthy to be so, but as a man of the common sort, born and devoted to obedience to public welfare, both by his deeds and by his words. He who should make account of my idle fancies to the prejudice of the pettiest law, or belief, or custom of his village, would greatly wrong himself, and me not less. For in what I say I warrant no assurance other than that it is what at that time I had in my thought—a disorderly and vacillating thought. I speak of every thing as matter for talk, and of nothing as matter for advice;[36] *nor am I ashamed, as they are, to confess that I do not know what I do not know.*[37] I should not be so bold in speaking if I claimed to be believed, and this was what I answered a great man who complained of the severity and contentiousness of my counsels. "Because you feel your mind bent and prepared in one direction, I put before you the other, with all the care I can, to enlighten your judgement, not to compel it. God guides the thoughts of your heart and will provide your choice. I am not so presumptuous as to desire even that my opinions should be impelling in a matter of such importance; my fortune has not prepared them for such potent and high decisions." In truth, I have not only a great number of traits,[38] but also many opinions which I should be willing that my son, if I had one, should dislike. What if the most truthful opinions be not always the most advantageous for man, whose composition is so irregular!

Apropos, or malapropos, it matters not which, it is a common proverb in Italy that he does not know Venus in her perfect sweetness who has not lain with the cripple. Chance or some particular incident has long ago put this saying into the mouths of the people; and it applies to males, as well as females. For the Queen of the Amazons replied to the Scythian who invited her love, *"The lame do it best"* (Greek proverb). In that feminine State, to escape the domination of the males, they used to cripple them in their earliest childhood; arms, legs, and other parts which gave them an advantage, were lamed, and the men were only used for the purpose for which we use the women over here.

I might have said that the disjointed motions of the cripple add some new kind of pleasure to the business, and a certain agreeable titillation to those who try it. But I have lately learned that the old Philosophy had even decided the question. It says that, as the legs and thighs of the lame woman do not, by reason of their imperfection, receive their due aliment, it follows that the genital parts, which lie above, are fuller, better nourished and more vigorous. Or perhaps that, as this defect prevents them taking exercise, those who are tainted with it do not waste so much strength and come fresher to the sports of Venus. Which is also the reason why the Greeks denounced the women-weavers as being hotter than others, by reason of their sedentary occupations which they perform without much bodily exercise.

Of Cripples

What can we not prove by arguing at this rate? Of the latter I might also say that the tremor which their work imparts to them, while thus seated, arouses and excites their feelings, as the shaking and jolting of their coaches does the ladies.

Do not these examples confirm what I said at the beginning, that our reasonings often anticipate the fact and that the extent of their jurisdiction is so boundless that they pass judgement and exert themselves in vacuity itself and about non-existent things? Besides the flexibility of our invention in devising explanations of all sorts of dreams, our imagination is equally ready to receive false impressions from very frivolous tokens. For example, on the mere authority of the ancient and general use of that proverb, I once made myself believe that I received more pleasure from a woman because she was not straight, and accordingly put down that deformity among the number of her charms.

Torquato Tasso, in the comparison that he makes of Italy and France, says that he noticed this: that our legs are more slender than those of Italian gentlemen; and he attributes the cause to our being constantly on horseback;[39] which is the very thing from which Suetonius draws a wholly different conclusion; for he says, on the contrary, that Germanicus had increased the size of his legs by constant use of the same exercise.[40] There is nothing so pliant and vagrant as our understanding; it is like the shoe of Theramenes, fitted for both feet;[41] whilst it is two-fold and various, subject-matters likewise are two-fold and various. "Give me a drachma of silver," said a cynic philosopher to Antigonus. "That is not the present of a king," he answered. "Give me then a talent." "That is not the present for a cynic."[42]

Of Cripples

Whether the heat opens many passages and hidden pores, by which the moisture may come into the young plants, or hardens the ground and contracts the gaping channels, so that fine rains may not injure it, or the keen power of the fierce-burning sun or the piercing cold of Boreas blast it.[43]

Every medallion has its reverse side.[44] That is why Clitomachus said of old that Carneades had outdone the labours of Hercules because he had eradicated from men acquiescence, that is, false opinions and rashness in judging.[45] This so vigourous conceit of Carneades sprang in my opinion from the impudence of those who in old days made profession of knowledge, and from their immoderate presumption. Æsop was put up for sale, with two other slaves. The buyer enquired of the first of these what he knew how to do; and he, to make himself valued, promised wonders[46]— that he knew this and that; the second answered as much or more for himself. When it came Æsop's turn, and he also was asked what he knew how to do, "Nothing," he said, "for these others have taken possession of every thing; they know every thing." Thus has it come about in the school of philosophy: the arrogance of those who attributed to the human mind capacity for all things gave occasion in others, from disdain and opposition, to the opinion that it is capable of nothing. The latter maintain the same extreme opinion of ignorance that the former maintain of knowledge, so that we can not deny that man is immoderate throughout, and that nothing stays him but necessity and inability to go further.

Chapter XII

OF PHYSIOGNOMY

ALMOST all the opinions that we hold are adopted by authority and on credit.[1] This is not amiss; we could not choose them more unwisely than by ourselves in times of such feebleness. The image of the discourses of Socrates which his friends have left us we approve only through respect for the general approbation, not from our judgement; they are not in accordance with our usages. If something of the same sort should be produced at this time, there are few men who would value it. We perceive as admirable only those things that are artificially keen and puffed up and inflated. Those that slip along with artlessness and simplicity easily escape so dull a sight as ours; they have a delicate and hidden beauty; it needs a clear and well-purified sight to discern that secret radiance. Is not artlessness, according to us, akin to foolishness and a quality to object to?

Socrates makes his mind move with a natural and familiar motion—thus speaks a peasant, thus speaks a woman; his talk always takes note of carters, joiners, cobblers, and masons;[2] and there are inductions and similitudes drawn from the most common and familiar actions of men; every one understands him. Under so mean a form we should

Of Physiognomy

never have plucked the nobility and splendour of his admirable conceptions—we who regard as flat and low all those ideas not supported by learning, who discern riches only in show and pomp. Our world is fashioned solely for ostentation; men are inflated only with wind, and are moved only by bounds, like footballs. This man[3] did not set before himself idle fancies; his aim was to supply us with matters and precepts which really and most directly are of service to life;

> To observe a measure and to hold to an end and to follow Nature.[4]

Likewise he was always one and the same,[5] and mounted, not by fits and starts. but by temperament, to a supreme state of vigour; or, to say better, he did not mount at all, but rather made vigour and obstacles and difficulties subservient to his primal and natural state.[6] In Cato we see clearly that his bearing is constrained much beyond that of common souls; in the brilliant actions of his life, and in his death, we always feel that he is mounted on the great horse. The other[7] treads the ground with an easy and ordinary gait, and carries on most useful discussions, and conducts himself in accordance with the regular course of human life both in death and in the most thorny difficulties that can occur.

It is fortunate that the man most worthy to be known and set before the world as an example is he of whom we have the most certain knowledge. The most clear-sighted men who ever lived have thrown light upon him. The witnesses that we have of him are admirable for their fidelity and for their competence. It is a great thing to have been

able to give such order to thoughts as simple as those of a
child that, without changing or stretching them, he has
brought forth from them the noblest conditions[8] of our
soul. He sets it forth as neither lofty nor rich: he represents
it merely as healthy, but, certainly, with a very cheerful
and genuine health. With these commonplace and natural
springs, with these ordinary, every-day ideas, he built up,
without excitement and without spurring himself, not only
the most settled but the most lofty and vigorous beliefs,
actions, and morals that ever were. It was he who brought
down human wisdom from the skies, where it was wasting
its time, to bestow it on mankind, where is its most appropriate and most laborious business. Observe him pleading before his judges; observe by what reasonings he arouses
his courage in the hazards of war, by what arguments he
fortifies his patience against calumny, tyranny, death, and
against his wife's temper; there is nothing in them borrowed
from art and from learning; the simplest souls recognise
therein their powers and their strength; it is not possible to
go back further and to descend lower.[9] He has done a great
kindness to human nature by shewing how much it is
capable of by itself.

We are, each of us, richer than we think, but we are
trained to borrow and to beg; we are taught to make more
use of what is others' than of our own. In nothing does
man know how to stop at the limit of his need. Pleasure,
wealth, power, he grasps of these more than he can hold;
his greed is not capable of moderation. I find that in eagerness for knowledge it is the same; he cuts out for himself
much more work than he can do and much more than he
has reason to do, making the utility of knowledge co-

Of Physiognomy

extensive with its subject-matter; *we are afflicted by excess of learning as of every thing else;*[10] and Tacitus has reason to praise the mother of Agricola for having curbed in her son a too eager appetite for learning.[11] Looked at steadily, it is a good thing, which has in it, like the other good things for man, much characteristic and innate vanity and weakness, which costs dear. Its acquisition is much more hazardous than that of any other food or drink; for of other things, what we have bought we carry home in some vessel, and there we have leisure to examine its value, how much and at what hour we shall use it. But learning we can not from the first put into any other vessel than our minds; we swallow it when we buy it, and leave the market-place either already infected or benefitted. There is some learning which only embarrasses and burdens us instead of giving us nourishment, and some again which, claiming to cure us, poisons us.

I have had pleasure in seeing men in some places take, from piety, a vow of ignorance, as well as of chastity, poverty, and penitence. This also is gelding our unruly appetites, to deaden the cupidity which spurs us to the study of books, and to deprive the mind of the pleasurable complacency which tickles us by the general belief in our learning. And it is a liberal fulfilment of the vow of poverty when poverty of the mind also is united with it. We need but very little learning to live at our ease; and Socrates teaches us that it exists in ourselves, and how to find it there and to make it of use to us. All the knowledge we have that is beyond what comes by Nature is almost idle and superfluous; it is much if it does not burden and disturb us more than it serves us. *There is need of little learning to make a good mind;*[12] our mind, a blundering and restless instrument, has feverish excesses. Collect your thoughts: you will find in yourself inborn reasonings about death—true reasonings and the best fitted to serve you at need; they are those which make a peasant and entire peoples die as firmly as a philosopher. Should I have died less cheerfully before I had read the Tusculans? I think not; and when I discover my real self,[13] I feel that my tongue has been enriched, my heart very little; that is as nature fashioned it for me, and it strengthens itself for the conflict, but only in a natural and usual way; books have served me not so much for instruction as for mental exercise.

What if learning, attempting to arm us with new means of defence against natural disadvantages, has more impressed on our imagination their greatness and their weight than its own reasonings and craft wherewith to shape ourselves? These are, indeed, refinements by which it rouses us often to no purpose. Observe even the most compressed and most judicious authors—how they strew about a sound reason many others that are trivial, and, when closely scanned, incorporeal; these are only sophistries which deceive us; but, inasmuch as it may be to our profit, I do not care to scrutinise them too much; there are herein many of this sort, in divers places, either borrowed or imitated. Thus we must be on our guard not to call strength that which is only prettiness, and solid what is only sharp, or good what is only beautiful. *Things that please more when tasted than when drunk.*[14] Not all that pleases nourishes.[15] *Where it is a matter, not of wits, but of the soul.*[16]

Witnessing the efforts of Seneca to make ready for death, seeing him labouring and sweating to resist and to encourage himself, and for so long a time struggling on his resting-place,[17] would have, for me, impaired his good name, had he not, when dying, very gallantly sustained it. His excitement was so ardent and so vehement that it shews that he was by disposition hot-blooded and impetuous *(a great soul speaks more calmly and serenely.*[18] *The mind is not of one colour and the soul of another.*[19] He must needs be convinced at his own expense), and shews somewhat that he was hard pressed by his adversaries. Plutarch's way, inasmuch as it is more disdainful and less constrained, is in my opinion so much the more virile and influential; I could easily believe that the movements of his soul were more assured and more steady. The one, more acute,[20] pricks us, and impels us with a start, chiefly touching the spirit. The other, more solid, ever instructs and sustains and strengthens us, touching more the understanding. The former carries away our judgement, the latter wins it. I have likewise seen other writings even more respected, which, in depicting the combat maintained against the thorns of the flesh, represent them as being so piercing, so powerful and invincible, that we, who are of the dregs of the people, have to wonder no less at the strangeness and unfamiliar force of the temptations described than at the resistance to them.

For what purpose do we arm ourselves with these weapons of learning? Look at the fields: the poor people whom we see here and there in them, stooping over their labour, know nothing of Aristotle and Cato, nothing of example or precept; from them does nature draw forth every day purer and more inflexible manifestations of firmness and patience than those which we are so carefully taught. How many do I constantly see who disregard poverty, how

many who desire death, or who meet it without alarm or
distress! He who is digging my garden buried this morning
his father or his son. The very names they give to maladies
sweeten and soften the severity. Phthisis is for them a cough,
dysentery a looseness, pleurisy a cold; and as gently as they
name them, so do they endure them. Their every-day toil
is interrupted only by very grievous sickness; only to die do
they take to their beds. *That simple and frank virtue has
been changed into an obscure and ingenious science.*[21]

I wrote this about the time that a heavy burden of our
troubles[22] rested with all its weight on me for several months.
On one side I had the enemy at my gates; on the other side,
marauders—worse enemies. *The struggle was not with
arms, but with crimes;*[23] and I experienced every sort of military outrage at once.

> There is a foe to be feared on the right hand and on
> the left, and he frightens both sides with an imminent
> danger.[24]

An unnatural war! Other wars are waged on foreign soil;
this one even against its own, preying upon and destroying
itself by its own poison. It is of so malign and ruinous a
nature that it ruins itself together with every thing else,
and rends and dismembers itself in its frenzy. We more
frequently see it melt away of itself than from lack of any
essential thing or by hostile force. All discipline evades it.
Its purpose is to cure sedition, and it is full of it; it desires
to chastise disobedience, and sets the example of it; and,
employed in defence of the laws, does its share of rebellion
against its own laws. Where do we find ourselves? Our own
medicine spreads infection!

Of Physiognomy

Our disease is aggravated by the aid we give it.[25]

It gains the upper hand and grows worse by treatment.[26]

All things right and wrong, confused by our evil
frenzy, have turned away from us the just mind of the
gods.[27]

In these general maladies we can distinguish at the beginning the well from the sick; but when they continue for any
time, as ours does, the whole body is affected by them from
head to heels; no part is exempt from corruption, for there
is no air which is inhaled so greedily, which so spreads and
penetrates, as does license. Our armies now are bound and
held together only by foreign cement; we are no longer
able to form a steadfast and well-governed corps of Frenchmen. What a disgrace! There is only so much discipline
as hired soldiers exhibit to us. As for ourselves, we conduct ourselves at discretion,[28] and each man at his own, not
at that of the leader; he has more to do within than without;[29] it is for him who commands to follow, to pay court,
to give way; for him alone to obey; all the rest are free and
disunited.

I like to see how much faint-heartedness and pusillanimity there is in ambition; through how much debasement
and servitude one must attain one's object. But I dislike to
see kindly natures, capable of dealing justly, every day become corrupted in managing and commanding this turmoil.
Long toleration engenders habit; habit, assent and imitation. We had a sufficiency of ill-conditioned souls without
spoiling those that were good and noble; consequently, if

1420

we last, there will hardly remain any to whom to entrust the
well-being of this realm, in case Fortune restores it to us.

Do not, at least, forbid this young man to come to
the rescue of a ruined age.[30]

What has become of the old precept that soldiers should
fear their commander more than the foe?[31] and this wonderful example: that an apple-tree happening to be enclosed
within the bounds of the camp of the Roman army, the
army was seen to move on the next day, leaving to the
owner the entire tale of his ripe and delicious apples?[32] I
should be glad if our young men, instead of using their
time in less profitable peregrinations and less honourable
methods of learning, should employ it, half in witnessing
naval warfare under some good captain-commander of
Rhodes,[33] half in becoming acquainted with the discipline of
the Turkish army; for it has many differences from ours,
and superiorities. One of these is that our soldiers become
more lawless when on expeditions, theirs more restrained
and circumspect; for trespasses or thefts from the common
people, which are punished by flogging in peace time, are in
time of war serious offences; thus, for an egg taken without
payment the fixed penalty is fifty blows with a cudgel; for
any thing else, however trivial, not necessary for nourishment, they are impaled or beheaded without delay.[34] I was
astonished to read in the history of Selim, the most cruel
conqueror who ever lived, that when he subjugated Egypt,
the beautiful gardens surrounding the city of Damascus,
which were all open and within the conquered territory, his
army being encamped on the very spot, were left unviolated
by the soldiers, for they had received no signal for pillage.[35]

1421

Of Physiognomy

But is there any ill in a government that it is worth while to combat by so deadly a drug?[36] Not even, said Favonius, the usurpation, by a tyrant, of possession[37] of a republic. And Plato likewise does not assent that a man should violate the repose of his country in order to cure it, and does not accept the reform which disturbs and endangers every thing, and which costs the blood and ruin of the citizens; declaring it to be the duty of an honest man, in such case, to let every thing alone, only praying God that he will lend his wonder-working hand; and he seems to take it ill of Dion, his great friend, that he had therein proceeded somewhat otherwise.[38] I was a Platonist to this extent before I knew that there had been such a man as Plato in the world. And even if this personage must be entirely refused association with us[39] (who, by the integrity of his thought, deserved by divine favour to penetrate so far into Christian light in the midst of the common darkness of the world in his time), I do not think it well becomes us to let ourselves be instructed by a pagan how great an impiety it is not to expect from God help that is purely his own, and without our coöperation. I often question whether, amongst so many people who meddle with such concerns, there was to be found none of so weak understanding as to be open to conviction[40] that he proceeded toward reformation by the worst of deformations; that he advanced toward his salvation by the most express causes we have of very certain damnation; that, by overturning the government, the magistracy, and the laws in whose guardianship God has placed him, filling fraternal hearts with parricidal hate, summoning to his aid devils and furies, he can bring succour to the sacrosanct mildness and justice of the divine law.

1422

Of Physiognomy

Ambition, avarice, cruelty, revenge, have not enough natural impetuosity of their own; let us attract them and stir them up by the high-sounding title of justice and devotion. There can not be imagined a worse aspect of things than when wickedness is legitimised and assumes, with the permission of the magistrate, the mantle of virtue. *There is nothing more deceitful in appearance than a corrupt religion, in which the will of the gods is a veil for crime;*[41] the extreme kind of injustice according to Plato is when that which is unjust is regarded as just.[42] The common people then[43] had much to endure: it was not a question of immediate losses only,—

> To such an extent is there confusion in the fields
> on every hand;—[44]

but future ones as well; the living had to suffer, those also who were not yet born. They were robbed, and, consequently, so was I, even of hope, being despoiled of all that they had laid up to live on for many years.

> What they can not carry off with them or take
> away, they destroy, and the wicked mob burns inoffensive huts.[45]

> There is no safety in walls, and the fields are laid
> waste by pillage.[46]

Besides this blow, I suffered others. I incurred the disadvantages which accompany moderation in such diseased conditions. I was ill treated on all hands; to the Ghibelline I was a Guelph, to the Guelph a Ghibelline; one of my poets says just this, but I know not where. The situation of my house and my intercourse with the men of my neighbourhood shewed me in one aspect, my life and my acts in another. No formal accusations were made, for there was nothing to take hold of: I never depart from the laws, and whosoever should have called me to account would have been found to be more guilty than I;[47] there were unspoken suspicions which circulated underhand, of which there is never a lack in so confused a medley, any more than of envious or foolish minds.

I commonly assist the injurious assumptions that Fortune scatters abroad against me, by a way that I have always had of shunning the justifying, excusing, or explaining myself, conceiving that to plead for my conscience is to compromise it; *for clear-sightedness is weakened by argument;*[48] and as if every one saw within me as clearly as I myself do, instead of retreating from the accusation I go to meet it, and rather heighten it by an ironical and mocking confession, if I am not entirely silent about it, as something unworthy of reply. But they who mistake this for overweening confidence feel scarcely less spite against me than those who mistake it for the weakness of an indefensible cause, especially those of high station, in whose eyes failure to bow down to them is the supreme offence, who are harsh to all justice that knows and feels itself, and is not submissive, humble, and suppliant; I have often run against that post. So it is that at what happened to me in those days an ambitious man would have hanged himself; so would an avaricious man. I care not at all for gain,—

> May I have what I now have, or even less; and may I live what is left of my life, if the gods will that there shall be any left,[49]—

1424

Of Physiognomy

but the losses that befall me from the misdoing of others, whether theft or violence, affect me almost as much as a man sick and suffering from avarice. The wound is immeasurably more bitter than the loss. A thousand diverse kinds of ills come upon me one by one; I should have endured them with more spirit all at once.[50]

I considered then to whom amongst my friends I could commit a necessitous and unfortunate old age. Having cast my eyes in every direction, I found myself bare. To let oneself fall headlong and from such a height, it must needs be into the arms of a steadfast, vigorous, and fortunate affection; these are rare, if there be any. Finally I recognised that the surest way was to entrust myself and my necessity to myself; and if it befell me to be but coldly in Fortune's favour, that I must commend myself the more earnestly to my own favour, must cling fast to myself, and consider myself the more closely. In all matters men throw themselves on external supports to spare their own, which alone are sure and alone powerful for him who knows how to arm himself with them; every one turns elsewhere and to the future, inasmuch as no one turns to himself.

And I considered that these were profitable disadvantages because, in the first place, bad scholars must be admonished by whipping when reasoning is not sufficient, even as we make a crooked stick straight by fire, and by force of wedges. I have for a very long time preached to myself to keep to myself and to hold aloof from foreign matters; yet am I forever turning my eyes aside; a salutation, a gracious word from a great personage, a kindly glance tempt me. God knows whether there is a scarcity of these nowadays, and what it means! I listen, moreover, without frowning to the

1425

bribes offered me to draw me into public view,[51] and I remonstrate so mildly that it seems as if I would more willingly suffer being overmastered. Now a spirit so intractable needs thrashing; and this vessel that warps and falls apart must be tightened up and brought together with lusty blows of the mallet and prevented from stealing away and escaping from itself.

In the second place, this unusual condition was useful as practice in preparing me for worse,—since I who, both by privilege of fortune and by the quality of my character,[52] hoped to be among the last, had come to be among the first overtaken by this tempest,—and instructing me betimes to coerce my life, and make it ready for a new condition. True liberty is having complete control of oneself. *He is most powerful who has himself in his own power.*[53]

In ordinary and quiet times we prepare for moderate and ordinary chances; but, in the confusion we have been in for thirty years, every Frenchman, whether as a private individual or as a citizen, sees himself every hour on the verge of the complete overthrow of his fortunes; proportionately must he keep his heart supplied with stronger and more vigorous provisions. Let us take it kindly of fate to have had us live in an age that is not inert and weak, or idle; a man who would not have been otherwise famous will become so by his ill-fortune.

As I seldom read in history of such disorders in other states without regretting that I was not able to be present, to observe them better, so my curiosity makes me in some sort enjoy seeing with my own eyes this noteworthy spectacle of our public death, its symptoms and its manner; and since it is out of my power to delay it, I am glad to be fated to look on at it and to instruct myself by it. So evidently do we seek to recognise even darkly and in the dramas of the stage the image of the tragic play of human fortune: it is not without compassion for what we hear; but our pain awakens our pleasure at the rarity of these woeful events. Nothing animates us which does not keenly touch us;[54] and good historians avoid, like stagnant water and dead sea, calm narratives, to recur to seditions and wars to which they know that we invite them.

I doubt if I can decently acknowledge at what little cost to the repose and tranquillity of my life I have passed more than half of it in the midst of the ruin of my country. I give myself a little too good a bargain in patience about events that do not touch me personally; and, as to self-pity, I consider not so much what is taken from me as what remains safe both within and without. There is a certain consolation in evading now one, now another, of the ills that successively glance at us sidelong, and strike hard elsewhere in our neighbourhood; as also in the fact that, in matters of public concern, the more widely extended my interest is, the weaker it is; moreover, it is half true, *that we feel as much of public calamities as concerns our private affairs;*[55] and the degree of health with which we set out was such that in itself it lessens the regret that we should have felt for it. It was health, but only in comparison with the sickness that has followed it. We have fallen from a great height; the corruption and brigandage which are found in conditions of dignity and in public service seem to me what is least endurable; to be robbed in a wood is less insulting than in a cautionary town.[56] It[57] was a general coherence of particular members, diseased one more than another, and the greater number affected with inveterate ulcers which no longer admitted of cure or asked for it.

This falling to pieces[58] therefore inspirited me rather than cast me down, by the help of my conscience, which bore itself not only tranquilly but proudly; and I found nothing for which to complain of myself. Likewise, as God never sends to mankind evils, any more than goods, wholly unmixed, my health in those days was more than usually good; and whilst without it I can do nothing, so with it there are few things that I can not do. It afforded me the means to awaken all my powers and to hide the harm done me,[59] which could easily have been greater; and I proved in my long-suffering that I had a good seat in fighting Fortune,[60] and that it would need a great shock to unhorse me. I do not say this to incite Fortune to make a more vigorous attack upon me; I am her servant, I hold out my hands to her; in God's name, let her be satisfied! Do I feel her assault? Indeed I do. As those who are overwhelmed and possessed by sadness are none the less permitted at intervals to touch in the dark some pleasure, and a smile escapes them, so I have enough power over myself to make my usual frame of mind tranquil and free from painful imaginings; but I allow myself to be surprised withal by fits and starts, by the stings of these unpleasant thoughts, which overcome me while I am arming myself to drive them away or struggle with them.

Behold another increase of evil which came upon me after the rest. Both without and within my house I was assailed by a plague of unexampled severity; for, as healthy bodies are subject to the most violent maladies inasmuch as they can be mastered only by them, so my very healthful climate,

Of Physiognomy

in which contagion, although in the neighborhood, has
never in the memory of man gained a foothold, becoming
poisoned, produced strange effects:

> The obsequies of old and young crowd pell-mell
> upon one another; no head does cruel Proserpine pass
> over.[61]

I had to endure this agreeable state of affairs—that the sight
of my house was appalling to me; every thing in it was
unguarded and at the mercy of any one who coveted it. I
myself, who am so hospitable, was most painfully seeking
a refuge for my family—a wandering family, a source of
terror to its friends and to itself, and of dismay wherever it
sought to establish itself; having to change its abode instantly if one of the band began to feel pain in the tip of a
finger. All maladies are at such time thought to be the
plague; no one gives himself the trouble to identify them.
And the best of the joke is that,[62] according to the rules of
the profession, whenever you go near any danger you must
be for forty days in anxiety regarding this evil, your imagination working upon you meanwhile after its fashion, and
even making you feverish.

All this would have affected me much less had I not been
compelled to feel the effects of other people's difficulties and
to serve six months, miserably, as a guide to that caravan;
for I carry in myself my preservatives—resolution and endurance. Fear of future danger,[63] which is especially dreaded
in this disease, disturbs me little, and if, being alone, I had
wished to take flight, it would have been a much bolder and
more distant one. It is a death which does not seem to me
among the worst: it is commonly short, faculties benumbed,

without pain, solaced by the general condition, without ceremonial, without mourning, without a crowd. But as for the souls of the neighbourhood, not a hundredth part of them can be saved.

You can see the domains of the shepherds deserted
and the pastures untenanted far and wide.[64]

In this locality my best revenue is from manual labor; the land that a hundred men used to work for me was long only stubble-fields.[65]

But what an example of resolution did we not see in the simplicity of this whole people! Generally, every one renounced care about life: the grapes remained hanging on the vines—the chief interest of the district; all unconcernedly making ready for death and awaiting its coming, this evening or to-morrow, with face and voice so little terrified that it seemed as if they had come to terms with this necessity and that it was a universal and inevitable condemnation. It is ever such; but with us how slight a hold has resolution in dying! The distance and difference of a few hours, the mere consideration of companionship, makes a difference in our apprehension of it. Regard these people: because they are all dying in the same month,—children and the young and the old,—they are astonished no more, they weep no more. I saw some who feared to remain behind as in a horrible solitude; and commonly I observed amongst them no other concern than about burials; it grieved them to see the bodies scattered over the fields at the mercy of wild beasts, which immediately multiplied there. How human caprices vary! The Neorites, a nation which Alexander subjugated, cast the bodies of their dead into the densest of their woods.

1430

there to be eaten; the only sepulture considered fortunate by them.[66] One man, in good health, dug his own grave; others laid themselves down in theirs while still living; and a workman of mine drew the earth down upon him with his hands and feet while dying. Was not this sheltering himself, to sleep more at his ease—an attempt somewhat similar in spirit to that of the Roman soldiers, who were found after the battle of Cannæ with their heads thrust into holes which they had dug and filled in with their own hands while they smothered?[67] In short, a whole nation was suddenly, by common action, settled in a way of living not inferior in firmness to any studied and agreed-upon resolution.

The greater part of the instructions of learning have, as regards encouraging us, more of pretence than of force, and more of ornament than of fruit. We have forsaken Nature, and we seek to teach her her lesson—she who guided us so happily and so safely; and meanwhile the traces of her instruction and what little remains of her image, by favour of ignorance, imprinted upon the life of this rustic crowd of rough men, learning is compelled every day to borrow, in order to make it a pattern to her disciples of perseverance, innocence, and tranquillity. It is a fine thing to see that these men, full of such great knowledge, have to imitate this ignorant simplicity, and to imitate it in the chief actions of virtue; and that our wisdom learns from the very beasts the instructions that are most useful in the most important and essential parts of our life: how it befits us to live and to die, how to manage our property, to love and bring up our children, to maintain justice—a singular testimony of human infirmity; and that this reason of ours, which we make use of as we like, ever finding some variety and novelty, leaves in us no apparent trace of Nature. And men have treated it as perfumers treat oil: they have adulterated it with so many argumentations and conceptions summoned from outside sources that it has become thereby vacillating and peculiar to each individual, and has lost its own unchanging and universal aspect;[68] and we must needs seek evidence of it in beasts subject neither to partiality and corruption, nor to diversity of opinion. It is, indeed, very true that they themselves do not always follow exactly the paths of Nature; but the distance that they stray from it is so slight that you can always see Nature's track; just as horses that are led by hand make many a bound and caper, but only to the length of their tether, and none the less always follow in the steps of him who guides them; and as the falcon flies when under the restraint of a leash.

Think upon exile, tortures, wars, diseases, shipwrecks,[69] *so that you may be a novice in no ill-fortune.*[70] Of what avail to us is the special interest which makes us occupy our mind beforehand with all the disturbances of human nature, and prepare ourselves, with so much toil, for meeting just those which perchance will not touch us?—*to be likely to suffer is as saddening as to have suffered;*[71] not only the blow harasses us, but the wind and the noise;[72] or, like completely insane people,—for surely it is insanity,—to go just now to have yourself whipped, because it may happen that Fortune will cause you to be whipped some day; and to put on your furred gown on St. John's Day[73] because you will need it at Christmas? Make yourself familiar in thought,[74] they say, with all ills that can befall you, especially the most extreme ones; thereby test yourself; thereby steady yourself. On the contrary, the easiest and the most natural way

1432

would be to relieve even your mind of them. They will not come soon enough [it is said]; their real existence does not last long enough; the mind must extend and prolong them; and incorporate them in itself beforehand, and cherish them, as if they did not sufficiently weigh upon our senses. "They will weigh heavily enough when they come," says one of the masters, not of some mild sect, but of the sternest; "meanwhile befriend yourself, believe what you like best."[75] "How does it avail you to go collecting and anticipating your ill-fortune, and to lose the present by dread of the future, and to be miserable now because you may be so in time?"[76] These are his words. Learning truly does us a good office by instructing us very exactly regarding the dimensions of evils,—

Sharpening men's wits with cares;[77]

it would be a pity if any part of their magnitude should escape our perception and knowledge.

It is certain that, for the most part, preparation for death has given more pain than physical suffering has done. It was truly said of old, and by a very judicious author, *Fatigue affects the senses less than thought.*[78] The perception of immediate death inspires us sometimes of itself with a sudden resolution no longer to avoid a wholly inevitable thing. Many gladiators in former times, after they had fought in a cowardly fashion, were seen to accept death courageously, offering their throat to their adversary's blade and inviting the stroke. The distant vision of death to come needs a deliberate firmness and one difficult, consequently, to have in readiness.[79] If you know not how to die, be not concerned: Nature will instruct you on the spot, plainly and sufficiently; she will do this business for you accurately; do not give it your attention.

> In vain, mortals, do you seek to know the uncertain hour of your death, and the path by which it is to come.[80]

> It is less painful to undergo suddenly certain ruin than to endure fear for a long time.[81]

We disturb life by anxiety about death, and death by anxiety about life. The one sharply pains us, the other affrights us. It is not against death that we prepare—that is too instantaneous a thing: a quarter of an hour of enduring harmless suffering does not deserve special precepts; to tell the truth, we prepare against the preparations for death. Philosophy orders us to have death always before our eyes, to foresee it, and to reflect upon it beforehand; and then gives us rules and precautions to be provided with, that this foresight and this reflection may not pain us. Thus do physicians, who throw us into illnesses that they may have occasion to employ their drugs and their skill.

If we have not known how to live, it is unjust to teach us how to die and to shape the end unlike what has gone before;[82] if we have known how to live steadfastly and calmly, we shall know how to die in like manner. They may boast of it as much as they please,—*the whole life of philosophers is a contemplation of death*,[83]—but it is my opinion that it is in truth the limit, but not the aim,[84] of life; it is its end, its extreme point, but not its object; life should have its own plans, its own designs; its proper study is how to order and conduct and endure itself. Amongst several other mat-

1434

ters included in the general and principal chapter of knowing how to live is this item of knowing how to die, and it
would be one of the lightest, did not our fears give it weight.

The lessons of simplicity, judged by their utility and by
their natural truth, are hardly inferior to those which learning teaches us. Men differ in feeling and in strength; they
must be guided to what is good for them, according to their
natures, and by different roads.

> Wherever the tempest carries me, I approach as a
> guest.[85]

I never find amongst my neighbours a peasant cogitating
with what bearing and confidence he may pass that last
hour; Nature teaches him to think of death only when he is
dying. And then it is with better grace than Aristotle, upon
whom death presses with two-fold force, both by its own
weight and from so prolonged preconsideration; wherefore
it was Cæsar's opinion that the least preconsidered death
was the happiest and the least burdened.[86] *He grieves more
than is necessary who grieves before it is necessary.*[87] The
bitterness of these imaginings is born of our searching; we
are always thus impeding ourselves, desiring to outstrip and
domineer over our natural limitations.[88] It is only for the
learned when in full health to dine the worse for this habit,
and to scowl at the image of death; the man of the people
has need neither of remedy nor of consolation save when the
shock comes and the stroke falls, and he gives it no attention except at the time of suffering from it.

Is it not true that, as we say, the stupidity and lack of
apprehension of the common man gives him this patience
with present ills and this profound indifference to sinister

1435

future events? that his soul, because he is more gross and obtuse, is less easily penetrated and excited? For God's sake, if it be so, let us henceforth teach stupidity: the best fruit that learning promises us is this, to which stupidity so gently leads her disciples.

We shall not lack good teachers, interpreters of natural simplicity; Socrates will be one of them, for, as I remember, he spoke about it in this sense[89] to the judges who were deliberating concerning his life: "I fear, sirs, that, if I beg you not to put me to death, I may convict myself of the charge of my accusers, which is that I pretend to more understanding than others, as having some more hidden knowledge of the things which are above us and below us. I know that I have neither been familiar with Death nor known her, nor have I ever seen any one who has had experience of her nature to instruct me thereon. They who fear her assume that they know her; for myself, I know neither what she is, nor what takes place in the other world. Perchance death is an indifferent thing, perchance desirable. It is to be believed, however, that, if it be a transmigration from one place to another, there is some amelioration in going to live with so many deceased great men and in being exempt from having longer to do with iniquitous and corrupt judges. If it be an annihilation of our existence, it is still an amelioration to enter upon a long and peaceful night; we find nothing sweeter in life than a tranquil and profound repose and sleep, without dreams.

"I carefully avoid those things which I know to be evil—such things as injuring one's neighbours and disobeying a superior, whether it be God or man; those things as to which I know not whether they be good or evil, I can not fear. If

Of Physiognomy

I am going to die and leave you living, only the gods see whether with you or with me it will be better. Therefore, so far as concerns me, you will order it as it may please you. But, according to my habit of counselling things just and profitable, I rightly say that, regarding your conscience, you will do better to set me free, if you do not see more clearly in my cause than I do myself; and judging according to my past actions, both public and private, according to my intentions, and according to the benefit which so many of our citizens, young and old, derive every day from my conversation, and the fruit that you all gather from me, you can not duly acquit yourselves toward my deserts except by ordaining that, considering my poverty, I be supported at the Prytenæum at public expense, which I have often known you to grant to others with less reason.

"Do not take it for obstinacy or disdain that I do not, as the custom is, supplicate you and attempt to excite your commiseration. I have friends and kinsfolk, not, as Homer says,[90] being begotten of wood or stone, any more than other men who are able to appear before you in tears and mourning; and I have three weeping children with whom to move you to pity; but I should disgrace our city if, at my age and with such a reputation for wisdom that I am now under prosecution therefor, I were to demean myself to such abject conduct. What would be said of other Athenians? I have ever admonished those who heard my words not to redeem life by a dishonourable act; and in my country's wars, at Amphipolis, at Potidæa, Delos, and elsewhere that I have been, I have shewn by deed how far I was from securing safety by shame. Furthermore, I should interfere with your duty and engage you in unsuitable acts; for it is not for my prayers to persuade you, but for the pure and solid reasons of justice. You have sworn to the gods to decide questions according to law;[91] it would seem as if I desired to suspect and accuse you of not believing that there are any gods; and I should testify against myself that I do not believe in them as I ought, if I distrusted their guidance and refused to leave my cause entirely in their hands. I do wholly trust them, and I hold it for certain that they will decide in this matter as will be most fitting for you and for me; good men, whether living or dead, have no reason to fear the gods."

Is not this a solid and sound way of pleading, but at the same time, while simple and honourable, of inconceivable loftiness, frank and just beyond all example, and uttered in such need! Truly he was wise to prefer it to that which the great orator Lysias had written for him,[92] excellently composed in judicial style, but unworthy for so noble a criminal. Could a suppliant word have been heard from the mouth of Socrates? Could that proud virtue have stooped at the height of its display? And would his rich and powerful nature have entrusted his defence to art, and, in his greatest effort, have renounced truth and simplicity, the ornaments of his speech, to adorn it with the fard, figures, and feignings of a pre-learned oration? He did very wisely, and quite in accordance with his nature, in not corrupting an incorruptible tenor of life[93] and so sacred an image of human character, to prolong by a year his decrepitude and wrong the immortal memory of that glorious close of life. He owed his life not to himself, but as an example, to the world. Would it not have been a public calamity if he had ended it in worthless and obscure fashion? Assuredly his own careless and indif-

Of Physiognomy

ferent consideration of his death deserved that posterity should consider it all the more in his stead; this it has done; and there is naught in justice so just as what Fortune ordained for his commendation. For the Athenians held in such abomination those who had been the cause of his death that they shunned them like excommunicated persons; they regarded as polluted whatever they had touched; at the bath-houses no one bathed with them; no one saluted them or held converse with them; so that, at last, unable longer to endure this public hatred, they hanged themselves.[94]

Though it may be thought that, having so many other examples in the sayings of Socrates which I might choose to make use of for my purpose, I have made an ill choice of this speech, and it may be judged to be far above common conceptions, yet I have made choice of it intentionally; for I judge otherwise and I maintain that in range and in simplicity this is a speech that touches on conditions much further back and deeper down[95] than ordinary conceptions; it represents, in its simple[96] courage and its childlike security, pure and primitive natural impressions and ignorance. For it may be believed that we have by nature fear of pain, but not of death on its own account; it is a part of our existence no less essential than is living. For what purpose should Nature have engendered in us hatred and horror of it, since it is of the greatest service to her in maintaining the succession and vicissitude of her works; and in this universal community[97] it conduces more to birth and increase than to loss or destruction?

Thus is the whole of things renewed.[98]

Of Physiognomy

One soul destroyed gives birth to a thousand souls.[99]

The passing away of one life is the passing on to a thousand others. Nature has made self-care and self-preservation instinctive in beasts. They go so far as to be afraid of their own impairment, of hurting and wounding themselves, of our shackling them and beating them—incidents subject to their senses and experience; but that we should kill them, this they can not be afraid of; neither have they the faculty to conceive of death and to form a judgement about it. Yet it is also said that they are seen not only to suffer death cheerfully (most heroes neigh when dying, and swans sing), but, still more, to seek it in their need, as is indicated by many stories of elephants.[100]

Besides, is not the method which Socrates makes use of here equally admirable for simplicity and vehemence? Truly, it is much more easy to talk like Aristotle and to live like Cæsar than to talk and live like Socrates. There lies the highest degree of perfection and of difficulty: art can not reach it. Now, our faculties are not thus trained; we neither put them to the test nor are aware of them; we invest ourselves with those of other men and let our own lie idle; as some one might say of me, that I have here simply made a collection of unfamiliar flowers, having myself supplied nothing but the thread that binds them.

I have indeed so far yielded to public opinion as to wear borrowed embellishments; but I do not intend them to cover me and hide me; that is the opposite of my design, which purposes to display only what is mine and what is mine by nature; and had I trusted myself, I should at all hazards have said nothing but from myself.[101] I load myself with them[102] more and more every day, beyond what I

1440

proposed, and beyond the original form of my work, in accordance with the whim of the age and from indolence. If this misbecomes me, as I believe, no matter; it may be of use to somebody else. A man may quote Homer and Plato who never saw them; and I myself have taken passages elsewhere than at their source. I can presently borrow if I please, without trouble and without skill,—having a thousand volumes about me in this room where I am writing,— from a dozen such scrap-collectors[103] of whose books I seldom turn the leaves, the wherewithal to inlay this treatise on Physiognomy. To stuff myself with citations, I need only the prefatory epistle of a German; and it is thus we seek a pleasing fame with which to cheat the foolish world.

These confections of commonplace, by which so many men make the most of their studies, are of little value save on commonplace subjects, and serve to point out things to us, not to guide us—a ridiculous fruit of learning, which Socrates censures so amusingly in Euthydemus.[104] I have seen books made about things never either studied or understood by the author, he entrusting to divers learned friends the investigation of this and that matter for the compilation, contenting himself for his share with having formed the plan and having by his dexterity bound together this bundle of supplies unknown to him; the ink and paper, at all events, are his. This is to buy or borrow a book, not to make it; it is to shew, not that you can make a book, but —whereof they might be in doubt—that you can not make one.

A president[105] boasted in my presence of having heaped up two hundred and more extraneous passages in an official decree; by proclaiming this, he annulled the renown it had won him; pusillanimous and absurd boasting, to my mind, on such a subject and from such a person.[106] I do the contrary, and amongst so many borrowings am very glad to be able now and then to conceal one, disguising it and shaping it to a new use, at the risk of letting it be said that it is from my failure to understand its original use; I give it with my hand some special aim, so that it may be the less wholly out of place. These others put their thefts on exhibition and reckon them up; so they keep on better terms with the law than I do. We naturalists[107] deem that the honour of invention is of great, even of incomparable, preference to the honour of quotation. Like those who steal horses, I paint their manes and tails, and sometimes I put out an eye; if their first master used them at an ambling pace, I make them trot, and use them as beasts of burden if they had served for riding.[108]

Had I desired to speak in learned fashion, I should have spoken sooner; I should have written at a time nearer my studies,[109] when I had more wit and more memory; and I should have trusted more to the vigour of that time of life than to this, if I had been inclined to make it my business to write. And what if the gracious boon which Fortune through the intervention of this work has lately presented me[110] could have befallen me at such a season instead of this, when it is equally desirable to possess and soon to be lost? Two of my acquaintances, men great in this capability, have in my opinion lost by half from having refused to put themselves forward at forty years of age, and waited till they were sixty. Maturity has its failings as immaturity has, and worse; and old age is as disadvantageous in this kind of work as in any other. Whoever places his decrepitude under pressure does a foolish thing, if he hopes thereby to squeeze out any products which have not the appearance of coming from[111] one who is unfortunate, or who is a dreamer, or drowsy. Our minds become less fluid, more dense, as we grow old. I deliver my ignorance pompously and abundantly, my knowledge in meagre and sorry fashion—the one incidentally and accidentally, the other expressly and principally; and I treat intentionally of nothing but nothing, nor of any other knowledge than that of ignorance.[112] I have chosen the time when I have before me the whole of my life, which I have to depict; what remains of it has more relation to death; and of my death itself, should I find it a talkative one as some do, I should still freely inform the world as I go hence.

Socrates was a perfect exemplar of all great qualities; I am vexed that his exterior chanced to be so unhandsome[113] as they say it was, and so unsuited to the beauty of his soul, he who was so enamoured of, so infatuated with, beauty. Nature did him a wrong. There is nothing more probable than the conformity and connection of the body and the mind. *It matters greatly to the soul in what sort of body it is placed; for there are many things in the body which sharpen the mind, many which blunt it.*[114] This writer is speaking of an unnatural ugliness and deformity of various parts; but we give the name of ugliness also to a mischance of feature, observed at first sight [but of which the impression passes], which is generally in the face, and offends us by the complexion, by a blemish, by an ungraceful look, or for some cause, often inexplicable, in different parts which are nevertheless well proportioned and perfect. The ugliness that clothed a very beautiful soul in Etienne La Boëtie

was of this category. This superficial ugliness, which none
the less governs the whole body,[115] is less prejudicial to the
condition of the mind, and has little significance in the
judgement of men. The other, more substantial, which is
called, more appropriately, deformity, more frequently
harms the inner nature; not every shoe of well-polished
leather, but every well-shaped shoe shews the shape of the
foot inside. It is not to be believed that this discordance
occurs without some accident that has interrupted the common course of things;[116] as Socrates said of his ugliness that
it would justly indicate an equal measure thereof in his
soul, had he not reformed that by education.[117] But, in so
saying, I hold that he was jesting according to his custom,
and never did so excellent a soul fashion itself.

I can not say often enough how highly I esteem beauty,
a quality potent and advantageous; he [118] called it a brief
tyranny; and Plato, the special advantage given by Nature.[119] We have none which surpasses it in influence; it
holds the first rank in the intercourse of mankind; it presents itself full face, charms and engrosses our judgement
with great authority and marvellous impressiveness. Phryne
would have lost her cause in the hands of an excellent advocate, had she not, opening her robe, corrupted her judges
by the splendour of her beauty.[120] And I observe that Cyrus,
Alexander, and Cæsar, those three masters of the world,
did not forget it in doing their great deeds, nor did Scipio.

The same word in Greek[121] includes both beauty and
goodness, and the Holy Spirit often calls persons good when
it means that they are beautiful. I will readily uphold the
order of the blessings of life according to the verses found
in some old poet, which Plato called trivial:[122] health,

beauty, wealth. Aristotle says that the right to command belongs to the beautiful, and, when there are any whose beauty approaches that of the images of the gods, veneration is due equally to them.[123] To one who asked him why men consorted oftener and longer with beautiful persons, he replied: "That question should be asked only by a blind man."[124] Most philosophers, and the greatest, paid for their instruction, and acquired wisdom by the mediation and favour of their beauty. Not only in the men who serve me, but in animals also, I consider it as very near to goodness. Yet it seems to me that this form and fashion of feature, and the lineaments from which others infer certain internal dispositions and our future fortunes, are matters which do not fall directly and simply under the heading of beauty and ugliness; no more than all good odour and freshness of air promise health, or all heavy or ill-smelling air promises infection in time of pestilence.

They who charge ladies with belying their beauty by their morals do not always hit the mark; for, as in a face which may not be too well made there may dwell an expression of honesty and trustworthiness, so, on the contrary, I have sometimes read between two lovely eyes threatening signs of a malign and dangerous nature. There are propitious physiognomies; and in a crowd of victorious enemies you will choose on the instant, from among men you never saw before, one rather than another to whom to surrender and to entrust your life, and not specially from considerations of beauty. A man's appearance is a weak guaranty; however, it has some significance; and had I the scourging of them, the sinners who belie and betray the promises which Nature stamped on their brow would be the most roughly treated; I would punish most sternly malice under a kindly aspect. It would seem that there are lucky and unlucky faces; and I think that it requires some skill to distinguish good-humoured from silly ones, stern from harsh, malicious from sad, scornful from melancholy, and other such neighbouring qualities. There are types of beauty not only haughty but sour; there are others that are sweet and, more than that, insipid. As to prophesying therefrom their future chances, those are matters which I leave unsettled.

I have accepted, as I have elsewhere said, very simply and unquestioningly[125] for myself this ancient precept—that we must not fail to follow Nature, and that the sovereign rule is to conform ourselves to her. I have not, as Socrates did, reformed my natural dispositions by the strength of my reason, and I have not at all interfered artfully with my inclination. I let myself continue even as I came hither: I combat nothing; my two dominant parts live of their own accord in peace and agreement; but my nurse's milk, thanks be to God! was moderately healthful and nourishing.

Shall I say this in passing—that I find a certain sort of pedantic integrity,[126] which almost alone is practised amongst us, to be held in higher esteem than it deserves, it being a slave to rules and constrained by hope and fear. I delight in it when of a kind that laws and religions do not make, but perfect and confirm; that feels capable of maintaining itself without assistance, springing up and rooted in us from the seed of universal reason implanted in every not inhuman man. This reasoning power, which straightens Socrates from his vicious bent, makes him obedient to the men and the gods who rule in his city—fearless in death, not because his soul is immortal, but because he is mortal.

Of Physiognomy

It is a ruinous instruction for any government, and much more harmful than astute and wily, which persuades the people that religious belief alone, and without good conduct,[127] is sufficient to satisfy divine justice. We are accustomed to seeing an enormous distinction between devotion and conscience.

I have an aspect which, both from outward appearance and from expression, wins favour,[128]—

What did I say—"I have"? Nay, I *had*, Chremes![129]

Alas! you see only the bones of a wasted body![130]—

and which makes a contrary show to that of Socrates. It has often happened to me that, solely on the strength of my appearance and my manner, persons who had no acquaintance with me have greatly trusted me, whether about their own affairs or about mine; and I have derived from it in foreign countries singular and unusual favours. But the two experiences that follow are perhaps worth narrating specially.

A certain person planned to take my household and me by surprise. His scheme was to come alone to my gate and demand admittance somewhat urgently. I knew him by name and had had reason to trust him as my neighbour and as a sort of relation. I had the gates opened to him as I do for every one. He appeared greatly terrified, his horse out of breath, quite overwrought. He told me this fable: that half a league away he had met with an enemy of his,— whom also I knew, and I had heard of their quarrel,—that this enemy had chased him hotly,[131] and that, being taken by surprise, in disarray, and much weaker in numbers, he

had fled to me for safety; that he was in great anxiety about
his followers, who, he said, he supposed were dead or prisoners, having been encountered in disorder, and far separated from one another.[132] I tried in all innocence to comfort
and encourage him and refresh him. Soon after, behold four
or five of his soldiers presented themselves in like condition
and affright; and then others, and afterward again others,
well equipped and well armed, to the number of twenty-
five or thirty, pretending that their enemy was at their heels.

This mysterious proceeding began to arouse my suspicion. I was not unaware what time I was living in, how
greatly my house might be coveted, and I had in mind
several examples of others of my acquaintance to whom the
same sort of misadventure had happened. However, considering that there was no gain in having begun with kindness if I did not so continue to the end, and not being able
to get rid of them without a complete breach, I took the
most natural and simplest course, as I always do, bidding
them come in: Also, in truth, I am by nature little distrustful and suspicious; I readily incline toward admitting excuses and the mildest interpretation; I take men as they
commonly are, and do not believe in perverse and unnatural
inclinations unless I am compelled to do so by strong evidence, any more than I believe in monstrosities and miracles.
And, furthermore, I am one who readily entrusts himself
to Fortune and lets himself go headlong into her arms;
whereof up to this hour I have had more reason to commend
than to reprove myself; and I have found her wiser and more
friendly to my concerns than I myself am. There have been
some actions in my life the conduct of which may justly be
called difficult, or, if you will, prudent. Of these, supposing

Of Physiognomy

a third part to have been my own, certainly two thirds are richly hers. We err, I think, in that we do not trust heaven enough about ourselves, but claim more for our own management than belongs to us; consequently, our plans so often lead us astray. Heaven is jealous of the extent we give to what is due to human prudence, to the prejudice of its own due, and limits this all the more because we amplify it.

These soldiers remained mounted in my courtyard, the leader with me in my hall, who would not have his horse stabled, saying that he should depart immediately as soon as he had news of his men. He found himself master of his undertaking, and it remained only to put it into execution. Often since then he has said—for he did not shrink from telling the tale—that my demeanour and my open-heartedness had wrested his treachery from his hands. He remounted his horse; his men, keeping their eyes constantly fixed upon him to see what signal he would make to them, were much amazed to see him ride away and abandon his advantage.

Another time, relying upon I know not what truce which had been published in our armies, I set off on a journey through a peculiarly ticklish region. My departure was no sooner known[133] than, lo and behold! three or four parties of horse from different places set out to catch me: one of them met me at the third stage, where I was attacked by fifteen or twenty masked gentlemen [well mounted and well armed][134] followed by a swarm of mounted bowmen. There I was, a prisoner and surrendered, carried off into the depths of a neighbouring forest, my horse taken from me, I myself stripped, my chests ransacked, my strong-box seized, and horses and retinue distributed amongst new masters.

1449

Of Physiognomy

We remained a long time in that thicket, disputing about the amount of my ransom, which they set so high that it clearly appeared that I was little known to them. They entered upon a lively debate about my life. In truth, there were many circumstances that warned me of the danger I was in.

> Then was there need of courage, Æneas; then was there need of a stout heart.[135]

I steadily maintained, on the strength of the truce, that I would yield them only the value of their plunderings, which was not to be despised, without promising other ransom. After two or three hours of this, they mounted me on a horse which had no power to run away, and committed me to the special charge of fifteen or twenty musketeers, and distributed my men among others, having ordered that they should lead us away as prisoners by different routes. When I had already gone two or three musket-shots from that place,—

> Having besought in prayer now Pollux and now Castor,[136]—

behold, a sudden and very unexpected change came over them. I saw the leader approach me with softer words, giving himself the trouble to search through the troop for my scattered possessions, and requiring the principal articles, so far as he could recover them, even to my strong-box, to be restored to me. The best present they made was, finally, my liberty; the rest was of little concern to me in those days.

Truly, I do not even know the true cause of so sudden a change, and of this reconsideration without any apparent

1450

reason, and of so miraculous a repentance, in such times, in a premeditated and considered enterprise, and one which through custom had become lawful—for I frankly avowed to them at the outset what party I belonged to and whither I was going. The chief man amongst them, who unmasked and told me his name (I should like to test, in my turn, what would be his conduct in such a mischance),[137] then said to me repeatedly that I owed this deliverance to my bearing, to the frankness and firmness of my language, which made me undeserving of such a misadventure; and asked security from me in a like case. It is possible that the divine goodness chose to use this whimsical means[138] for my preservation; it saved me again the next day from other worse snares of which these very persons had warned me. The last of these two gentlemen is still living to tell the tale; the first was killed not long ago.

If my aspect did not answer for me, if people did not read in my eyes and in my voice the simplicity of my intention, I should not have lived so long without quarrels and without giving offence, considering my indiscreet freedom of saying at random whatever comes into my head and of judging things rashly. This habit may justly appear uncivil and unsuited to our custom; but I have never met with any one who deemed it insulting and malicious, or who was stung by my freedom if he had it from my own mouth; reported words have a different sound and a different sense. Besides, I hate no man, and I am so loath to give offence that I can not do it even in the interest of reason itself; and when there has been occasion for me to sentence criminals, I have preferred to fail in justice; *so that I am desirous that sins should not be committed, rather than brave enough to punish them when committed.*[139] Some one, it is said, reproached Aristotle for having been too merciful to a wicked man. "I have indeed," he said, "been merciful to this man, but not to his wickedness."[140] Judgements are ordinarily exasperated to severity by horror of the crime. That very emotion chills my judgement; horror of the murder that has taken place makes me fear to cause a second; and the ugliness of the past cruelty makes me abhor any imitation of it. To me, who am a man of no importance,[141] may be applied what was said of Charillus, King of Sparta: "He can not be good, since he is not bad to the wicked."[142] Or thus, for Plutarch presents him in these two ways, as he does a thousand other matters, differently and contrariwise: "He must indeed be a good man, since he is good even to the wicked."[143] As, in lawful actions, it annoys me to busy myself about them when they concern persons to whom they are displeasing, so, to speak the truth, in unlawful ones I am not conscientious enough about them when they concern persons who welcome them.

Chapter XIII

OF EXPERIENCE

THERE is no desire more natural than the desire for knowledge. We make trial of all means that can lead us to it. When reasoning fails us, we then make use of experience,—

> Through various practices experience has brought forth art, example pointing the way,[1]—

which is a much feebler and lower means; but truth is so great a thing that we must not disdain any medium that leads us to it. Reason has so many shapes that we know not which to take hold of; experience has no less. The conclusions that we seek to draw from the comparison of events are not reliable, inasmuch as events are always dissimilar. There is no quality so universal in their appearance as diversity and variety. The Greeks and the Latins and ourselves all make use of the similitude of the egg as the most perfect example of the kind; none the less, there have been men, notably one at Delphi,[2] who detected marks of difference in eggs so that he never took one for another, and, having many hens, could tell which had laid a certain egg. Dissimilarity enters of necessity into our works; no skill

1453

can attain similitude. Neither Perrozet, nor any other, can so carefully polish and whiten the backs of his cards that some gamblers do not distinguish them when merely passing through the hands of another. Resemblance does not make things so much the same as dissemblance makes them different.[3] Nature has constrained herself to make nothing other than any thing else.[4]

Yet little to my liking is that man's opinion who thought by the multitude of laws to curb the authority of judges by marking the limits of their actions;[5] he did not perceive that there is as much freedom and scope in the interpretation of laws as in making them. And they make fools of themselves who think to lessen our discussions and to check them by referring us to the express words of the Bible; because our minds find no less spacious a field in criticising the meaning of others than in putting forward their own; and as if there were less animosity and bitterness in glossing than in inventing. We see how mistaken he was, for we have in France more laws than all the rest of the world put together, and more than would be needed to govern all the world of Epicurus; *as we once suffered from crimes, so we now suffer from laws;*[6] and yet we have left so much for our judges to consider and decide, that there was never freedom of action so powerful and so uncontrolled. What have our lawmakers gained by selecting a hundred thousand kinds of special acts and attaching to them a hundred thousand laws? Such a number is in no proportion to the infinite diversity of human actions. The multiplication of our contrivings will never equal the variation of examples. Add to these a hundred times as many, still it will never come to pass that amongst future events any one in all that vast num-

Of Experience

ber of selected and recorded events will fall in with one to which it can be joined and paired so exactly that there will not remain some circumstance and diversity which will require a different consideration of judgement. There is little relation between our actions, which are in perpetual mutation, and fixed and unchanging laws. The most desirable, the most simple and general, are the most rare; and I believe that it would be better to have none at all than to have them in such numbers as we have.

Nature gives us always happier laws than those we give ourselves; witness the description by the poets of the Golden Age and the condition in which we see those nations to be living which have no other laws. Observe those who employ as their only judges in their controversies the first passers-by travelling amongst their mountains;[7] and others, on market-day, choose one of themselves, who decides on the spot all their lawsuits. What risk would there be in having the wisest men thus settle our disputes according to circumstances and at sight, without being bound by precedents and consequences? For every foot its own shoe. King Ferdinand, when sending out colonies to the Indies, wisely provided that they should take thither no lawyers,[8] for fear that lawsuits might multiply in that new world, jurisprudence being a science productive, by its nature, of altercation and division.[9] He judged with Plato that lawyers and doctors are a bad provision for a country.[10]

How is it that our ordinary language, so simple for every other purpose, becomes obscure and unintelligible in a contract and a testament; and that a man who expresses himself very clearly in whatever else he says and writes can find no way of declaring his meaning in these which does not

Of Experience

fall into uncertainty and contradiction, if it be not that the chief men of this art, applying themselves with peculiar care to selecting solemn words and forming sentences arranged with art, have so weighed every syllable and so minutely examined every sort of combination, that they are seen to be all bewildered and confused by the infinite number of figures and very minute divisions which no longer can be brought under any rule and prescribed order or to any certain understanding. *Whatsoever is divided until it is only dust becomes confused.*[11] Who has not seen children trying to separate a mass of quicksilver into a number of parts? The more they press it and push it and strive to control it, the more they fret the liberty of that generous metal; it eludes their skill and divides and scatters itself indefinitely. It is the same in this case; for by the sub-division of these subtleties we are taught to increase our doubts; we are put in the way of magnifying and diversifying difficulties; they are amplified and dispersed. By the sowing of questions and the reshaping of them, the world is made to fructify and abound in uncertainty and in dispute; as the soil becomes more fertile, the more it is broken up and deeply dug. *Learning creates difficulties.*[12] We doubted with Ulpian and we still doubt with Bartolus and Baldus.[13] There is need of effacing the traces of this infinite diversity of opinions, far from decking ourselves out in them and passing them on to posterity.

I know not what to say to it, but it is evident from experience that so many interpretations dissipate the truth and destroy it. Aristotle wrote to be understood; if he failed, still less will a less able man, and an outsider, succeed than he who sets forth his own conception. We work

1456

Of Experience

over some matter and increase its volume by diluting it; of one subject we make a thousand, and, multiplying and subdividing, we fall into the infinity of atoms of Epicurus. Never did two men judge alike of the same thing, and it is impossible to find two opinions exactly similar, not only in different men but in the same man at different times. I often find grounds for doubt in passages which the commentary has not deigned to touch upon. I stumble more easily in a level country, like certain horses I know which trip more frequently on a smooth road.

Who would not say that commentaries increase doubts and ignorance, since there is to be found no book, human or divine, with which the world concerns itself, of which the interpretation does away with the difficulty? The hundredth commentary hands it over to the following one, even more full of thorns and rough places than the first had found it. When is it ever agreed amongst us that "this book contains enough in itself; there is now nothing more to be said"? This is most manifest in chicanery; we give lawful authority to innumerable doctors of law, innumerable decrees, and as many interpretations. Nevertheless, do we find any end to the needs of interpreting? Is there seen herein any progress and advance toward tranquillity? Do we need fewer advocates and judges than when the mass of law was still in its first infancy? On the contrary, we obscure and bury the understanding of it. We can no longer get at it except by permission of many fences and barriers. Men do not recognise the natural disease of their mind: it does nothing but ferret and search, and is incessantly beating the bush and idly obstructing and impeding itself by its work, and stifles itself therein like our silk-worms; *there*

Of Experience

is a mouse in the pitch.[14] It thinks that it beholds far off I know not what glimmer of light and fancied truth; but whilst the mind hastens thither, so many difficulties block its path with obstacles and new quests, that they turn it from the path and bewilder it; not unlike what happened to Æsop's dogs, which, discovering what looked like a dead body floating in the sea, not being able to approach it, undertook to drink up all the water in order to make a dry passage to it, and so choked themselves.[15] This is in accord with what one Crates said of the writings of Heraclitus, that they need for a reader a good swimmer who would not be swallowed up by the depth of their teaching.[16]

It is only personal weakness that makes us content with what others, or we ourselves, have found in this chase after knowledge; a man of more ability will not be content with it. There is always a place for one who follows us, yes, and for following ourselves, and a different road to take. There is no end to our investigation; our end is in the other world. It is a sign of diminished power when the mind is content —or a sign of weariness. No generous spirit stands still within itself; it always reaches forward and goes beyond its strength; it has sallies not equalled by its deeds; if it does not advance and press on, if it does not take its stand and give blows and dash hither and yon,[17] it is but half alive. Its pursuits are without limit and without method; its aliment is wonder, search, and ambiguity; which Apollo[18] sufficiently made evident, speaking always to us with double meanings, obscurely and indirectly, not feasting us, but cheating and occupying us. It has an irregular, perpetual movement, without object. Its conceptions incite and follow and reproduce one another.

1458

Of Experience

So in a running stream one wave we see
After another roll incessantly.
And as they glide, each will successively
Pursue the other, each the other fly:
By this wave that is e'er pushed on, and this
By that continually preceded is:
The water still does into water go,
Still the same brook, but different waters flow.

There is more ado with interpreting interpretations than
with interpreting the things themselves, and more books
about books than about any other subject; we do nothing
but comment on each other. Every thing swarms with commentaries; of authors there is a great dearth. Is not the chief
and most famous learning of our times learning to understand the learned? Is it not the common and final object of
all studies? Our opinions are grafted one on another; the
first serves as a stalk for the second, the second for the third;
in like manner we clamber up from step to step, and it
therefore happens that the one who has mounted highest has
often more honour than desert; for, mounted on the shoulders of the penultimate, he is, after all, only the least little
bit higher.

How often, and perchance foolishly, have I enlarged my
book to speak of itself! Foolishly, if it were only for this
reason, that it befits me to remember what I say of others
who do likewise: "That those so frequent glances at their
works testify to a heart trembling with love; and that the
even contemptuous rudeness with which they batter them
is but the pretty way and affection of maternal regard," as
Aristotle points out, in whose eyes to overvalue and to un-

Of Experience

dervalue oneself often arise from one and the same quality of arrogance.[19] As for my excuse, it is this: that I should be allowed more liberty than others in this matter, inasmuch as of set purpose I write of myself and of my writings, as of my other actions; that my theme turns upon itself; I know not whether this will be accepted.

In Germany I saw that Luther left behind him as many schisms and dissensions—yes, more—about the uncertainty of his opinions, as he himself raised about the Holy Scripture. Our discussion is verbal; I ask what Nature means, what Pleasure, Circle, and *Substitution*.[20] The question is one of words and is paid back in like manner. A stone is a body; but he who should urge, "And body, what is that?" — "Substance." — "And substance, what?" — and so on, would at last drive the respondent to the end of his dictionary. One word is exchanged for another word, often less understood; I know better what Man is than what Animal is, or Mortal, or Reasonable. To satisfy one doubt, they give me three; it is the head of Hydra. Socrates asked Memnon[21] what virtue was. "There is," said Memnon, "the virtue of man and of woman, of a magistrate and of a private person, of a child and of an old man." "This is excellent!" cried Socrates; "we were in search of one virtue and you bring us a swarm of them." We impart one question, we are given in return a hive full. As no event and no bodily form wholly resembles another, so none is wholly different from another. A happy mingling on the part of nature! If our faces were not similar, we could not distinguish man from beast; if they were not dissimilar, we could not distinguish man from man.[22] All things are connected by some similitude; every example halts, and the relation apparent from experience is always feeble and imperfect; we have to add comparison to it by some tie. Thus it is that the laws do their work and adapt themselves to each one of our affairs by some wire-drawn, forced, and roundabout interpretation.

Since ethical laws, which look to the individual duty of each of us separately, are so difficult to frame as we see that they are, it is no wonder if those which control so many individuals are even more so. Consider the form of this justice[23] which rules us: it is a very witness to human imbecility, so much contradiction and error is there in it. What we find to be lenity and severity in justice—and we find so much of both that I know not whether what lies between is as often found therein—are unhealthy and unjust features of the real body and substance of justice. Some peasants come to me in haste, to inform me that they have just left, in a forest belonging to me, a man with countless wounds, who is still breathing, and who begged them, for pity's sake, to give him water and to help him rise. They say they dared not go near him, but ran away, for fear the officers of justice would catch them, and, as happens to those found near a murdered man, they would be called in question about this mishap, to their total ruin, as they had neither the ability nor the money to defend their innocence. What should I say to them? It is certain that that humane service would have brought them into trouble.

How many innocent people have we discovered who have been punished, I will say without fault on the part of the judges, and how many have there been whom we have not discovered? This has happened in my day: certain men were condemned to death for homicide, the sentence being agreed upon and determined, although not actually pronounced. At

Of Experience

this juncture, the judges were advised, by the officials of a subordinate court in the neighbourhood, that they held in custody prisoners who had openly confessed this homicide and cast unquestionable light on the whole business. None the less, they deliberated whether they should suspend and postpone the execution of the sentence passed upon those first accused; they discussed the unusualness of the case and its consequences in the way of hindering judgements; that, the condemnation being passed according to law, the judges had no power to revoke it. In short, the poor devils were sacrificed to the formulas of justice. Philip,[24] or some other, dealt with a similar dilemma in this wise: by a considered judgement he had sentenced one man to pay heavy damages to another. The truth coming to light some time after, he found that he had decided unjustly. On one side was the legitimate power of the facts of the case, on the other side the legitimate power of judicial forms;[25] he to some degree satisfied both, by letting the sentence stand and recompensing out of his own purse the loss of the condemned party. But it was with a reparable accident that he had to deal. My men were irreparably hanged. How many condemnations I have seen more criminal than the crime!

All this brings to my mind these ancient opinions: that he must needs do wrong in details, who desires to do right in sum and substance, and injustice in small things who desires to succeed in doing justice in great things;[26] that human justice is formed on the same model as the art of healing, according to which whatever is useful is also just and honourable;[27] and what was maintained by the Stoics, that Nature herself proceeds in opposition to justice in most of her works; and what the Cyrenaics maintained, that there is nothing inherently lawful,[28] that customs and laws constitute justice; and the Theodorians, who consider theft, sacrilege, every kind of licentiousness, lawful for the sage, if he knows it to be profitable to him.[29]

There is no remedy: I am in this like Alcibiades, that I will never appear personally, if I can avoid it, before a man who can decide as to my face,[30] when my honour and my life may depend more on the skill and care of my attorney than on my innocence. I would trust myself to a form of justice that would recognise my well-doing as well as my wrong-doing, when I should have as much to hope as to fear. Indemnity is not sufficient recompense for a man who does better than not doing amiss. Our justice offers us but one of its hands, and that the left; let him be who he may, he comes off with loss.

In the kingdom of China, whose government and whose arts, without intercourse with and knowledge of ours, surpass ours in many kinds of excellence, and whose history teaches me how much more spacious and various the world is than either the ancients or we ourselves discover, the officials deputed by the prince to inspect the condition of his provinces, whilst they punish those who are guilty of malversation in their functions, also remunerate with simple liberality those who have conducted themselves therein better than is ordinary and beyond the necessity of their duty; those under examination present themselves, not only to be guaranteed from loss, but to gain something; not simply to be paid, but to receive gifts.[31]

No judge has yet, thanks be to God! spoken as a judge to me in any cause whatsoever, whether my own or another's, criminal or civil; nor has any prison received me, even as a visitor. My imagination makes the sight of one disagreeable to me, even from outside. I am so infatuated with liberty that, were I forbidden access to some corner of the Indies, I should in consequence live less at my ease; and so long as I can find open land and air elsewhere, I will never cower in a place where I must be hidden. Good God! how ill could I endure the condition in which I see so many people—fettered to one part of this realm, deprived of the right to enter the chief cities and of access to the courts, and of the use of the public roads, for having quarrelled with our laws! If those under which I live should even shake their finger at me by way of menace, I should instantly go elsewhere, no matter where, to seek others. All my small prudence in these civil wars in which we are engaged is employed to the end that they shall not interfere with my liberty to go and come.

Now the laws maintain their credit, not because they are just, but because they are laws: this is the mystical basis of their authority; they have no other, and this serves them well. They are often made by fools;[32] more often by men who, from hatred for equality, lack a sense of equity; but always by men, fruitless and vacillating fabricators. There is nothing so awkwardly and abundantly faulty as the laws, or so commonly. Whosoever obeys them because they are just does not obey them for what he justly should. Our own French laws to some degree lend a helping hand, by their irregularity and lack of order, to the confusion and corruption which are seen in their administration and execution. What is commanded is so perplexing and unsettled that there is some excuse both for disobedience and for blunders of interpretation, of administration, and of observance.

Of Experience

Whatever then may be the fruits we may gain from experience, that which we derive from outside examples will hardly be of much service for our education, if we profit so little by that which comes to ourselves, which is more familiar to us, and is surely sufficient to instruct us in what we need.

I study myself more than any other subject; this is my metaphysic, this is my physic.[33]

> By what art God rules the mansion of the universe;
> whence comes the rising moon, and whither it sets, and
> whence each month, with horns joined, returns to its
> full; where the winds overwhelm the sea; what regions
> Eurus seizes with his blast, and why water always turns
> into clouds; and whether a day will come which will
> overthrow the towers of the universe . . . seek, you
> whom the toil of the universe disturbs.[34]

In this universe,[35] I allow myself to be led ignorantly and carelessly by the general law of the world; I shall understand it well enough when I feel it; my learning can not make any alteration in its course; it will not change itself for me; that is folly to hope for; and it is greater folly to be thereby disturbed, since it is necessarily uniform, manifest, and common to all. The goodness and competence of him who governs us discharges us wholly and entirely from concern about government; philosophic investigations and reflections serve only as food for our curiosity. The philosophers, with a great appearance of reason,[36] refer us to the rules of Nature; but those have nothing to do with such sublime knowledge; these thinkers falsify them and present us with Nature's face printed too high in colour and too artificialised,[37] whence arise many different portraitures of an unchanging subject.

Of Experience

As she has furnished us with feet for walking, so has she with wisdom to guide us through life; a wisdom not so subtle, sturdy, and ostentatious as that which they devise, but suitable for us, easy, quiet, and salutary, and which does very well what the other talks of, for him who has the good-fortune to know how to use it simply and properly, that is to say, naturally. To entrust oneself most entirely to Nature is to entrust oneself to her most wisely. Oh, how pleasant and soft a pillow is ignorance and incuriosity, whereon to rest a well-formed head!

I should prefer to understand myself well by study of myself rather than of Plato.[38] From my own experience I find enough to make me wise were I a good scholar. He who brings to memory the violence of his past anger, and how far that excitement carried him, sees the ugliness of that passion more plainly than Aristotle, and conceives a juster hatred of it. He who calls to mind the ills that he has incurred and those that have threatened him, and the trivial occasions that have moved him from one state to another, thereby prepares himself for future changes and for the examination of his condition. Cæsar's life furnishes no clearer example for us than our own; both as emperor and as a man of the people,[39] his is always a life that all human chances affect. Let us but listen to it: we say to ourselves every thing of which we have chief need. Is not the man who remembers having been very many times mistaken in his judgement a fool not to become forever after distrustful of it? When I find myself convicted by another's argument of holding a false opinion, I do not so much learn from what he says to me that is new, and about my ignorance in that special matter,—that would be little gain,—as I learn in general my weakness and the treachery of my understanding, whence I derive the reformation of the whole mass. In all my other errors I do likewise, and am conscious of great benefit to my life from this rule. I do not consider the species and the individual instance as a stone over which I have stumbled. I learn to suspect my steps, and trust to amend my manner of walking. To learn that you have said or done a foolish thing is to learn only that; you must learn that you are nothing but a fool—knowledge much more ample and more important.

The mistakes my memory has so often made, even when most certain of itself, are not idly wasted; in vain does it now swear to me and assure me—I shake my ears; the first opposition to its testimony throws me into suspense, and I should not dare to trust it about any thing important, or warrant it about the doings of another; and were it not that [I see nothing but lying and that][40] what I do from lack of memory others do even oftener from lack of good faith, I should always, in matters of fact, take the truth from another's mouth rather than from my own. If every one should watch closely the mental effects and the circumstances of the passions which lord over him, as I have done those of the one to which I am subject, he would see them coming and would abate their impetuosity and their force a little; they do not always seize us by the collar suddenly: there are threats, and degrees:

> As when the waves begin to whiten beneath the wind's first breath, and the sea rises little by little and lifts its surges higher, and then from the lowest depths rises to the stars.[41]

In me, judgement occupies a magisterial seat; at least it

Of Experience

carefully endeavours to do so; it allows natural inclinations to take their course, both of hate and of friendship, yes, and that which I feel for myself, without being itself thereby changed and corrupted. If it can not reform the other parts to its mind, at least it does not allow itself to be deformed by them: it plays its game by itself.

The admonition to every man to know himself must have important results, since the god of knowledge and light[42] had it placed on the front of his temple as comprising all that he could counsel us. Plato likewise says that wisdom is naught else but the following out of that injunction,[43] and Socrates, in Xenophon, confirms it in detail.[44] The difficulties and obscurities in every branch of learning are perceived only by those who have entered therein; for it indeed requires some degree of intelligence to be able to notice that one does not know; and we must attempt to push open a door, to learn that it is closed to us. From this is derived this platonic paradox: that neither those who have knowledge need to seek information, inasmuch as they have knowledge; nor those who have not knowledge, inasmuch as, in order to seek information, one must know what one seeks information about.[45] And so, in the matter of knowing oneself, the fact that every one is seen to be so decided and satisfied about himself, and that every one thinks that he is sufficiently enlightened about himself, is a proof that no man is in the least enlightened about himself, as Socrates teaches Euthydemus.[46]

I, who practise no other profession, find in myself a depth and variety so infinite that the fruit of my learning only makes me feel how much I still have to learn. I owe to my weakness, so often acknowledged, my tendency to modera-

1468

Of Experience

tion, my obedience to beliefs prescribed to me, my constant coldness with regard to opinions, and my avoidance of extremes,[47] and my hatred of that troublesome and quarrelsome arrogance which believes wholly in itself and trusts in itself, the capital enemy of order and of truth. Do but hear them lord it: the first foolish things that they put forward they utter in the manner in which religion and laws are established. *Nothing is more shameful than that assertion and acquiescence should precede knowledge and comprehension.*[48] Aristarchus said that in ancient times there were scarcely seven wise men in the world, and that in his day scarcely seven ignorant ones were to be found.[49] Have we not more reason than he to say this in our time? Assertion and obstinate persistence in assertion are common signs of stupidity and ignorance. Let a man tumble on his nose a hundred times a day: he will be seen on his high horse, as determined and headstrong as before; you would say that there has been infused into him meanwhile some new spirit and force of understanding, and that it has been with him as of old with that son of the earth[50] who recovered his vigour and was strengthened by his fall;

> Whose weakened limbs, when they have touched his mother, are strong with renewed vigour.[51]

Does not this stubborn blockhead think to take on a new wit when he takes up a new controversy? It is from my knowledge of myself that I cast reproach on human ignorance, which is, in my opinion, the most unfailing part of the school of the world. Those who will not infer it in themselves from so vain an example as mine or as their own, let them, present my ideas in general terms and gropingly—as

Of Experience

the philosopher Antisthenes said to his disciples: "Let us go, you and me, and hearken to Socrates; there I shall be a learner with you"; and, maintaining thereby that dogma of the Stoic sect, that virtue was enough to make a life fully happy and in need of nothing else, he added, "Save of the force of Socrates."[53]

The prolonged attention that I give to considering myself trains me to judge passably of others also; and there are few things of which I speak more happily and more excusably. It happens to me often to see and distinguish the conditions of my friends more accurately than they themselves do. I have astonished a man by the pertinence of my description and have warned him against himself. Having accustomed myself from my youth to behold my life exhibited in the lives of others, I have acquired a thoughtful nature in this; and, when I give my mind to it, I allow few things about me which may serve this purpose to escape my notice: man's demeanour, humours, talk. I study every thing—what I should avoid, what I should imitate. Thus I discover in my friends, by their outward manifestations, their inward inclinations, not so as to arrange this infinite variety of actions, so diverse and unconnected, under certain kinds and heads, but so as clearly to distribute my apportionings and divisions into recognised classes and compartments;

> But it is impossible to count the number of their species, and to tell their names.[54]

Men of learning utter and indicate their ideas more specifically and in detail. I, who see in these matters only so much as custom, without order, acquaints me with about them, present my ideas in general terms and gropingly—as in this place. I pronounce my judgement in desultory phrases; it is something that can not be said all at once and in its entirety. Connection and conformity are not found in such souls as ours, mean and commonplace. Wisdom is a solid and entire structure, of which every part has its station and bears its mark. *Only wisdom is wholly complete in itself.*[55] I leave it to artists—and I know not whether they will succeed in a matter so mixed up, so minute and fortuitous—to marshal in companies this infinite diversity of visages and to stay our mutability and bring order into it. Not only do I find it difficult to connect our actions one with another, but, each by itself, I find it difficult properly to designate it by some principal quality, so ambiguous and varicoloured are they in different lights. What is noted as unusual in Perseus, the King of Macedonia, that his intelligence, limiting itself to no one condition, wandering through all kinds of life, exhibiting such flighty and erratic habits that neither by himself nor by any other man whatsoever was he to be known,[56] seems to me to be true of very nearly all men. And, beyond reach of all, I have known another of the same type to whom I think that this description could be more fitly applied: no medium position, but forever throwing himself from one to the other extreme from unconjecturable causes; following no course without a cross-way, and wonderful contrariety; no simple force; so that the most probable conception that can be formed any day about him is that he was aiming and studying to make himself known by being unknowable.

We need very good ears to hear ourselves judged of freely; and since there are few who can stand it without being stung, they who venture to undertake it with us shew a peculiar effect of friendship for us; for it is to love soundly to undertake to wound and offend in order to benefit. I find it difficult to pass judgement on him in whom the bad qualities exceed the good ones. Plato enjoins three qualities for him who desires to examine the soul of another: knowledge, good-will, boldness.[57]

I have sometimes been asked what service I should have considered myself fit for if any one had thought to make use of me while I was of the suitable age,—

> Whilst better blood gave me strength, and old age
> had not yet sprinkled my temples with grey.[58]

"For no service," I replied; and I freely forgive myself for not being able to do any thing which enslaves me to another. But I would have told my master the truth about himself, and would have criticised his morals, had he so wished; not as a whole, by scholastic teachings, which I do not at all know and from which I do not see that there springs any genuine reformation in those who do know them; but by watching his character step by step, at every opportunity, and judging of it at sight, simply and naturally, part by part; shewing him what he is in common opinion, setting myself in opposition to his flatteries. There is no one of us who would not be of less worth than kings, were he thus constantly corrupted, as they are, by this rabble. What! even Alexander, so great both as king and as philosopher, could not protect himself from them! I should have had enough fidelity and judgement and frankness for that. It would be a nameless office—otherwise it would fail of its effect and its seemliness; and it is a task which can not be played indifferently by all men; for even truth itself is not privileged to be employed at all times and in all ways; its use, wholly noble as it is, has its bounds and limits. It often happens, as the world is, that we utter it in the ear of a prince, not only fruitlessly, but harmfully, and even unjustly; and I can not be made to believe that a godly admonition may not be badly applied, and that the importance of the substance should not often yield to the importance of the form.

I would choose for this business a man satisfied with his station,—

Who is willing to be what he is, and prefers nothing else,[59]—

and of medium station by birth; inasmuch as, on the one hand, he would not be afraid to touch his master's heart to the quick, dreading to lose the continuance of his advancement; and on the other hand, being of medium condition of life, he would have more easy intercourse with all sorts of people. I should wish this position given to one man only; for to scatter the privilege of such freedom and intimacy among many would engender a harmful lack of reverence; yes, and from that one man I should exact, above all else, the fidelity of silence.

A king is not to be believed when, for glory's sake, he boasts of his firmness in meeting the attack of his enemy, if, for his benefit and amendment, he can not suffer the freedom of a friend's words, which have no other purpose than to open his ears, the rest of their effect being in his own hands. Now there is no condition of men who have as great need as these of true and free admonitions. They lead a public life and have to conform to the ideas of so many on-lookers that, as it is the custom to let them hear nothing to divert them from their path, they become unconsciously entangled in the hatred and detestation of their peoples, often from causes which they would have been able to avoid, even with no prejudice to their pleasures, if they had been warned and set right in time. Commonly their favourites consider themselves rather than their masters; and it is well for them that they do, inasmuch as, in truth, most offices of true friendship are, with regard to the sovereign, difficult and hazardous to attempt; so that there is need, not only of much affection and of frankness, but also of courage.[60]

In fine, all this medley which I scribble here is but a record of the essays of my life, which, for inward health, is a good enough example for instruction taken hindside foremost.[61] But as for bodily health, no one can furnish more useful experience than I, who present it in its purity, in no wise corrupted or altered by art and by theory.[62] Experience is rightly on its own dung-hill as regards medicine, about which reason leaves the whole field open to it. Tiberius said that whosoever had lived twenty years should answer to himself as to what things were harmful or salutary for him, and should guide himself without medicine.[63] And he might have learned this from Socrates, who, carefully enjoining upon his disciples the study of their health as a very important study, added that it was easy for a man of intelligence, taking care about exercise and eating and drinking, to discern better than any physician what was good or bad for him.[64] Indeed, medicine professes always to take experience as a test of its working; so that Plato had reason for saying that, to be truly a physician, it was requisite that he who undertook this office should have had all the maladies he proposed to cure, and should have passed through all the chances and conditions which he must judge.[65] It is well that they should themselves have the pox if they would know how to treat it. Truly I would trust myself to such a one: for the others treat us as he does who, seated at his table, paints the sea, the reefs, and the harbours, and there, in all security, manœuvres the model of a ship; let him face the real thing, he knows not which way to turn. They describe our ills as a town crier does a lost horse or dog: of such a colour, such a size, and such ears; but put it before him, and he does not know it.

For God's sake, let medicine one day give me some good and perceptible assistance; see how sincerely I will cry out,

As last I salute a science that gives results![66]

The arts which promise to keep the body in health and the soul in health promise us much; but withal there are none which keep their promises less. And in our day those amongst us who profess these arts shew less results thereof than any other men. We may say of them, at most, that they sell medicinal drugs; but that they are physicians, that we can not say [when we look at them and those who are governed by them.][67] I have lived long enough to think well of the mode of life which has carried me so far; for any one who would like to taste it, I have made trial of it; I am his taster.[68] Here are a few particulars, as memory may supply me with them. I have no habits which have not varied according to circumstances, but I record those which I have seen most frequently in operation, which have had most possession of me to the present time.

My manner of life is the same in sickness as in health: the same bed, the same hours, the same food, and the same drinks are of service to me. I add nothing at all save moderation as to the more or less, according to my strength and my appetite. Health for me means maintaining my wonted condition not turned from its course. I see that sickness makes me leave it in one direction; if I put trust in physicians, they will turn me out of it in another; and by fate and by art, there I am out of the right road. I believe nothing more confidently than this: that I can not be harmed by the use of things to which I have been so long accustomed. It is habit that gives such shape to our lives as it pleases; it is all in all there; it is the potion of Circe, which changes our nature as it deems best. How many nations, and our near neighbours, think absurd any fear of evening dampness which is so manifestly harmful to us! And our watermen and our peasants laugh at it. You make a German ill if you give him a mattress to sleep on, as an Italian with a feather-bed, and a Frenchman without bed-curtains and a fire. The stomach of a Spaniard can not bear eating what we eat, nor ours drinking what the Swiss drink. A German at Augusta[69] amused me by attacking the discomforts of our fireplaces on the same ground which we commonly make use of in condemnation of their stoves; for, in truth, that unaired heat and the smell of the over-heated material of which they are made gives a headache to most people who are not accustomed to it— not to me. But after all, this heat, being even and constant and wide-spreading, without flame, without smoke, without the wind that because of the openness of our chimneys blows down on us, can in many other respects be favourably compared with ours. Why do we not copy the Roman architecture? For it is said that in ancient time fires were not made in the houses but outside them and below them; whence the heat was carried through the whole dwelling by pipes passed between the walls, which circle about the places that were to be warmed; which I have seen clearly described, I know not where, in Seneca.[70] This German, hearing me praise the agreeableness and beauties of his city, which certainly deserves it, began to commiserate me because I had to leave it; and among the first disagreeable things that he mentioned was the heaviness of head which the chimneys elsewhere would cause me. He had heard some one make this complaint and attached it to us, being unable, because he was accustomed to it, to detect it in his own house. All heat that comes from fire weakens and oppresses me; yet Evenus said that fire was the best spice of life.[71] I choose any other way to escape cold.

We dislike wines near the bottom of the cask; in Portugal these lees are thought delicious and are the beverage of princes. In fine, each nation has many customs and usages which are not only unknown but appear barbarous and extraordinary to other nations. What shall we do with the people who accept only printed evidence, who do not believe men if they be not in a book, or the truth if it be not of due age? We dignify our follies when we put them into type. There is much more weight for such people if you say, "I have read it," than if you say, "I have heard it said." But I, who no more disbelieve a man's mouth than his pen, and who know that men write as inconsiderately as they talk, and who think as highly of this age as I do of a bygone age, I quote a friend of mine as readily as I do Aulus Gellius or Macrobius, and what I have seen as what they have written. And as it is held of virtue that it is no greater for being of long standing, so I believe of truth that it is none the wiser for being older. I often say that it is pure foolishness that makes us run after foreign and scholastic examples; their abundance in these days is as in the times of Homer and Plato. But is it not that we seek the honour of the quotation more than the truth of the matter, as if it were nobler to borrow our proofs from the shop of Vascosan or Plantin than from what we see in our village? or really, in truth, that we have not the wit to examine and make the most of what happens before our eyes, and to judge it keenly enough to bring it forward as an example? for if we say that we lack authority to give weight to our testimony, we speak from the purpose; since, in my opinion, from the most commonplace things, and the most usual and familiar, if we can see them in the right light,[72] may be conceived the greatest miracles of Nature and the most wonderful examples, particularly on the subject of human actions.

Now, as bearing upon my theme, putting aside the examples that I know of from books, and what Aristotle says of Andron the Argian, that he crossed the arid sands of Libya without drinking,[73] a gentleman who has acquitted himself worthily in many employments said, in my presence, that he had travelled from Madrid to Lisbon in the heat of summer without drinking. He is in vigorous health for his age, and there is nothing extraordinary in his habits of life but this—that he goes two or three months, even a year, so he told me, without drinking. He is sometimes thirsty, but he lets it pass and maintains that it is an appetite which easily weakens of itself; and he drinks more from whim than from need or for pleasure.

Here is another case. It is not long ago that I found one of the most learned men in France, among those of no mean

Of Experience

fortune, studying in the corner of a room, shut off by hangings, and above him his servants in unrestrained uproar.[74] He told me, and Seneca says almost the same of himself,[75] that he profited by this racket, as if, battered by the noise, he withdrew his mind and confined himself the more within himself for contemplation, and that that storm of voices drove his thoughts inward. When a student at Padua, his study was for so long a time near the clatter of coaches and the tumult of the market-place, that he trained himself not only to despise noise, but to make use of it for the service of his studies. Socrates replied to Alcibiades, when he wondered how he could endure the constant noisiness of his wife's obstinacy, "As those do who are accustomed to the common sound of wheels drawing water."[76] I am quite the opposite: my mind is sensitive and quick to take flight; when it is engaged with itself, the least buzzing of a fly is death to it.

In his youth Seneca was so bitten, after the example of Sextius, with the idea of eating nothing that had not been killed[77] that he went without that sort of food for a year, with pleasure, as he says, and renounced the habit only to avoid being suspected of borrowing this rule from certain new religions which disseminated it. He adopted at the same time the injunctions of Attalus, not to lie on mattresses into which the body sinks, and till his old age he used those which do not yield to the body;[78] what the habit of his time caused to be considered austerity in him, our time regards as effeminacy.

Consider the difference between the manner of life of my farm-servants and my own; the Scythians and Indians are no further removed from my ability and my habit. I know

that I have withdrawn children from begging, to enter my
service, who very soon after have forsaken me and my
kitchen and my livery, simply to return to their former life;
and I found one of them afterward collecting mussels from
the garbage-heap for his dinner, whom neither by prayers
nor by threats could I divert from the relish and pleasure that
he found in indigence. Beggars have their nobleness and
their delights like the rich, and, it is said, their dignities and
political orders. The effect of wontedness can make acceptable to us, not only such manner of life as it pleases (but
the wise say that we must fix our minds on the best, which
custom will forthwith make easy for us[79]), but also change
and variation, which is the noblest and most useful of its
teachings. The best of my bodily dispositions is that I am
flexible and far from opinionative; I have some inclinations
more personal and ordinary and more agreeable than others;
but with very little effort I turn away from them and slip
easily into a contrary course. A young man should break in
upon his rules, to arouse his energy and keep it from becoming flavourless and inert; and there is no course of life
so foolish and feeble as that which is guided by rules and
discipline.

> When it pleases him to ride to the first mile-stone,
> he chooses the hour from a book; if he has rubbed the
> corner of his eye, and it itches, he seeks a remedy only
> after he has consulted his horoscope.[80]

If he trusts my advice, he will often plunge even into excesses; otherwise the slightest over-indulgence undoes him;
he becomes tiresome and disagreeable in social relations.
The quality least befitting a well-bred man is fastidiousness

1480

and being bound to a particular way; it is particular if it be not pliable and yielding. It is humiliating to fail to do from lack of ability, or not to dare to do, what you see your comrades do. Let such men stay in their kitchen. In all other men it is unseemly; but in a man-at-arms it is vicious and intolerable; for he, as Philopœmen was wont to say, should accustom himself to every diversity and inequality of life.[81]

Although I have been fashioned as much as possible to liberty and indifference, yet so it is that, as I grow old, having from heedlessness become fixed in certain ways (my age is beyond instruction and has henceforth nothing to consider save to uphold itself), habit has now unconsciously so stamped its impress on me in certain matters that I call deviation from it excess; and I can not without an effort either sleep in the daytime, or take any thing between meals, or eat breakfast, or go to bed until a long time, say three hours, after supper, or procreate except before sleep, or standing, or remain sweaty, or quench my thirst with water alone or wine alone, or remain long bare-headed, or have my hair cut after dinner; and I should do without my gloves with as much discomfort as without my shirt, and without washing on leaving the table and on rising, and without a canopy and curtains to my bed, as being very necessary things. I could dine without a cloth; but very uncomfortably without white napkins, as the Germans do; I soil them more than they and the Italians do, and make little use of spoon and fork. I regret that we have not followed a custom that I have seen introduced after the example of kings: that napkins be changed with each course, as plates are. We know of that hard-working soldier Marius that, as he grew old, he became so fastidious about his way of drink-

ing that he would drink only from a special cup of his own.[82]
China and silver cups I dislike in comparison with glass.[83]
For my part, I allow myself to take a fancy even to a certain
shape of glasses, and do not willingly drink from a common
glass any more than from a common hand; any metal cup
I dislike in comparison with a clear and transparent material;
let my eyes taste also according to their capacity.

I owe many such niceties to habit. Nature has also, on
the other hand, brought me hers: as the not being able to
tolerate two full meals a day without overloading my
stomach; or entire absence from one of the meals without
being filled with wind, my mouth being dry, and my appetite dull; the being harmed by long exposure to night air;
for in recent years when, in military service, fatigue duty
lasts all night, as commonly happens, after five or six hours
my stomach begins to trouble me, together with a violent
headache, and I can not go to daybreak without vomiting.
When others go off to breakfast I go away to sleep, and after
that I am as lively as before. I had always understood that
the dew did not fall except in the evening; but having, of
late years, known familiarly and for a long time a gentleman who is imbued with the belief that the dew is heavier
and more dangerous when the sun is sinking, an hour or two
before it sets, when he carefully avoids it, and makes no account of the night dew, he has almost persuaded me, not so
much by his talk as by his feelings.

How is it? Does mere doubt and enquiry strike our
imagination and change us? They who wholly yield to these
inclinations draw upon themselves complete ruin, and I am
sorry for many a gentleman who, through the folly of his
physician, has imprisoned himself[84] while he was still young

and sound. It would be much more worth while to suffer from a cold than to lose forever, by unfamiliarity, the intercourse of common life, a matter of such frequent occurrence. That is a vexatious sort of learning which discredits the pleasantest hours of the day. Let us lengthen our hold in every possible way; for the most part we become enured to the matter by persistence, and rectify our nature, as Cæsar did the falling sickness, by dint of scorning and bribing it.[85] We should devote ourselves to the best rules, but not be enslaved by them; for it is not these, if there are any, to which to be in bondage and servitude is profitable.

Kings and philosophers obey Nature's call, and ladies too. A man who lives in the public eye is obliged to observe the conventions; I, who am an obscure and private individual, enjoy every dispensation that Nature allows. As a soldier and a Gascon I may be allowed a little indiscretion. Wherefore I will say of that action that it must be relegated to certain fixed and night hours, to which we should force and subject ourselves by habit, as I have done; but not, as I have done in my declining years, pamper ourselves by being tied for this function to a particularly comfortable place and seat, and make it a burden by prolongation and luxury.

And yet in the dirtiest functions is it not in some measure excusable to require more care and cleanliness? *Man is by Nature a cleanly and dainty animal.*[86] It is the one function of Nature that I can best bear to put off. I have known many soldiers to be inconvenienced by the irregularity of their bowels; whilst I and mine never miss the moment of our assignation, which is on leaping out of bed, unless we are disturbed by some urgent occupation or some serious malady.

So, as I was saying, my opinion is that those who are sick

can not better find safety than by keeping quietly on in the course of life in which they have been bred and brought up; change, whatever it may be, causes trouble and injury. It is not to be believed[87] that chestnuts are injurious to a native of Perigord or of Lucca, and milk and cheese to mountain-dwellers. They are ordered a mode of life, not only new, but opposed to their accustomed one; a change which a man in health could not stand. Prescribe water for a seventy-year-old Breton; confine a seaman in a heated room; forbid walking to a Basque footman; they are deprived of motion and, at last, of air and light.

> Is it so important to live? . . . We are compelled to deprive our minds of things to which we are accustomed, and, in order to live, we cease to live. Shall I regard those as living, for whom the air that we breathe and the very light by which we are guided are made oppressive?[88]

If such measures do no other good, they do at least this: they prepare the patients for death in good season, by sapping their life little by little and narrowing their use of it.

Both in health and in sickness I readily let myself go according to those appetites that are insistent. I give great authority to my desires and inclinations. I do not like to cure an ill by an ill; I hate remedies that are more disturbing than the disease. To be under subjection to the colic and under subjection to abstinence from the pleasure of eating oysters are to me two ills; the malady nips us in one direction, the regimen in another. Since we are in danger of disappointment, let us risk it rather in pursuit of pleasure. The world does the opposite, and thinks nothing profitable which is not

Of Experience

painful; it is suspicious of facility. My appetite, fortunately enough, has in many things accommodated and adjusted itself of its own accord to the health of my stomach; the pungency and piquancy of sauces was agreeable to me when I was young; later, my stomach becoming tired of them, my taste forthwith followed suit. Wine is harmful for the sick; it is the first thing for which my mouth feels distaste—an invincible distaste. Whatever I take that is disagreeable to me harms me, and nothing harms me that I take hungrily and gladly. I have never been harmed by doing what was truly agreeable to me; and indeed I have made medical opinion give way very largely to my pleasure; and as a young man,

> When Cupid, gay in saffron shift,
> Would hover round with playful wiles,[89]—

I yielded, as wantonly and thoughtlessly as any other, to the desire that held me captive;

> And held my own with glory,[90]—

My love, however, was more constant and enduring than vigorous;

> I scarce remember reaching six.[91]

It is, indeed, distressing and wonderful to me to have to confess at what a tender age I first chanced to come under Cupid's subjection. It was, indeed, a chance, for it was long before the age of choice and knowledge. I cannot remember so far back. And my lot may be wedded to that of Quartilla, who had no recollection of her maidenhood.

Of Experience

Precocious hairs and beard blossomed,
A mother's admiration.[92]

The physicians modify, usually with good results, their rules according to the vehemence of their patients' cravings. The great desire in question must be put down to Nature, however monstrous and vicious we may imagine it to be. And then, how much does it need to satisfy the imagination? In my opinion that faculty is all important, at least more so than any other. The most grievous and the most common ills are those that fancy puts upon me. I like this Spanish saying from several points of view, *God defend me from myself.*[93]

When I am ill I am sorry not to have some craving that will give me this pleasure of satisfying it; medicine would find it hard to turn me from it. I feel the same when I am well; I see hardly any thing more to hope and wish for. It is pitiful when even the power of wishing becomes weak and languid.

The science of medicine is not so established that we are without authority, whatever we may do; it changes according to the climate and according to the moon's phases, according to Farnel[94] and according to l'Escale.[95] If your physician does not think it wise for you to sleep, to take wine, or such and such meat, do not be troubled, I will find you another who will not be of his opinion; the diversity of medical arguments and opinions includes every variety of form. I saw a wretched sick man, half-dying, and fainting with intolerable thirst, in the hope of a cure; and he was laughed at later by another physician who condemned this advice as harmful. Had he not made good use of his pain? There died lately of the stone a man of this profession, who had resorted to extreme abstinence to withstand his malady; his associates say that that fasting, on the contrary, had drained his body and hardened the gravel in his kidney.

I have observed when I have been wounded[96] or ill, that talking stirs and harms me as much as any disturbance does. Using my voice costs me dear and wearies me; for it is loud and vigorous, so that, when I have had to talk privately of affairs of importance, with great men, I have often given them the trouble to tell me to speak low.

This story deserves that I should interrupt myself. Some one in a certain Greek school was talking loudly, as I do. The master of ceremonies sent to him to speak lower. "Let him send me," he replied, "the tone in which he wishes me to speak." The other answered that he should take his tone from the ears of him to whom he spoke.[97] That was well said, provided this be understood: "Speak according to what your business is with your listener"; for if it means, "Let it suffice you that he hears you," or "Regulate yourself by him," I do not find it reasonable. The voice, by its tone and action, conveys some expression and signification of my meaning; it is for me to govern it as representing me. There is a voice for instruction, a voice for flattery or for reprimandment. I would have my voice not only reach my listener, but perchance strike him and pierce him through. When I berate my servant in a harsh and cutting tone, it would be well for him to say to me, "Speak more softly, master, I hear you plainly." *There is a certain sort of voice adapted to the hearing, not so much by its volume, as by its suitableness.*[98] The uttered word pertains half to him who speaks, half to him who hears. The latter should prepare to receive it in the direction of its impulse; as, with those playing tennis, he who receives the ball shifts his place and makes ready for it according as he sees him move who makes the stroke, and according to the nature of the stroke.[99]

Experience has taught me this also: that we ruin ourselves by impatience. Evils have their lifetime and their limits, their maladies and their health. The constitution of maladies is shaped on the same pattern as the constitution of animals; their destiny and their length of days are allotted to them from their birth. He who tries imperiously to shorten them by force, by crossing their course, prolongs and multiplies them, and irritates instead of assuaging them.[100] I am of Crantor's opinion,[101] that we ought not obstinately to resist evils in reckless fashion, or to succumb to them from want of vigour, but that we should naturally yield to them according to their character and our own. We should give free passage to maladies; and I find that they tarry less long with me, who let them do as they will; and some of those which are deemed most obstinate and tenacious have left me, by their own subsidence, without the help of medicine and against its rules. Let us leave a little for Nature to do, who understands her affairs better than we. "But that man died of it." So will you die, if not of that disease, of another; and how many have not escaped death from it with three doctors by their side!

Example is a dim looking-glass, all containing and with many meanings.[102] If the medicine be a pleasant one, take it; it is always so much present pleasure. I shall not be stayed either by its name or its colour if it be delicious and appetising; pleasure is one of the chief kinds of profit. I have allowed to grow old and die a natural death within me, colds and gouty tendencies,[103] relaxation of the bowels, palpitations of the heart, sick headaches, and other mischances, which have left me when I had half enured myself to entertaining them. One can exorcise them better by courtesy than by defiance. We must patiently endure the laws of our condition; we have to grow old, to become feeble, to be ill, in spite of all medicine. That is the first teaching that the Mexicans give their children when, as they come forth from the mother's womb, they greet them thus: "Child, you have come into the world to endure; endure, suffer, and be silent."

It is not just to complain because that has happened to some one which may happen to every one. *Be indignant if any thing unjust is decreed against you alone.*[104] Behold an old man who asked God to keep him in perfect and vigorous health, that is to say, to bring back his youth:

Fool, why do you vainly ask for these things in your childish prayers?[105]

Is it not folly? His state does not comport with it. Gout, the stone, indigestion, are signs of long years, as heat, rain, and winds are of long journeys. Plato does not believe that Æsculapius would take the trouble to provide by rules for prolonging life in a wasted and feeble body, useless for his country, useless for his occupation, and for begetting sound and robust children; and he does not deem such care compatible with the divine justice and wisdom which guides all things toward usefulness.[106] My good friend, all is at an end; you can not be put to rights; at most you can be plastered over and propped up a bit, and it will prolong your wretchedness by some few hours.

Of Experience

Not otherwise does he who wishes to support a
building about to fall place various props against it,
until the fatal day when the whole structure falls apart,
and drags down the props with the rest.[107]

We must learn to suffer what can not be avoided. Our life,
like the harmony of the world, is composed of contrary
things, also of diverse tones, sweet and harsh, keen and dull,
soft and solemn. If a musician should like only some of
them, what would it mean? It is necessary for him to know
how to employ them all in common, and blend them; and so
must we the goods and the ills which are consubstantial with
our life.[108] Our existence can not subsist without this commixture, and one set of elements is not less essential than the
other. To attempt to kick against natural necessity is to shew
like folly with Ctesiphon, who undertook by kicking to deal
with his mule.[109]

I seldom seek advice about the changes for the worse that
I feel, for men of this kind are presumptuous when they
have you at their mercy; they stuff your ears with their
prognostications; and once, surprising me unawares when
weakened by illness, they treated me harmfully with their
dogmatism and their magisterial phiz, at one time threatening me with severe pains, and again, with approaching
death. I was neither cast down nor moved from my position
by this, but I was jostled and pushed; if my judgement was
neither changed nor disturbed, at least it was embarrassed;
there is always agitation and strife.

Now, I treat my imagination as gently as I can, and
would relieve it if I could from all difficulty and contest. It
must be helped and flattered, and deceived when possible.

Of Experience

My mind is fit for this office; it finds no lack of specious evidence on all sides. Could it persuade what it preaches, it would help me happily. Will you have an example? It says that it is for my good that I have the stone; that buildings of my age naturally have to suffer some leakage (the time comes when they begin to open at the joints, and are unlike themselves;[110] it is a common necessity, and no unusual miracle would be performed for me; I pay in this way the dues of old age, and I could not do so more cheaply); [it says] that the companionship I have should console me, I having met with the most ordinary mischance of the men of my day (I see them everywhere afflicted by the same sort of malady, and association with them does me honour, inasmuch as this malady readily attacks the great; it is essentially noble and dignified); [it says] that of the men who are stricken with it there are few who get off with better terms, since it costs them the discomfort of an unpleasant course of treatment and the annoyance of taking medicinal drugs every day, whereas I owe improvements solely to my good-fortune; for some common broths of eringa[111] or Turk's herb, which I have taken two or three times as a compliment to ladies who, more sweetly than my malady is bitter, have presented me with half of theirs, have seemed to me equally easy to take and worthless in effect. Other men have to pay a thousand vows to Æsculapius and as many crowns to their physician for an easy and abundant discharge of gravel, which I frequently obtain by the favour of nature. Even the decorum of my bearing in company is not disturbed by this, and I hold my water ten hours and as long as a healthy man.

"The dread of this malady," it says, "used to terrify thee formerly when it was unknown to thee.[112] The outcries and despair of those who aggravate it by their impatience engendered horror of it in thee. It is a malady that affects the organs with which thou hast most transgressed. Thou art a conscientious man;

The undeserved hardship is the one to be lamented;[113]

consider this chastisement; it is very mild compared with others, and of a paternal kindness; consider the lateness of its coming; it incommodes and occupies only that season of thy life which, in any case, is already ruined and sterile, having given room to the excesses and pleasures of thy youth, as by mutual agreement. The fear of this malady, and the compassion for it that the people feel, serve thee as occasion for pride—a quality which, although thou hast purged thy judgement of it and hast cured thy conversation of it, thy friends can still recognise some trace of in thy nature. It is pleasant to hear it said of oneself: 'There is strength for you! there is patience!' Thou art seen sweating with the effort, turning pale, flushing, trembling, vomiting even to blood, suffering strange contractions and convulsions, dropping at times great tears from thine eyes, discharging a thick, black, alarming urine, or having it stopped by a sharp rough-edged stone, which cruelly tears and stings the neck of the penis; talking meanwhile with those present, with thy usual countenance, jesting at moments with ladies,[114] taking thy share in serious talk, making excuses for thy suffering, and belittling thy endurance. Dost thou remember those men of bygone times who hungrily sought out ills, to keep their courage in breath and exercise? Assume that Nature carries and casts thee into this glorious school, which thou wouldst never have entered of thine own free will. If thou dost tell me that this is a dangerous and deadly malady, what others are not so? For it is a medical deception to except some maladies which they say do not lead straight to death: what does it matter whether they go thither by accident, or whether they slide and slip easily into the path that leads to it? But thou diest not because thou art sick, thou diest because thou art living;[115] death kills thee without the aid of sickness, and for some persons sicknesses have kept death away; they have lived the longer because it seemed to them that they were about to die; moreover, as with wounds, there are diseases also that are medicinal and salutary.

"Colic often has no less long a life than we; there are men with whom it has continued from their childhood to their extreme old age; and had they not left its company, it was ready to attend them further; thou dost kill it oftener that it kills thee. And if it should put before thee the image of near-by death, would it not be doing a good office to a man so old, to turn him to meditation upon his end? And, what is more, thou no longer hast any reason for recovery; whether or no, very soon the necessity common to all will summon thee. Consider how skillfully and gently it disgusts thee with life and loosens thy hold upon the world, not compelling thee by its tyrannical subjection,—like so many other ill conditions that are seen in old men, which keep them continually and without remission enchained by weaknesses and pains,—but it instructs thee by warnings resumed at intervals, intermingling with them long pauses and respites, as if to give thee opportunity to meditate and to rehearse its lesson at thine ease. To give thee opportunity to judge aright, and to be resolved like a brave man, it puts before thee the state of thy whole condition as regards both good and ill, and, in one and the same day, a life sometimes very cheerful and sometimes unendurable. If thou dost not embrace death, at least thou dost touch her hand once a month; whence thou mayst the more hope that she will one day surprise thee without warning, and that, being so often led even to the place of embarkation, confident that thou art still on the accustomed terms, some morning thou and thy confidence will be unexpectedly carried across the water. One has no reason to complain of maladies that fairly divide the time with health."

I am grateful to fortune in that it assails me so often with the same kind of weapons; it shapes me to them and trains me to them by custom, enures and habituates me to them. I know now very nearly how much it will cost me to be rid of them.[116] In default of natural memory, I create one of paper; and when some new symptom appears in my disease, I note it down; whence it happens that at this day, having passed through almost every sort of experience, if something surprising threatens me, by turning over these little loose records, like Sibylline leaves, I do not fail to find in my past experience some favourable prognostic to console me. Wontedness also helps me to hope better things of the future; for this action of clearing out having so long continued, it is to be believed that nature will not change this course, and that no worse condition will result from it than what I now endure. Moreover, the character of this disease is not ill suited to my quick and unanticipating[117] disposition. When it attacks me mildly, it frightens me, for it is to stay long; but by its nature it has vigorous and spirited excesses; it shakes me to the utmost for a day or two. My kidneys lasted for forty years without impairment; it is almost fourteen

Of Experience

years since their condition changed.[118] Evils as well as goods
have their period. Perchance this misfortune is near its end.
Age diminishes the heat of my stomach; its digestion being
therefore less perfect, it sends this crude matter to my kidneys; why may not, in like manner, the heat of my kidneys
be diminished in turn so that they may no longer solidify
my phlegm, and nature may set about finding some other
channel of purgation? Years have evidently drained from
me some discharges; why not these excrements which
furnish material for the gravel?

But is any ecstasy comparable to that sudden change,
when, from extreme pain, I pass with lightning speed, by
the voiding of my stone, to the beautiful light of health,
free and full, as comes to pass in our sudden and most
severe attacks of colic? Is there aught in the pain endured
that is a counterpoise to the pleasure of so sudden an amendment? How much more beautiful health appears to me
after sickness, so near, so in actual contact, that I can recognise them in each other's presence, in their fullest equipment, in which they array themselves emulously, as if to
oppose and thwart each the other. Quite as the Stoics say,
that the vices are introduced with profit to give value and
support to virtue,[119] so we may say, with better reason and
less bold conjecture, that nature has given us pain for the
honour and service of pleasure and comfort. When Socrates,
after his fetters had been removed, felt a delicate enjoyment
from the itching which their weight had caused in his legs,
he took pleasure in considering the close alliance between
pain and pleasure, how they are associated in an inevitable
union, so that in turn they follow and engender each other;
and he exclaimed that the excellent Æsop might have

1495

Of Experience

derived from this consideration a fit subject for a fine fable.[120]

The worst that I see about other diseases is that they are not so serious in their immediate effect as they are in their result; one is a year in recovering, all the while full of weakness and dread; there is so much chance and so many degrees in getting back to safety, that there is no end to it. Before you have been unmuffled, first from an outer cap and then from your skull-cap, before fresh air has been allowed you, and wine and your wife and melons, it is great luck if you have not relapsed into some new misery. This disease has this privilege, that it carries itself clean off, whereas the others always leave behind some impress or change which renders the body susceptible to new ills, and lend a hand one to another. Those diseases are excusable which content themselves with their possession of us, without extending it and without introducing their after effects; but courteous and gracious are those whose passing brings us some profitable consequence. Since I have had the colic, I find myself more free from other symptoms of trouble, it seems to me, than I was before; and I have had no fever since then. I infer that my severe and frequent vomitings purge me, and also that my loss of appetite and the singular fasts I keep, digest my peccant humours, and that nature discharges in these stones what is superfluous and harmful. Do not tell one that it is a medicine too dearly bought; what about the many evil-smelling potions, cauterisings, incisions, sudorifics, setons, dietings, and so many methods of cure which often bring death to us because we can not sustain their violence and unseasonableness! Therefore, when I am attacked, I take it as medicine; when I am exempt, I take it as a lasting and complete deliverance.

1496

Of Experience

Here is still another act of grace on the part of my disease, and one peculiar to it, namely, that it almost plays its game by itself and lets me play mine, or it holds on only from lack of courage on my part; when at its worst, I have kept on horseback for ten hours. Simply suffer; you have not to follow any other treatment; play at any game, dine, run, do this and also do that if you can, your diversion will be more serviceable than harmful. Say as much to one who has smallpox, or gout, or a rupture. Other maladies are more universally obligatory; they constrain our actions much more, disturb our whole system, and involve in consideration of them the whole condition of life. This one simply pinches the skin; it leaves your understanding and your will at your disposal, and your tongue and feet and hands; it arouses you rather than stupefies you. The mind is smitten by a burning fever, and overthrown by an epilepsy, and put out of joint by a severe headache, and in fine paralysed by all maladies which injure the whole body and its nobler organs. By this disease the mind is not attacked; if things go wrong with her, hers be the blame; she betrays herself, abandons herself, and disables herself. It is only fools who allow themselves to be persuaded that this hard and solid substance which is concocted in our kidneys can be dissolved by potions; and so, when it stirs, there is nothing to do but give it passage; for that matter, it will take it.

I observe also this special convenience in this disease—that it is one about which we have little to guess at; we are dispensed from the disturbance which other maladies cause us from uncertainty as to their origin and conditions and progress—an infinitely painful disturbance. We have no

Of Experience

need of doctoral consultation and interpretation; our sensations tell us both what it is and where it is. By such arguments, both strong and weak, I try, as Cicero did with the malady of old age,[121] to lull to sleep and divert my imagination, and to anoint its sores. If they are worse to-morrow, to-morrow we will provide other shifts.

Let this be true: suppose that still again the slightest motion forces pure blood from my kidneys. What of that? I cease not to move about as before and to ride after my hounds with youthful ardour and pride; and I consider that I have complete mastery over so important a matter when it costs me no more than a dull heaviness and discomfort in that region; it is some large stone which presses upon and uses up the substance of my kidneys, and my life, and which I expel by slow degrees, not without some natural pleasurable sensation, as an excrement henceforth superfluous and troublesome. Now, if I feel something giving way, do not expect me to busy myself in examining my pulse and my urine to derive from them some unpleasant anticipation; I shall feel the evil quickly enough without prolonging it by the evil of fear. He who dreads suffering already suffers what he dreads; added to which, the dubitation and ignorance of those who take upon them to explain the means of Nature and her internal progressions, and the many false prognostics of their art, should make us understand that her methods are utterly unknown; there is great uncertainty, variety, and obscurity as to what she promises or threatens. Save old age, which is an indubitable sign of the approach of death, I see in all other happenings few signs of the future upon which we can base our divination.

I judge myself only by real sensation, not by reasoning.

Of Experience

What would be the use, since I desire to bring to the situation nothing save expectation and patience? Would you know how much I gain by that? Look at those who do otherwise and who rely upon so many different persuasions and counsels; how often the imagination without the body[122] makes them suffer! Many a time, when in safety and free from these dangerous mishaps, I have found pleasure in describing them to physicians as then coming upon me; I have sustained the verdict of their terrible conclusions quite at my ease, and thereafter remained so much the more beholden to God for his favour, and better informed as to the worthlessness of that profession.

There is nothing that should be so enjoined upon the young as activity and alertness; our life is only in movement. I bestir myself with difficulty and am slow in every thing: in rising, in going to bed, at my meals; seven o'clock is early for me, and where I rule, I neither dine before eleven nor sup till after six. I formerly attributed the cause of the fevers and sicknesses that I fell into to the heaviness and indolence that long sleep had brought upon me; and I have always repented going to sleep again after waking in the morning. Plato condemns excess in sleeping more than excess in drinking.[123] I like to sleep on a hard bed and alone, yes, without a woman, in kingly fashion, rather well covered. My bed is never warmed, but since I have grown old I am given, when I need them, cloths to keep my feet and my stomach warm. They found fault with Scipio the Great for sleeping too much, in my opinion, for no other reason than that it vexed them that there was nothing else to find fault with in him.[124] If I am particular about any thing in my habits, it is rather about the kind of bed than aught

Of Experience

else; but I accommodate myself in general to necessity as
well as any other man. Sleep has filled a large part of my
life, and I continue at my present age to sleep eight or nine
hours together. I sometimes abandon with profit this slothful propensity, and am evidently the better for doing so;
I feel somewhat the effort of the change, but it is over in
three days. And I see few men who can live with less sleep
when need is, or who are more constantly in motion, or to
whom fatigue-duty[125] is less burdensome. My body is
capable of steady activity, but not of an impetuous and
sudden kind. I avoid nowadays violent exercises which
make me sweat; my limbs become tired before they become
warm. I can stand on my feet all day long, and walking is
not irksome to me; but from my early youth I have never
liked to go through city streets[126] except in the saddle; on
foot I muddy myself to the thighs, and small men are likely
to be jostled and elbowed because their appearance does not
attract attention;[127] and I like to rest, whether lying or sitting, with my legs as high as my seat, or higher.

There is no employment so agreeable as that of a soldier,
an employment both noble in performance,—for the most
powerful, most generous, and proudest of all virtues is
valour,—and noble in its source; there is no form of usefulness more righteous or more unlimited than the protection of the repose and grandeur of one's country. The
companionship of so many men, noble, young, active, gives
you pleasure, as do the frequent sight of so many terrible
spectacles; the freedom of that natural intercourse and a
virile and unceremonious mode of life; the variety of innumerable differing actions; the brave harmony of martial
music that supports you and excites alike the ear and the

soul; the honour of this employment, even its severity and its difficulty, which Plato regards as of so little importance that in his *Republic* he gives a share in it to women and children.[128]

You summon yourself, a volunteer, to special duties and risks, according as you judge their brilliancy and importance, and you see when life itself is pardonably employed therein,—

The thought comes that it is a beautiful thing to die in arms.[129]

To fear the common risks that concern so great a multitude, and not to dare what is dared by so many kinds of souls, and a whole people, is for a mean heart, debased beyond measure. Companionship gives steadiness even to children. If others surpass you in learning, in charm, in strength, in fortune, you can blame outside causes for it; but to be inferior to them in stoutness of soul—for that you have only yourself to blame. Death is more abject, more dull and disagreeable, in a bed than when fighting; fevers and apoplexies are as painful and deadly as a musket-shot. Whosoever would be able to bear valiantly the mischances of ordinary life would not have to increase his courage on becoming a soldier. *To live, my Lucilius, is to be a soldier.*[130]

I do not recall ever having had an irritated skin; scratching is truly the pleasantest of natural gratifications and nearest at hand; but repentance for it is too troublesomely close. I use it most for my ears, which have attacks of itching inside.

I was born with all my senses sound almost to perfection. My stomach is comfortably good, as is my head, and generally they remain so, and so does my breathing, through my attacks of fever. I have passed the age which some nations, not without reason, fixed as being so justly the limit of life that they did not allow it to be exceeded; yet do I still have times of revival, although uncertain and brief, so complete that there is little lacking of the health and painlessness of my youth. I say nothing about animation and vigour; there is no reason that it[131] should accompany me beyond its bounds.

> I can no longer expose myself on the threshold to the rain from heaven.[132]

My face and my eyes immediately reveal my condition. All my changes begin there, and seem a little sharper than in fact they are. I am often commiserated by my friends before I feel the reason for it. My mirror does not startle me; for even in my youth it happened more than once that I had an unusual colour and general appearance of ill presage,[133] without great harm; so that the physicians who found no inward cause to account for that outward change attributed it to the mind and to some secret passion which was preying upon me within. They were mistaken. If my body was as much ruled by me as my mind is, we should travel a little more at ease. My mind was at that time not only free from trouble, but full of satisfaction and enjoyment, as it is usually, half by its nature, half by design;

> And the infection of my sick mind does not harm my body.[134]

I hold that this temperament of my mind has many a time lifted up the body when it was downcast; that is often droop-

ing, and the other, if not gay, is at least in a tranquil state
of repose. I had a quartan fever for four or five months,
which quite changed my appearance; my mind was always,
not at ease, but cheerful. If the pain is external, feebleness
and langour scarcely sadden me. I know of many bodily
weaknesses, dreadful even to name, which I should fear less
than a thousand passions and agitations of mind which I
see everywhere. I resign myself to run no more; it is enough
that I can crawl, nor do I complain of the natural decay that
possesses me,—

Who is surprised at a goitre in the Alps?[135]

any more than I regret that my length of life is not as long
and sound as that of an oak.

I have no grudge against my imagination; I have had
few thoughts in my life which have so much as interrupted
my slumber, unless those of desire, which aroused me without discomforting me. I seldom dream, and then it is of
fantastic, chimerical things, produced usually by amusing
thoughts, absurd rather than melancholy; and I hold that
it is true that dreams are faithful interpreters of our inclinations, but that there is skill in assorting and understanding them.

It is little wonder that the things which men use in
life, and think about and look after and see and do,
when they are awake, they see in dreams.[136]

Plato says, moreover, that it is the office of prudence to
draw from them prophetic instructions for the future.[137] I
see nothing in that save the marvellous experiences related
by Socrates, Xenophon, and Aristotle, men of unimpeach-

able authority.[138] Histories relate that the Atlantes[139] never
dreamed, and that they never ate any thing which had been
killed;[140] this last fact I add inasmuch as it is, perchance,
the reason why they do not dream; for Pythagoras ordered
food to be prepared in a certain way to make dreams appropriate to the occasion.[141] Mine are gentle and cause in me
heither motions of the body nor vocal utterances. I have
seen in the course of my life many persons extraordinarily
excited by them. The philosopher Theon walked when
dreaming, and likewise the servant of Pericles, even on the
roof and ridge-pole of the house.[142]

At table I rarely make a choice, but take the first and
nearest dish, and I change reluctantly from one flavour to
another. The crowding of dishes and courses is to me as
disagreeable as any other crowd. I am easily satisfied with
a few dishes, and I detest the opinion of Favorinus, that at
a banquet the dish for which you have an appetite must be
taken from you and a new one always substituted for it;
and that that is a most niggardly supper-party at which the
guests are not satiated with the rumps of various birds, and
that only the beccafico deserves to be eaten whole.[143] I make
constant use of salt meat, yet I like bread better unsalted,
and my baker prepares no other kind for my table, contrary to the customs of the country. In my childhood, I
had to be corrected chiefly for my refusal of things which
are commonly best liked at that age—sugar-plums, preserves, and cakes. My tutor fought against this aversion to
dainties as being due to a form of daintiness; and it is in
fact nothing else than a delicacy of taste, whatever it may
be affected by.[144] He who rids a child of a certain special and
persistent liking for brown bread and bacon, or for garlic,

cures him of daintiness. There are those who appear as if
it were hard, and required patience, to go without beef and
ham, when they have partridges; this gives them pleasure;[145] this is the daintiness of the dainty, it is the fastidiousness of an easy lot, which finds usual and familiar things
distasteful; *whereby luxury mocks at the tedium of riches.*[146]
To fail to find good cheer in what is so to another, to have
special regard to one's diet, is the essence of this defect;

> If you are afraid to dine on all kinds of vegetables
> from a dish of moderate size.[147]

There is, indeed, this difference, that it is better to limit
one's desire to the things most easily to be had; but it is
always a defect, to be limited. I used to call a kinsman of
mine fastidious, who, from having lived in our galleys, had
unlearned the use of our beds, and the habit of undressing
when he went to sleep.

If I had male children, I should readily wish for them my
own fortune; the good father whom God gave me, to whom
I can offer naught save the recognition of his kindness,—
but that certainly of the liveliest,—sent me from my cradle
to be brought up in a little village of his, and kept me there
whilst I was at nurse and even longer, fashioning me to the
most humble and simple way of living. *A great part of liberty is a well-ordered stomach.*[148] Never assume yourself,
and still less give to your wives, the charge of their[149] nurture; leave it to fortune to shape them under general and
natural laws; leave it to habit to train them to frugality and
hardship, so that they may have rather to descend from
harsh conditions than ascend to them. My father's idea
aimed also at another purpose—to connect me with the

Of Experience

people and with the condition of men who need our assistance; and he judged that I should be inclined to look rather toward him who holds out his arms to me than toward him who turns his back on me. And it was for this reason also that he selected, to hold me at the font, persons of the most lowly fortunes, in order to bind and attach me to them.

His plan has not succeeded at all badly; I readily associate with men of humble condition, whether because there is more vanity in so doing, or from innate compassion, which in me is infinitely powerful. The party condemned by me in our civil wars I shall condemn the more bitterly if it becomes flourishing and prosperous; it will be in a way to conciliate me somewhat, if I see it depressed and crushed. How gladly I contemplate the noble spirit of Chelonis, daughter and wife of kings of Sparta. Whilst Cleombrotus her husband, during the commotion in his city, had the advantage over Leonidas her father, she was a good daughter and joined her father in his exile, in his wretchedness setting herself in opposition to the victor. Fortune changing, we see her, her will changing with their fortune, bravely take her place by the side of her husband, whom she followed wherever his disasters carried him, having, it seems to me, no other desire than to unite herself to the party where she was most needed and where she most evinced her compassion.[150] I incline more naturally to the example of Flaminius, who gave himself to those who needed him more than to those who could benefit him,[151] than I do to that of Pyrrhus, ready to humble himself before the great and to lord it over the lowly.[152]

Long sitting at table is wearisome and harmful to me; for, because I formed this habit when a child, for lack of

1506

something better to do, I eat as long as I am at table; therefore, at my own house, although our meals are of the shortest, I prefer to sit down a little after the others, after the habit of Augustus;[153] but I do not imitate him in leaving the table before the others. On the contrary, I like to be quiet for a long while afterward, and to listen to talk, provided that I take no part in it; for it tires me and injures me to use my voice when my stomach is full; whilst I find the exercise of talking loud and disputing before meals very healthful and agreeable. The ancient Greeks and Romans were wiser than we, assigning to eating, which is a principal action of life, several hours of the day and the better part of the night, if some other unusual employment did not keep them from it; eating and drinking less hastily than we, who do every thing post-haste, and protracting that natural pleasure more at leisure and by habit, intermixing with it different kinds of profitable and agreeable intercourse.

Those whose concern it is to take care of me can easily take away from me what they consider to be injurious to me; for about such things I never desire, or find lacking, what I do not see; but, on the other hand, they waste their time in preaching abstinence to me about the things before me; so that, when I wish to fast, I must be separated from the other diners and have just so much put before me as there is need of for a dietary repast;[154] for if I sit down at the table, I forget my resolution. When I order a change in the preparation of some dish, my people know that it means that my appetite has failed, and that I shall not touch it. I like all those things little cooked that can bear it, and I like them very tender, and even, as to many, changed in their smell. Toughness is the only thing in general that annoys

Of Experience

me (as for any other quality, I am as indifferent and as patient as any man I have known); so that, contrary to common taste, even among fish it happens that I find some too fresh and too hard. It is not the fault of my teeth, which have always been good even to excellence, and which old age only now begins to threaten. I learned in childhood to rub them with my napkin in the morning and also on going to and leaving the table.

God is gracious to those from whom he withdraws life by degrees; that is the sole benefit from old age; the final death will be so much the less complete and less hurtful; it will kill only a half or a quarter of a man. Here is a tooth which has just fallen out painlessly, of itself; it was the natural term of its duration, and that part of my being, and many other parts, amongst those which were the most active and held highest rank during my years of vigour, are already dead, and others half dead. Thus it is that I melt away and escape from myself. What folly would it be for my understanding to regard the beginning of the coming fall, already so far advanced, as if it were from the top.[155] I do not hope for such a fate. In truth, I derive my chief consolation as to my death, in thinking that it will be of a reasonable and natural kind, and that I can henceforth neither demand nor hope for other than unwarranted kindness from destiny. Men persuade themselves that in former times we had longer lives as well as greater stature; but they are deceived, and Solon, who was of those old days, fixes the extreme duration of life at seventy years.[156] I, who have so greatly revered in all things that *excellent mediocrity*[157] of ancient times, and who have so regarded the mean as the most perfect measure—shall I lay claim to a measureless

and prodigious old age? Whatever happens in opposition
to the course of Nature may be unpleasant; but what happens in accordance with Nature must always be agreeable;
*all things that are done according to Nature are to be ac-
counted as good;*[158] for this reason, as Plato says, the death
that comes by wounds or disease is violent; but that which
overtakes us led by old age is the easiest of all and in some
degree delightful.[159] *Young men die by violence, old men
of maturity.*[160]

Death is mingled and confused with our life everywhere;
decay anticipates its hour and insinuates itself even into the
very course of our progress. I have portraits of myself at
five-and-twenty, and at five-and-thirty years of age; I compare them with the one of to-day: in how many ways are
they no longer me! How much more distant my present
aspect is from those than from that of my death! It is too
great an abuse of Nature to drag her so far that she is constrained to quit us, and to abandon our guidance, our eyes,
our teeth, our legs, and all the rest, to the mercy of external
and solicited health, and, weary of following us, to resign
us into the hands of art.

I am not extremely fond of either salads or fruit, except
melons. My father detested every sort of sauce; I like them
all. Overeating does me harm; but as to quality, I have as
yet no certain knowledge that any thing eatable is injurious
to me; as also I pay no attention to the full moon, new
moon, or autumn and springtime. There are irregular and
unknown processes within us—as to radishes, for example:
at first I found them good for me, then disagreeable, and
now good again. In many things I perceive that my stomach
and my appetite thus vary; I have changed from white wine

to red, and then from red to white. I am fond of fish, and make Lent of Shrove-tide,[161] and fast days of feast days. I believe what some people say, that it is more easy of digestion than flesh. As I make it a point of conscience not to eat meat on fish day, so does my taste bid me not to mix fish with flesh: the contrast seems to me too great.

In my youth I used sometimes to go without a meal, either to sharpen my appetite for the morrow (for, as Epicurus fasted and ate sparingly to accustom his enjoyment in it to dispense with profusion,[162] I, on the contrary, do this to train my enjoyment to profit better by profusion and to make more lively use of it), or to maintain my strength to serve in some action of body or mind (for both become cruelly sluggish with repletion, and above all things I detest that senseless coupling of a goddess so wholesome and alert with that windy, belching little god, all puffed up with the fumes of his liquor), or to cure my sick stomach, or because there was no fit company; for I say, with this same Epicurus, that it needs not to consider so much what we eat as with whom we eat;[163] and I applaud Chilo for not choosing to promise to go to Periander's banquet before he had been told who the other guests would be.[164] No dish is so agreeable to me, no sauce so appetising, as the pleasure derived from the company. I believe that it is healthier to eat more slowly and less at a time and to eat more often, but I like to give appetite and hunger their due; I should have no pleasure in being forced to three or four meagre meals, straggling through the day, like medicine. Who would assure me that the ready appetite which I had this morning I shall find again at supper? Let us, old men especially, seize the first opportune moment that comes to us; let us leave hopes and

Of Experience

prognostications to the almanack-makers. The last fruit of my health is pleasure; let us cling to the first that comes, present and known. I avoid persistency in these laws for fasting; he who wishes a mode of action to be of service to him, let him shun continuing in it; we become hardened to it, our powers fall asleep in it; six months later you will have so wonted your stomach to it that your only profit will be the having lost the freedom of using it otherwise without harm.

I have my legs and thighs no more warmly clad in winter than in summer—simply a silk stocking. I have gone so far to guard against colds as to keep my head warmer, and, because of my colic, my stomach; my maladies became accustomed to it in a few days and scorned my ordinary precautions. I got from a skull-cap to a night-cap, and, out of doors, from a common cap to a quilted hat.[165] The wadding of my doublet now serves only to give it shape; it is of no use unless I add to it the skin of a hare or a vulture, with a skull-cap on my head. Follow this gradation and you will go a fine pace. I shall do nothing of the sort; I would gladly recede from the beginning I have made, if I dared. If you fall into some new discomfort, this alteration for the better is of no further use to you; you are accustomed to it; you must seek another change. Thus are they ruined who allow themselves to become entangled in enforced regulations, and who are superstitiously bound to them; they need still more of them, and yet more again, and still others; there is no end.

It is much more convenient for our employment and our pleasure to do as the ancients did—go without dinner and postpone eating heartily until the hour of retirement and rest, without interrupting the day; so I used formerly to do. I have learned since by experience that, on the contrary, it is better to dine at mid-day, and that digestion goes on better when one is awake. I am but little subject to being thirsty, whether I am well or ill; when ill, my mouth is apt to be dry, but without thirst, and ordinarily I drink only from the desire that comes to me with eating, and far on in the meal. I drink pretty well for a man of common make: in summer and at an appetising meal I not only go beyond the limits of Augustus, who drank precisely three times,[166] but, not to infringe the rule of Democritus, who forbade stopping at four as an unlucky number,[167] I go on at times to five —about three half-pints; for small glasses are my favourite, and it pleases me to empty them, which others avoid doing as unseemly. I weaken my wine, often with a half, some times with a third, as much water; and when I am in my own house, following an old custom which my father's physician prescribed for my father and himself, what I need is mixed in the buttery some hours before it is served. It is said that Cranaus, King of the Athenians,[168] was the first to follow this practice of diluting wine; whether useful or no, I have heard debated. I consider it more proper and more healthful that children should not make use of wine until after sixteen or eighteen years of age. The most customary and common form of life is the most excellent; any peculiarity, it seems to me, should be avoided, and I should as much detest a German who mixed water with his wine as a Frenchman who drank his pure. Public custom gives the law in such matters.

I dread a heavy atmosphere and I mortally detest smoke, —the first repairs that I hastened to make in my house were to the chimneys and privies, the common and intolerable defect of old buildings,—and I count amongst the severities of war the thick clouds of dust in which we are buried all day long in hot weather. My respiration is free and easy; and my colds generally pass away without affecting the lungs and without a cough. The severity of summer is more harmful to me than that of winter; for, besides the discomforts of the heat, which is less remediable than that of cold, and besides the force of the sun's rays on the head, my eyes are hurt by any brilliant light; I could not now dine sitting opposite a burning, blazing fire. In the days when I was more in the habit of reading, I used to place a piece of glass over the page, to deaden the whiteness of the paper, and obtained much relief. I do not know [at fifty-four years of age] [169] the use of spectacles, and I see as far as I ever did and as any other; it is true that, toward nightfall, I begin to feel difficulty and inability in reading, a use of my eyes which has always been hard on them, especially at night. Here is one step down, barely perceptible; I shall take another, a second to a third, a third to a fourth, so gently that I shall be stark blind before I am aware of the failure and old age of my sight, so skilfully do the Fates untwist our lives! I am likewise in doubt whether my hearing is hesitating about growing dull; and you will see that, when I have half lost it, I shall still lay the blame on the voices of those who speak to me; we must force the soul to exert itself, to make it perceive how it ebbs away.

My gait is quick and firm; and I know not which of the two, my mind or my body, I can with most difficulty keep quiet. [170] The preacher is a good friend to me who can compel my attention through a whole sermon. In places of

Of Experience

ceremony, where every one is so stiffened in bearing, where I have seen the ladies keep even their eyes so fixed, I can never succeed in preventing some part of me from being always restless; although I am seated, I am not settled[171] [and as for gesticulation, I am rarely to be found without a stick in my hand, whether on horseback or on foot].[172] As the chambermaid of Chrysippus the philosopher said of her master that he was drunk only in his legs, for he was wont to keep them moving in whatever position he was (and she said it at a time when, his companions being excited by wine, he felt no effect from it),[173] so it might be said of me, from childhood, that either insanity or quicksilver is in my feet, since I so naturally keep them moving and shifting, wherever I put them.

To eat greedily, as I do, is unmannerly, besides being harmful to health, and, indeed, to pleasure. I often bite my tongue, sometimes my fingers, in my haste. Diogenes, observing a child who was eating dust, gave his tutor a buffet.[174] There were men at Rome who taught the art of eating gracefully as well as that of so walking.[175] I lose from hasty eating the opportunity to talk, which is such a pleasant seasoning of a repast, provided that the talk be appropriate, amusing, and brief.

There is jealousy and envy between our pleasures: they clash and get in one another's way. Alcibiades, a man who well understood how to make good cheer, banished even music from the table because it might disturb the charm of discourse, for the reason which Plato ascribes to him, that it is a custom amongst ordinary men to summon to their festivals players of instruments, and singers, for lack of the good discourse and agreeable conversation with which

Of Experience

men of understanding know how to entertain one another.[176] Varro requires these things in an entertainment:
an assemblage of persons charming in appearance and agreeable in intercourse who are neither dumb nor loquacious;
neatness and delicacy in the viands and the place, and
pleasant weather.[177] The art of good public entertainment
is one demanding not a little skill and not a little luxury;[178]
neither great generals nor great philosophers have disdained
to know and practise it. My imagination has given into the
keeping of my memory three such occasions, which chance
made sovereignly delightful to me at different times in my
more blooming years.[179] My present state debars me from
the enjoyment of them, for each guest furnishes for himself
the principal charm and flavour of the occasion by the appropriate temper of body and mind in which he is. I, who
carry myself close to the ground,[180] detest that inhuman
wisdom which would make us disdain and be hostile to the
care of the body.

I deem it equally wrong to accept natural pleasures unwillingly and to accept them too willingly. Xerxes was a
simpleton who, enwrapped in all mortal pleasures, offered
a reward to him who should find others for him;[181] but
scarcely less of a simpleton is he who curtails those pleasures which nature has found for him. They must be neither
sought nor shunned; they must be received. I receive them
somewhat more courteously and graciously, and very readily
let myself follow my natural inclination. We have no occasion to exaggerate their emptiness: it makes itself sufficiently felt and sufficiently manifest, thanks to our feeble,
kill-joy spirit, which disgusts us with them as with itself. It
treats both itself and whatsoever it receives, sometimes now,

1515

sometimes then,[182] according to its own insatiable, errant, and versatile nature.

Unless the vessel is clean, whatever you pour into it turns sour.[183]

I, who boast of embracing so carefully and so fully all the conveniences of life, find therein, when I look into them thus closely, almost nothing but wind. But what of that! We are wind throughout; and the wind, wiser than we, takes pleasure in rustling and blowing, and is content with its own function, with no desire for stability or solidity, qualities not belonging to it.

The pure pleasures of the imagination, as well as its pains, some say are our greatest emotions, as the scales of Critolaus indicated.[184] It is no wonder: the imagination fashions them as she will and cuts them out of the whole cloth. Every day I see signal and, perchance, desirable examples of this. But I, being of a mixed and clumsy composition, can not be so fully engrossed by this one simple object,[185] that I do not grossly abandon myself to present pleasures of human and universal sway, perceived by the mind and by the senses conveyed to the mind.[186] The Cyrenaic philosophers maintain that, like physical suffering, bodily pleasures are the more powerful, both as being twofold and as being more in accordance with reason.[187] There are some, as Aristotle says, who with savage stupidity shew aversion to them;[188] I know others who do the like from ambition.[189] Why do they not also renounce breathing? Why do they not live on what belongs to them alone [with no aid from their accustomed conditions],[190] and refuse light because it is gratuitous, costing them no invention and no strength.

Of Experience

Let them try what it is to be supported by Mars or Pallas or Mercury, instead of Venus, Ceres and Bacchus. Such boastful moods may fashion for themselves some satisfaction—for what can not the fancy do for us? but they have no sign of wisdom.[191] Will they not, as they lie with their wives, seek the quadrature of the circle? I detest being enjoined to have my mind in the clouds, when my body is at table. I would not have the mind nailed there or wallow there, but I would have it sit there, not recline.

Aristippus pleaded only for the body, as if we had no soul; Zeno embraced only the soul, as if we had no body;[192] both mistakenly. Pythagoras, they say, adopted a philosophy that was all contemplation, Socrates one that was all character and action; Plato found the mean between the two.[193] But they say this only by way of talk. And the true mean is found in Socrates; and Plato is more Socratic than Pythagorean, and it becomes him better.

When I dance, I dance; when I sleep, I sleep; aye, and when I walk by myself in a fine orchard, if my thoughts are busied part of the time with outside occurrences, I bring them back to the walk, to the orchard, to the charm of that solitude, and to myself. Nature has maternally arranged that the actions which she has imposed on us for our needs should also be pleasurable to us; and she invites us to them, not only by reason, but by appetite. It is detrimental to break her rules. When I see Cæsar, or Alexander, at the height of his great labours, so fully enjoy human and bodily pleasures, I do not say that it is a relaxing of his soul; I say that he tightens it, subjecting by strength of spirit these violent occupations and toilsome thoughts to the habits of every-day life.

They had been wise, had they believed that here was

their ordinary vocation, there the extraordinary one. We are great fools! "He passed his life in idleness," we say; "I have done nothing to-day." What! have you not lived? That is not only the fundamental, but the most noble, of your occupations. "If I had been given occasion to deal with great matters, I might have shown what I could do." Have you been able to meditate on your life and arrange it? then you have done the greatest of all works. Nature, to manifest and express herself, demands nothing of Fortune: she manifests herself equally in all ranks, and behind curtains as without one. Have you learned to compose your character? you have done more than he who has composed books. Have you learned to lay hold of repose? you have done more than he who has laid hold of empires and cities. Man's great and glorious master-work is to live befittingly; all other things— to reign, to lay up treasure, to build—are at the best mere accessories and aids.[194]

I take pleasure in seeing the general of an army at the foot of a breach which he proposes presently to assault, lending himself completely and with a free mind to his dinner and to conversation with his friends; and in seeing Brutus, when heaven and earth had conspired against him and Roman liberty, steal from his rounds some hours of the night, to read and abridge Polybius in all freedom.[195] It is for small souls, buried under the weight of affairs, not to know how to free themselves therefrom entirely; not to know how to leave them and return to them.

Ye brave men, who have often suffered with me worse things, now drown your cares in wine; to-morrow we will journey again over the boundless sea.[196]

1518

Of Experience

Whether it be in mockery or in earnest that the theological and Sorbonic wine has passed into a proverb, and their feast as well, I think there is reason that they should dine the more agreeably and gaily because they have employed the morning profitably and seriously in the occupation of their schools. The consciousness of having well spent the other hours is a good and savoury condiment of the repast. Thus have wise men lived: and that inimitable striving after virtue which amazes us in one and the other Cato, that nature stern even to inopportuneness, gently submitted to the laws of human condition, and found pleasure in those of Venus and Bacchus, according to the precepts of their sect, which demands that the perfectly wise man be as skilled and well versed in the practice of pleasure as in any other duty of life; *that he who has a delicate judgement have also a delicate palate.*[197]

Relaxation and facility, it seems to me, miraculously honour and best befit a strong and generous mind. Epaminondas did not think that to join in the dancing of the youths of his city, to sing and play upon instruments and to be attentively interested in these things, would detract from the honour of his glorious victory or from the perfect reformation of character that was his.[198] And amongst all the admirable actions of the younger Scipio (all things considered, the first of the Romans),[199] there is nothing which imparts to him a greater charm than to see him gaily and boyishly trifling, picking up and selecting shells on the seashore, and playing with Lælius at *Cornichon va devant;*[200] and in bad weather amusing and pleasing himself by writing comedies about the most common and vulgar actions of men.[201] And with his head full of that marvellous enterprise against Hannibal

1519

and Africa, visiting the schools in Sicily and attending lectures on philosophy so much as to arm to the teeth the blind jealousy of his enemies at Rome.[202] I am exceedingly vexed that the finest pair of lives in Plutarch, the lives of these two great men, was one of the first to be lost.[203] Nor is there any thing more noteworthy in the life of Socrates than that, when he was quite old, he found time to be instructed in dancing and in playing on musical instruments, and considered the time well employed.[204] This same man was seen to stand in a trance an entire day and night, in the presence of the whole Greek army, surprised and preoccupied by some profound thought.[205] He was seen, the first amongst so many valiant men of the army, to rush to the assistance of Alcibiades when overwhelmed by the enemy, to shield him with his body, and deliver him from the throng by main force of arms.[206] In the battle at Delos, when Xenophon had been thrown from his horse, Socrates raised and rescued him;[207] and of all the people of Athens, exasperated like himself at so shameful a spectacle, he presented himself the first to rescue Theramenes, whom the Thirty Tyrants were leading to death by their satellites; nor would he desist from this bold undertaking save at the remonstrance of Theramenes himself, although he was followed by but two in all.[208] He was known, when solicited by a fair one of whom he was enamoured, to maintain, if need were, a strict abstinence.[209] He was seen constantly to march in war-time, and to walk upon ice, bare-footed; to wear the same garment in winter and in summer; to surpass all his comrades in patient endurance of toil; to eat not otherwise at a banquet than at his own table.[210] He was seen for twenty-seven years to endure, with unchanging bearing, hunger, poverty, the indocility of his children, the scratches of his wife, and, finally, calumny, tyranny, prison, fetters, and poison. But were this man challenged to drink in a contest as a duty of courtesy, he it was in all the army who had the best of it;[211] and he refused neither to play for nuts with the children nor to ride a hobby-horse with them; and he did it well, for all actions, says philosophy, equally befit and equally honour the wise man. There are grounds for presenting the image of this personage in all patterns and shapes of perfection, and we should never be weary of doing so. There are very few complete and spotless examples of life, and our education is wronged by setting before us every day weak and imperfect ones, scarcely of value in a single direction, which rather draw us backward, rather corrupting than correcting.

Man deceives himself;[212] we move much more easily by going by way of the ends, where the boundary acts as check and guide, than along the broad and open mid-way, and guided by skill rather than by nature; but also much less nobly and commendably. The grandeur of the soul comes not so much in striving for height and for advance as in knowing how to order and circumscribe itself; it considers great whatsoever is sufficient, and shews its loftiness by caring more for medium things than for eminent ones.[213] There is nothing so fine and so justifiable as to play the man well and duly; nor any knowledge so difficult as the knowing how to live this life well; and the most inhuman of our diseases is to despise our being. He who would set his soul apart, let him do it boldly, if he can, when the body is in evil case, to free it from the contagion; at other times, on the contrary, let it assist and favour the body and not decline to share in its natural pleasures, but delight in them conjugally, bringing to them moderation, if it be the wiser, for fear lest, through indiscretion, the pleasures become unpleasing. Excess is the pest of pleasure, and self-restraint is not its scourge, it is its spice. Eudoxus, who placed pleasure as the sovereign good, and his companion, who held it at so high value, tasted it in its most charming sweetness by means of self-restraint, which in them was singular and exemplary.[214] I enjoin my soul to regard both pain and pleasure with an eye equally under control, *for a swelling of the soul in joy is as blameworthy as its contraction in grief,*[215] and equally firm; but regarding the one cheerfully and the other austerely, and, according to its ability, as desirous to stretch out the one as to contract the other.[216]

To view sanely what is good, results in viewing sanely what is evil, and pain has something not to be shunned in its gentle beginning, and pleasure something to be shunned in its final excess. Plato couples them together[217] and considers it to be the duty of fortitude to combat equally pain and the immoderate and enchanting blandishments of pleasure.[218] They are two fountains from which whosoever —it may be city, man, or beast—draws when and as much as possible, is very fortunate; the one we must take as medicine and as a necessity, more sparingly; the other from thirst, but not to drunkenness.[219] Pain and pleasure, love and hatred, are the first things of which a child is sensible; if, when reason comes, these things are governed by it, that is virtue.[220]

I have a vocabulary of my own; I pass the time, when it is bad and disagreeable; when it is good, I do not desire to pass it, I savour it and detain it; we must hurry over what is bad, and rest in what is good. These common phrases, "pas-

Of Experience

time" and "passing the time," represent the custom of those prudent folk who think that they can make no better use of life than to glide through it and evade it, to pass it, to shun it, and so far as in them lies, to ignore it and fly from it as a troublesome and contemptible sort of thing. But I recognise it to be otherwise, and I find it valuable and agreeable even in its last stages, in which I now hold it; and Nature has put it into our hands surrounded with circumstances so favourable that we have only ourselves to blame if it harasses us and escapes us unprofitably. *A fool's life is thankless, anxious, concerned wholly with the future.*[221] Nevertheless, I prepare myself to lose it without regret, as a thing by its nature subject to be lost, not as being annoying and irksome. On the other hand, to dislike to die rightly befits only those who take pleasure in living. There is husbandry in the enjoyment of life; I enjoy it twice as much as others do, for the proportion of enjoyment depends on the more or less care we give it. At this hour especially, when I perceive my life as so brief in point of time, I desire to enlarge it and increase it in weight; I desire to check the promptitude of its flight by the promptitude of my grasp, and by the vigour of my use of it to counterbalance the speed of its flow; in proportion as my possession of life is shorter, I must needs make it deeper and fuller.

Others feel the charm of contentment and prosperity; I feel it as they do, but not merely in passing and gliding along; it must be studied, relished, and meditated upon, that we may render for it adequate thanks to him who grants it to us. They enjoy other pleasures as they do that of sleep, without recognising them. To the end that even sleep should not escape me thus stupidly, I have in other days found it well that I should be disturbed in my sleep, in order that I might catch sight of it. I hold consultation between a pleasure and myself;[222] I do not skim over it; I sound it and bend my reason, grown peevish and averse, to receive it. Do I find myself in a tranquil frame of mind? Is there some pleasure that tickles me? I do not let it play tricks with my senses, I associate my soul with it, not to be entangled therein, but to enjoy herself; not therein to be lost, but to be found; making use of her, for her part, to regard herself in this prosperous condition, to weigh and to estimate this good-fortune, and to amplify it. She measures how much she owes to God for being at rest in her conscience and in other inner perturbations, in having the body in natural health, enjoying in an orderly and suitable fashion the exercise of the easy and agreeable functions whereby it is his pleasure, of his grace, to compensate the sorrow with which his justice in its turn smites us; how much it is worth to her to be so situated that, wherever she turns her eyes, the sky is serene about her: no desire, no fear or doubt which troubles the air; no difficulty, past, present, or future, over which her imagination does not pass scatheless. Much light is thrown on this consideration by the comparison of different conditions: thus I represent to myself in a thousand aspects those who are carried away and overthrown by chance or by their own error, and also those more akin to me who receive their good-fortune negligently and carelessly. These are people who really "pass their time"; they pass beyond the present and what they possess, to wait upon hope, and for shadows and vain images which fancy puts before them,—

Like the images which, men say, flit about after death, or the visions that mock our senses in sleep,[223]—

1524

which hasten and prolong their flight, the more they are
followed after. The fruit and the object of their pursuit is
to pursue; as Alexander said that the end of his labour was
to labour,[224]—

> Believing that nothing was done so long as any
> thing remained to be done.[225]

For my own part, then, I love life and cultivate it, as it
has pleased God to bestow it upon us. I have no desire that
it should be without the need of eating and drinking, and
it would seem to me to err not less excusably to desire that
that necessity might be double; *a wise man is a most earnest
seeker of the treasures of Nature;*[226] or that we should support ourselves simply by putting into the mouth a little of
the drug by which Epimenides deprived himself of appetite
and nourished himself;[227] or that we should stupidly beget
children by the fingers or the heels, but, reverently speaking, that we might also beget them by the fingers and the
heels voluptuously; or that the body should be without desire and without pleasing excitement—those are ungrateful
and iniquitous lamentations. I heartily and gratefully accept
what Nature has done for me, and take pleasure in it and
am satisfied with it. It does wrong to that great and all-
powerful Giver to despise his gift, to impair it and deface it;
being all good, he has made all things good; *every thing
that is according to Nature is worthy of esteem.*[228]

Of the opinions of philosophy, I embrace more freely
those which are most solid, that is to say, most human and
most natural to us;[229] my judgements are, conformably to
my character, unassuming and humble. Philosophy plays
the child to my thinking when she betakes herself to logic-

chopping[230] to preach to us that it is an unnatural alliance to marry the divine with the terrestrial, the reasonable with the unreasonable, the harsh with the indulgent, the upright with the crooked; that carnal enjoyments partake of the brute, unworthy to be tasted by the wise man—the sole pleasure he may derive from the possession of a young wife; that it is the pleasure his conscience feels in performing a due action, like putting on his boots for a necessary ride. Its disciples could have had no more reason and vigour in ravishing their wives than in such teaching. This is not what Socrates says, the teacher of philosophy and our instructor: he prizes bodily pleasure as he ought, but he places above this that of the mind as having more strength, steadiness, facility, variety, and dignity. This pleasure, according to him, does not by any means stand alone (he is not so irrational) but is simply first; for him, moderation tempers, not opposes, pleasure.

Nature is a gentle guide, but not more gentle than prudent and just. *We should enter into the nature of things and see thoroughly what it demands.*[231] I seek everywhere her track; we have confused it with artificial traces; and that sovereign good of the Academic and Peripatetic sects, which is to live according to nature, becomes from this cause difficult to limit and explain; and that of the Stoics, akin to it, which is to concur with Nature. Is it not an error to consider some actions less worthy because they are necessary? Truly they will not drive it out of my head that the marriage of pleasure and necessity is very suitable, for which, says one of the ancients, the gods always conspire.[232] Wherefore shall we disunite by separation a fabric woven of so close and fraternal a correspondence? On the contrary, let us confirm

it by mutual services; let the mind arouse and vivify the dulness of the body, the body check the frivolity of the mind
and steady it. *Surely he who praises the nature of the soul
as the highest good, and condemns the nature of the flesh as
an evil, seeks the soul carnally and shuns the flesh carnally,
since he does it from human vanity, not from divine truth.*[233]

There is in this gift bestowed upon us by God no part
undeserving our attention; we must account for it to a hair.
And a mandate to man to conduct himself according to his
condition is explicit, direct, and very important; and the
Creator has given it to us seriously and sternly. Authority
alone can influence an ordinary intellect, and it has the more
weight in a foreign tongue; let us make use of it here. *Who
will not say that it is the nature of folly to do in a slothful
and stubborn way what is to be done, to drive the body in
one direction, the soul in another, and to be torn apart by
the most contrary movements?*[234]

So then, as proof, make some one tell you some day the
thoughts and fancies that he admits into his head and for
which he turns his thoughts from a good repast and regrets
the hour that he spends in eating: you will find that there
is nothing so insipid in all the food on your table as this fine
communing with his soul (for the most part it would be better worth while for us really to sleep, than to keep awake);
and you will find that his thoughts and intentions are worth
less than your dish of hash. Were they the mental raptures
of Archimedes himself—what then? I do not here touch
upon, and do not confuse with monkey-like men such as we
ourselves are, occupied with vain desires and cogitations,
those venerable souls uplifted by the ardour of devotion and
religious feeling to a constant and scrupulous meditation

upon divine things; who, anticipating, by force of a lively and vehement hope, the habit of eternal nourishment, the final aim and last step of Christian desires and the sole constant and incorruptible pleasure, scorn to pay heed to our necessitous, shifting, and ambiguous needs, and readily resign to the body the care and use of sensual and temporal food. This [235] is a study of special honour. Between you and me, these are things that I have always seen to be singularly accordant: super-celestial beliefs and sub-terrestrial morals. Our studies are all of this world, and of the things of this world the most natural are the best.[236]

Æsop, that great man, saw his master make water as he walked. "What," said he, "must we do that as we run?"[237] Use our time as best we may, there will still be much left that is unemployed and ill employed. Our mind apparently has too few other hours to do its business without disassociating itself from the body for that brief space which it requires for its need. There are men who desire to put themselves outside themselves and escape from being men; it is mere foolishness; instead of transforming themselves into angels, they transform themselves into beasts; instead of uplifting themselves, they degrade themselves. Those transcendent humours terrify me like lofty and inaccessible places; and nothing is so difficult for me to swallow in the life of Soccrates as his trances and his dæmon, and nothing so human in Plato as that because of which they say that he was called divine. And of our branches of knowledge those seem to me to be the most earthly and low which are highest mounted; and I find nothing so despicable and so mortal in the life of Alexander as his fancies about his immortalisation.[238] Philotas quipped him amusingly by his rejoinder. He had congratulated him by letter on the oracle of Jupiter Ammon, which had placed him amongst the gods. "So far as you are concerned, I am very glad about it; but there is ground for pitying men who have to live with a man and obey him, who surpasses and is not content with the proportions of a man."[239]

> It is because you submit to the gods that you rule.[240]

The admirable inscription with which the Athenians commemorated the visit of Pompeius to their city is conformable with my thoughts:

> Thou art a god inasmuch as thou dost recognise thyself to be a man.[241]

It is an absolute and, as it were, divine perfection to be able to enjoy obediently one's existence. We seek other conditions because we do not understand the use of our own, and go outside of ourselves because we know not what is taking place. Much good does it do us to mount on stilts, for on stilts we must still walk with our legs; and on the loftiest throne in the world we sit only on our buttocks. The finest lives are, to my thinking, those which are conformed to the common human model, with regularity, with nothing wonderful or extravagant. Old age, indeed, needs to be treated a little more gently. Let us commend it to that God who is the protector of health and wisdom, but cheerful and companionable.

> Grant, I pray, son of Latona, that I enjoy in full health, and with mind unimpaired, the goods that have been prepared for me; and that my old age be not unhonoured, nor lack the lyre.[242]